TO TERRA...

Volume 1

KEIKO TAKEMIYA

VERTICAL.

Translation—Dawn T. Laabs
Production—Hiroko Mizuno
Shinobu Sato

Copyright © 2007 by Keiko Takemiya
Translation Copyright © 2007 by Dawn T. Laabs and Vertical, Inc.

Published by Vertical, Inc., New York.

Originally serialized in Japanese as *Tera he...*
in *Gekkan manga shonen*, Asahi Sonorama, 1977-80.

ISBN 1-932234-67-5 / 978-1-932234-67-1

Manufactured in the United States of America

Vertical, Inc.
www.vertical-inc.com

TO TERRA...

VOLUME 1

PART 1

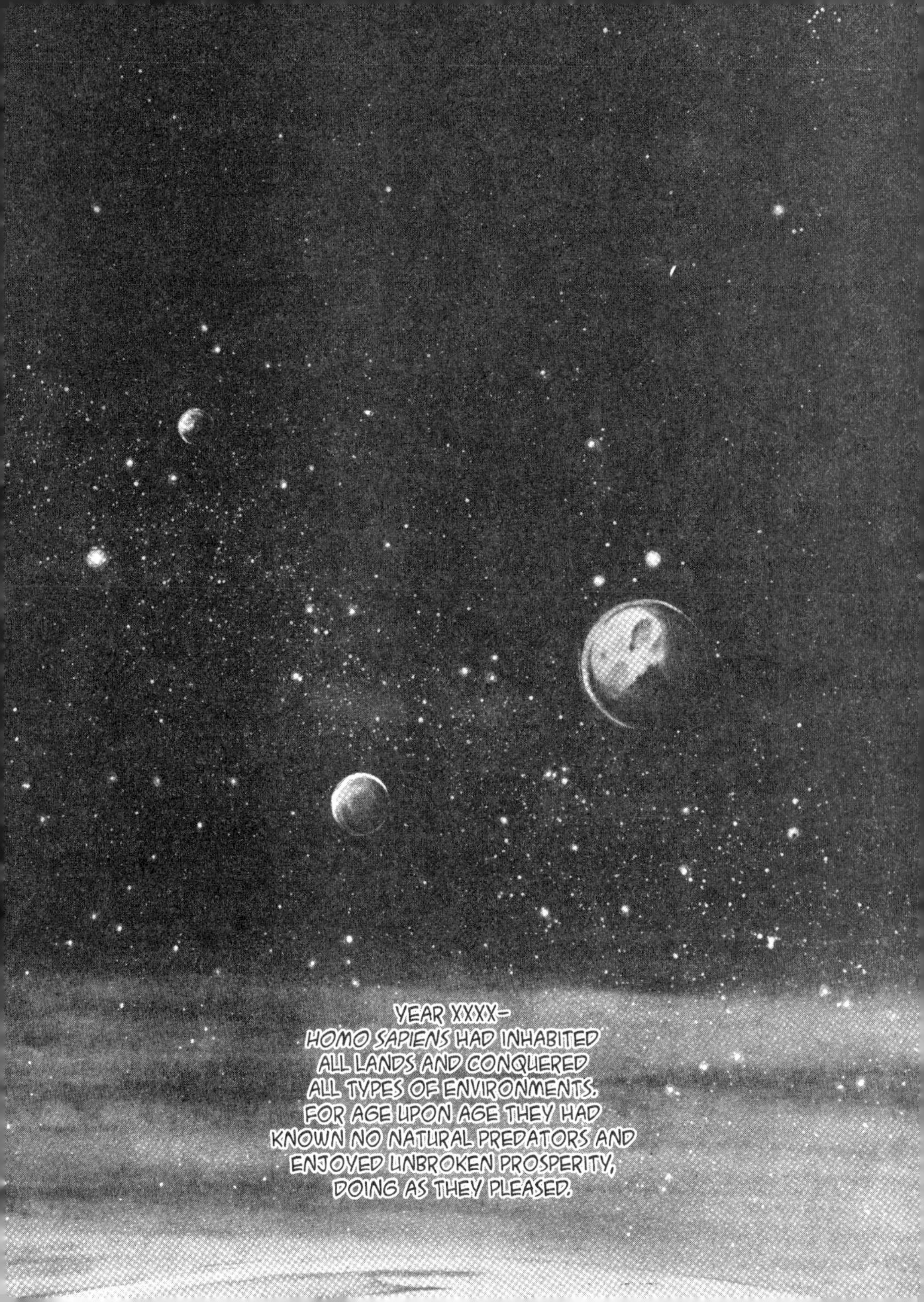
YEAR XXXX—
HOMO SAPIENS HAD INHABITED ALL LANDS AND CONQUERED ALL TYPES OF ENVIRONMENTS. FOR AGE UPON AGE THEY HAD KNOWN NO NATURAL PREDATORS AND ENJOYED UNBROKEN PROSPERITY, DOING AS THEY PLEASED.

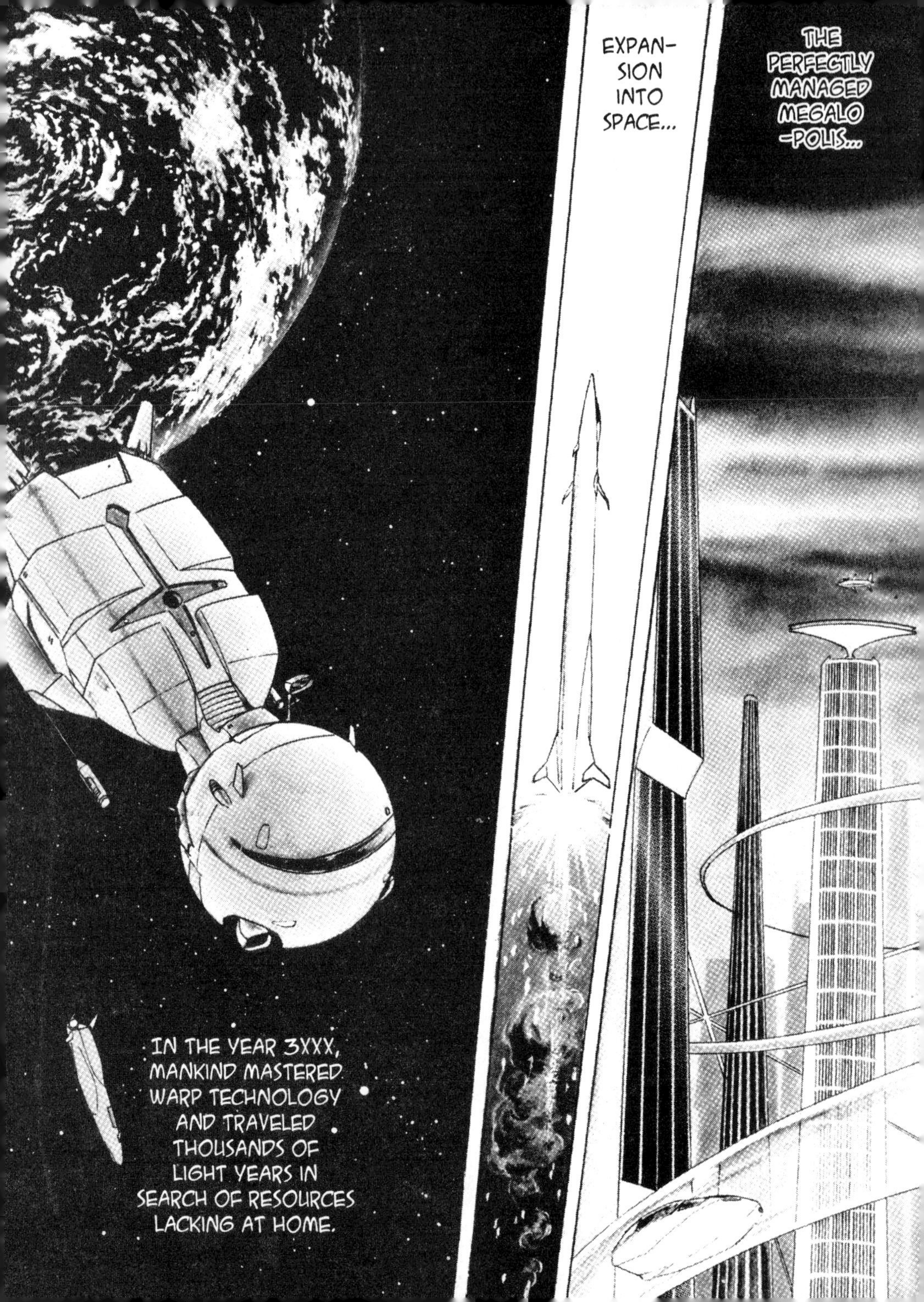
THE PERFECTLY MANAGED MEGALO-POLIS...
EXPAN-SION INTO SPACE...
IN THE YEAR 3XXX, MANKIND MASTERED WARP TECHNOLOGY AND TRAVELED THOUSANDS OF LIGHT YEARS IN SEARCH OF RESOURCES LACKING AT HOME.

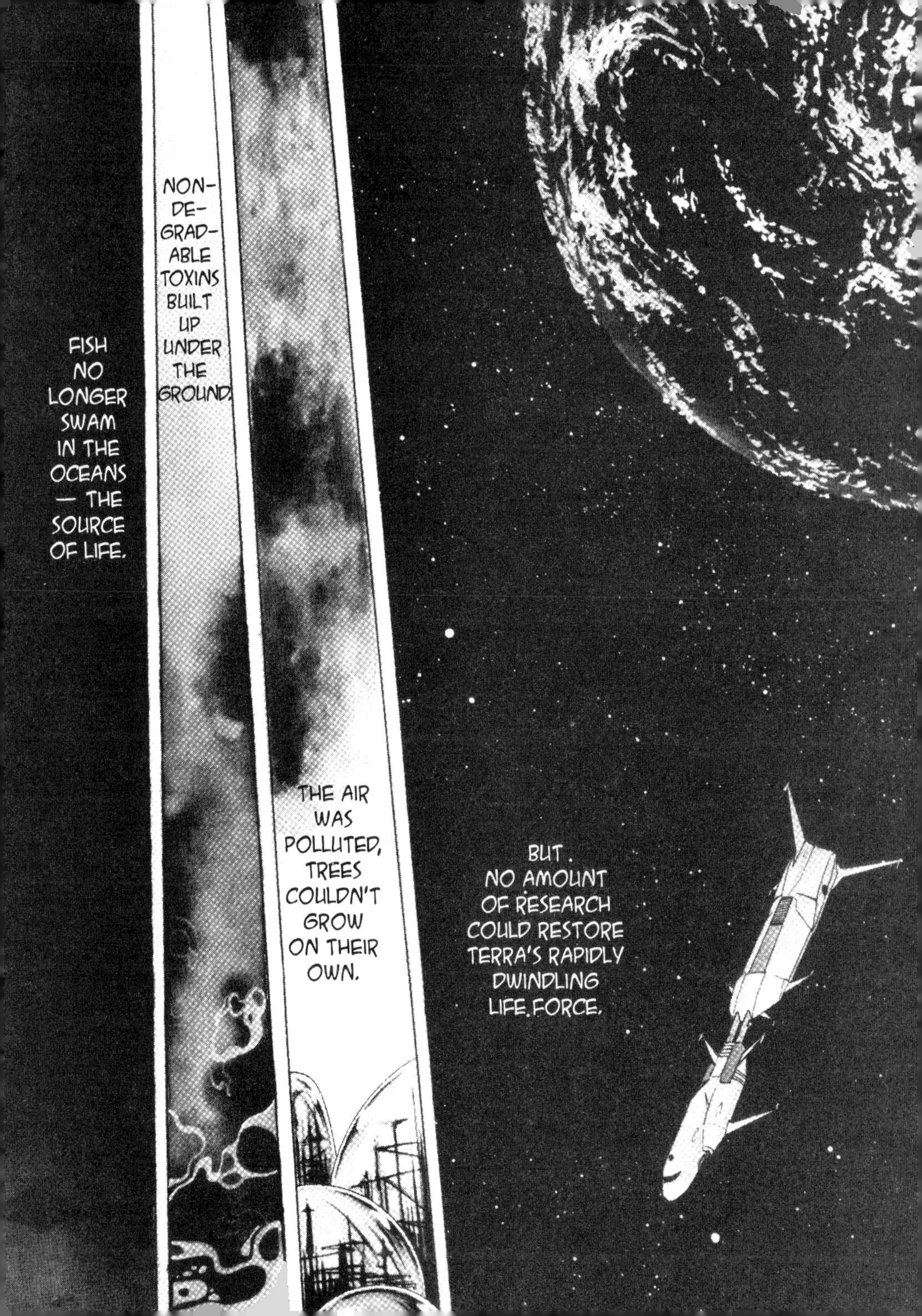
FISH NO LONGER SWAM IN THE OCEANS — THE SOURCE OF LIFE.
NON-DE-GRAD-ABLE TOXINS BUILT UP UNDER THE GROUND.
THE AIR WAS POLLUTED, TREES COULDN'T GROW ON THEIR OWN.
BUT . NO AMOUNT OF RESEARCH COULD RESTORE TERRA'S RAPIDLY DWINDLING LIFE FORCE.

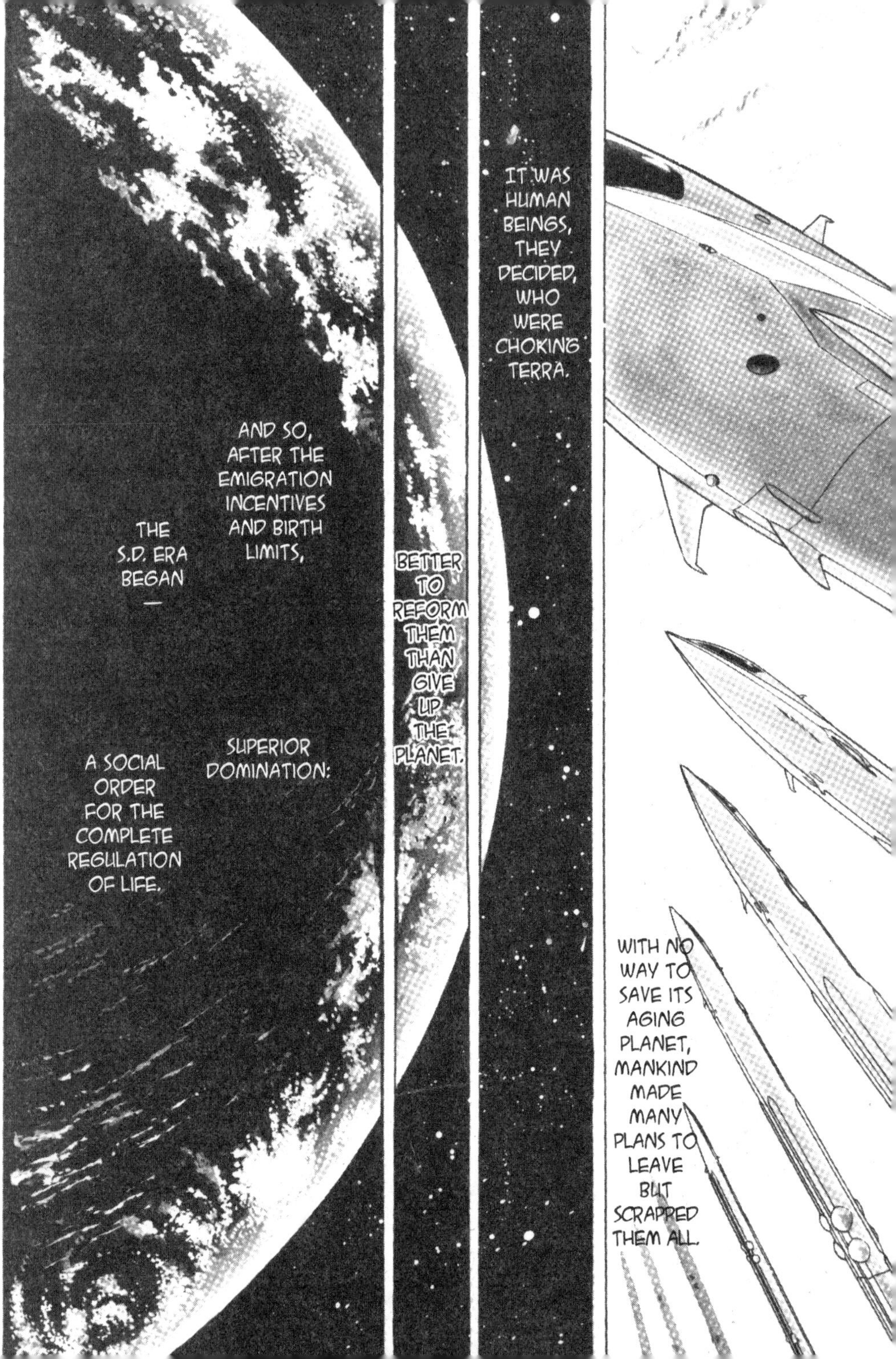
WITH NO WAY TO SAVE ITS AGING PLANET, MANKIND MADE MANY PLANS TO LEAVE BUT SCRAPPED THEM ALL.
IT WAS HUMAN BEINGS, THEY DECIDED, WHO WERE CHOKING TERRA.
BETTER TO REFORM THEM THAN GIVE UP THE PLANET.
AND SO, AFTER THE EMIGRATION INCENTIVES AND BIRTH LIMITS,
THE S.D. ERA BEGAN —
SUPERIOR DOMINATION:
A SOCIAL ORDER FOR THE COMPLETE REGULATION OF LIFE.

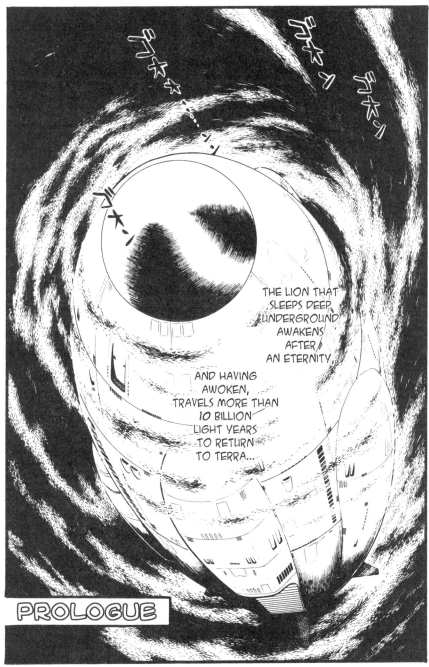

THE LION THAT SLEEPS DEEP UNDERGROUND AWAKENS AFTER AN ETERNITY.

AND HAVING AWOKEN, TRAVELS MORE THAN 10 BILLION LIGHT YEARS TO RETURN TO TERRA...

PROLOGUE

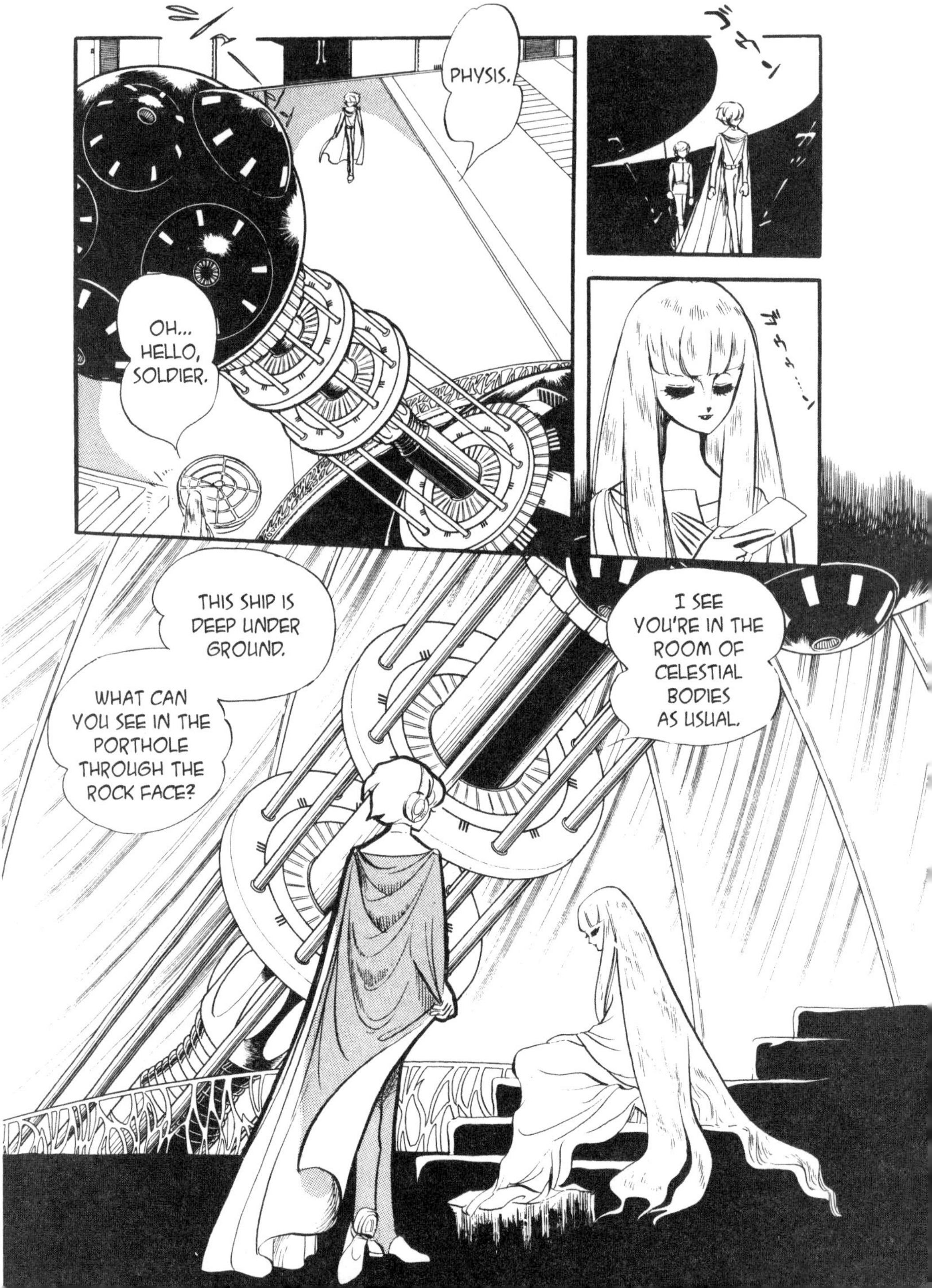
PHYSIS.
OH... HELLO, SOLDIER.
I SEE YOU'RE IN THE ROOM OF CELESTIAL BODIES AS USUAL.
THIS SHIP IS DEEP UNDER GROUND.
WHAT CAN YOU SEE IN THE PORTHOLE THROUGH THE ROCK FACE?

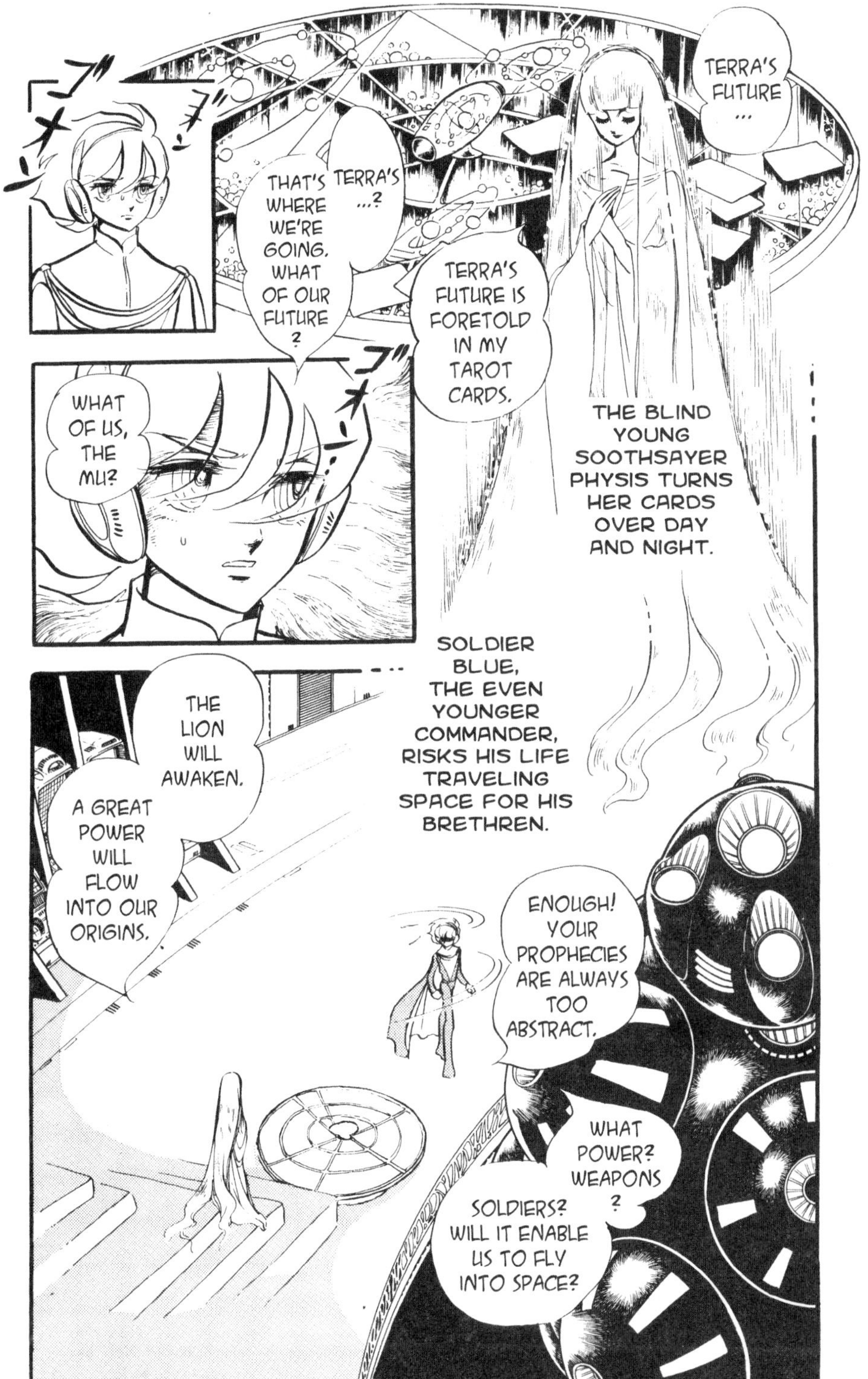
TERRA'S FUTURE ...
TERRA'S ...?
THAT'S WHERE WE'RE GOING. WHAT OF OUR FUTURE?
TERRA'S FUTURE IS FORETOLD IN MY TAROT CARDS.
WHAT OF US, THE MU?
THE BLIND YOUNG SOOTHSAYER PHYSIS TURNS HER CARDS OVER DAY AND NIGHT.
SOLDIER BLUE, THE EVEN YOUNGER COMMANDER, RISKS HIS LIFE TRAVELING SPACE FOR HIS BRETHREN.
THE LION WILL AWAKEN.
A GREAT POWER WILL FLOW INTO OUR ORIGINS.
ENOUGH! YOUR PROPHECIES ARE ALWAYS TOO ABSTRACT.
WHAT POWER? WEAPONS?
SOLDIERS? WILL IT ENABLE US TO FLY INTO SPACE?

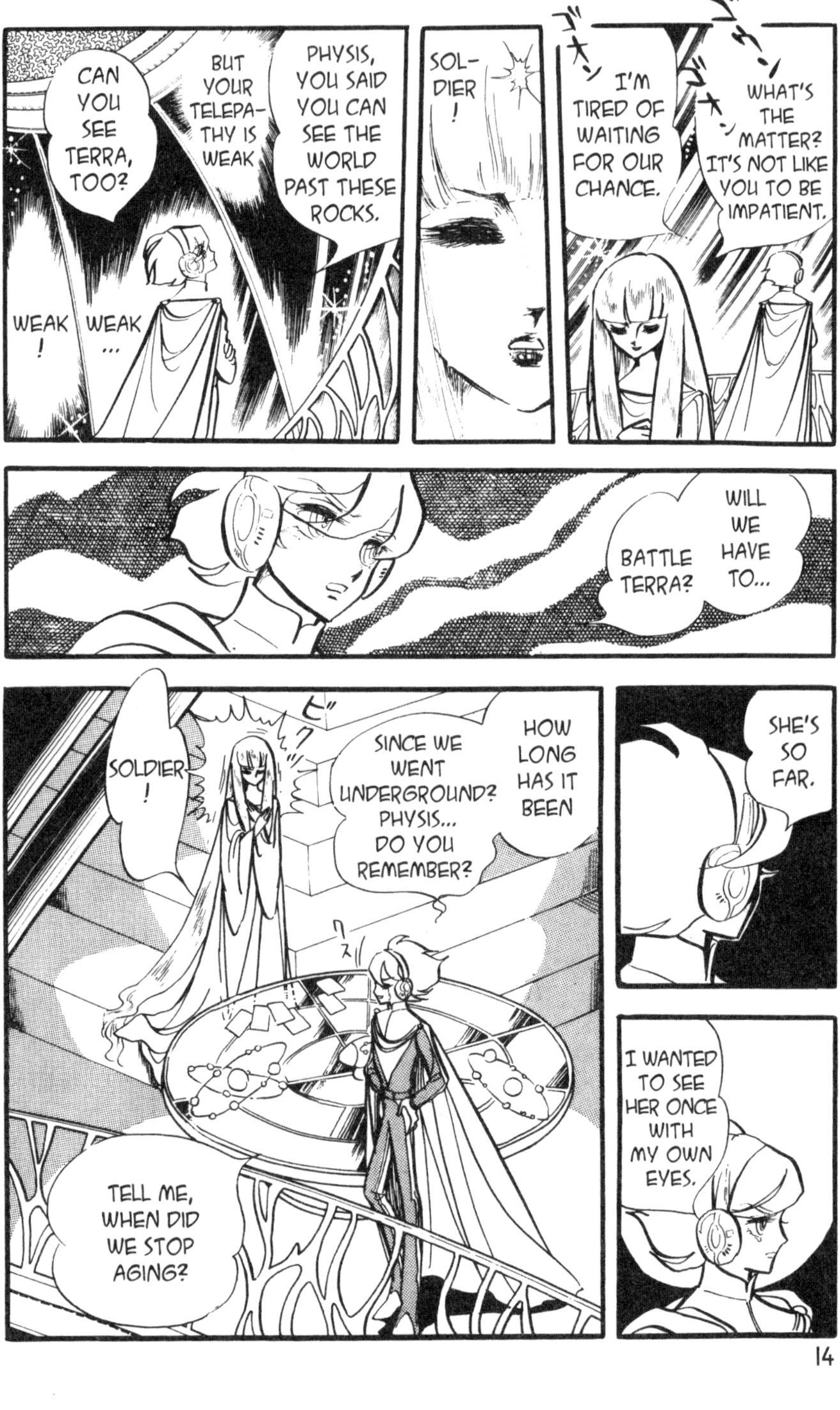

WHAT'S THE MATTER? IT'S NOT LIKE YOU TO BE IMPATIENT.
I'M TIRED OF WAITING FOR OUR CHANCE.
SOL-DIER!
PHYSIS, YOU SAID YOU CAN SEE THE WORLD PAST THESE ROCKS.
BUT YOUR TELEPA-THY IS WEAK
CAN YOU SEE TERRA, TOO?
WEAK...
WEAK!
WILL WE HAVE TO...
BATTLE TERRA?
SHE'S SO FAR.
I WANTED TO SEE HER ONCE WITH MY OWN EYES.
HOW LONG HAS IT BEEN
SINCE WE WENT UNDERGROUND? PHYSIS... DO YOU REMEMBER?
SOLDIER!
TELL ME, WHEN DID WE STOP AGING?

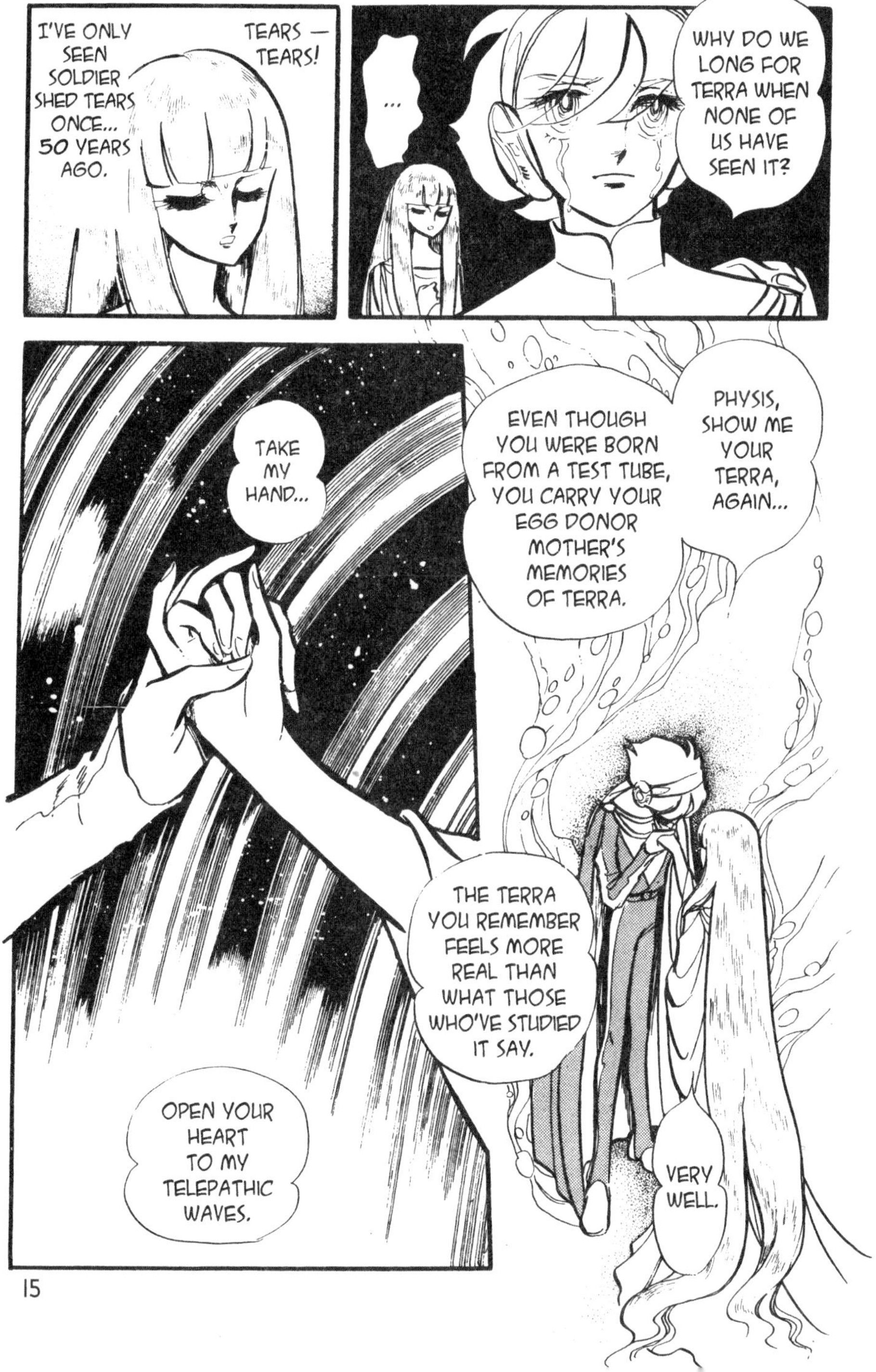
WHY DO WE LONG FOR TERRA WHEN NONE OF US HAVE SEEN IT?
...
TEARS — TEARS!
I'VE ONLY SEEN SOLDIER SHED TEARS ONCE... 50 YEARS AGO.
PHYSIS, SHOW ME YOUR TERRA, AGAIN...
EVEN THOUGH YOU WERE BORN FROM A TEST TUBE, YOU CARRY YOUR EGG DONOR MOTHER'S MEMORIES OF TERRA.
THE TERRA YOU REMEMBER FEELS MORE REAL THAN WHAT THOSE WHO'VE STUDIED IT SAY.
VERY WELL.
TAKE MY HAND...
OPEN YOUR HEART TO MY TELEPATHIC WAVES.

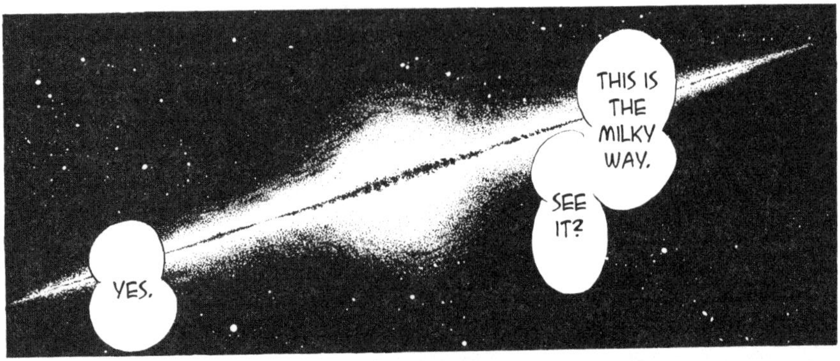
THIS IS THE MILKY WAY.
SEE IT?
YES.

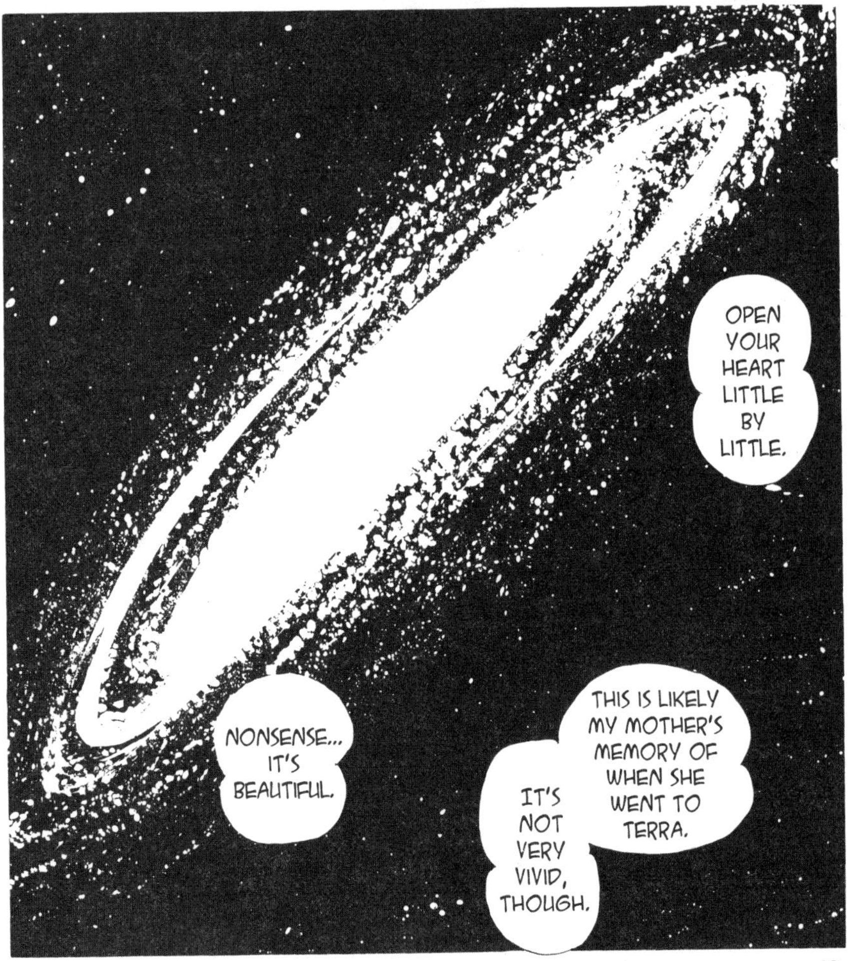
OPEN YOUR HEART LITTLE BY LITTLE.
THIS IS LIKELY MY MOTHER'S MEMORY OF WHEN SHE WENT TO TERRA.
IT'S NOT VERY VIVID, THOUGH.
NONSENSE... IT'S BEAUTIFUL.

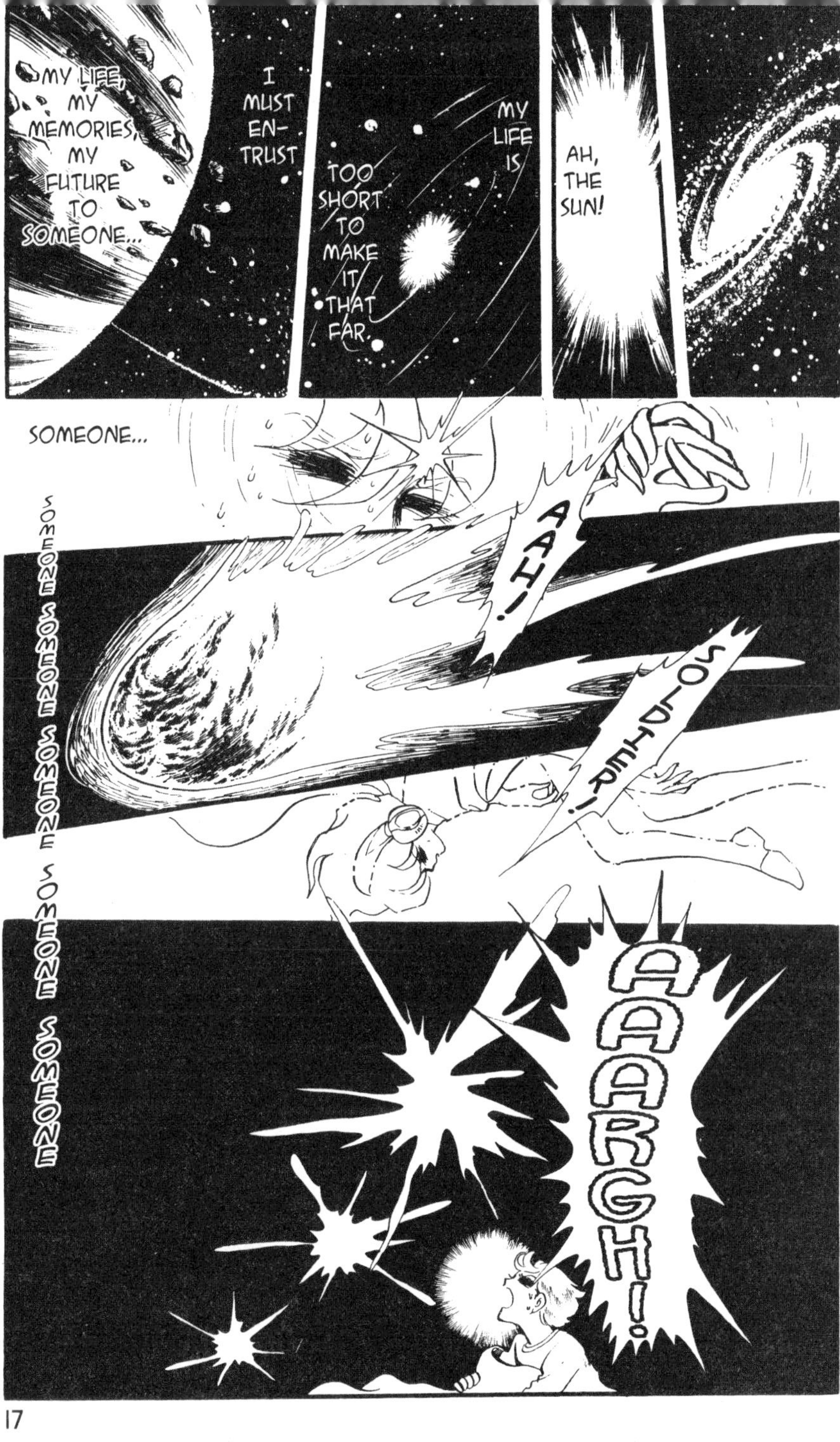
AH, THE SUN!
MY LIFE IS TOO SHORT TO MAKE IT THAT FAR.
I MUST EN-TRUST
MY LIFE, MY MEMORIES, MY FUTURE TO SOMEONE...
AAH!
SOLDIER!
SOMEONE...
SOMEONE SOMEONE SOMEONE SOMEONE SOMEONE SOMEONE
AAARGH!

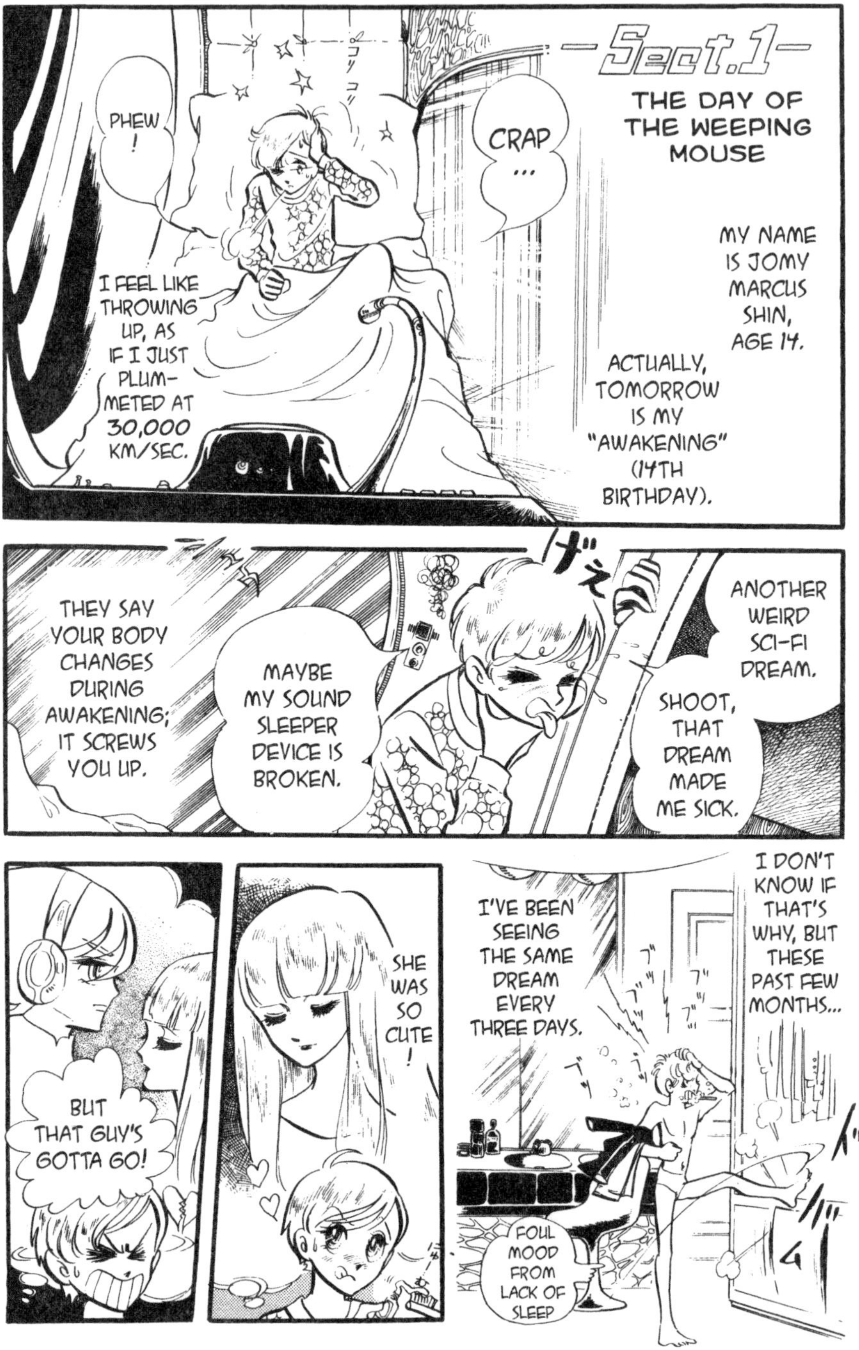
—Sect.1—
THE DAY OF THE WEEPING MOUSE
MY NAME IS JOMY MARCUS SHIN, AGE 14.
ACTUALLY, TOMORROW IS MY "AWAKENING" (14TH BIRTHDAY).
CRAP ...
PHEW !
I FEEL LIKE THROWING UP, AS IF I JUST PLUM-METED AT 30,000 KM/SEC.
ANOTHER WEIRD SCI-FI DREAM.
SHOOT, THAT DREAM MADE ME SICK.
MAYBE MY SOUND SLEEPER DEVICE IS BROKEN.
THEY SAY YOUR BODY CHANGES DURING AWAKENING; IT SCREWS YOU UP.
I DON'T KNOW IF THAT'S WHY, BUT THESE PAST FEW MONTHS...
I'VE BEEN SEEING THE SAME DREAM EVERY THREE DAYS.
FOUL MOOD FROM LACK OF SLEEP
SHE WAS SO CUTE!
BUT THAT GUY'S GOTTA GO!

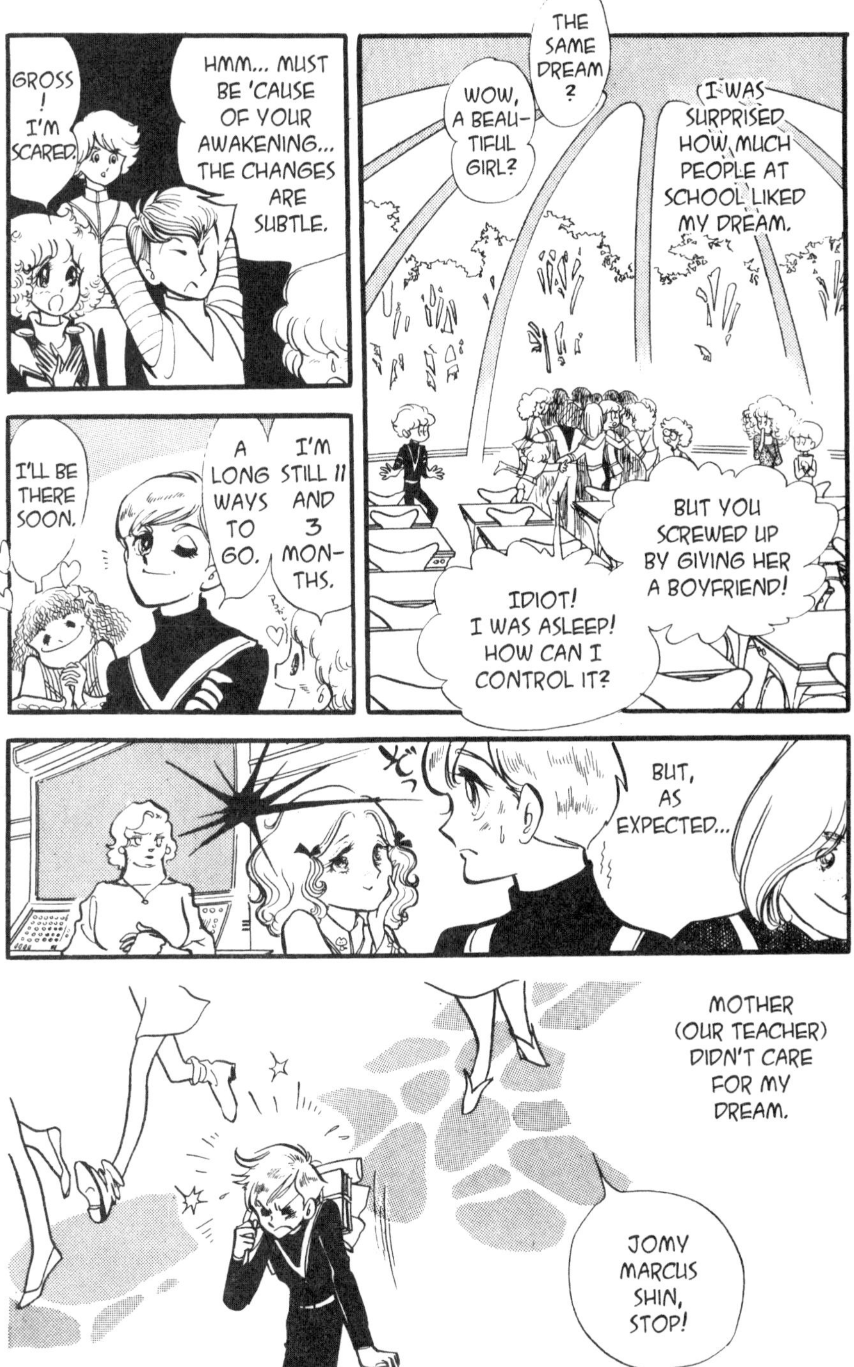
I WAS SURPRISED HOW MUCH PEOPLE AT SCHOOL LIKED MY DREAM.
THE SAME DREAM?
WOW, A BEAU-TIFUL GIRL?
BUT YOU SCREWED UP BY GIVING HER A BOYFRIEND!
IDIOT! I WAS ASLEEP! HOW CAN I CONTROL IT?
HMM... MUST BE 'CAUSE OF YOUR AWAKENING... THE CHANGES ARE SUBTLE.
GROSS! I'M SCARED.
I'M STILL 11 AND 3 MON-THS.
A LONG WAYS TO GO.
I'LL BE THERE SOON.
BUT, AS EXPECTED...
MOTHER (OUR TEACHER) DIDN'T CARE FOR MY DREAM.
JOMY MARCUS SHIN, STOP!

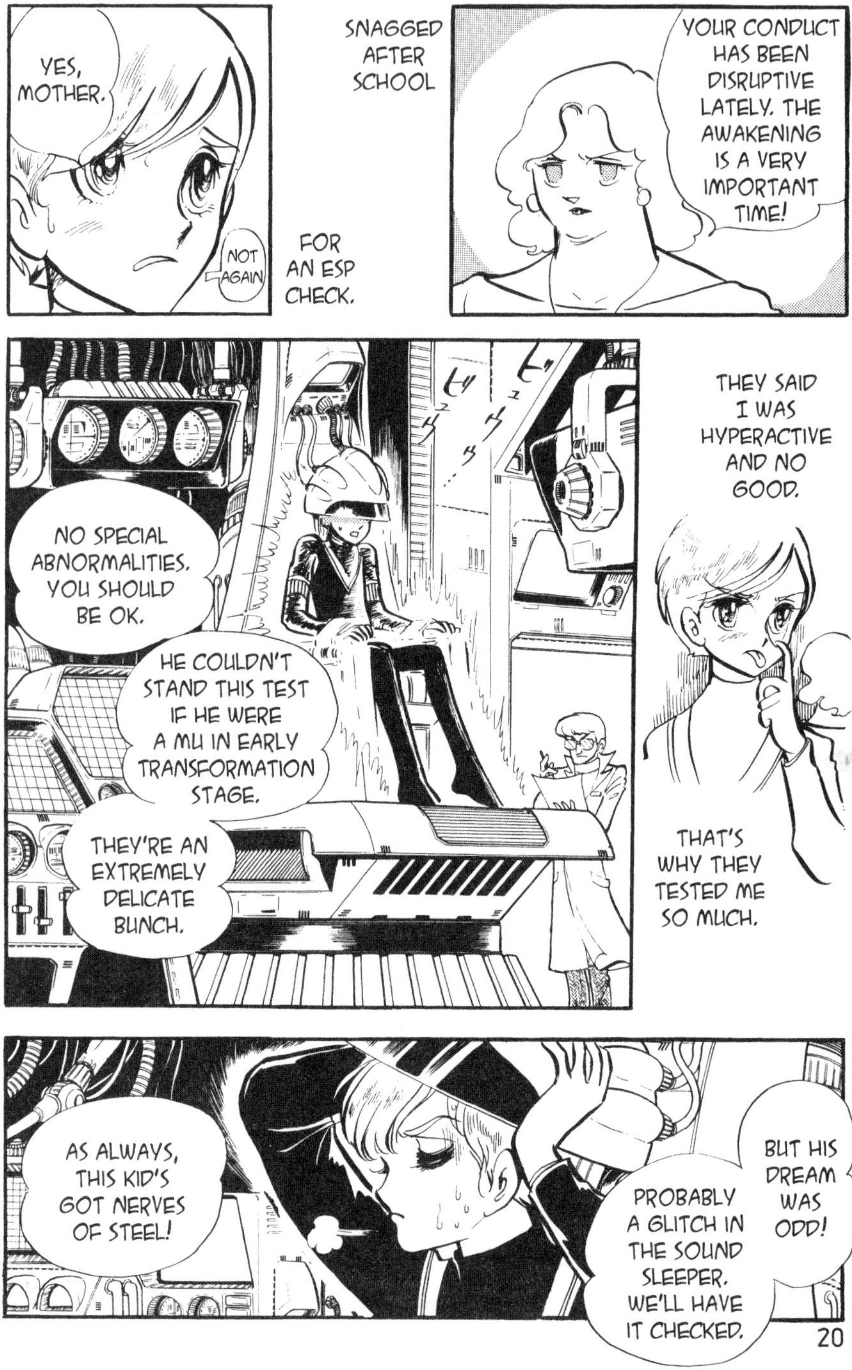
SNAGGED AFTER SCHOOL
FOR AN ESP CHECK.
YOUR CONDUCT HAS BEEN DISRUPTIVE LATELY. THE AWAKENING IS A VERY IMPORTANT TIME!
YES, MOTHER.
NOT AGAIN
THEY SAID I WAS HYPERACTIVE AND NO GOOD.
THAT'S WHY THEY TESTED ME SO MUCH.
NO SPECIAL ABNORMALITIES. YOU SHOULD BE OK.
HE COULDN'T STAND THIS TEST IF HE WERE A MU IN EARLY TRANSFORMATION STAGE.
THEY'RE AN EXTREMELY DELICATE BUNCH.
BUT HIS DREAM WAS ODD!
PROBABLY A GLITCH IN THE SOUND SLEEPER. WE'LL HAVE IT CHECKED.
AS ALWAYS, THIS KID'S GOT NERVES OF STEEL!

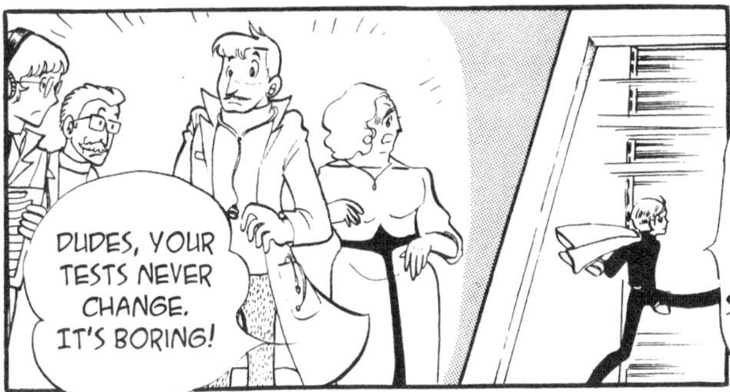
HUMPH! SORRY I'M SO TOUGH AND THICK-SKINNED.
DUDES, YOUR TESTS NEVER CHANGE. IT'S BORING!

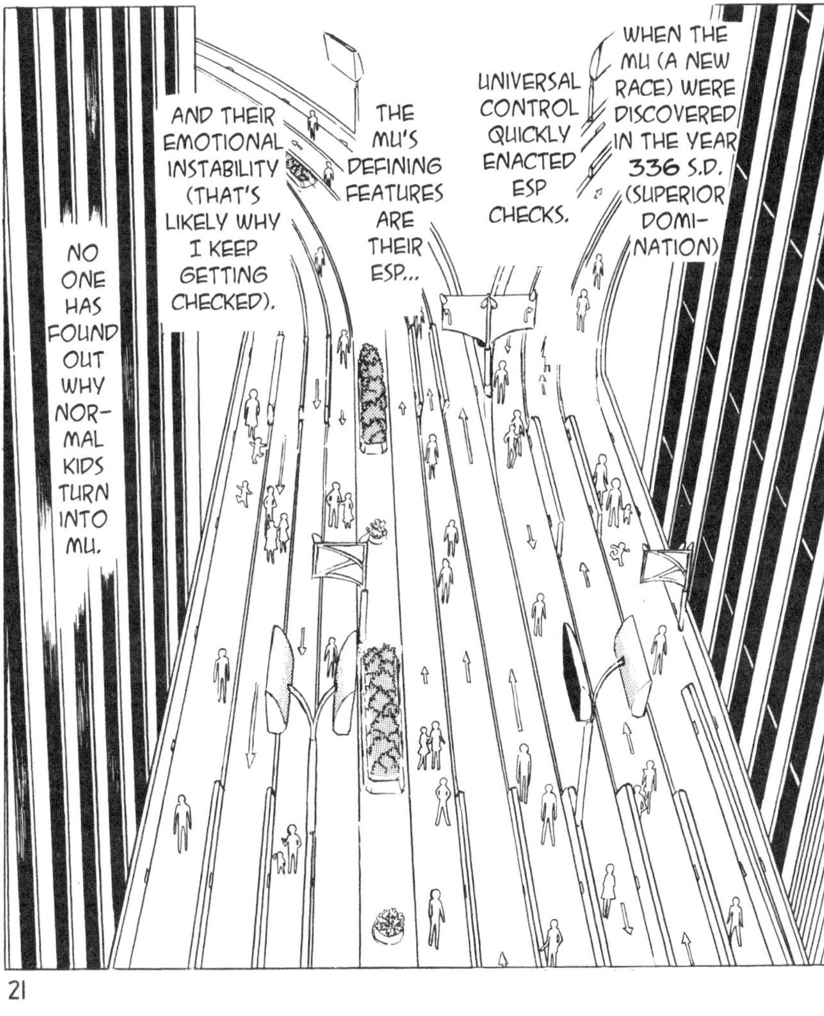
WHEN THE MU (A NEW RACE) WERE DISCOVERED IN THE YEAR 336 S.D. (SUPERIOR DOMI-NATION)
UNIVERSAL CONTROL QUICKLY ENACTED ESP CHECKS.
THE MU'S DEFINING FEATURES ARE THEIR ESP...
AND THEIR EMOTIONAL INSTABILITY (THAT'S LIKELY WHY I KEEP GETTING CHECKED).
NO ONE HAS FOUND OUT WHY NOR-MAL KIDS TURN INTO MU.

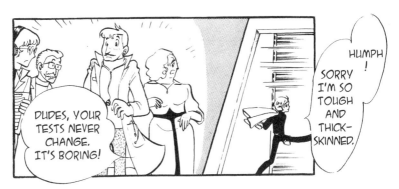

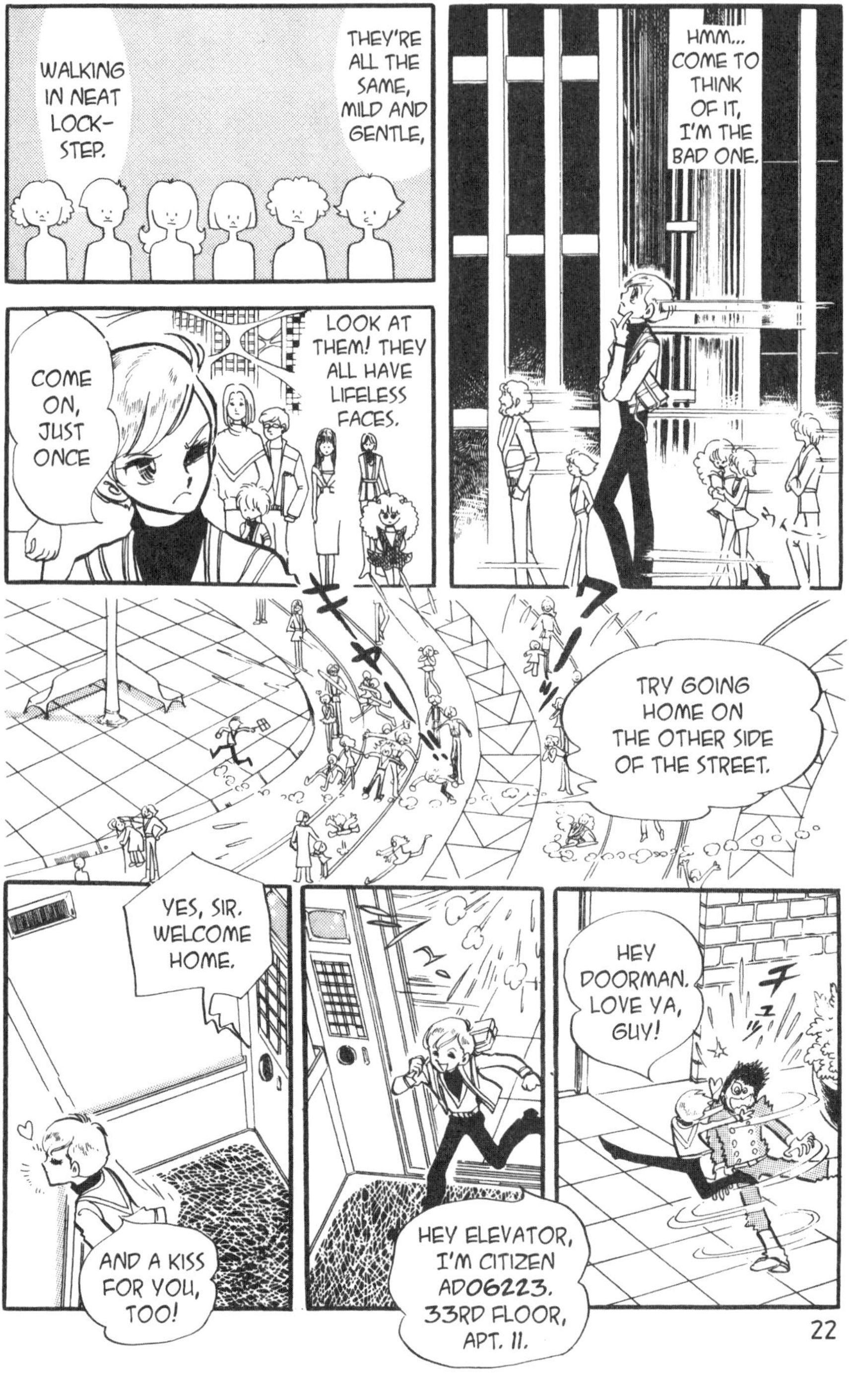
HMM... COME TO THINK OF IT, I'M THE BAD ONE.
THEY'RE ALL THE SAME, MILD AND GENTLE,
WALKING IN NEAT LOCK-STEP.
LOOK AT THEM! THEY ALL HAVE LIFELESS FACES.
COME ON, JUST ONCE
TRY GOING HOME ON THE OTHER SIDE OF THE STREET.
HEY DOORMAN. LOVE YA, GUY!
HEY ELEVATOR, I'M CITIZEN AD06223. 33RD FLOOR, APT. 11.
YES, SIR. WELCOME HOME.
AND A KISS FOR YOU, TOO!

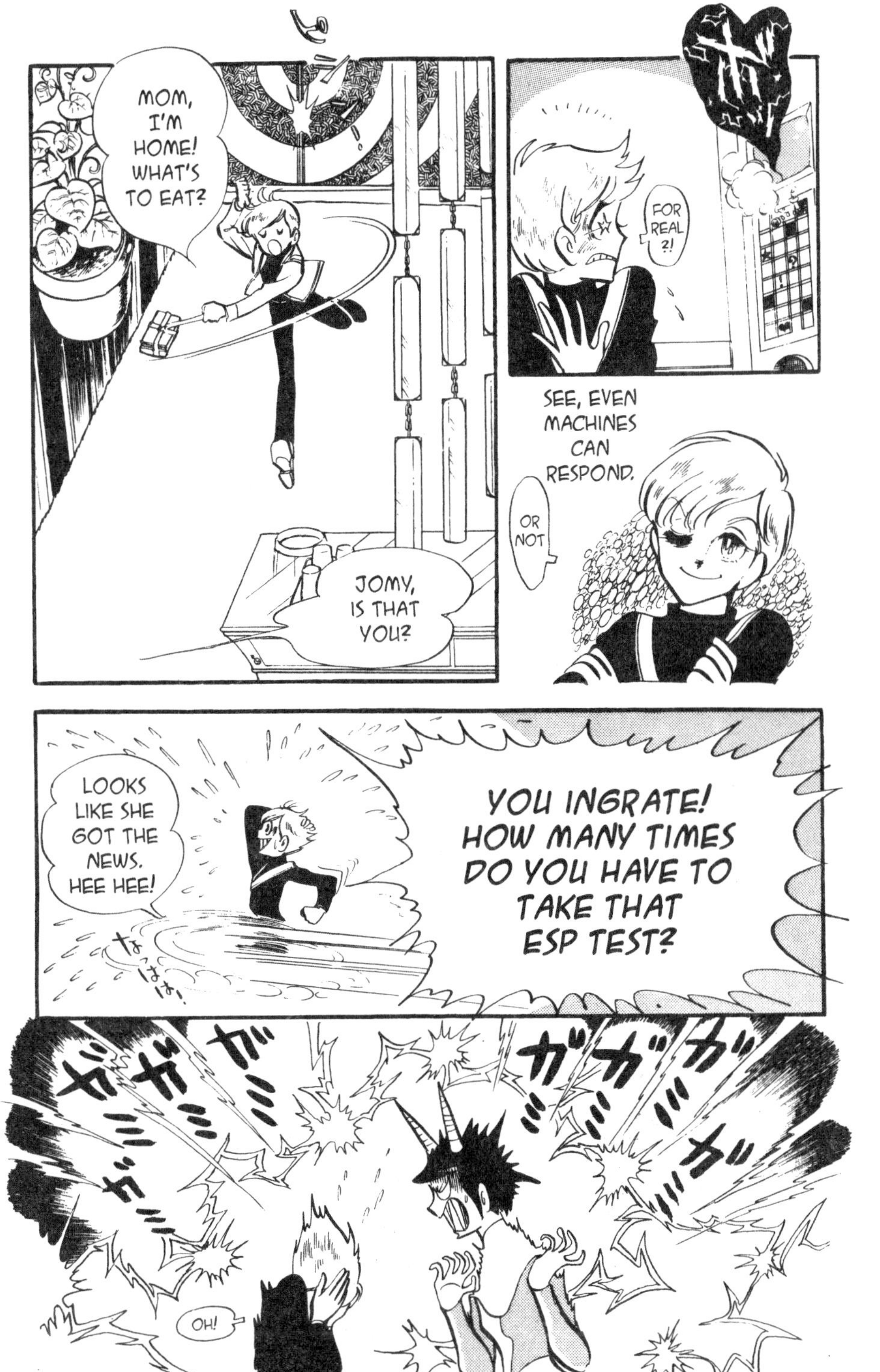
FOR REAL?!
SEE, EVEN MACHINES CAN RESPOND.
OR NOT
MOM, I'M HOME! WHAT'S TO EAT?
JOMY, IS THAT YOU?
YOU INGRATE! HOW MANY TIMES DO YOU HAVE TO TAKE THAT ESP TEST?
LOOKS LIKE SHE GOT THE NEWS. HEE HEE!
OH!

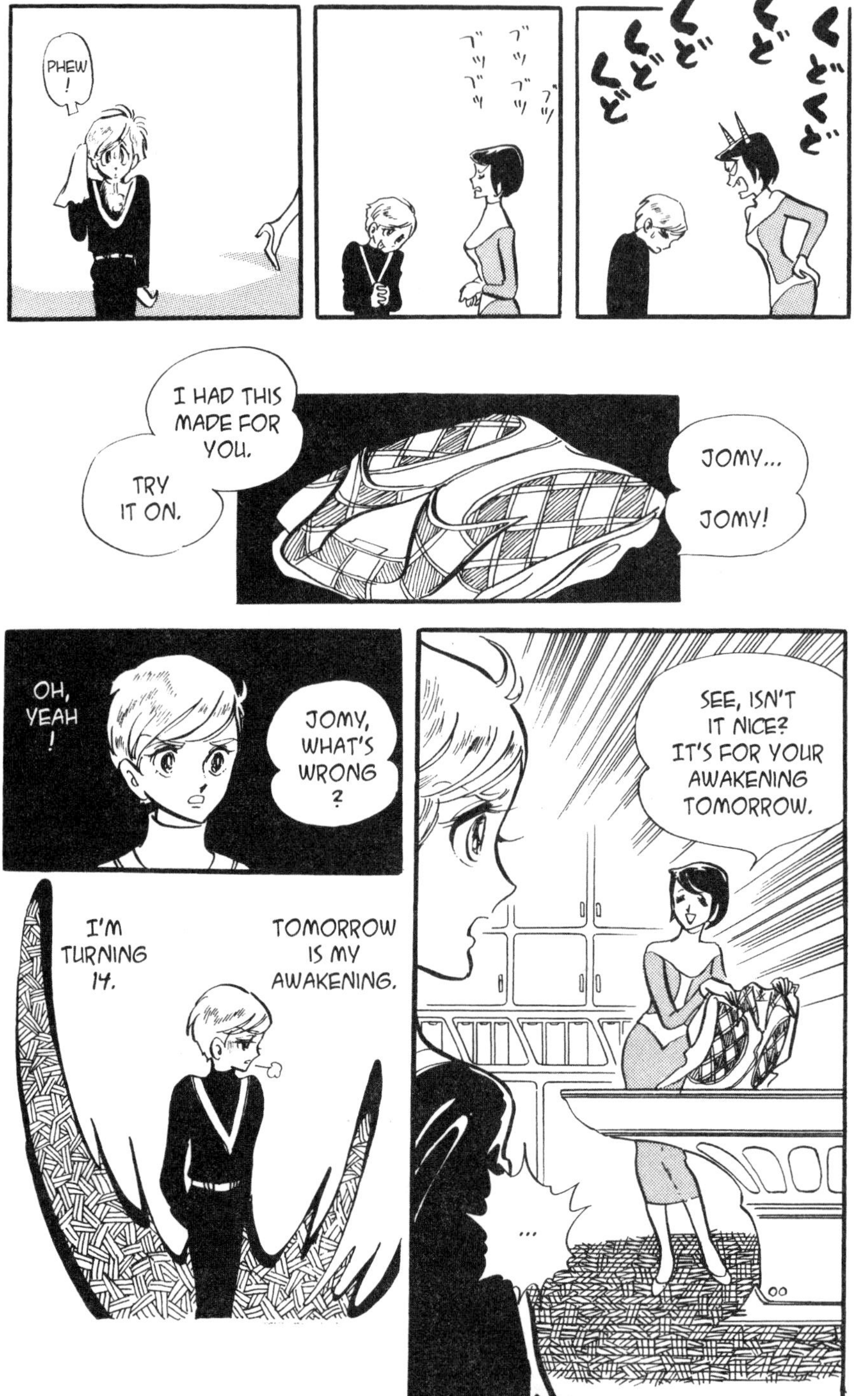
くどくど
くど
くど
くどくど
ブツブツ
ブツブツ
ブツブツ
PHEW!
JOMY...
JOMY!
I HAD THIS MADE FOR YOU.
TRY IT ON.
SEE, ISN'T IT NICE? IT'S FOR YOUR AWAKENING TOMORROW.
...
JOMY, WHAT'S WRONG?
OH, YEAH!
TOMORROW IS MY AWAKENING.
I'M TURNING 14.

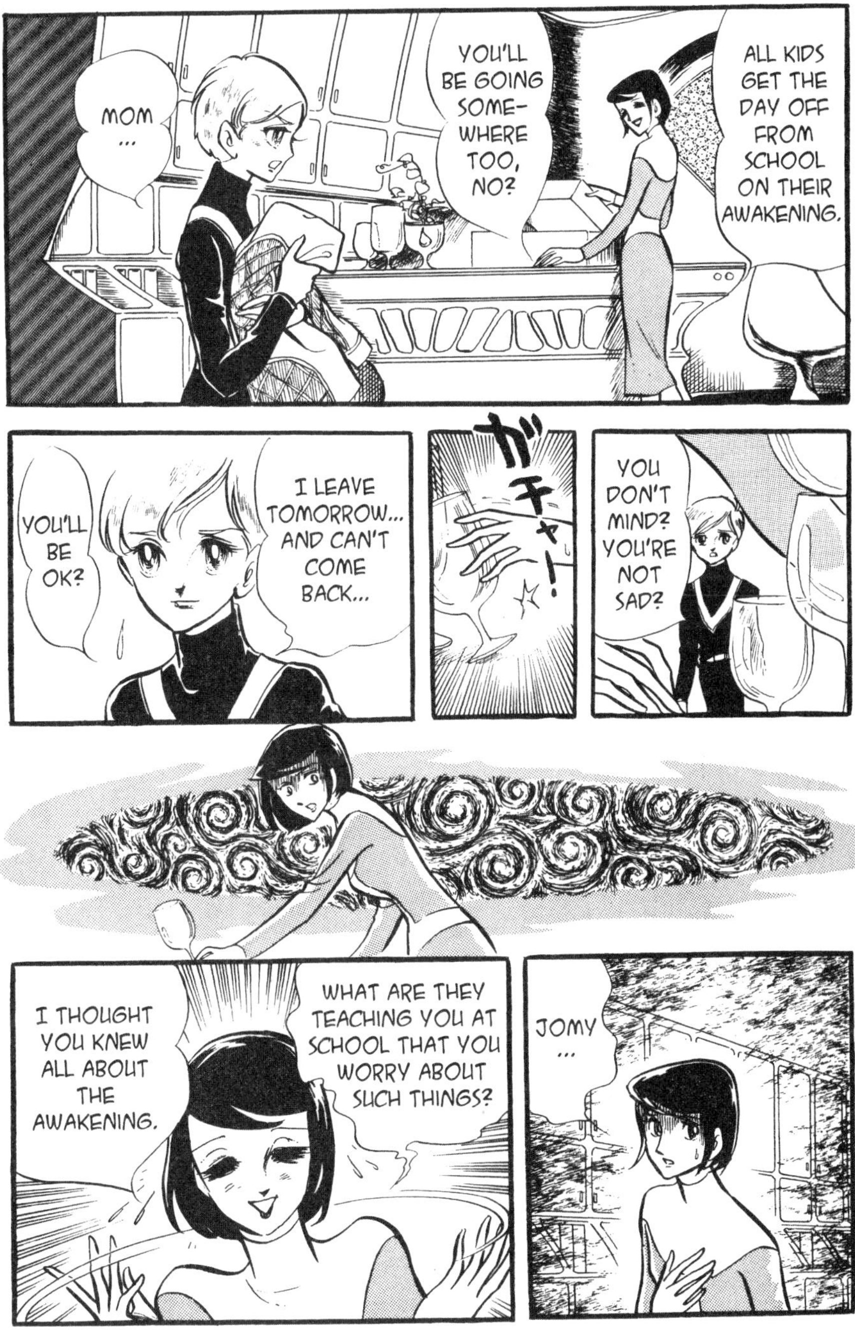
ALL KIDS GET THE DAY OFF FROM SCHOOL ON THEIR AWAKENING.
YOU'LL BE GOING SOME-WHERE TOO, NO?
MOM ...
YOU DON'T MIND? YOU'RE NOT SAD?
ガチャー!
I LEAVE TOMORROW... AND CAN'T COME BACK...
YOU'LL BE OK?
JOMY ...
WHAT ARE THEY TEACHING YOU AT SCHOOL THAT YOU WORRY ABOUT SUCH THINGS?
I THOUGHT YOU KNEW ALL ABOUT THE AWAKENING.

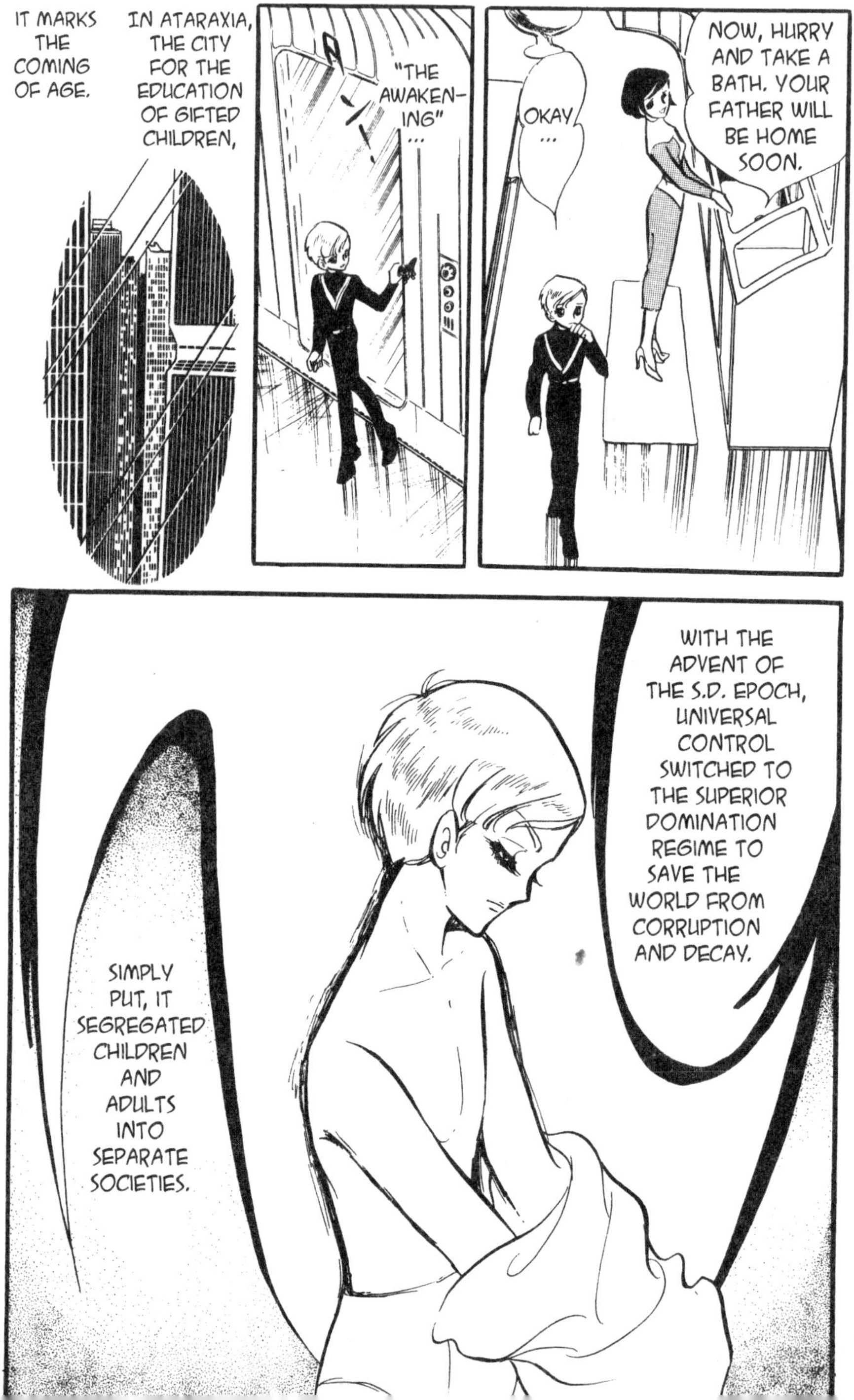
NOW, HURRY AND TAKE A BATH. YOUR FATHER WILL BE HOME SOON.
OKAY ...
"THE AWAKENING" ...
IN ATARAXIA, THE CITY FOR THE EDUCATION OF GIFTED CHILDREN,
IT MARKS THE COMING OF AGE.
WITH THE ADVENT OF THE S.D. EPOCH, UNIVERSAL CONTROL SWITCHED TO THE SUPERIOR DOMINATION REGIME TO SAVE THE WORLD FROM CORRUPTION AND DECAY.
SIMPLY PUT, IT SEGREGATED CHILDREN AND ADULTS INTO SEPARATE SOCIETIES.

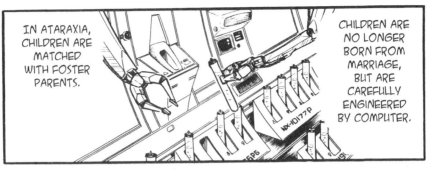

CHILDREN ARE NO LONGER BORN FROM MARRIAGE, BUT ARE CAREFULLY ENGINEERED BY COMPUTER.
IN ATARAXIA, CHILDREN ARE MATCHED WITH FOSTER PARENTS.
TODAY, IT'S EVEN POSSIBLE FOR SOPHISTICATED ANDROIDS TO REAR CHILDREN.
CHILDREN ARE ALWAYS UNDER THE STRICT SUPERVISION OF UNIVERSAL CONTROL.
THEY ARE EDUCATED AND LEAD HEALTHY LIVES INSULATED FROM BAD INFLUENCES.
THEY ARE RASIED TO BE "IMMACULATE" CHILDREN WHO WILL PURIFY ADULT SOCIETY.
HELLO? UNIVERSAL CONTROL?

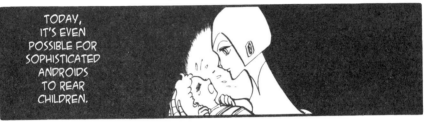

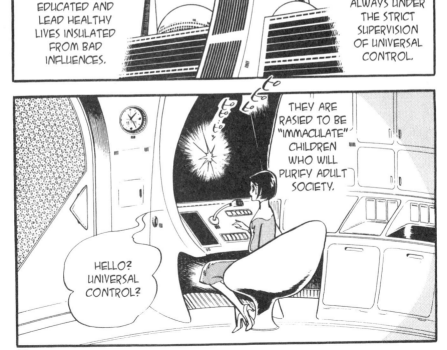

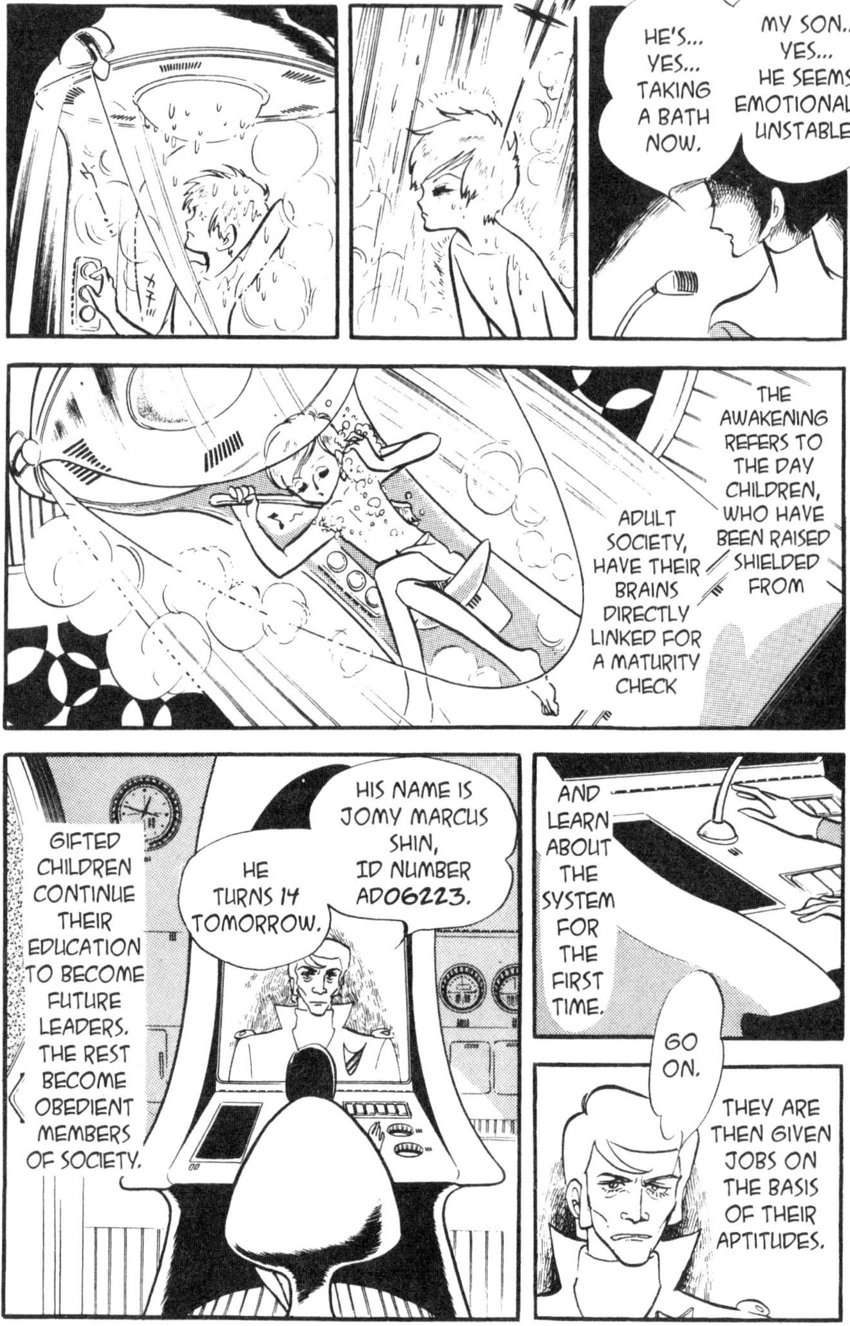
MY SON... YES... HE SEEMS EMOTIONALLY UNSTABLE.
HE'S... YES... TAKING A BATH NOW.
THE AWAKENING REFERS TO THE DAY CHILDREN, WHO HAVE BEEN RAISED SHIELDED FROM
ADULT SOCIETY, HAVE THEIR BRAINS DIRECTLY LINKED FOR A MATURITY CHECK
AND LEARN ABOUT THE SYSTEM FOR THE FIRST TIME.
GO ON.
THEY ARE THEN GIVEN JOBS ON THE BASIS OF THEIR APTITUDES.
HIS NAME IS JOMY MARCUS SHIN, ID NUMBER AD06223.
HE TURNS 14 TOMORROW.
GIFTED CHILDREN CONTINUE THEIR EDUCATION TO BECOME FUTURE LEADERS. THE REST BECOME OBEDIENT MEMBERS OF SOCIETY.

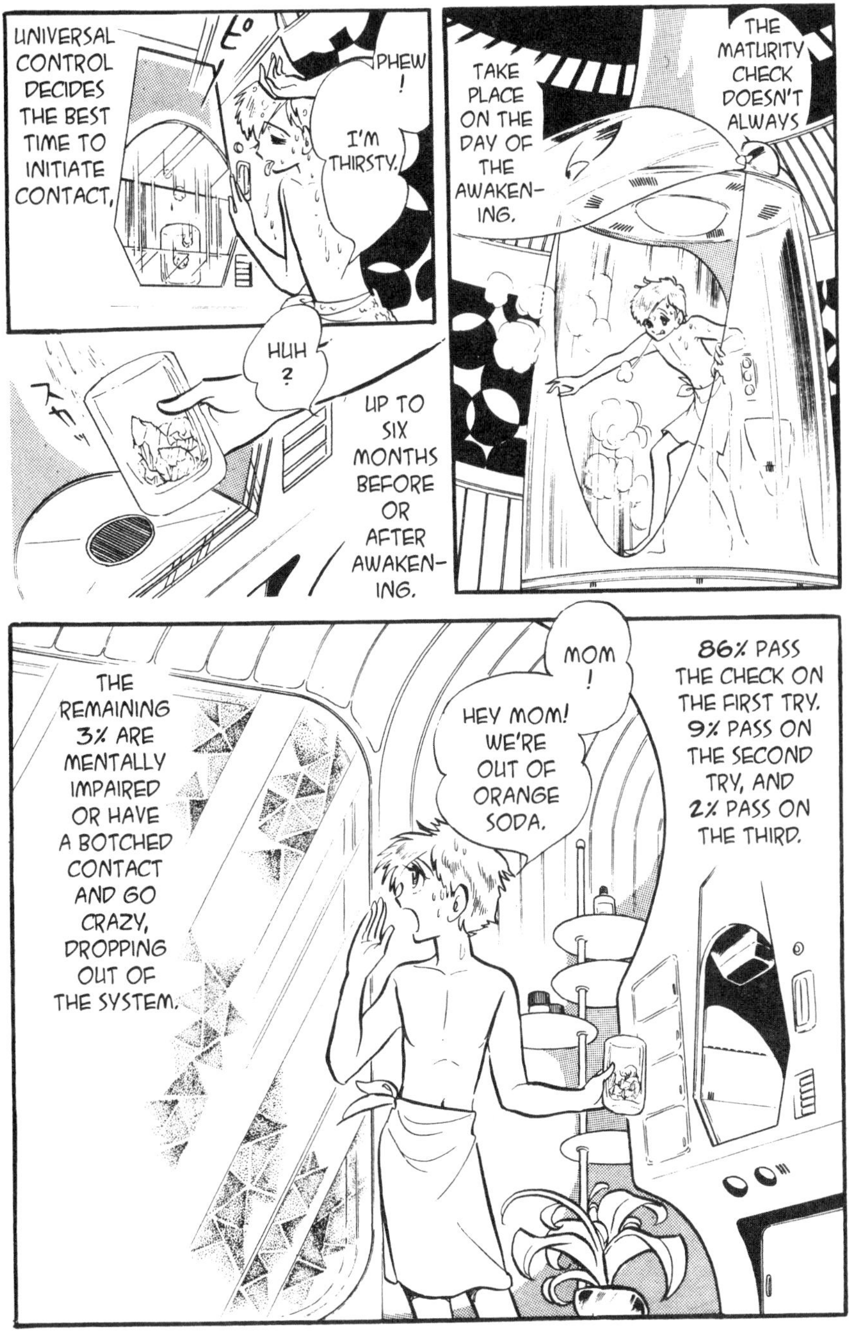
THE MATURITY CHECK DOESN'T ALWAYS
TAKE PLACE ON THE DAY OF THE AWAKEN-ING.
UNIVERSAL CONTROL DECIDES THE BEST TIME TO INITIATE CONTACT,
PHEW!
I'M THIRSTY.
HUH?
UP TO SIX MONTHS BEFORE OR AFTER AWAKEN-ING.
86% PASS THE CHECK ON THE FIRST TRY. 9% PASS ON THE SECOND TRY, AND 2% PASS ON THE THIRD.
MOM!
HEY MOM! WE'RE OUT OF ORANGE SODA.
THE REMAINING 3% ARE MENTALLY IMPAIRED OR HAVE A BOTCHED CONTACT AND GO CRAZY, DROPPING OUT OF THE SYSTEM.

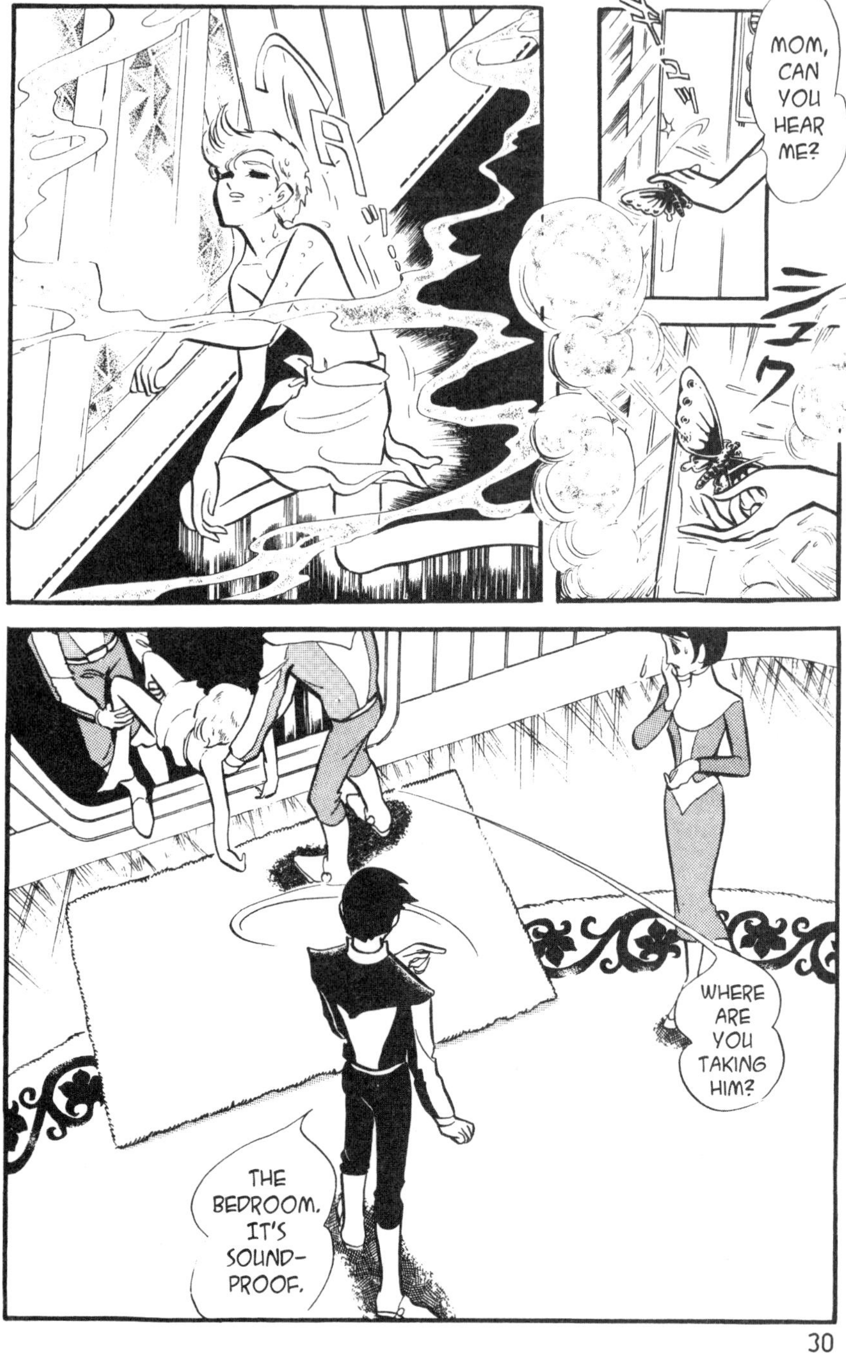
MOM, CAN YOU HEAR ME?
シュワ
WHERE ARE YOU TAKING HIM?
THE BEDROOM. IT'S SOUND-PROOF.

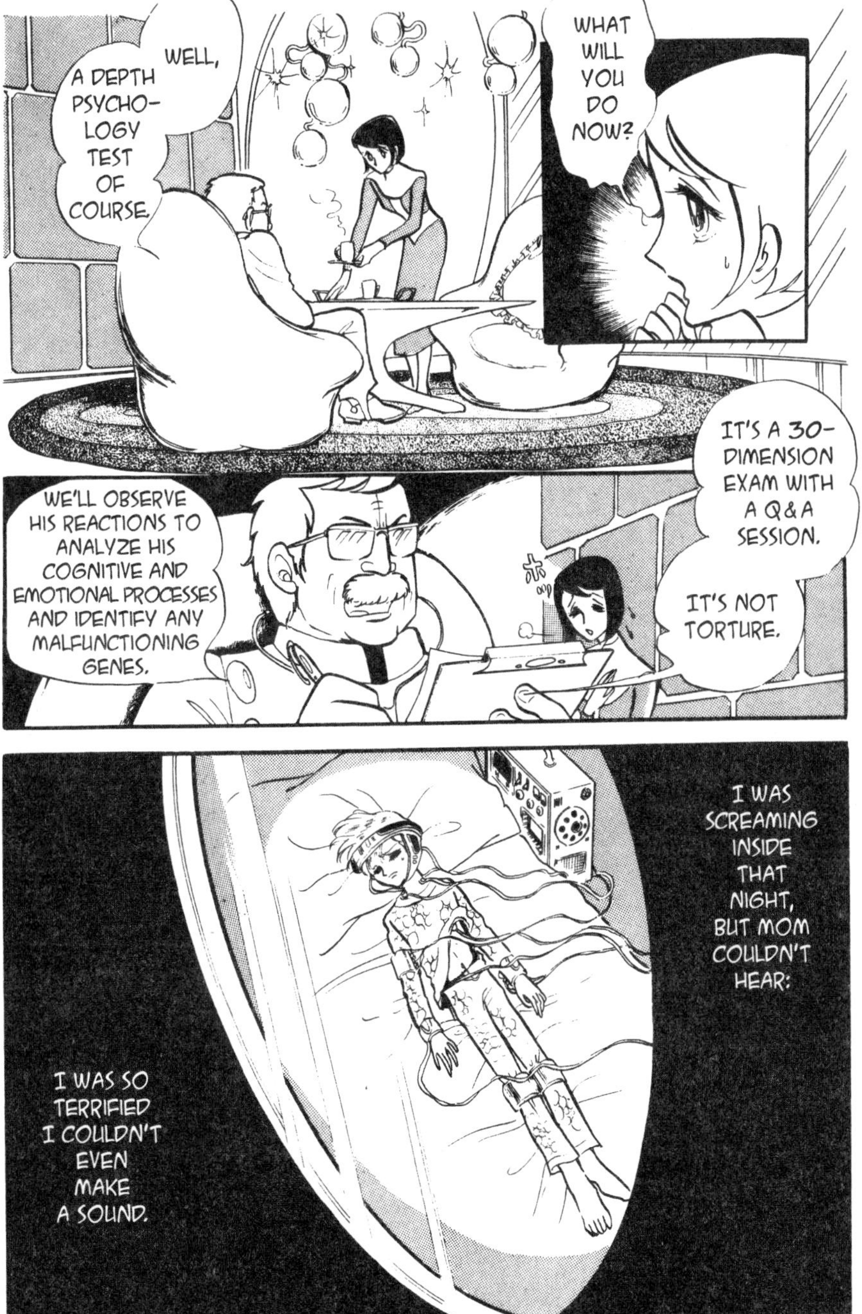
WHAT WILL YOU DO NOW?
WELL, A DEPTH PSYCHOLOGY TEST OF COURSE.
IT'S A 30-DIMENSION EXAM WITH A Q&A SESSION.
IT'S NOT TORTURE.
WE'LL OBSERVE HIS REACTIONS TO ANALYZE HIS COGNITIVE AND EMOTIONAL PROCESSES AND IDENTIFY ANY MALFUNCTIONING GENES.
I WAS SCREAMING INSIDE THAT NIGHT, BUT MOM COULDN'T HEAR:
I WAS SO TERRIFIED I COULDN'T EVEN MAKE A SOUND.

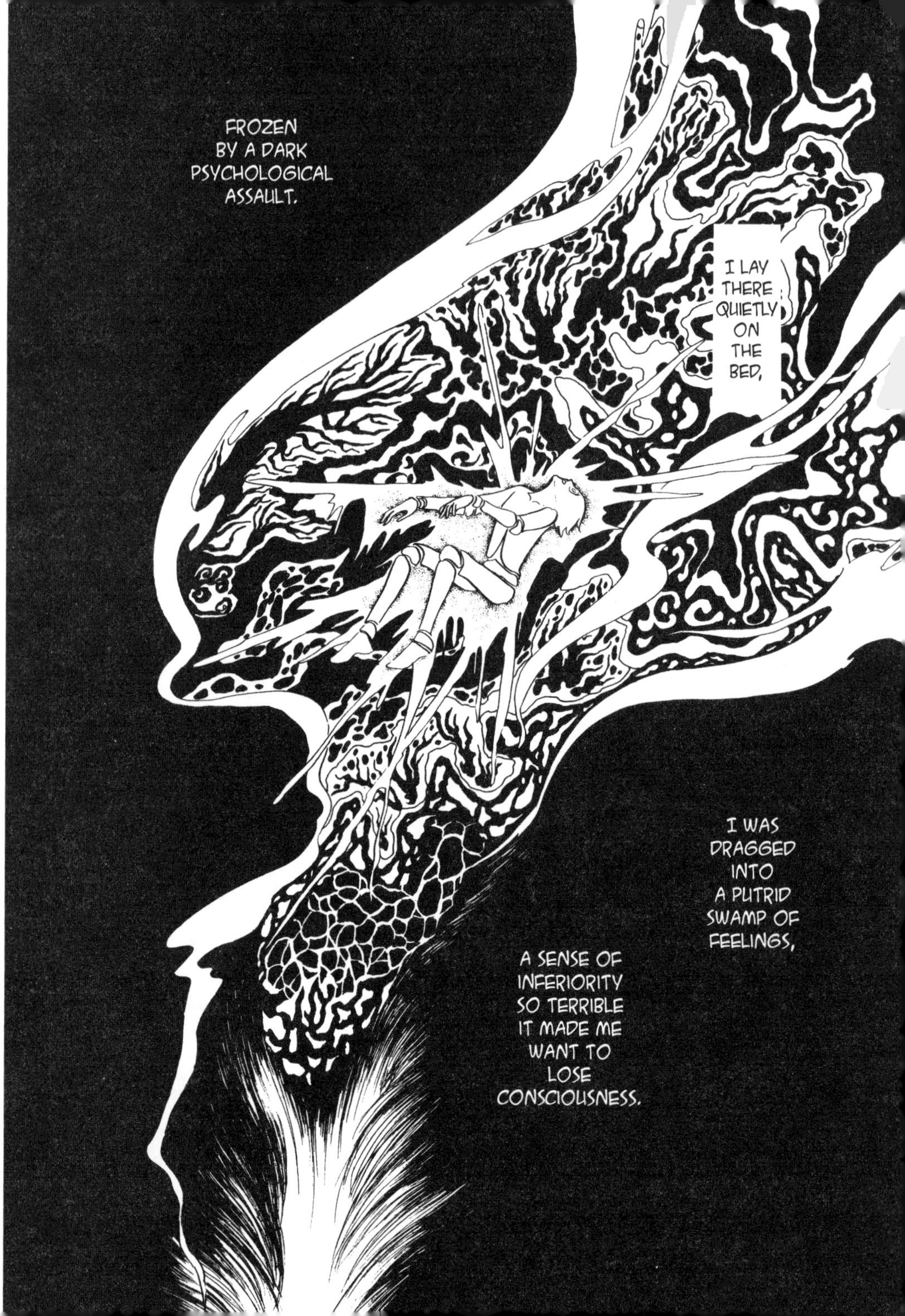
I LAY THERE QUIETLY ON THE BED,
FROZEN BY A DARK PSYCHOLOGICAL ASSAULT.
I WAS DRAGGED INTO A PUTRID SWAMP OF FEELINGS,
A SENSE OF INFERIORITY SO TERRIBLE IT MADE ME WANT TO LOSE CONSCIOUSNESS.

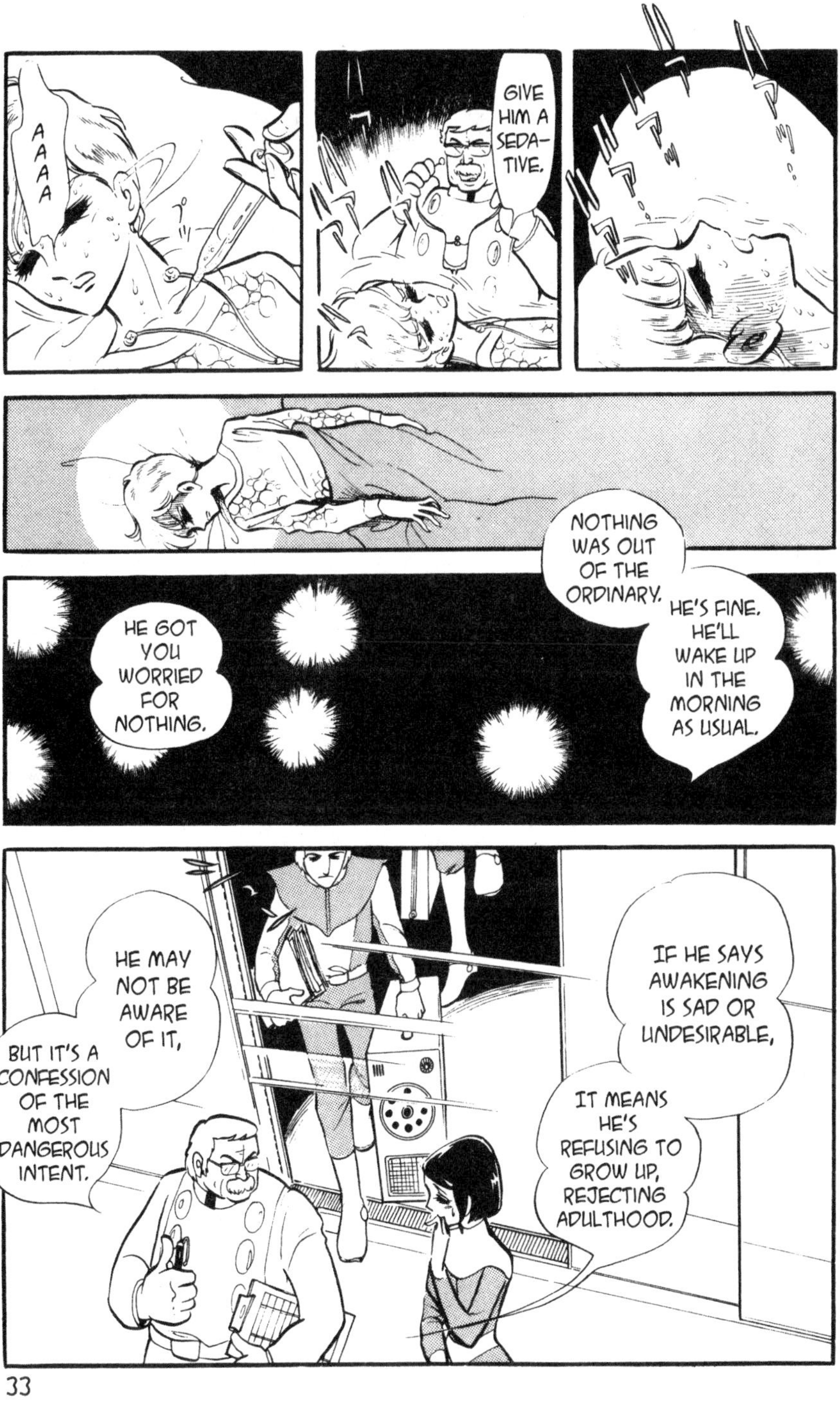
GIVE HIM A SEDATIVE.
AAAA
NOTHING WAS OUT OF THE ORDINARY.
HE'S FINE. HE'LL WAKE UP IN THE MORNING AS USUAL.
HE GOT YOU WORRIED FOR NOTHING.
IF HE SAYS AWAKENING IS SAD OR UNDESIRABLE,
IT MEANS HE'S REFUSING TO GROW UP, REJECTING ADULTHOOD.
HE MAY NOT BE AWARE OF IT,
BUT IT'S A CONFESSION OF THE MOST DANGEROUS INTENT.

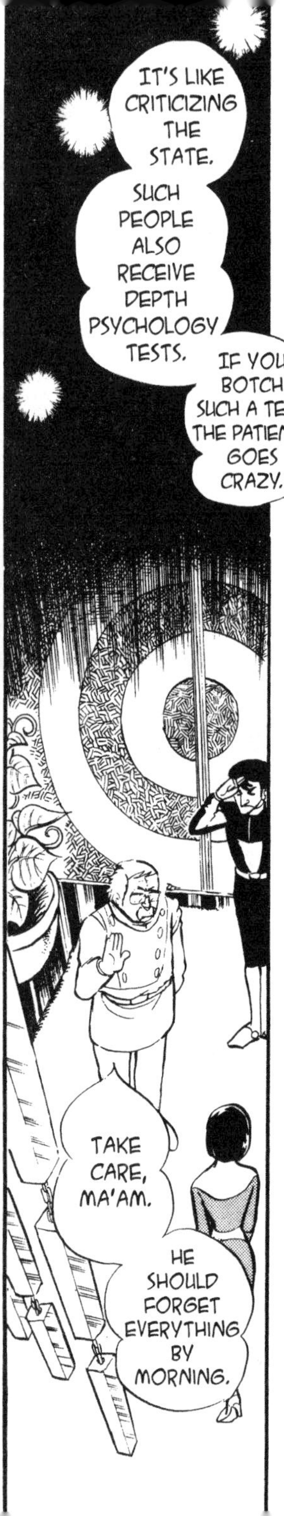
IT'S LIKE CRITICIZING THE STATE.
SUCH PEOPLE ALSO RECEIVE DEPTH PSYCHOLOGY TESTS.
IF YOU BOTCH SUCH A TEST, THE PATIENT GOES CRAZY.
TAKE CARE, MA'AM.
HE SHOULD FORGET EVERYTHING BY MORNING.
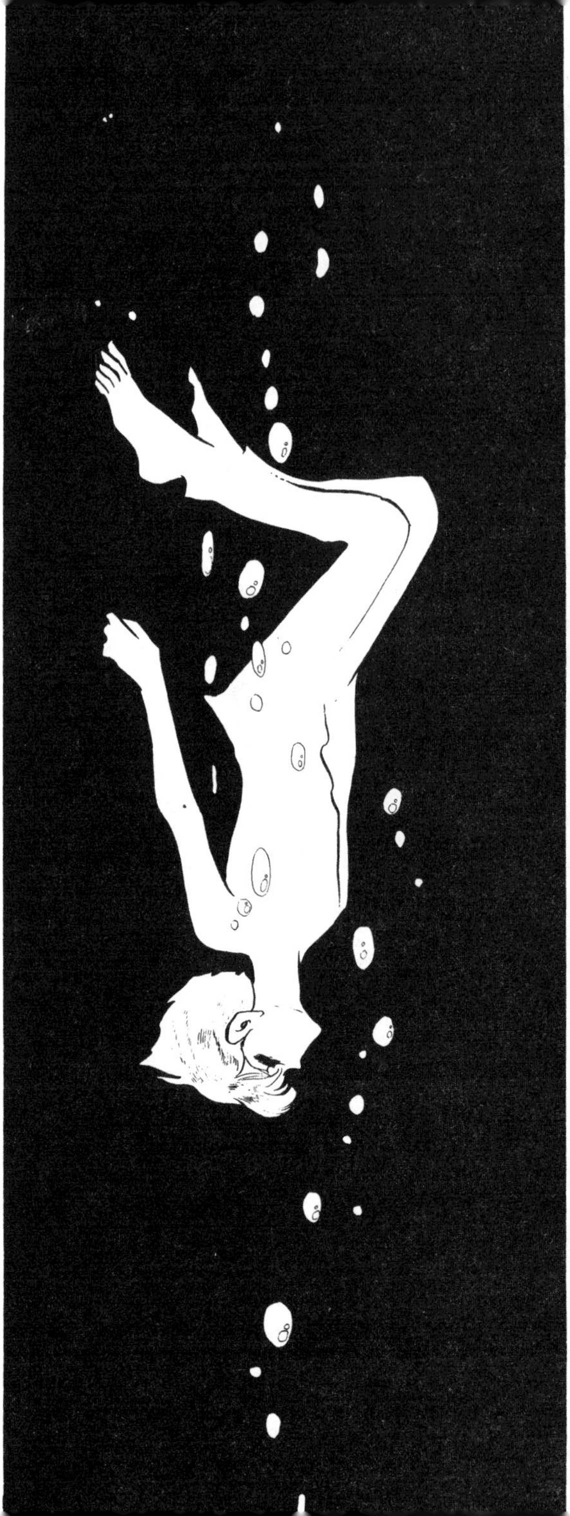

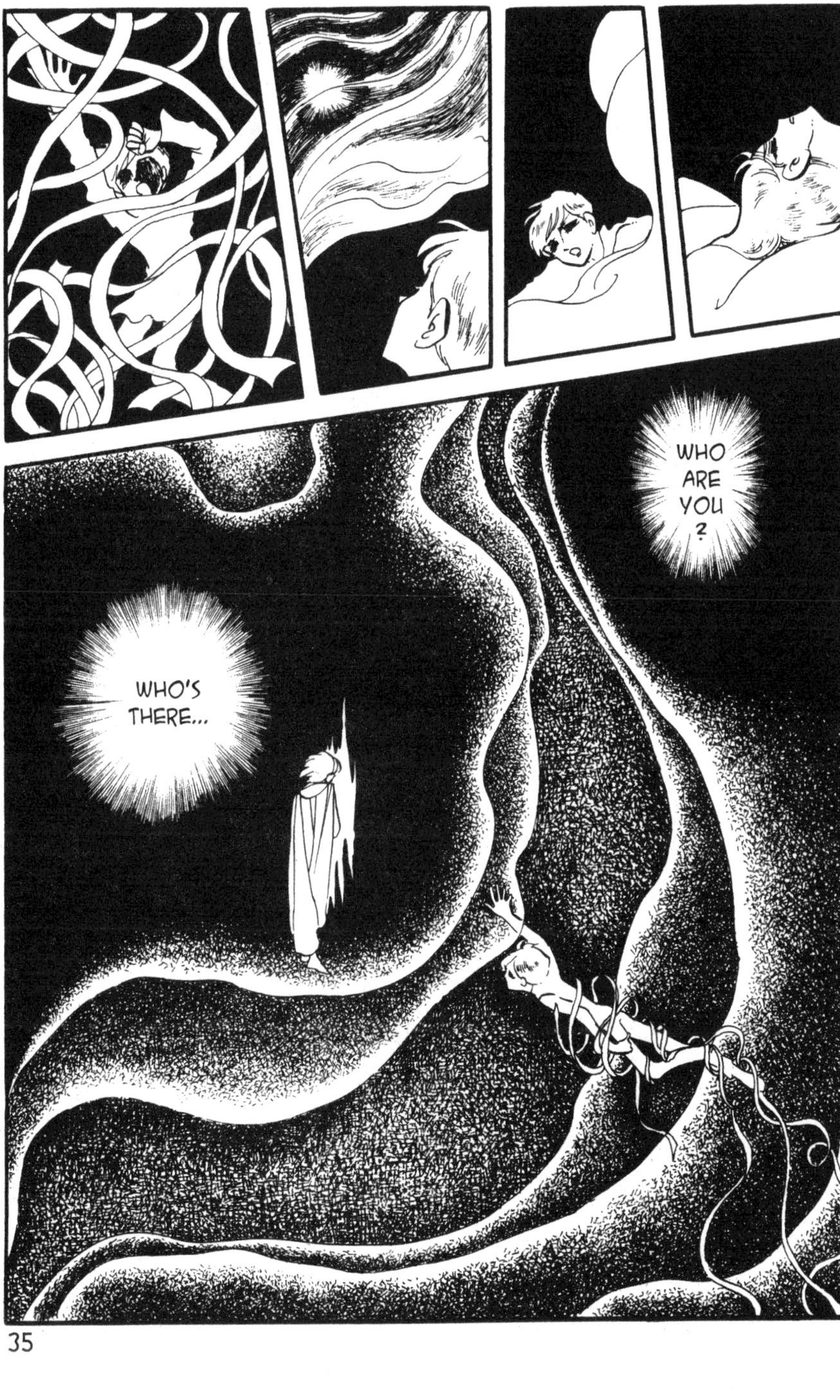
WHO ARE YOU ?
WHO'S THERE...

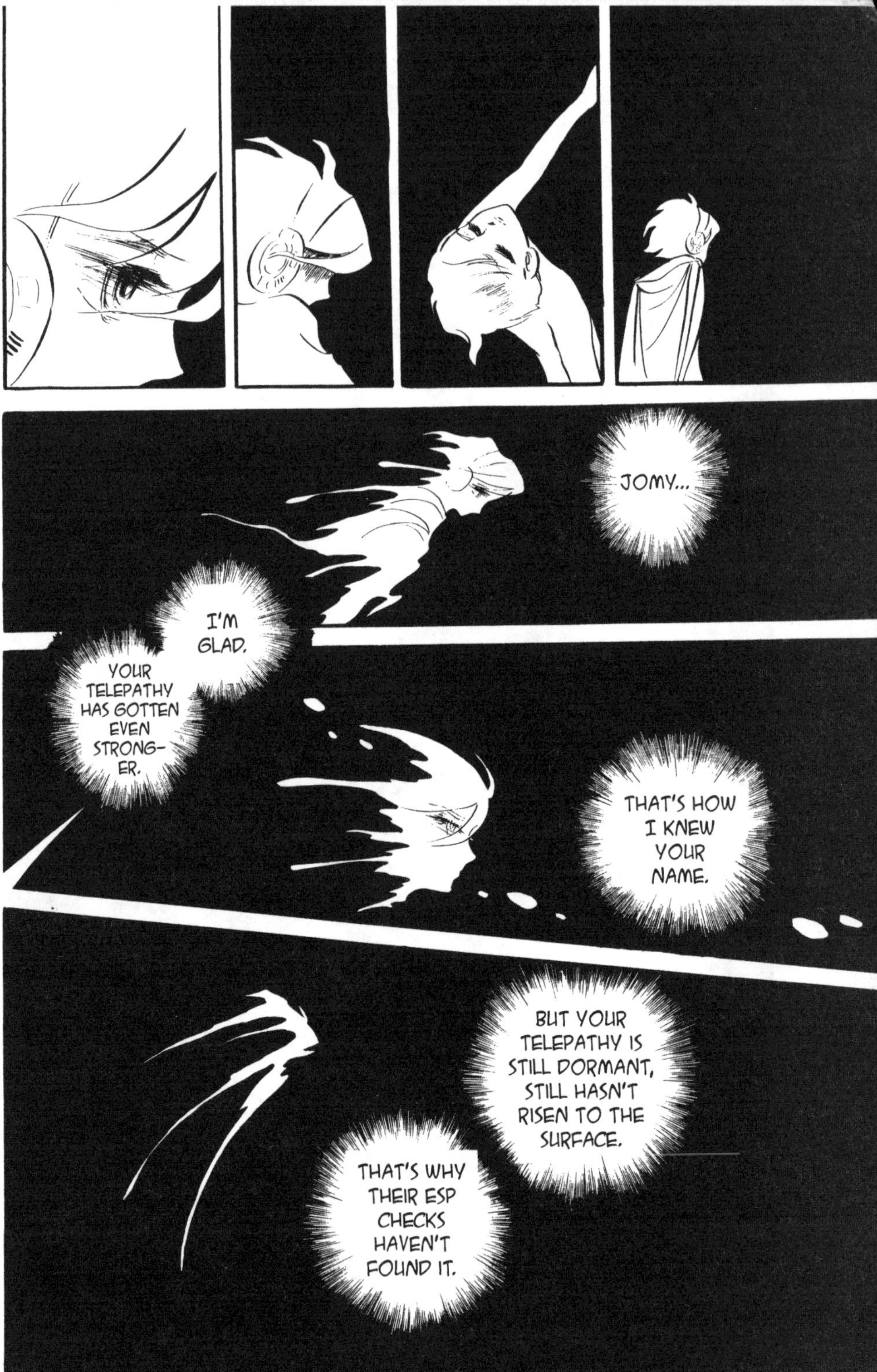
JOMY...
I'M GLAD.
YOUR TELEPATHY HAS GOTTEN EVEN STRONG-ER.
THAT'S HOW I KNEW YOUR NAME.
BUT YOUR TELEPATHY IS STILL DORMANT, STILL HASN'T RISEN TO THE SURFACE.
THAT'S WHY THEIR ESP CHECKS HAVEN'T FOUND IT.

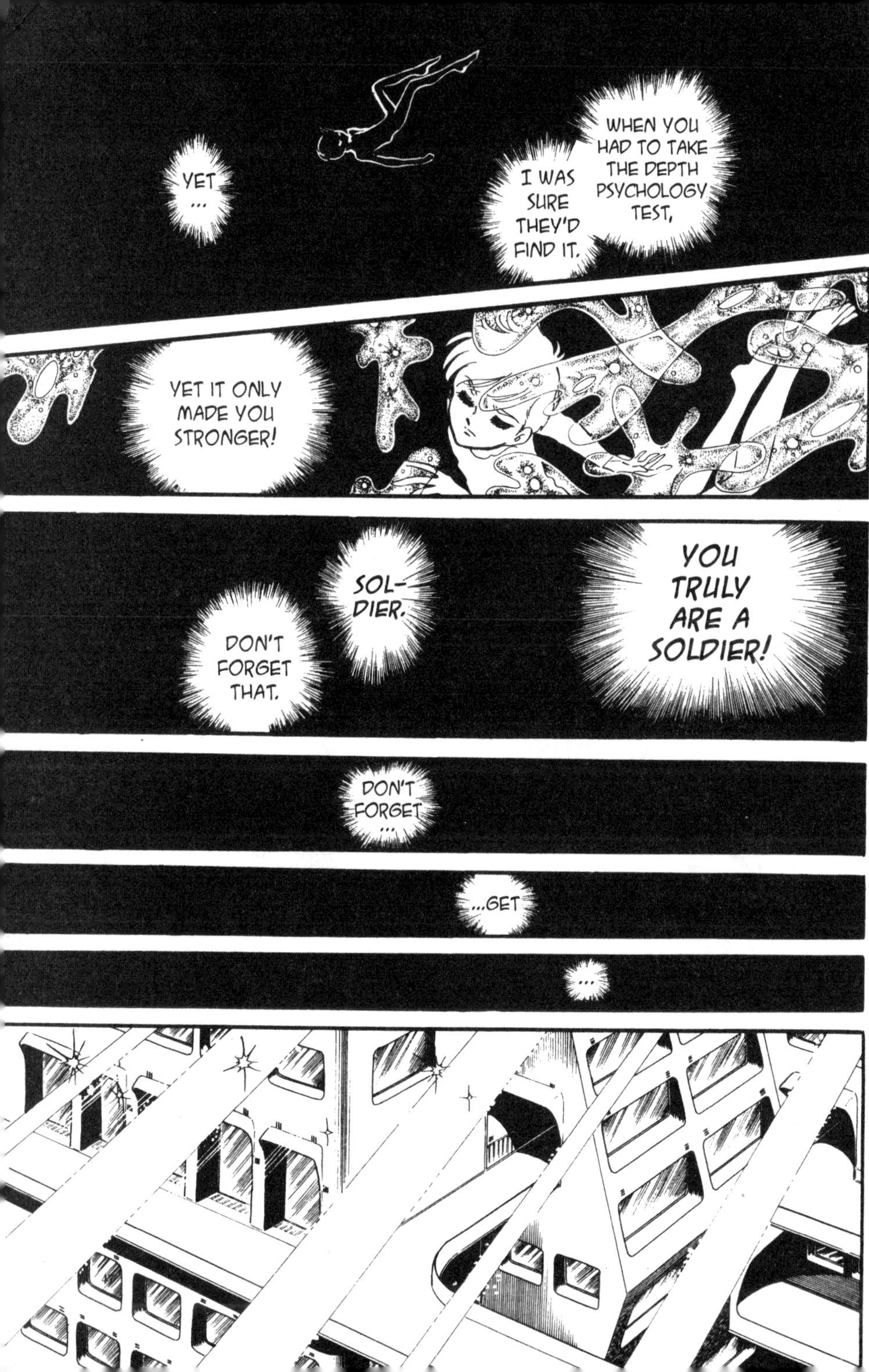
WHEN YOU HAD TO TAKE THE DEPTH PSYCHOLOGY TEST,
I WAS SURE THEY'D FIND IT.
YET ...
YET IT ONLY MADE YOU STRONGER!
YOU TRULY ARE A SOLDIER!
SOL- DIER.
DON'T FORGET THAT.
DON'T FORGET ...
...GET
...

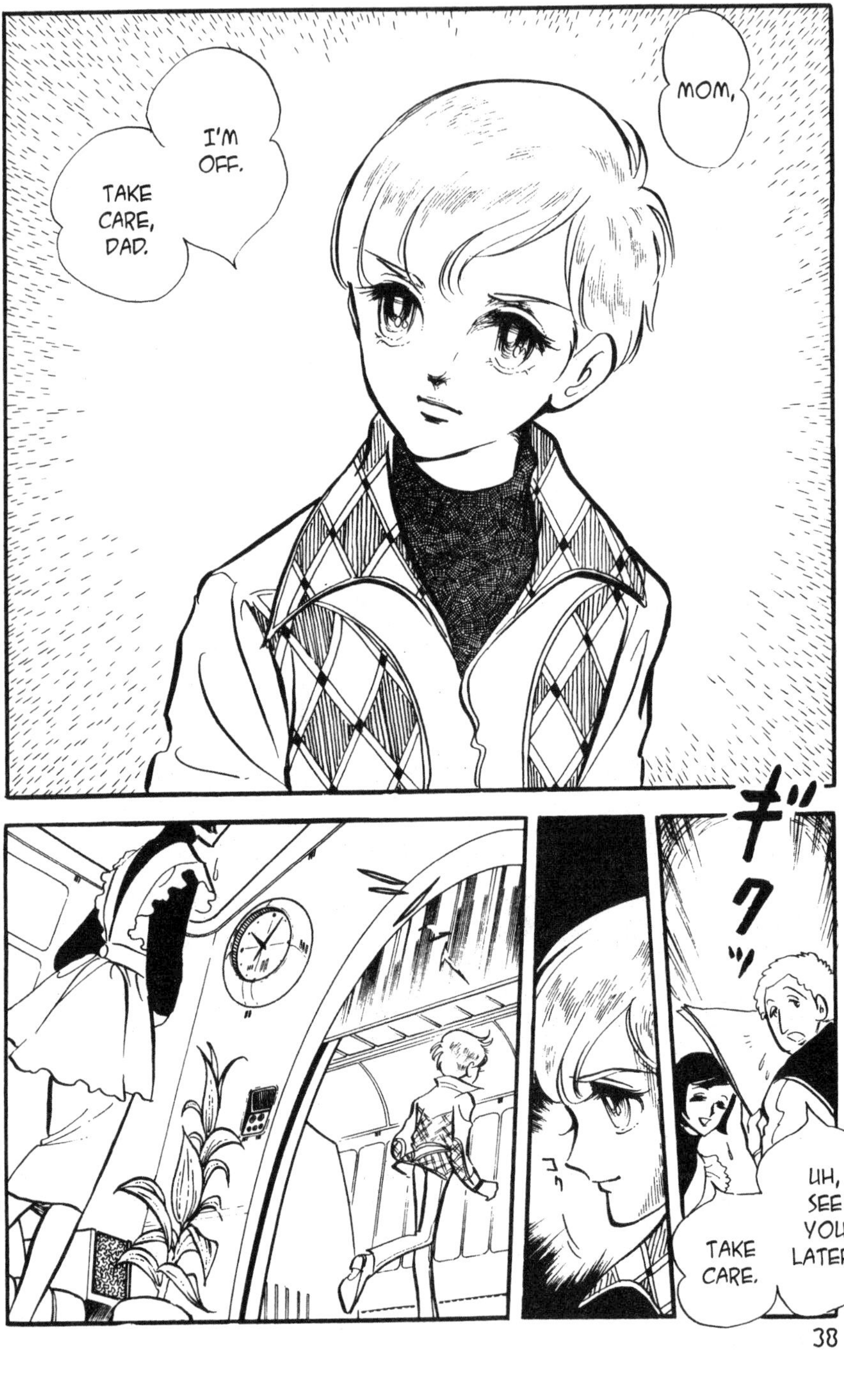
MOM,
I'M OFF.
TAKE CARE, DAD.
ギクッ
UH, SEE YOU LATER.
TAKE CARE.

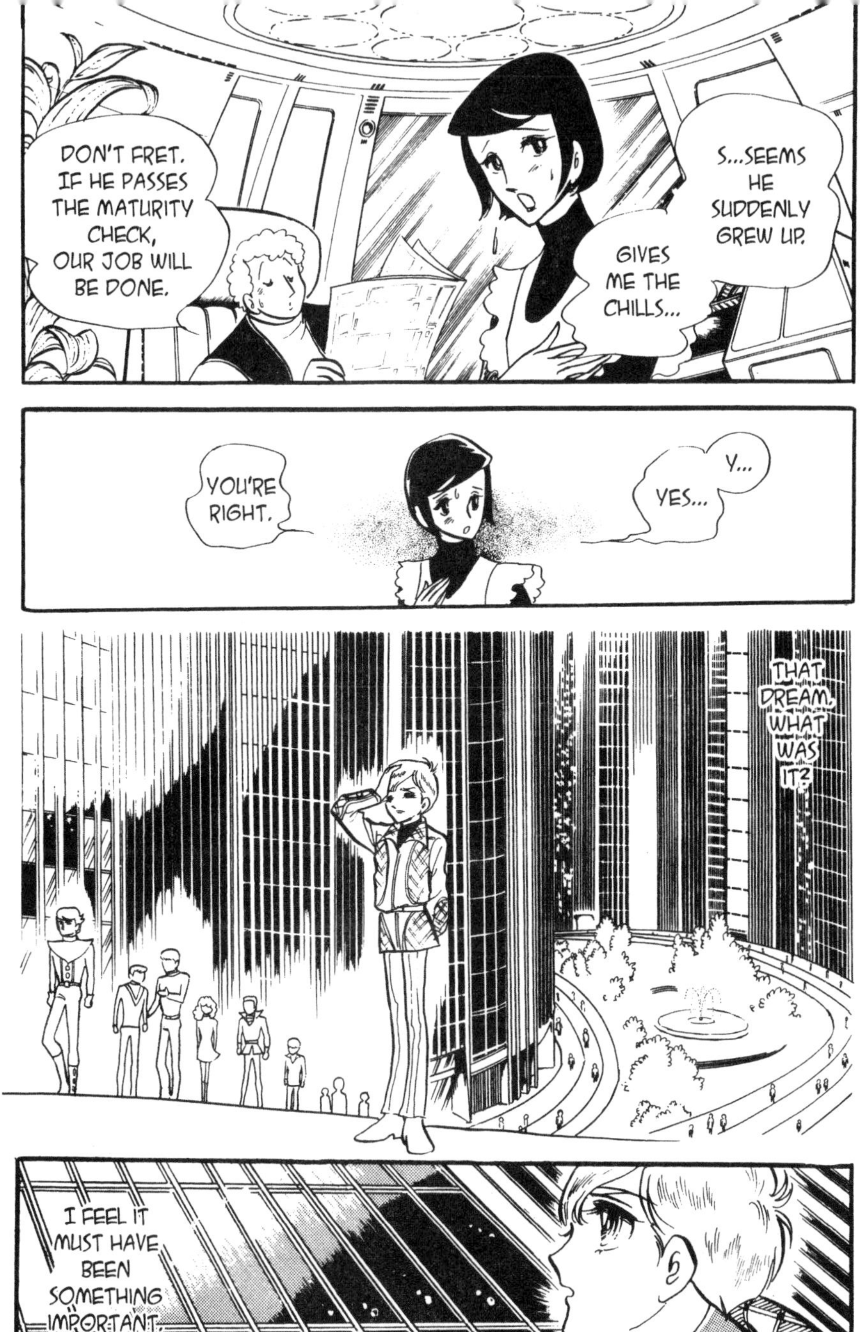
S...SEEMS HE SUDDENLY GREW UP.
GIVES ME THE CHILLS...
DON'T FRET. IF HE PASSES THE MATURITY CHECK, OUR JOB WILL BE DONE.
Y...
YES...
YOU'RE RIGHT.
THAT DREAM, WHAT WAS IT?
I FEEL IT MUST HAVE BEEN SOMETHING IMPORTANT.

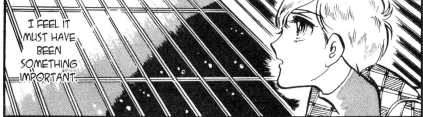

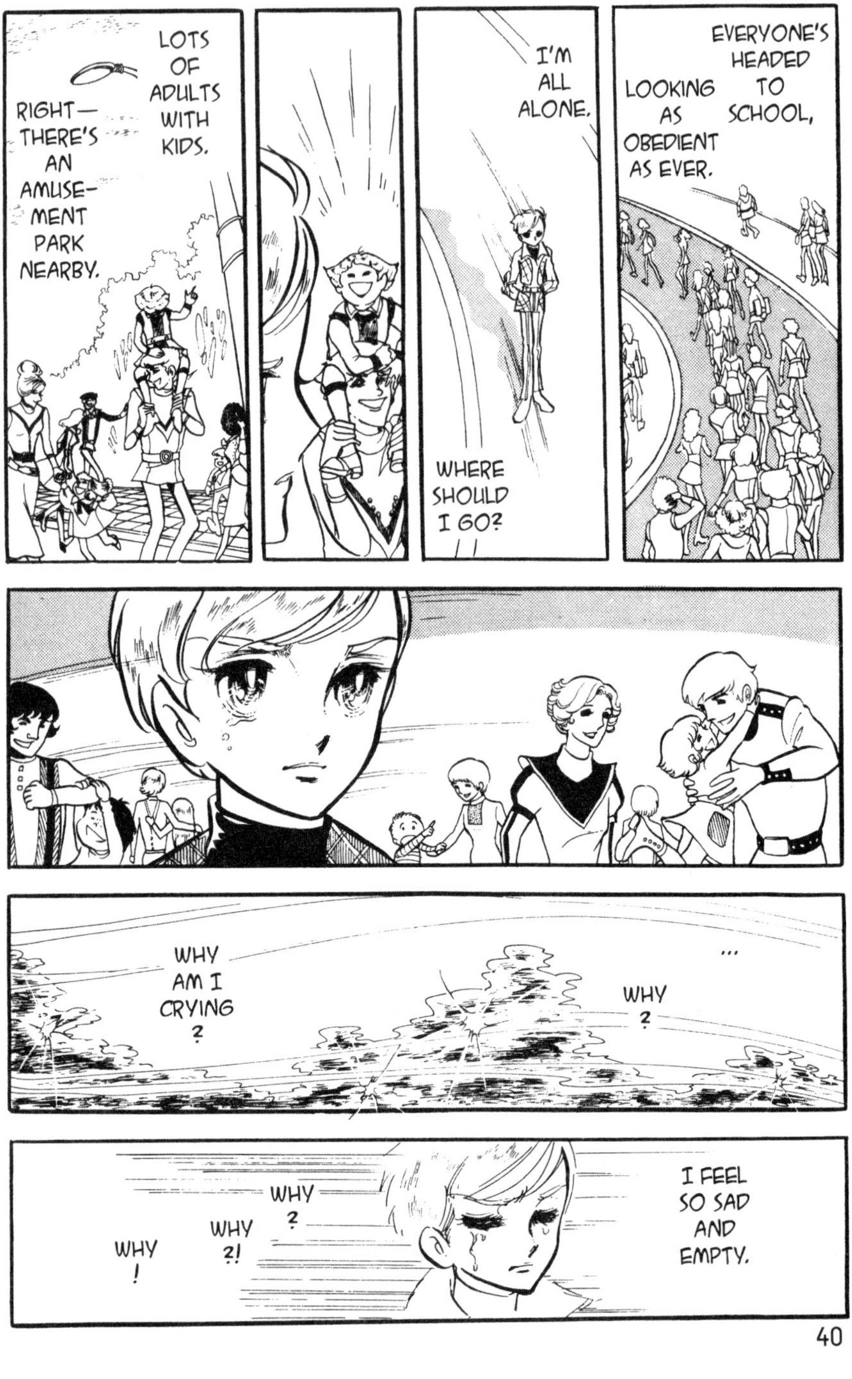
EVERYONE'S HEADED TO SCHOOL,
LOOKING AS OBEDIENT AS EVER.
I'M ALL ALONE.
WHERE SHOULD I GO?
LOTS OF ADULTS WITH KIDS.
RIGHT— THERE'S AN AMUSEMENT PARK NEARBY.
...
WHY?
WHY AM I CRYING?
I FEEL SO SAD AND EMPTY.
WHY?
WHY?!
WHY!

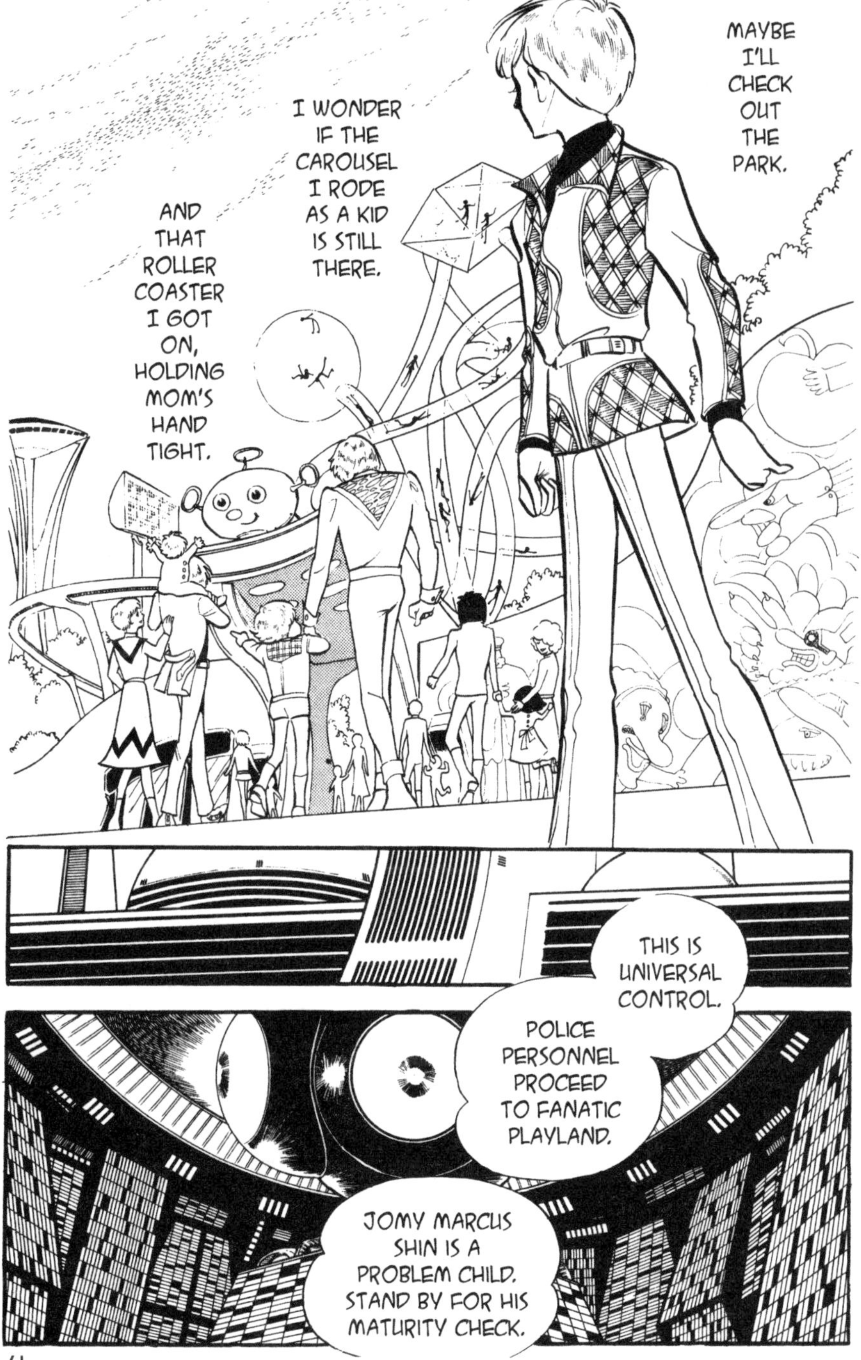
MAYBE I'LL CHECK OUT THE PARK.
I WONDER IF THE CAROUSEL I RODE AS A KID IS STILL THERE.
AND THAT ROLLER COASTER I GOT ON, HOLDING MOM'S HAND TIGHT.
THIS IS UNIVERSAL CONTROL.
POLICE PERSONNEL PROCEED TO FANATIC PLAYLAND.
JOMY MARCUS SHIN IS A PROBLEM CHILD. STAND BY FOR HIS MATURITY CHECK.

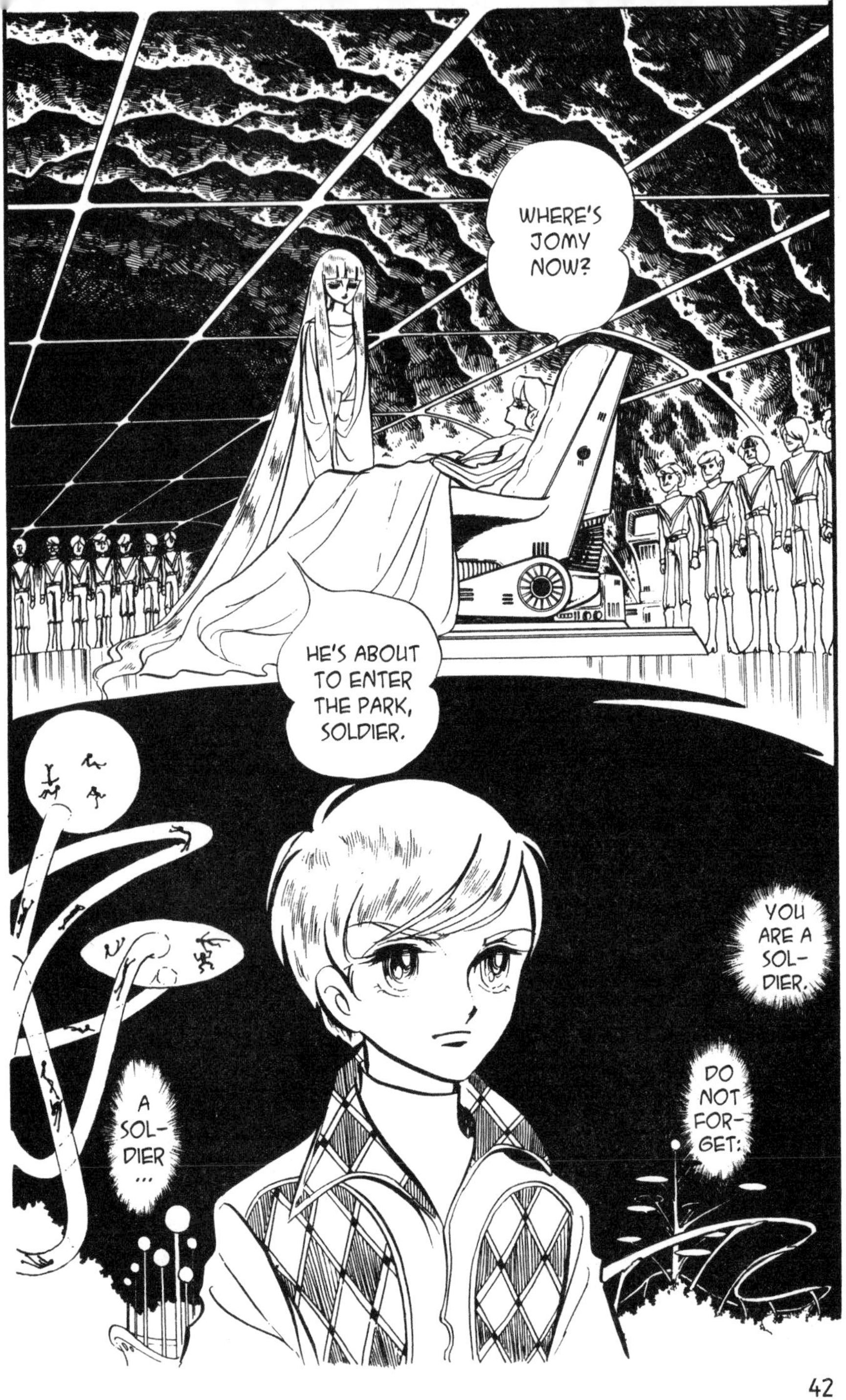
WHERE'S JOMY NOW?
HE'S ABOUT TO ENTER THE PARK, SOLDIER.
YOU ARE A SOL-DIER.
DO NOT FOR-GET:
A SOL-DIER ...

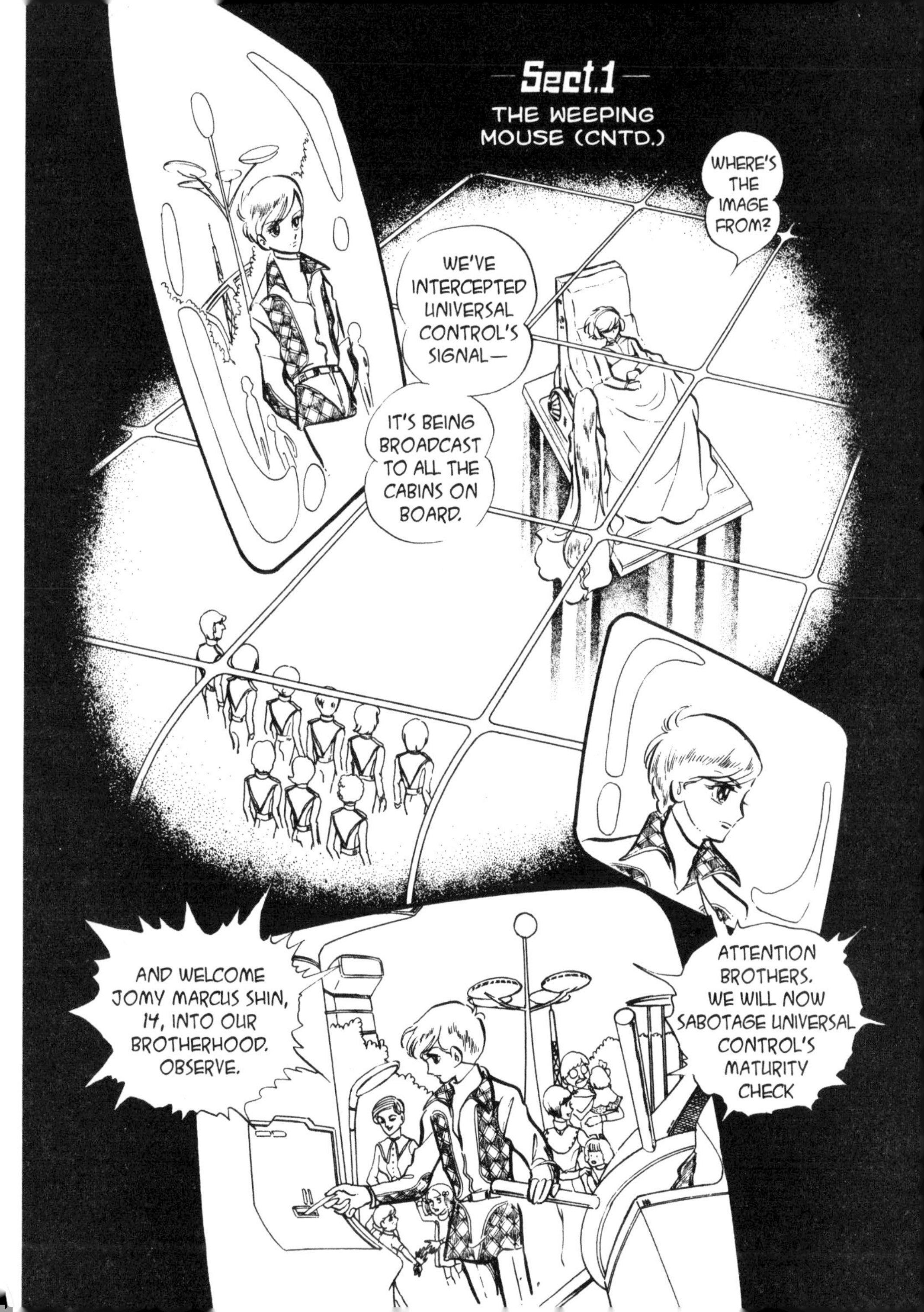
Sect.1
THE WEEPING MOUSE (CNTD.)
WHERE'S THE IMAGE FROM?
WE'VE INTERCEPTED UNIVERSAL CONTROL'S SIGNAL—
IT'S BEING BROADCAST TO ALL THE CABINS ON BOARD.
ATTENTION BROTHERS. WE WILL NOW SABOTAGE UNIVERSAL CONTROL'S MATURITY CHECK
AND WELCOME JOMY MARCUS SHIN, 14, INTO OUR BROTHERHOOD. OBSERVE.

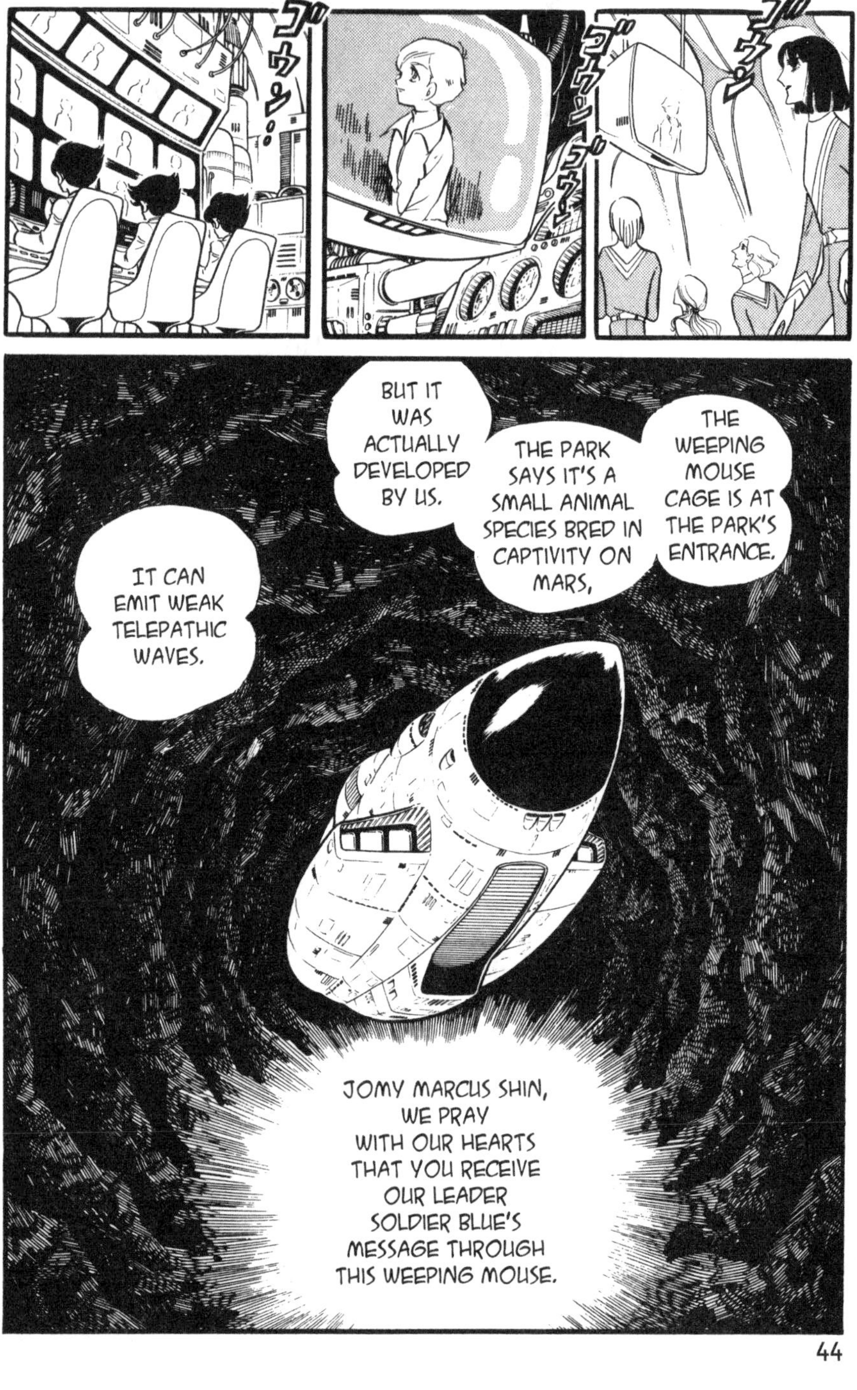
ゴウン
ゴウン ゴウン ゴウン
ゴウン…
THE WEEPING MOUSE CAGE IS AT THE PARK'S ENTRANCE.
THE PARK SAYS IT'S A SMALL ANIMAL SPECIES BRED IN CAPTIVITY ON MARS,
BUT IT WAS ACTUALLY DEVELOPED BY US.
IT CAN EMIT WEAK TELEPATHIC WAVES.
JOMY MARCUS SHIN, WE PRAY WITH OUR HEARTS THAT YOU RECEIVE OUR LEADER SOLDIER BLUE'S MESSAGE THROUGH THIS WEEPING MOUSE.

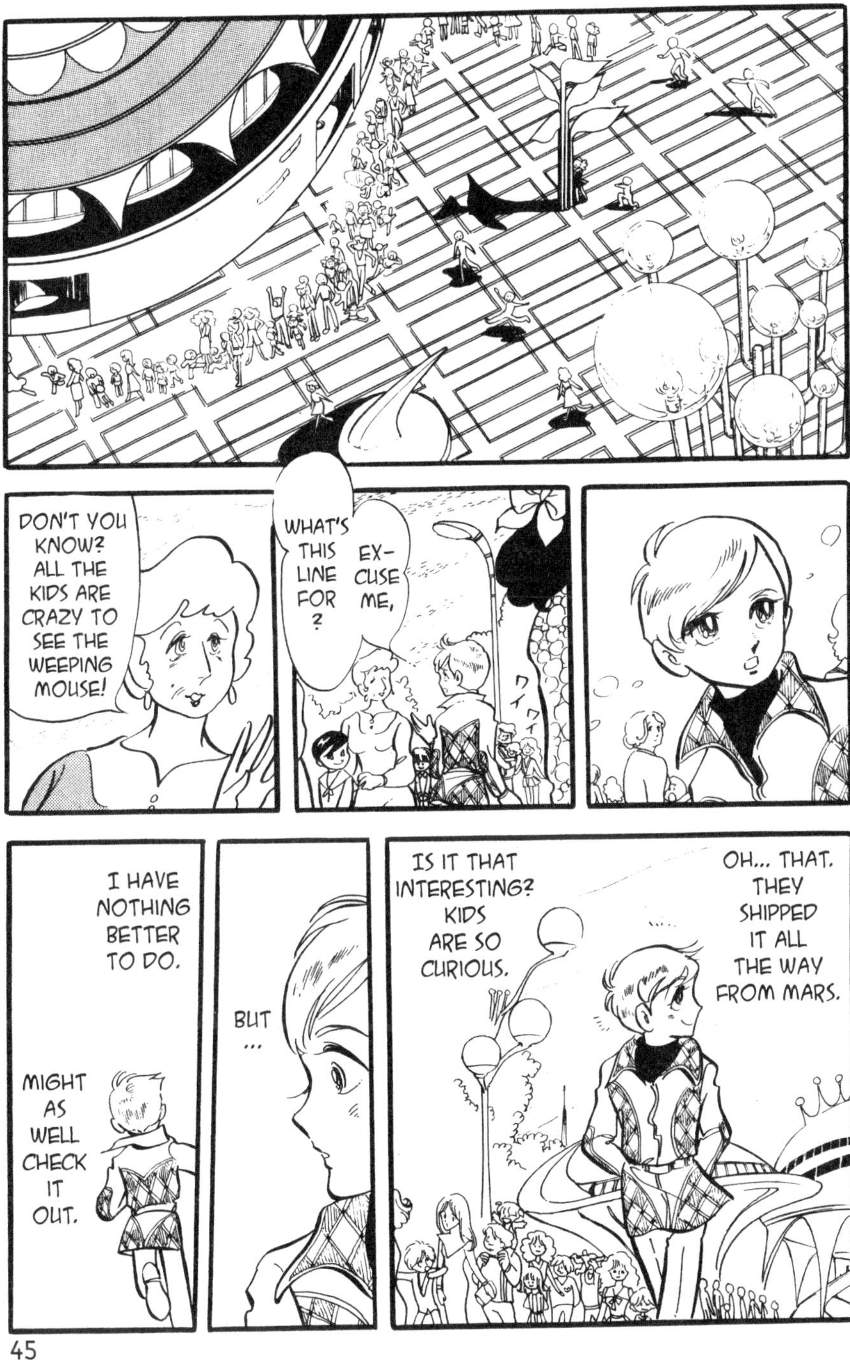
EX-CUSE ME,
WHAT'S THIS LINE FOR?
ワイワイ
DON'T YOU KNOW? ALL THE KIDS ARE CRAZY TO SEE THE WEEPING MOUSE!
OH... THAT. THEY SHIPPED IT ALL THE WAY FROM MARS.
IS IT THAT INTERESTING? KIDS ARE SO CURIOUS.
....
BUT ...
I HAVE NOTHING BETTER TO DO.
MIGHT AS WELL CHECK IT OUT.

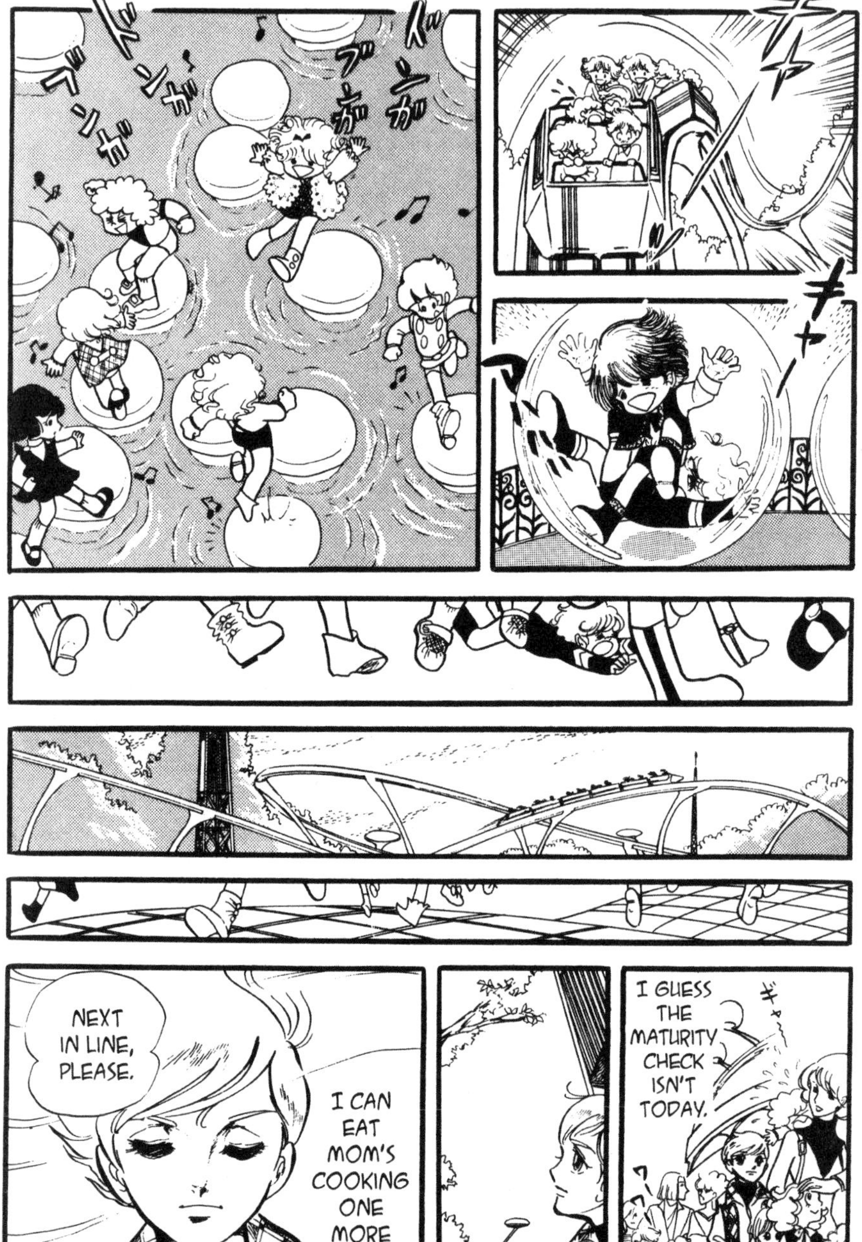
I GUESS THE MATURITY CHECK ISN'T TODAY.
NEXT IN LINE, PLEASE.
I CAN EAT MOM'S COOKING ONE MORE TIME.

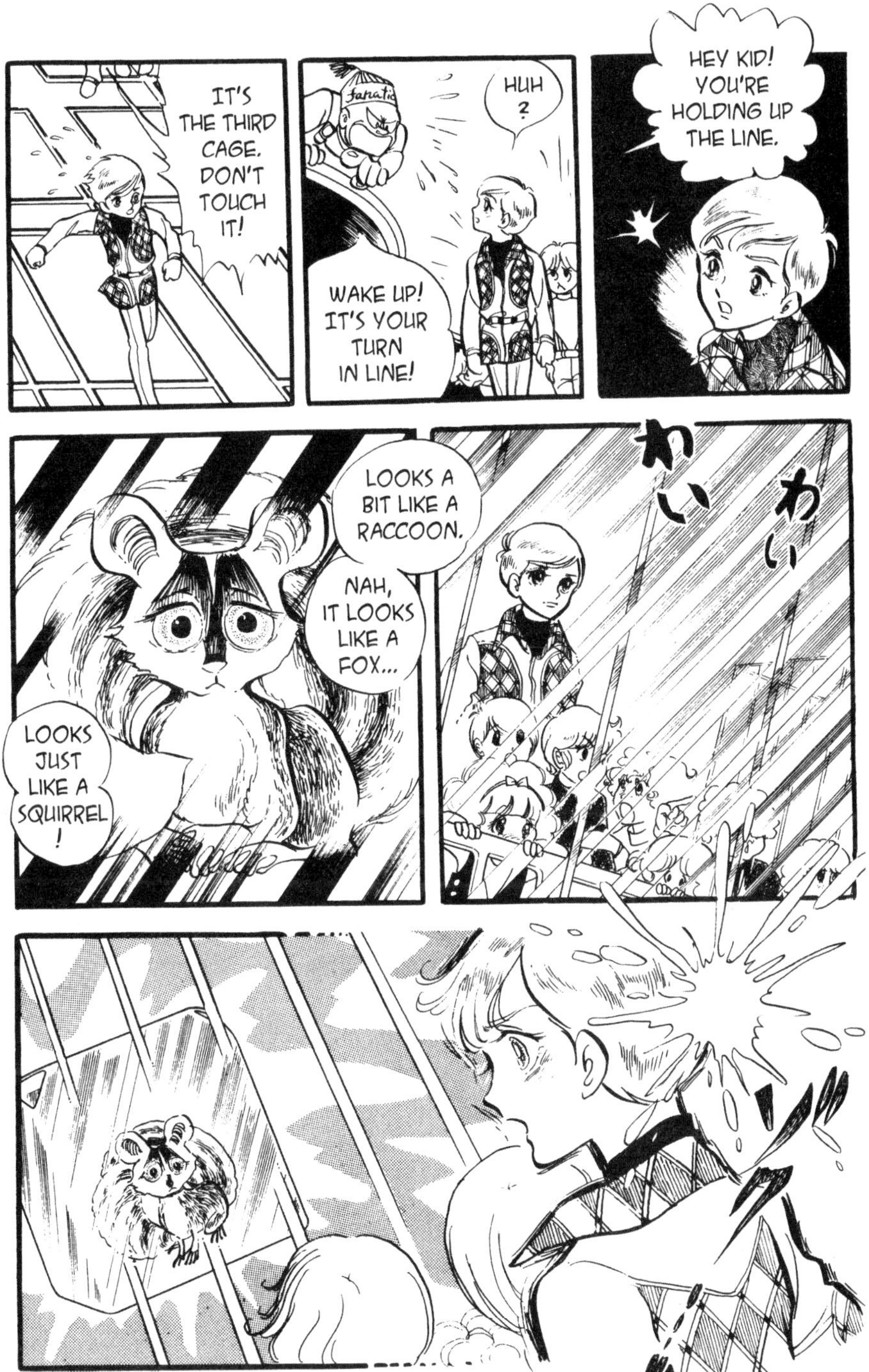
HEY KID! YOU'RE HOLDING UP THE LINE.
HUH ?
WAKE UP! IT'S YOUR TURN IN LINE!
IT'S THE THIRD CAGE. DON'T TOUCH IT!
わい
わい
LOOKS A BIT LIKE A RACCOON.
NAH, IT LOOKS LIKE A FOX...
LOOKS JUST LIKE A SQUIRREL !

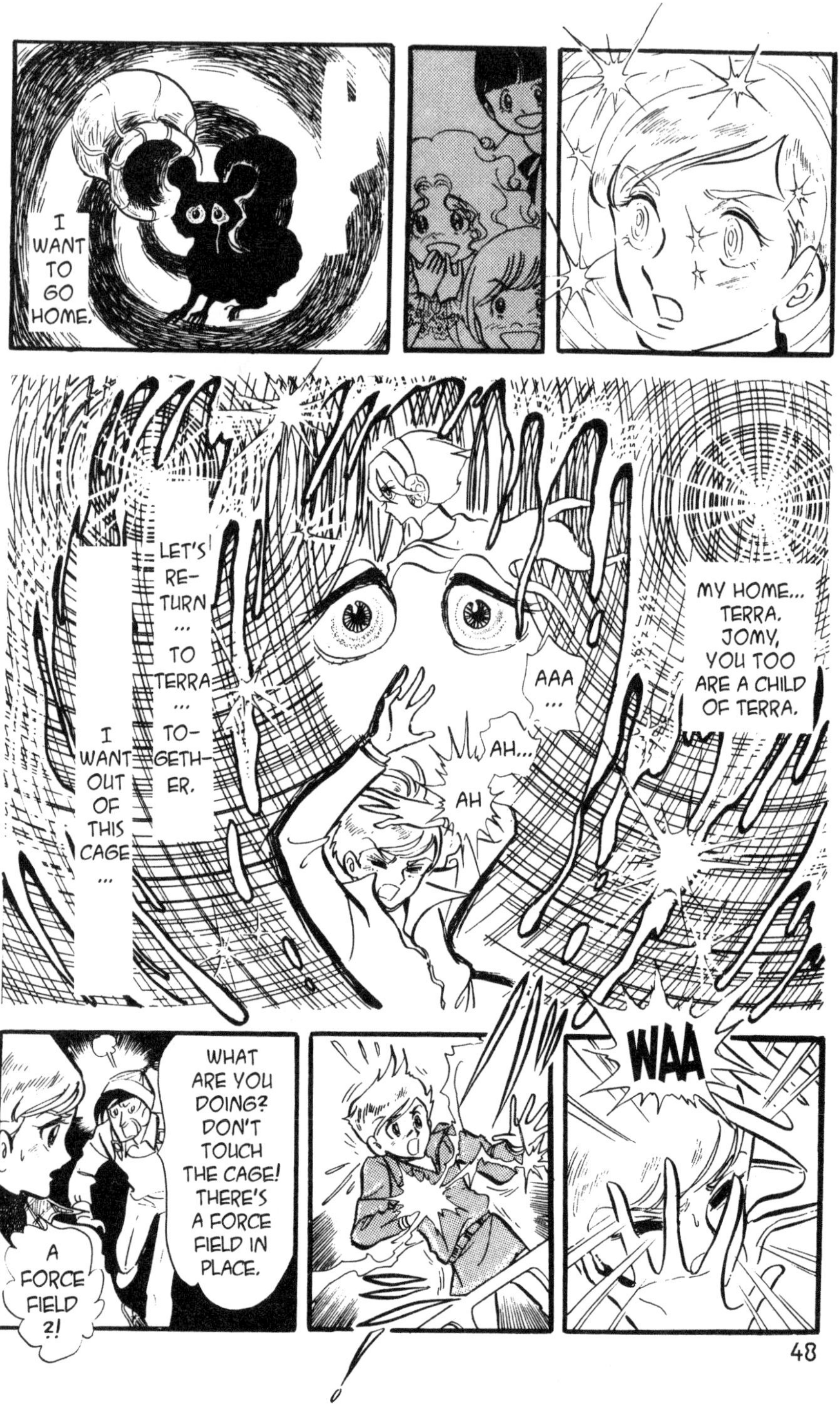
I WANT TO GO HOME.
MY HOME... TERRA. JOMY, YOU TOO ARE A CHILD OF TERRA.
AAA ...
AH...
AH
LET'S RETURN ... TO TERRA ... TOGETHER.
I WANT OUT OF THIS CAGE ...
WAA
WHAT ARE YOU DOING? DON'T TOUCH THE CAGE! THERE'S A FORCE FIELD IN PLACE.
A FORCE FIELD ?!

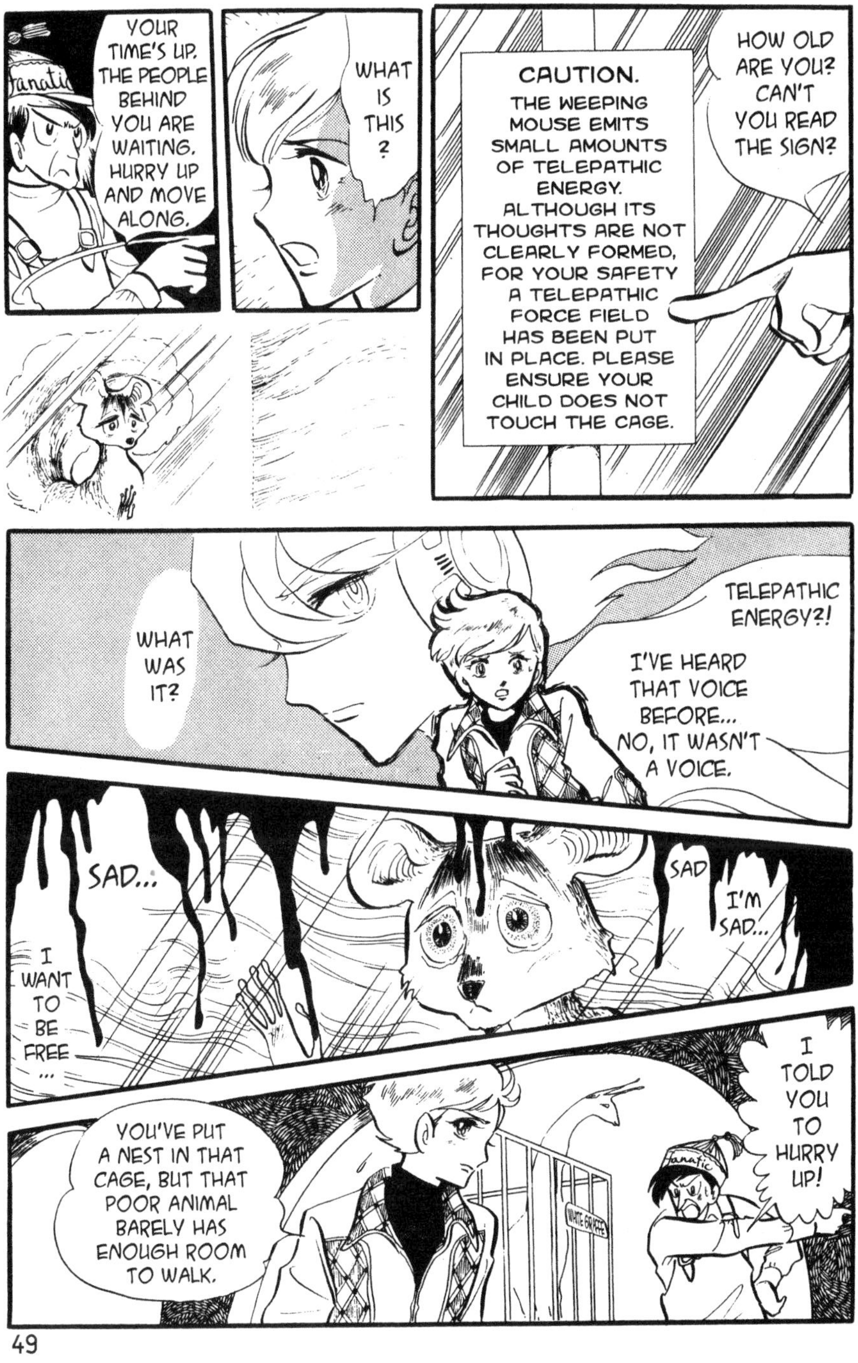
HOW OLD ARE YOU? CAN'T YOU READ THE SIGN?
CAUTION.
THE WEEPING MOUSE EMITS SMALL AMOUNTS OF TELEPATHIC ENERGY. ALTHOUGH ITS THOUGHTS ARE NOT CLEARLY FORMED, FOR YOUR SAFETY A TELEPATHIC FORCE FIELD HAS BEEN PUT IN PLACE. PLEASE ENSURE YOUR CHILD DOES NOT TOUCH THE CAGE.
WHAT IS THIS?
YOUR TIME'S UP. THE PEOPLE BEHIND YOU ARE WAITING. HURRY UP AND MOVE ALONG.
Fanatic
TELEPATHIC ENERGY?!
I'VE HEARD THAT VOICE BEFORE... NO, IT WASN'T A VOICE.
WHAT WAS IT?
SAD
I'M SAD...
SAD...
I WANT TO BE FREE...
I TOLD YOU TO HURRY UP!
Fanatic
YOU'VE PUT A NEST IN THAT CAGE, BUT THAT POOR ANIMAL BARELY HAS ENOUGH ROOM TO WALK.

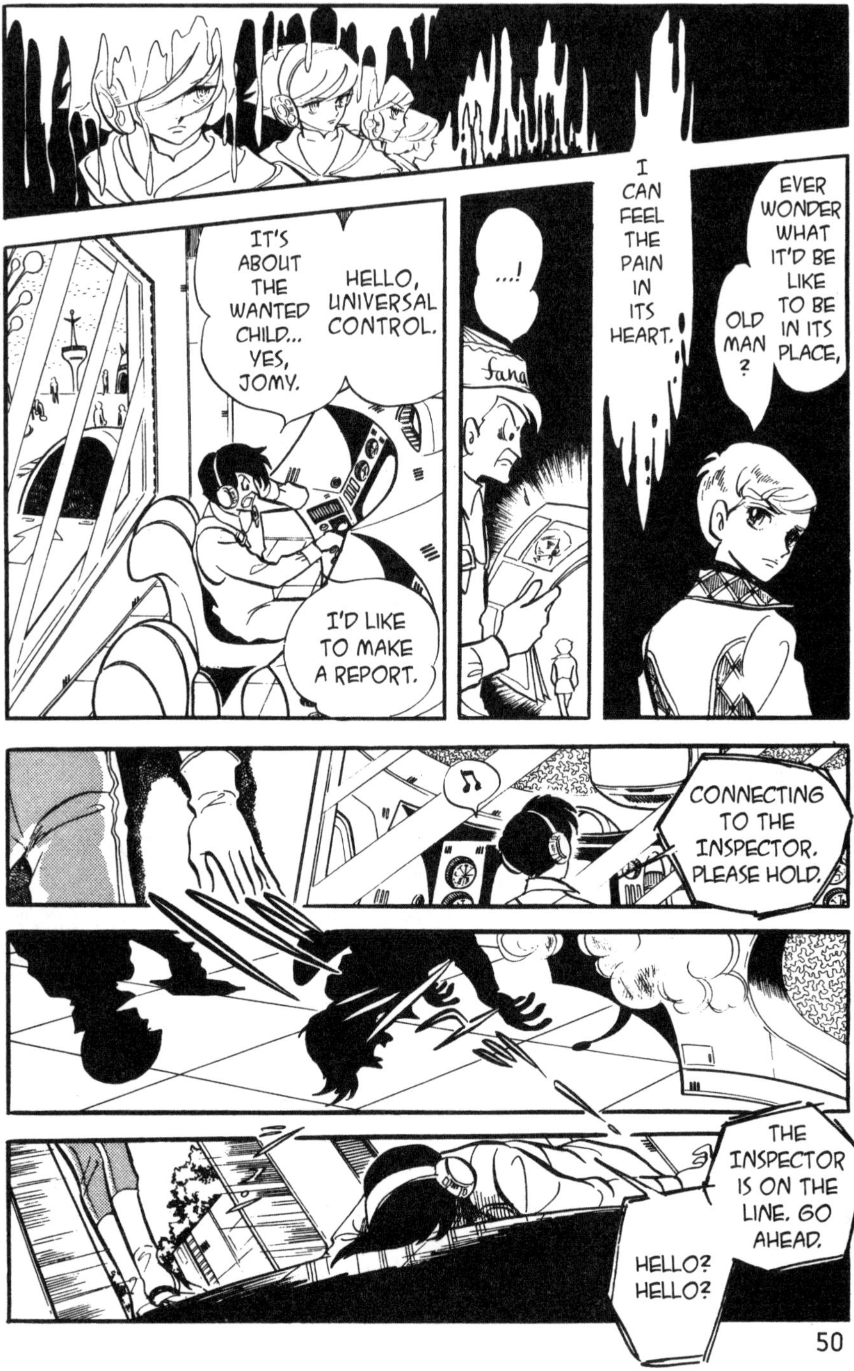
EVER WONDER WHAT IT'D BE LIKE TO BE IN ITS PLACE,
OLD MAN?
I CAN FEEL THE PAIN IN ITS HEART.
...!
HELLO, UNIVERSAL CONTROL.
IT'S ABOUT THE WANTED CHILD... YES, JOMY.
I'D LIKE TO MAKE A REPORT.
CONNECTING TO THE INSPECTOR. PLEASE HOLD.
THE INSPECTOR IS ON THE LINE. GO AHEAD.
HELLO? HELLO?

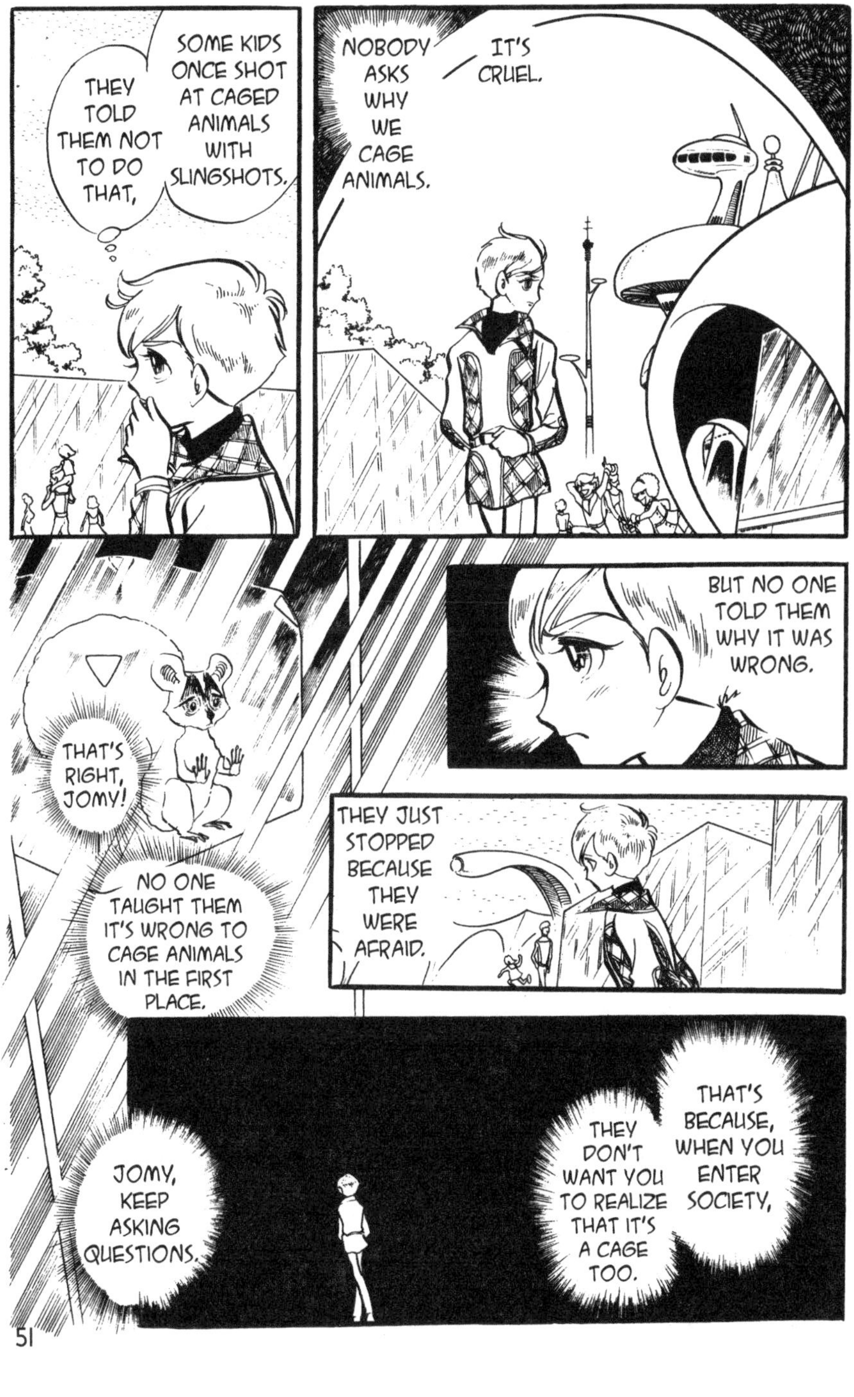
IT'S CRUEL.
NOBODY ASKS WHY WE CAGE ANIMALS.
SOME KIDS ONCE SHOT AT CAGED ANIMALS WITH SLINGSHOTS.
THEY TOLD THEM NOT TO DO THAT,
BUT NO ONE TOLD THEM WHY IT WAS WRONG.
THEY JUST STOPPED BECAUSE THEY WERE AFRAID.
THAT'S RIGHT, JOMY!
NO ONE TAUGHT THEM IT'S WRONG TO CAGE ANIMALS IN THE FIRST PLACE.
THAT'S BECAUSE, WHEN YOU ENTER SOCIETY,
THEY DON'T WANT YOU TO REALIZE THAT IT'S A CAGE TOO.
JOMY, KEEP ASKING QUESTIONS.

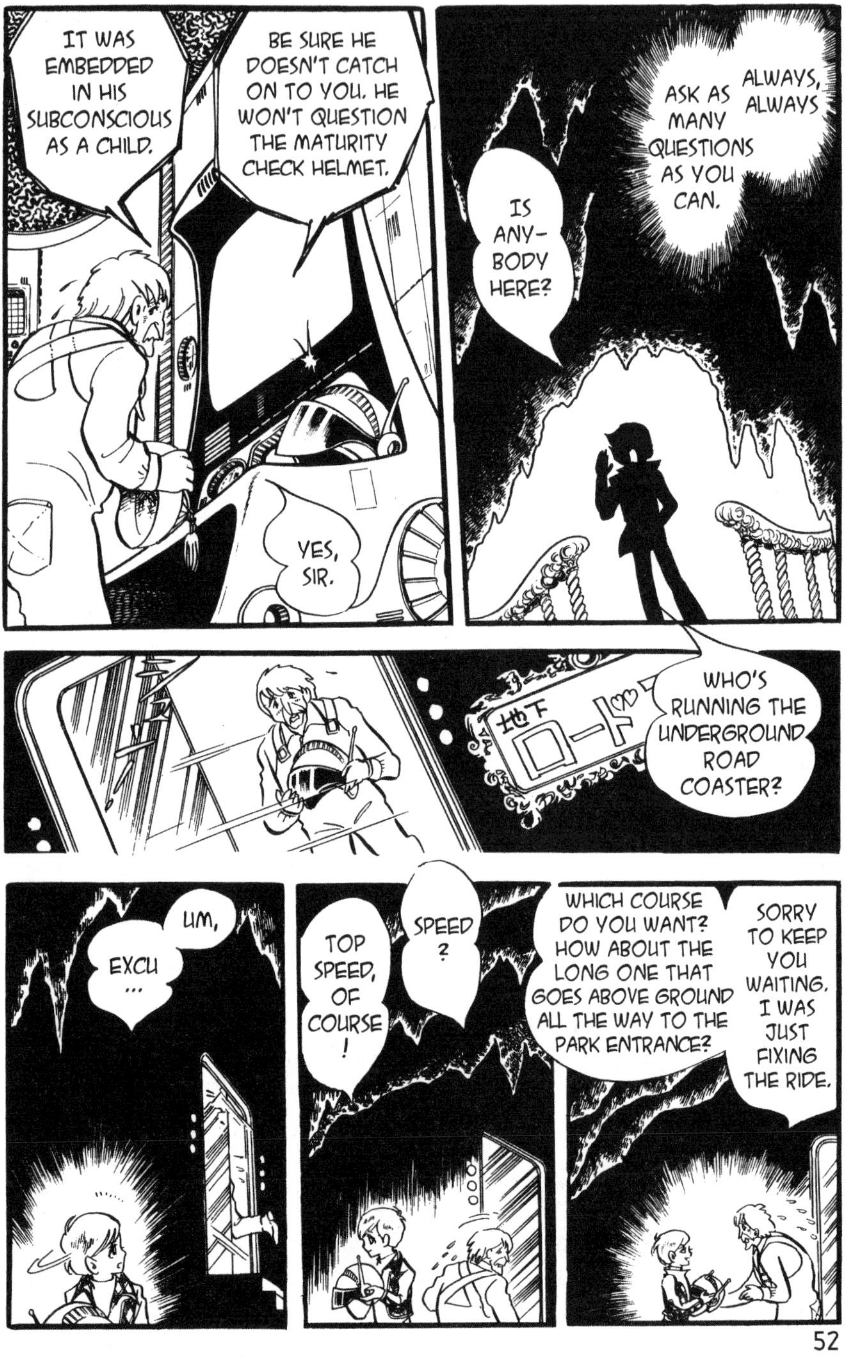
ALWAYS, ALWAYS ASK AS MANY QUESTIONS AS YOU CAN.
IS ANYBODY HERE?
BE SURE HE DOESN'T CATCH ON TO YOU. HE WON'T QUESTION THE MATURITY CHECK HELMET.
IT WAS EMBEDDED IN HIS SUBCONSCIOUS AS A CHILD.
YES, SIR.
WHO'S RUNNING THE UNDERGROUND ROAD COASTER?
地下
ロード
SORRY TO KEEP YOU WAITING. I WAS JUST FIXING THE RIDE.
WHICH COURSE DO YOU WANT? HOW ABOUT THE LONG ONE THAT GOES ABOVE GROUND ALL THE WAY TO THE PARK ENTRANCE?
SPEED?
TOP SPEED, OF COURSE!
UM,
EXCU...

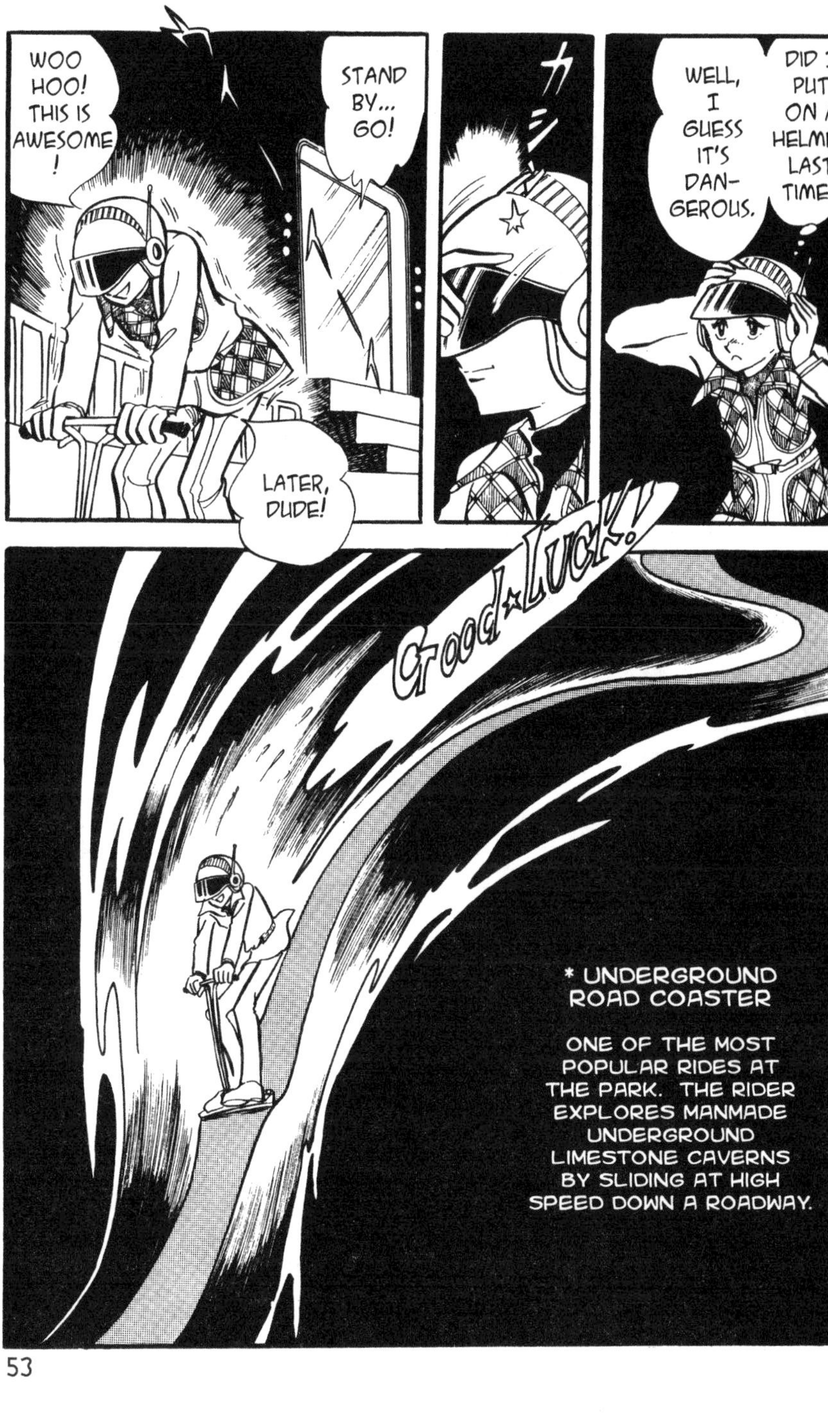
DID I PUT ON A HELMET LAST TIME?
WELL, I GUESS IT'S DAN-GEROUS.
STAND BY... GO!
WOO HOO! THIS IS AWESOME!
LATER, DUDE!
Good☆LUCK!
* UNDERGROUND ROAD COASTER
ONE OF THE MOST POPULAR RIDES AT THE PARK. THE RIDER EXPLORES MANMADE UNDERGROUND LIMESTONE CAVERNS BY SLIDING AT HIGH SPEED DOWN A ROADWAY.

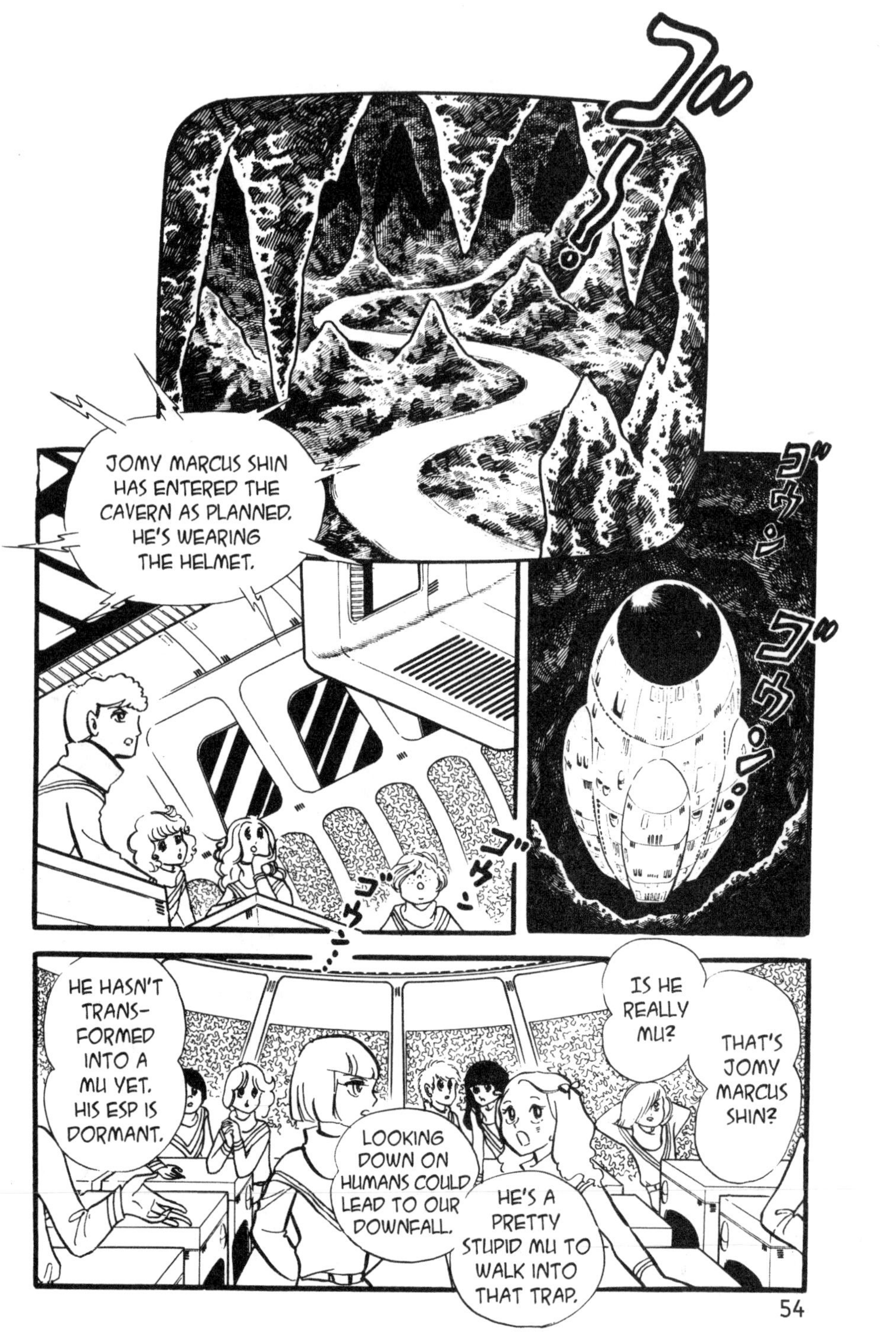
JOMY MARCUS SHIN HAS ENTERED THE CAVERN AS PLANNED. HE'S WEARING THE HELMET.
THAT'S JOMY MARCUS SHIN?
IS HE REALLY MU?
HE HASN'T TRANS-FORMED INTO A MU YET. HIS ESP IS DORMANT.
HE'S A PRETTY STUPID MU TO WALK INTO THAT TRAP.
LOOKING DOWN ON HUMANS COULD LEAD TO OUR DOWNFALL.

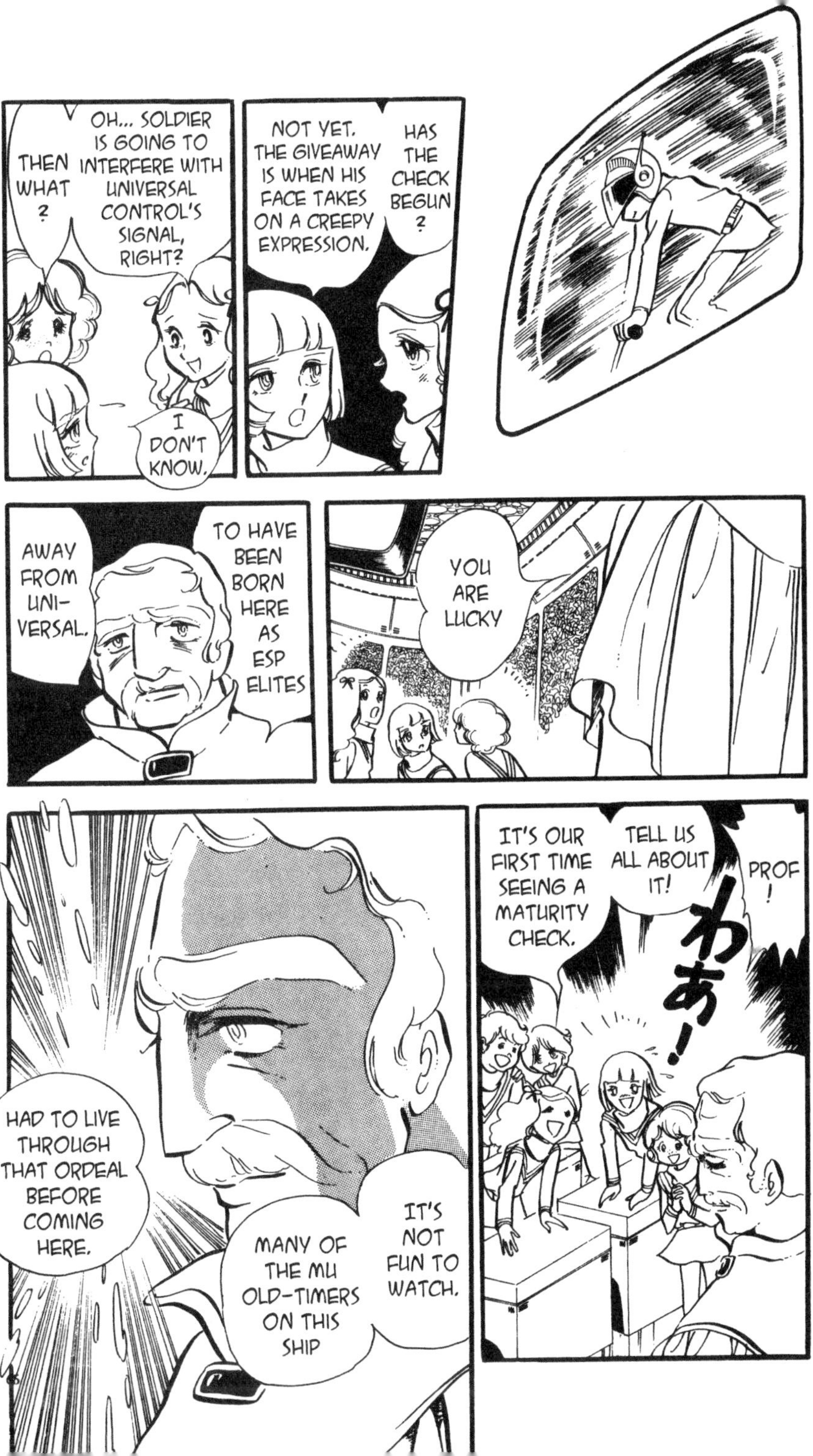
HAS THE CHECK BEGUN?
NOT YET. THE GIVEAWAY IS WHEN HIS FACE TAKES ON A CREEPY EXPRESSION.
OH... SOLDIER IS GOING TO INTERFERE WITH UNIVERSAL CONTROL'S SIGNAL, RIGHT?
THEN WHAT?
I DON'T KNOW.
YOU ARE LUCKY
TO HAVE BEEN BORN HERE AS ESP ELITES
AWAY FROM UNI-VERSAL.
PROF!
TELL US ALL ABOUT IT!
IT'S OUR FIRST TIME SEEING A MATURITY CHECK.
わあ!
IT'S NOT FUN TO WATCH.
MANY OF THE MU OLD-TIMERS ON THIS SHIP
HAD TO LIVE THROUGH THAT ORDEAL BEFORE COMING HERE.

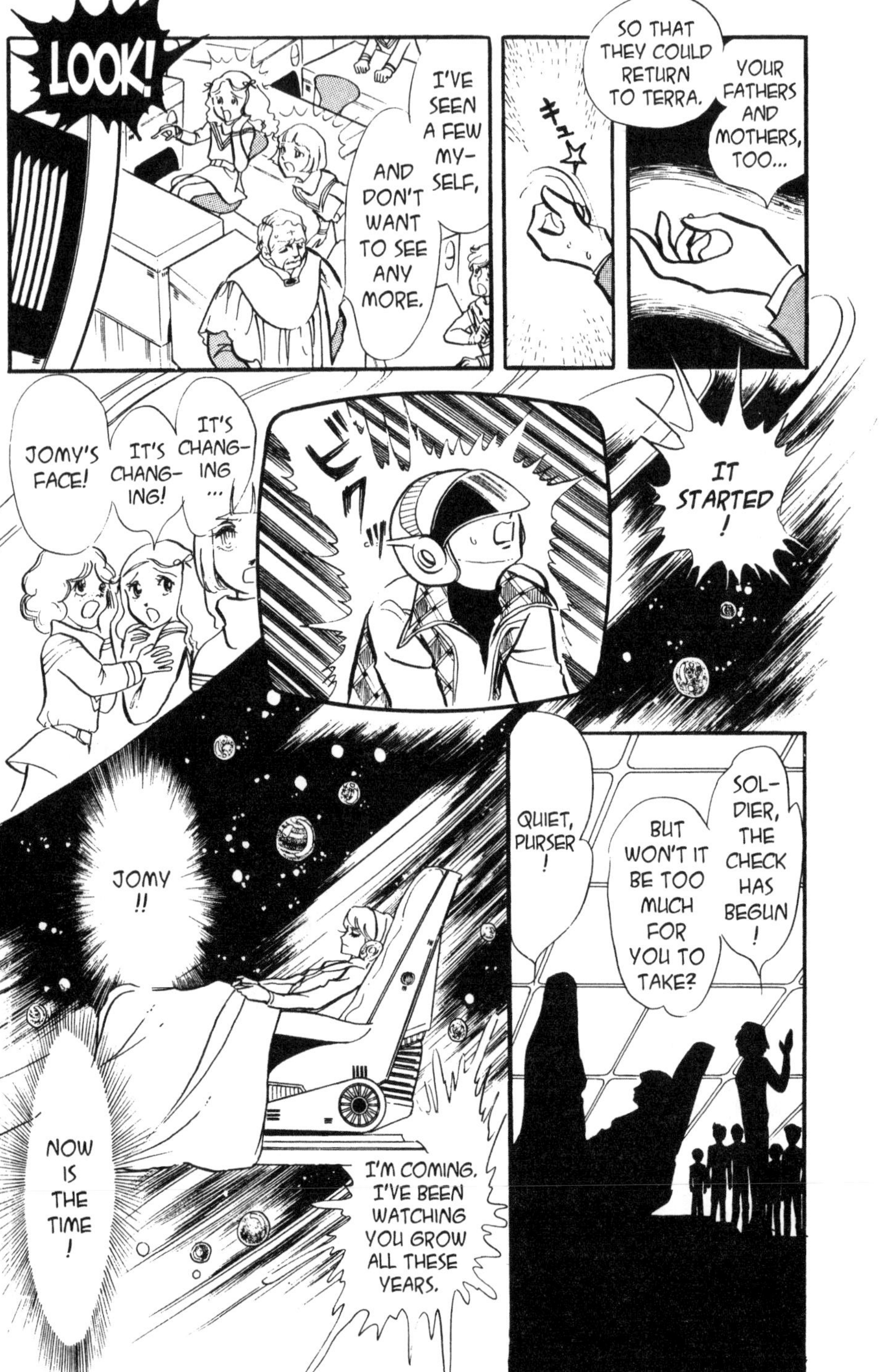
YOUR FATHERS AND MOTHERS, TOO...
SO THAT THEY COULD RETURN TO TERRA.
キュ
I'VE SEEN A FEW MY-SELF,
AND DON'T WANT TO SEE ANY MORE.
LOOK!
IT STARTED!
ビク
IT'S CHANG-ING...
IT'S CHANG-ING!
JOMY'S FACE!
SOL-DIER, THE CHECK HAS BEGUN!
BUT WON'T IT BE TOO MUCH FOR YOU TO TAKE?
QUIET, PURSER!
JOMY!!
I'M COMING. I'VE BEEN WATCHING YOU GROW ALL THESE YEARS.
NOW IS THE TIME!

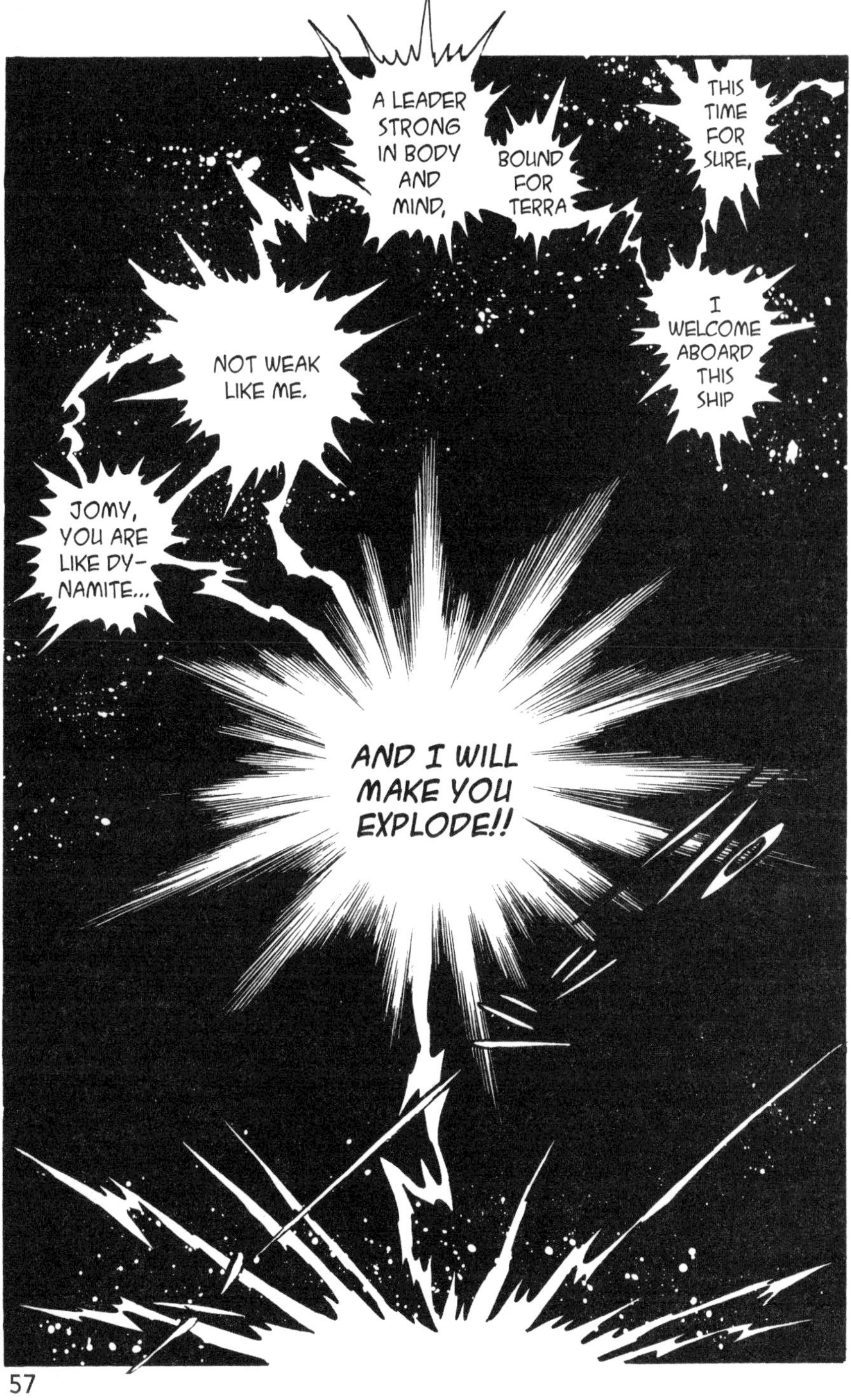
THIS TIME FOR SURE,
I WELCOME ABOARD THIS SHIP
BOUND FOR TERRA
A LEADER STRONG IN BODY AND MIND,
NOT WEAK LIKE ME.
JOMY, YOU ARE LIKE DY-NAMITE...
AND I WILL MAKE YOU EXPLODE!!

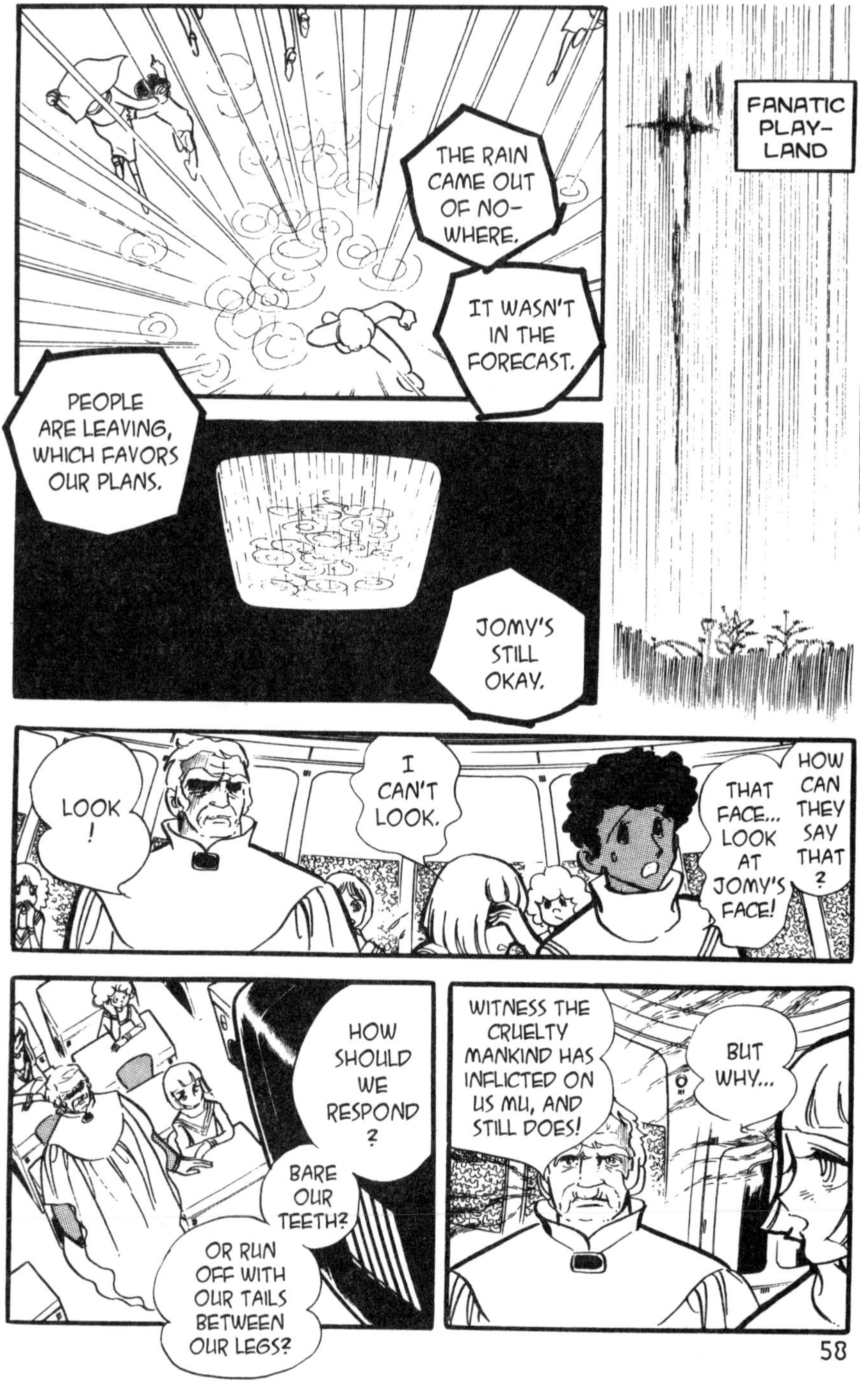
FANATIC PLAY-LAND
THE RAIN CAME OUT OF NO-WHERE.
IT WASN'T IN THE FORECAST.
PEOPLE ARE LEAVING, WHICH FAVORS OUR PLANS.
JOMY'S STILL OKAY.
HOW CAN THEY SAY THAT?
THAT FACE... LOOK AT JOMY'S FACE!
I CAN'T LOOK.
LOOK!
BUT WHY...
WITNESS THE CRUELTY MANKIND HAS INFLICTED ON US MU, AND STILL DOES!
HOW SHOULD WE RESPOND?
BARE OUR TEETH?
OR RUN OFF WITH OUR TAILS BETWEEN OUR LEGS?

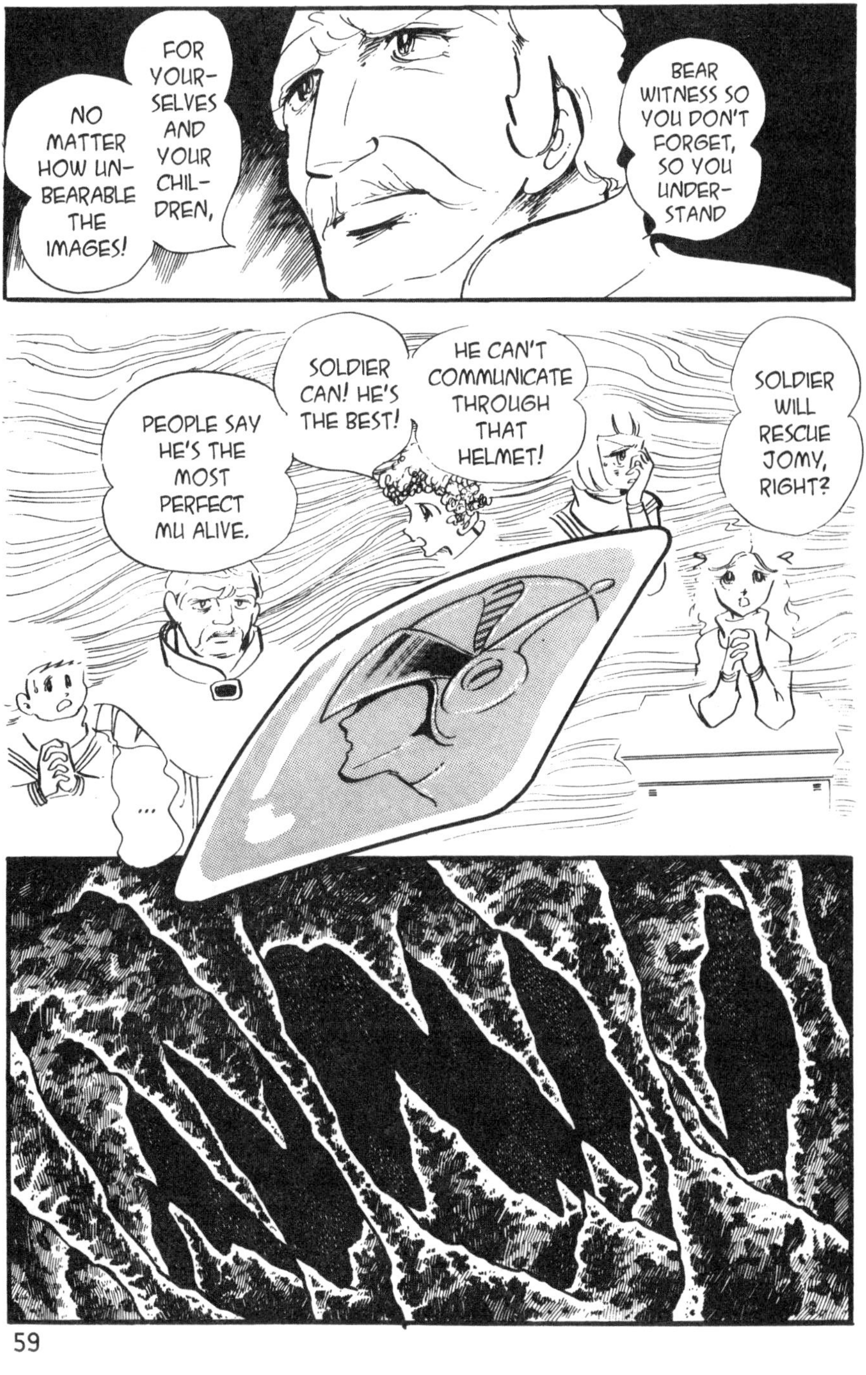
BEAR WITNESS SO YOU DON'T FORGET, SO YOU UNDERSTAND
FOR YOURSELVES AND YOUR CHILDREN,
NO MATTER HOW UNBEARABLE THE IMAGES!
SOLDIER WILL RESCUE JOMY, RIGHT?
HE CAN'T COMMUNICATE THROUGH THAT HELMET!
SOLDIER CAN! HE'S THE BEST!
PEOPLE SAY HE'S THE MOST PERFECT MU ALIVE.
...

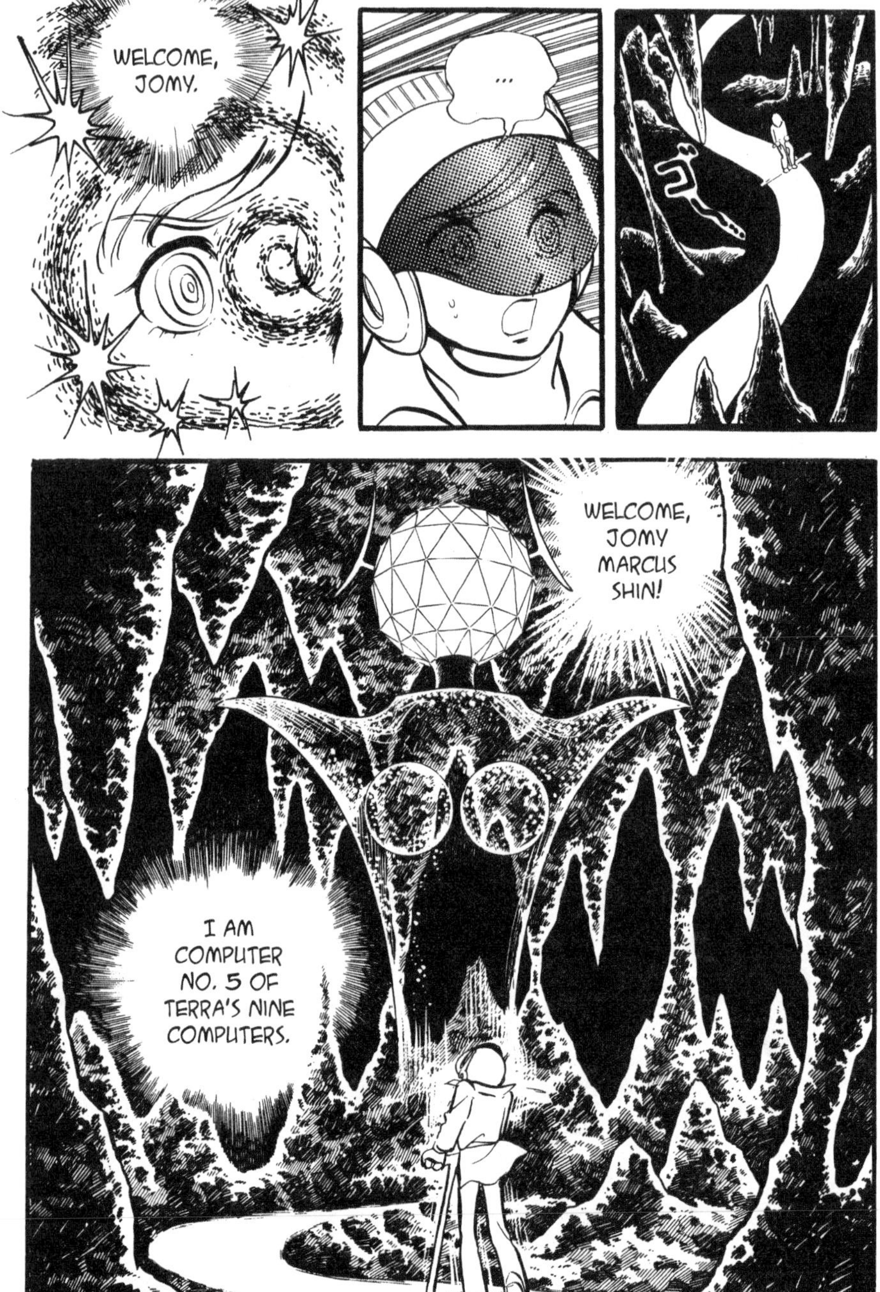
...
WELCOME, JOMY.
WELCOME, JOMY MARCUS SHIN!
I AM COMPUTER NO. 5 OF TERRA'S NINE COMPUTERS.

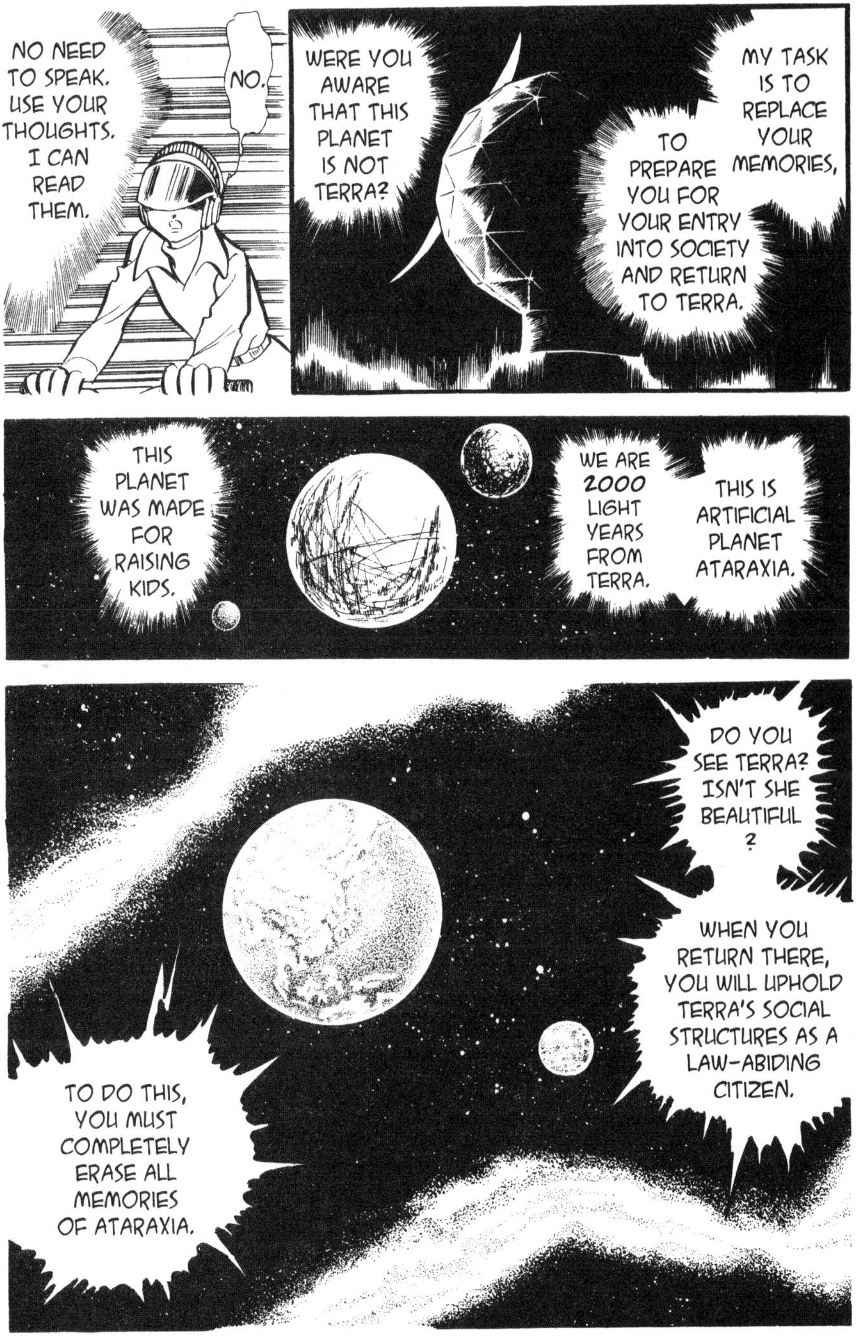
MY TASK IS TO REPLACE YOUR MEMORIES,
TO PREPARE YOU FOR YOUR ENTRY INTO SOCIETY AND RETURN TO TERRA.
WERE YOU AWARE THAT THIS PLANET IS NOT TERRA?
NO.
NO NEED TO SPEAK. USE YOUR THOUGHTS. I CAN READ THEM.
THIS IS ARTIFICIAL PLANET ATARAXIA.
WE ARE 2000 LIGHT YEARS FROM TERRA.
THIS PLANET WAS MADE FOR RAISING KIDS.
DO YOU SEE TERRA? ISN'T SHE BEAUTIFUL?
WHEN YOU RETURN THERE, YOU WILL UPHOLD TERRA'S SOCIAL STRUCTURES AS A LAW-ABIDING CITIZEN.
TO DO THIS, YOU MUST COMPLETELY ERASE ALL MEMORIES OF ATARAXIA.

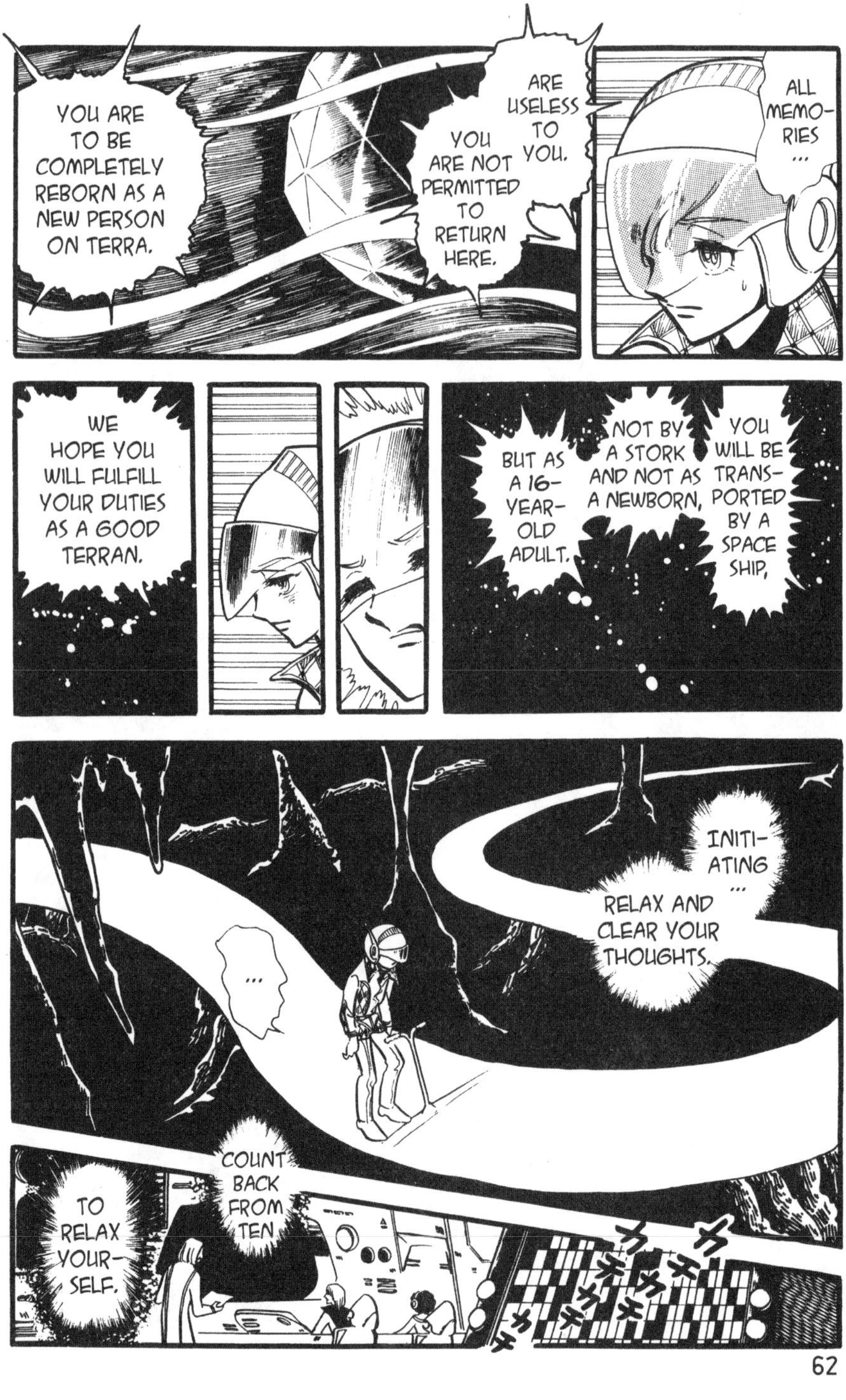
ALL MEMORIES ...
ARE USELESS TO YOU.
YOU ARE NOT PERMITTED TO RETURN HERE.
YOU ARE TO BE COMPLETELY REBORN AS A NEW PERSON ON TERRA.
YOU WILL BE TRANSPORTED BY A SPACE SHIP,
NOT BY A STORK AND NOT AS A NEWBORN,
BUT AS A 16-YEAR-OLD ADULT.
WE HOPE YOU WILL FULFILL YOUR DUTIES AS A GOOD TERRAN.
INITIATING ...
RELAX AND CLEAR YOUR THOUGHTS.
...
COUNT BACK FROM TEN
TO RELAX YOURSELF.

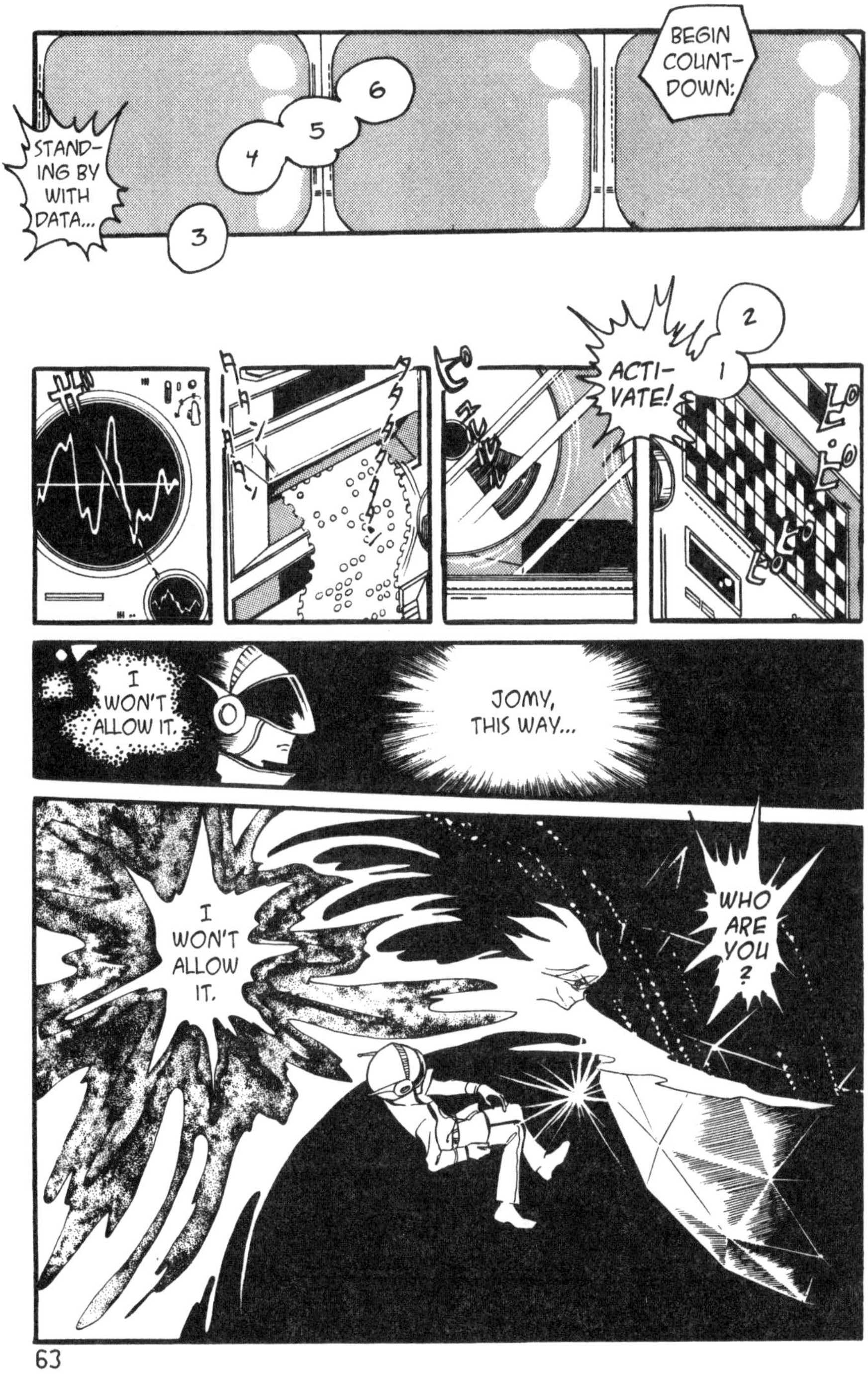

BEGIN COUNT-DOWN:
6
5
4
3
STANDING BY WITH DATA...
2
1
ACTIVATE!
JOMY, THIS WAY...
I WON'T ALLOW IT.
WHO ARE YOU?
I WON'T ALLOW IT.

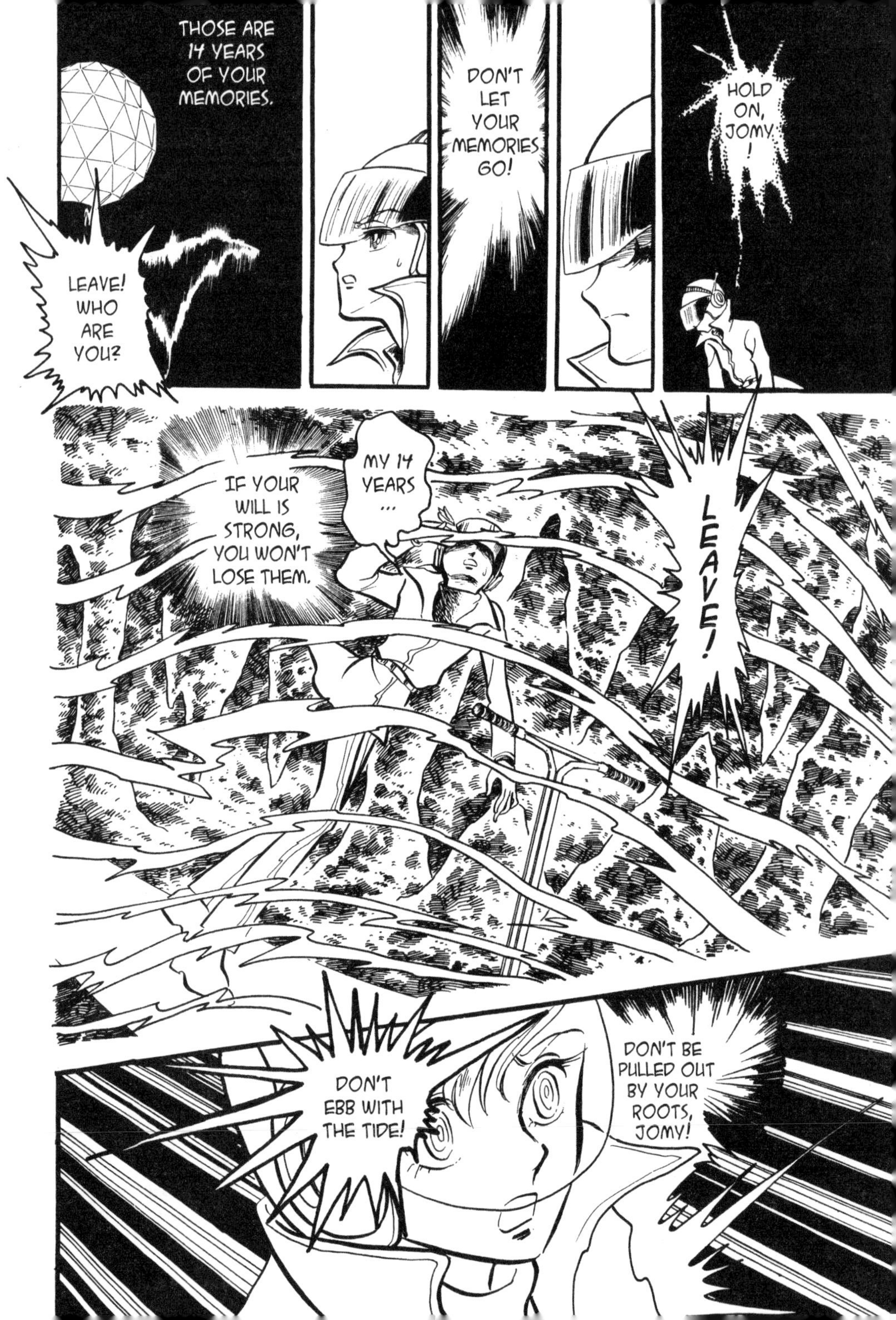
HOLD ON, JOMY!
DON'T LET YOUR MEMORIES GO!
THOSE ARE 14 YEARS OF YOUR MEMORIES.
LEAVE! WHO ARE YOU?
LEAVE!
MY 14 YEARS...
IF YOUR WILL IS STRONG, YOU WON'T LOSE THEM.
DON'T BE PULLED OUT BY YOUR ROOTS, JOMY!
DON'T EBB WITH THE TIDE!

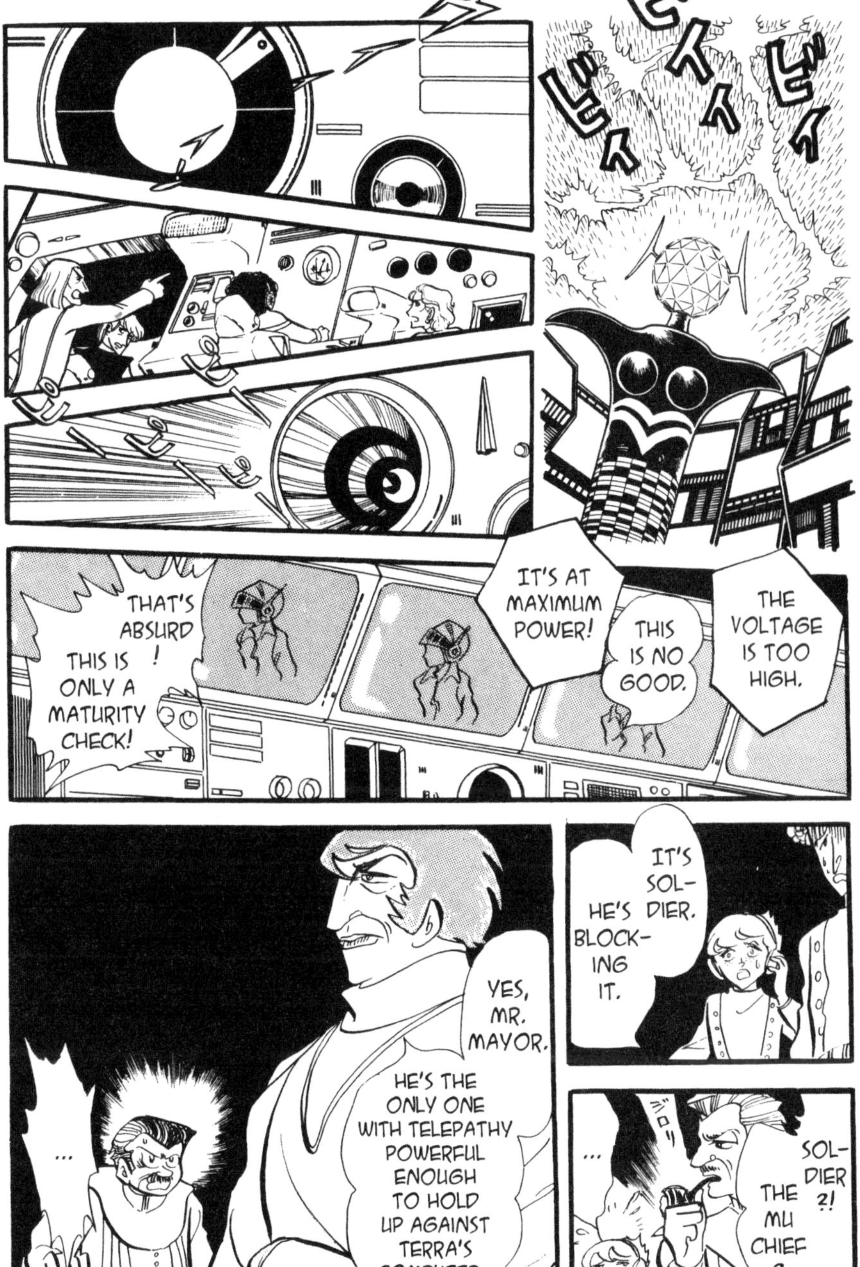
THE VOLTAGE IS TOO HIGH.
THIS IS NO GOOD.
IT'S AT MAXIMUM POWER!
THAT'S ABSURD!
THIS IS ONLY A MATURITY CHECK!
IT'S SOL-DIER.
HE'S BLOCK-ING IT.
SOL-DIER?!
THE MU CHIEF?
ジロリ
...
YES, MR. MAYOR.
HE'S THE ONLY ONE WITH TELEPATHY POWERFUL ENOUGH TO HOLD UP AGAINST TERRA'S COMPUTER.
...

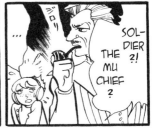

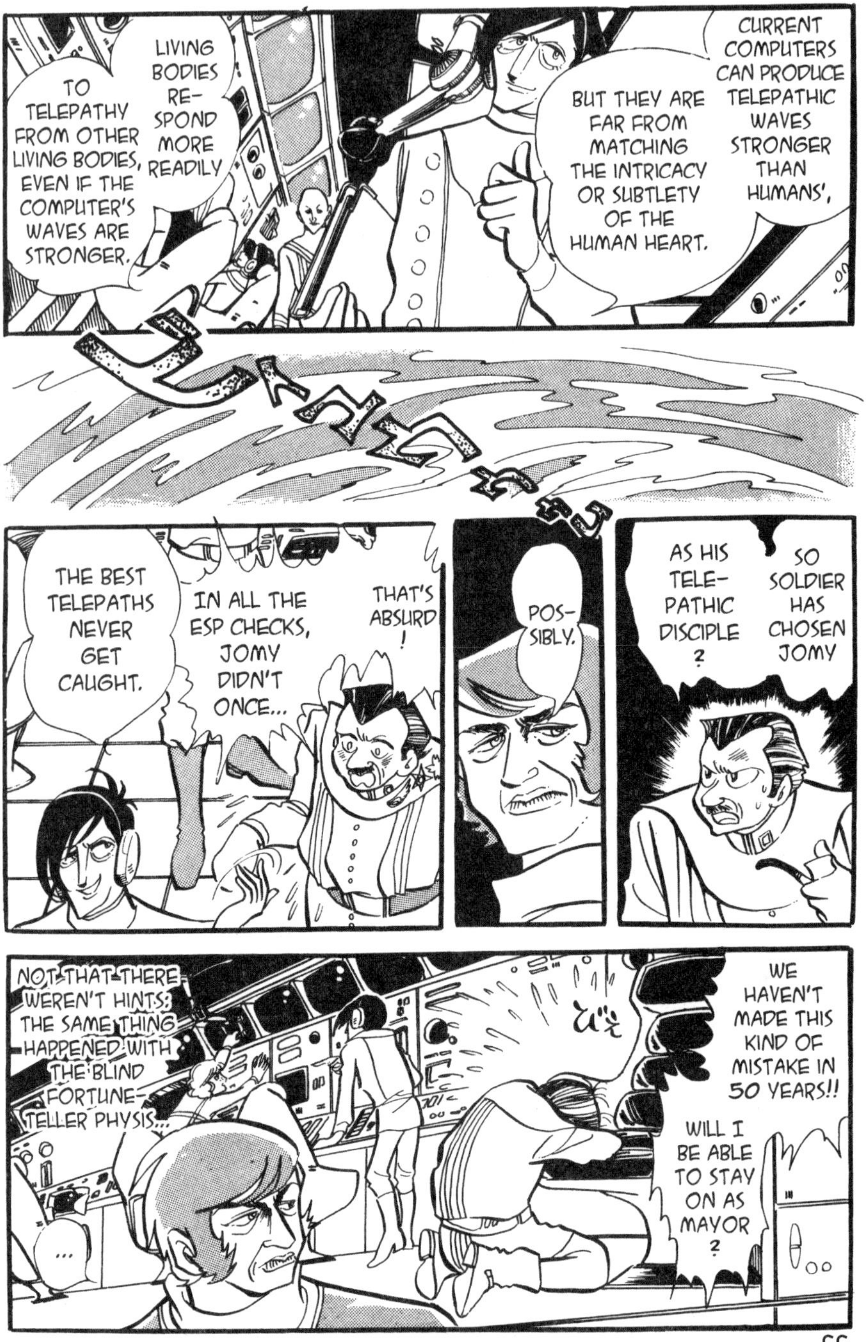
CURRENT COMPUTERS CAN PRODUCE TELEPATHIC WAVES STRONGER THAN HUMANS',
BUT THEY ARE FAR FROM MATCHING THE INTRICACY OR SUBTLETY OF THE HUMAN HEART.
LIVING BODIES RE-SPOND MORE READILY
TO TELEPATHY FROM OTHER LIVING BODIES, EVEN IF THE COMPUTER'S WAVES ARE STRONGER.
SO SOLDIER HAS CHOSEN JOMY
AS HIS TELE-PATHIC DISCIPLE?
POS-SIBLY.
THAT'S ABSURD!
IN ALL THE ESP CHECKS, JOMY DIDN'T ONCE...
THE BEST TELEPATHS NEVER GET CAUGHT.
WE HAVEN'T MADE THIS KIND OF MISTAKE IN 50 YEARS!!
WILL I BE ABLE TO STAY ON AS MAYOR?
NOT THAT THERE WEREN'T HINTS: THE SAME THING HAPPENED WITH THE BLIND FORTUNE-TELLER PHYSIS...
...

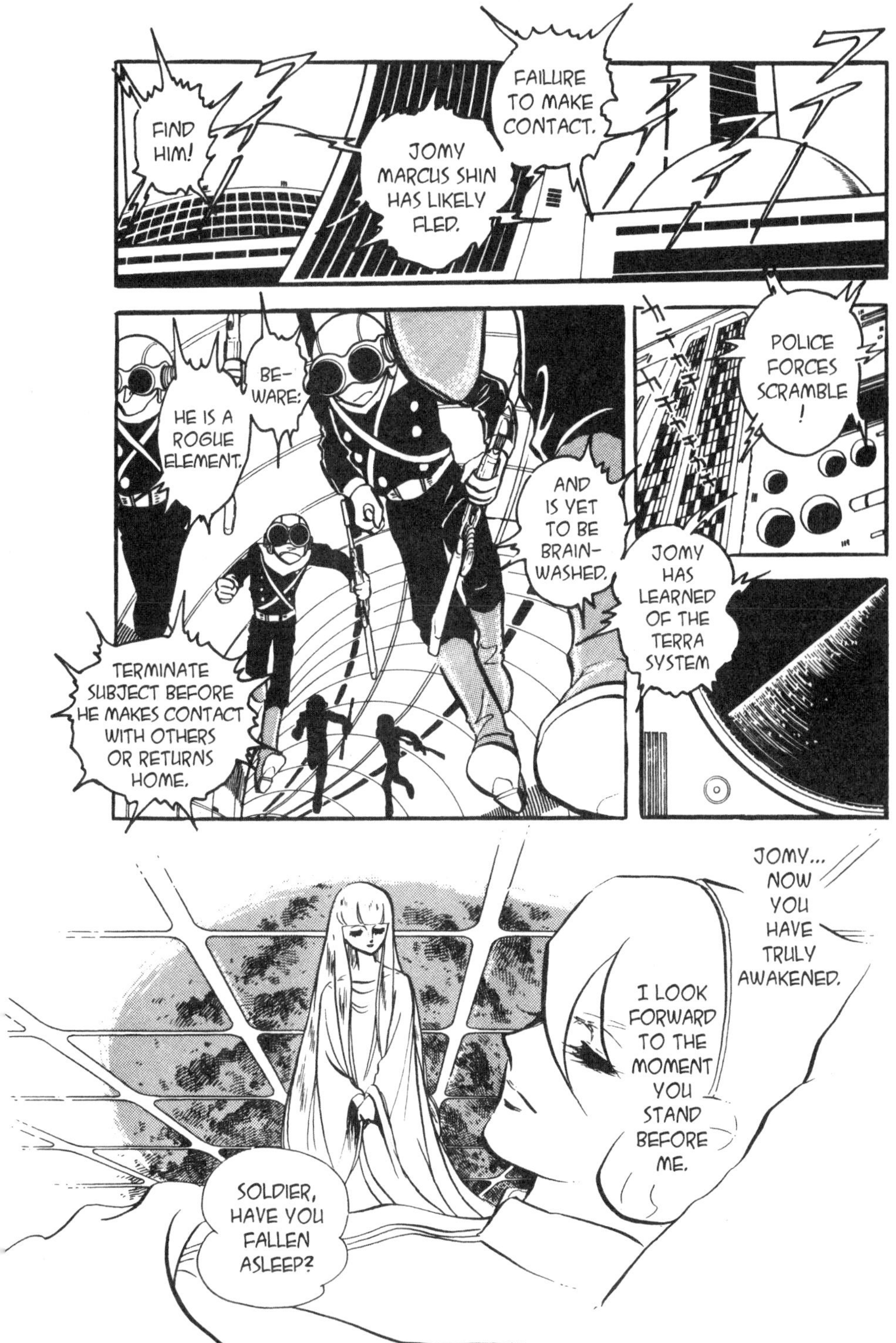
FAILURE TO MAKE CONTACT.
JOMY MARCUS SHIN HAS LIKELY FLED.
FIND HIM!
POLICE FORCES SCRAMBLE!
JOMY HAS LEARNED OF THE TERRA SYSTEM
AND IS YET TO BE BRAIN-WASHED.
BE-WARE:
HE IS A ROGUE ELEMENT.
TERMINATE SUBJECT BEFORE HE MAKES CONTACT WITH OTHERS OR RETURNS HOME.
JOMY... NOW YOU HAVE TRULY AWAKENED.
I LOOK FORWARD TO THE MOMENT YOU STAND BEFORE ME.
SOLDIER, HAVE YOU FALLEN ASLEEP?

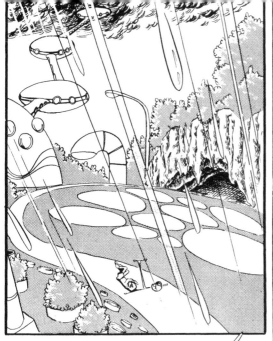

THAT'S
COLD
!

UGH
...

THE LION THAT
SLEEPS DEEP
UNDERGROUND
AWAKENS AFTER
AN ETERNITY, AND
HAVING AWOKEN,
TRAVELS MORE
THAN 10 BILLION
LIGHT YEARS
TO RETURN
TO TERRA...

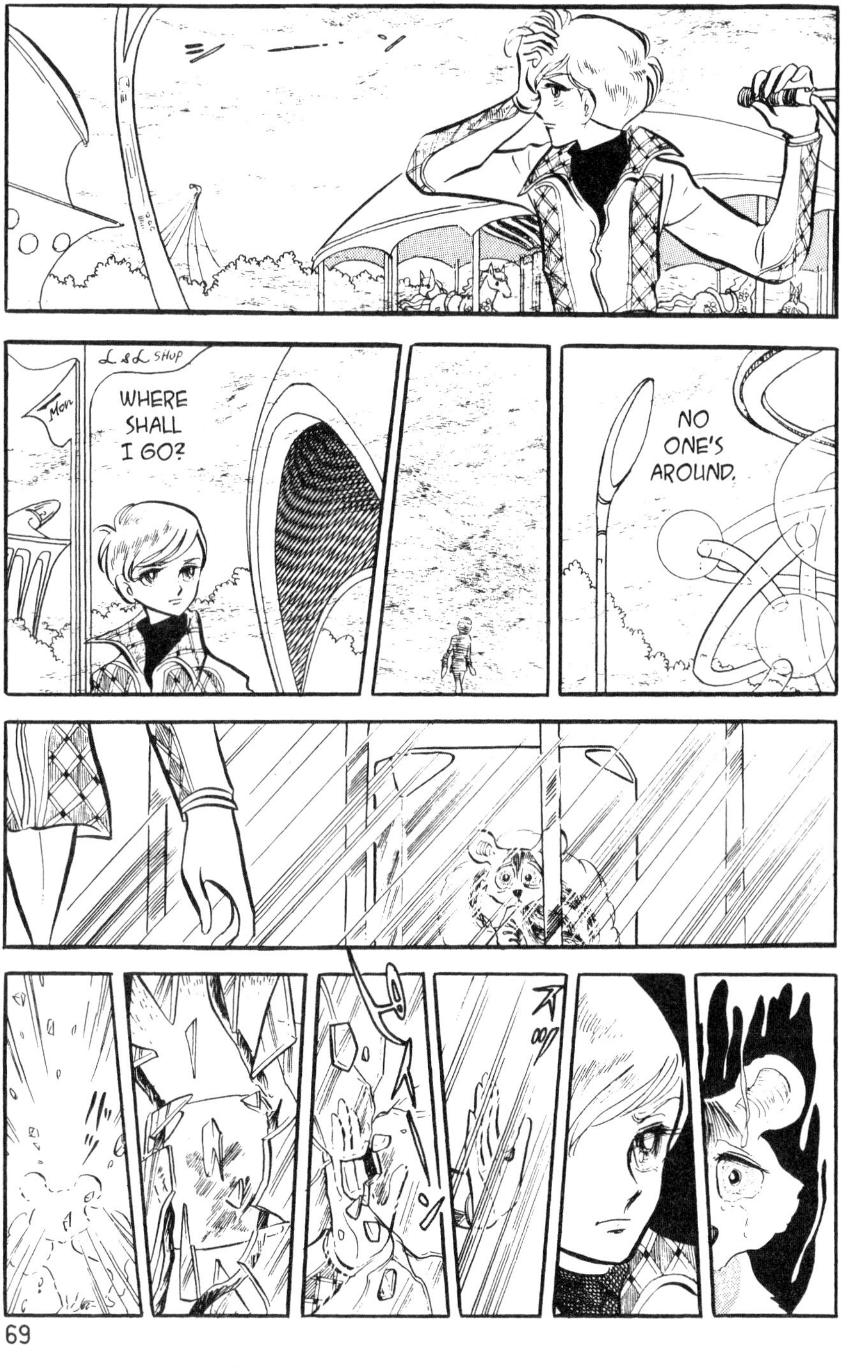
NO ONE'S AROUND.
L & L SHOP
WHERE SHALL I GO?
Mon

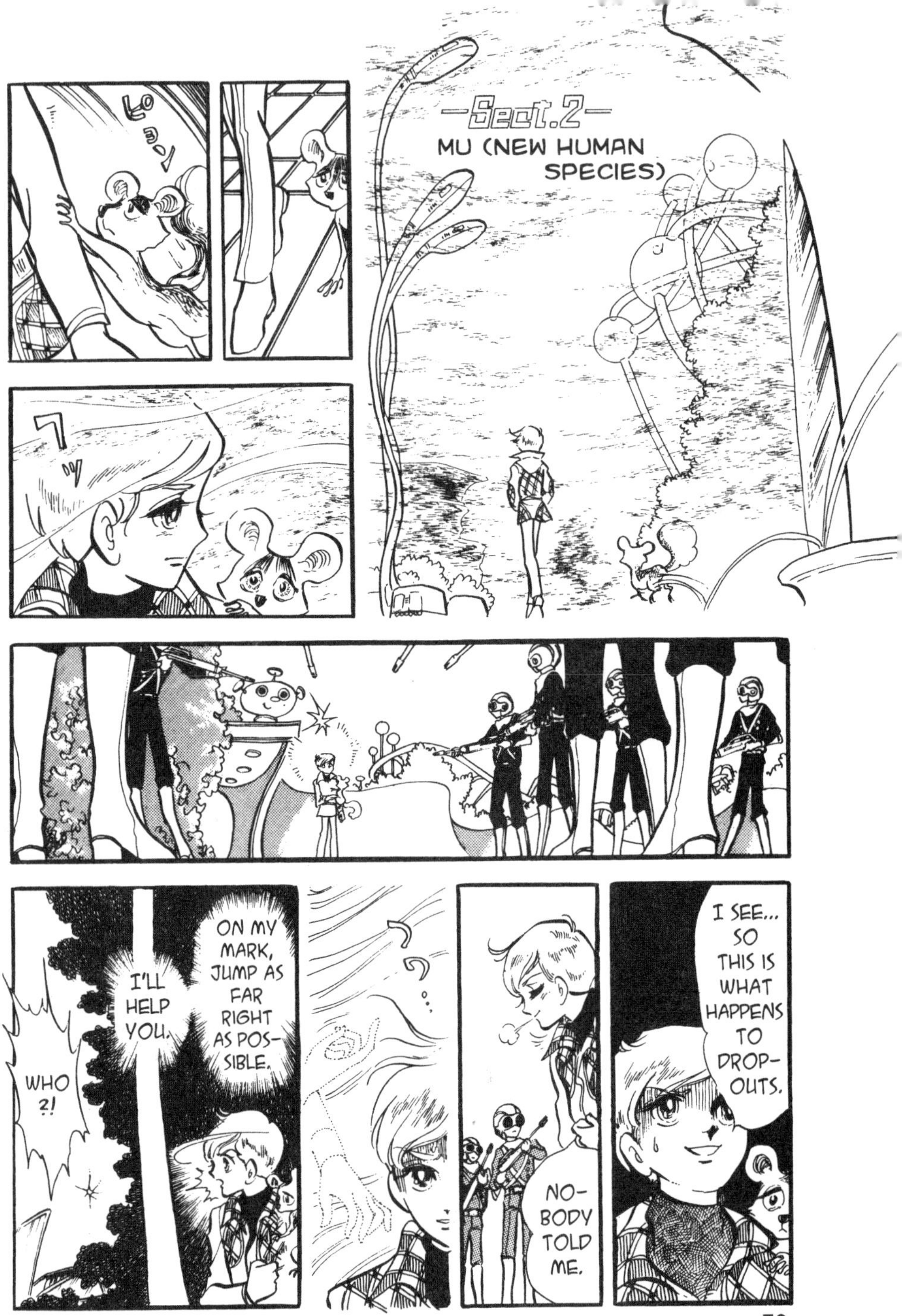
—Sect.2—
MU (NEW HUMAN SPECIES)
ピョン
I SEE... SO THIS IS WHAT HAPPENS TO DROP-OUTS.
NO-BODY TOLD ME.
ON MY MARK, JUMP AS FAR RIGHT AS POS-SIBLE.
I'LL HELP YOU.
WHO?!

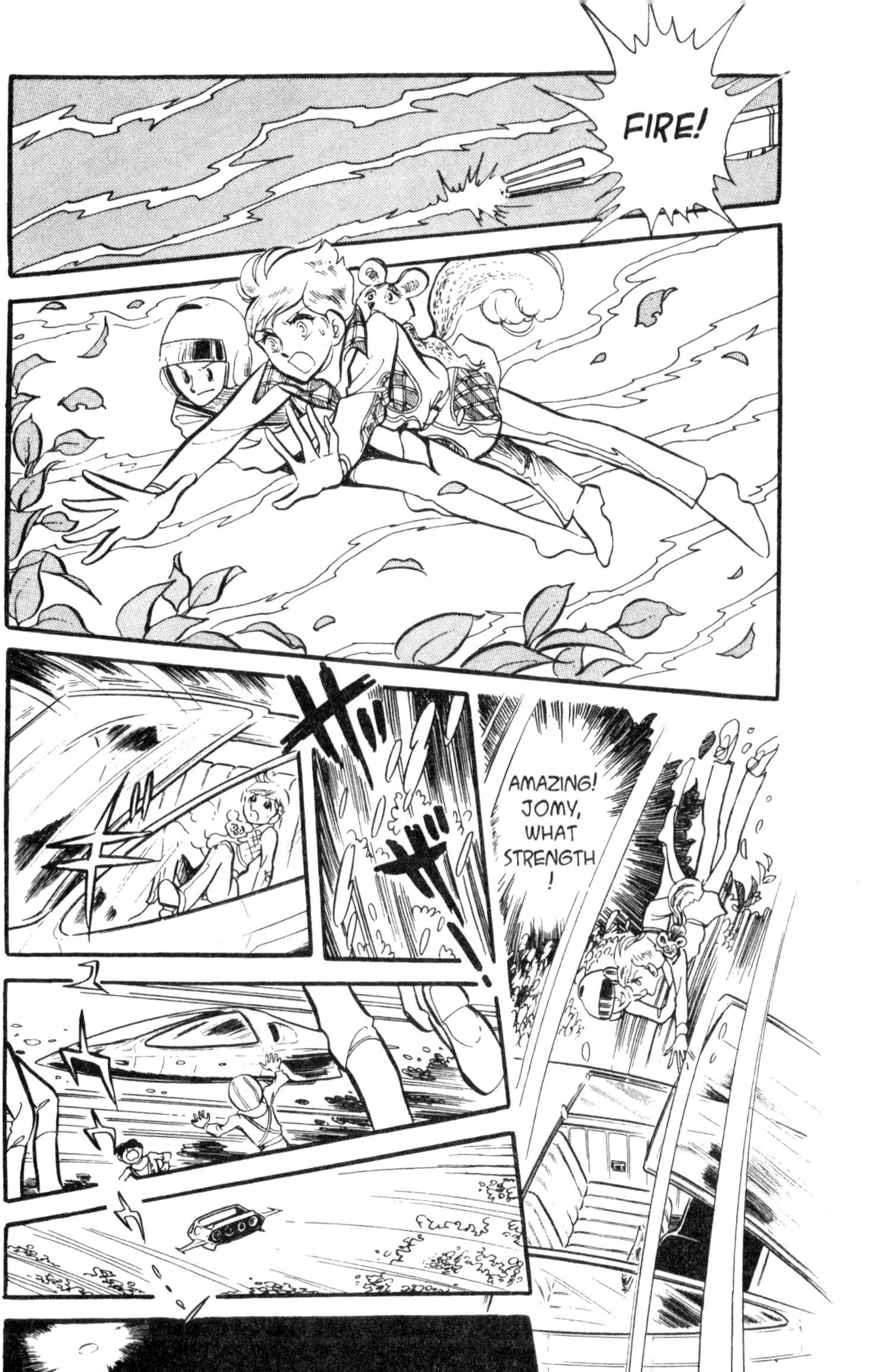
FIRE!
AMAZING! JOMY, WHAT STRENGTH!

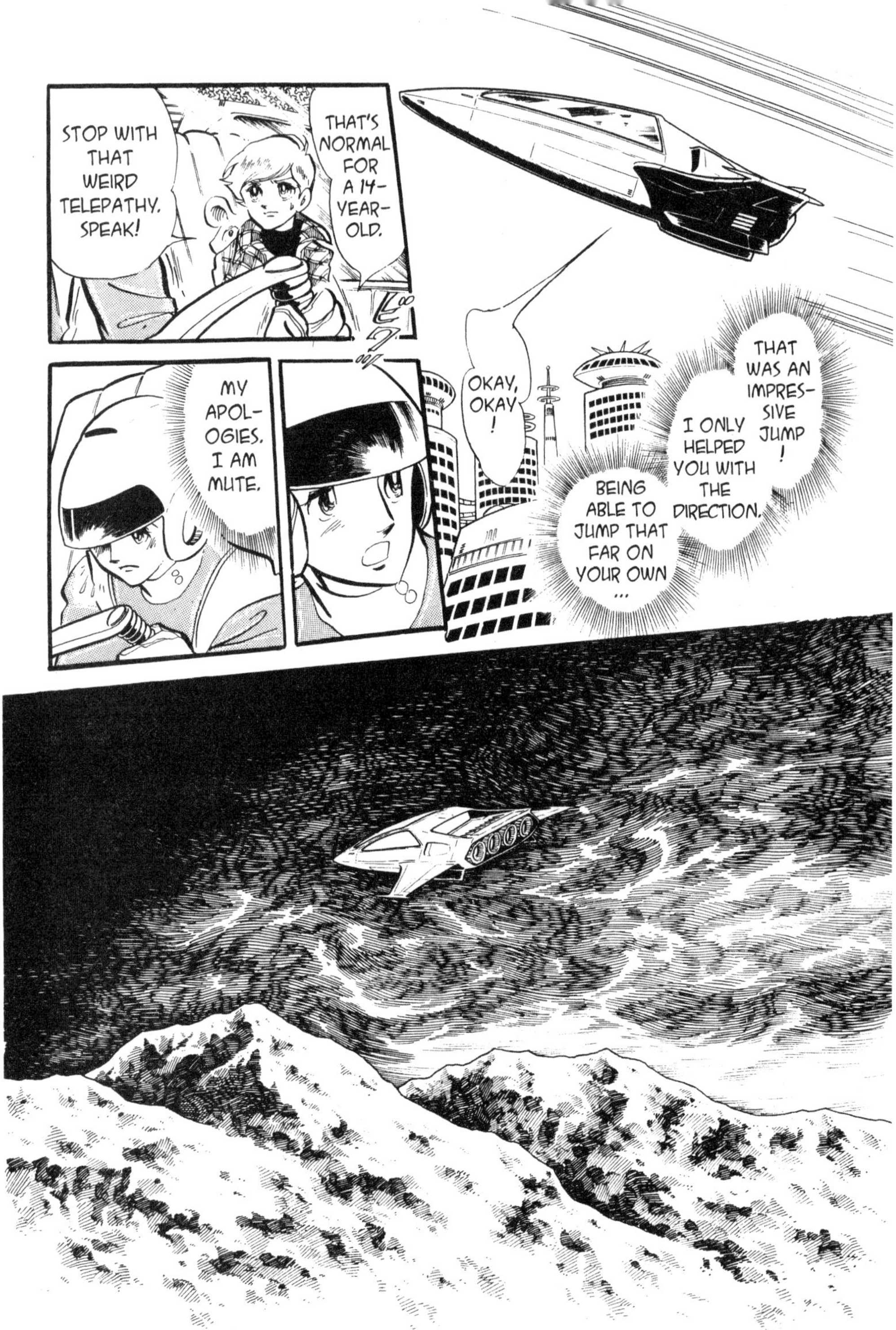
THAT WAS AN IMPRESSIVE JUMP!
I ONLY HELPED YOU WITH THE DIRECTION.
BEING ABLE TO JUMP THAT FAR ON YOUR OWN...
OKAY, OKAY!
THAT'S NORMAL FOR A 14-YEAR-OLD.
STOP WITH THAT WEIRD TELEPATHY. SPEAK!
MY APOLOGIES. I AM MUTE.

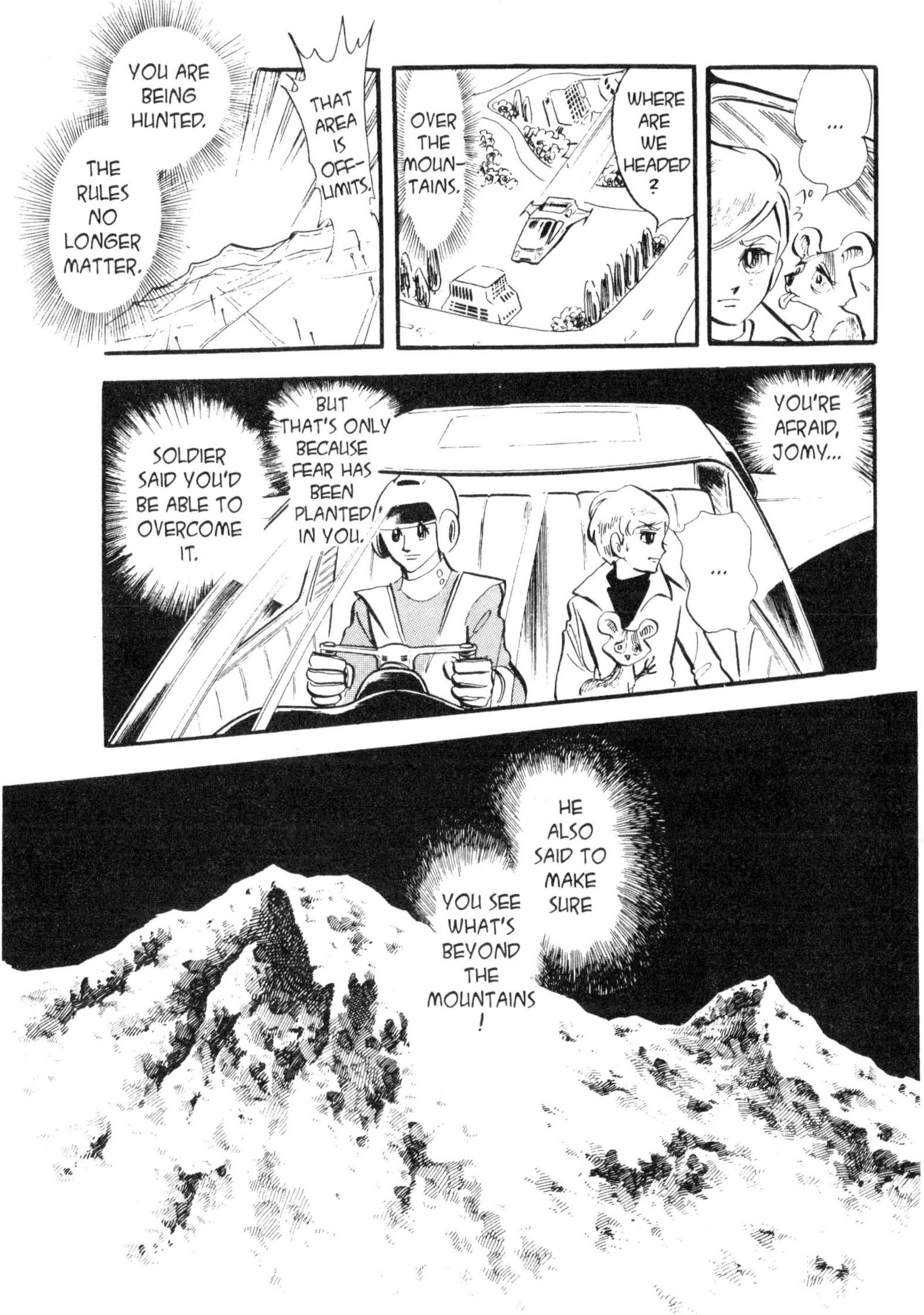
...
WHERE ARE WE HEADED?
OVER THE MOUNTAINS.
THAT AREA IS OFF-LIMITS.
YOU ARE BEING HUNTED.
THE RULES NO LONGER MATTER.
YOU'RE AFRAID, JOMY...
...
BUT THAT'S ONLY BECAUSE FEAR HAS BEEN PLANTED IN YOU.
SOLDIER SAID YOU'D BE ABLE TO OVERCOME IT.
HE ALSO SAID TO MAKE SURE
YOU SEE WHAT'S BEYOND THE MOUNTAINS!

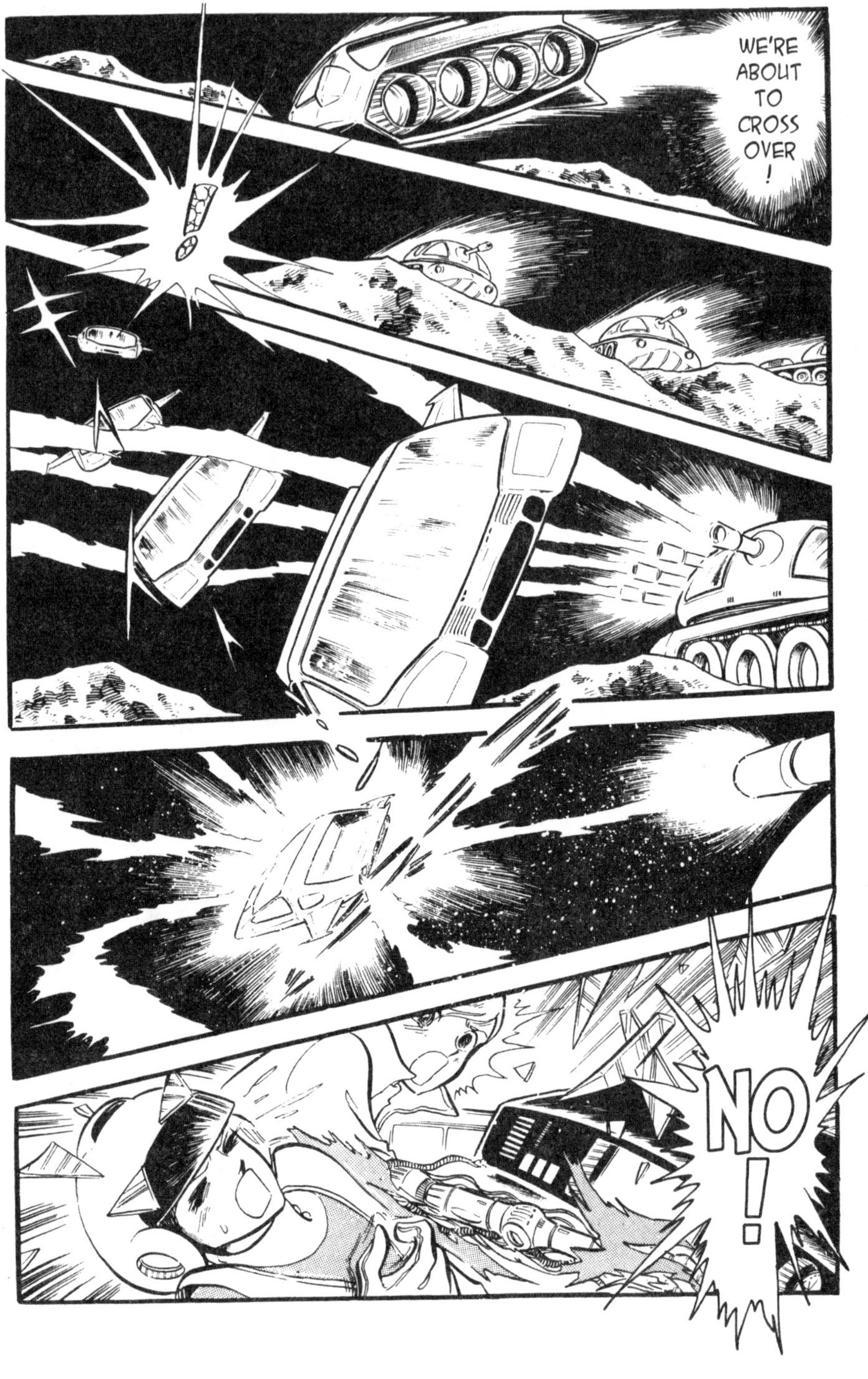
WE'RE ABOUT TO CROSS OVER!
NO!

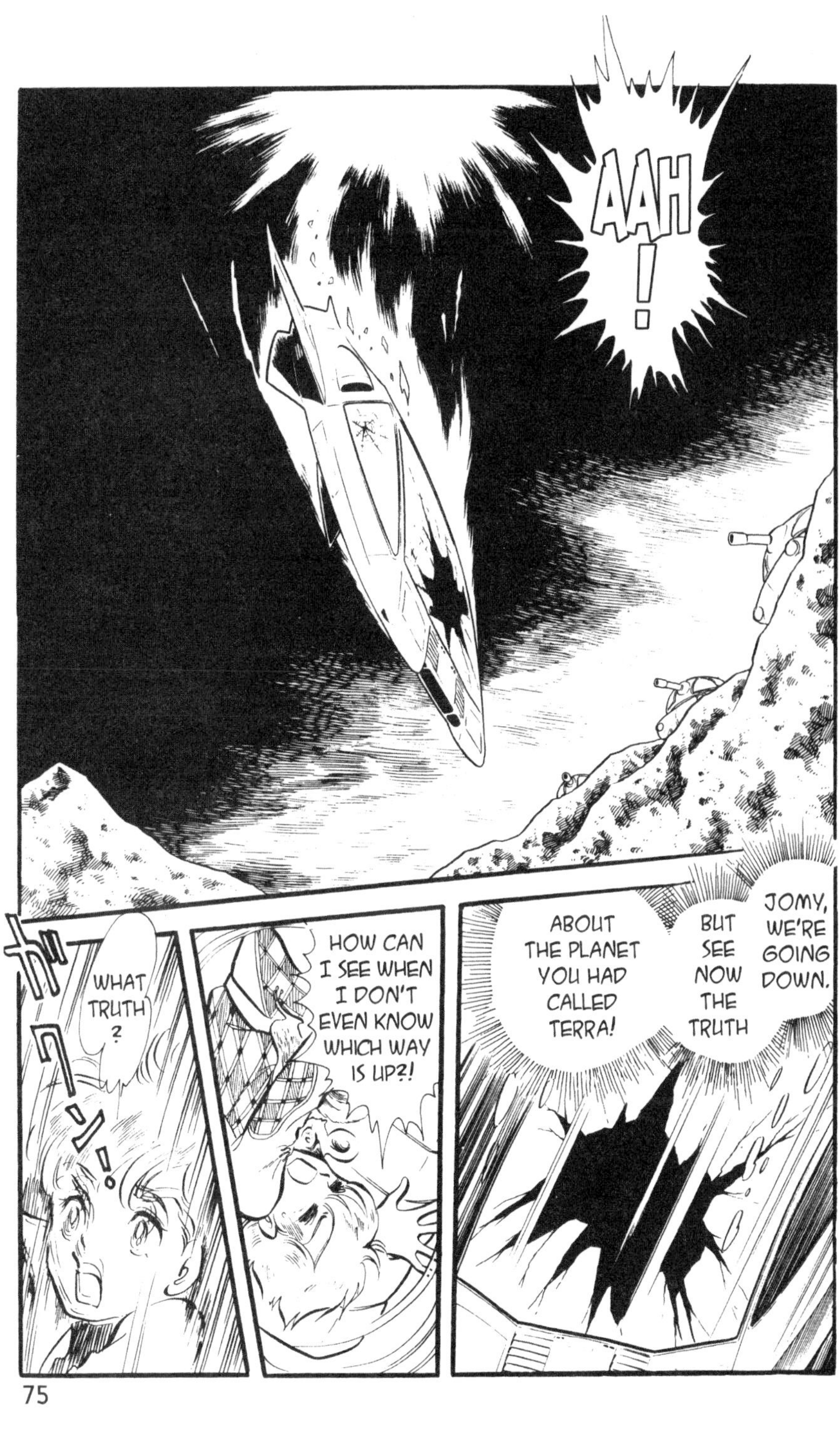
AAH!
JOMY, WE'RE GOING DOWN.
BUT SEE NOW THE TRUTH
ABOUT THE PLANET YOU HAD CALLED TERRA!
HOW CAN I SEE WHEN I DON'T EVEN KNOW WHICH WAY IS UP?!
WHAT TRUTH?

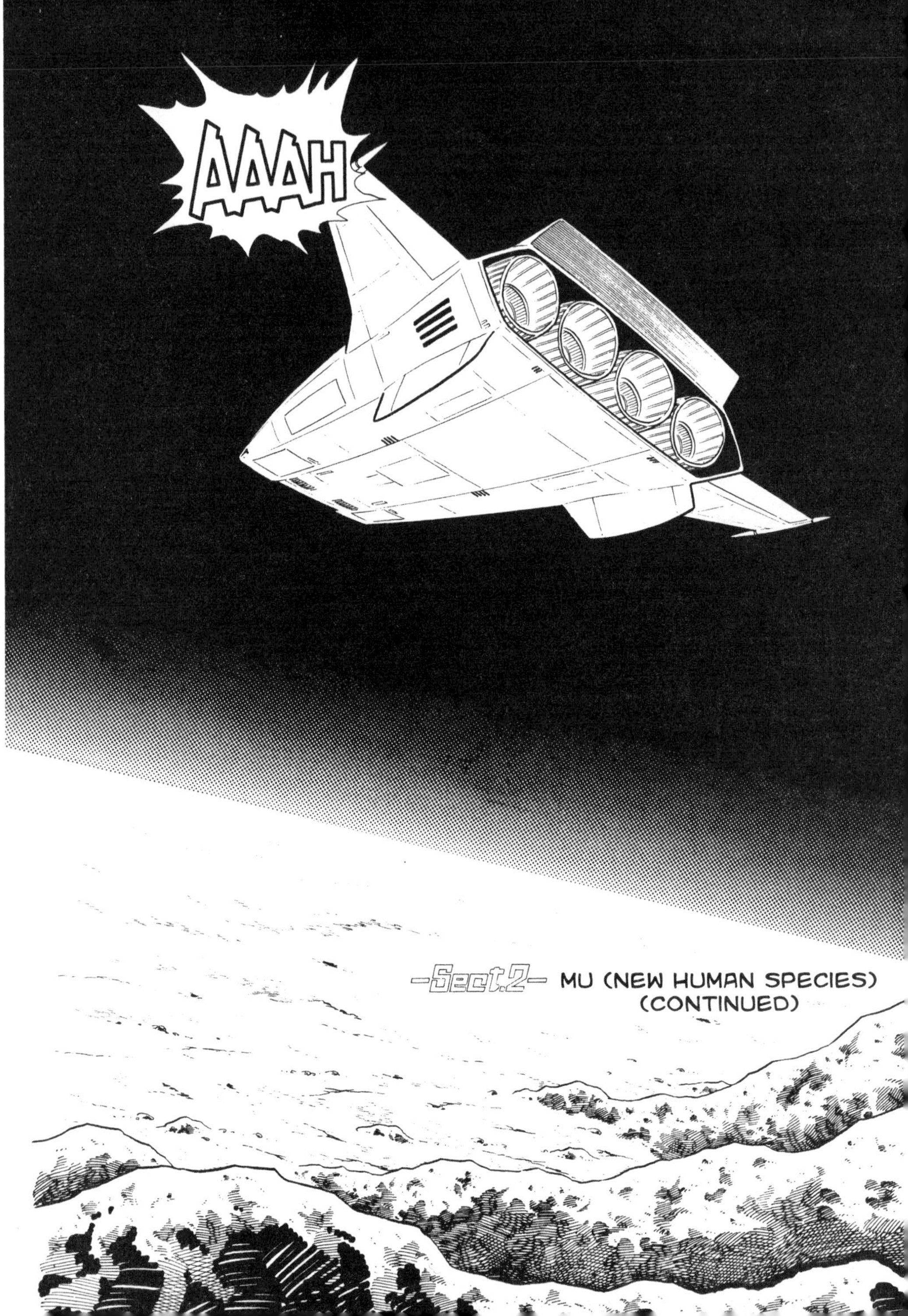
AAAH
-Sect.2- MU (NEW HUMAN SPECIES)
(CONTINUED)

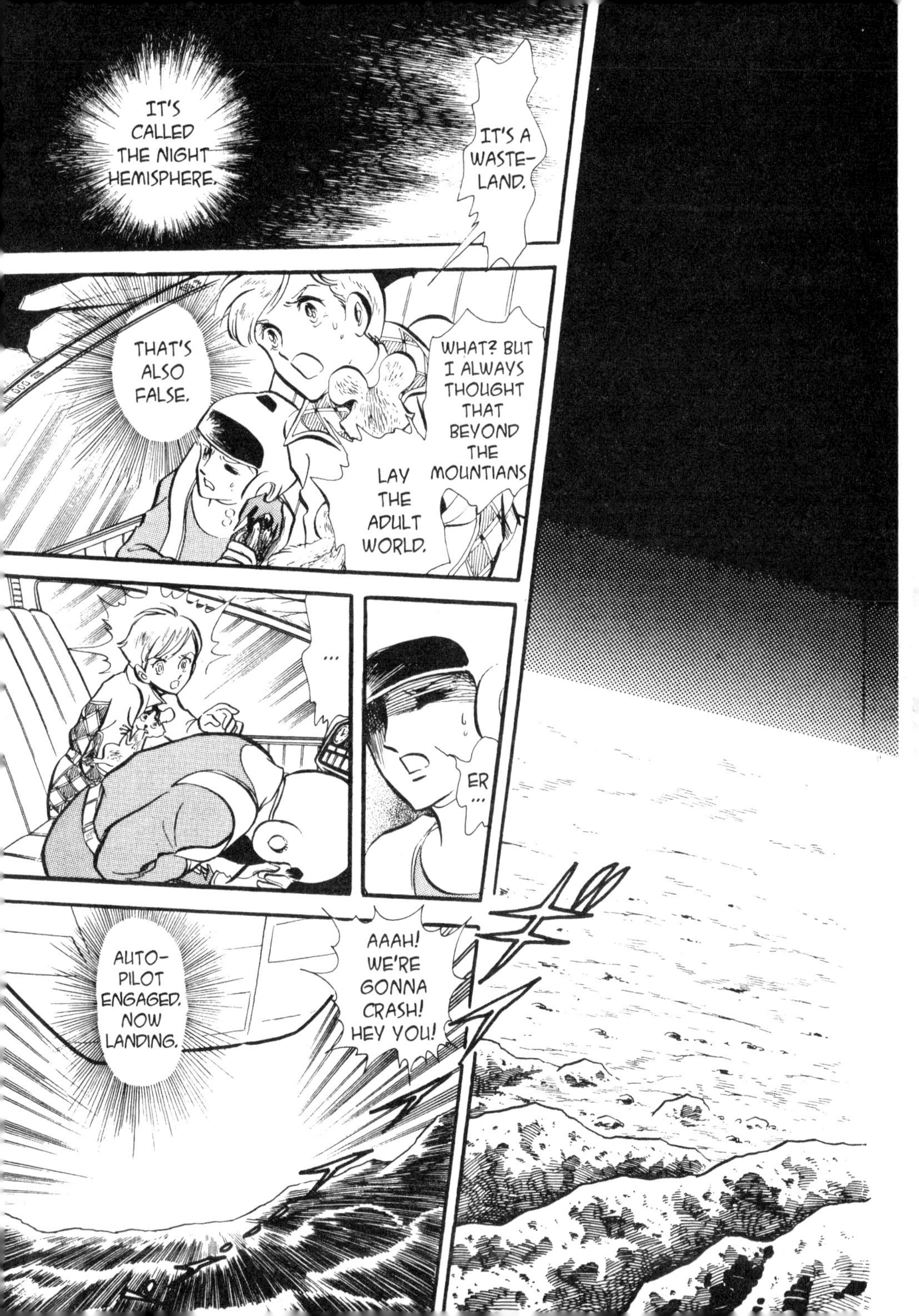
IT'S A WASTE-LAND.
IT'S CALLED THE NIGHT HEMISPHERE.
WHAT? BUT I ALWAYS THOUGHT THAT BEYOND THE MOUNTIANS
LAY THE ADULT WORLD.
THAT'S ALSO FALSE.
ER...
...
AAAH! WE'RE GONNA CRASH! HEY YOU!
AUTO-PILOT ENGAGED. NOW LANDING.

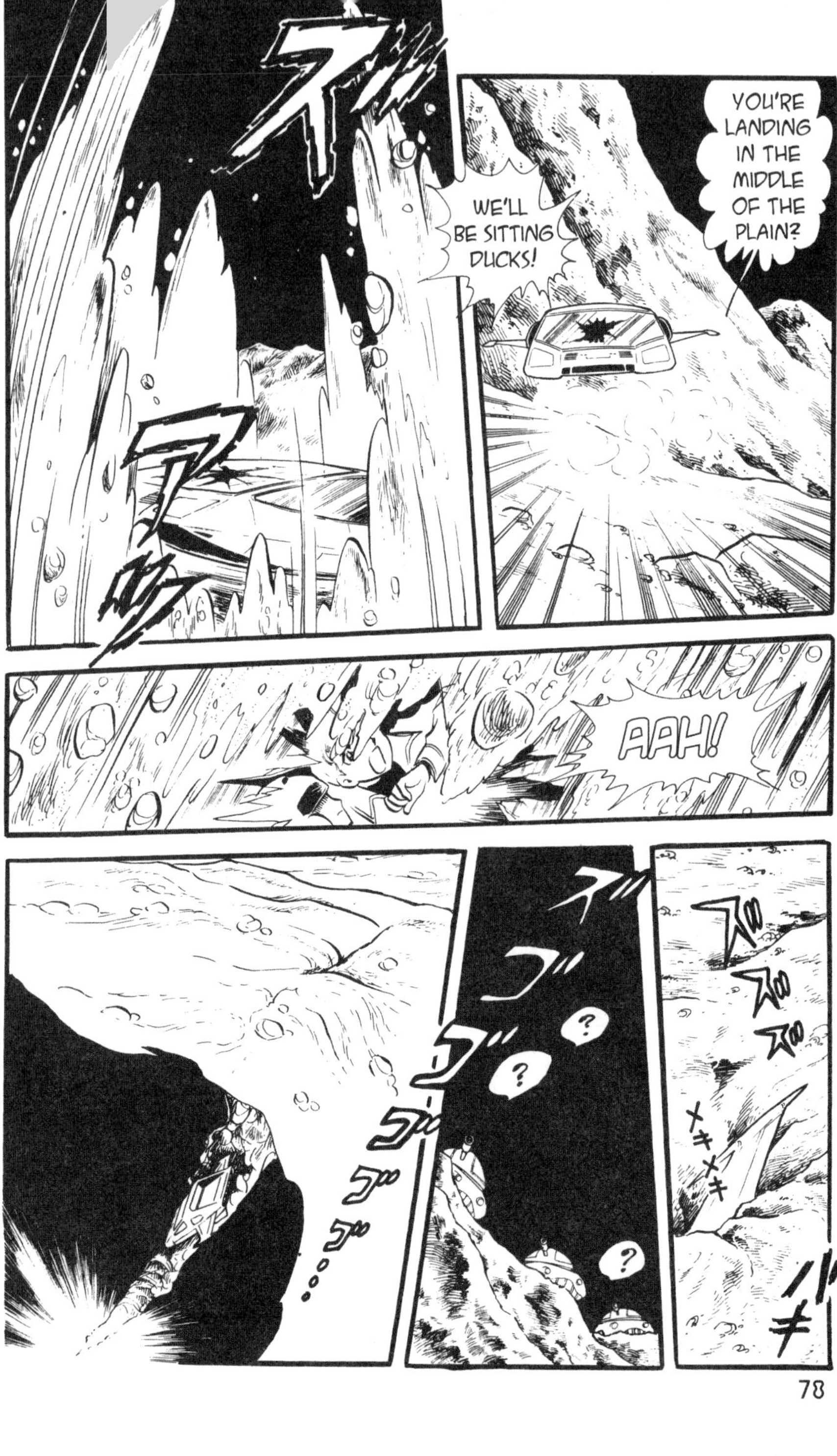
YOU'RE LANDING IN THE MIDDLE OF THE PLAIN?
WE'LL BE SITTING DUCKS!
AAH!
メキメキ

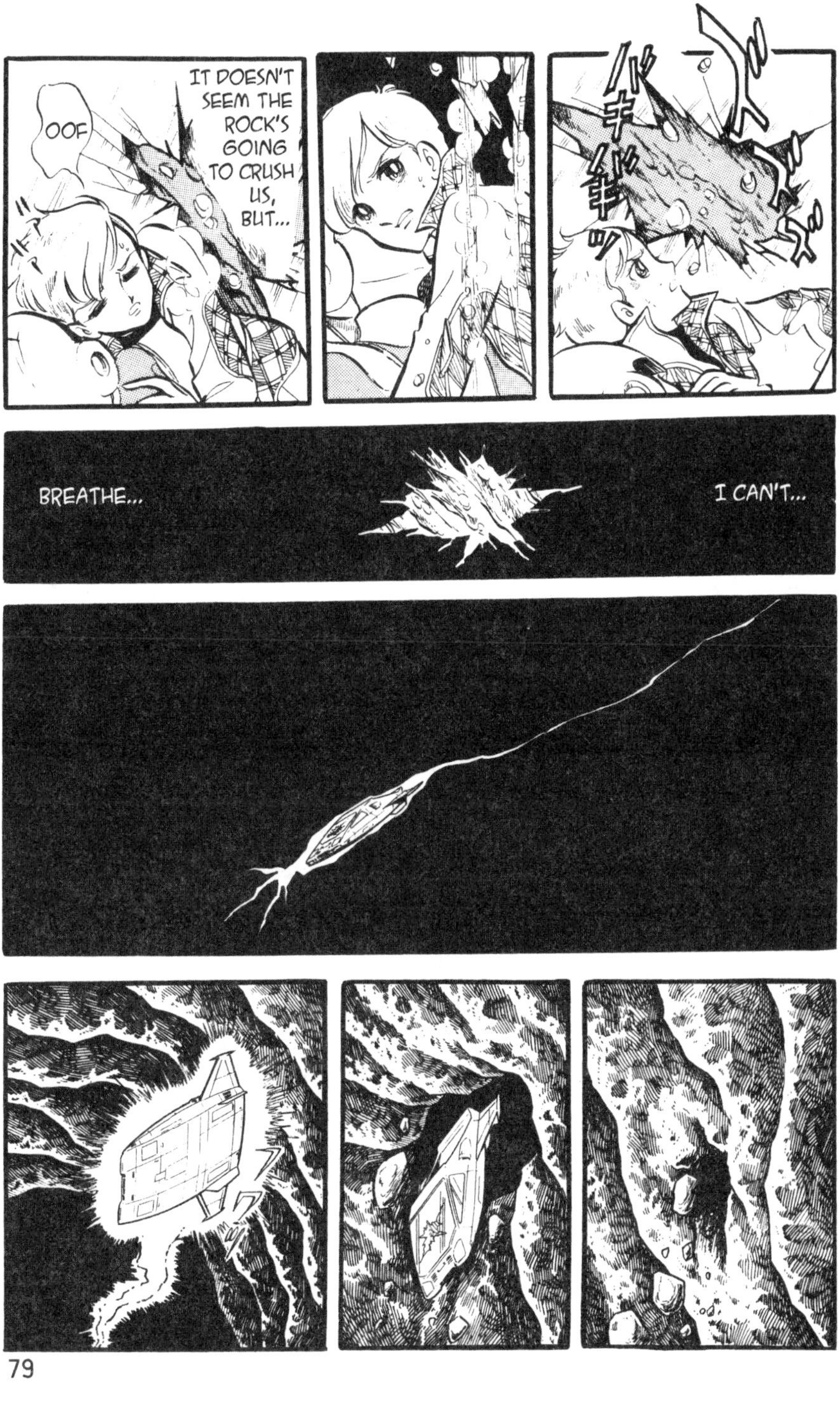
IT DOESN'T SEEM THE ROCK'S GOING TO CRUSH US, BUT...
OOF
I CAN'T...
BREATHE...

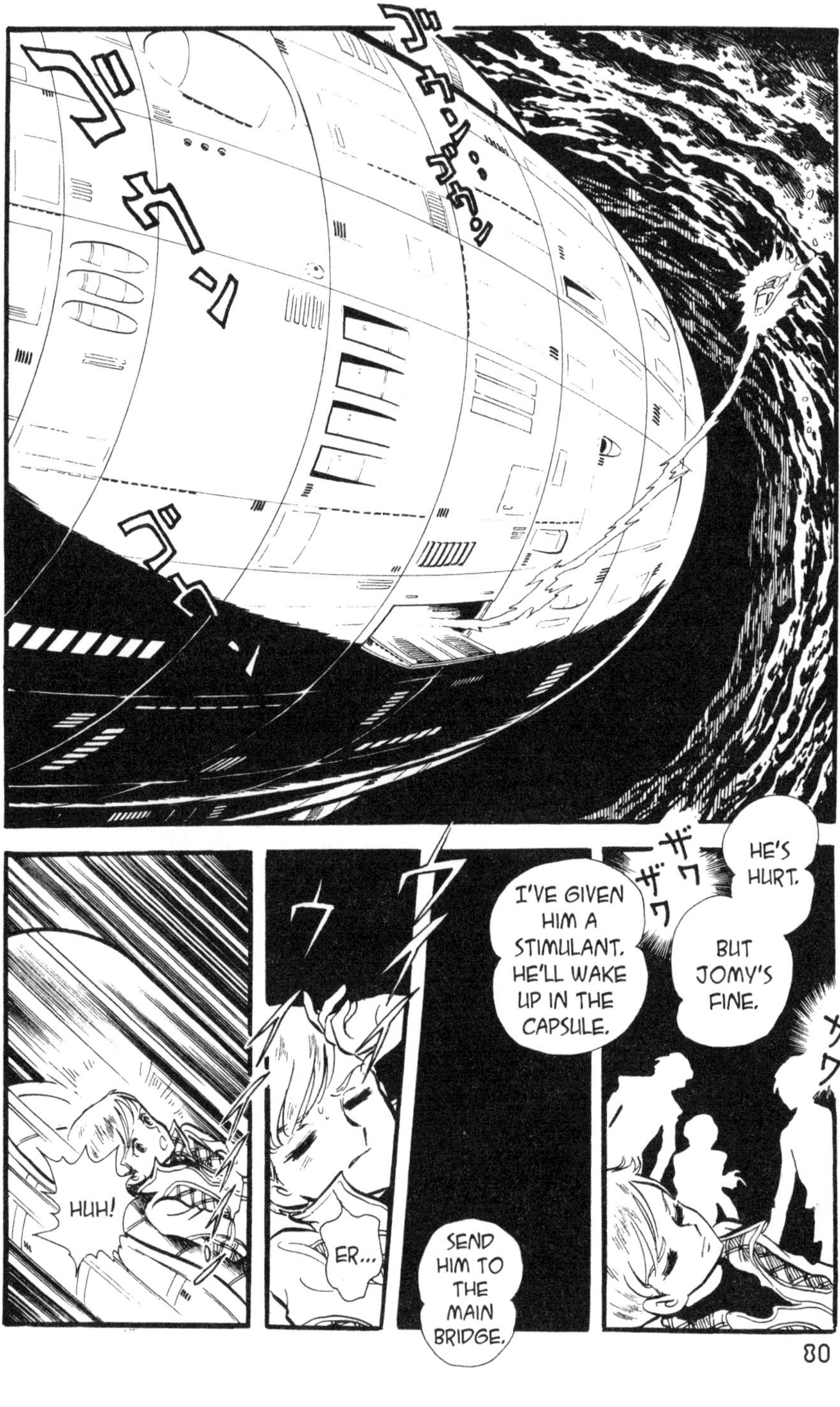
ザワ
ザワ
HE'S HURT.
BUT JOMY'S FINE.
I'VE GIVEN HIM A STIMULANT. HE'LL WAKE UP IN THE CAPSULE.
ザワ
ER...
SEND HIM TO THE MAIN BRIDGE.
HUH!

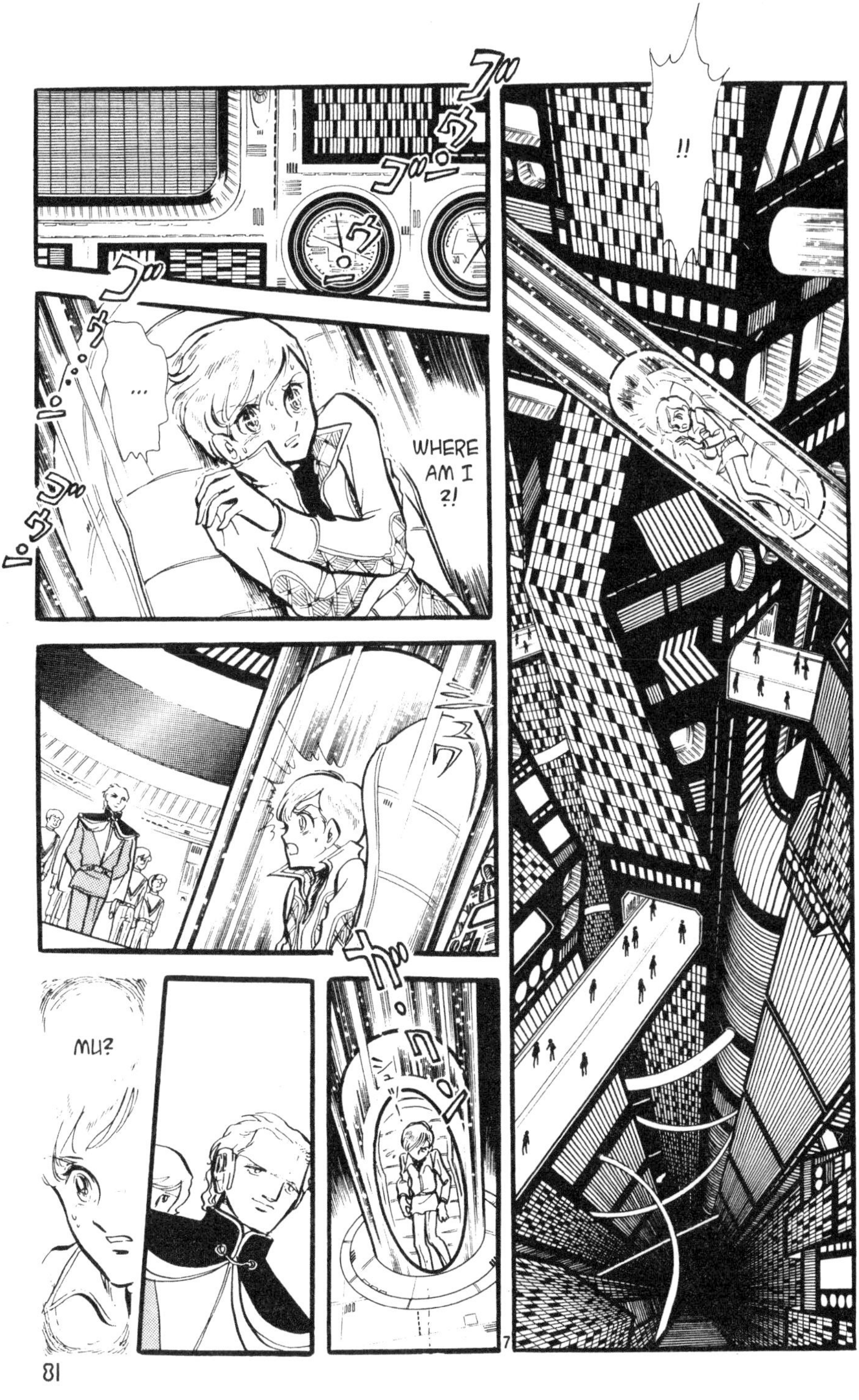
!!
...
WHERE AM I ?!
MU?

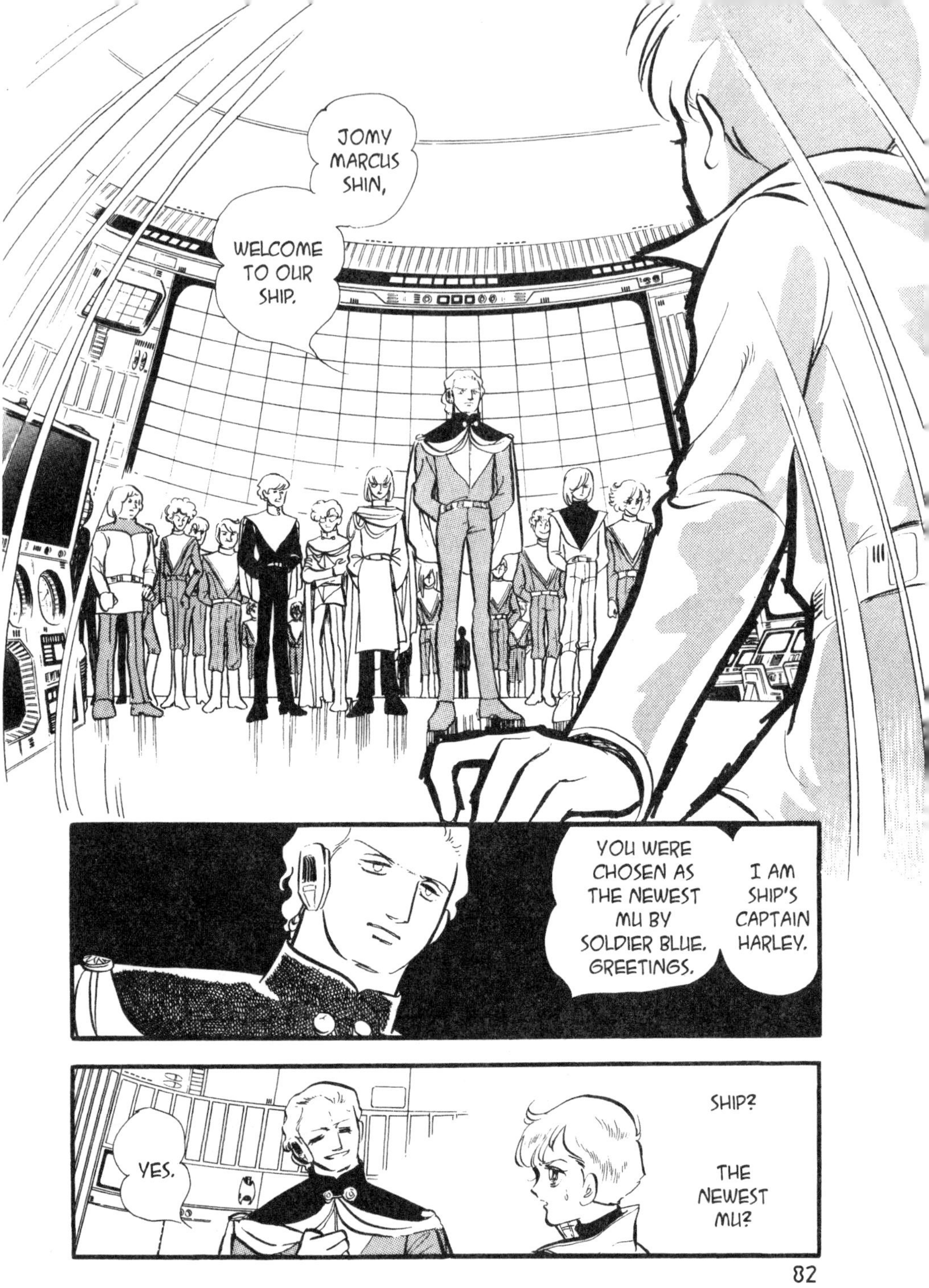
JOMY MARCUS SHIN,
WELCOME TO OUR SHIP.
I AM SHIP'S CAPTAIN HARLEY.
YOU WERE CHOSEN AS THE NEWEST MU BY SOLDIER BLUE. GREETINGS.
SHIP?
THE NEWEST MU?
YES.

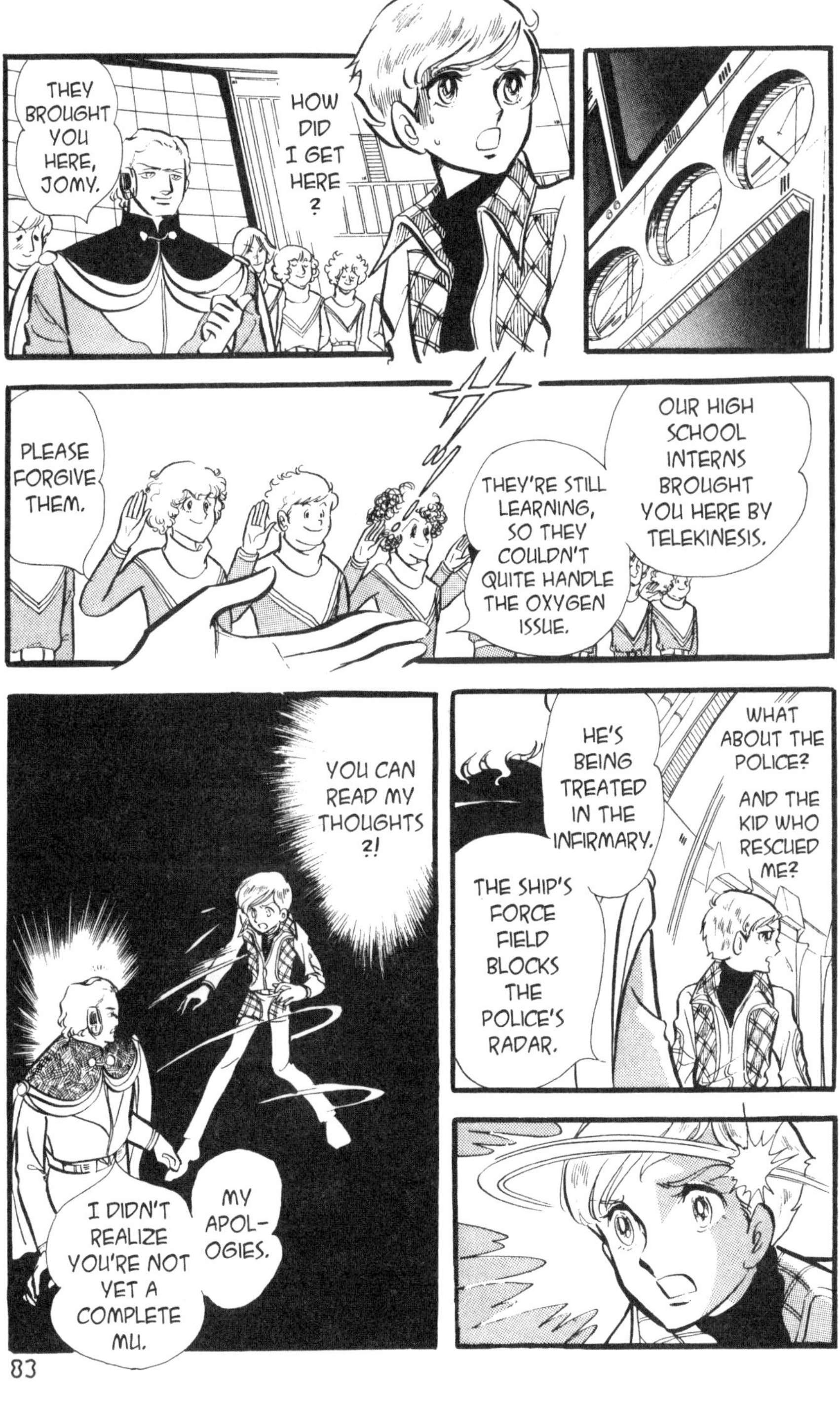
HOW DID I GET HERE?
THEY BROUGHT YOU HERE, JOMY.
OUR HIGH SCHOOL INTERNS BROUGHT YOU HERE BY TELEKINESIS.
THEY'RE STILL LEARNING, SO THEY COULDN'T QUITE HANDLE THE OXYGEN ISSUE.
PLEASE FORGIVE THEM.
WHAT ABOUT THE POLICE?
AND THE KID WHO RESCUED ME?
HE'S BEING TREATED IN THE INFIRMARY.
THE SHIP'S FORCE FIELD BLOCKS THE POLICE'S RADAR.
YOU CAN READ MY THOUGHTS?!
MY APOLOGIES.
I DIDN'T REALIZE YOU'RE NOT YET A COMPLETE MU.

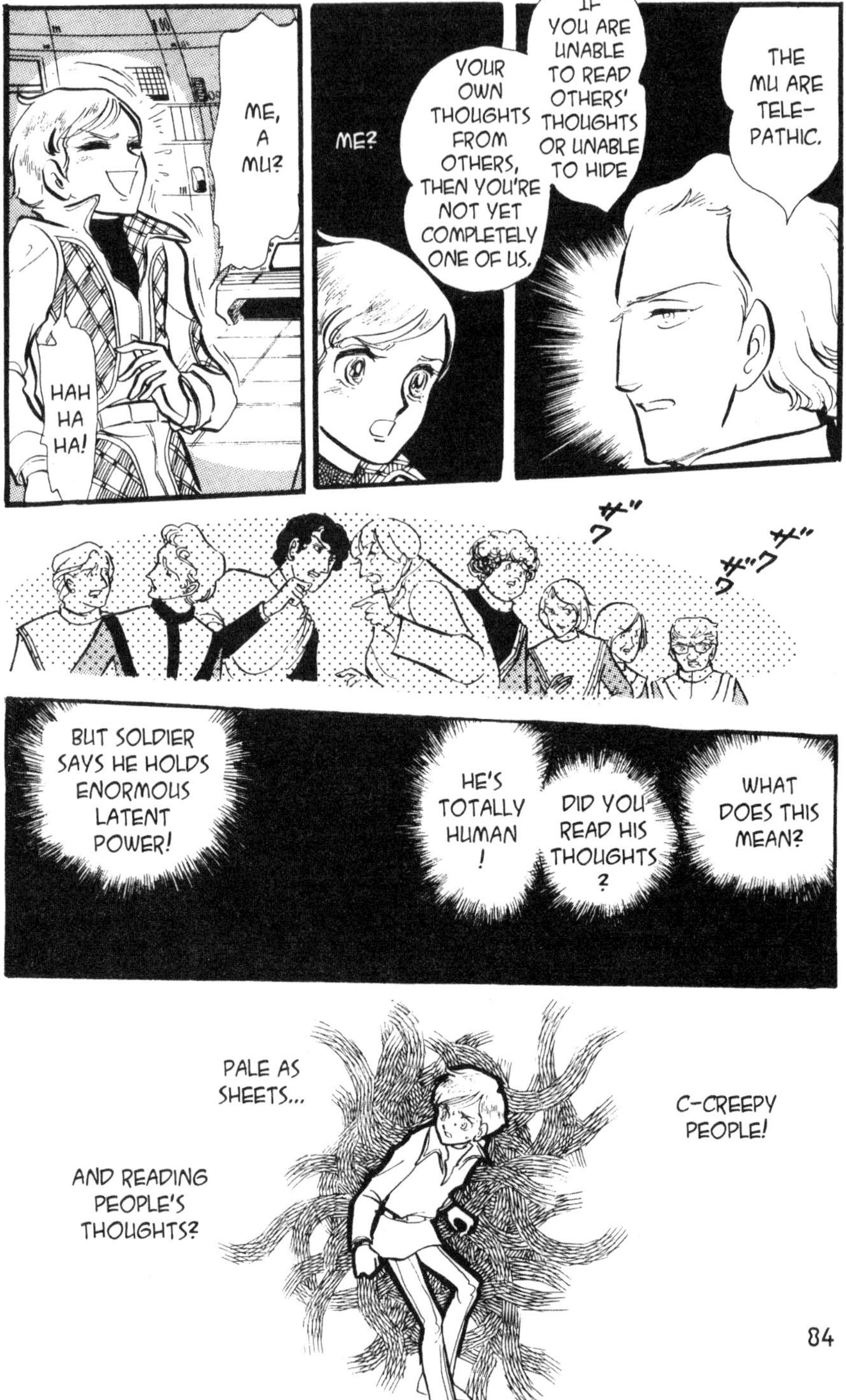
THE MU ARE TELE-PATHIC.
IF YOU ARE UNABLE TO READ OTHERS' THOUGHTS OR UNABLE TO HIDE
YOUR OWN THOUGHTS FROM OTHERS, THEN YOU'RE NOT YET COMPLETELY ONE OF US.
ME?
ME, A MU?
HAH HA HA!
ザワ
ザワ ザワ
WHAT DOES THIS MEAN?
DID YOU READ HIS THOUGHTS?
HE'S TOTALLY HUMAN!
BUT SOLDIER SAYS HE HOLDS ENORMOUS LATENT POWER!
C-CREEPY PEOPLE!
PALE AS SHEETS...
AND READING PEOPLE'S THOUGHTS?

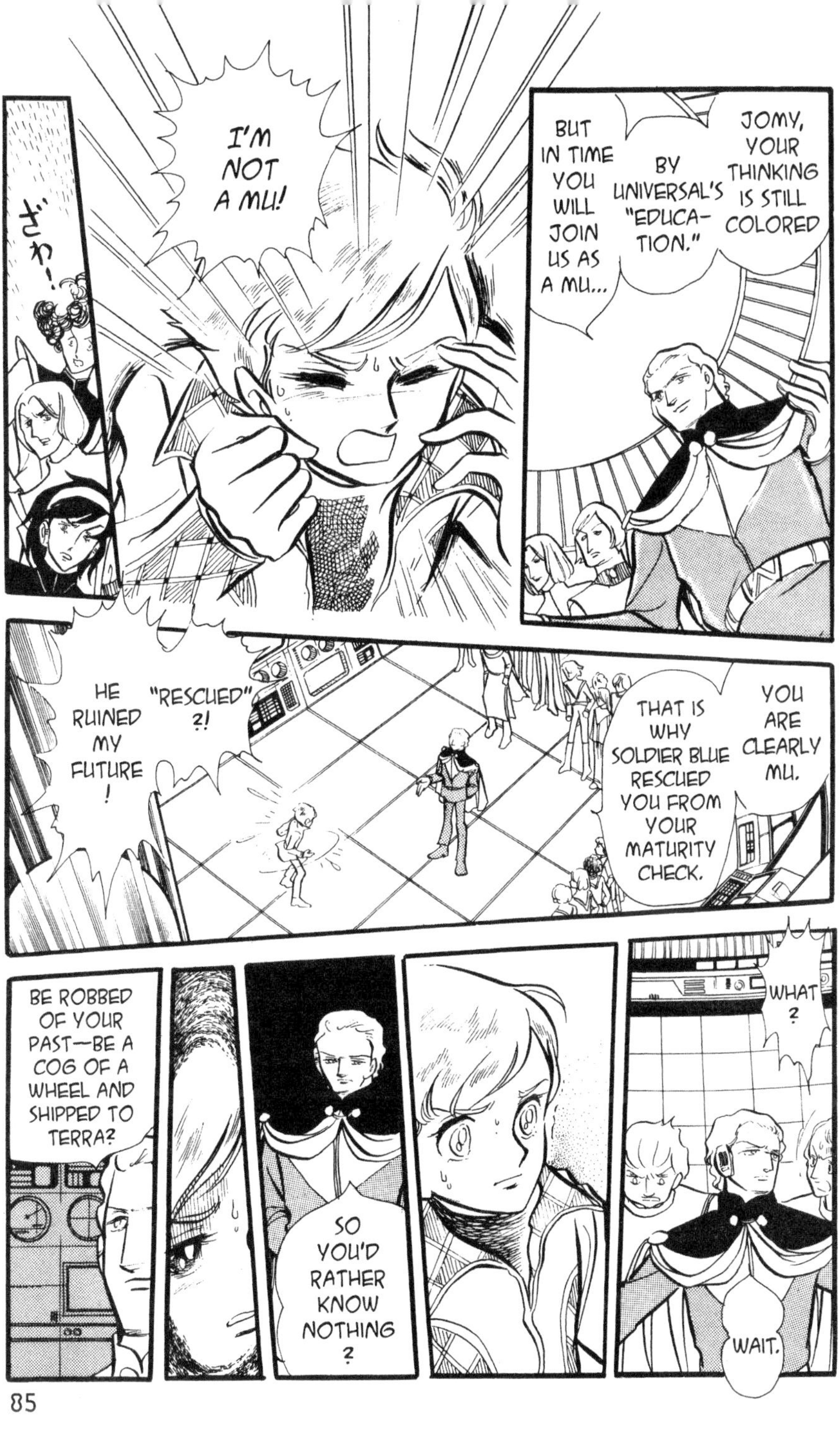
JOMY, YOUR THINKING IS STILL COLORED
BY UNIVERSAL'S "EDUCATION."
BUT IN TIME YOU WILL JOIN US AS A MU...
I'M NOT A MU!
ざわ！
YOU ARE CLEARLY MU.
THAT IS WHY SOLDIER BLUE RESCUED YOU FROM YOUR MATURITY CHECK.
"RESCUED"?!
HE RUINED MY FUTURE!
WHAT?
WAIT.
SO YOU'D RATHER KNOW NOTHING?
BE ROBBED OF YOUR PAST—BE A COG OF A WHEEL AND SHIPPED TO TERRA?

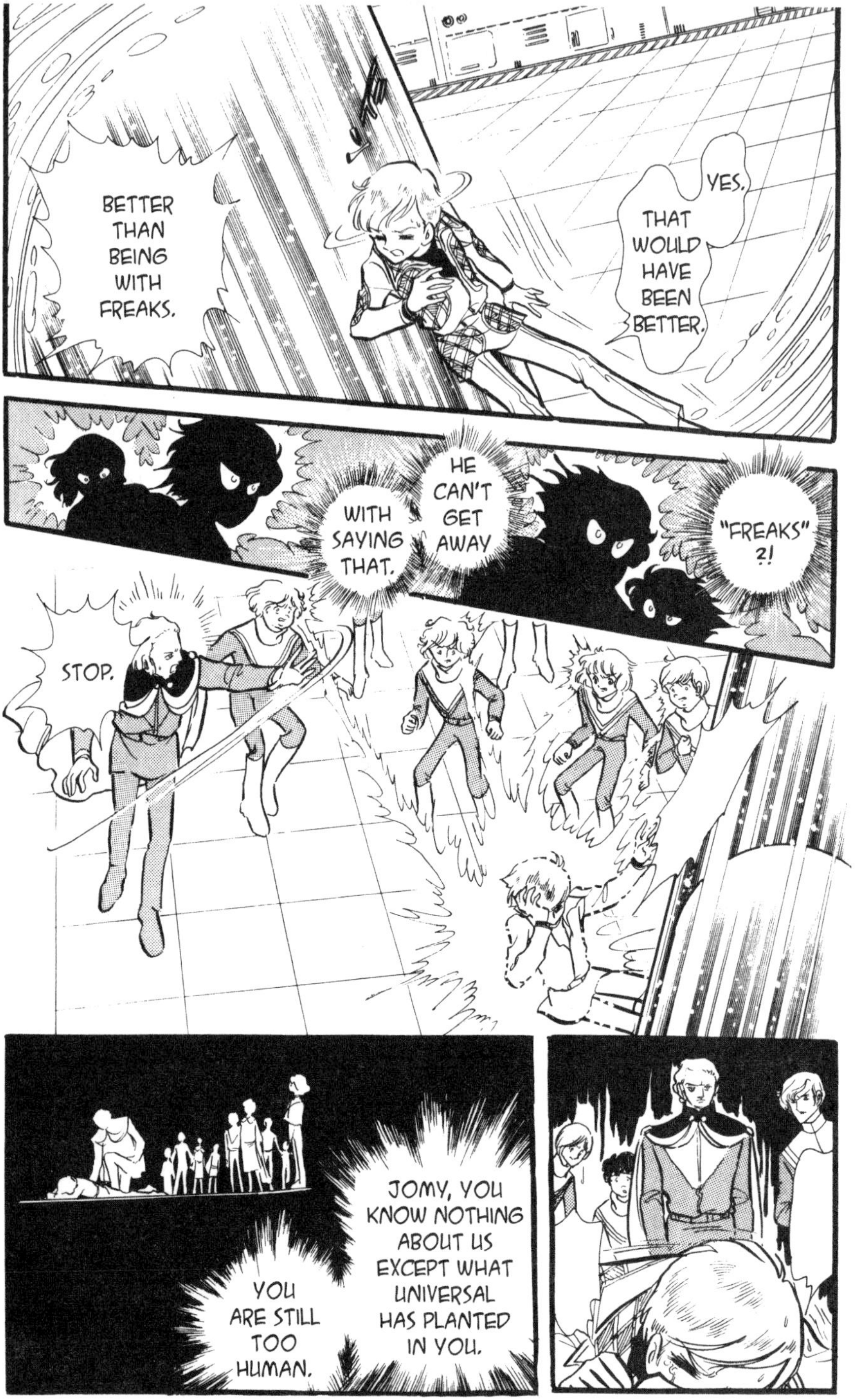
YES. THAT WOULD HAVE BEEN BETTER.
BETTER THAN BEING WITH FREAKS.
"FREAKS" ?!
HE CAN'T GET AWAY WITH SAYING THAT.
STOP.
JOMY, YOU KNOW NOTHING ABOUT US EXCEPT WHAT UNIVERSAL HAS PLANTED IN YOU.
YOU ARE STILL TOO HUMAN.

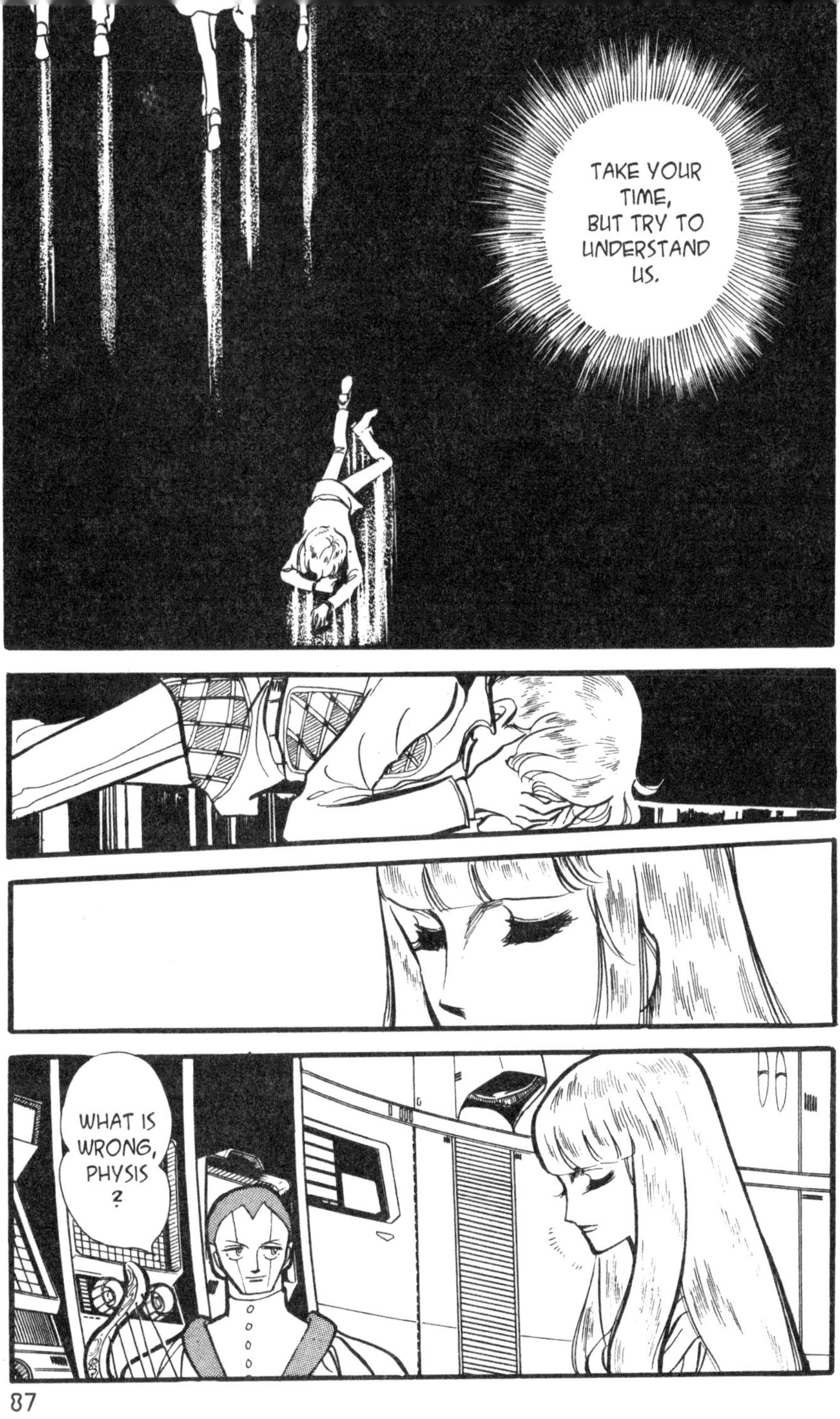
TAKE YOUR TIME, BUT TRY TO UNDERSTAND US.
WHAT IS WRONG, PHYSIS ?

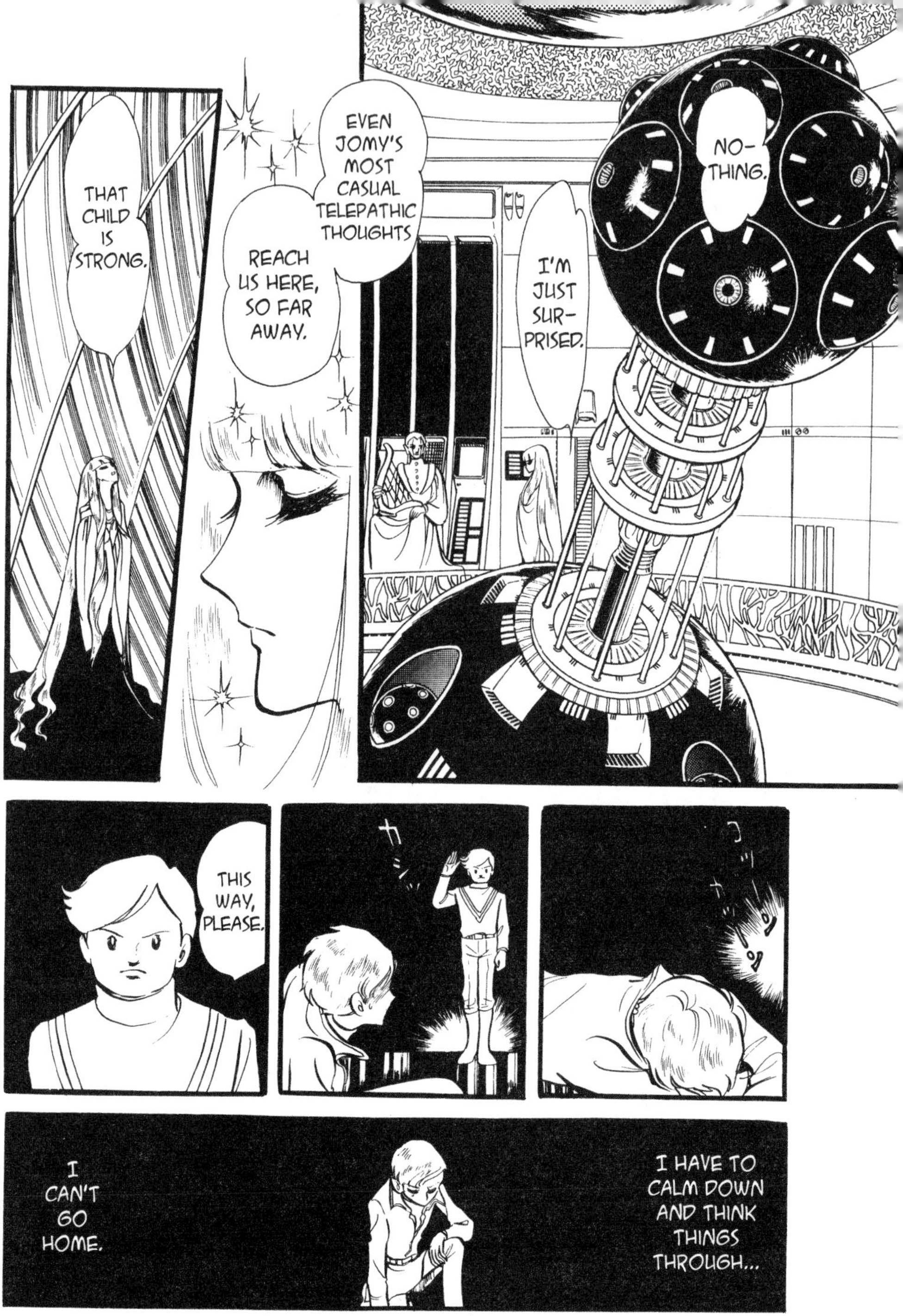
NO-THING.
I'M JUST SUR-PRISED.
EVEN JOMY'S MOST CASUAL TELEPATHIC THOUGHTS
REACH US HERE, SO FAR AWAY.
THAT CHILD IS STRONG.
THIS WAY, PLEASE.
I HAVE TO CALM DOWN AND THINK THINGS THROUGH...
I CAN'T GO HOME.

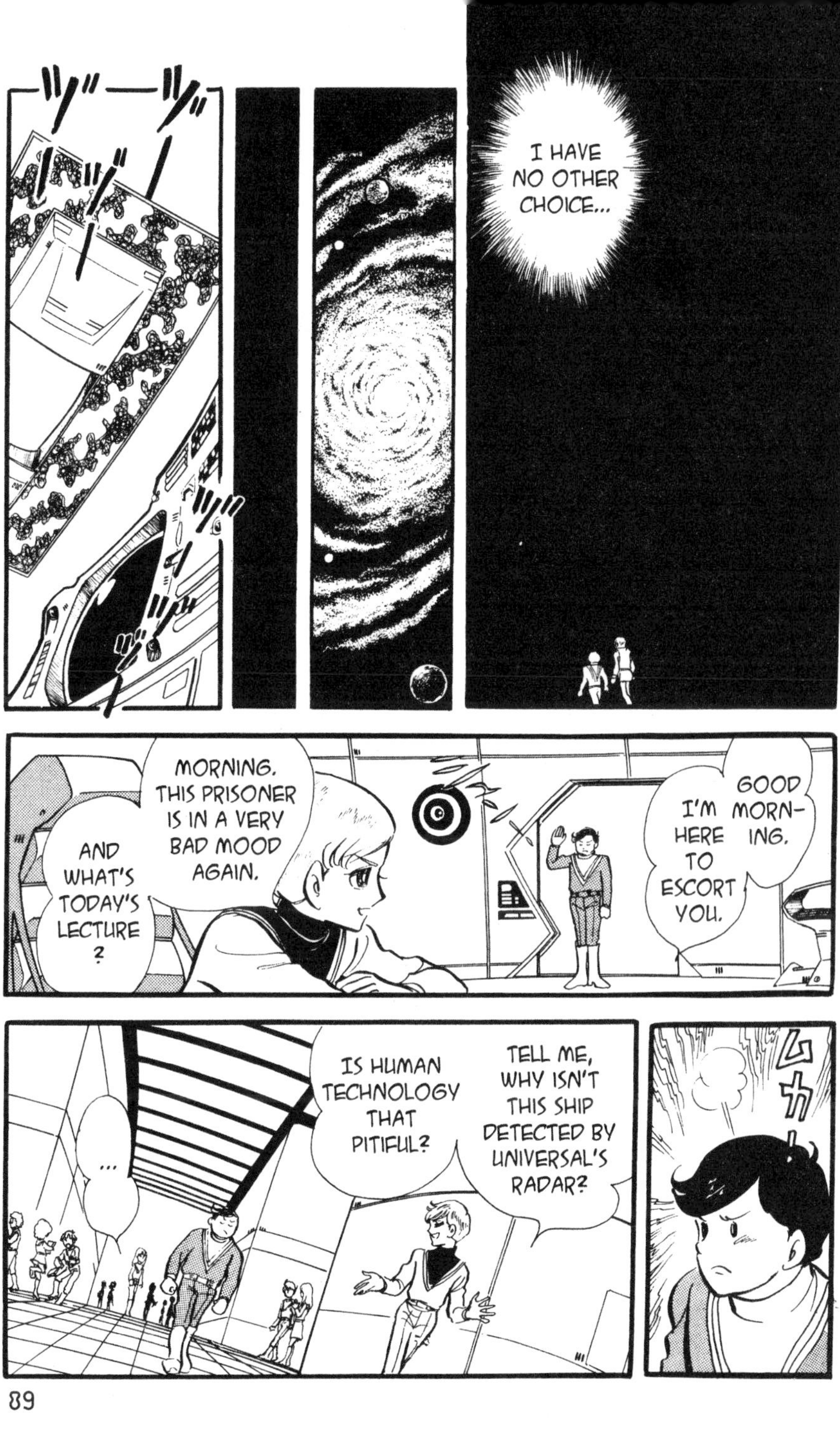
I HAVE NO OTHER CHOICE...
GOOD MORNING.
I'M HERE TO ESCORT YOU.
MORNING. THIS PRISONER IS IN A VERY BAD MOOD AGAIN.
AND WHAT'S TODAY'S LECTURE?
ムカ
TELL ME, WHY ISN'T THIS SHIP DETECTED BY UNIVERSAL'S RADAR?
IS HUMAN TECHNOLOGY THAT PITIFUL?
...

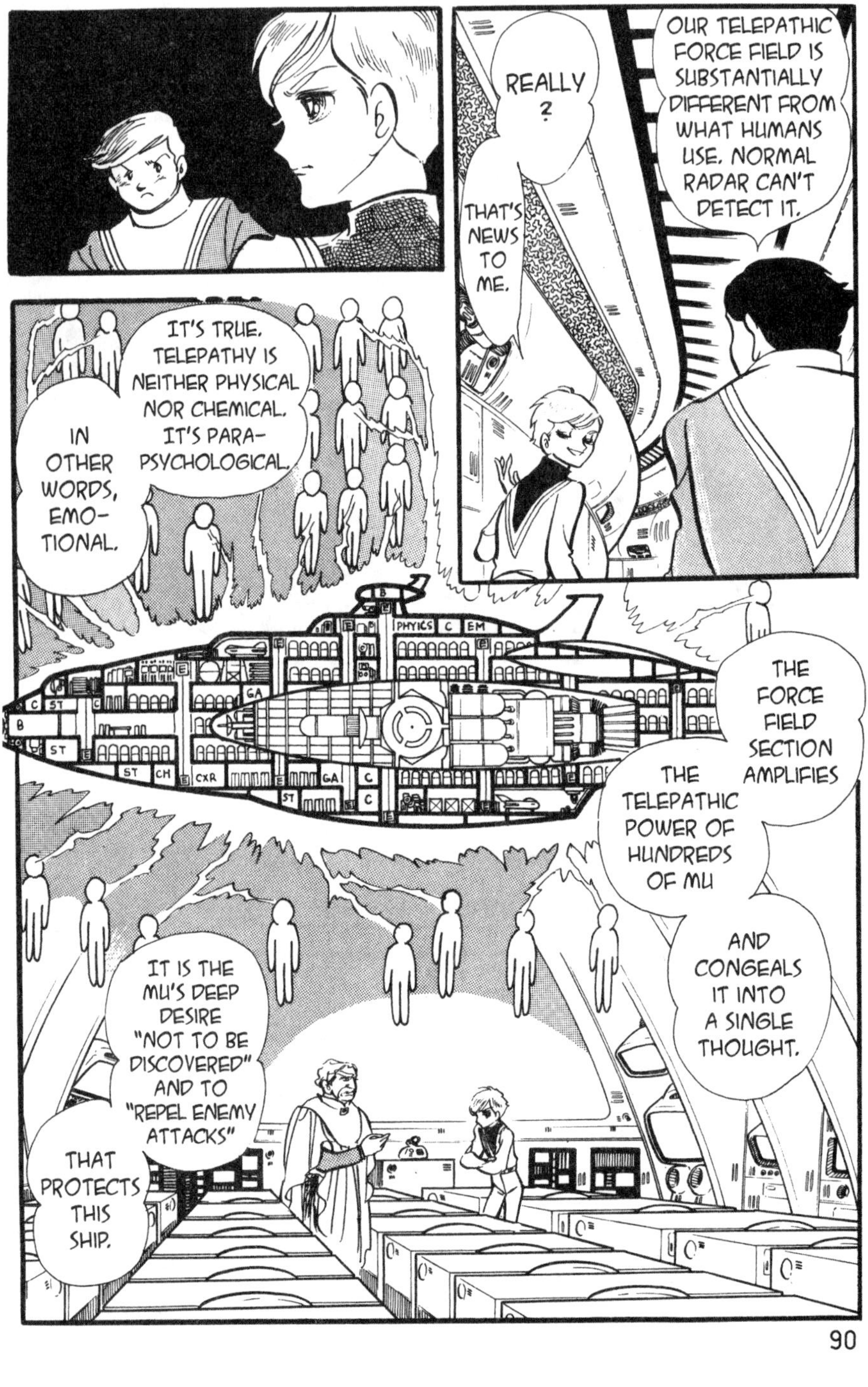

OUR TELEPATHIC FORCE FIELD IS SUBSTANTIALLY DIFFERENT FROM WHAT HUMANS USE. NORMAL RADAR CAN'T DETECT IT.
REALLY?
THAT'S NEWS TO ME.
IT'S TRUE. TELEPATHY IS NEITHER PHYSICAL NOR CHEMICAL. IT'S PARA-PSYCHOLOGICAL.
IN OTHER WORDS, EMO-TIONAL.
THE FORCE FIELD SECTION AMPLIFIES
THE TELEPATHIC POWER OF HUNDREDS OF MU
AND CONGEALS IT INTO A SINGLE THOUGHT.
IT IS THE MU'S DEEP DESIRE "NOT TO BE DISCOVERED" AND TO "REPEL ENEMY ATTACKS"
THAT PROTECTS THIS SHIP.

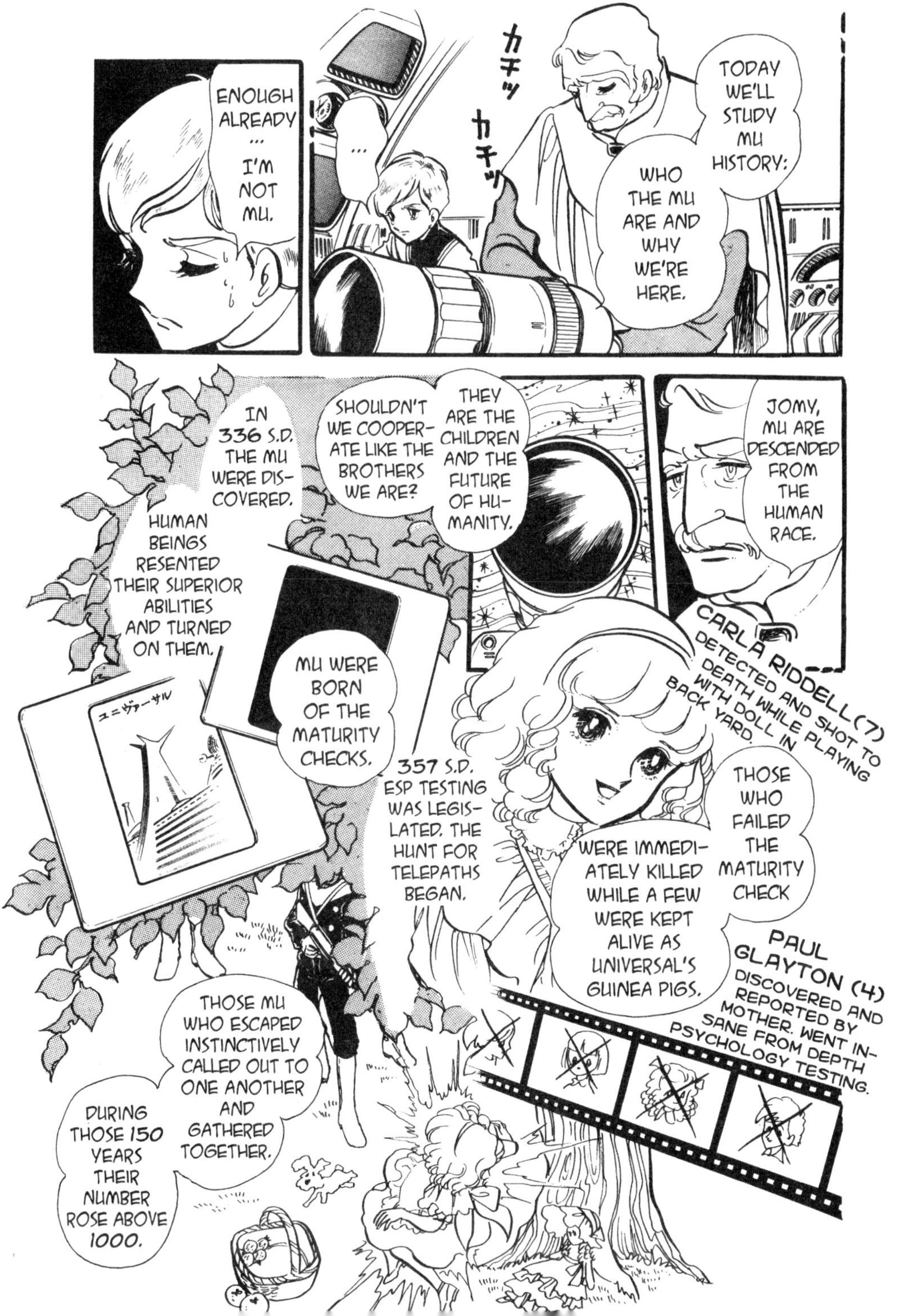
カチッ
カチッ
TODAY WE'LL STUDY MU HISTORY:
WHO THE MU ARE AND WHY WE'RE HERE.
...
ENOUGH ALREADY ... I'M NOT MU.
JOMY, MU ARE DESCENDED FROM THE HUMAN RACE.
THEY ARE THE CHILDREN AND THE FUTURE OF HUMANITY.
SHOULDN'T WE COOPERATE LIKE THE BROTHERS WE ARE?
IN 336 S.D. THE MU WERE DISCOVERED.
HUMAN BEINGS RESENTED THEIR SUPERIOR ABILITIES AND TURNED ON THEM.
CARLA RIDDELL (7) DETECTED AND SHOT TO DEATH WHILE PLAYING WITH DOLL IN BACK YARD.
MU WERE BORN OF THE MATURITY CHECKS.
ユニヴァーサル
357 S.D. ESP TESTING WAS LEGISLATED. THE HUNT FOR TELEPATHS BEGAN.
THOSE WHO FAILED THE MATURITY CHECK
WERE IMMEDIATELY KILLED WHILE A FEW WERE KEPT ALIVE AS UNIVERSAL'S GUINEA PIGS.
PAUL GLAYTON (4) DISCOVERED AND REPORTED BY MOTHER. WENT INSANE FROM DEPTH PSYCHOLOGY TESTING.
THOSE MU WHO ESCAPED INSTINCTIVELY CALLED OUT TO ONE ANOTHER AND GATHERED TOGETHER.
DURING THOSE 150 YEARS THEIR NUMBER ROSE ABOVE 1000.

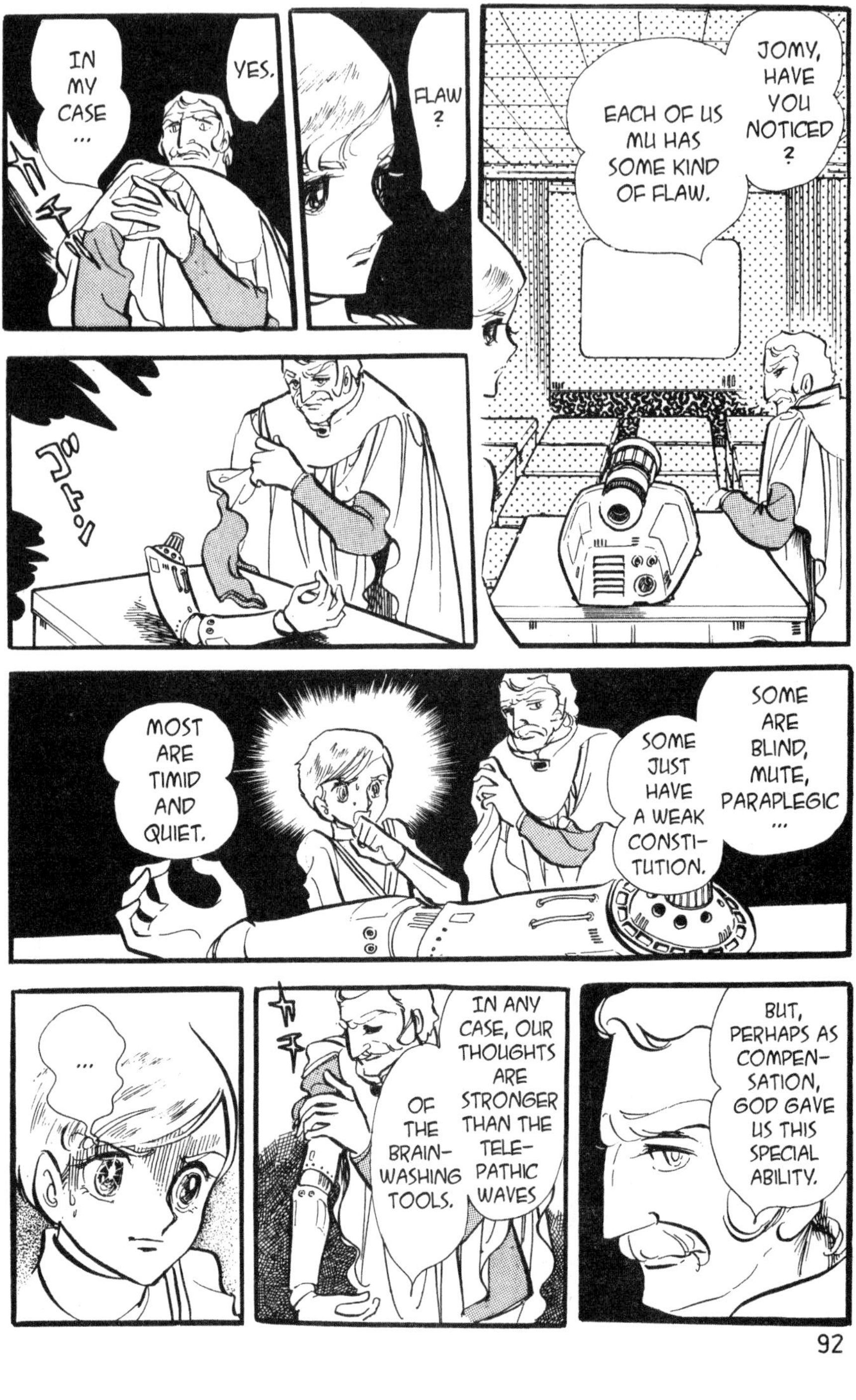
JOMY, HAVE YOU NOTICED?
EACH OF US MU HAS SOME KIND OF FLAW.
FLAW?
YES.
IN MY CASE...
SOME ARE BLIND, MUTE, PARAPLEGIC...
SOME JUST HAVE A WEAK CONSTI-TUTION.
MOST ARE TIMID AND QUIET.
BUT, PERHAPS AS COMPEN-SATION, GOD GAVE US THIS SPECIAL ABILITY.
IN ANY CASE, OUR THOUGHTS ARE STRONGER THAN THE TELE-PATHIC WAVES
OF THE BRAIN-WASHING TOOLS.
...

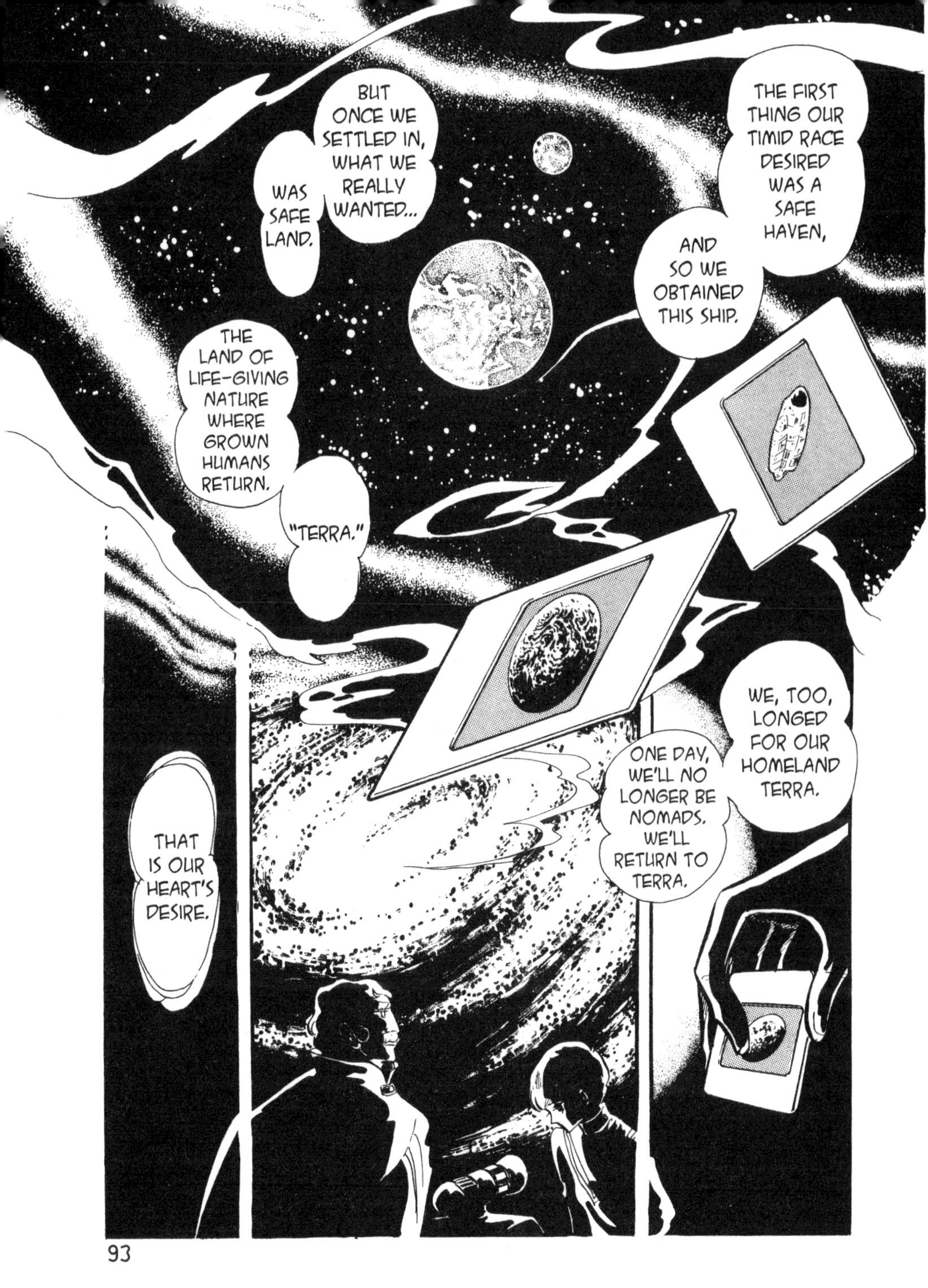
THE FIRST THING OUR TIMID RACE DESIRED WAS A SAFE HAVEN,
AND SO WE OBTAINED THIS SHIP.
BUT ONCE WE SETTLED IN, WHAT WE REALLY WANTED...
WAS SAFE LAND.
THE LAND OF LIFE-GIVING NATURE WHERE GROWN HUMANS RETURN.
"TERRA."
WE, TOO, LONGED FOR OUR HOMELAND TERRA.
ONE DAY, WE'LL NO LONGER BE NOMADS. WE'LL RETURN TO TERRA.
THAT IS OUR HEART'S DESIRE.

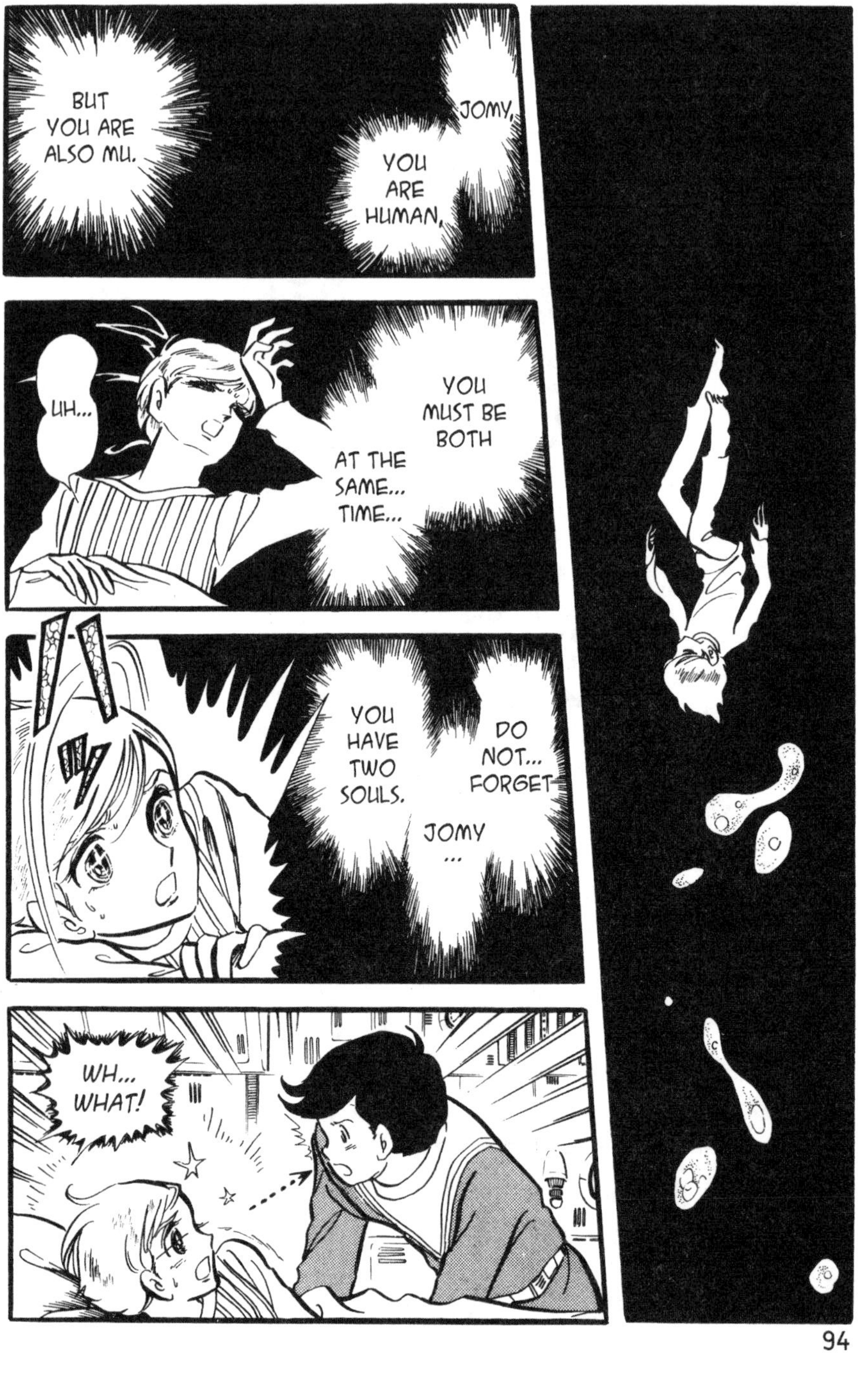
JOMY,
YOU ARE HUMAN,
BUT YOU ARE ALSO MU.
YOU MUST BE BOTH
AT THE SAME... TIME...
UH...
DO NOT... FORGET
YOU HAVE TWO SOULS.
JOMY ...
WH... WHAT!

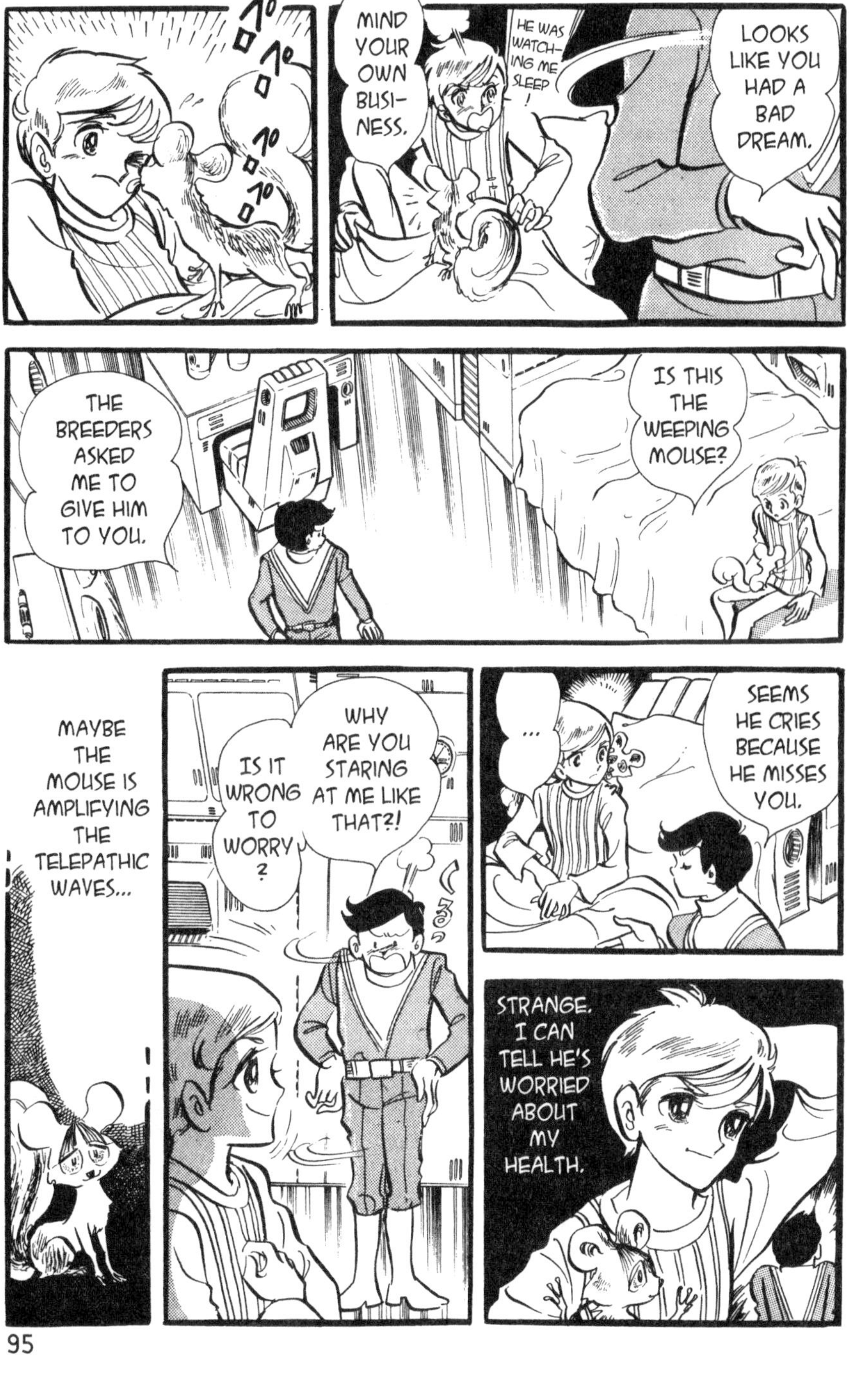

LOOKS LIKE YOU HAD A BAD DREAM.
HE WAS WATCHING ME SLEEP!
MIND YOUR OWN BUSINESS.
IS THIS THE WEEPING MOUSE?
THE BREEDERS ASKED ME TO GIVE HIM TO YOU.
SEEMS HE CRIES BECAUSE HE MISSES YOU.
...
STRANGE. I CAN TELL HE'S WORRIED ABOUT MY HEALTH.
WHY ARE YOU STARING AT ME LIKE THAT?!
IS IT WRONG TO WORRY?
くるっ
MAYBE THE MOUSE IS AMPLIFYING THE TELEPATHIC WAVES...

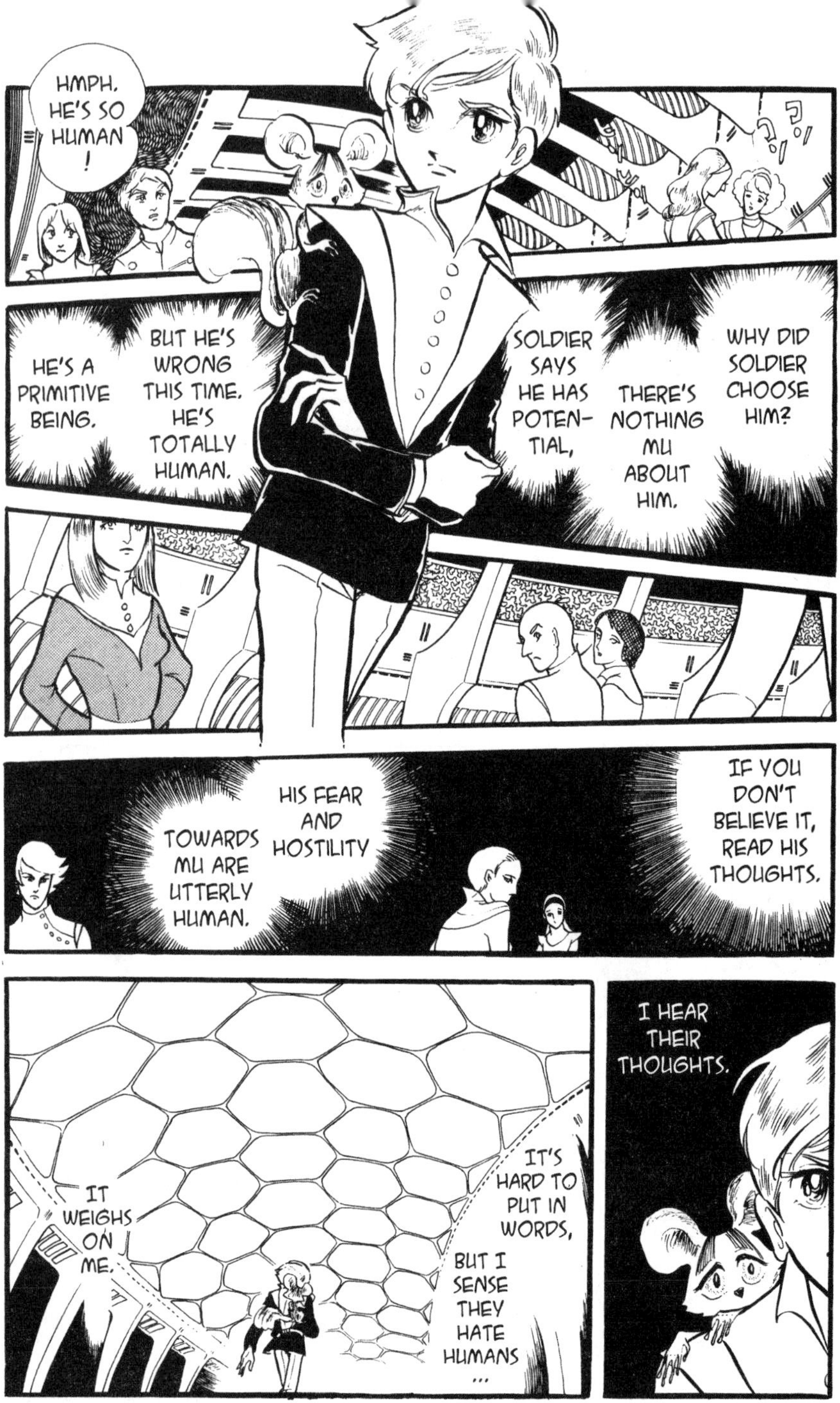
HMPH. HE'S SO HUMAN!
WHY DID SOLDIER CHOOSE HIM?
THERE'S NOTHING MU ABOUT HIM.
SOLDIER SAYS HE HAS POTEN-TIAL,
BUT HE'S WRONG THIS TIME. HE'S TOTALLY HUMAN.
HE'S A PRIMITIVE BEING.
IF YOU DON'T BELIEVE IT, READ HIS THOUGHTS.
HIS FEAR AND HOSTILITY
TOWARDS MU ARE UTTERLY HUMAN.
I HEAR THEIR THOUGHTS.
IT'S HARD TO PUT IN WORDS,
BUT I SENSE THEY HATE HUMANS ...
IT WEIGHS ON ME.

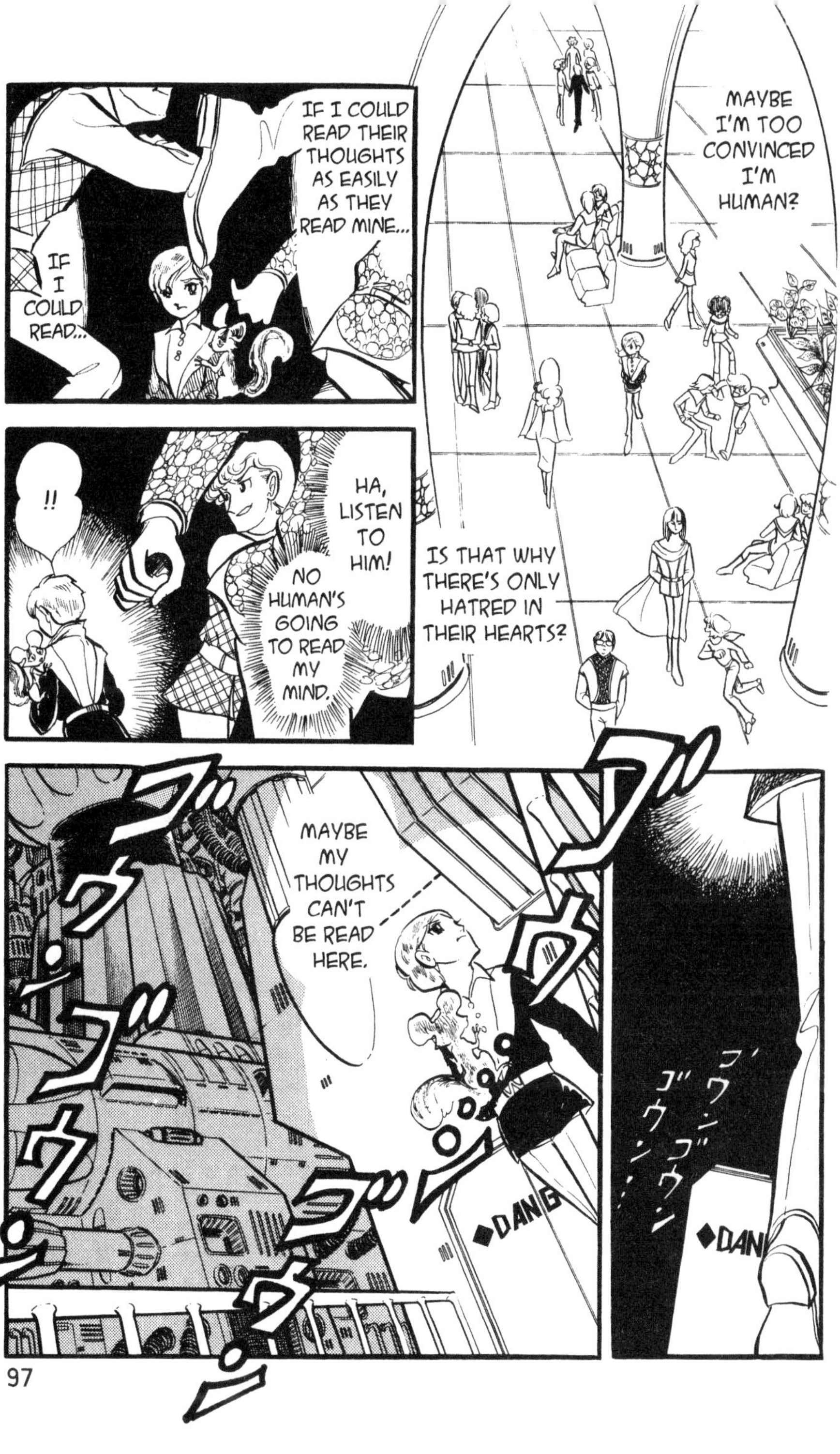
MAYBE I'M TOO CONVINCED I'M HUMAN?
IS THAT WHY THERE'S ONLY HATRED IN THEIR HEARTS?
IF I COULD READ THEIR THOUGHTS AS EASILY AS THEY READ MINE...
IF I COULD READ...
HA, LISTEN TO HIM!
NO HUMAN'S GOING TO READ MY MIND.
!!
ゴウンゴウン
ゴウンゴウン……
DAN
MAYBE MY THOUGHTS CAN'T BE READ HERE.
DANG

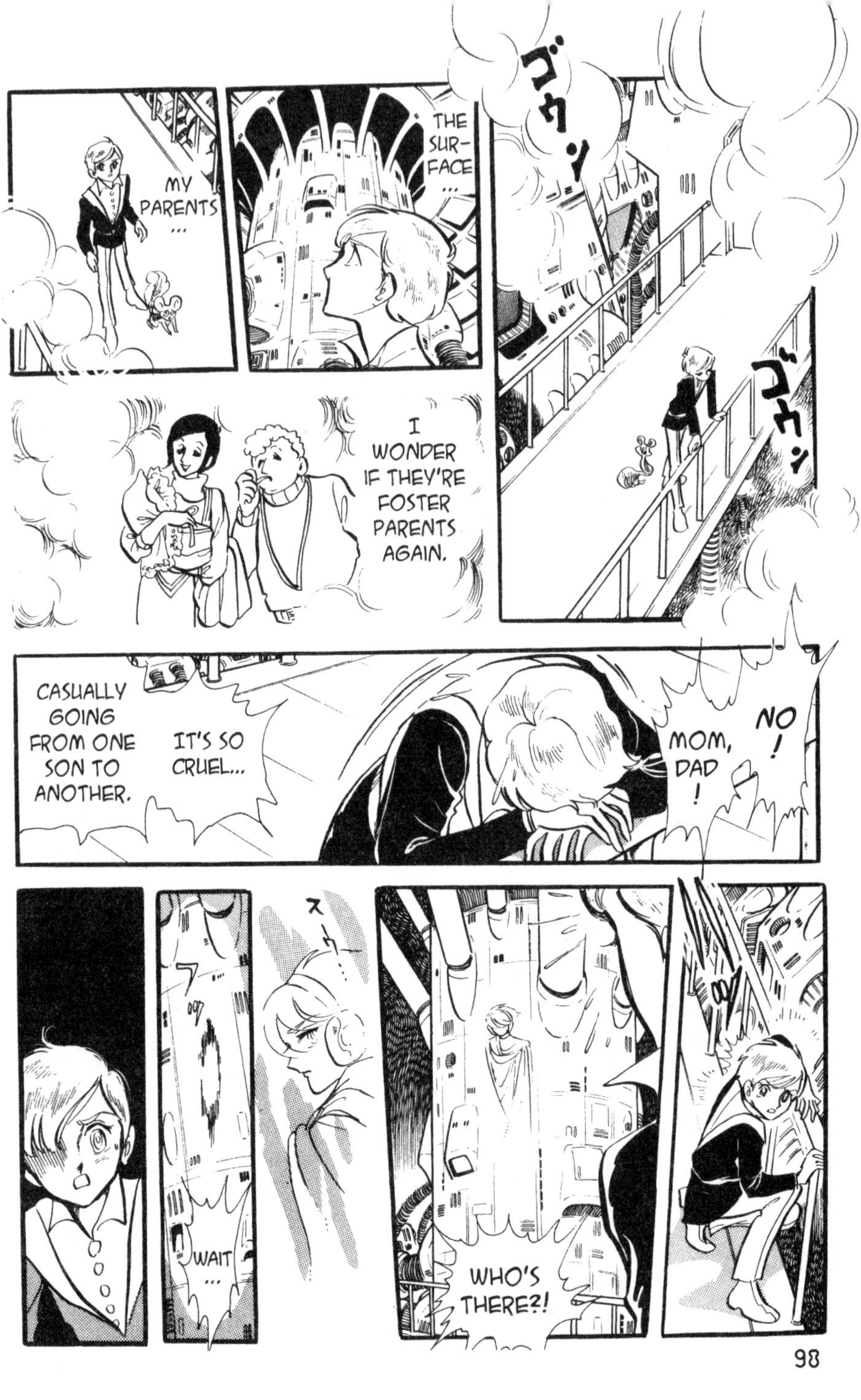
ゴウン
ゴウン
THE SUR-FACE ...
MY PARENTS ...
I WONDER IF THEY'RE FOSTER PARENTS AGAIN.
NO!
MOM, DAD!
IT'S SO CRUEL...
CASUALLY GOING FROM ONE SON TO ANOTHER.
WHO'S THERE?!
スー...
WAIT ...

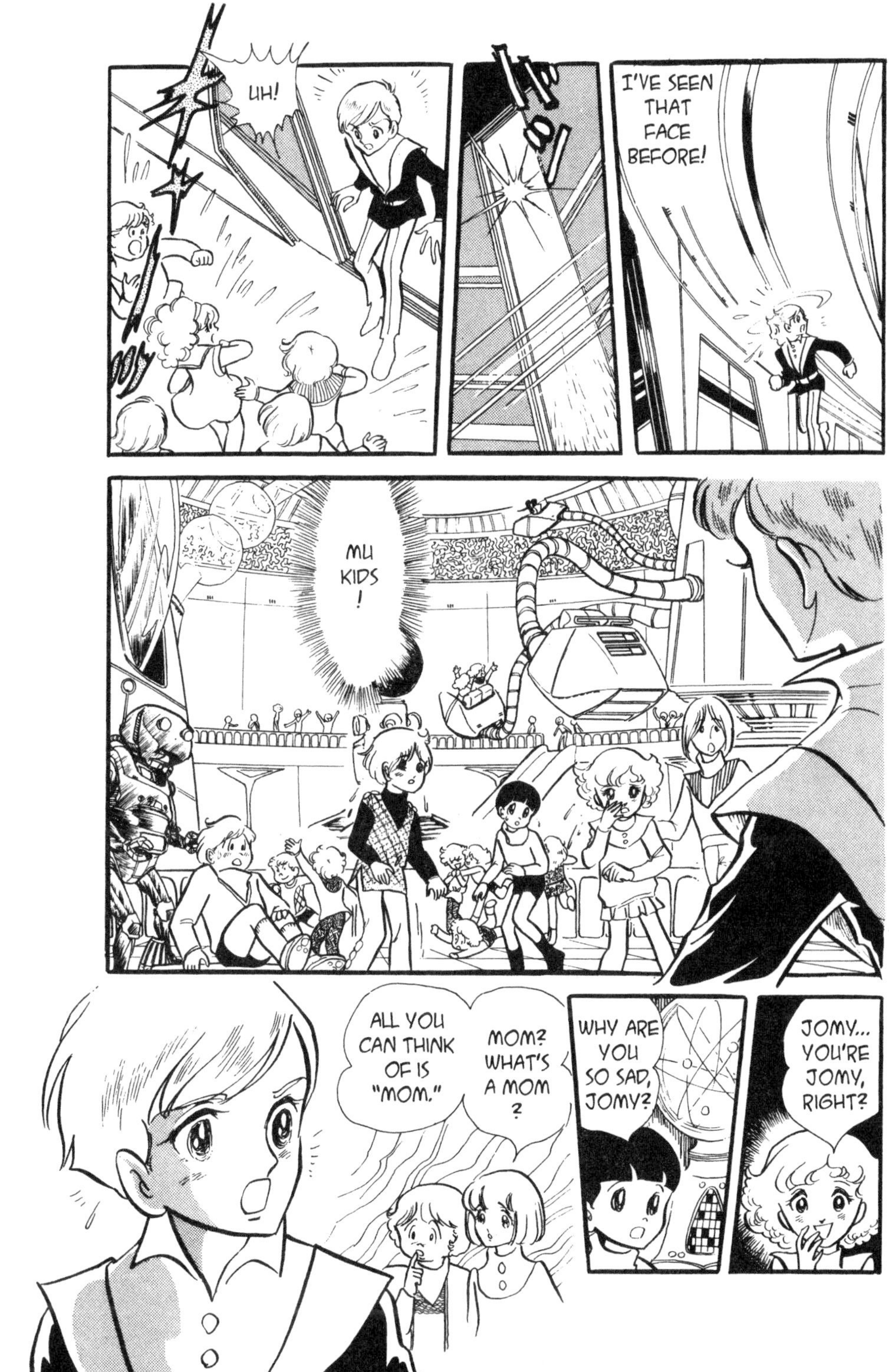
I'VE SEEN THAT FACE BEFORE!
UH!
MU KIDS!
JOMY... YOU'RE JOMY, RIGHT?
WHY ARE YOU SO SAD, JOMY?
MOM? WHAT'S A MOM?
ALL YOU CAN THINK OF IS "MOM."

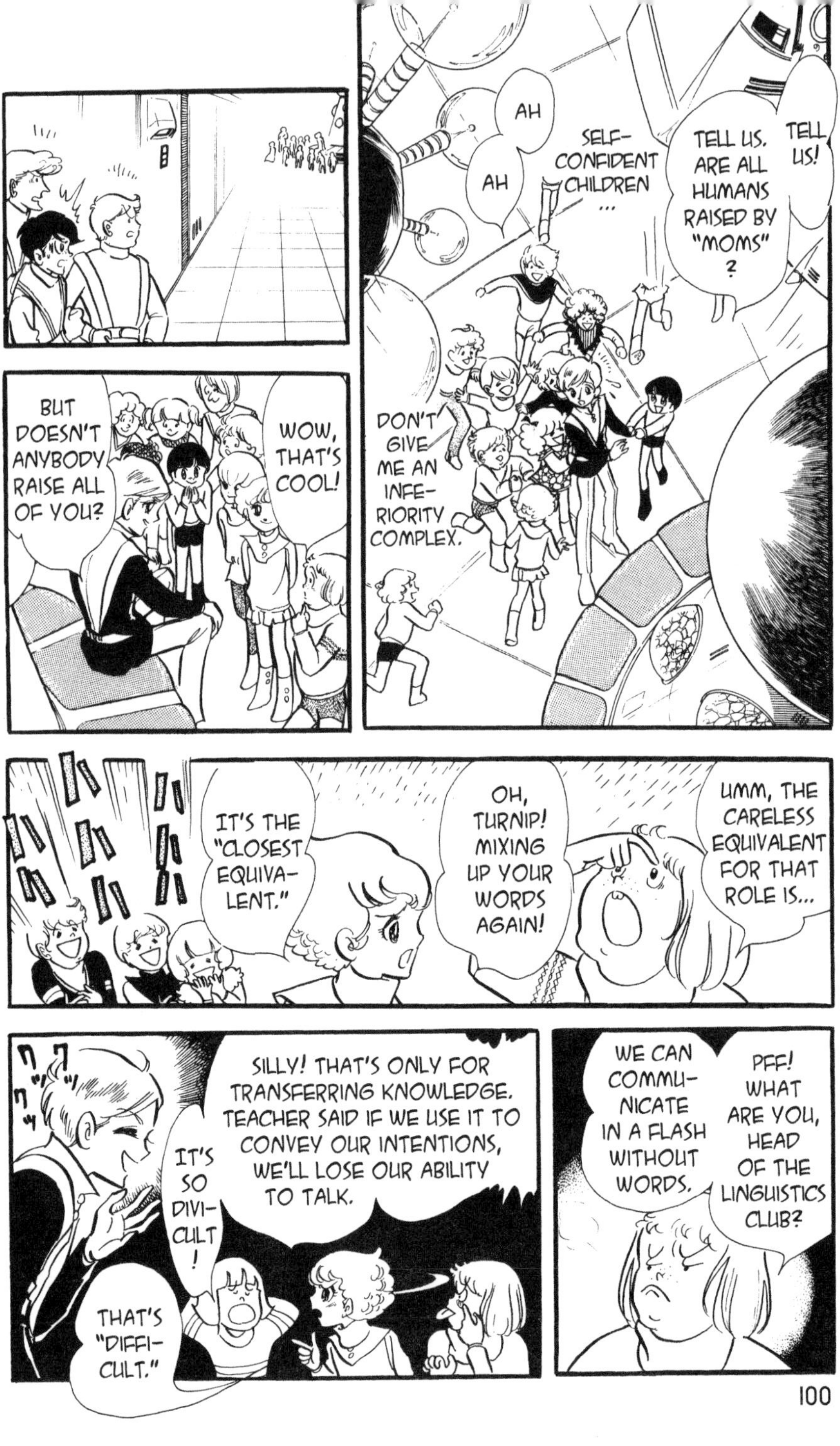
TELL US!
TELL US. ARE ALL HUMANS RAISED BY "MOMS"?
SELF-CONFIDENT CHILDREN ...
AH
AH
DON'T GIVE ME AN INFERIORITY COMPLEX.
WOW, THAT'S COOL!
BUT DOESN'T ANYBODY RAISE ALL OF YOU?
UMM, THE CARELESS EQUIVALENT FOR THAT ROLE IS...
OH, TURNIP! MIXING UP YOUR WORDS AGAIN!
IT'S THE "CLOSEST EQUIVALENT."
PFF! WHAT ARE YOU, HEAD OF THE LINGUISTICS CLUB?
WE CAN COMMUNICATE IN A FLASH WITHOUT WORDS.
SILLY! THAT'S ONLY FOR TRANSFERRING KNOWLEDGE. TEACHER SAID IF WE USE IT TO CONVEY OUR INTENTIONS, WE'LL LOSE OUR ABILITY TO TALK.
IT'S SO DIVICULT!
THAT'S "DIFFICULT."

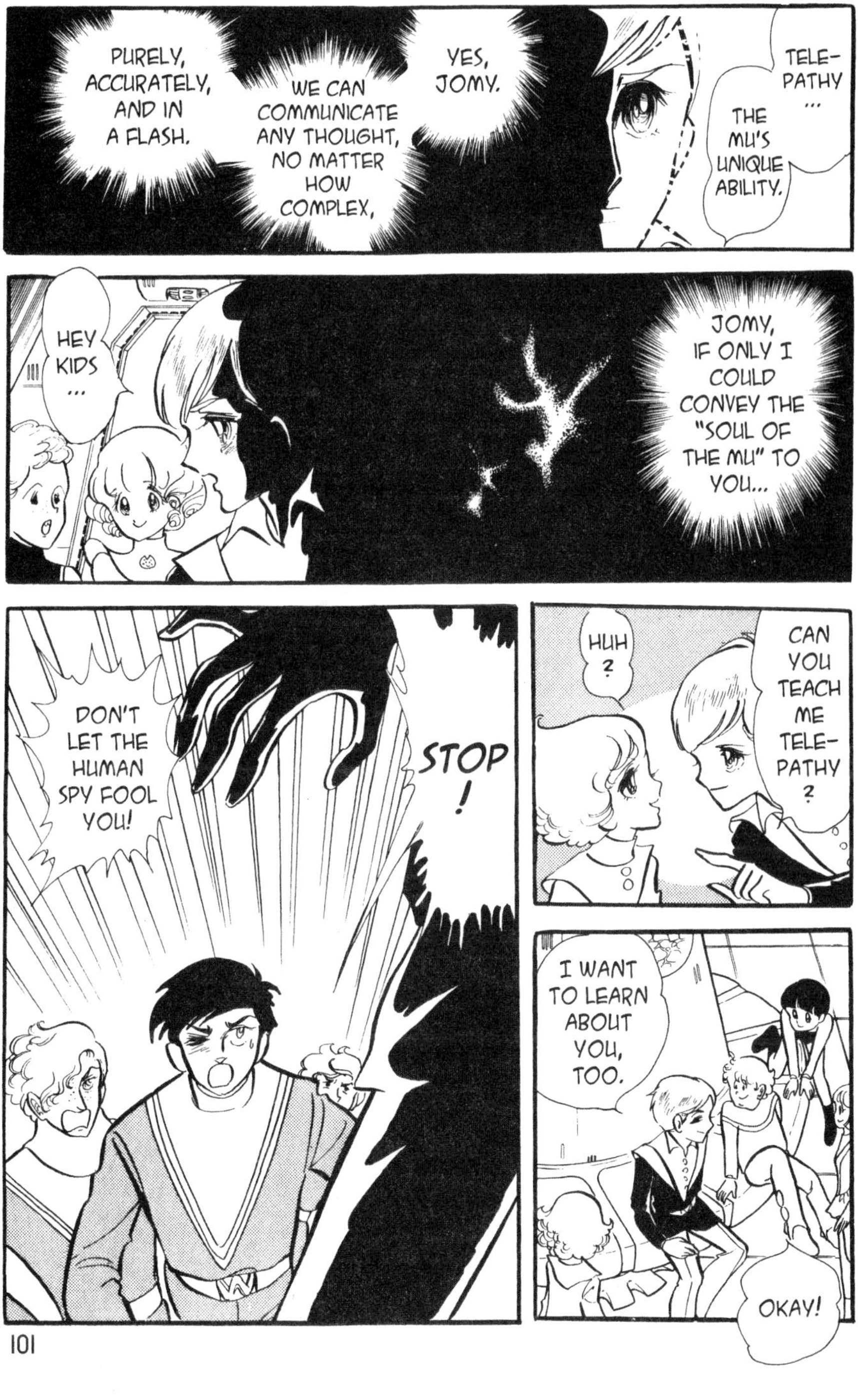
TELE-PATHY ...
THE MU'S UNIQUE ABILITY.
YES, JOMY.
WE CAN COMMUNICATE ANY THOUGHT, NO MATTER HOW COMPLEX,
PURELY, ACCURATELY, AND IN A FLASH.
JOMY, IF ONLY I COULD CONVEY THE "SOUL OF THE MU" TO YOU...
HEY KIDS ...
CAN YOU TEACH ME TELE-PATHY ?
HUH ?
I WANT TO LEARN ABOUT YOU, TOO.
OKAY!
STOP !
DON'T LET THE HUMAN SPY FOOL YOU!

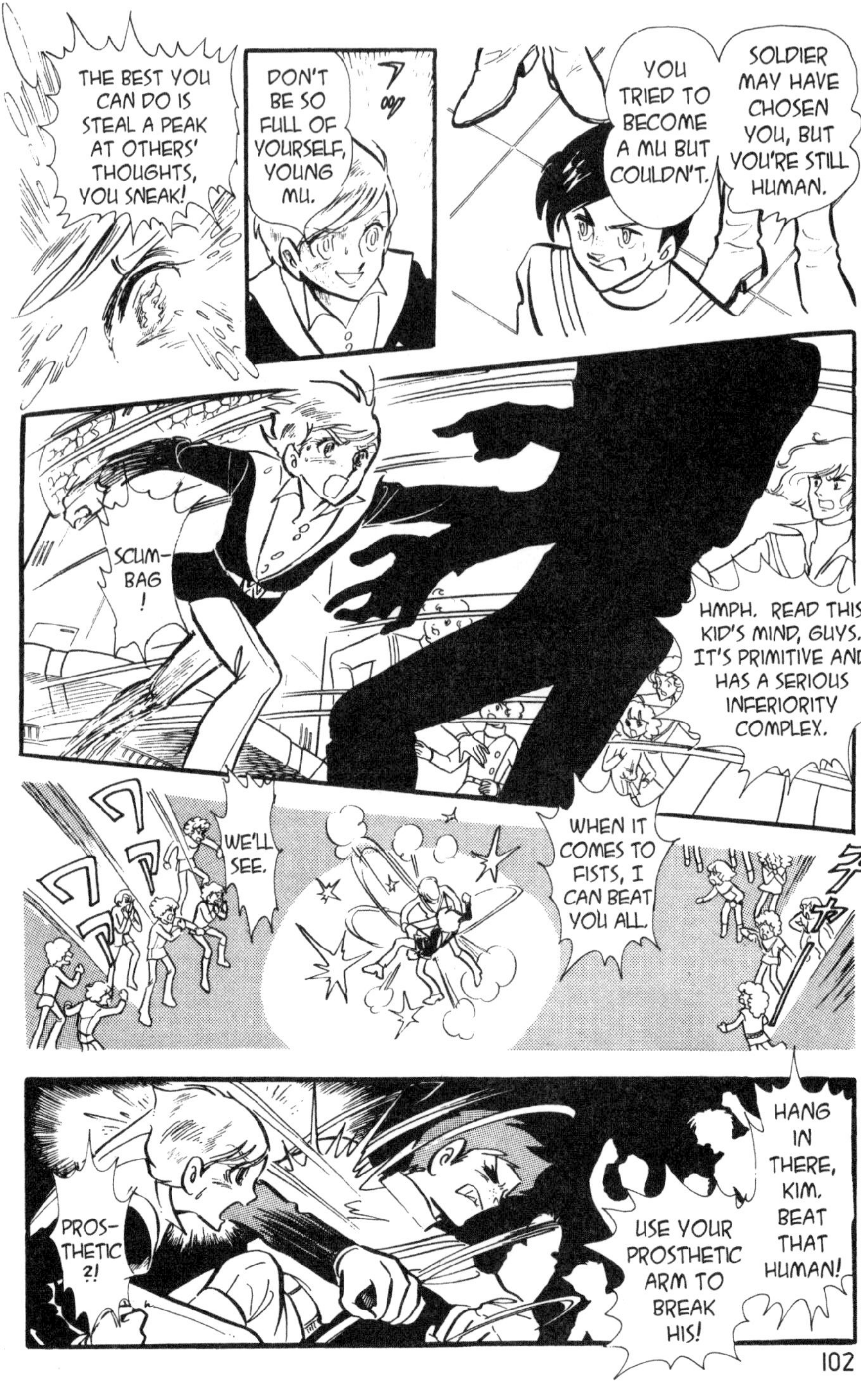
SOLDIER MAY HAVE CHOSEN YOU, BUT YOU'RE STILL HUMAN.
YOU TRIED TO BECOME A MU BUT COULDN'T.
DON'T BE SO FULL OF YOURSELF, YOUNG MU.
THE BEST YOU CAN DO IS STEAL A PEAK AT OTHERS' THOUGHTS, YOU SNEAK!
HMPH. READ THIS KID'S MIND, GUYS. IT'S PRIMITIVE AND HAS A SERIOUS INFERIORITY COMPLEX.
SCUM-BAG!
WHEN IT COMES TO FISTS, I CAN BEAT YOU ALL.
WE'LL SEE.
HANG IN THERE, KIM. BEAT THAT HUMAN!
USE YOUR PROSTHETIC ARM TO BREAK HIS!
PROS-THETIC?!

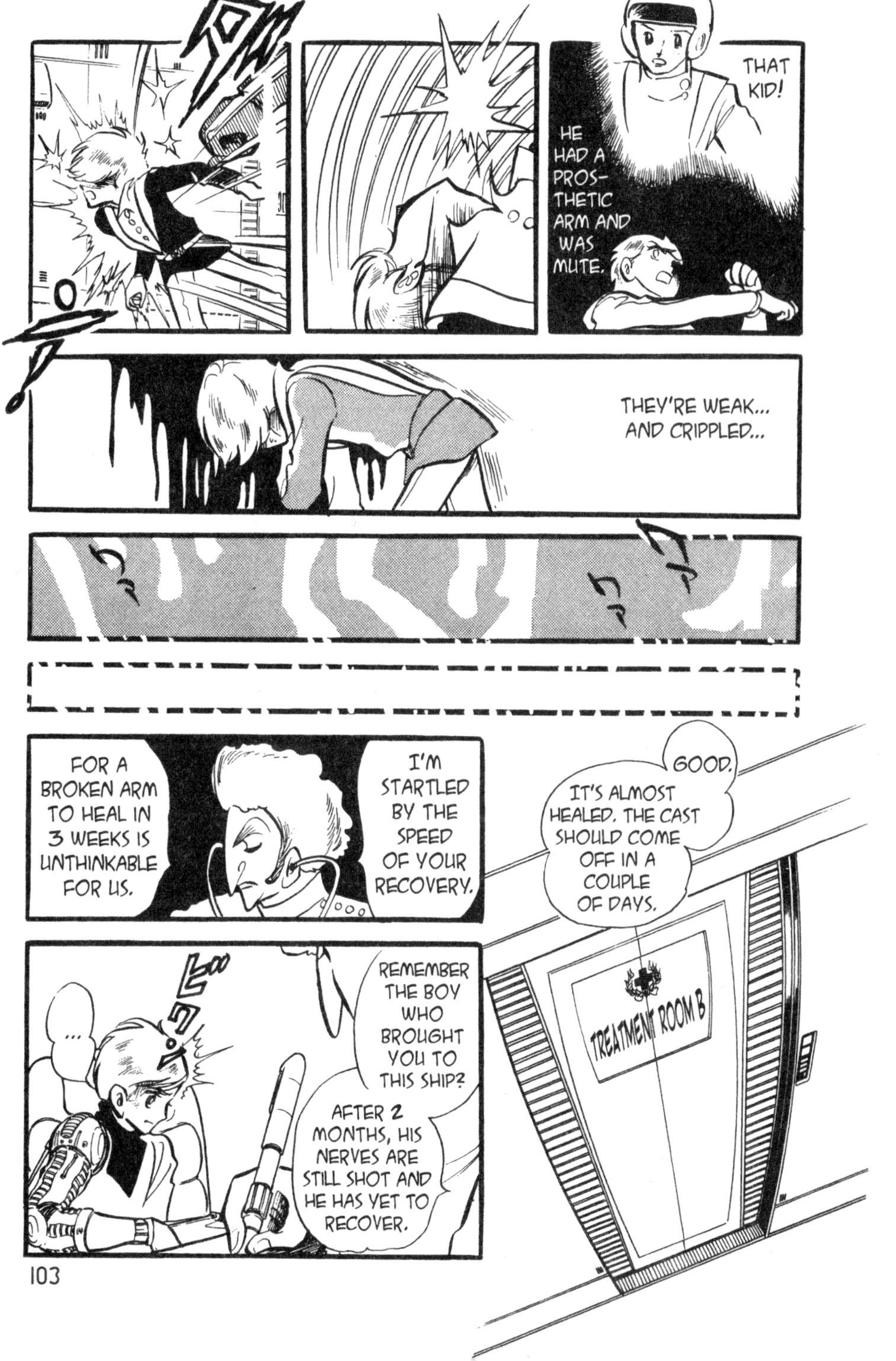
THAT KID!
HE HAD A PROSTHETIC ARM AND WAS MUTE.
THEY'RE WEAK... AND CRIPPLED...
GOOD.
IT'S ALMOST HEALED. THE CAST SHOULD COME OFF IN A COUPLE OF DAYS.
TREATMENT ROOM B
I'M STARTLED BY THE SPEED OF YOUR RECOVERY.
FOR A BROKEN ARM TO HEAL IN 3 WEEKS IS UNTHINKABLE FOR US.
REMEMBER THE BOY WHO BROUGHT YOU TO THIS SHIP?
AFTER 2 MONTHS, HIS NERVES ARE STILL SHOT AND HE HAS YET TO RECOVER.
...

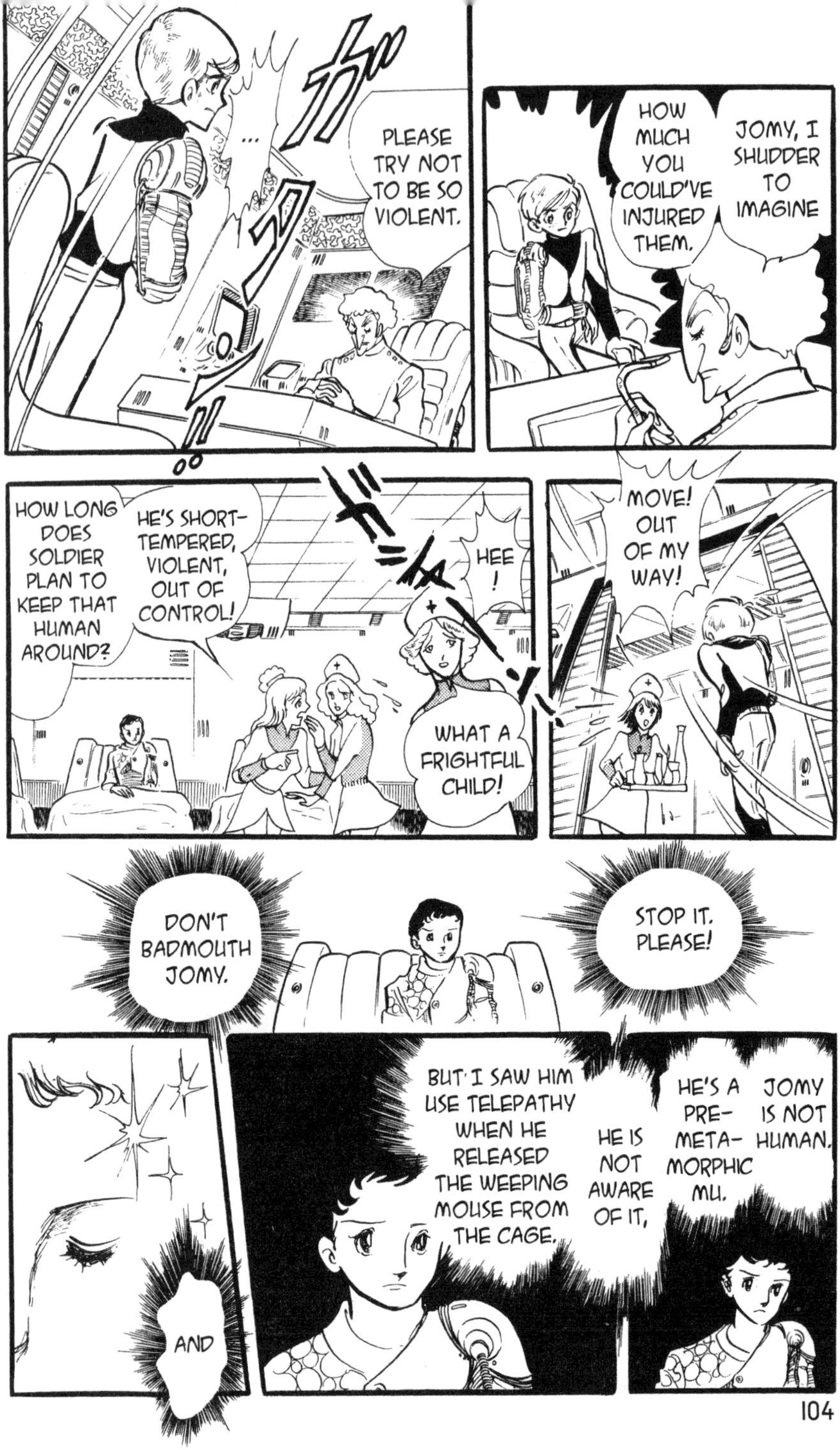
JOMY, I SHUDDER TO IMAGINE
HOW MUCH YOU COULD'VE INJURED THEM.
PLEASE TRY NOT TO BE SO VIOLENT.
...
MOVE! OUT OF MY WAY!
HEE!
WHAT A FRIGHTFUL CHILD!
HE'S SHORT-TEMPERED, VIOLENT, OUT OF CONTROL!
HOW LONG DOES SOLDIER PLAN TO KEEP THAT HUMAN AROUND?
STOP IT. PLEASE!
DON'T BADMOUTH JOMY.
JOMY IS NOT HUMAN.
HE'S A PRE-METAMORPHIC MU.
HE IS NOT AWARE OF IT,
BUT I SAW HIM USE TELEPATHY WHEN HE RELEASED THE WEEPING MOUSE FROM THE CAGE.
AND

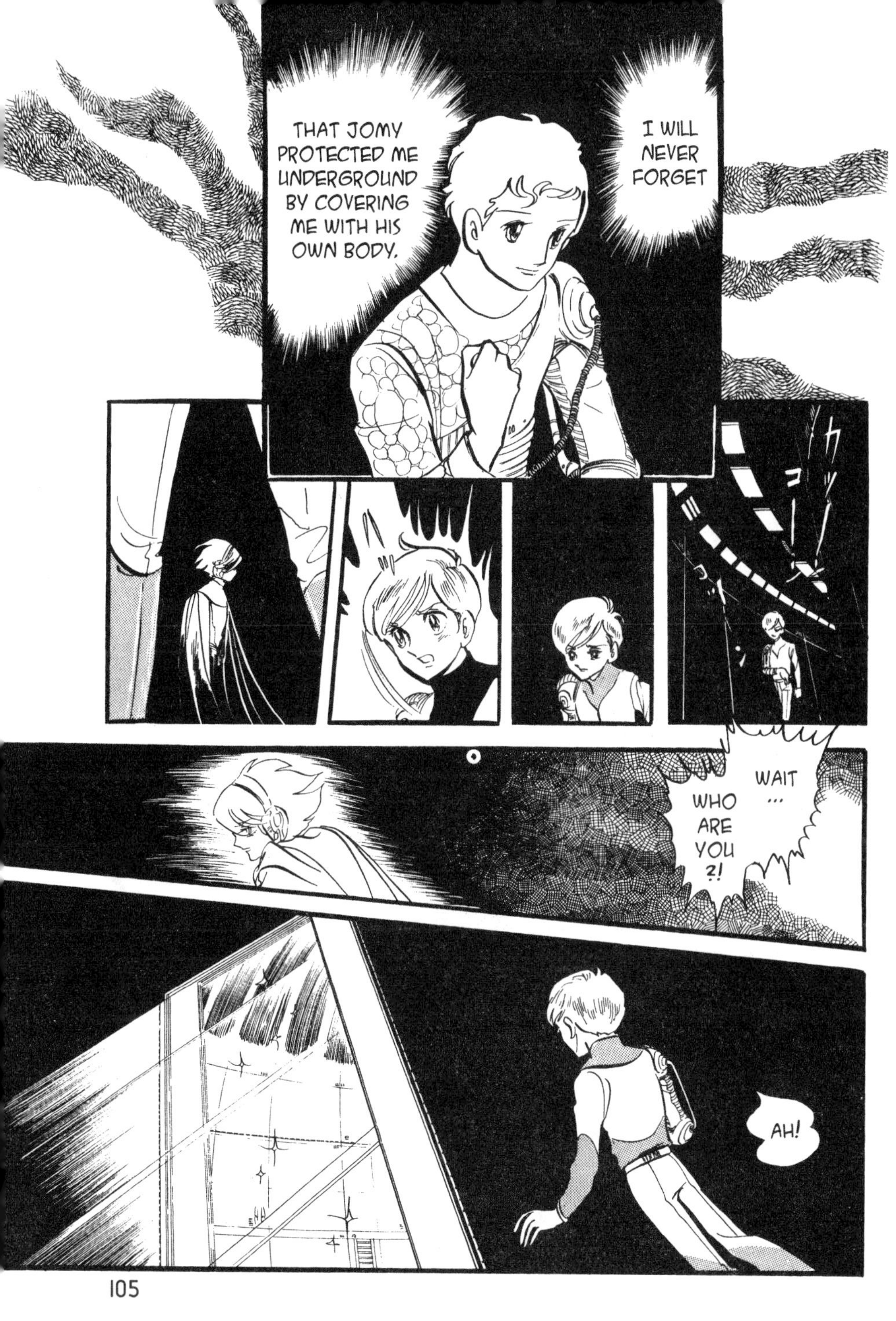
I WILL NEVER FORGET
THAT JOMY PROTECTED ME UNDERGROUND BY COVERING ME WITH HIS OWN BODY.
カッ
WAIT ...
WHO ARE YOU ?!
AH!

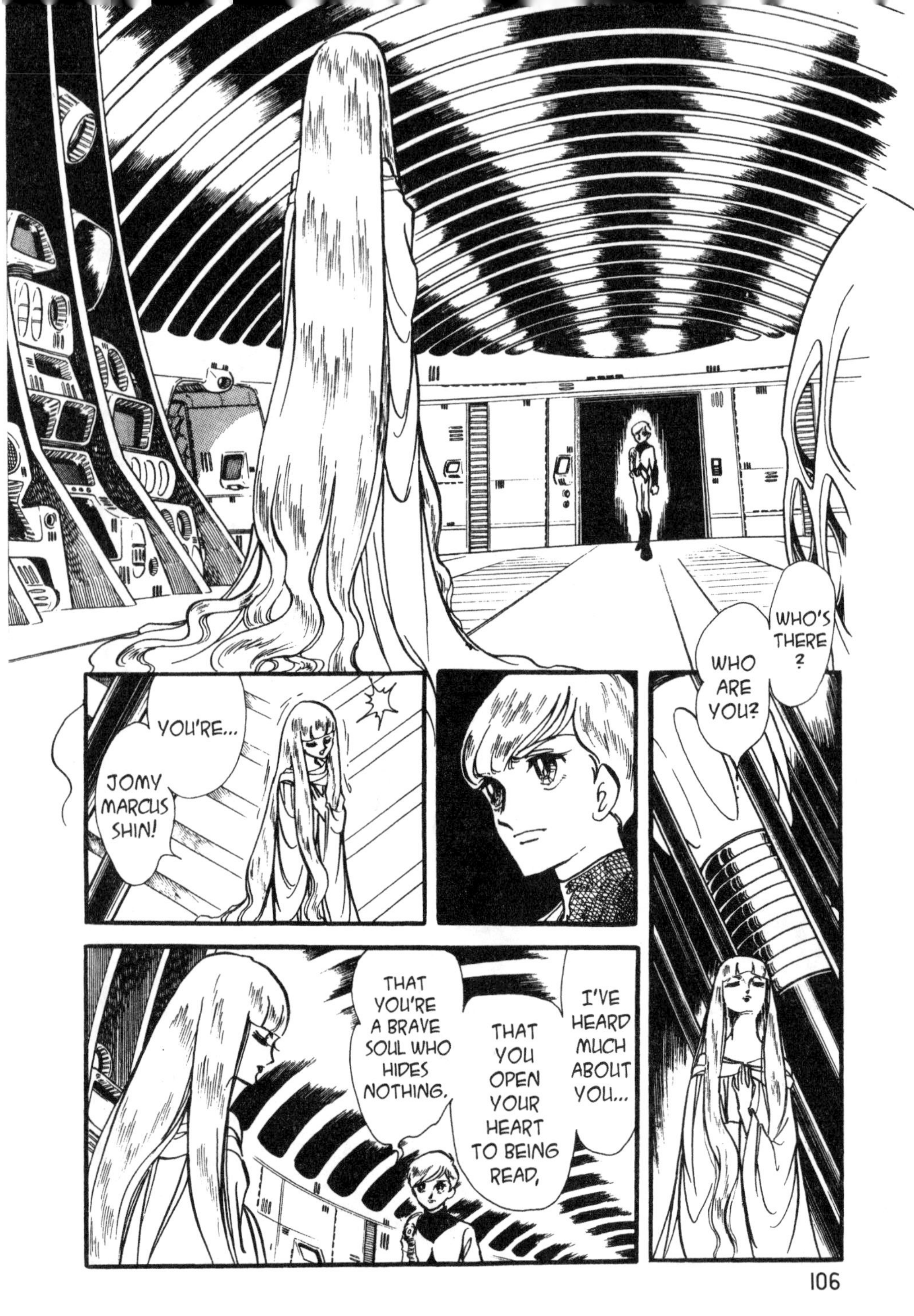
WHO'S THERE?
WHO ARE YOU?
YOU'RE...
JOMY MARCUS SHIN!
I'VE HEARD MUCH ABOUT YOU...
THAT YOU OPEN YOUR HEART TO BEING READ,
THAT YOU'RE A BRAVE SOUL WHO HIDES NOTHING.

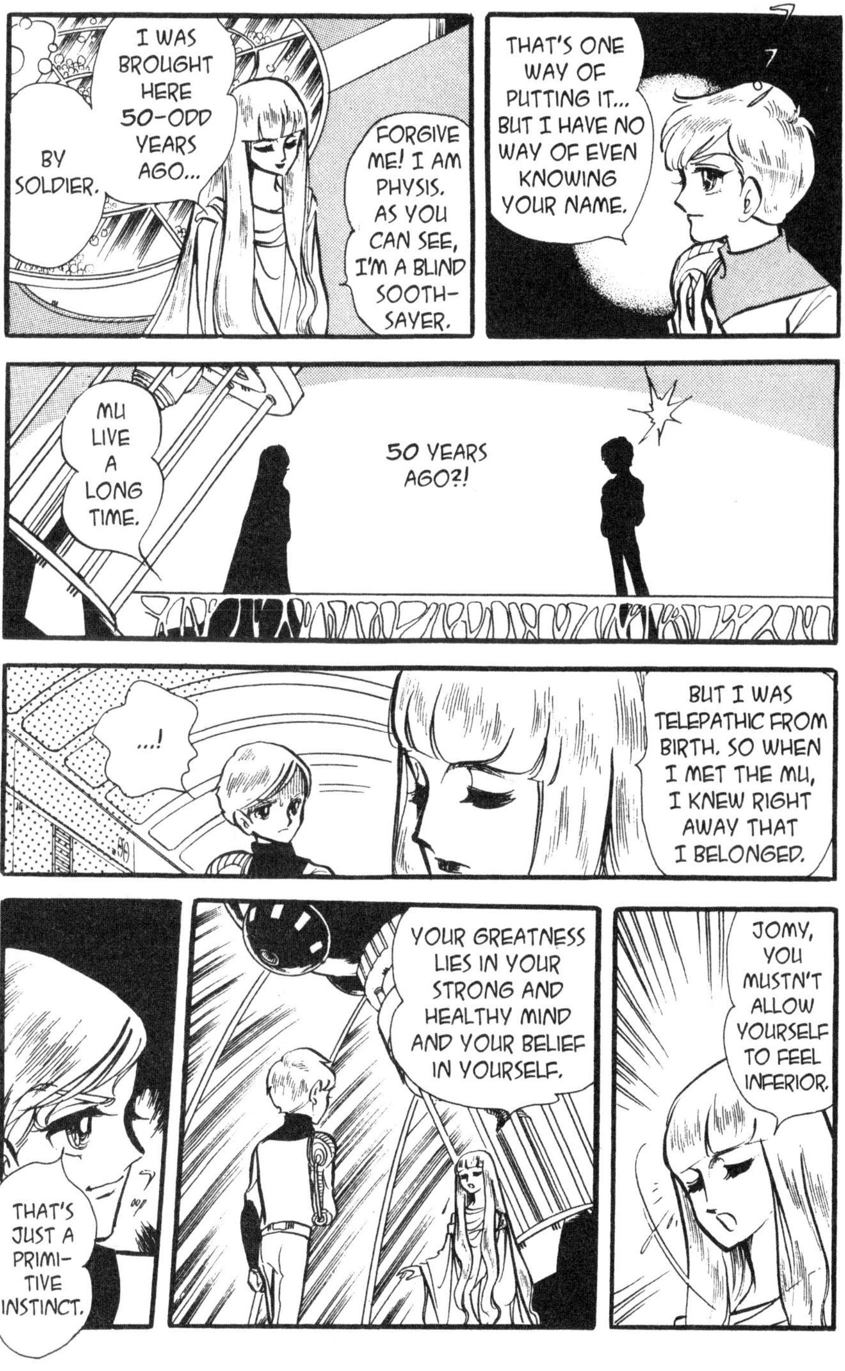
THAT'S ONE WAY OF PUTTING IT... BUT I HAVE NO WAY OF EVEN KNOWING YOUR NAME.
FORGIVE ME! I AM PHYSIS. AS YOU CAN SEE, I'M A BLIND SOOTHSAYER.
I WAS BROUGHT HERE 50-ODD YEARS AGO...
BY SOLDIER.
50 YEARS AGO?!
MU LIVE A LONG TIME.
BUT I WAS TELEPATHIC FROM BIRTH, SO WHEN I MET THE MU, I KNEW RIGHT AWAY THAT I BELONGED.
...!
JOMY, YOU MUSTN'T ALLOW YOURSELF TO FEEL INFERIOR.
YOUR GREATNESS LIES IN YOUR STRONG AND HEALTHY MIND AND YOUR BELIEF IN YOURSELF.
THAT'S JUST A PRIMITIVE INSTINCT.

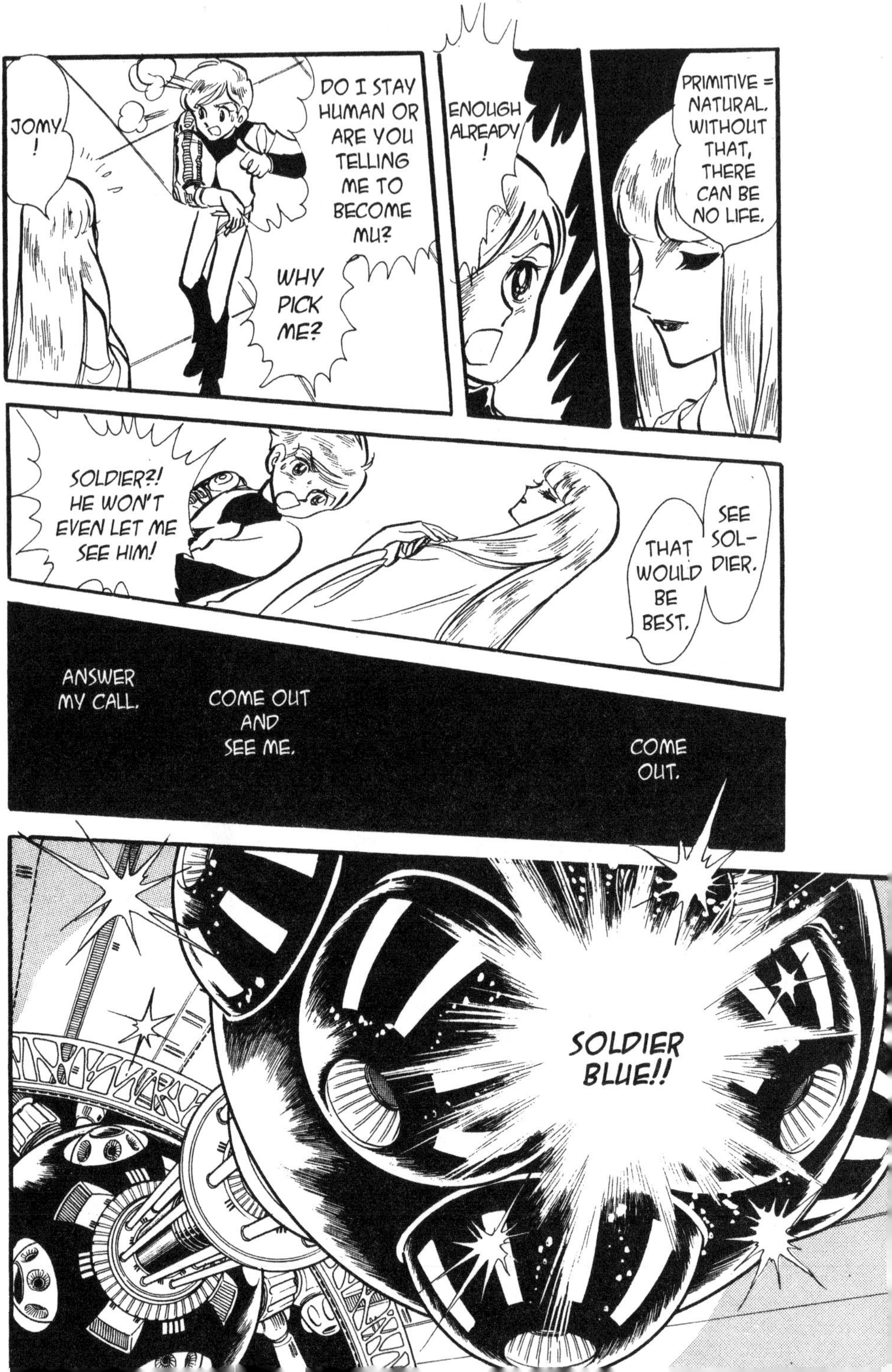
PRIMITIVE = NATURAL. WITHOUT THAT, THERE CAN BE NO LIFE.
ENOUGH ALREADY!
DO I STAY HUMAN OR ARE YOU TELLING ME TO BECOME MU?
WHY PICK ME?
JOMY!
SEE SOLDIER.
THAT WOULD BE BEST.
SOLDIER?! HE WON'T EVEN LET ME SEE HIM!
COME OUT.
COME OUT AND SEE ME.
ANSWER MY CALL.
SOLDIER BLUE!!

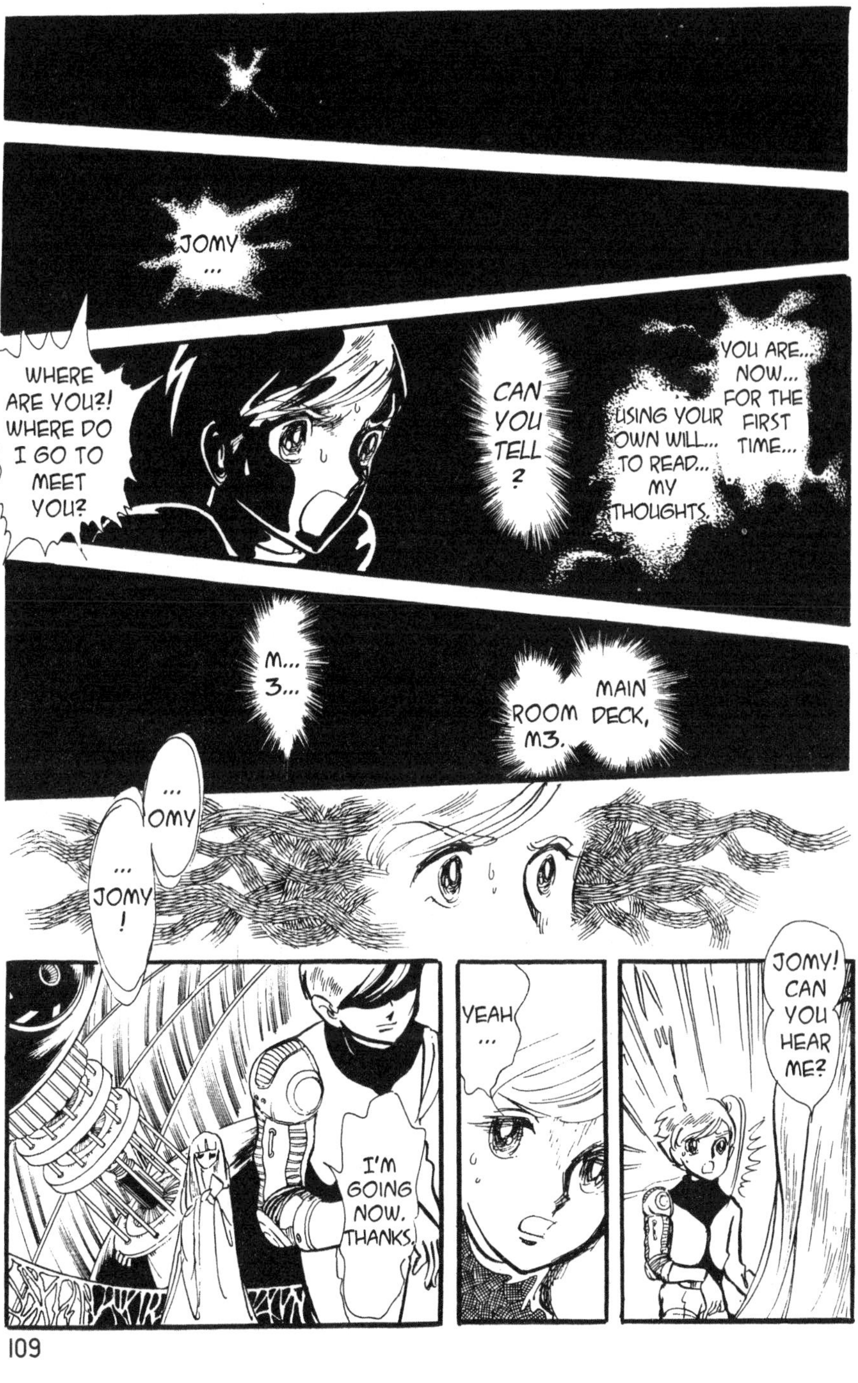
JOMY ...
YOU ARE... NOW... FOR THE FIRST TIME...
USING YOUR OWN WILL... TO READ... MY THOUGHTS.
CAN YOU TELL?
WHERE ARE YOU?! WHERE DO I GO TO MEET YOU?
MAIN DECK, ROOM M3.
M... 3...
... OMY
... JOMY!
JOMY! CAN YOU HEAR ME?
YEAH ...
I'M GOING NOW. THANKS.

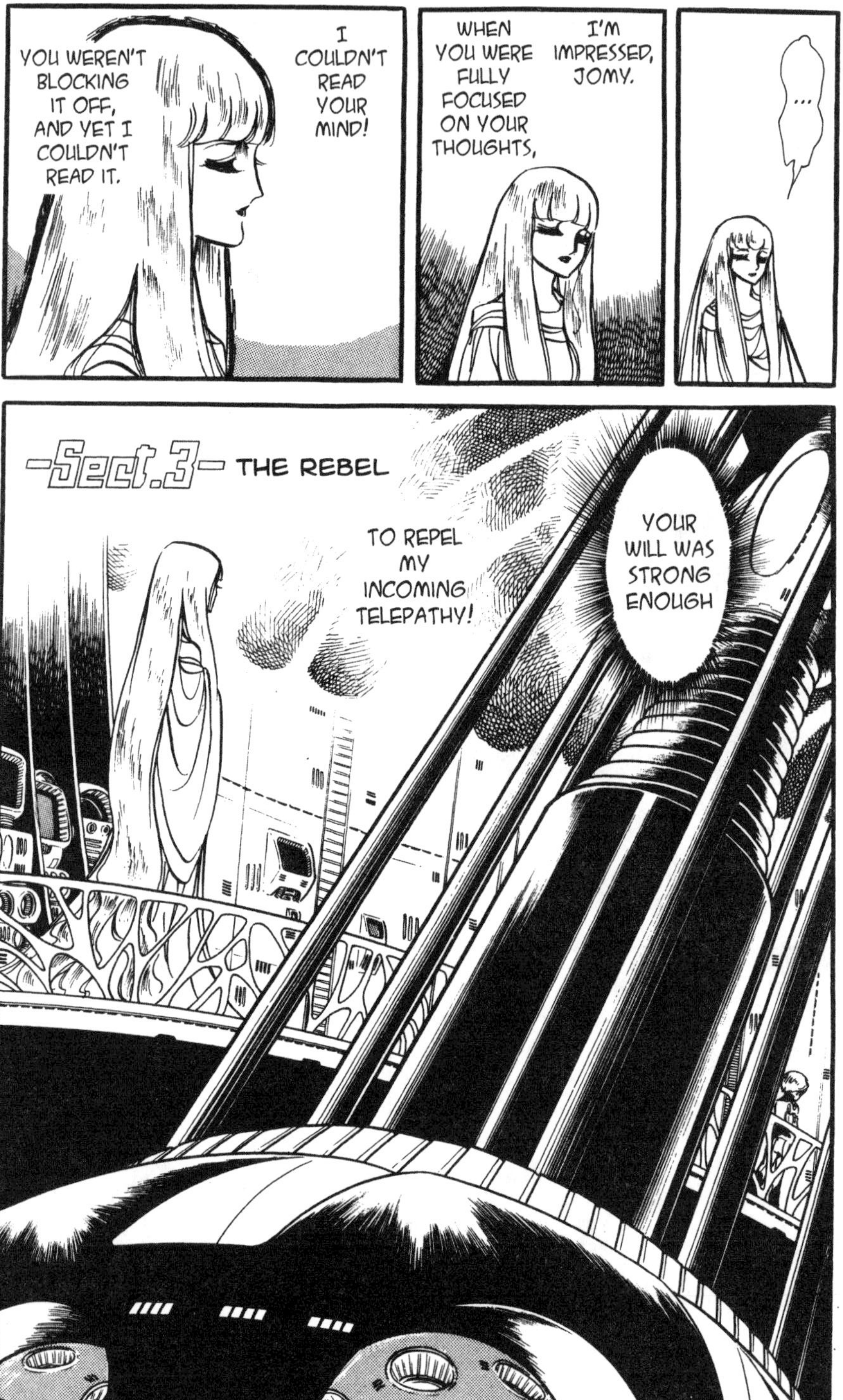
...
I'M IMPRESSED, JOMY.
WHEN YOU WERE FULLY FOCUSED ON YOUR THOUGHTS,
I COULDN'T READ YOUR MIND!
YOU WEREN'T BLOCKING IT OFF, AND YET I COULDN'T READ IT.
YOUR WILL WAS STRONG ENOUGH
TO REPEL MY INCOMING TELEPATHY!
-Sect.3- THE REBEL

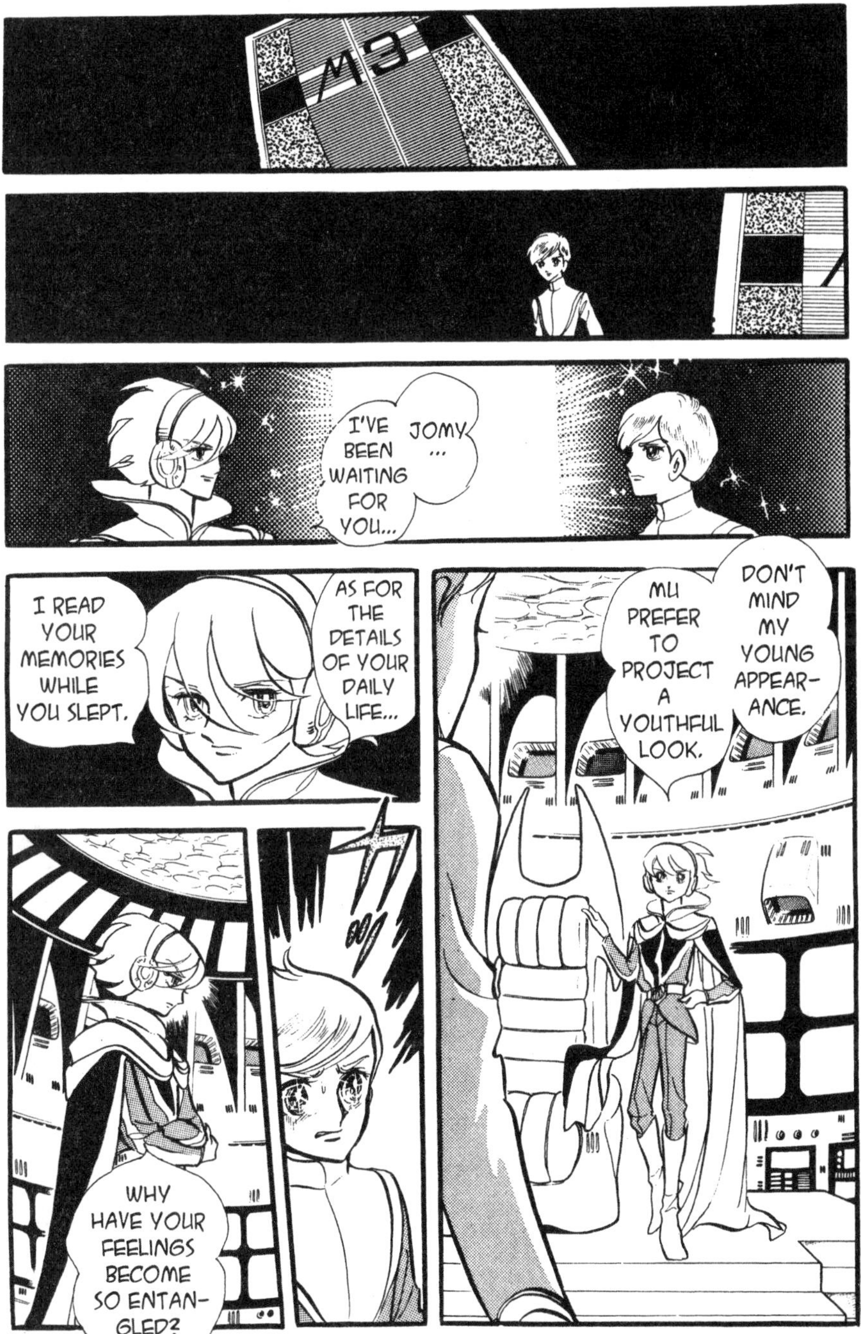
M3
JOMY...
I'VE BEEN WAITING FOR YOU...
DON'T MIND MY YOUNG APPEARANCE.
MU PREFER TO PROJECT A YOUTHFUL LOOK.
AS FOR THE DETAILS OF YOUR DAILY LIFE...
I READ YOUR MEMORIES WHILE YOU SLEPT.
WHY HAVE YOUR FEELINGS BECOME SO ENTANGLED?

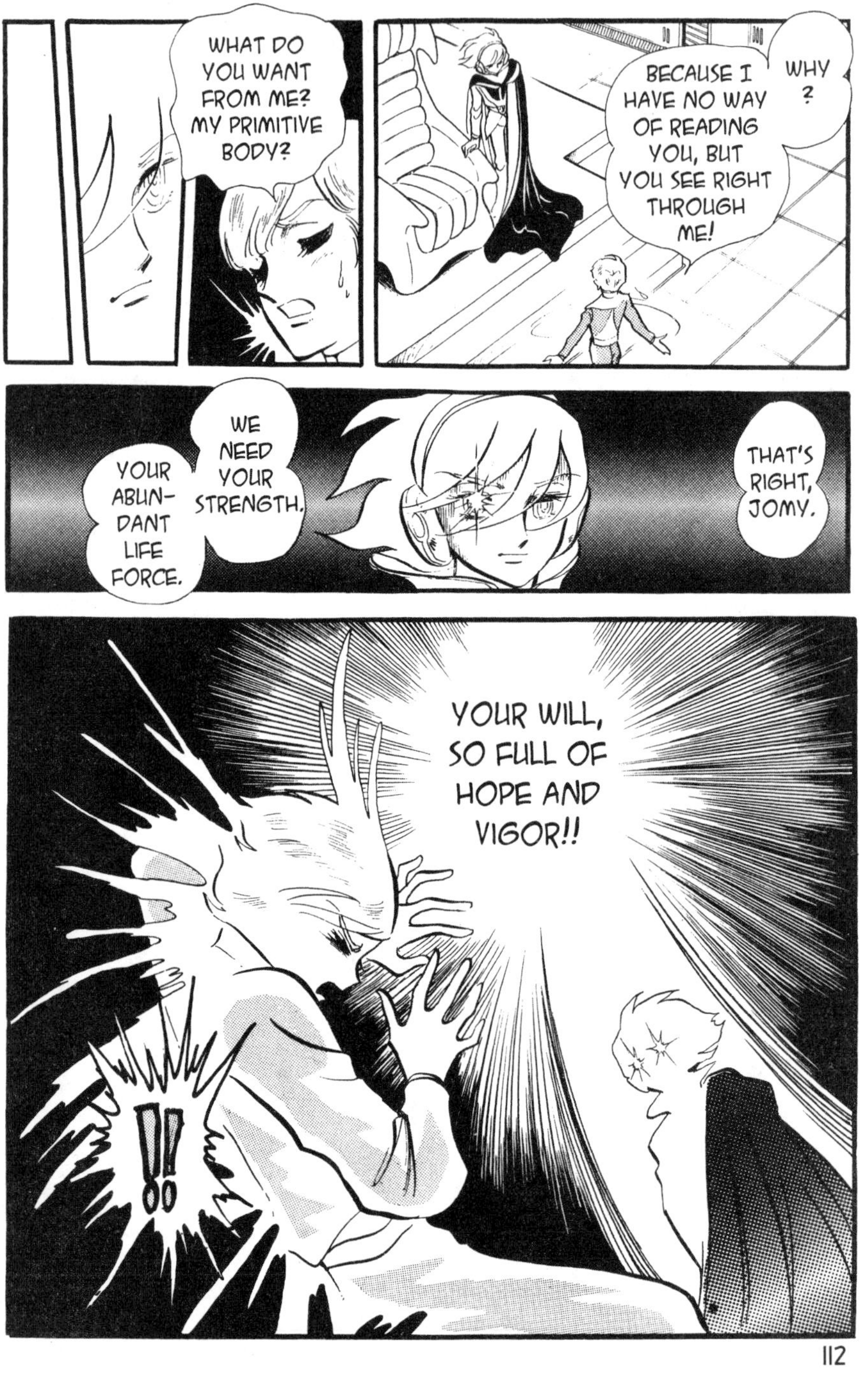
WHY?
BECAUSE I HAVE NO WAY OF READING YOU, BUT YOU SEE RIGHT THROUGH ME!
WHAT DO YOU WANT FROM ME? MY PRIMITIVE BODY?
THAT'S RIGHT, JOMY.
WE NEED YOUR STRENGTH.
YOUR ABUN-DANT LIFE FORCE.
YOUR WILL, SO FULL OF HOPE AND VIGOR!!
!!

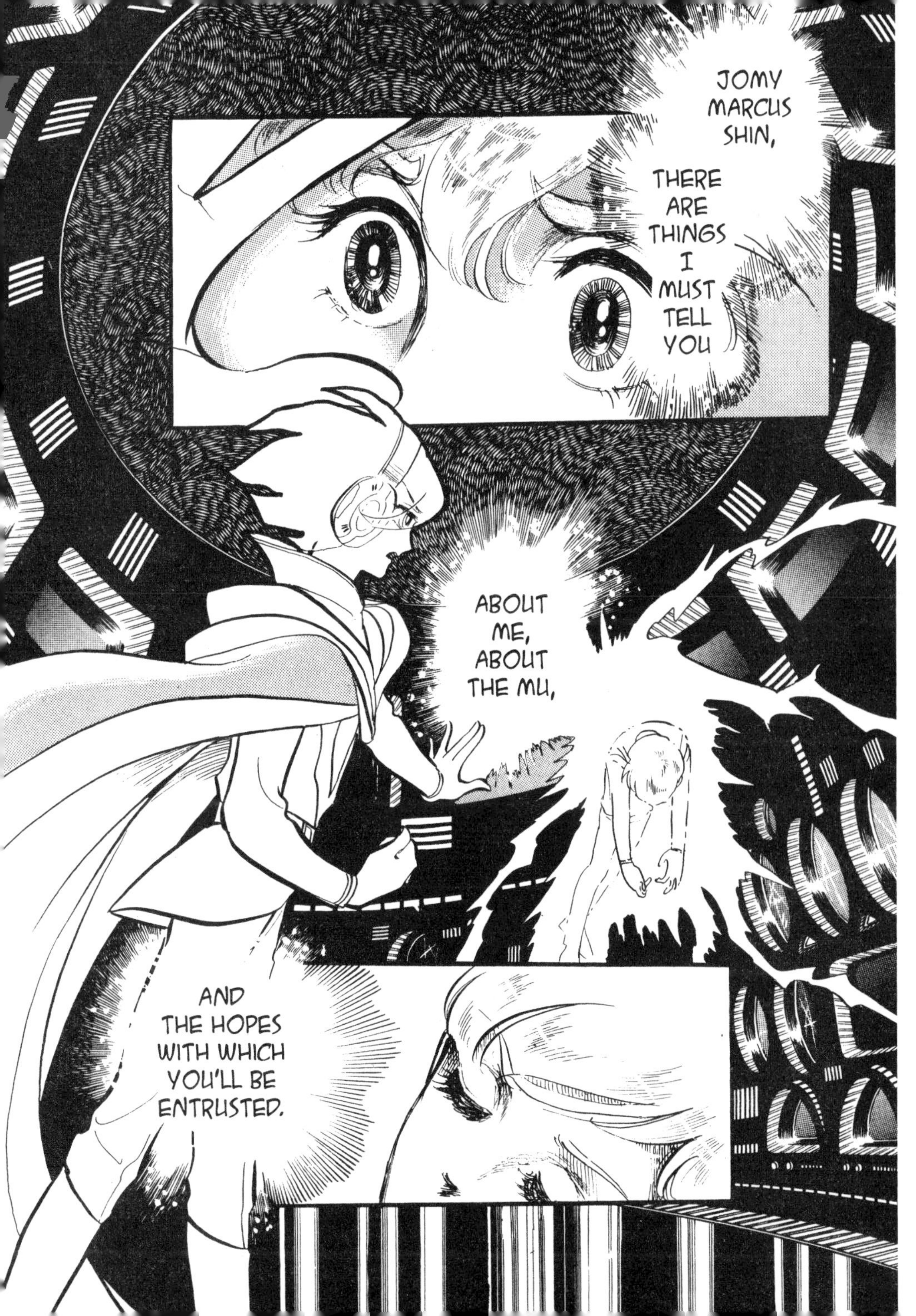
JOMY MARCUS SHIN,
THERE ARE THINGS I MUST TELL YOU
ABOUT ME, ABOUT THE MU,
AND THE HOPES WITH WHICH YOU'LL BE ENTRUSTED.

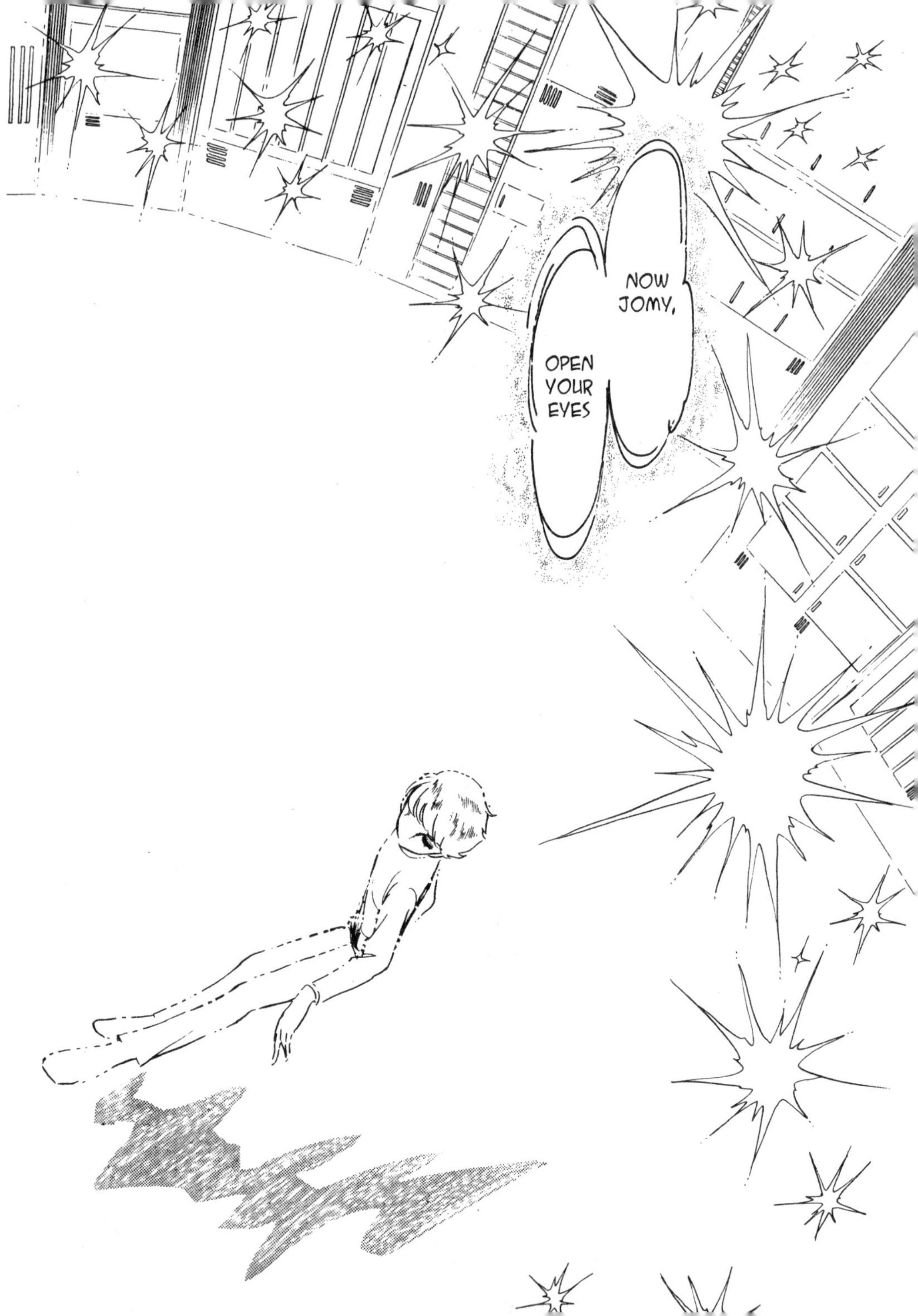
NOW JOMY,
OPEN YOUR EYES

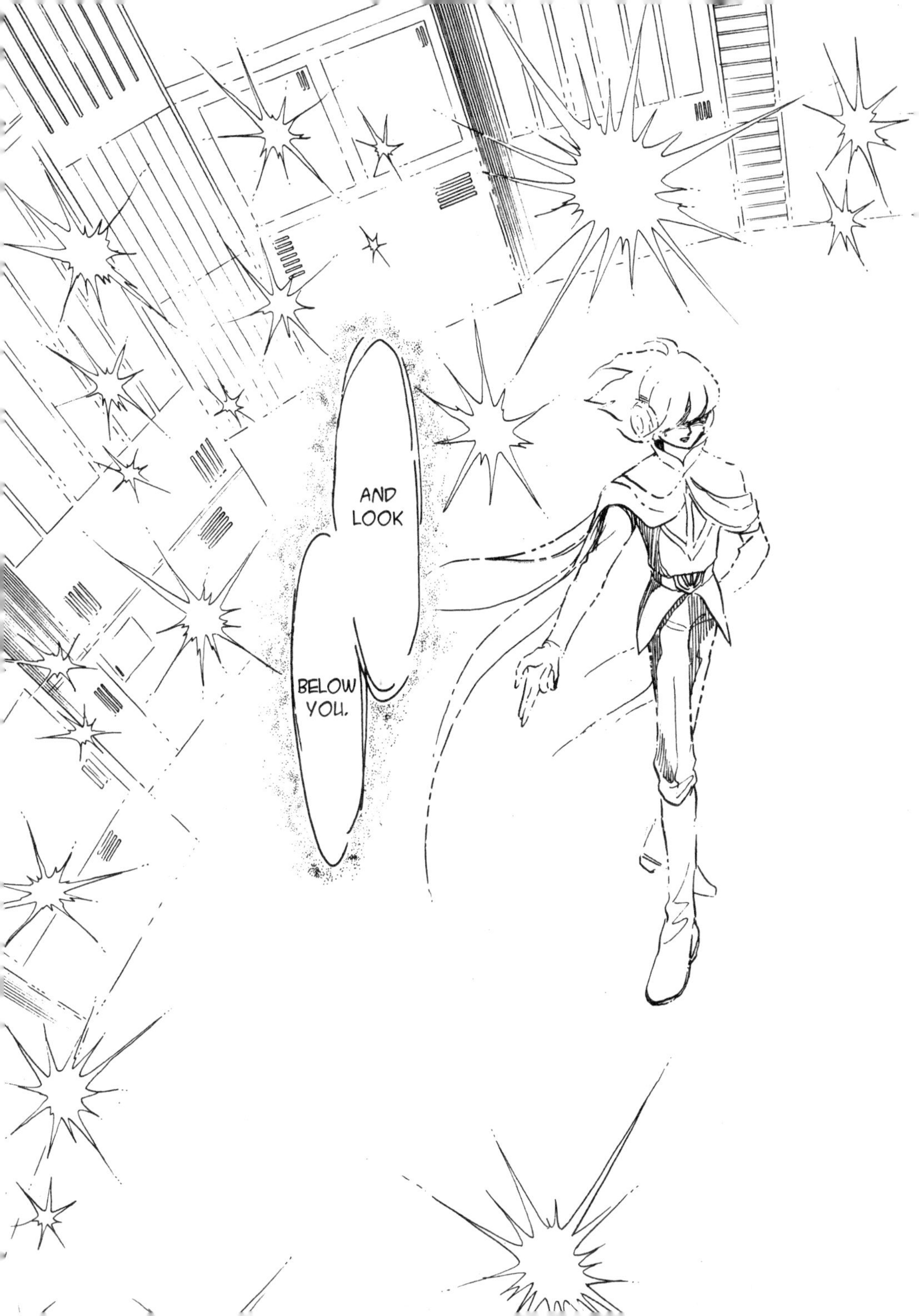
AND LOOK
BELOW YOU.

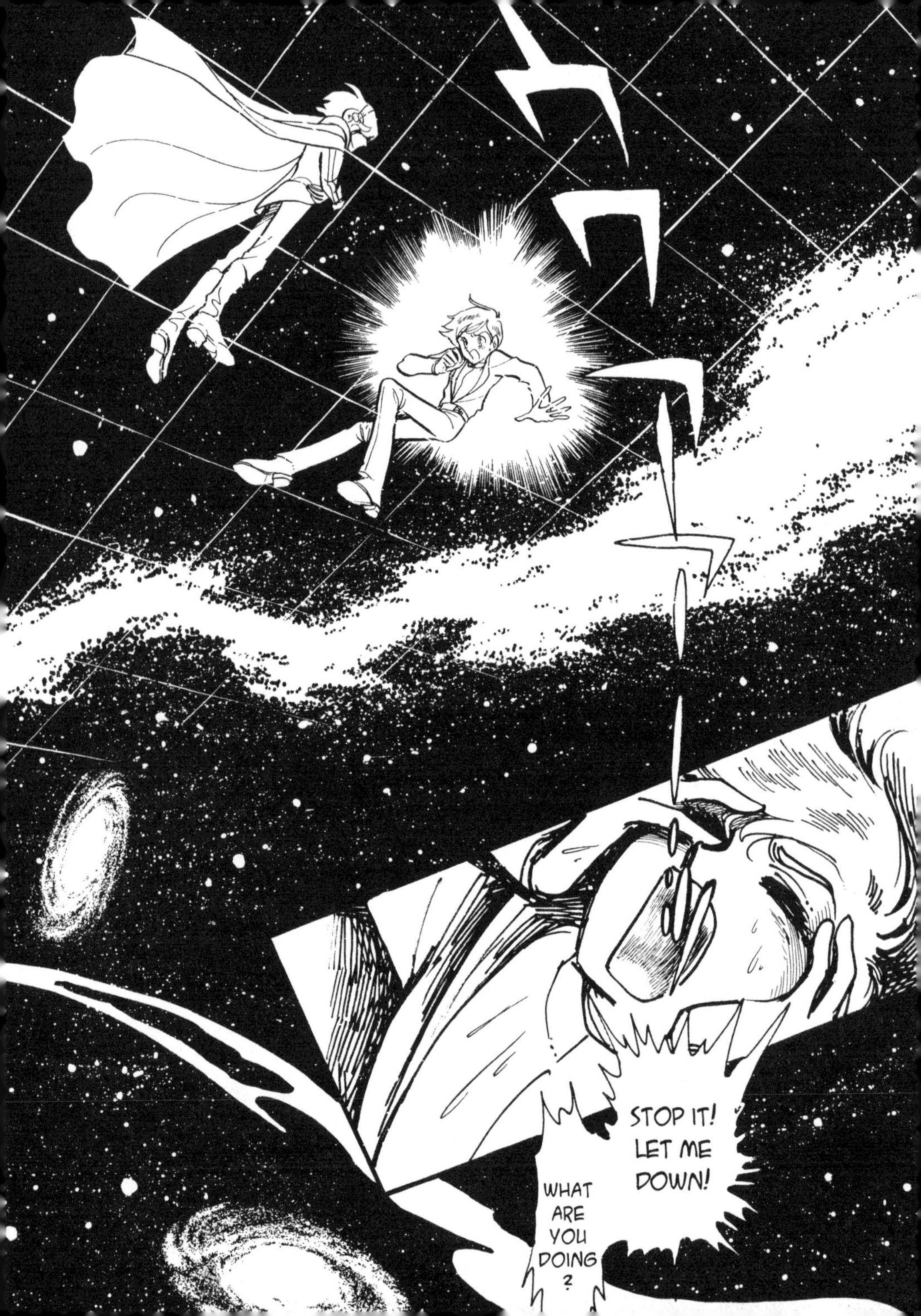
STOP IT! LET ME DOWN!
WHAT ARE YOU DOING?

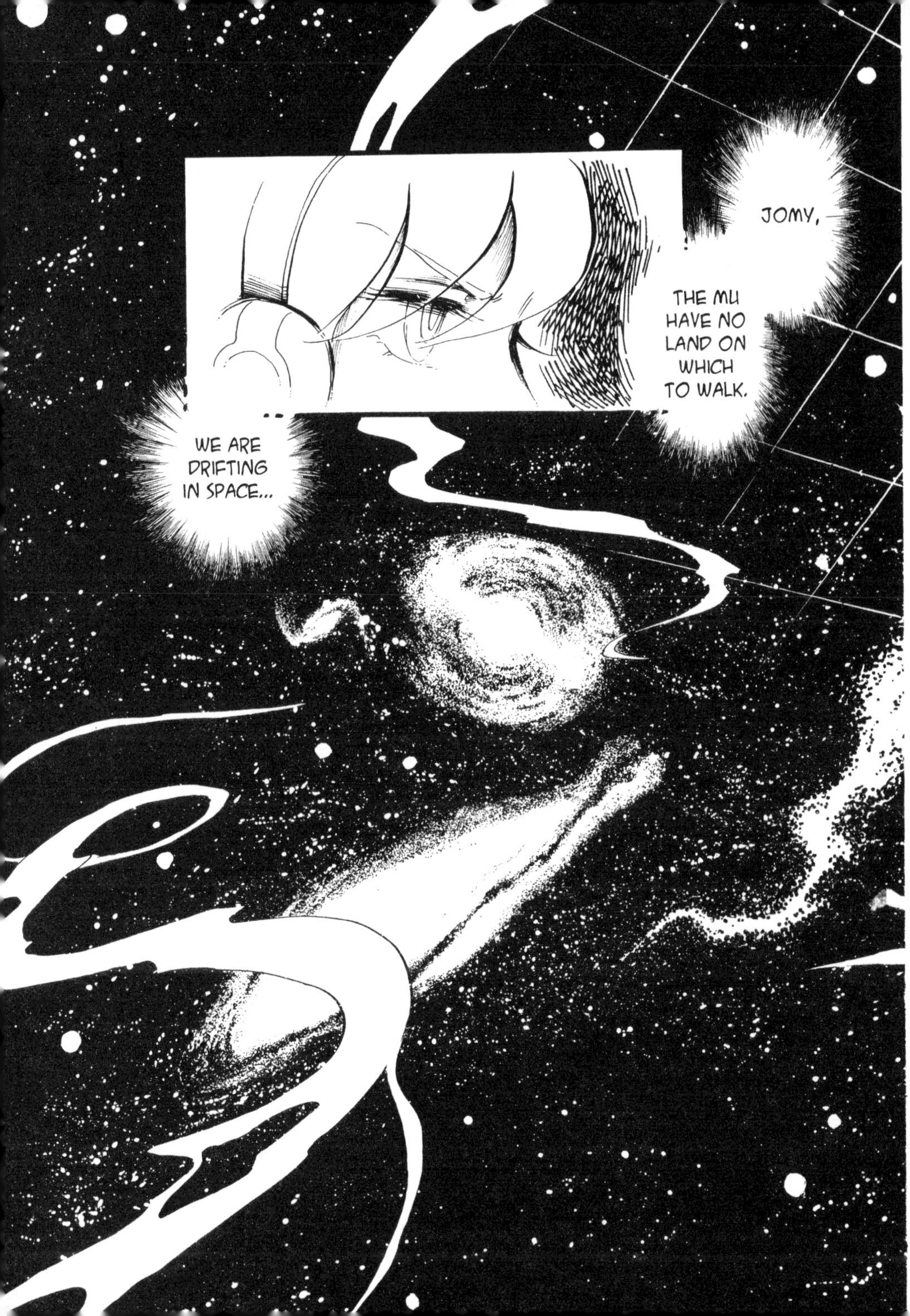
JOMY,
THE MU HAVE NO LAND ON WHICH TO WALK.
WE ARE DRIFTING IN SPACE...

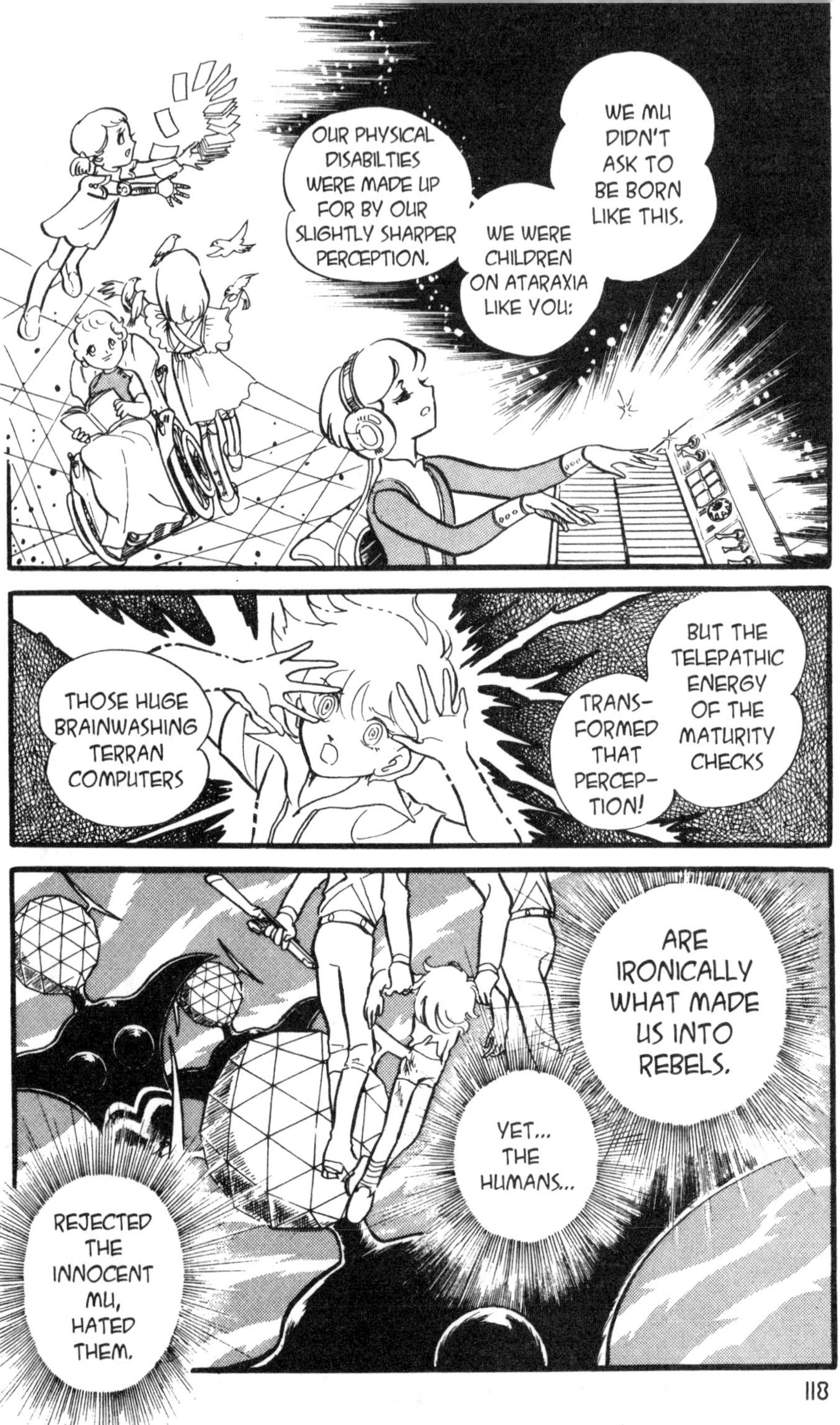
WE MU DIDN'T ASK TO BE BORN LIKE THIS.
WE WERE CHILDREN ON ATARAXIA LIKE YOU:
OUR PHYSICAL DISABILTIES WERE MADE UP FOR BY OUR SLIGHTLY SHARPER PERCEPTION.
BUT THE TELEPATHIC ENERGY OF THE MATURITY CHECKS
TRANS-FORMED THAT PERCEP-TION!
THOSE HUGE BRAINWASHING TERRAN COMPUTERS
ARE IRONICALLY WHAT MADE US INTO REBELS.
YET... THE HUMANS...
REJECTED THE INNOCENT MU, HATED THEM.

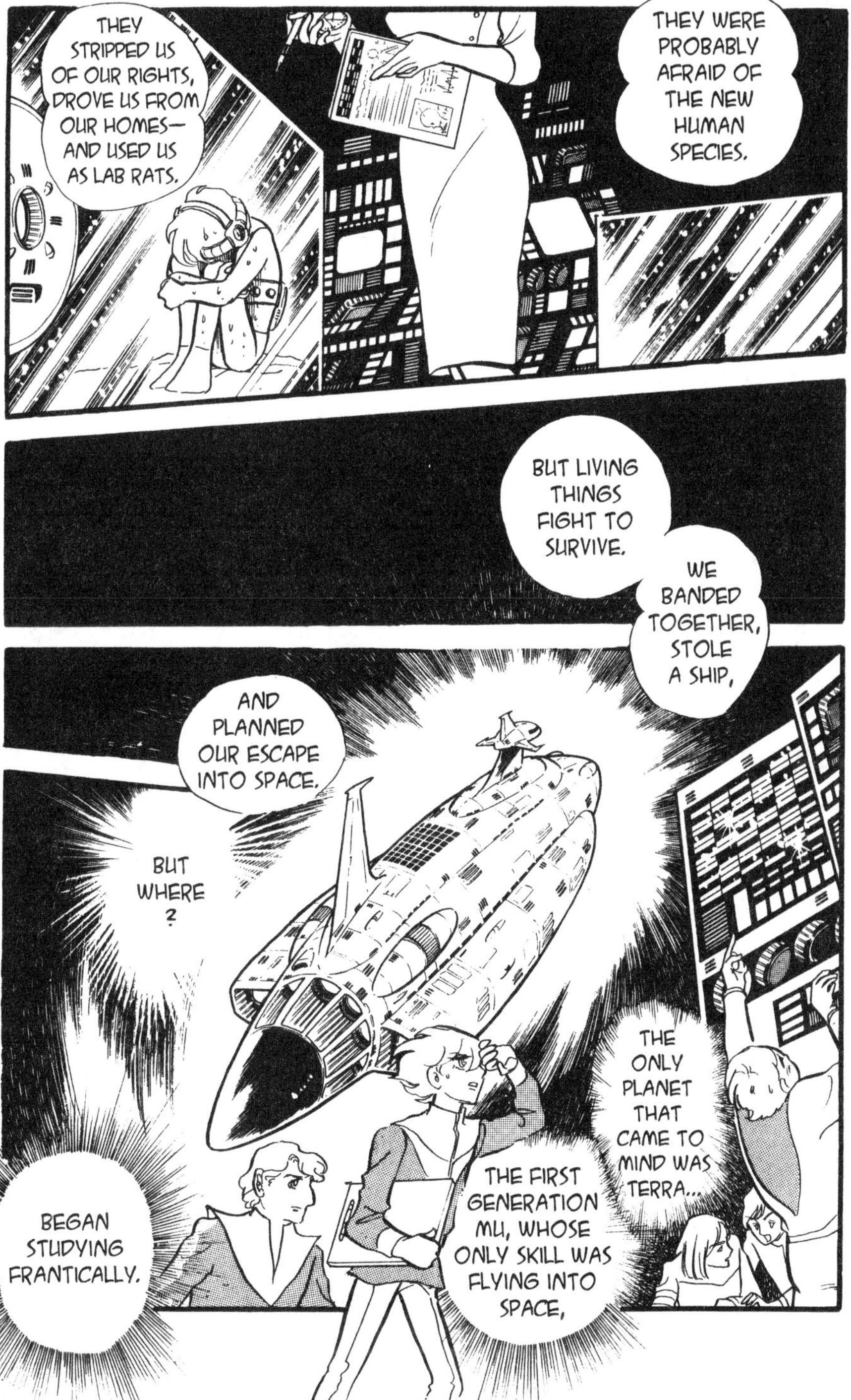
THEY WERE PROBABLY AFRAID OF THE NEW HUMAN SPECIES.
THEY STRIPPED US OF OUR RIGHTS, DROVE US FROM OUR HOMES—AND USED US AS LAB RATS.
BUT LIVING THINGS FIGHT TO SURVIVE.
WE BANDED TOGETHER, STOLE A SHIP,
AND PLANNED OUR ESCAPE INTO SPACE.
BUT WHERE?
THE ONLY PLANET THAT CAME TO MIND WAS TERRA...
THE FIRST GENERATION MU, WHOSE ONLY SKILL WAS FLYING INTO SPACE,
BEGAN STUDYING FRANTICALLY.

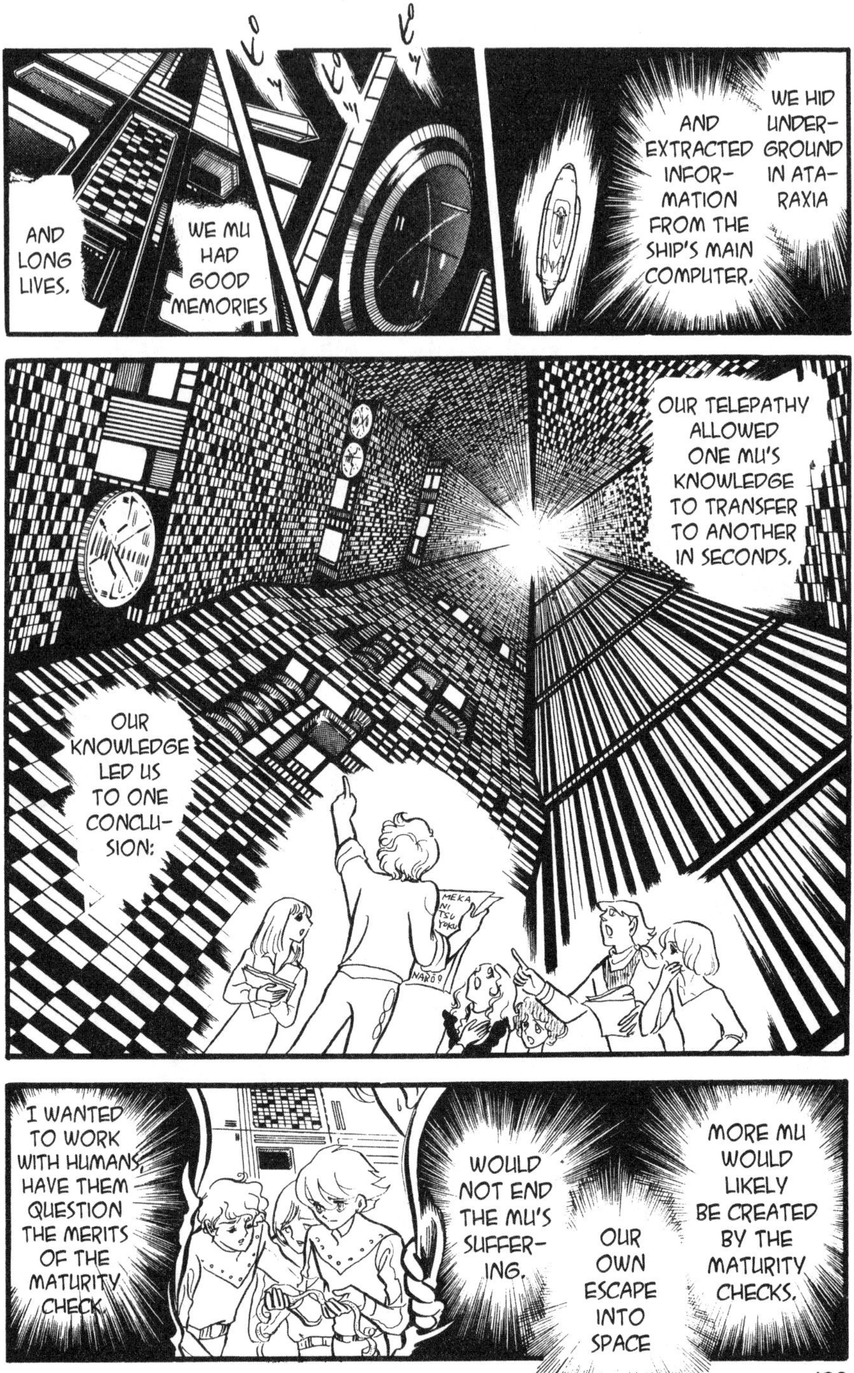
WE HID UNDER-GROUND IN ATA-RAXIA
AND EXTRACTED INFOR-MATION FROM THE SHIP'S MAIN COMPUTER.
WE MU HAD GOOD MEMORIES
AND LONG LIVES.
OUR TELEPATHY ALLOWED ONE MU'S KNOWLEDGE TO TRANSFER TO ANOTHER IN SECONDS.
OUR KNOWLEDGE LED US TO ONE CONCLU-SION:
MORE MU WOULD LIKELY BE CREATED BY THE MATURITY CHECKS.
OUR OWN ESCAPE INTO SPACE
WOULD NOT END THE MU'S SUFFER-ING.
I WANTED TO WORK WITH HUMANS, HAVE THEM QUESTION THE MERITS OF THE MATURITY CHECK.

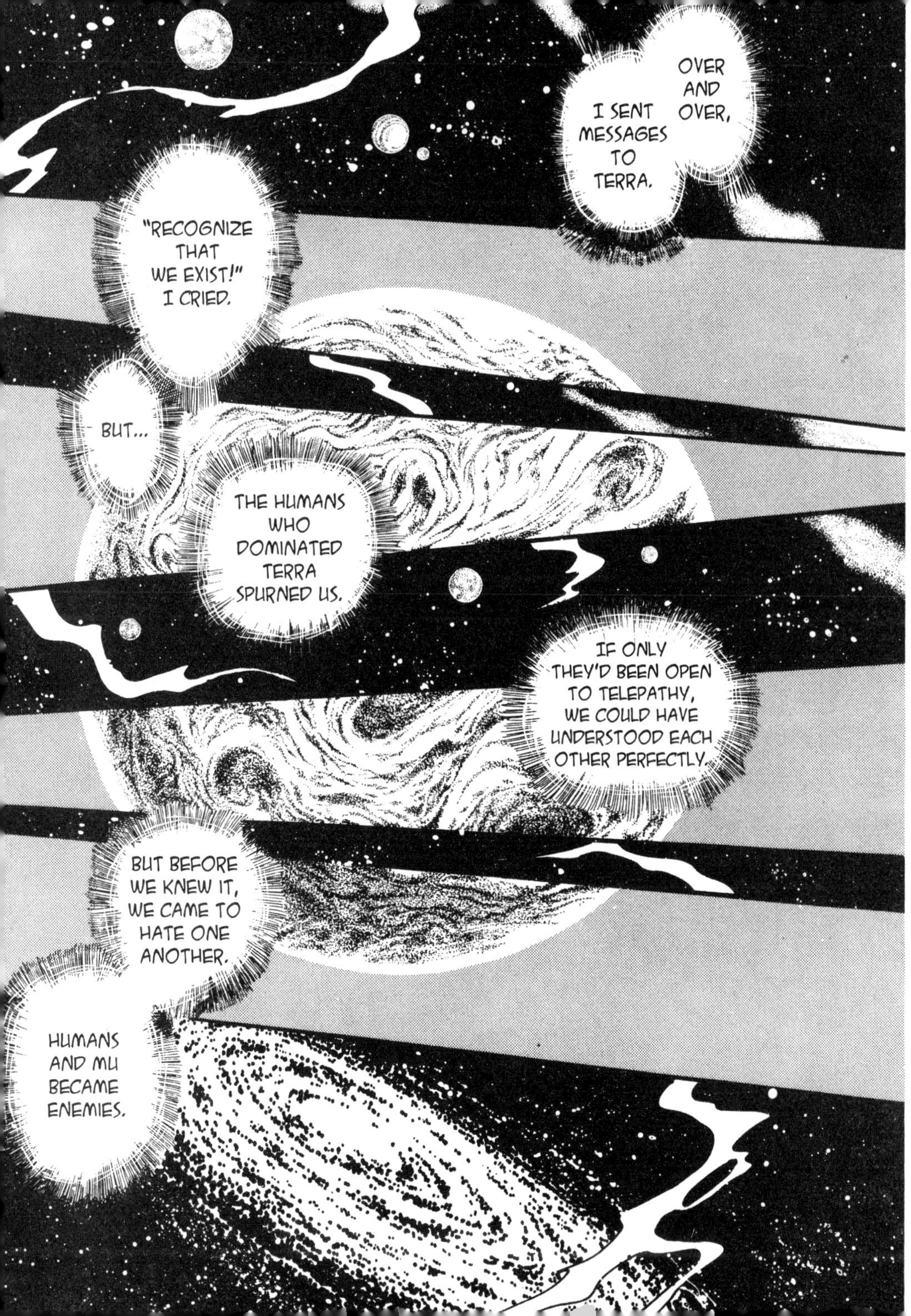
OVER AND OVER, I SENT MESSAGES TO TERRA.
"RECOGNIZE THAT WE EXIST!" I CRIED.
BUT...
THE HUMANS WHO DOMINATED TERRA SPURNED US.
IF ONLY THEY'D BEEN OPEN TO TELEPATHY, WE COULD HAVE UNDERSTOOD EACH OTHER PERFECTLY.
BUT BEFORE WE KNEW IT, WE CAME TO HATE ONE ANOTHER.
HUMANS AND MU BECAME ENEMIES.

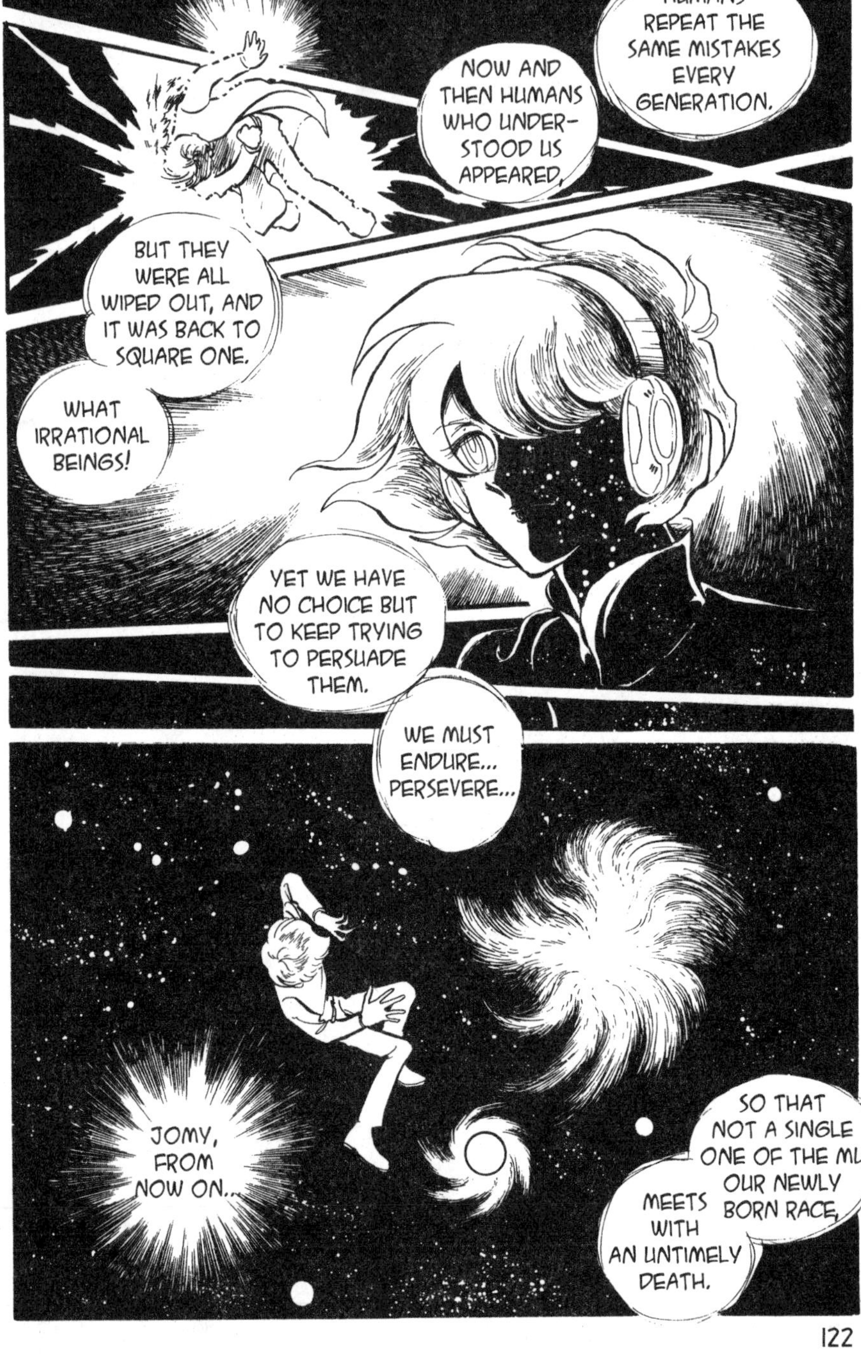
HUMANS REPEAT THE SAME MISTAKES EVERY GENERATION.
NOW AND THEN HUMANS WHO UNDER-STOOD US APPEARED,
BUT THEY WERE ALL WIPED OUT, AND IT WAS BACK TO SQUARE ONE.
WHAT IRRATIONAL BEINGS!
YET WE HAVE NO CHOICE BUT TO KEEP TRYING TO PERSUADE THEM.
WE MUST ENDURE... PERSEVERE...
SO THAT NOT A SINGLE ONE OF THE MU, OUR NEWLY BORN RACE,
MEETS WITH AN UNTIMELY DEATH.
JOMY, FROM NOW ON...

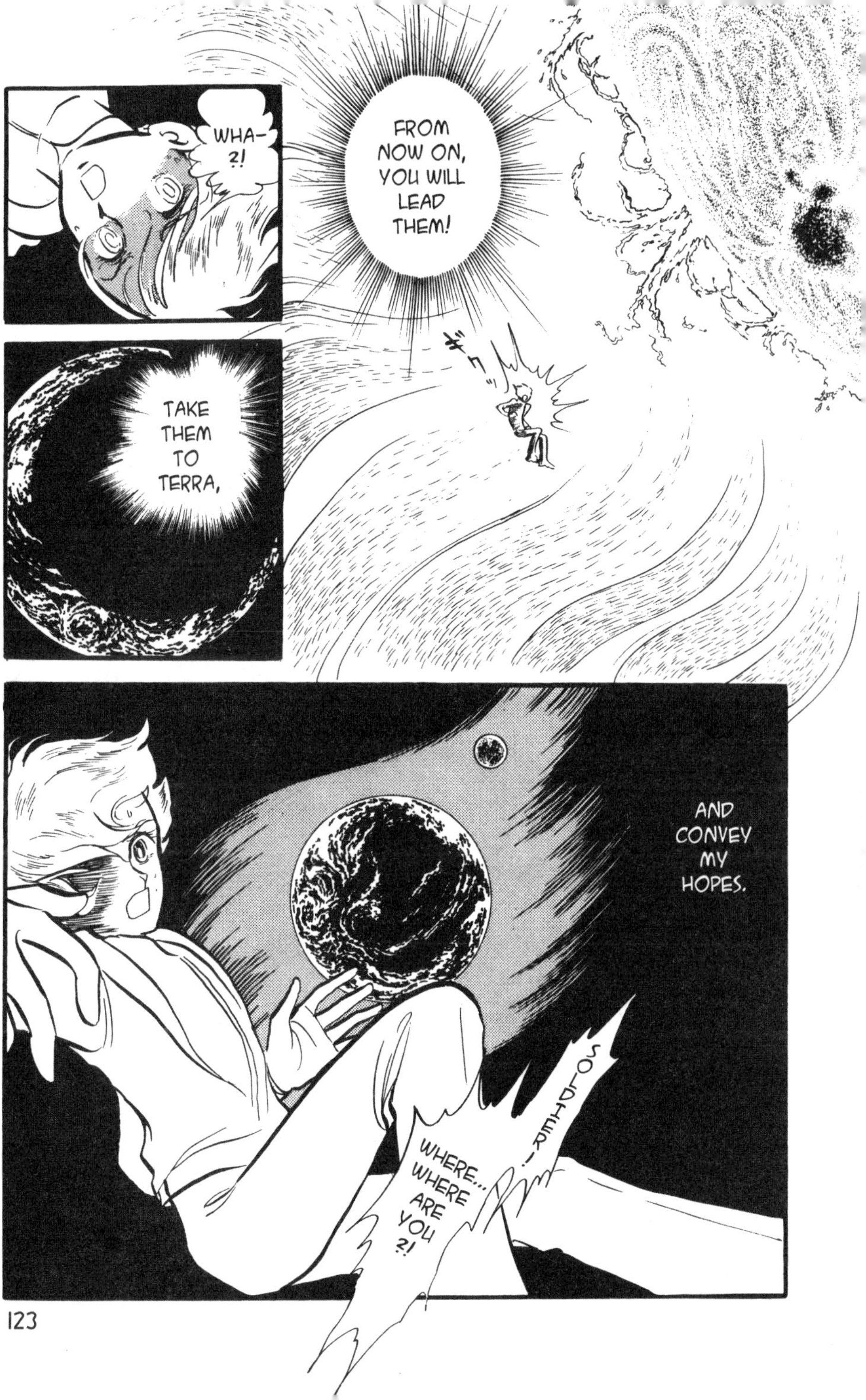
FROM NOW ON, YOU WILL LEAD THEM!
ギクッ
WHA-?!
TAKE THEM TO TERRA,
AND CONVEY MY HOPES.
SOLDIER...
WHERE... WHERE ARE YOU?!

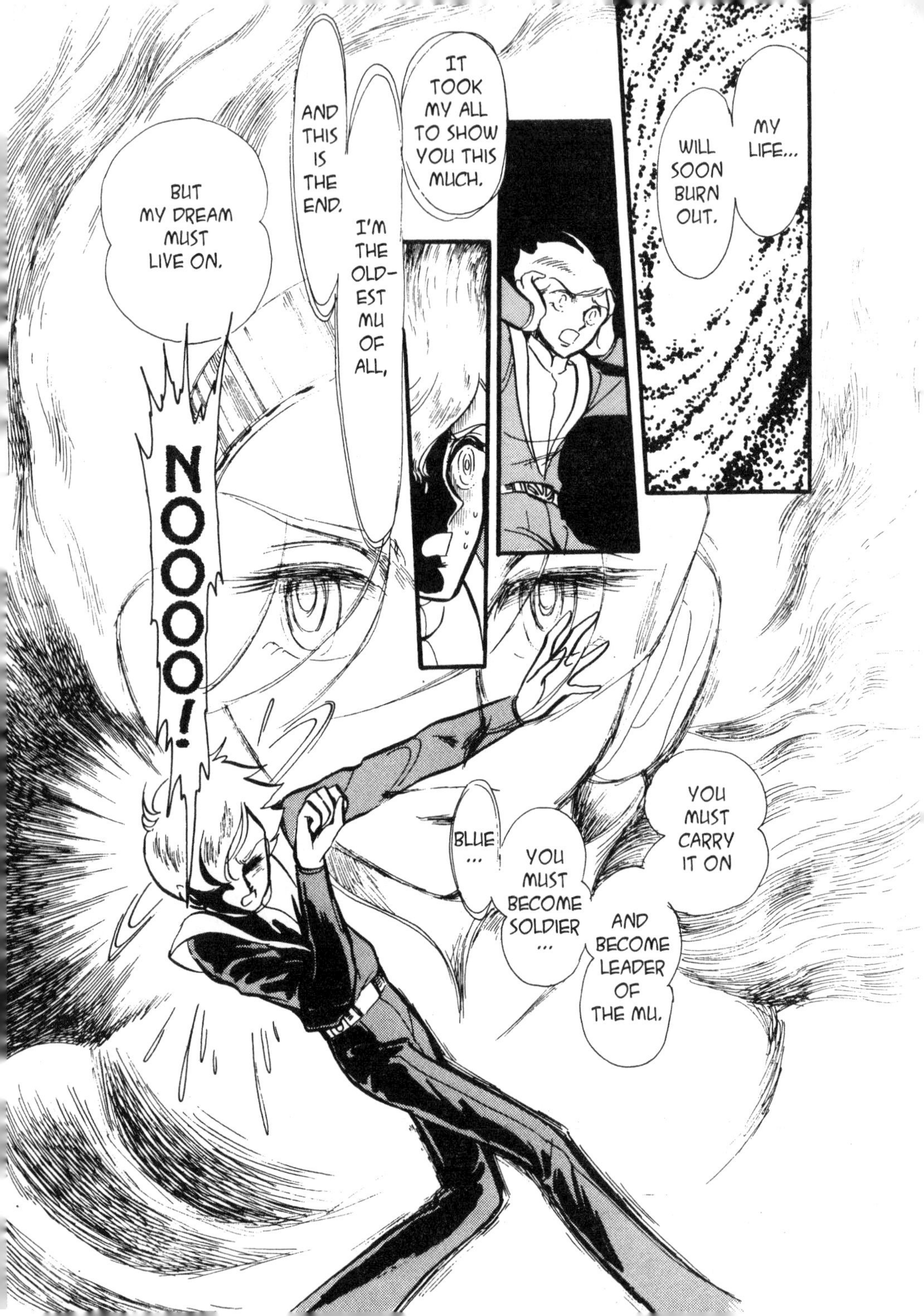
MY LIFE...
WILL SOON BURN OUT.
IT TOOK MY ALL TO SHOW YOU THIS MUCH.
AND THIS IS THE END.
I'M THE OLDEST MU OF ALL,
BUT MY DREAM MUST LIVE ON.
BLUE...
YOU MUST BECOME SOLDIER...
YOU MUST CARRY IT ON
AND BECOME LEADER OF THE MU.
NOOOO!

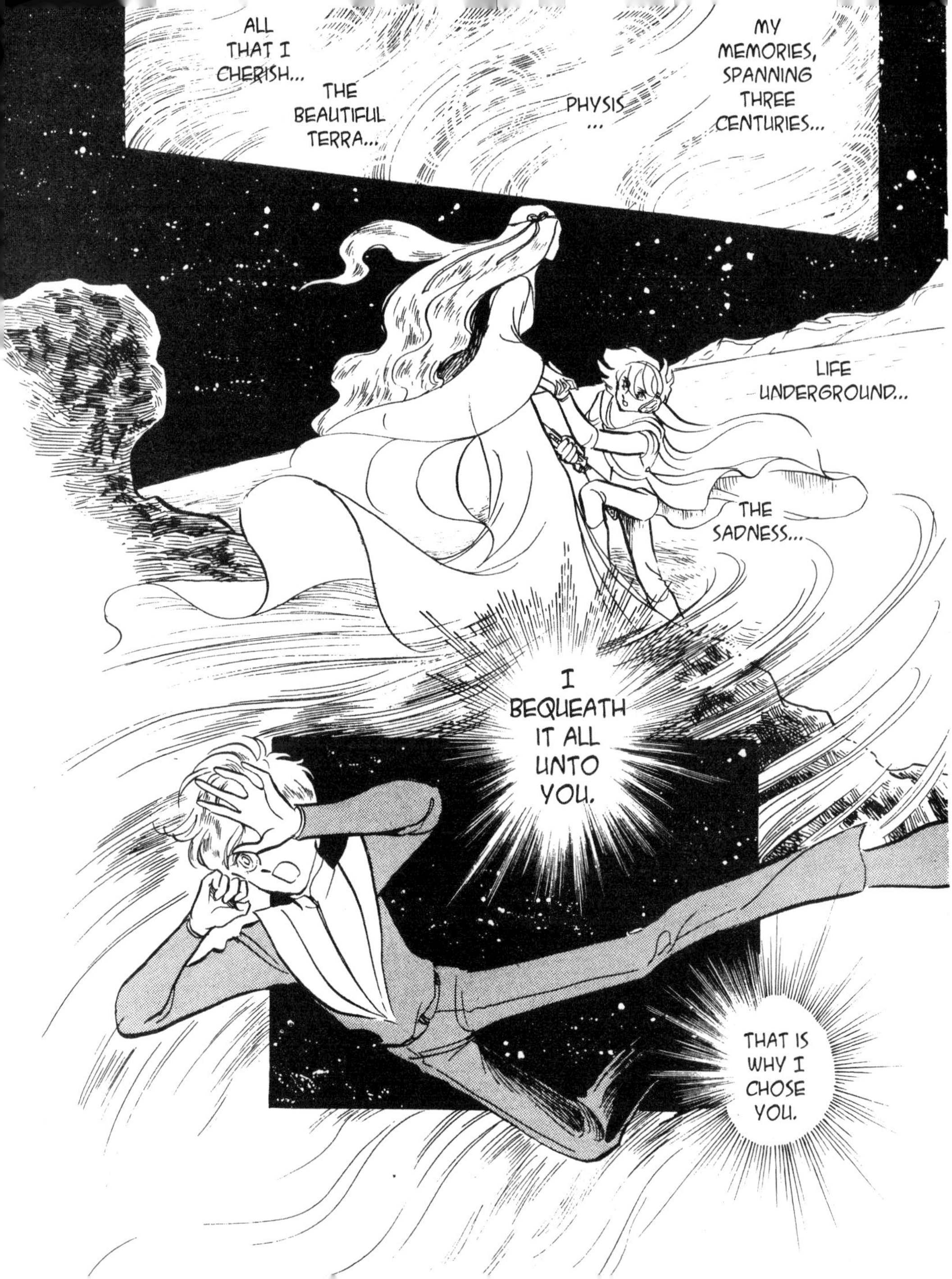
MY MEMORIES, SPANNING THREE CENTURIES...
PHYSIS ...
THE BEAUTIFUL TERRA...
ALL THAT I CHERISH...
LIFE UNDERGROUND...
THE SADNESS...
I BEQUEATH IT ALL UNTO YOU.
THAT IS WHY I CHOSE YOU.

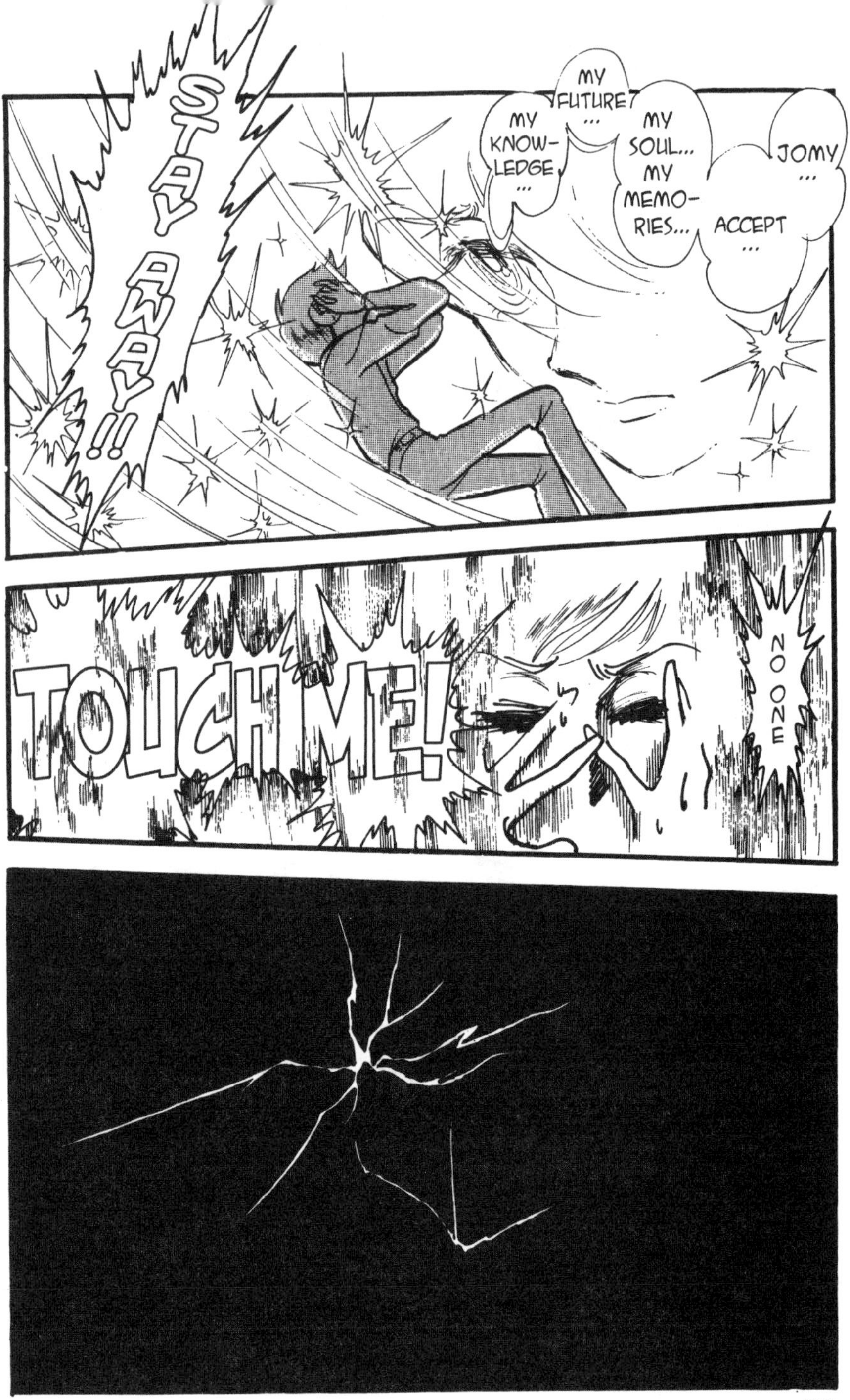
JOMY ...
ACCEPT ...
MY SOUL... MY MEMORIES...
MY FUTURE? ...
MY KNOWLEDGE ...
STAY AWAY!!
NO ONE
TOUCH ME!

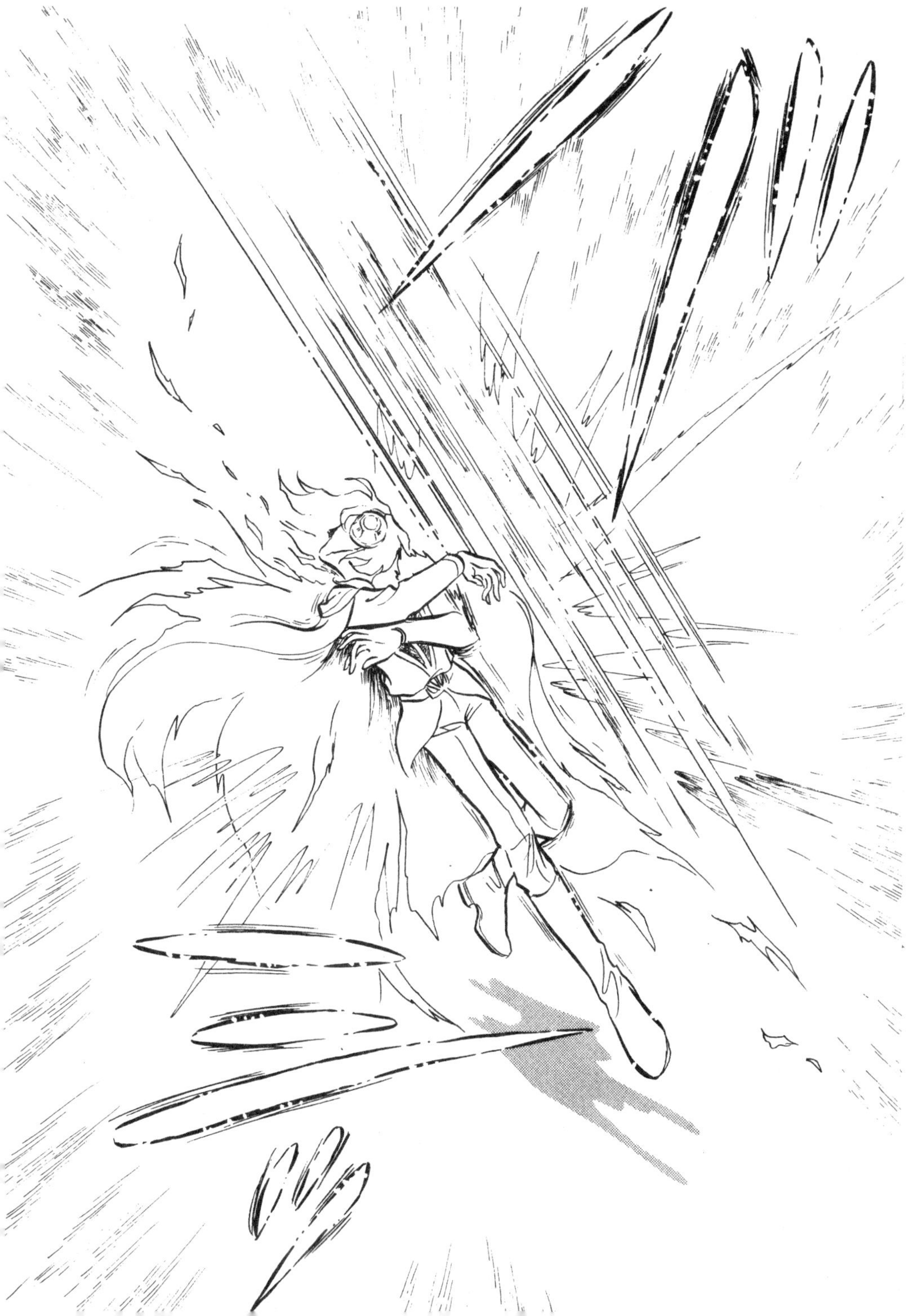

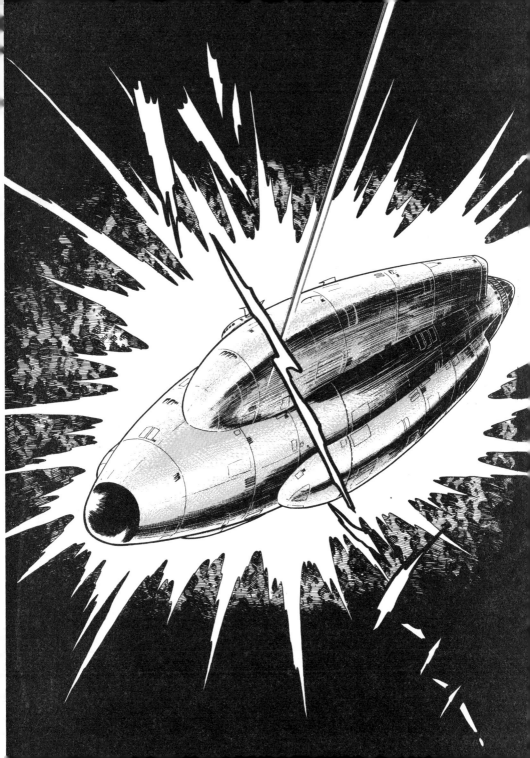

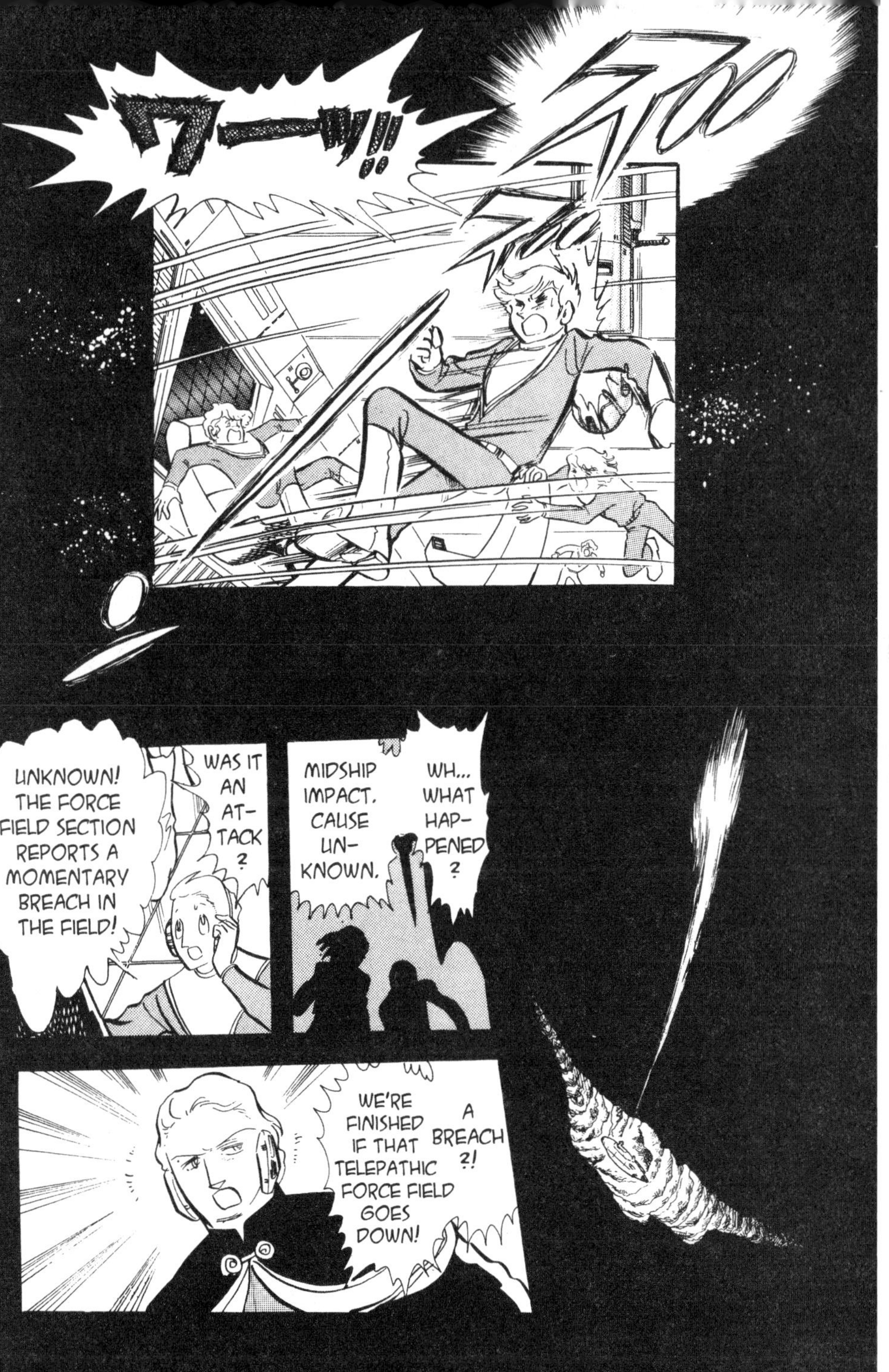
ワーッ!!
WH... WHAT HAP-PENED?
MIDSHIP IMPACT. CAUSE UN-KNOWN.
WAS IT AN AT-TACK?
UNKNOWN! THE FORCE FIELD SECTION REPORTS A MOMENTARY BREACH IN THE FIELD!
A BREACH?!
WE'RE FINISHED IF THAT TELEPATHIC FORCE FIELD GOES DOWN!

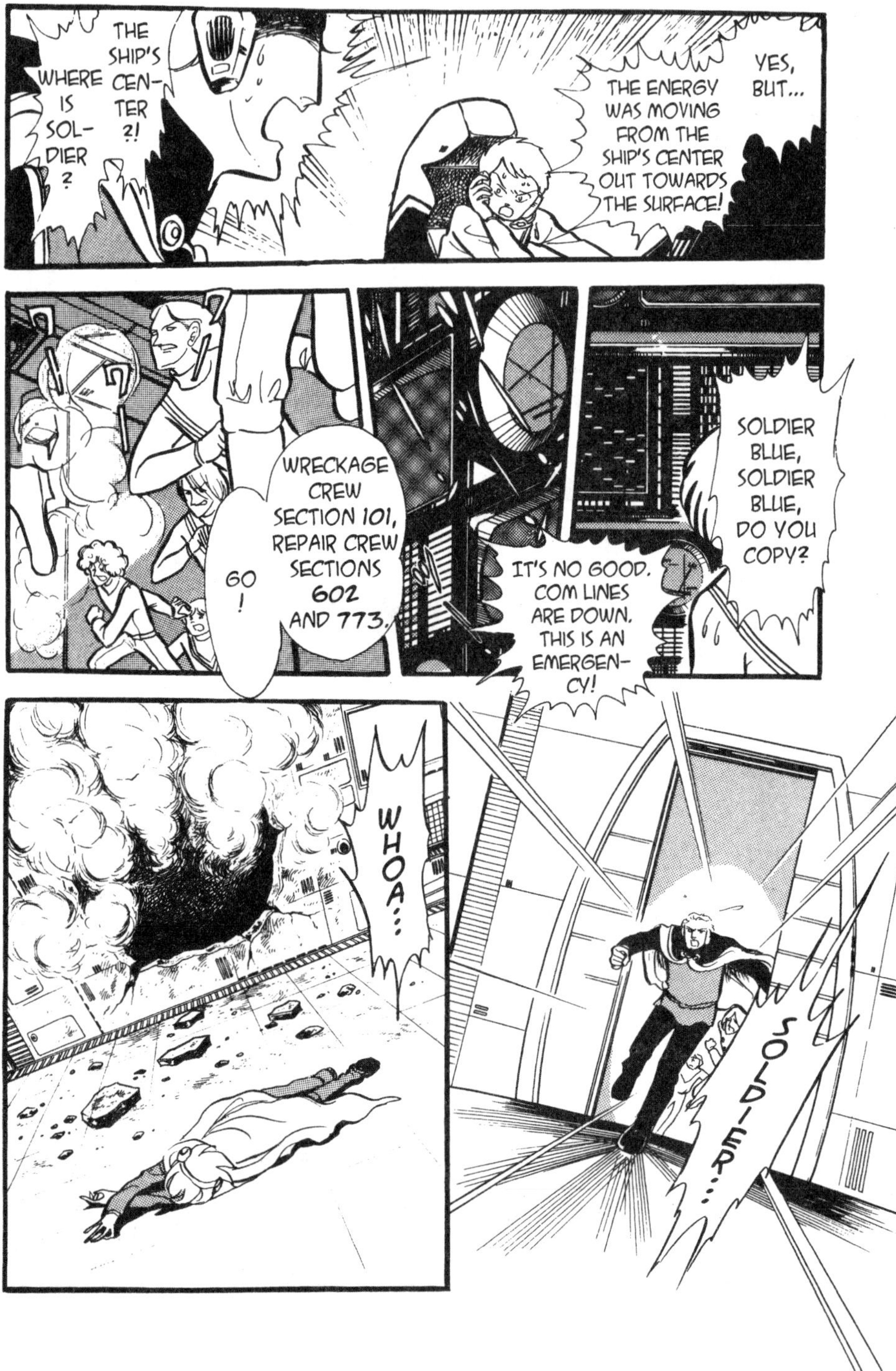
YES, BUT...
THE ENERGY WAS MOVING FROM THE SHIP'S CENTER OUT TOWARDS THE SURFACE!
THE SHIP'S CEN-TER?!
WHERE IS SOL-DIER?
SOLDIER BLUE, SOLDIER BLUE, DO YOU COPY?
IT'S NO GOOD. COM LINES ARE DOWN. THIS IS AN EMERGEN-CY!
WRECKAGE CREW SECTION 101, REPAIR CREW SECTIONS 602 AND 773.
GO!
SOLDIER...
WHOA...

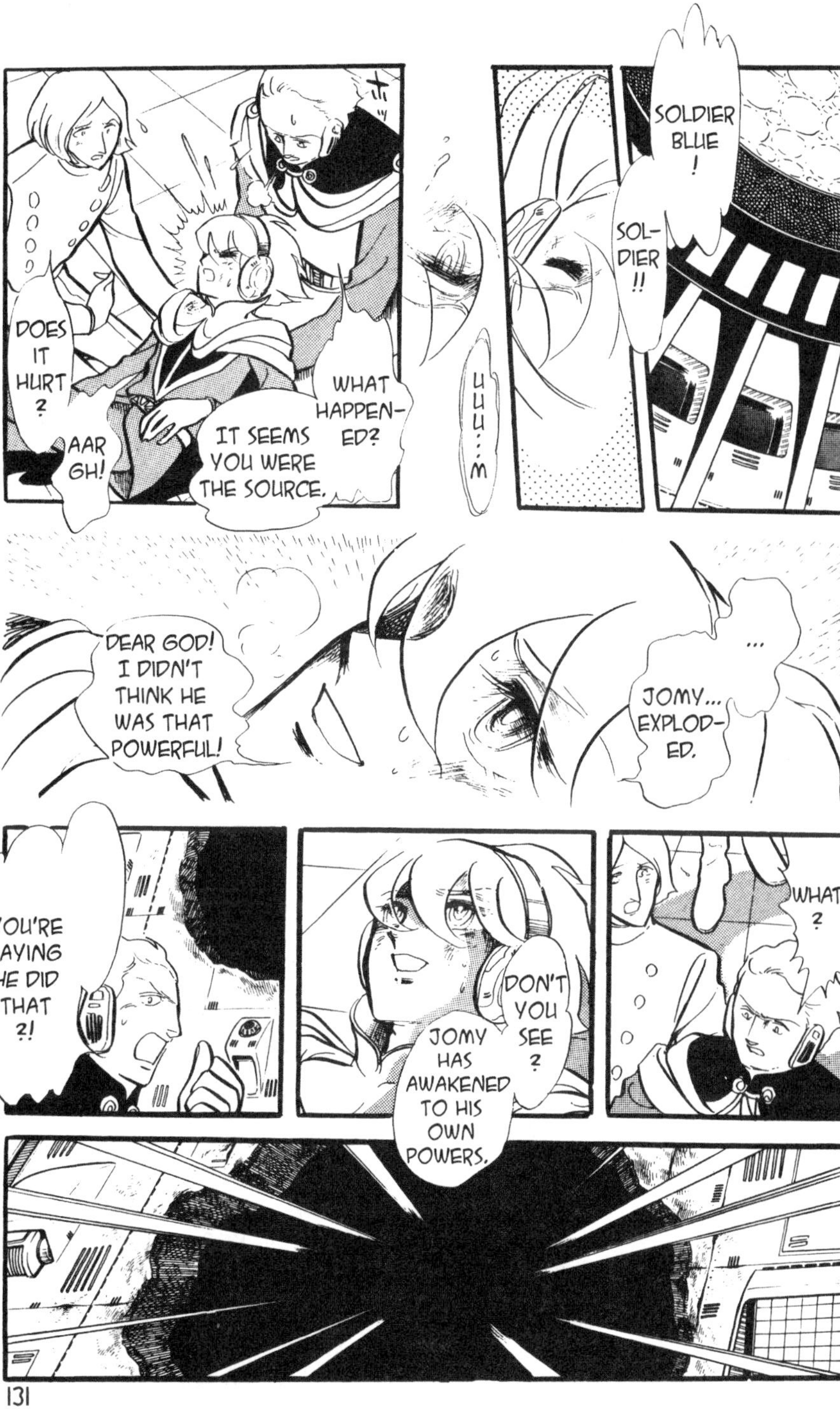
SOLDIER BLUE !
SOL-DIER !!
UUU...M
WHAT HAPPEN-ED?
IT SEEMS YOU WERE THE SOURCE.
DOES IT HURT?
AAR GH!
...
JOMY... EXPLOD-ED.
DEAR GOD! I DIDN'T THINK HE WAS THAT POWERFUL!
WHAT?
DON'T YOU SEE?
JOMY HAS AWAKENED TO HIS OWN POWERS.
YOU'RE SAYING HE DID THAT?!

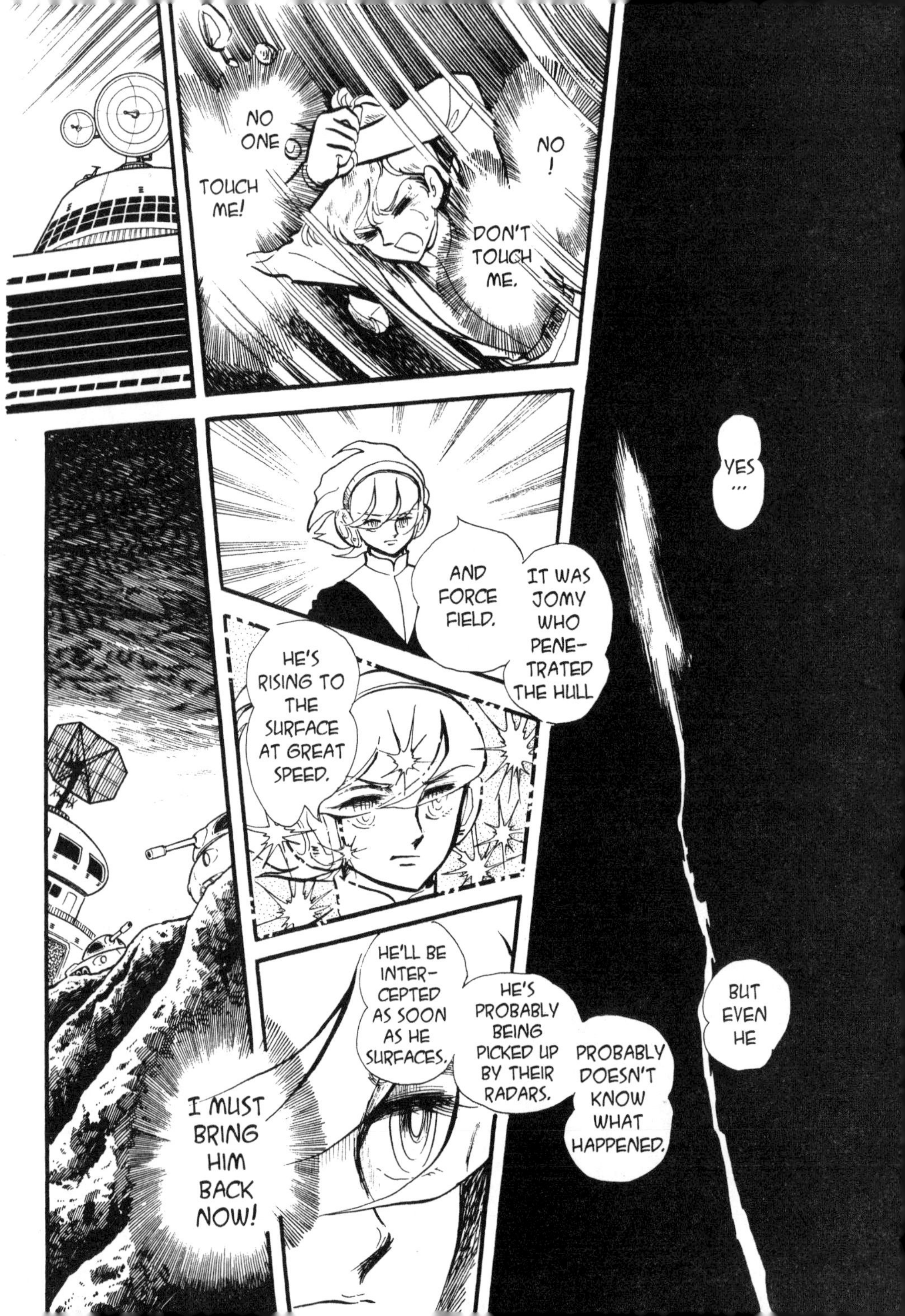
YES...
BUT EVEN HE
PROBABLY DOESN'T KNOW WHAT HAPPENED.
NO!
DON'T TOUCH ME.
NO ONE TOUCH ME!
IT WAS JOMY WHO PENE-TRATED THE HULL
AND FORCE FIELD.
HE'S RISING TO THE SURFACE AT GREAT SPEED.
HE'S PROBABLY BEING PICKED UP BY THEIR RADARS.
HE'LL BE INTER-CEPTED AS SOON AS HE SURFACES.
I MUST BRING HIM BACK NOW!

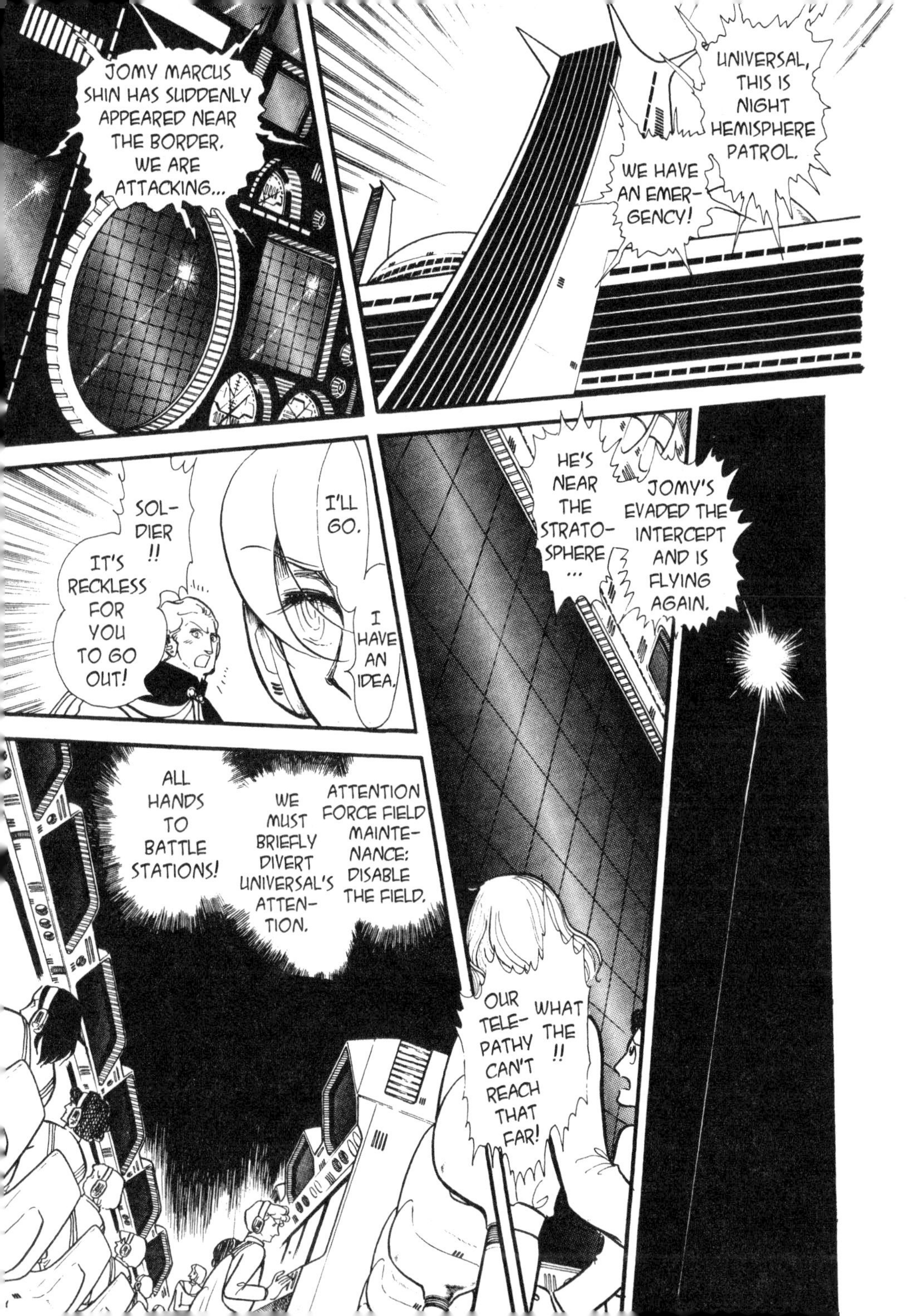
UNIVERSAL, THIS IS NIGHT HEMISPHERE PATROL.
WE HAVE AN EMER-GENCY!
JOMY MARCUS SHIN HAS SUDDENLY APPEARED NEAR THE BORDER. WE ARE ATTACKING...
JOMY'S EVADED THE INTERCEPT AND IS FLYING AGAIN.
HE'S NEAR THE STRATO-SPHERE ...
I'LL GO.
I HAVE AN IDEA.
SOL-DIER !!
IT'S RECKLESS FOR YOU TO GO OUT!
WHAT THE !!
OUR TELE-PATHY CAN'T REACH THAT FAR!
ATTENTION FORCE FIELD MAINTE-NANCE: DISABLE THE FIELD.
WE MUST BRIEFLY DIVERT UNIVERSAL'S ATTEN-TION.
ALL HANDS TO BATTLE STATIONS!

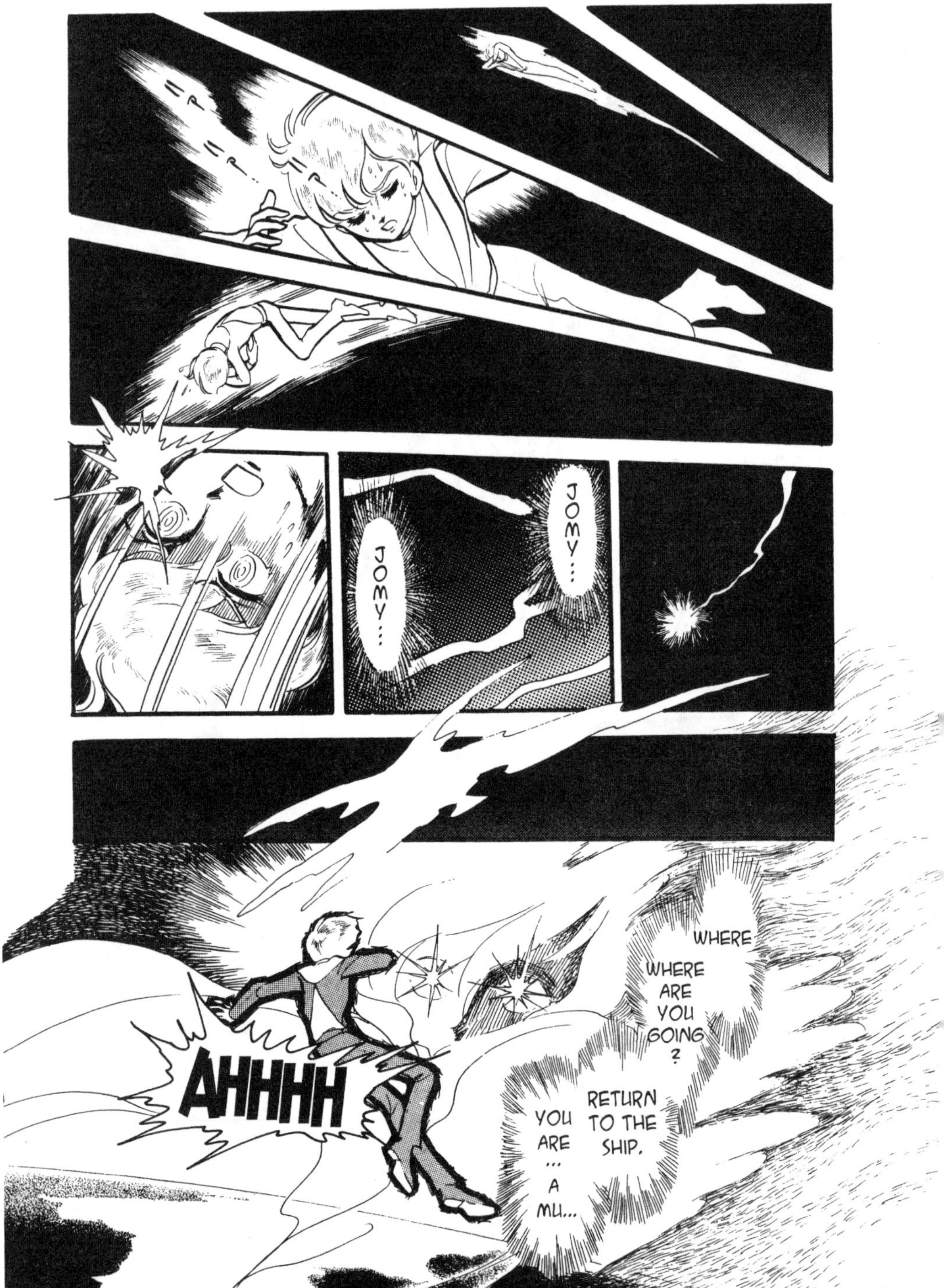
JOMY...
JOMY...
WHERE
WHERE ARE YOU GOING?
RETURN TO THE SHIP.
YOU ARE ... A MU...
AHHHH

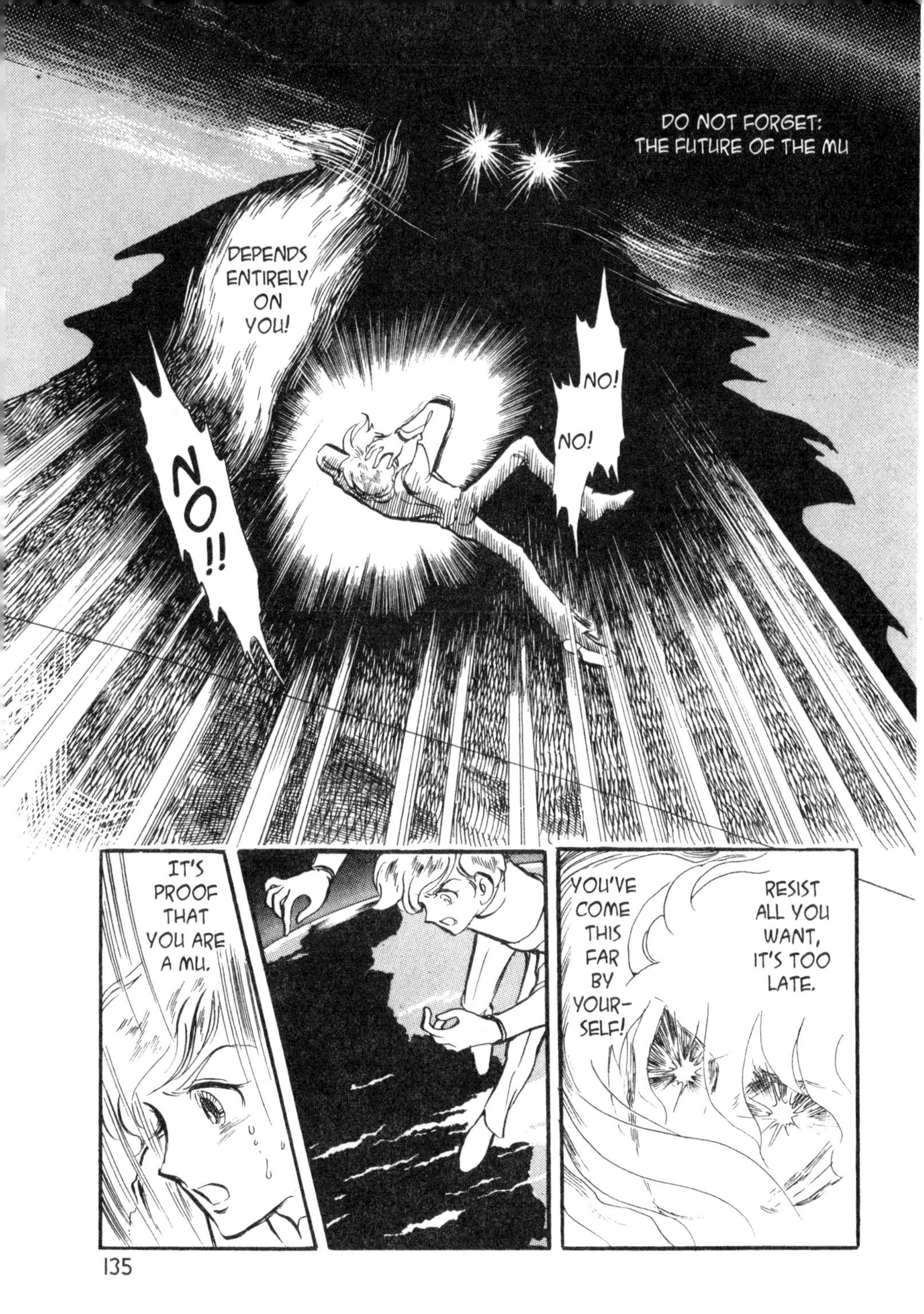
DO NOT FORGET: THE FUTURE OF THE MU
DEPENDS ENTIRELY ON YOU!
NO!
NO!
NO!!
RESIST ALL YOU WANT, IT'S TOO LATE.
YOU'VE COME THIS FAR BY YOUR-SELF!
IT'S PROOF THAT YOU ARE A MU.

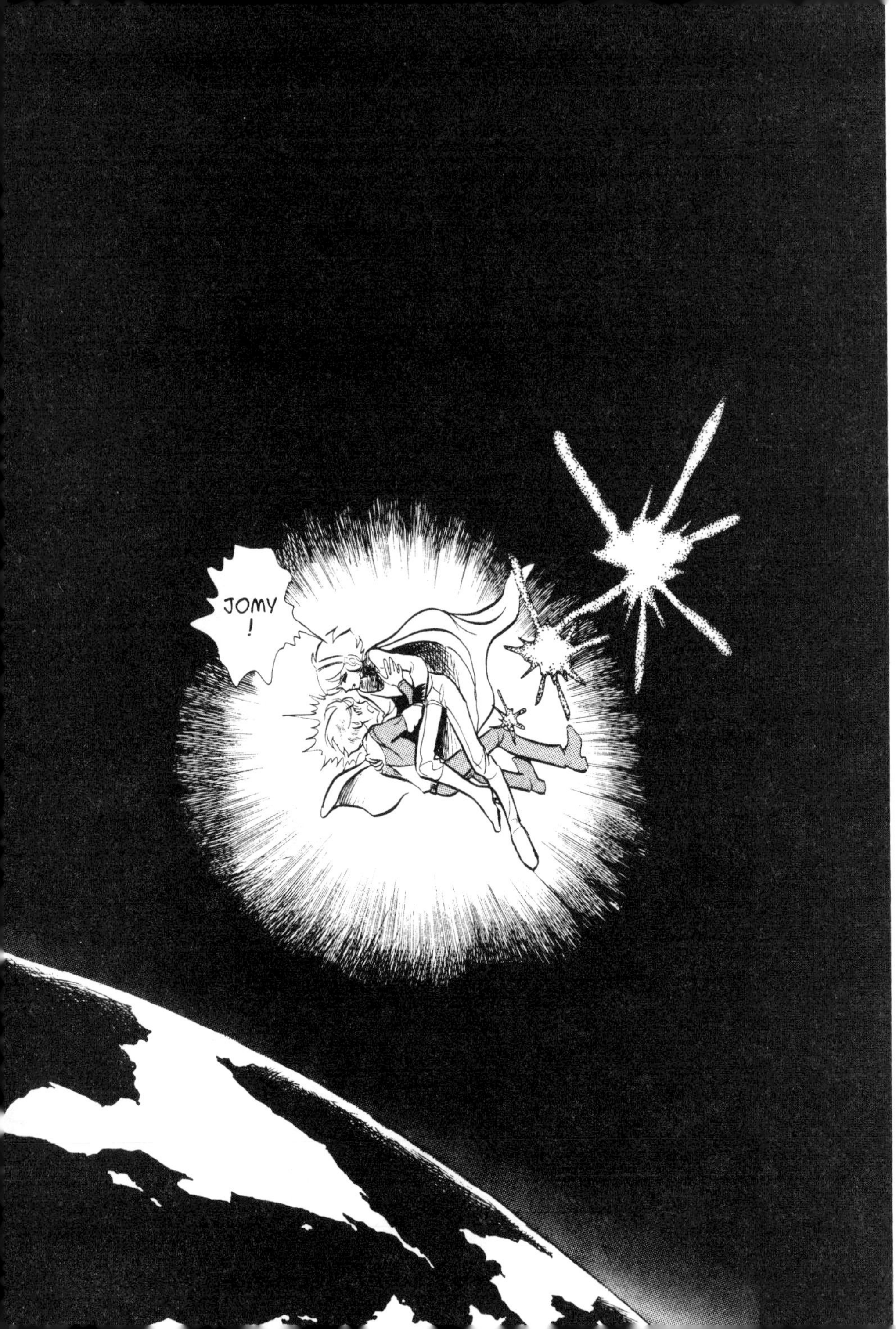
JOMY!

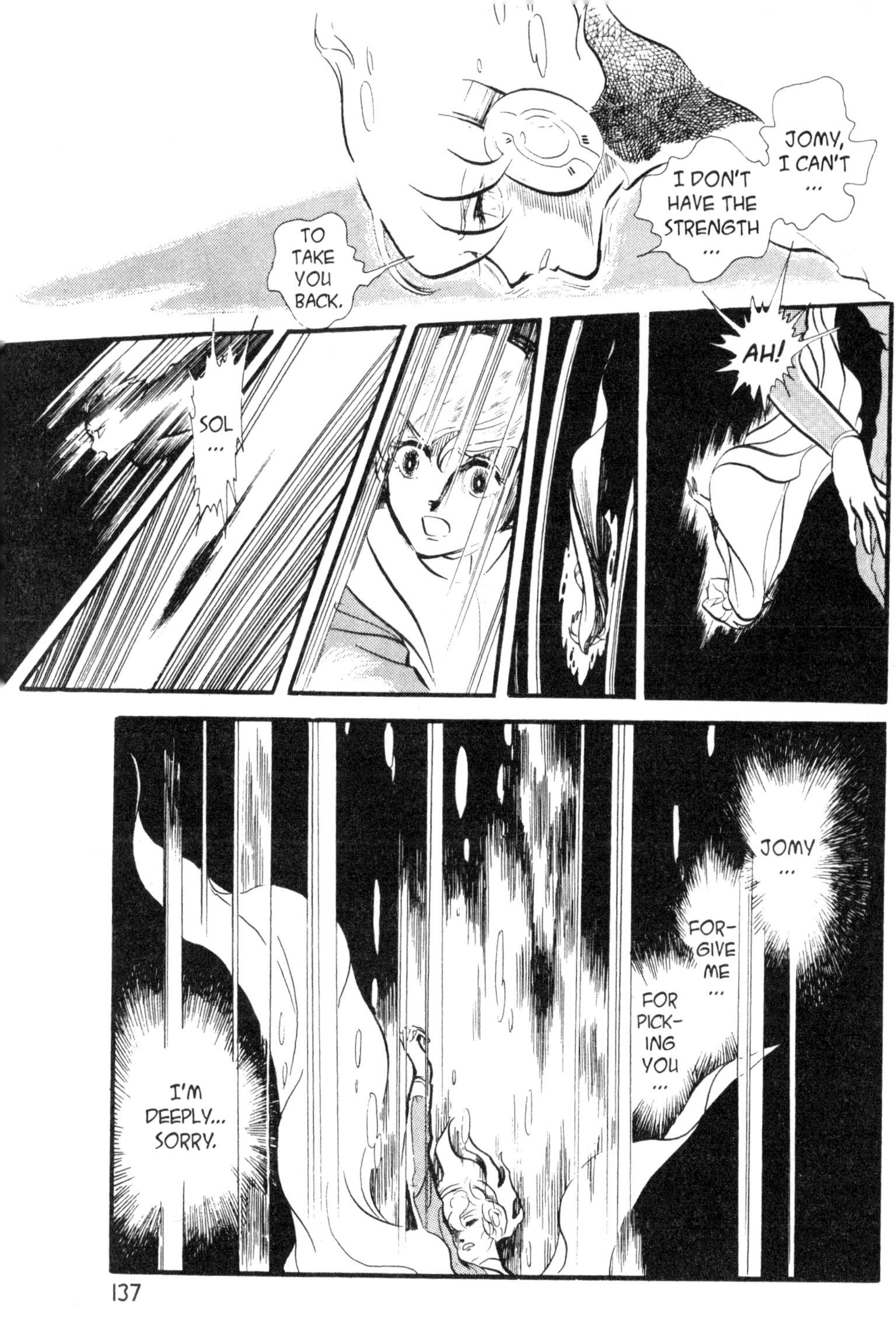
JOMY, I CAN'T ...
I DON'T HAVE THE STRENGTH ...
TO TAKE YOU BACK.
AH!
SOL ...
JOMY ...
FOR-GIVE ME ...
FOR PICK-ING YOU ...
I'M DEEPLY... SORRY.

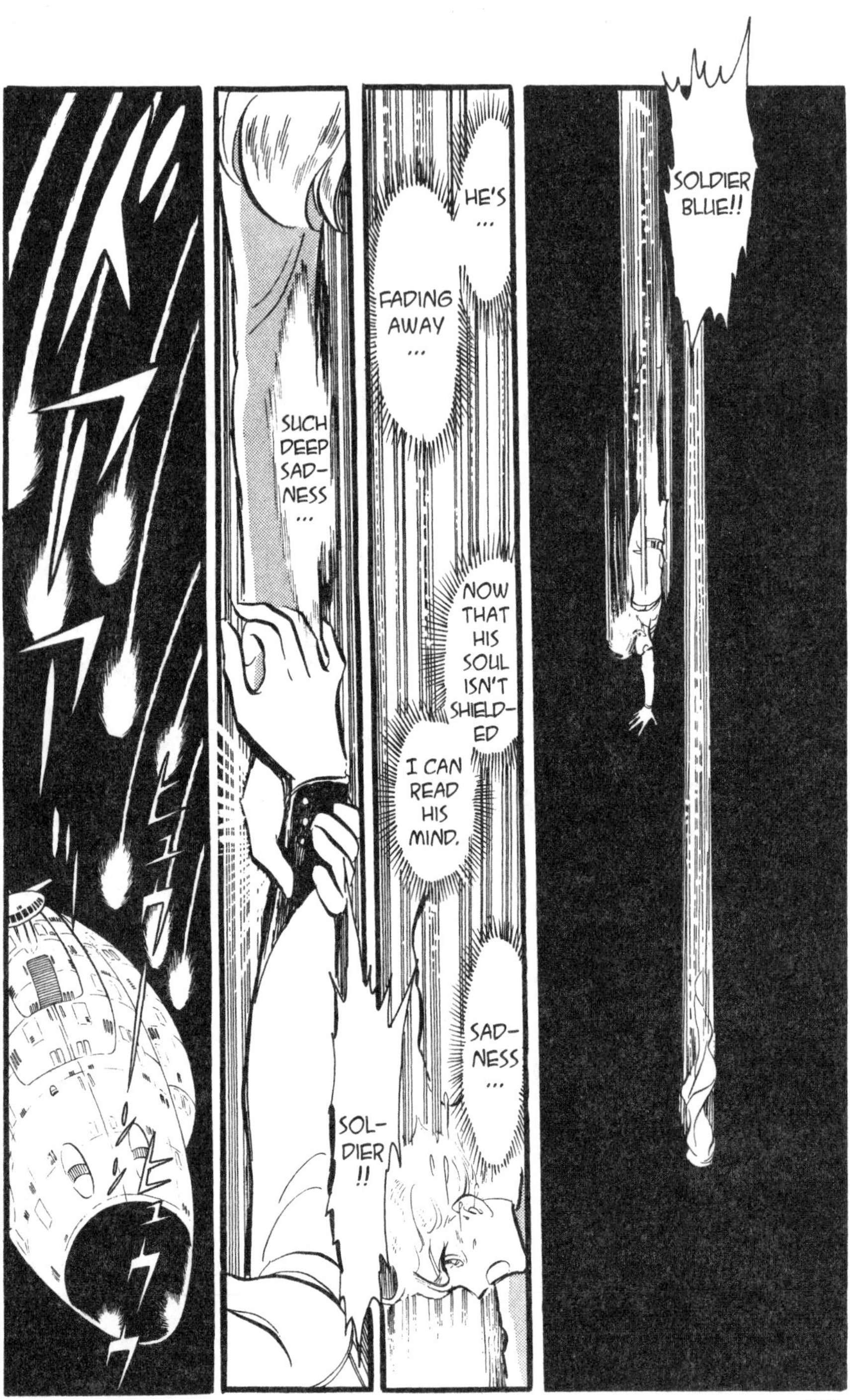
SOLDIER BLUE!!
HE'S ...
FADING AWAY ...
NOW THAT HIS SOUL ISN'T SHIELD-ED
I CAN READ HIS MIND.
SAD-NESS ...
SUCH DEEP SAD-NESS ...
SOL-DIER !!

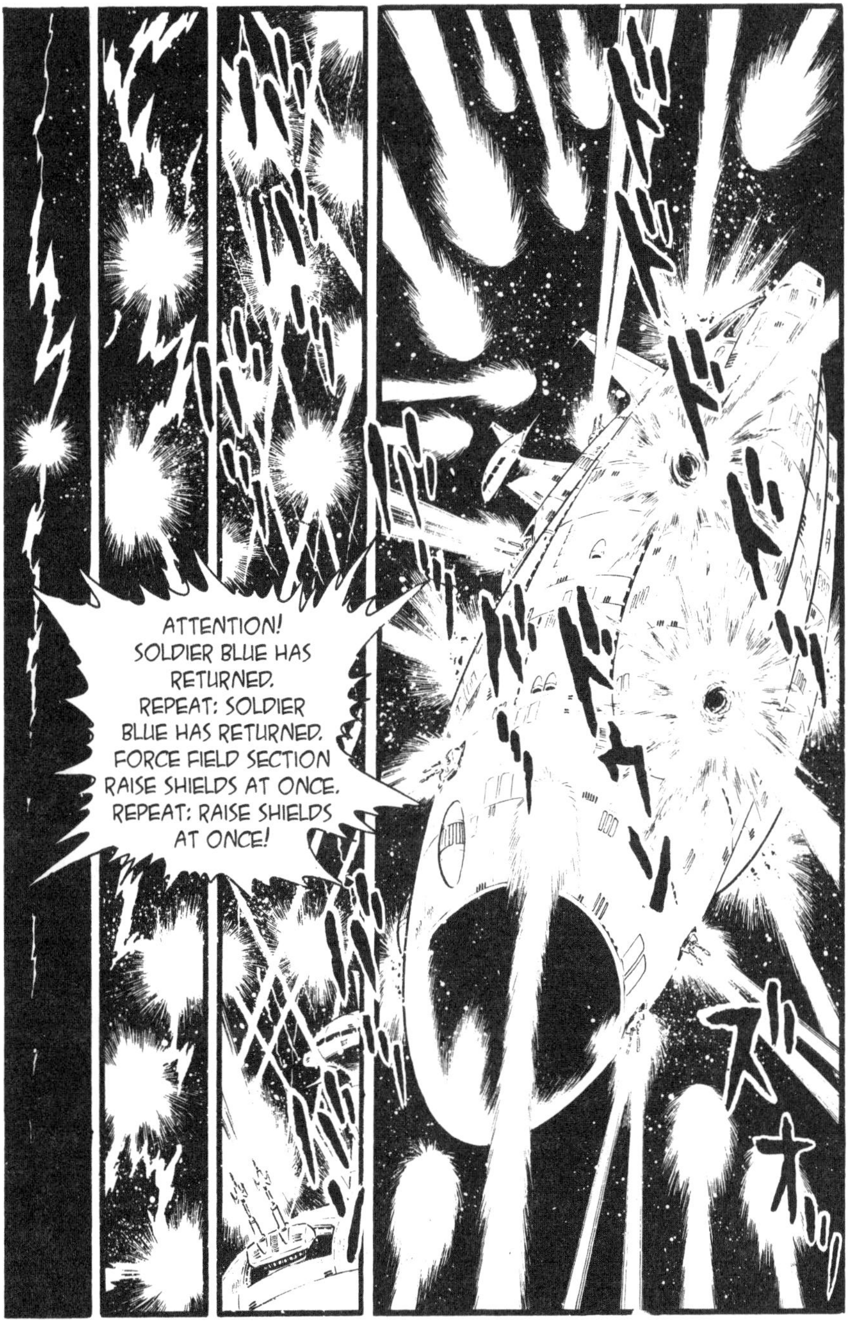
ATTENTION! SOLDIER BLUE HAS RETURNED. REPEAT: SOLDIER BLUE HAS RETURNED. FORCE FIELD SECTION RAISE SHIELDS AT ONCE. REPEAT: RAISE SHIELDS AT ONCE!

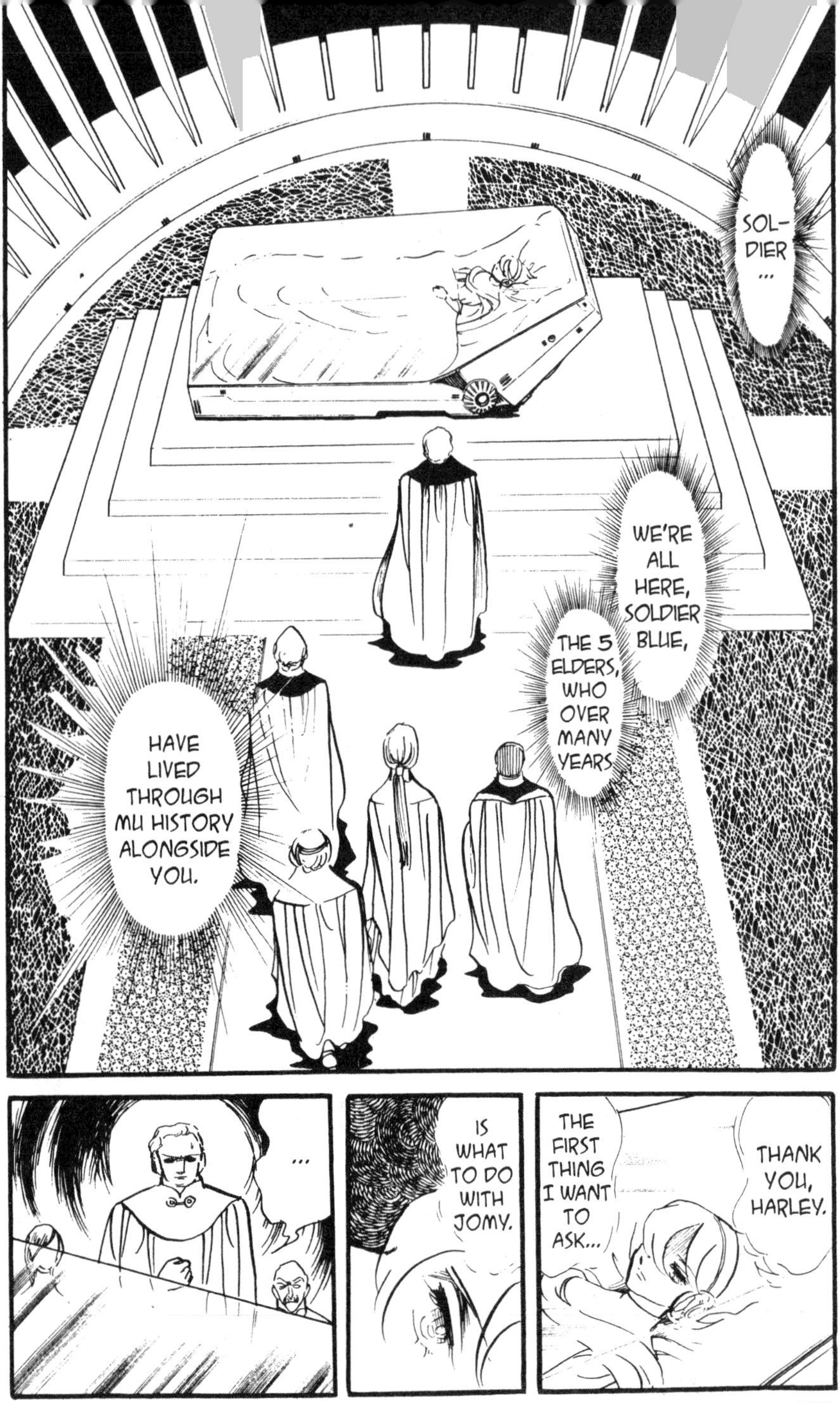
SOL-DIER ...
WE'RE ALL HERE, SOLDIER BLUE,
THE 5 ELDERS, WHO OVER MANY YEARS
HAVE LIVED THROUGH MU HISTORY ALONGSIDE YOU.
THANK YOU, HARLEY.
THE FIRST THING I WANT TO ASK...
IS WHAT TO DO WITH JOMY.
...

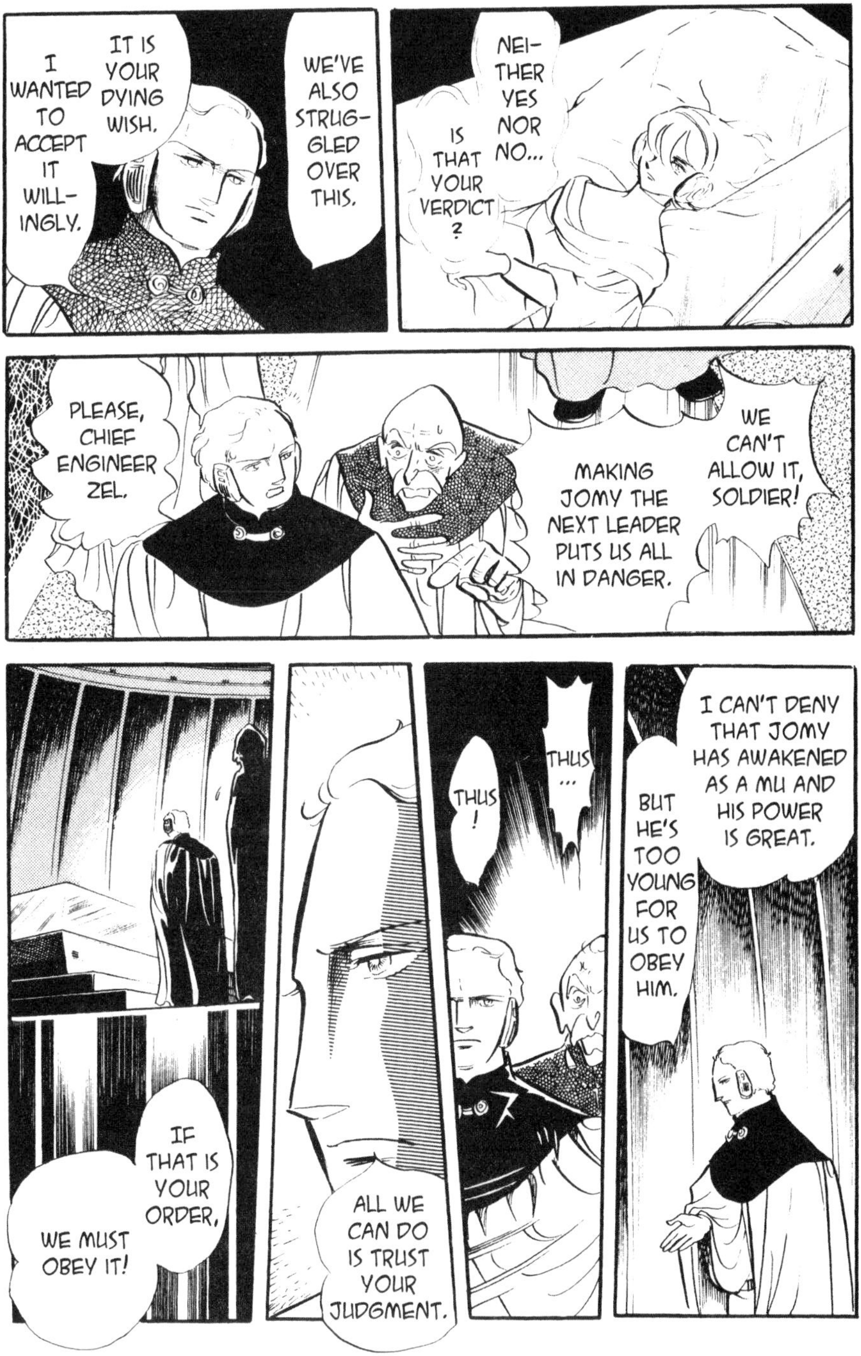
NEITHER YES NOR NO...
IS THAT YOUR VERDICT?
WE'VE ALSO STRUGGLED OVER THIS.
IT IS YOUR DYING WISH.
I WANTED TO ACCEPT IT WILLINGLY.
WE CAN'T ALLOW IT, SOLDIER!
MAKING JOMY THE NEXT LEADER PUTS US ALL IN DANGER.
PLEASE, CHIEF ENGINEER ZEL.
I CAN'T DENY THAT JOMY HAS AWAKENED AS A MU AND HIS POWER IS GREAT.
BUT HE'S TOO YOUNG FOR US TO OBEY HIM.
THUS...
THUS!
ALL WE CAN DO IS TRUST YOUR JUDGMENT.
IF THAT IS YOUR ORDER,
WE MUST OBEY IT!

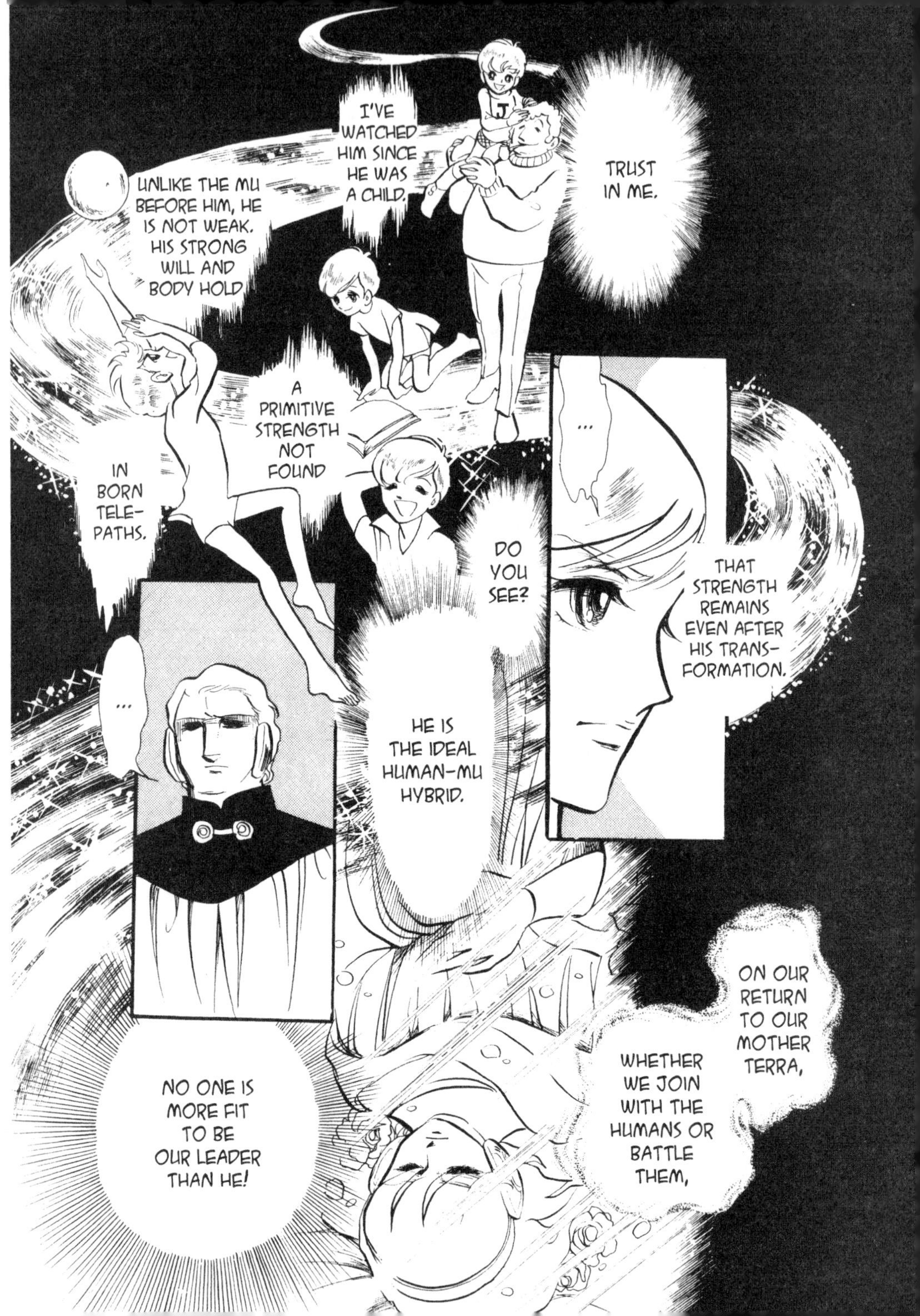
TRUST IN ME.
I'VE WATCHED HIM SINCE HE WAS A CHILD.
UNLIKE THE MU BEFORE HIM, HE IS NOT WEAK. HIS STRONG WILL AND BODY HOLD
A PRIMITIVE STRENGTH NOT FOUND
IN BORN TELE-PATHS.
...
THAT STRENGTH REMAINS EVEN AFTER HIS TRANS-FORMATION.
DO YOU SEE?
HE IS THE IDEAL HUMAN-MU HYBRID.
...
ON OUR RETURN TO OUR MOTHER TERRA,
WHETHER WE JOIN WITH THE HUMANS OR BATTLE THEM,
NO ONE IS MORE FIT TO BE OUR LEADER THAN HE!

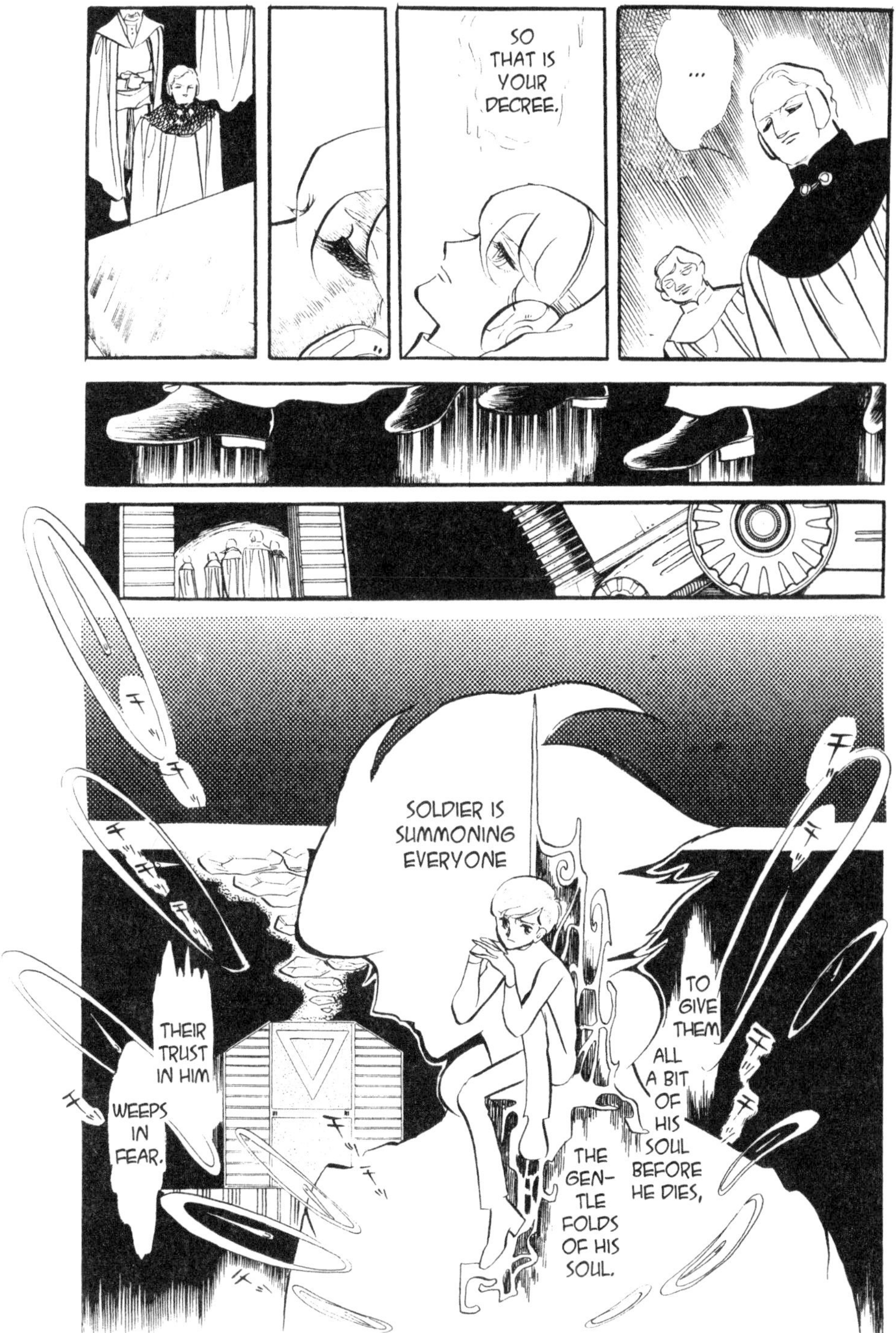
...
SO THAT IS YOUR DECREE.
SOLDIER IS SUMMONING EVERYONE
TO GIVE THEM ALL A BIT OF HIS SOUL BEFORE HE DIES,
THE GEN-TLE FOLDS OF HIS SOUL.
THEIR TRUST IN HIM
WEEPS IN FEAR.

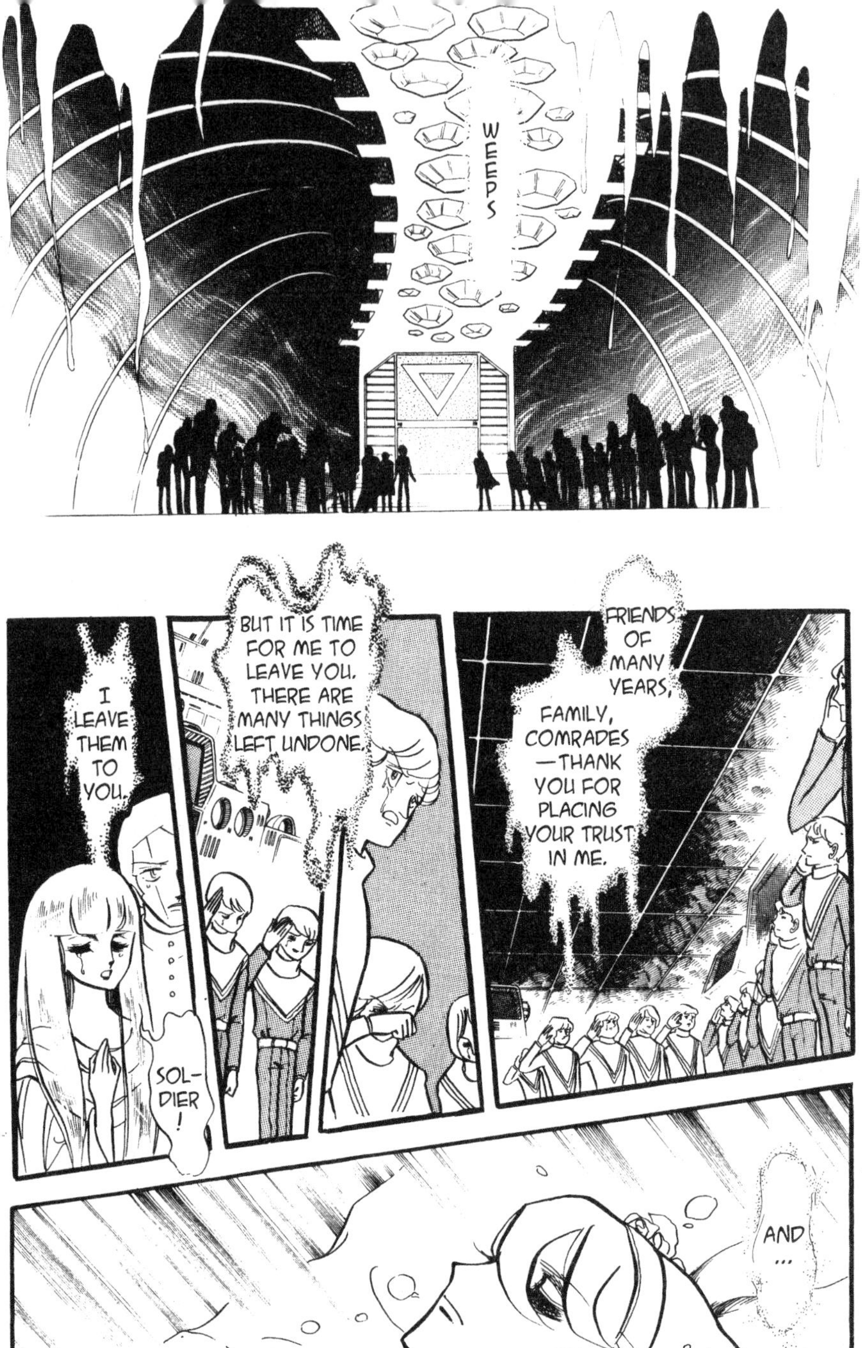
WEEPS
FRIENDS OF MANY YEARS, FAMILY, COMRADES—THANK YOU FOR PLACING YOUR TRUST IN ME.
BUT IT IS TIME FOR ME TO LEAVE YOU. THERE ARE MANY THINGS LEFT UNDONE.
I LEAVE THEM TO YOU.
SOL-DIER!
AND ...

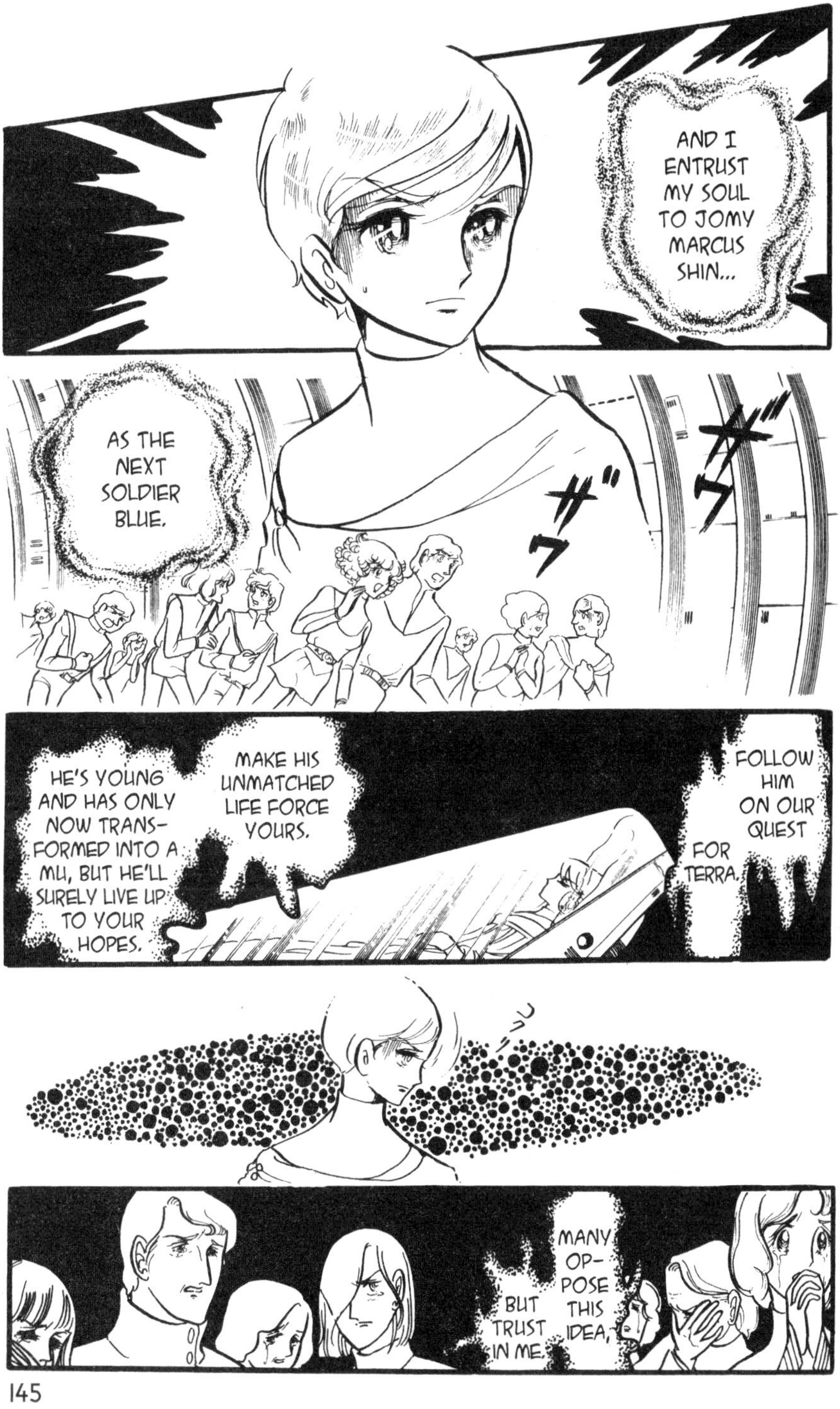
AND I ENTRUST MY SOUL TO JOMY MARCUS SHIN...
ザワ
ザワ
AS THE NEXT SOLDIER BLUE.
FOLLOW HIM ON OUR QUEST FOR TERRA.
MAKE HIS UNMATCHED LIFE FORCE YOURS.
HE'S YOUNG AND HAS ONLY NOW TRANS-FORMED INTO A MU, BUT HE'LL SURELY LIVE UP TO YOUR HOPES.
MANY OP-POSE THIS IDEA,
BUT TRUST IN ME.

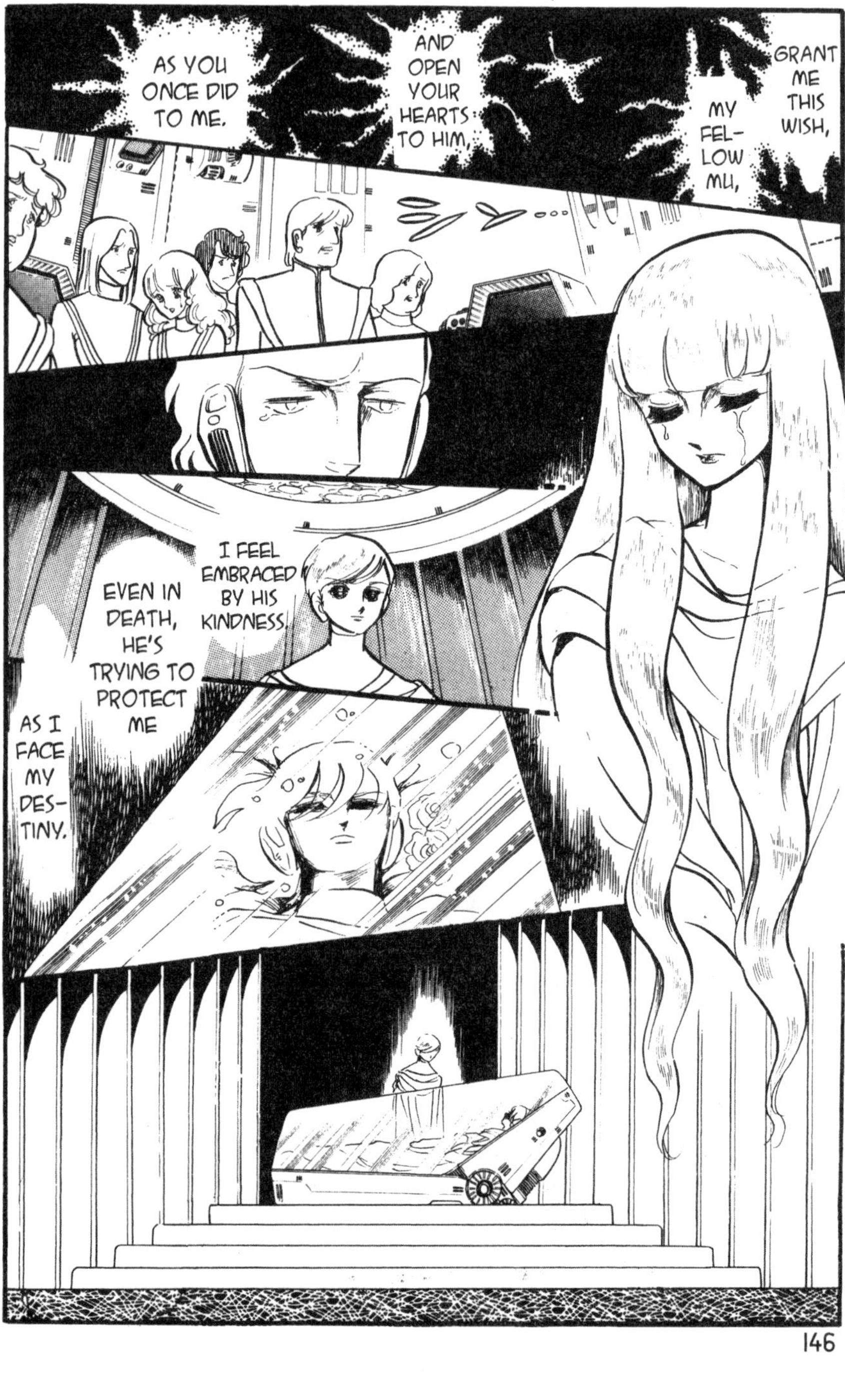
GRANT ME THIS WISH,
MY FEL- LOW MU,
AND OPEN YOUR HEARTS TO HIM,
AS YOU ONCE DID TO ME.
I FEEL EMBRACED BY HIS KINDNESS.
EVEN IN DEATH, HE'S TRYING TO PROTECT ME
AS I FACE MY DES- TINY.

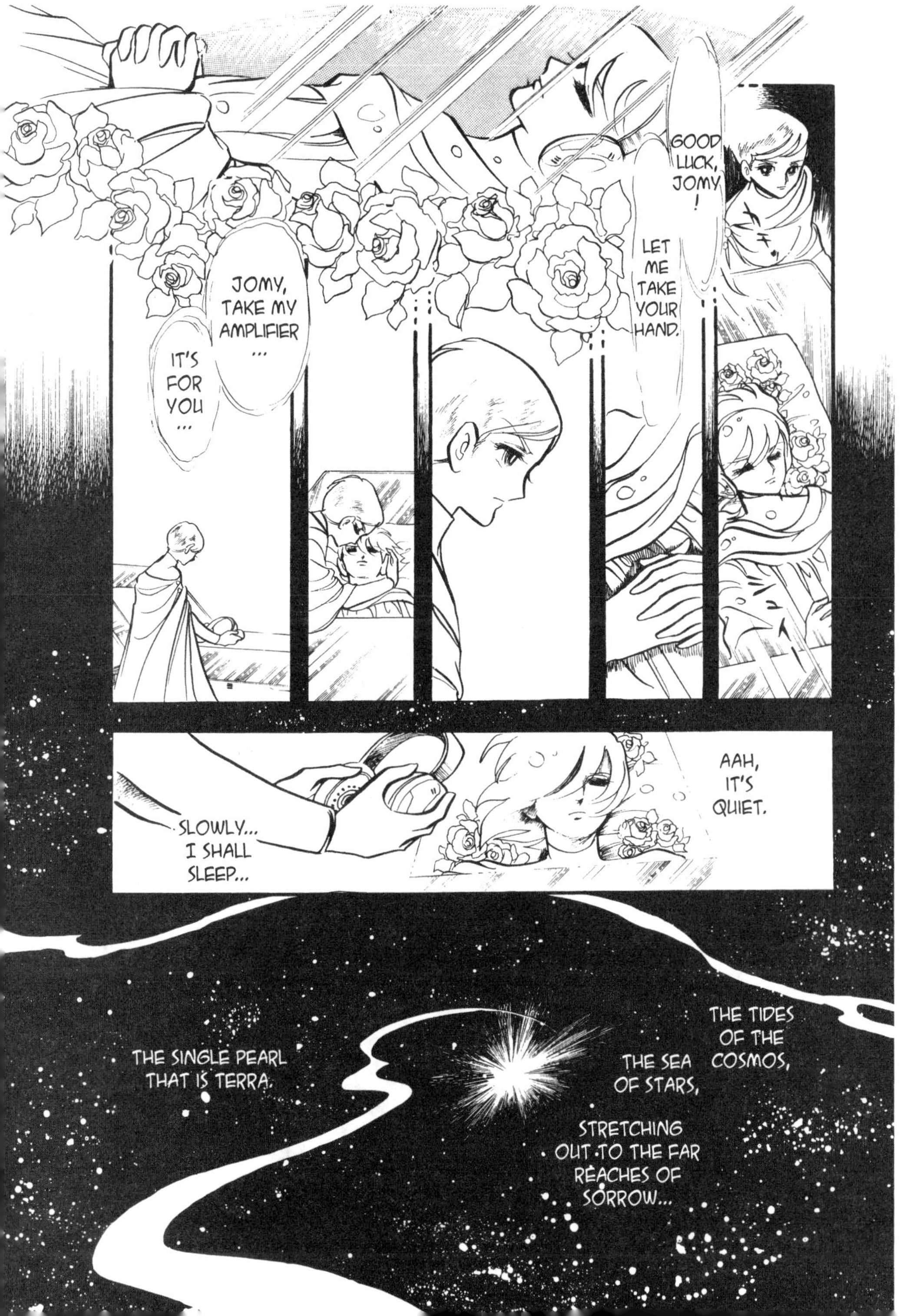
GOOD LUCK, JOMY!
LET ME TAKE YOUR HAND.
JOMY, TAKE MY AMPLIFIER...
IT'S FOR YOU...
AAH, IT'S QUIET.
SLOWLY... I SHALL SLEEP...
THE TIDES OF THE COSMOS,
THE SEA OF STARS,
STRETCHING OUT TO THE FAR REACHES OF SORROW...
THE SINGLE PEARL THAT IS TERRA.

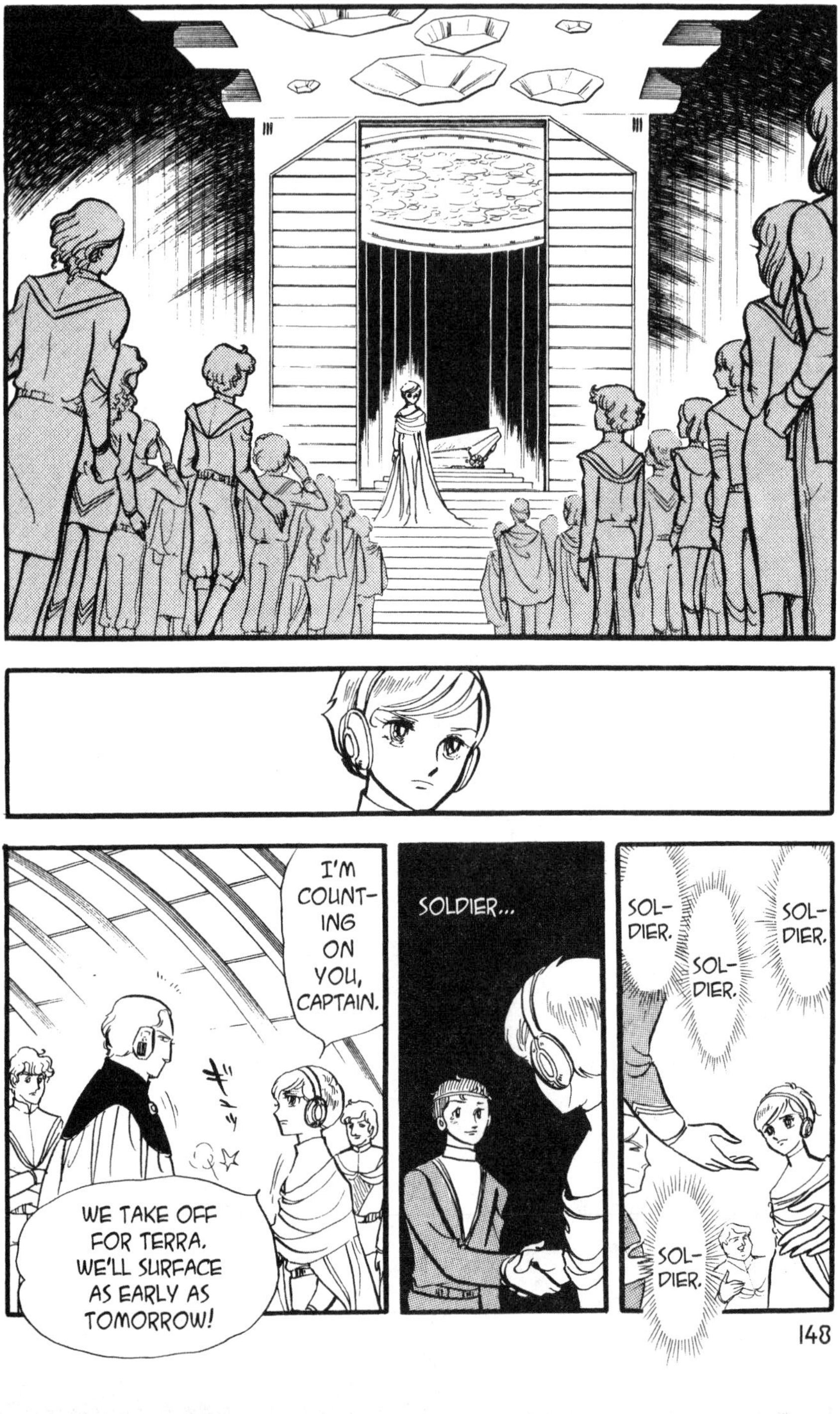
SOL-DIER.
SOL-DIER.
SOL-DIER.
SOL-DIER.
SOLDIER...
I'M COUNTING ON YOU, CAPTAIN.
WE TAKE OFF FOR TERRA. WE'LL SURFACE AS EARLY AS TOMORROW!

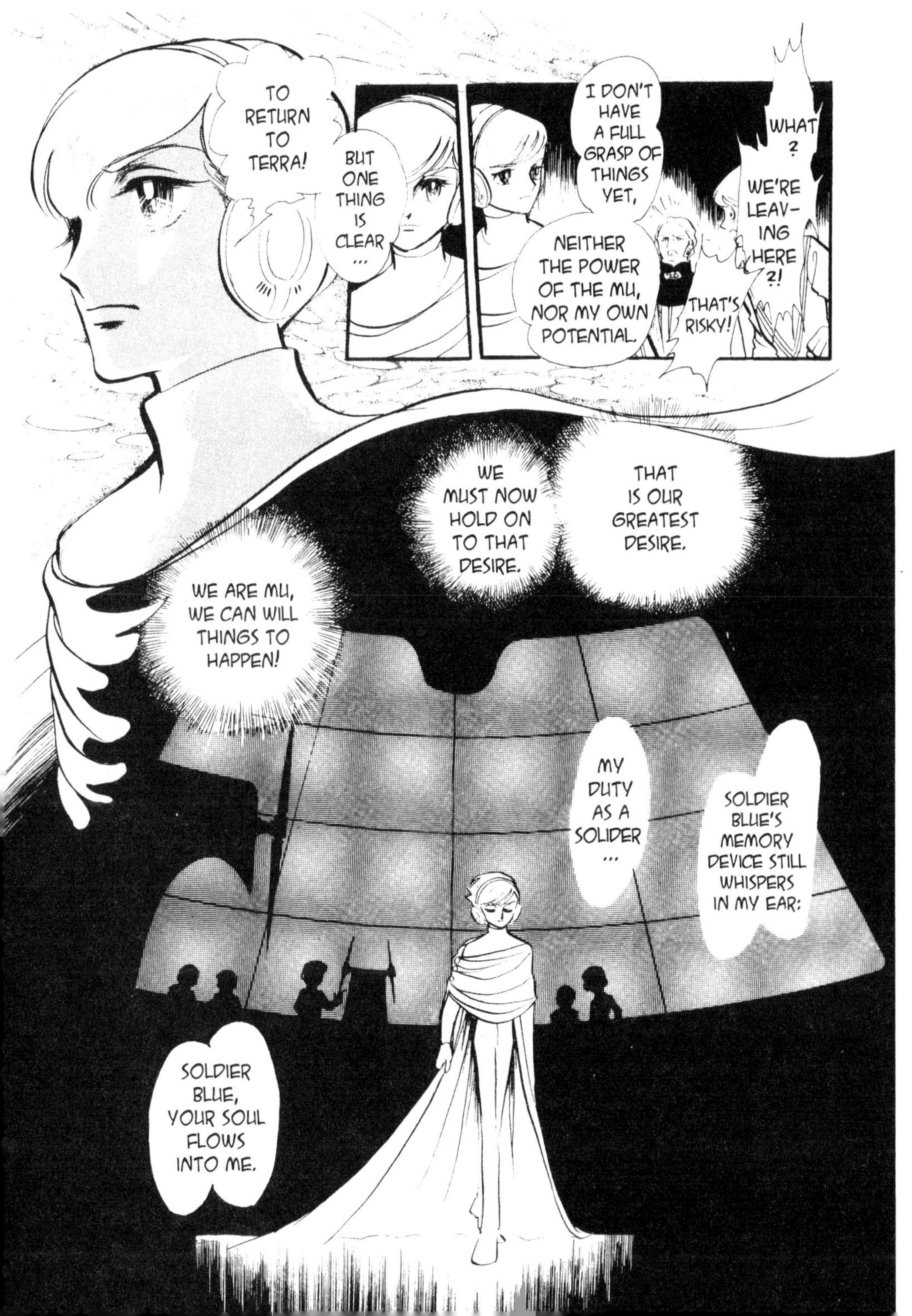

WHAT? WE'RE LEAVING HERE?!
THAT'S RISKY!
I DON'T HAVE A FULL GRASP OF THINGS YET,
NEITHER THE POWER OF THE MU, NOR MY OWN POTENTIAL.
BUT ONE THING IS CLEAR...
TO RETURN TO TERRA!
THAT IS OUR GREATEST DESIRE.
WE MUST NOW HOLD ON TO THAT DESIRE.
WE ARE MU, WE CAN WILL THINGS TO HAPPEN!
SOLDIER BLUE'S MEMORY DEVICE STILL WHISPERS IN MY EAR:
MY DUTY AS A SOLIDER...
SOLDIER BLUE, YOUR SOUL FLOWS INTO ME.

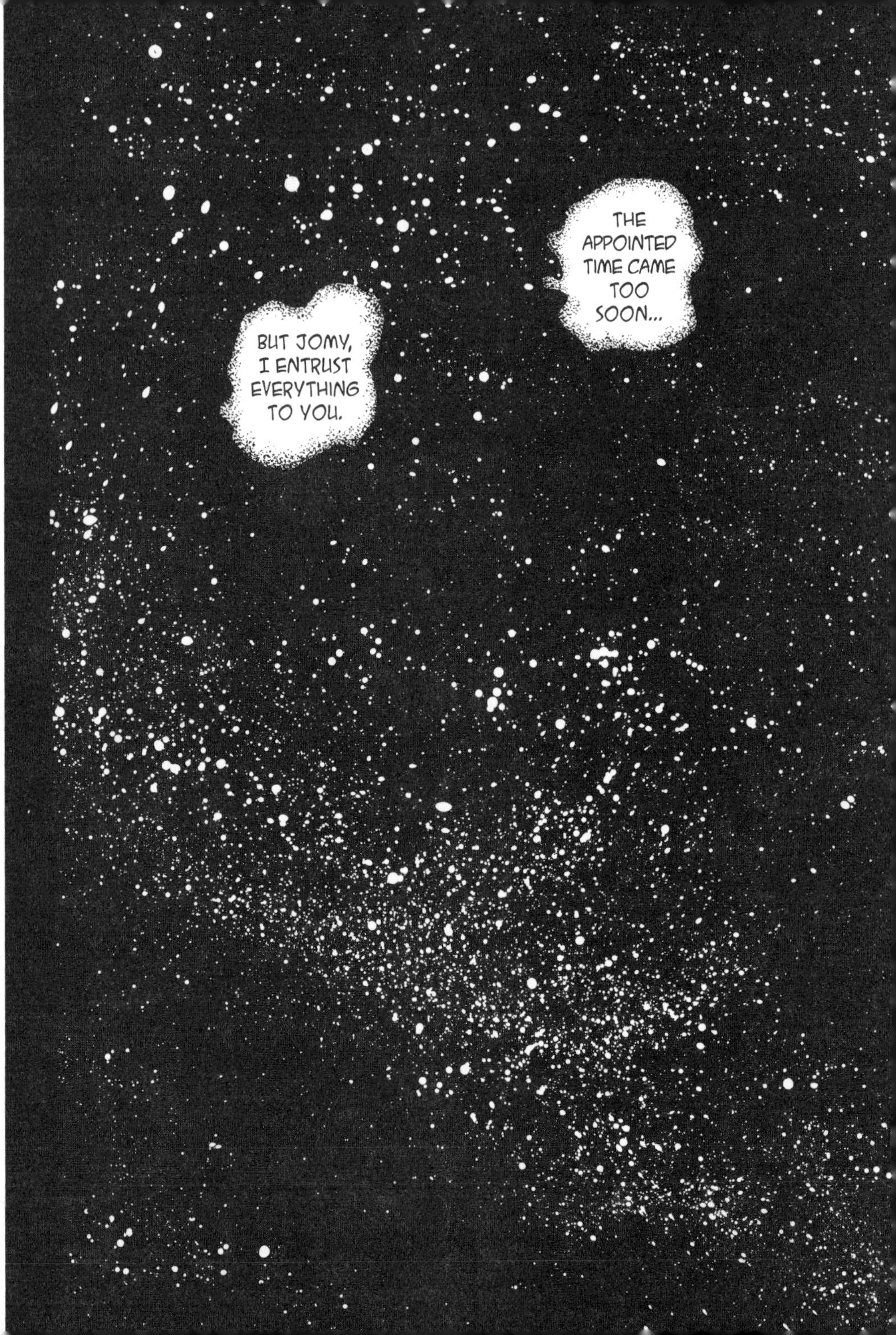
THE APPOINTED TIME CAME TOO SOON...
BUT JOMY, I ENTRUST EVERYTHING TO YOU.

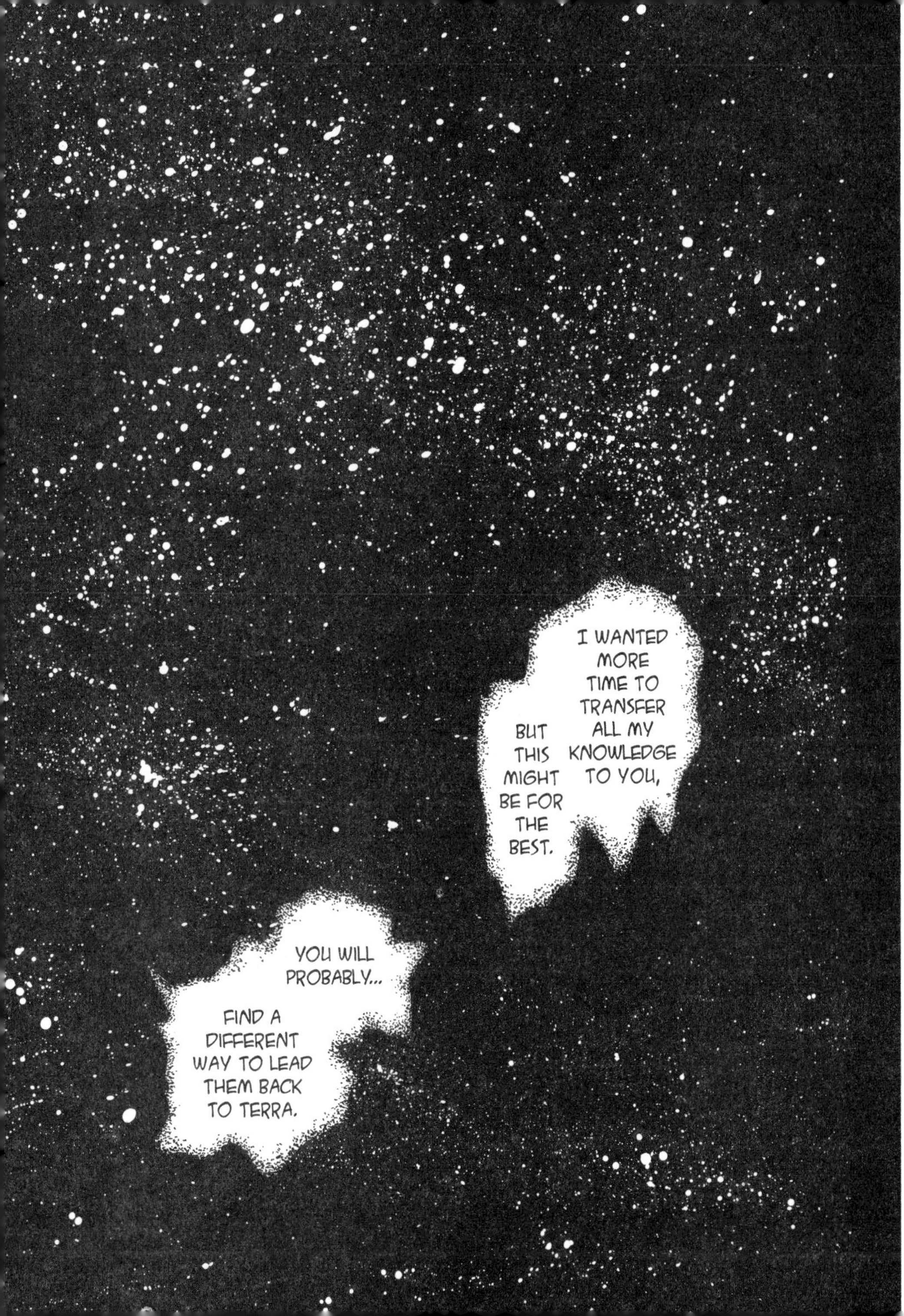
I WANTED MORE TIME TO TRANSFER ALL MY KNOWLEDGE TO YOU,
BUT THIS MIGHT BE FOR THE BEST.
YOU WILL PROBABLY...
FIND A DIFFERENT WAY TO LEAD THEM BACK TO TERRA.

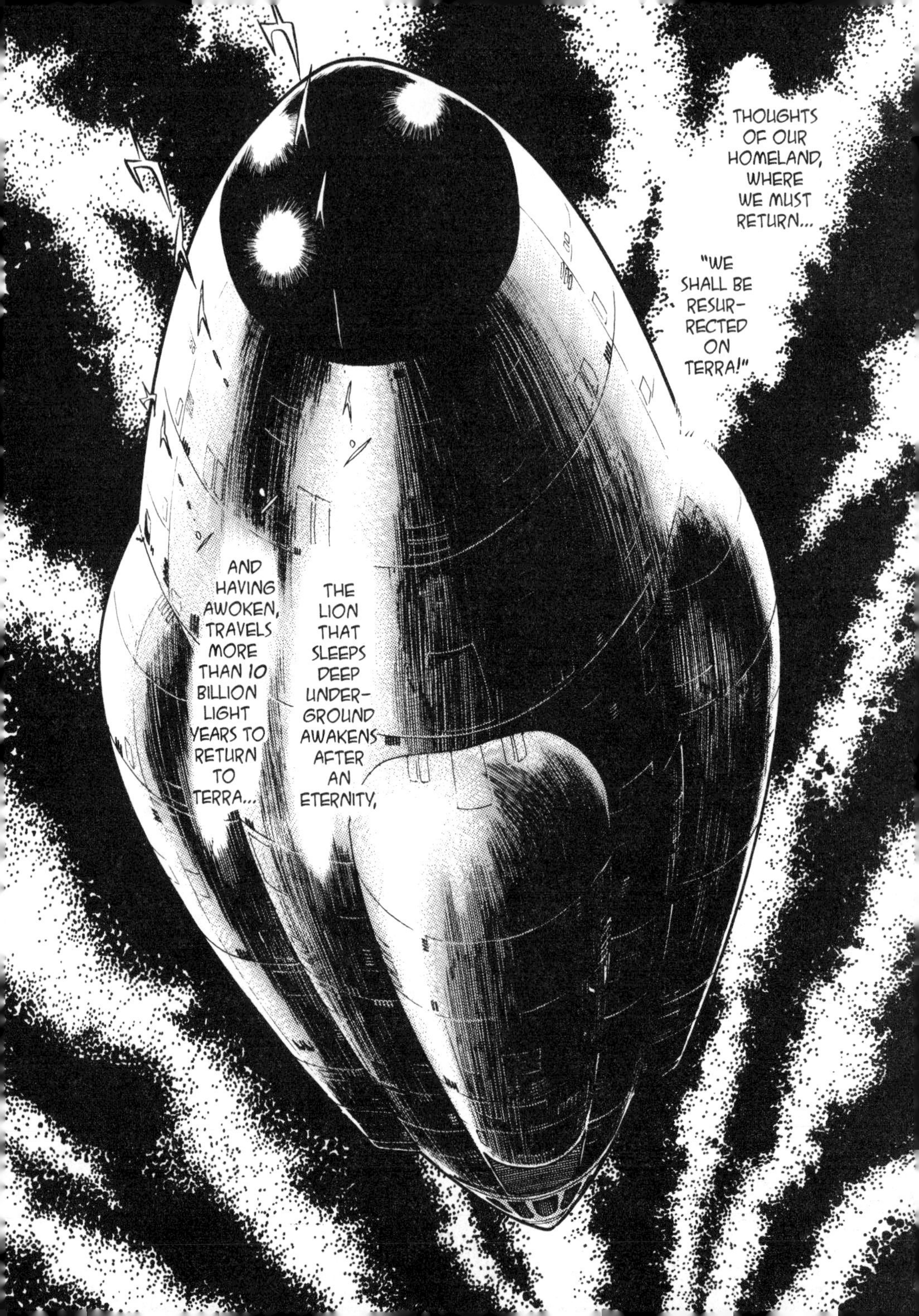
THOUGHTS OF OUR HOMELAND, WHERE WE MUST RETURN...
"WE SHALL BE RESUR-RECTED ON TERRA!"
THE LION THAT SLEEPS DEEP UNDER-GROUND AWAKENS AFTER AN ETERNITY,
AND HAVING AWOKEN, TRAVELS MORE THAN 10 BILLION LIGHT YEARS TO RETURN TO TERRA...

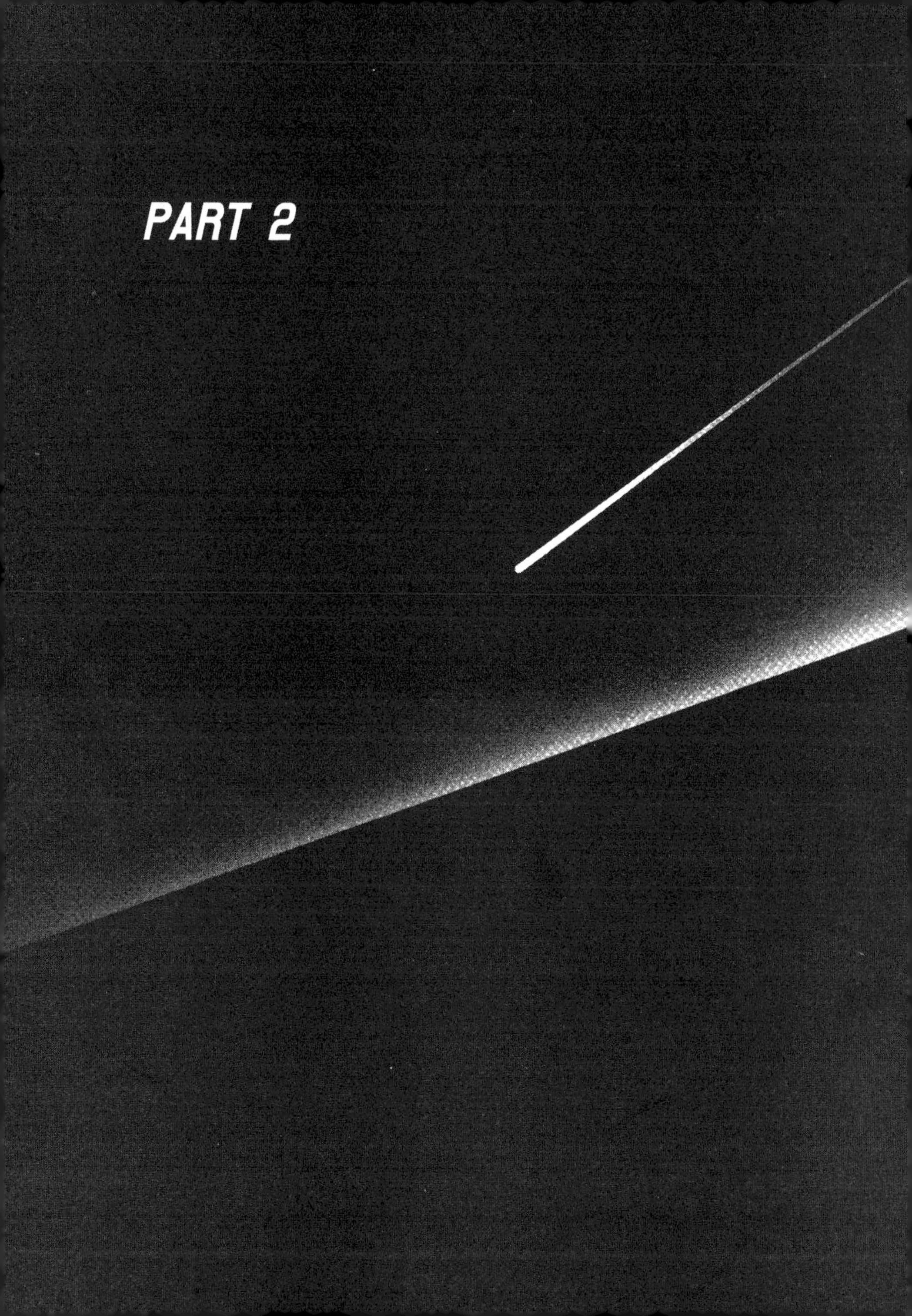
PART 2

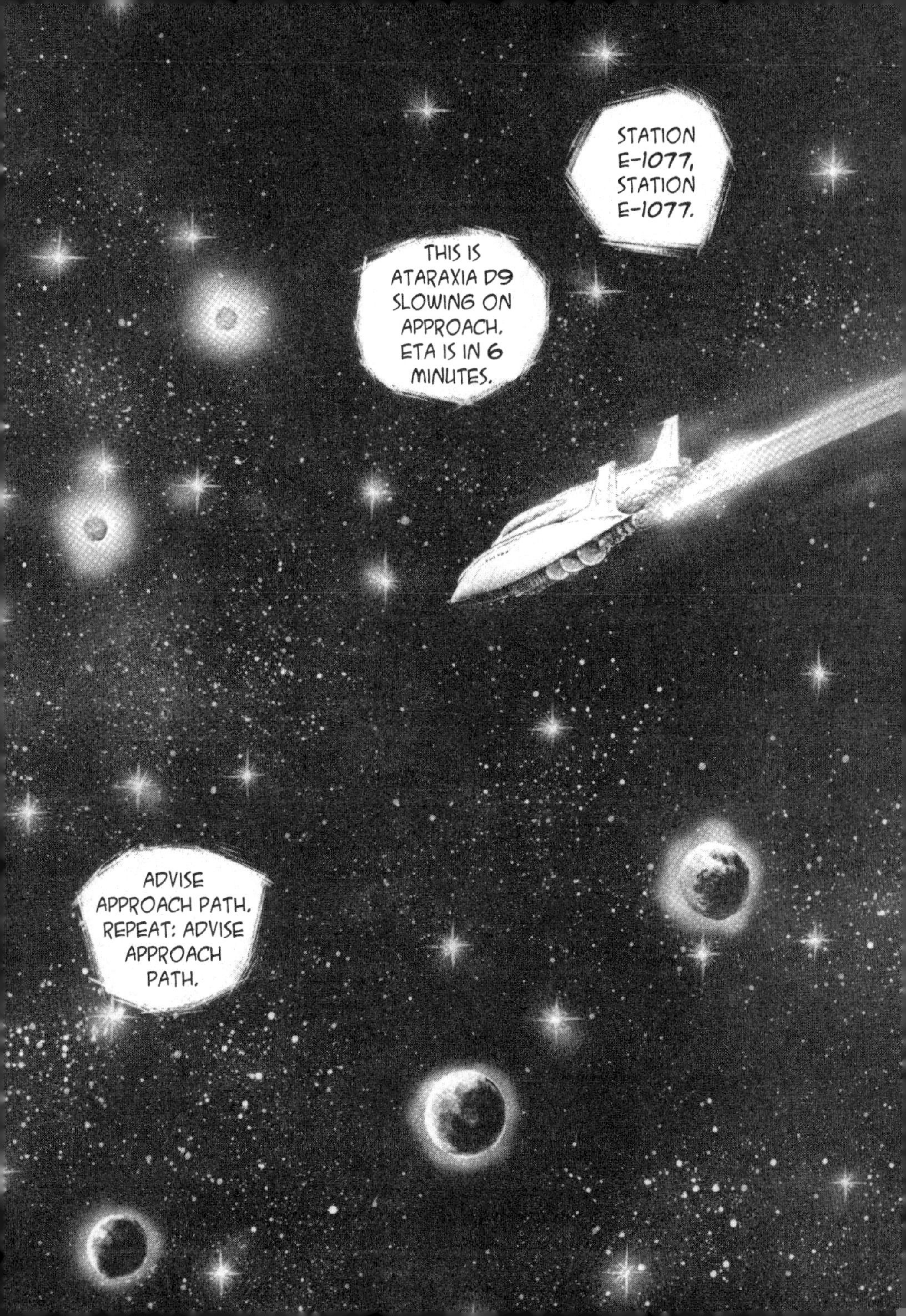
STATION E-1077, STATION E-1077.
THIS IS ATARAXIA D9 SLOWING ON APPROACH. ETA IS IN 6 MINUTES.
ADVISE APPROACH PATH. REPEAT: ADVISE APPROACH PATH.

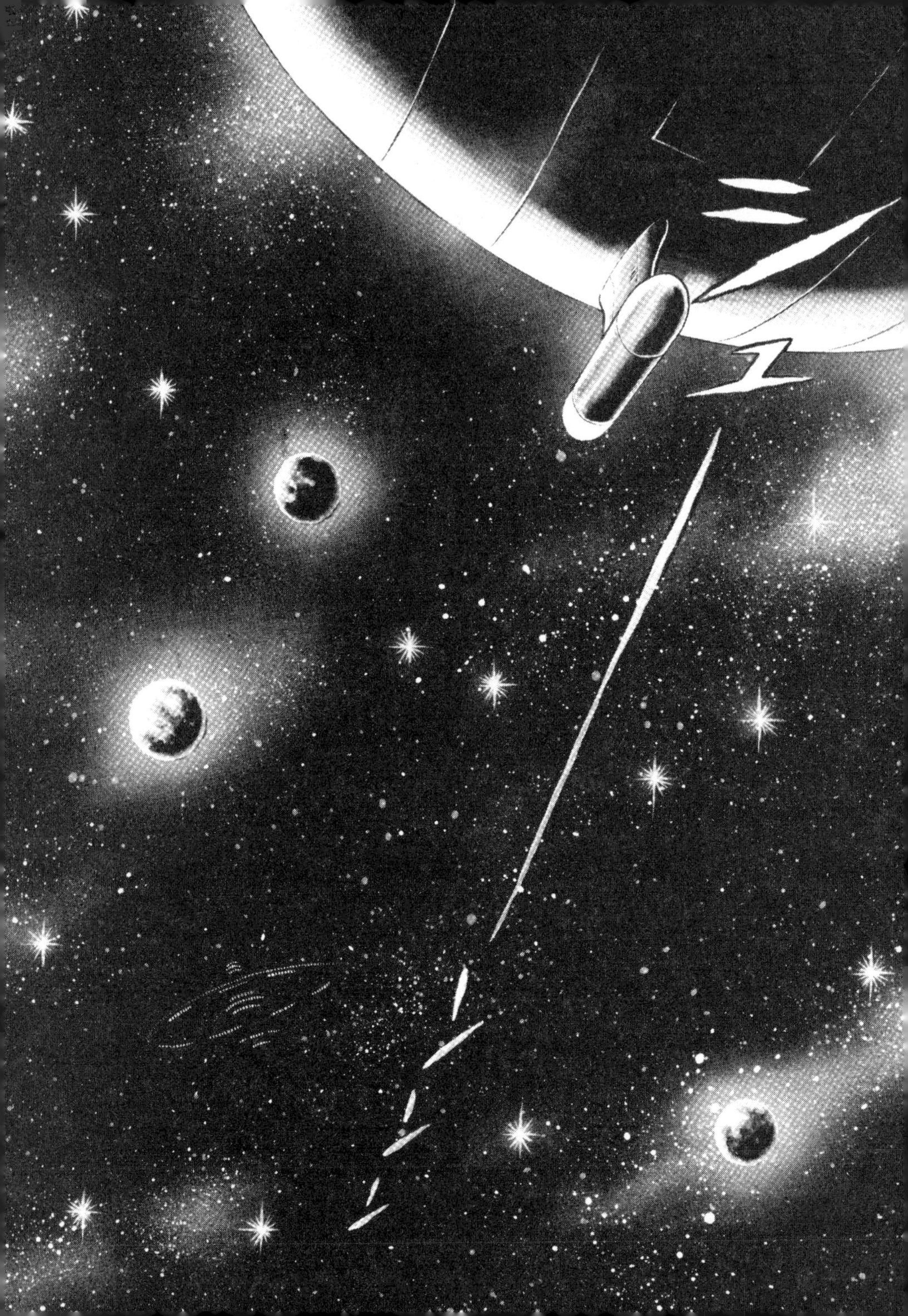

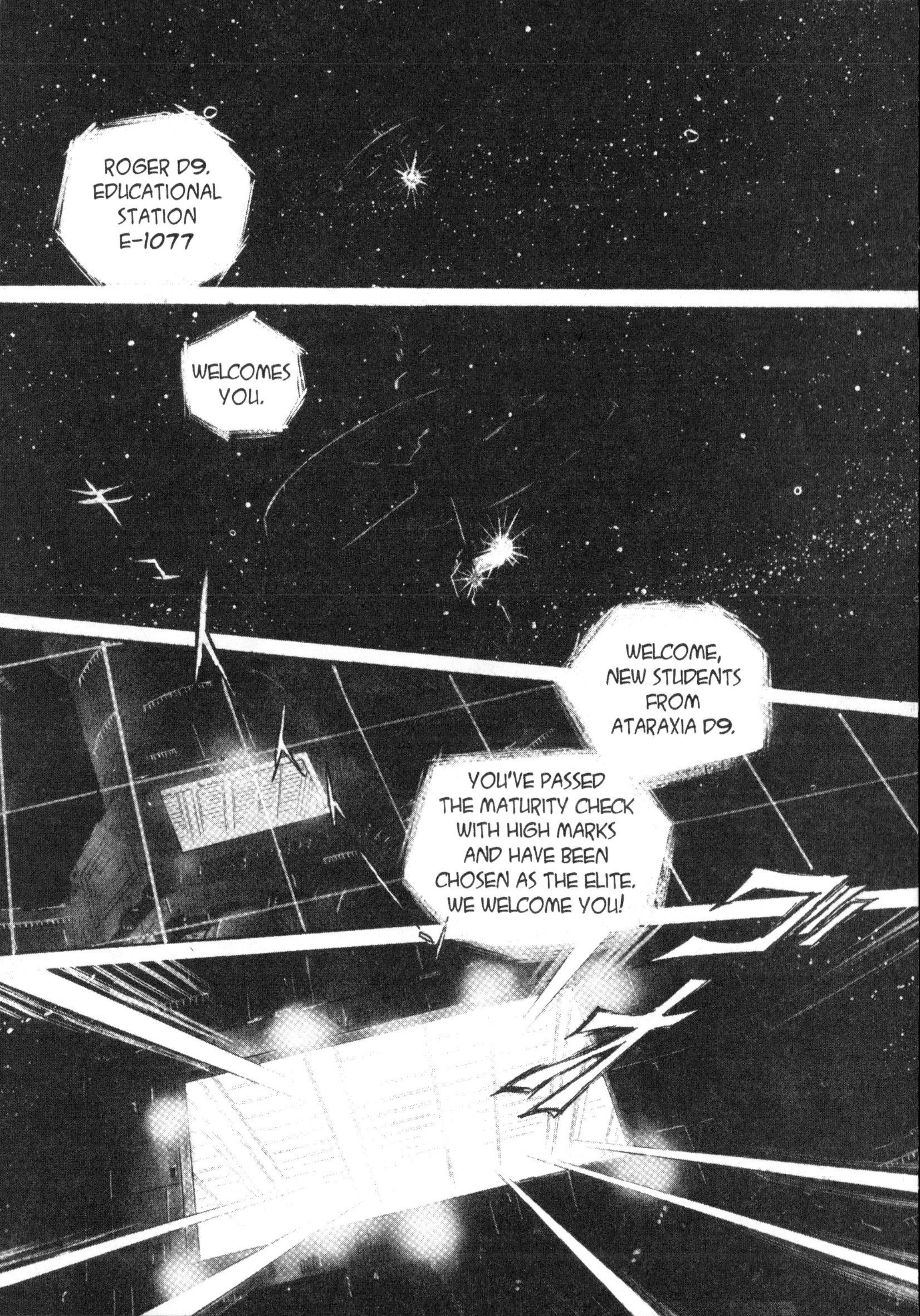
ROGER D9. EDUCATIONAL STATION E-1077
WELCOMES YOU.
WELCOME, NEW STUDENTS FROM ATARAXIA D9.
YOU'VE PASSED THE MATURITY CHECK WITH HIGH MARKS AND HAVE BEEN CHOSEN AS THE ELITE. WE WELCOME YOU!

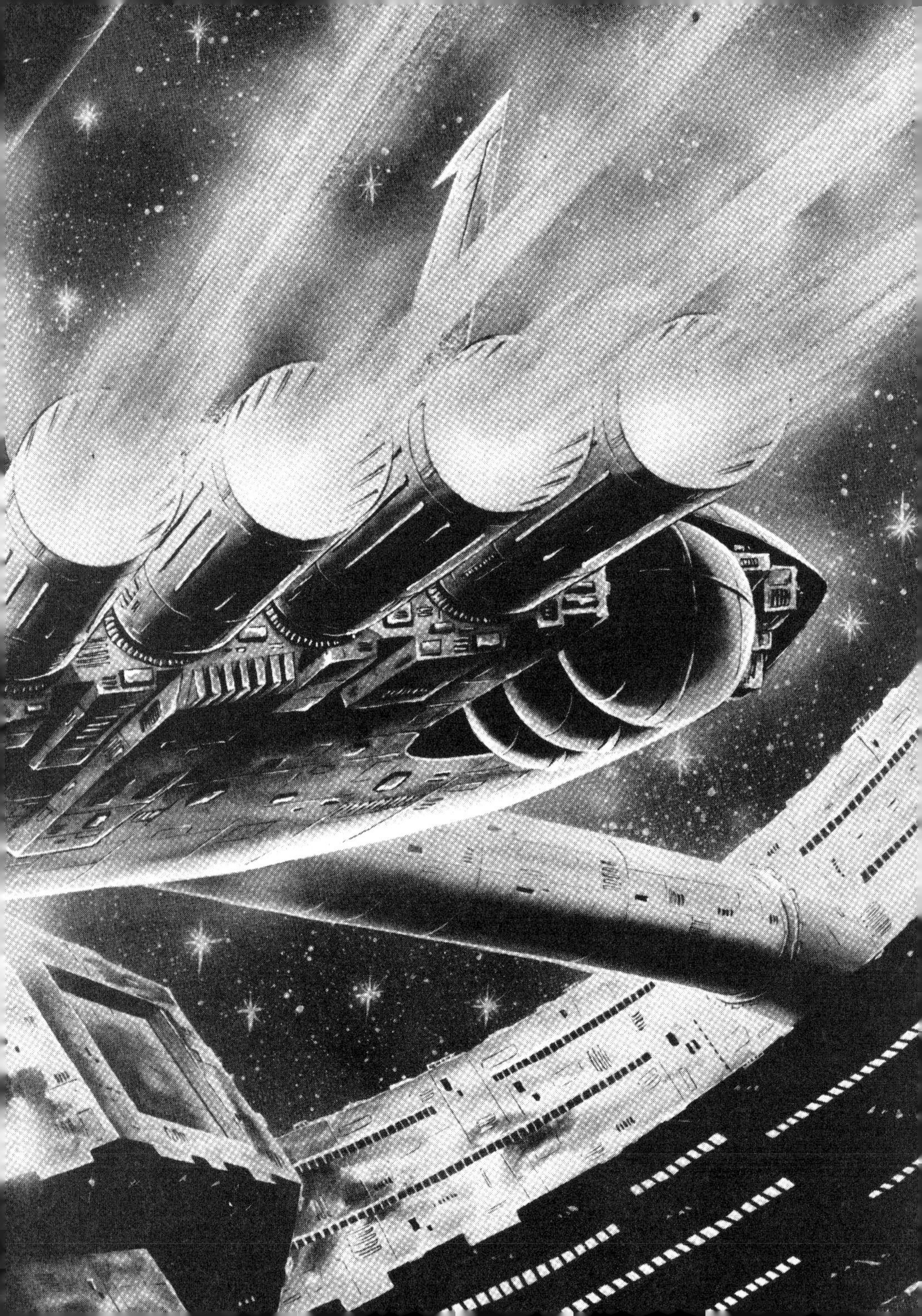

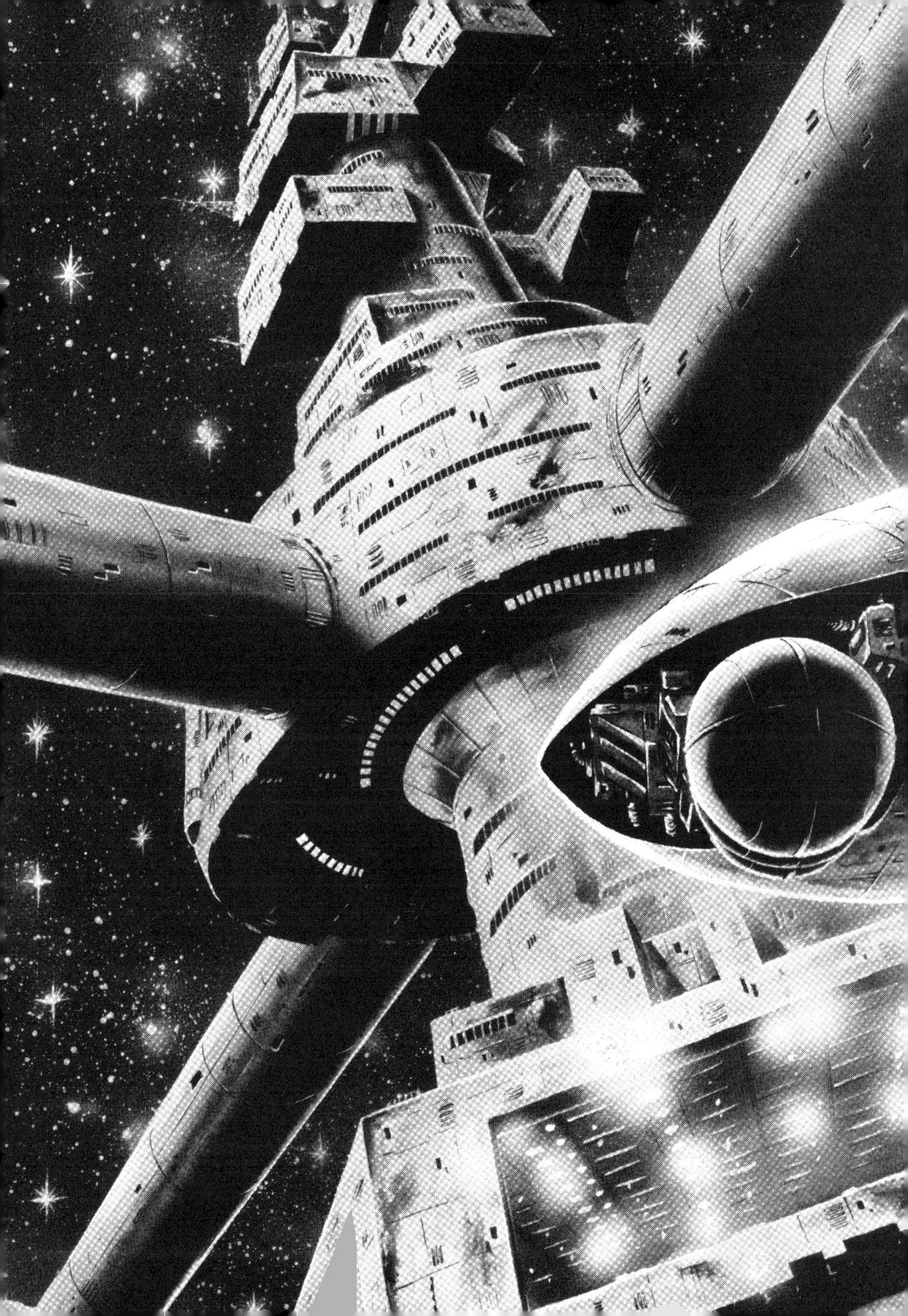

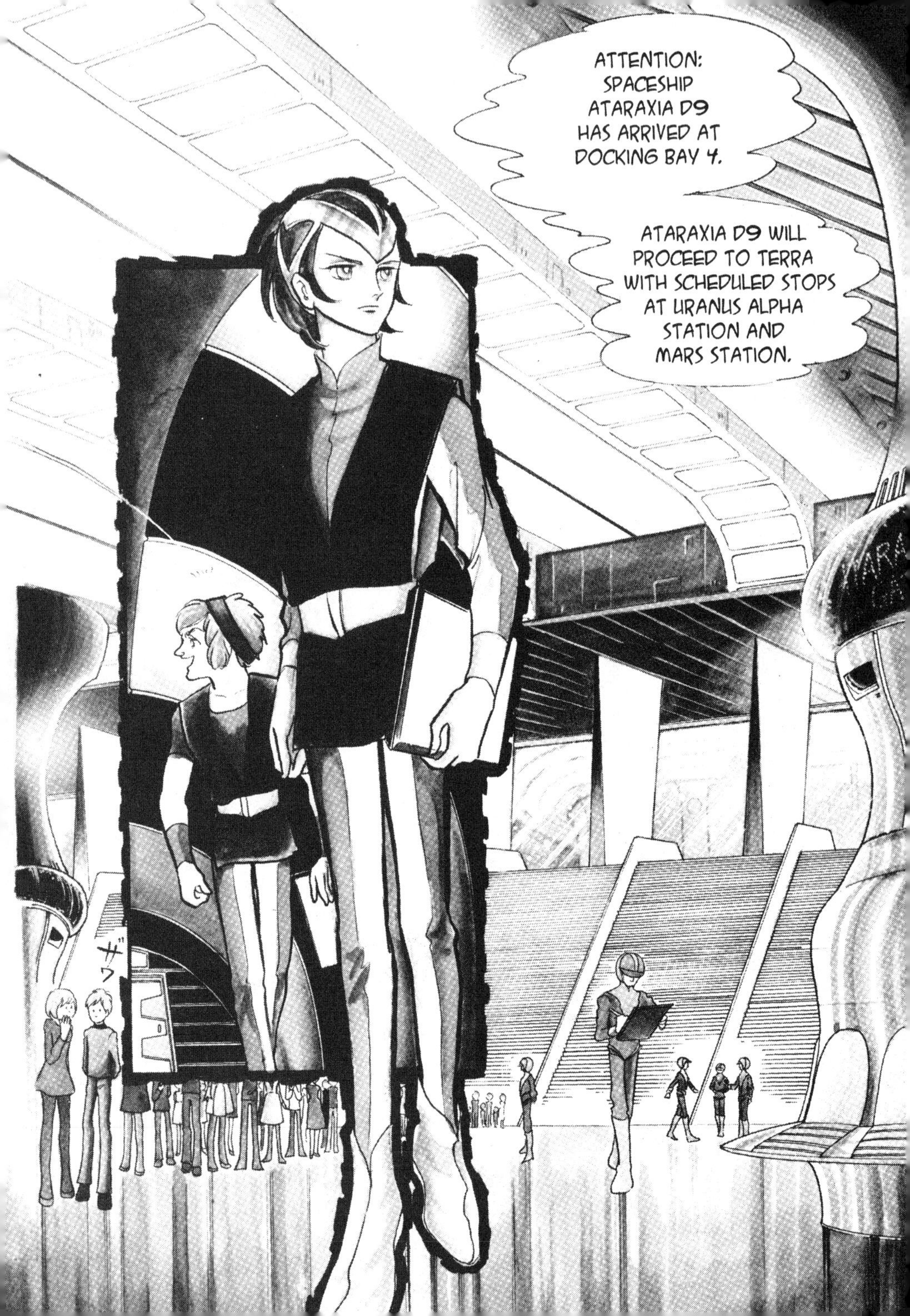
ATTENTION: SPACESHIP ATARAXIA D9 HAS ARRIVED AT DOCKING BAY 4.
ATARAXIA D9 WILL PROCEED TO TERRA WITH SCHEDULED STOPS AT URANUS ALPHA STATION AND MARS STATION.

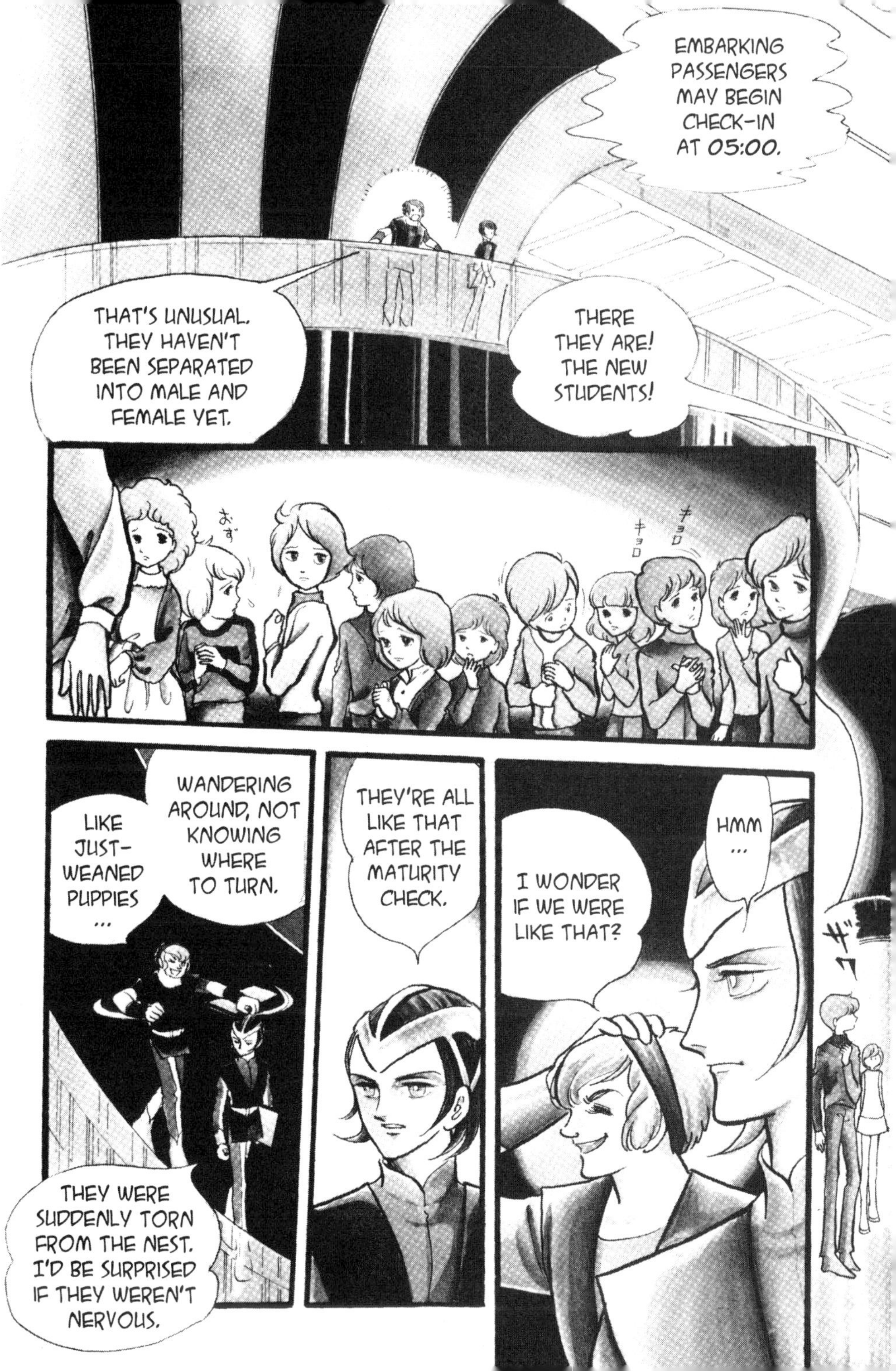
EMBARKING PASSENGERS MAY BEGIN CHECK-IN AT 05:00.
THERE THEY ARE! THE NEW STUDENTS!
THAT'S UNUSUAL. THEY HAVEN'T BEEN SEPARATED INTO MALE AND FEMALE YET.
キョロ
キョロ
おず
HMM ...
I WONDER IF WE WERE LIKE THAT?
THEY'RE ALL LIKE THAT AFTER THE MATURITY CHECK.
WANDERING AROUND, NOT KNOWING WHERE TO TURN.
LIKE JUST-WEANED PUPPIES ...
THEY WERE SUDDENLY TORN FROM THE NEST. I'D BE SURPRISED IF THEY WEREN'T NERVOUS.

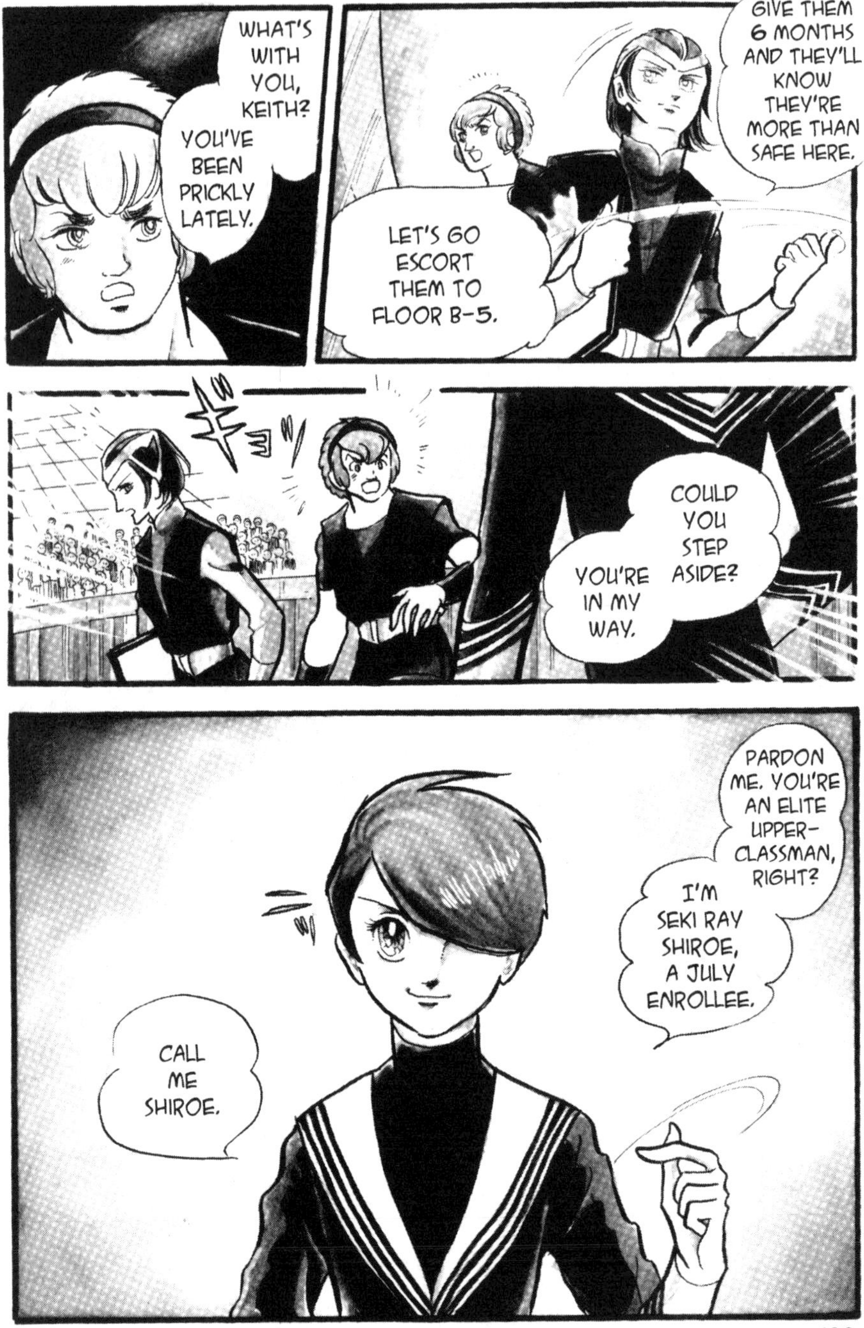
GIVE THEM 6 MONTHS AND THEY'LL KNOW THEY'RE MORE THAN SAFE HERE.
LET'S GO ESCORT THEM TO FLOOR B-5.
WHAT'S WITH YOU, KEITH?
YOU'VE BEEN PRICKLY LATELY.
COULD YOU STEP ASIDE?
YOU'RE IN MY WAY.
PARDON ME. YOU'RE AN ELITE UPPER-CLASSMAN, RIGHT?
I'M SEKI RAY SHIROE, A JULY ENROLLEE.
CALL ME SHIROE.

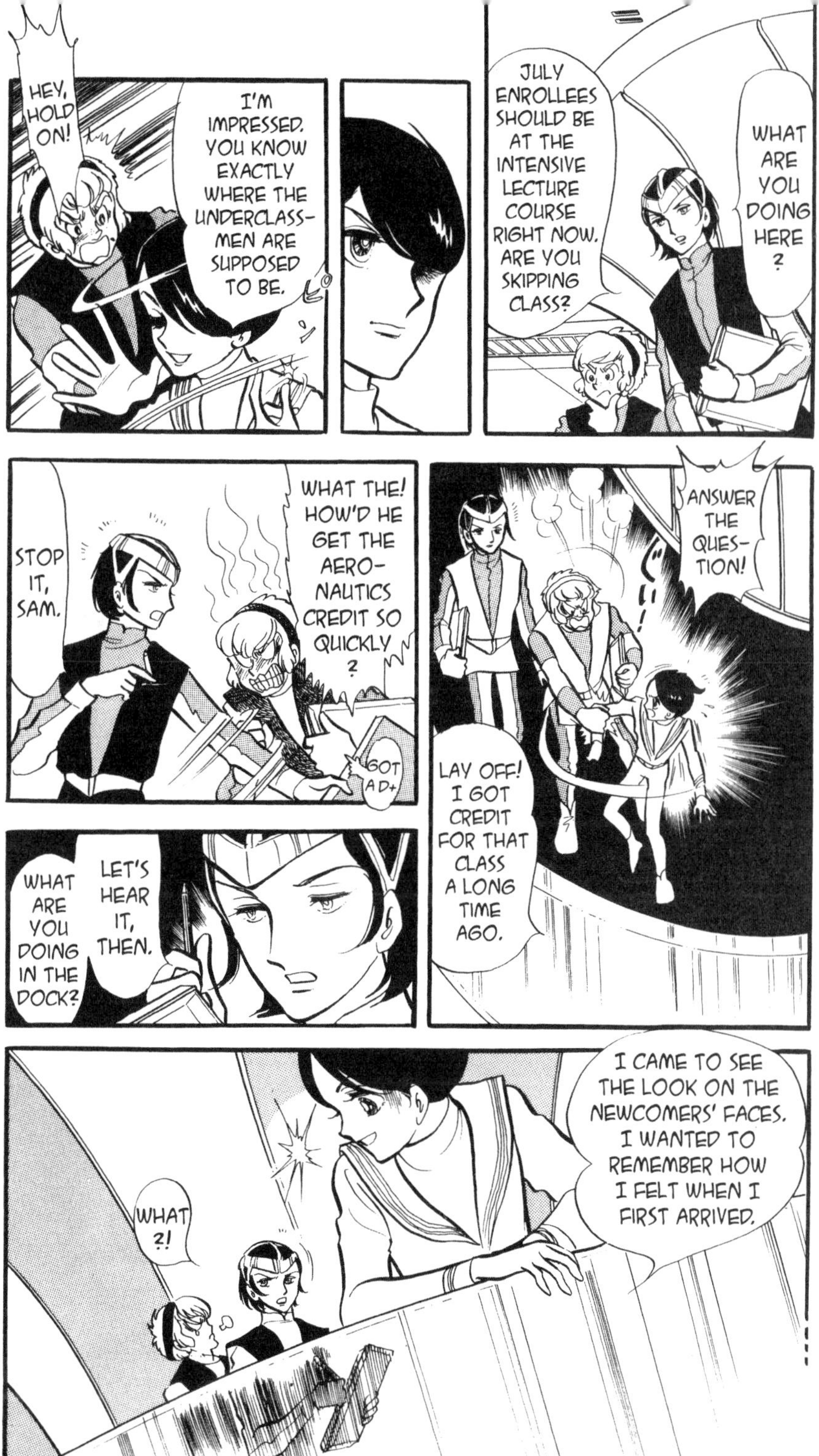
WHAT ARE YOU DOING HERE?
JULY ENROLLEES SHOULD BE AT THE INTENSIVE LECTURE COURSE RIGHT NOW. ARE YOU SKIPPING CLASS?
I'M IMPRESSED. YOU KNOW EXACTLY WHERE THE UNDERCLASSMEN ARE SUPPOSED TO BE.
HEY, HOLD ON!
ANSWER THE QUESTION!
LAY OFF! I GOT CREDIT FOR THAT CLASS A LONG TIME AGO.
WHAT THE! HOW'D HE GET THE AERONAUTICS CREDIT SO QUICKLY?
STOP IT, SAM.
GOT A D+
LET'S HEAR IT, THEN.
WHAT ARE YOU DOING IN THE DOCK?
I CAME TO SEE THE LOOK ON THE NEWCOMERS' FACES. I WANTED TO REMEMBER HOW I FELT WHEN I FIRST ARRIVED.
WHAT?!

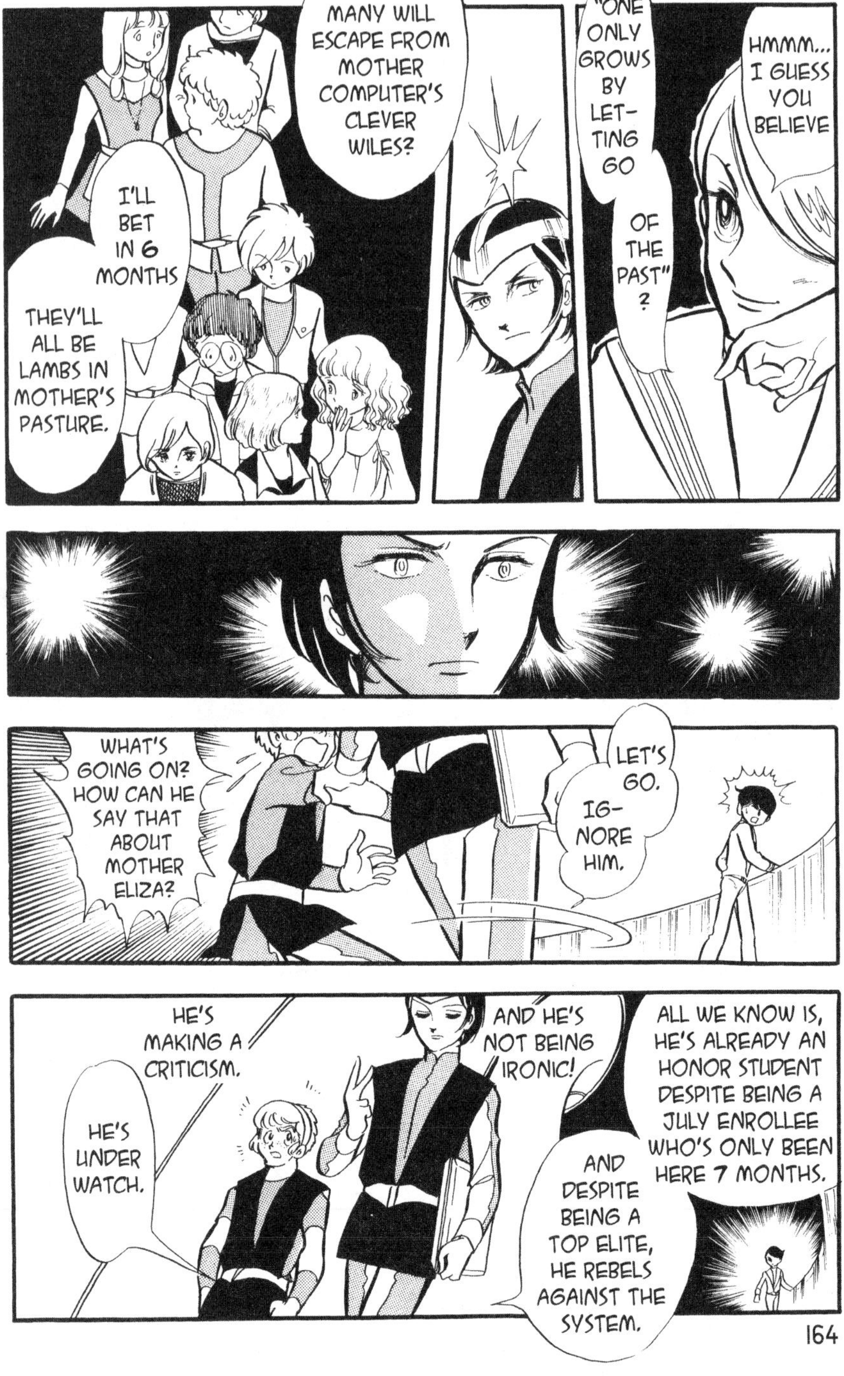
HMMM... I GUESS YOU BELIEVE
"ONE ONLY GROWS BY LETTING GO OF THE PAST"?
HOW MANY WILL ESCAPE FROM MOTHER COMPUTER'S CLEVER WILES?
I'LL BET IN 6 MONTHS
THEY'LL ALL BE LAMBS IN MOTHER'S PASTURE.
LET'S GO. IGNORE HIM.
WHAT'S GOING ON? HOW CAN HE SAY THAT ABOUT MOTHER ELIZA?
ALL WE KNOW IS, HE'S ALREADY AN HONOR STUDENT DESPITE BEING A JULY ENROLLEE WHO'S ONLY BEEN HERE 7 MONTHS.
AND DESPITE BEING A TOP ELITE, HE REBELS AGAINST THE SYSTEM.
AND HE'S NOT BEING IRONIC!
HE'S MAKING A CRITICISM.
HE'S UNDER WATCH.

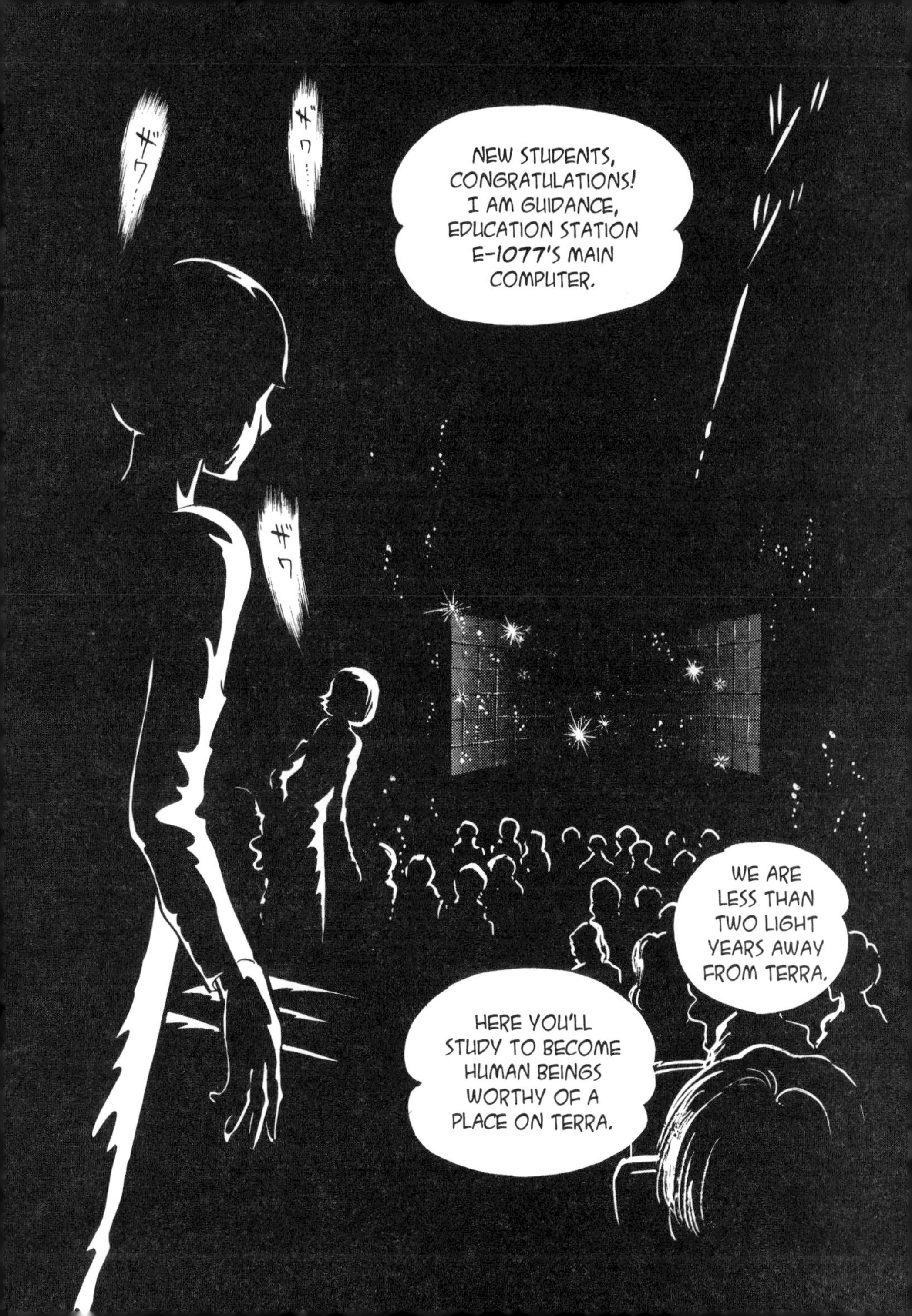

NEW STUDENTS, CONGRATULATIONS! I AM GUIDANCE, EDUCATION STATION E-1077'S MAIN COMPUTER.
ザワ…
ザワ…
ザワ
WE ARE LESS THAN TWO LIGHT YEARS AWAY FROM TERRA.
HERE YOU'LL STUDY TO BECOME HUMAN BEINGS WORTHY OF A PLACE ON TERRA.

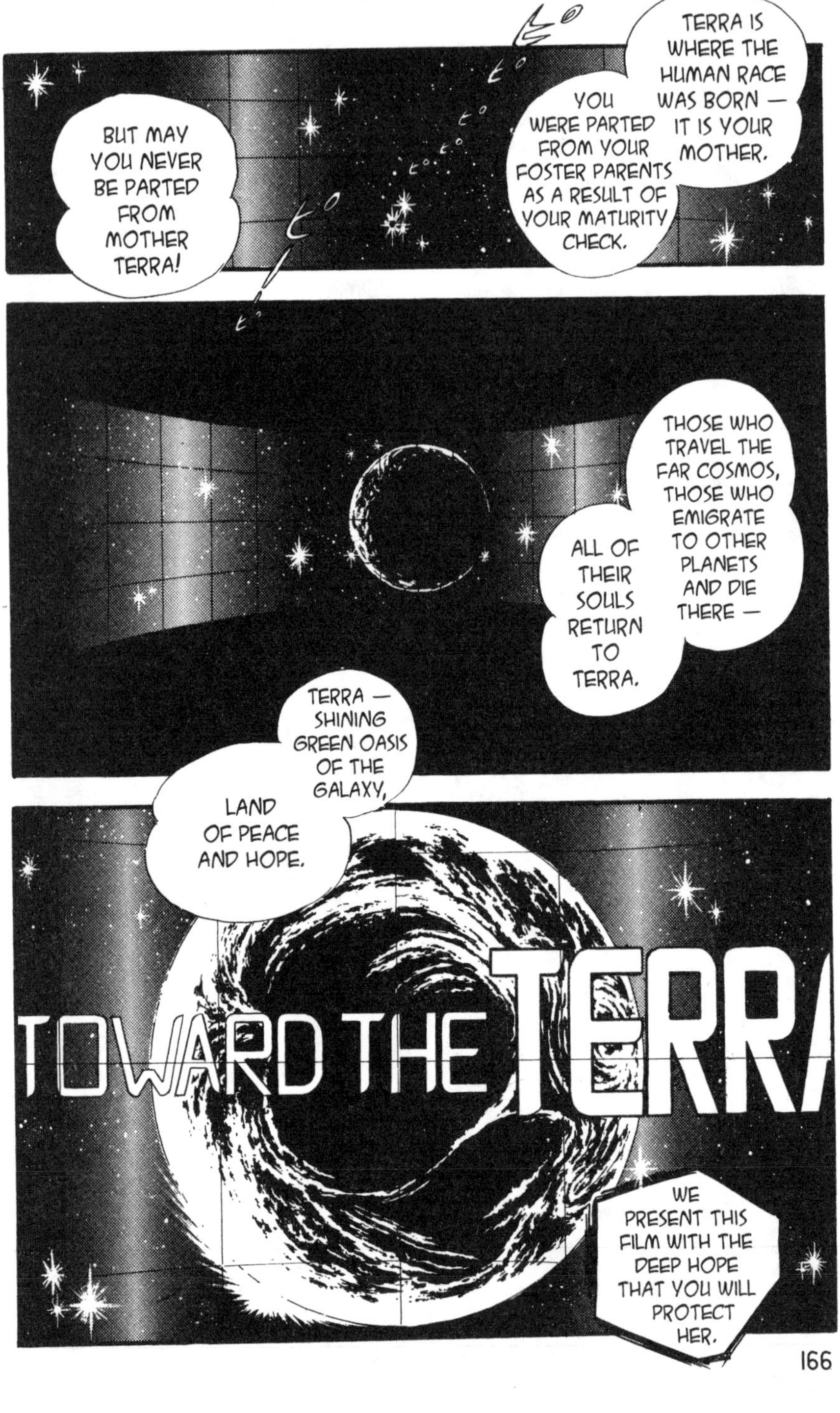
TERRA IS WHERE THE HUMAN RACE WAS BORN — IT IS YOUR MOTHER.
YOU WERE PARTED FROM YOUR FOSTER PARENTS AS A RESULT OF YOUR MATURITY CHECK.
BUT MAY YOU NEVER BE PARTED FROM MOTHER TERRA!
THOSE WHO TRAVEL THE FAR COSMOS, THOSE WHO EMIGRATE TO OTHER PLANETS AND DIE THERE —
ALL OF THEIR SOULS RETURN TO TERRA.
TERRA — SHINING GREEN OASIS OF THE GALAXY,
LAND OF PEACE AND HOPE.
TOWARD THE TERR
WE PRESENT THIS FILM WITH THE DEEP HOPE THAT YOU WILL PROTECT HER.

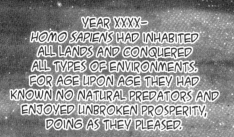

YEAR XXXX—
HOMO SAPIENS HAD INHABITED
ALL LANDS AND CONQUERED
ALL TYPES OF ENVIRONMENTS.
FOR AGE UPON AGE THEY HAD
KNOWN NO NATURAL PREDATORS AND
ENJOYED UNBROKEN PROSPERITY,
DOING AS THEY PLEASED.

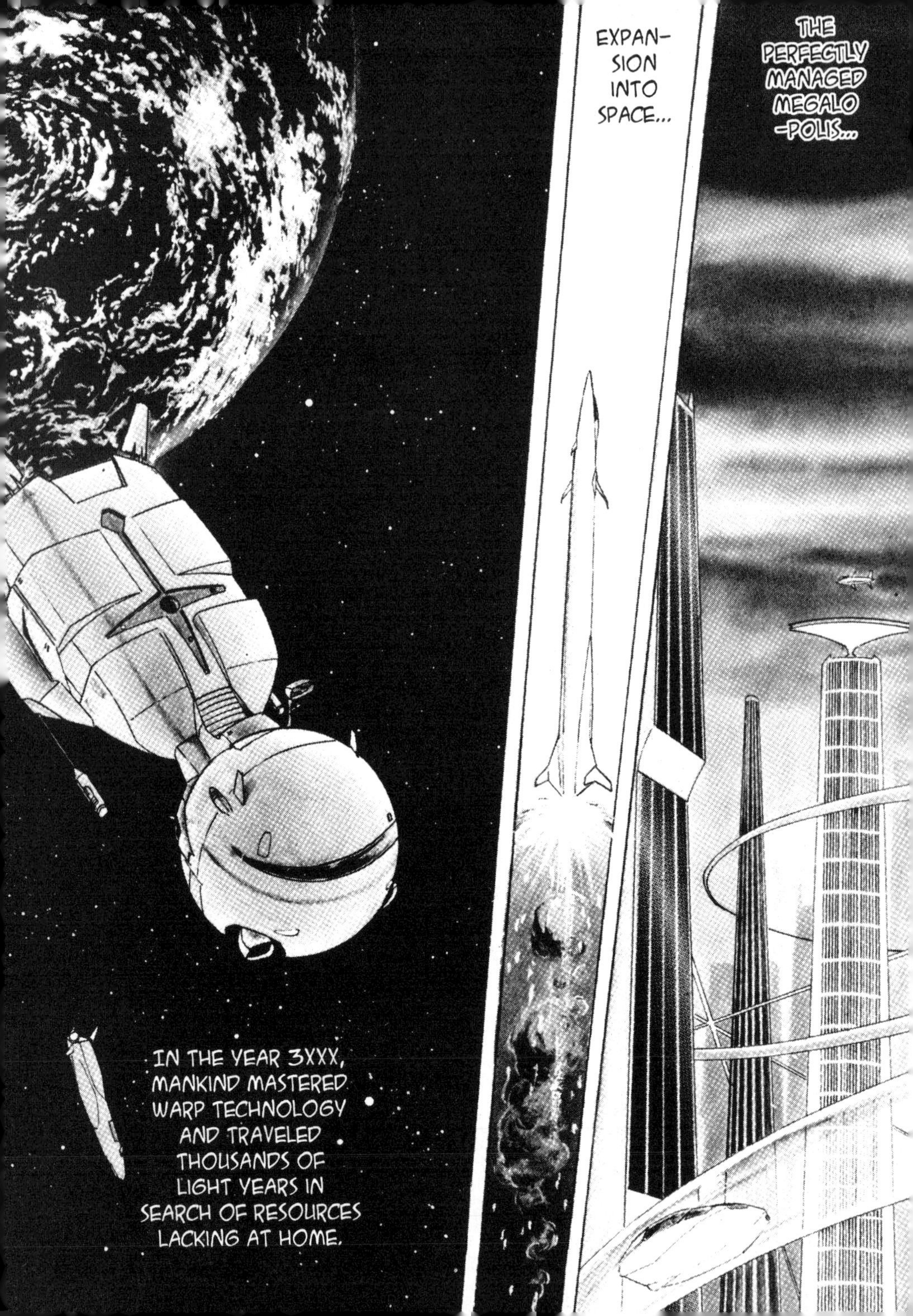
THE PERFECTLY MANAGED MEGALO-POLIS...
EXPAN-SION INTO SPACE...
IN THE YEAR 3XXX, MANKIND MASTERED WARP TECHNOLOGY AND TRAVELED THOUSANDS OF LIGHT YEARS IN SEARCH OF RESOURCES LACKING AT HOME.

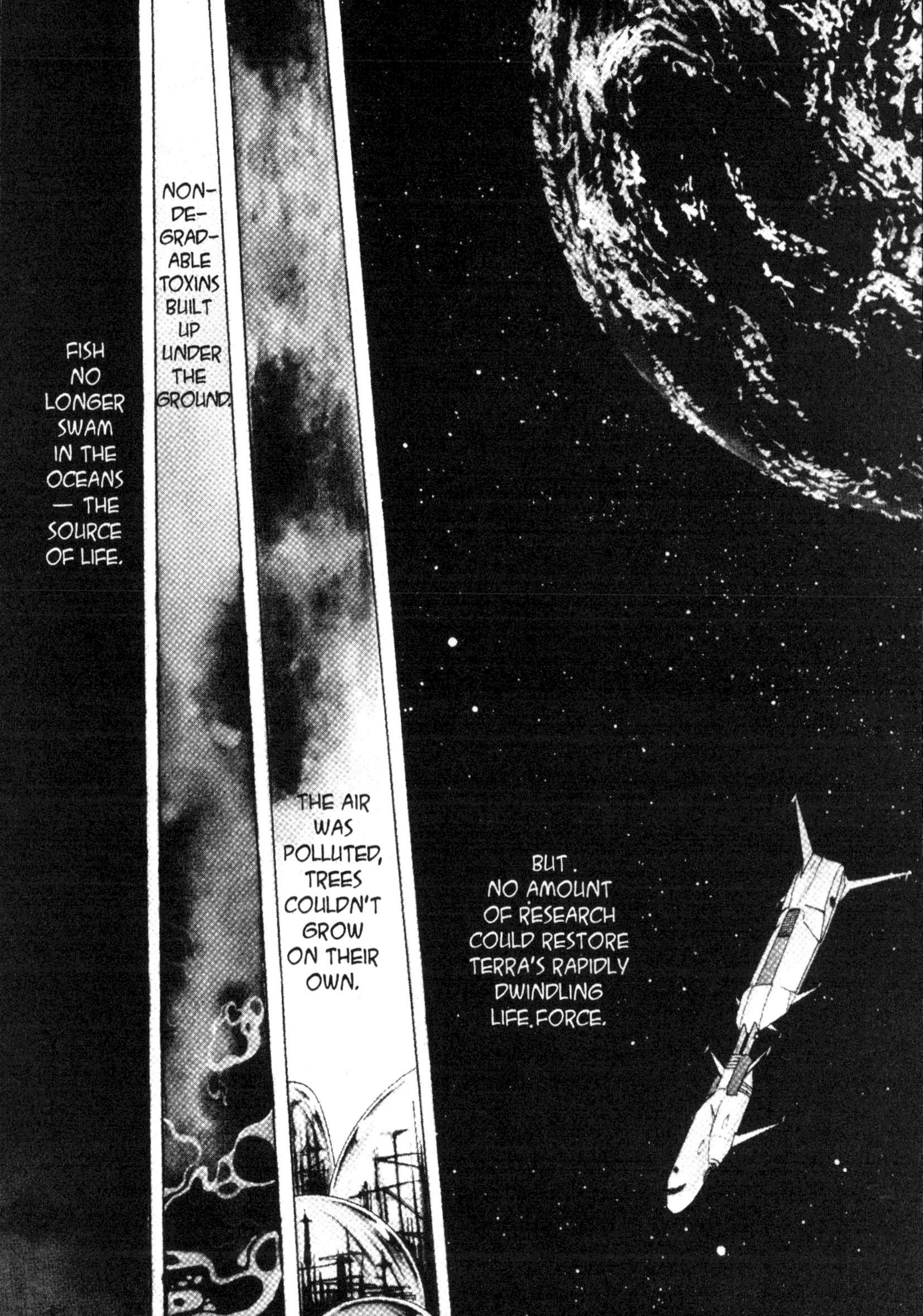
FISH NO LONGER SWAM IN THE OCEANS — THE SOURCE OF LIFE.
NON-DE-GRAD-ABLE TOXINS BUILT UP UNDER THE GROUND.
THE AIR WAS POLLUTED, TREES COULDN'T GROW ON THEIR OWN.
BUT . NO AMOUNT OF RESEARCH COULD RESTORE TERRA'S RAPIDLY DWINDLING LIFE FORCE.

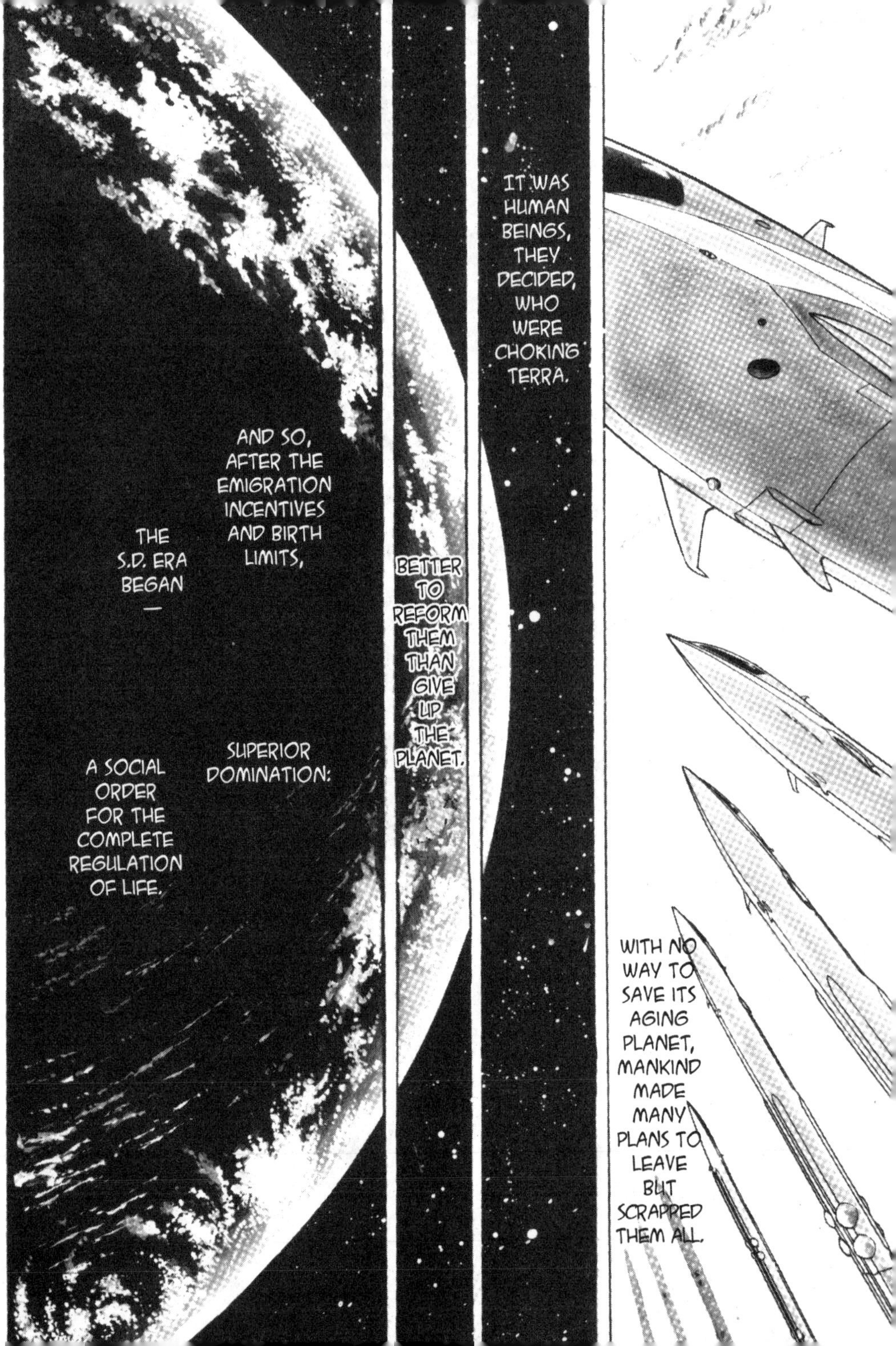
WITH NO WAY TO SAVE ITS AGING PLANET, MANKIND MADE MANY PLANS TO LEAVE BUT SCRAPPED THEM ALL.
IT WAS HUMAN BEINGS, THEY DECIDED, WHO WERE CHOKING TERRA.
BETTER TO REFORM THEM THAN GIVE UP THE PLANET.
AND SO, AFTER THE EMIGRATION INCENTIVES AND BIRTH LIMITS,
THE S.D. ERA BEGAN —
SUPERIOR DOMINATION:
A SOCIAL ORDER FOR THE COMPLETE REGULATION OF LIFE.

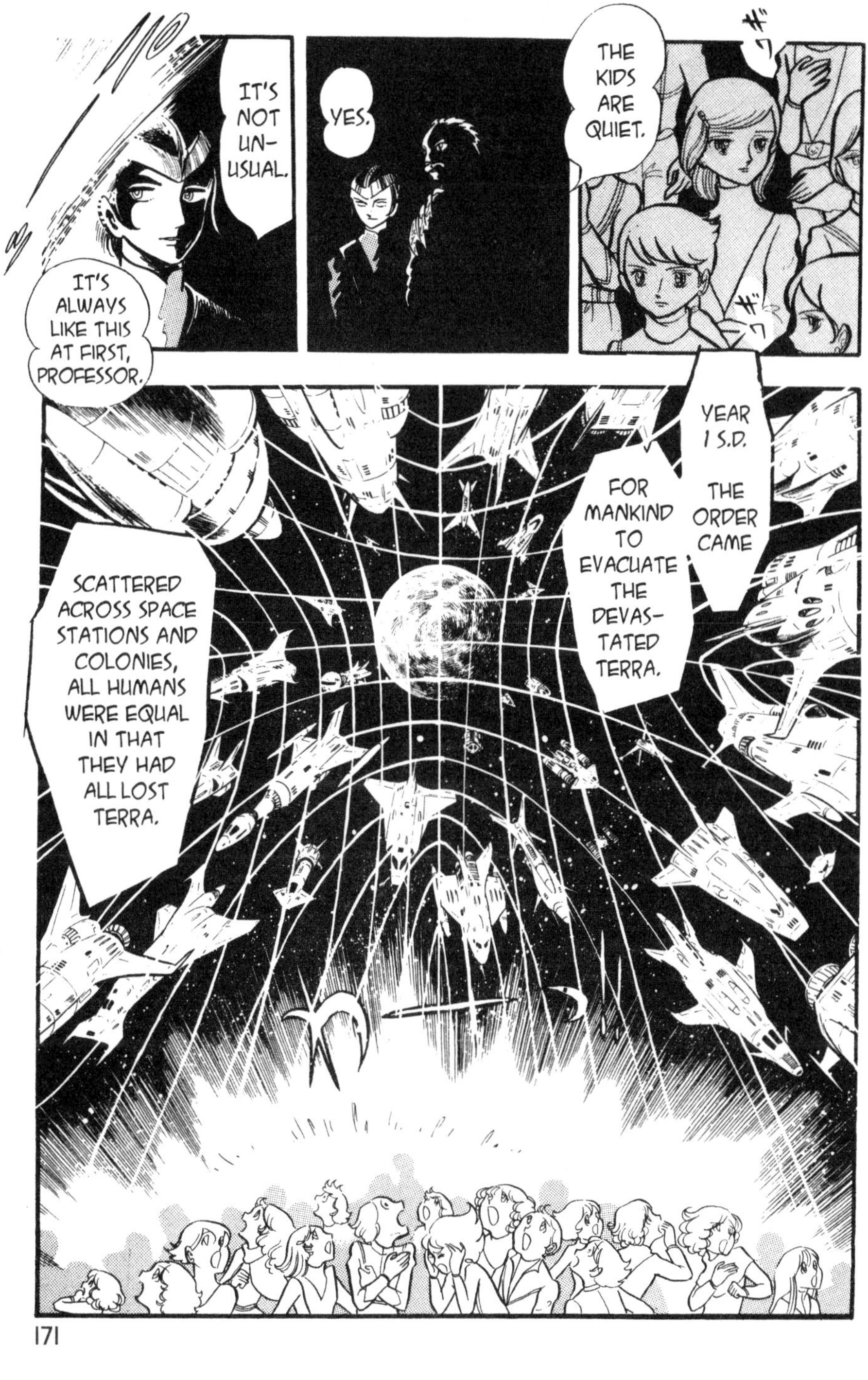
ザワ
THE KIDS ARE QUIET.
ザワ
YES.
IT'S NOT UN-USUAL.
IT'S ALWAYS LIKE THIS AT FIRST, PROFESSOR.
YEAR 1 S.D.
THE ORDER CAME
FOR MANKIND TO EVACUATE THE DEVAS-TATED TERRA.
SCATTERED ACROSS SPACE STATIONS AND COLONIES, ALL HUMANS WERE EQUAL IN THAT THEY HAD ALL LOST TERRA.

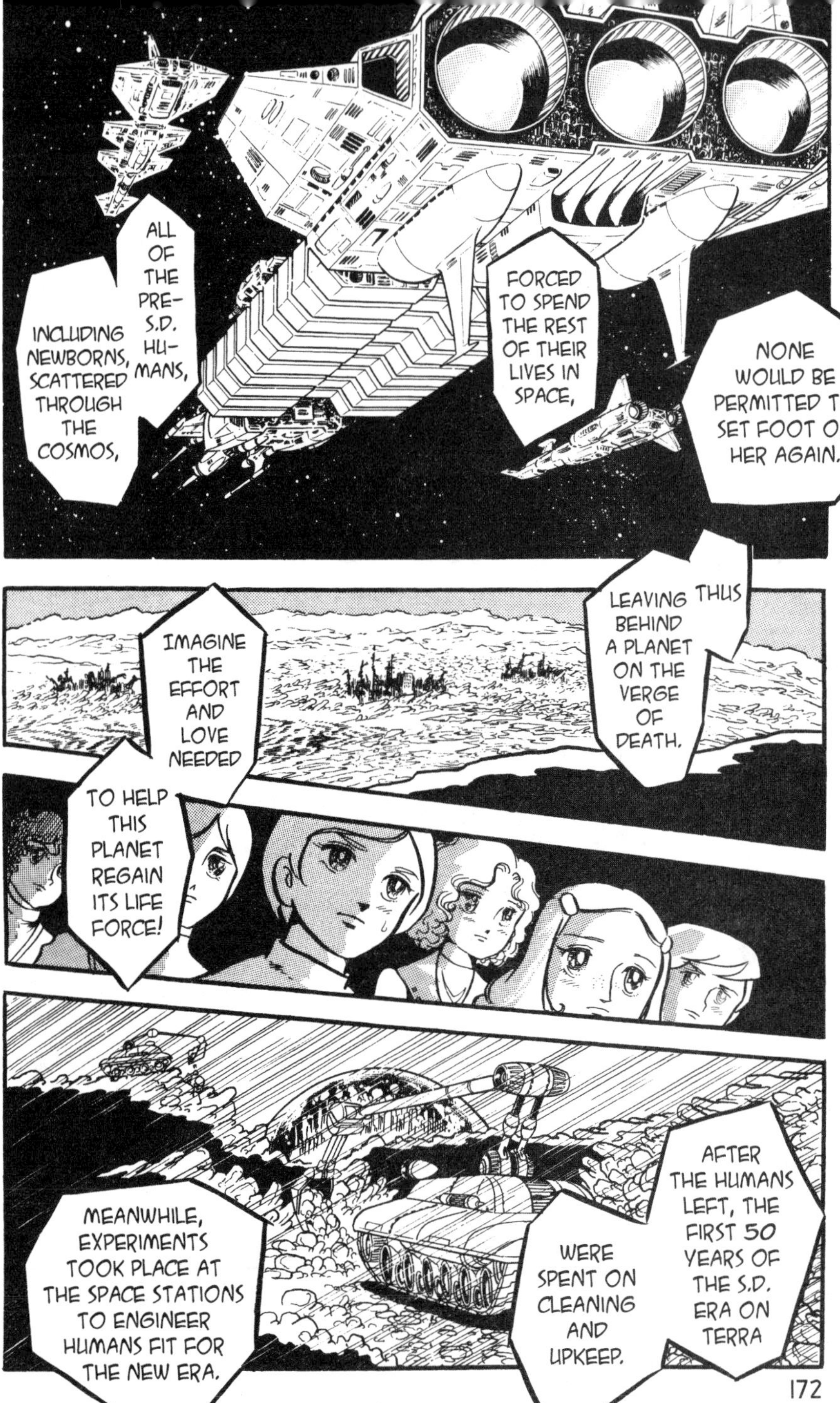
NONE WOULD BE PERMITTED TO SET FOOT ON HER AGAIN.
FORCED TO SPEND THE REST OF THEIR LIVES IN SPACE,
ALL OF THE PRE-S.D. HUMANS,
INCLUDING NEWBORNS, SCATTERED THROUGH THE COSMOS,
THUS LEAVING BEHIND A PLANET ON THE VERGE OF DEATH.
IMAGINE THE EFFORT AND LOVE NEEDED
TO HELP THIS PLANET REGAIN ITS LIFE FORCE!
AFTER THE HUMANS LEFT, THE FIRST 50 YEARS OF THE S.D. ERA ON TERRA
WERE SPENT ON CLEANING AND UPKEEP.
MEANWHILE, EXPERIMENTS TOOK PLACE AT THE SPACE STATIONS TO ENGINEER HUMANS FIT FOR THE NEW ERA.

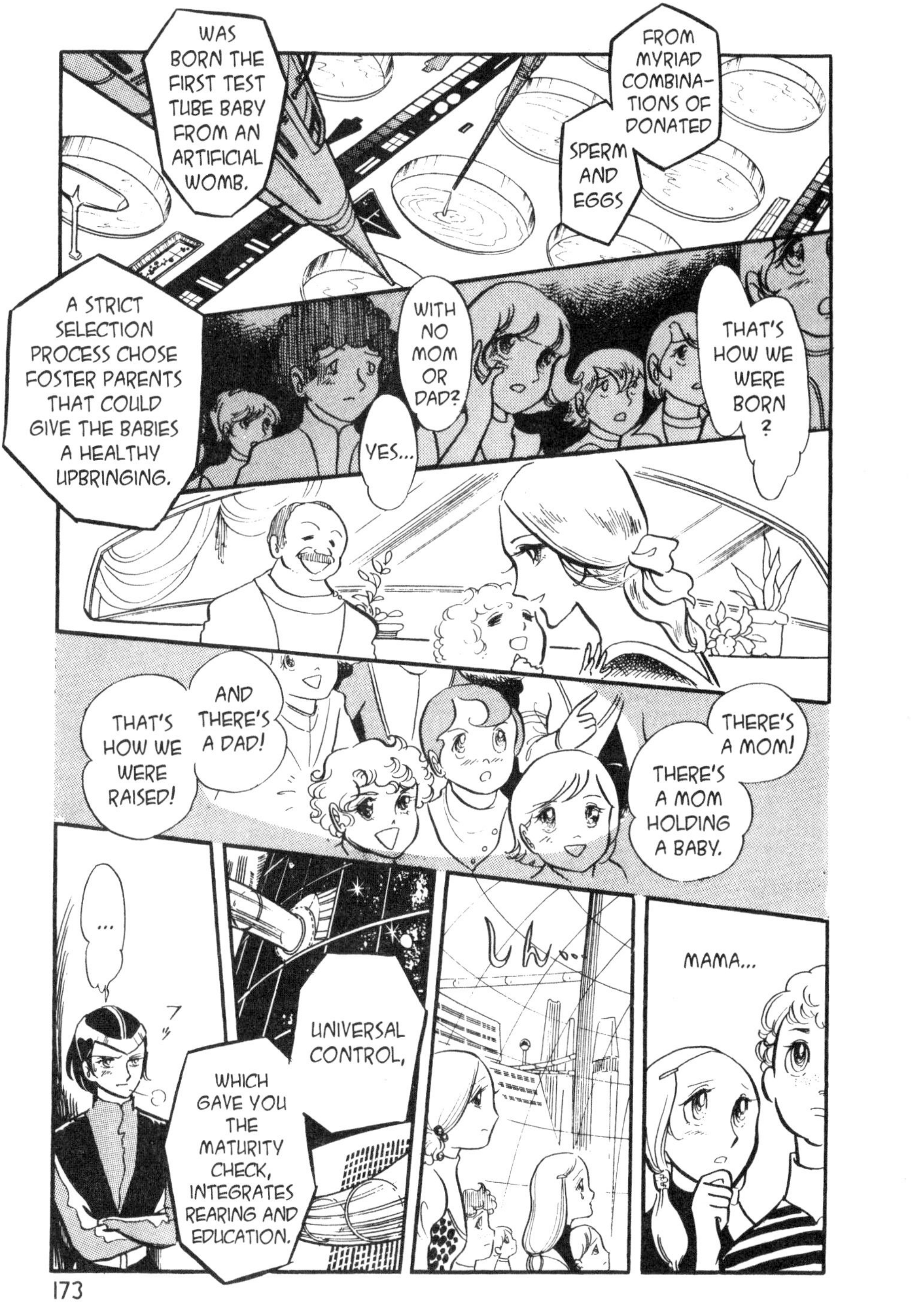
FROM MYRIAD COMBINATIONS OF DONATED
SPERM AND EGGS
WAS BORN THE FIRST TEST TUBE BABY FROM AN ARTIFICIAL WOMB.
THAT'S HOW WE WERE BORN?
WITH NO MOM OR DAD?
YES...
A STRICT SELECTION PROCESS CHOSE FOSTER PARENTS THAT COULD GIVE THE BABIES A HEALTHY UPBRINGING.
THERE'S A MOM!
THERE'S A MOM HOLDING A BABY.
AND THERE'S A DAD!
THAT'S HOW WE WERE RAISED!
MAMA...
しん...
UNIVERSAL CONTROL,
WHICH GAVE YOU THE MATURITY CHECK, INTEGRATES REARING AND EDUCATION.
...

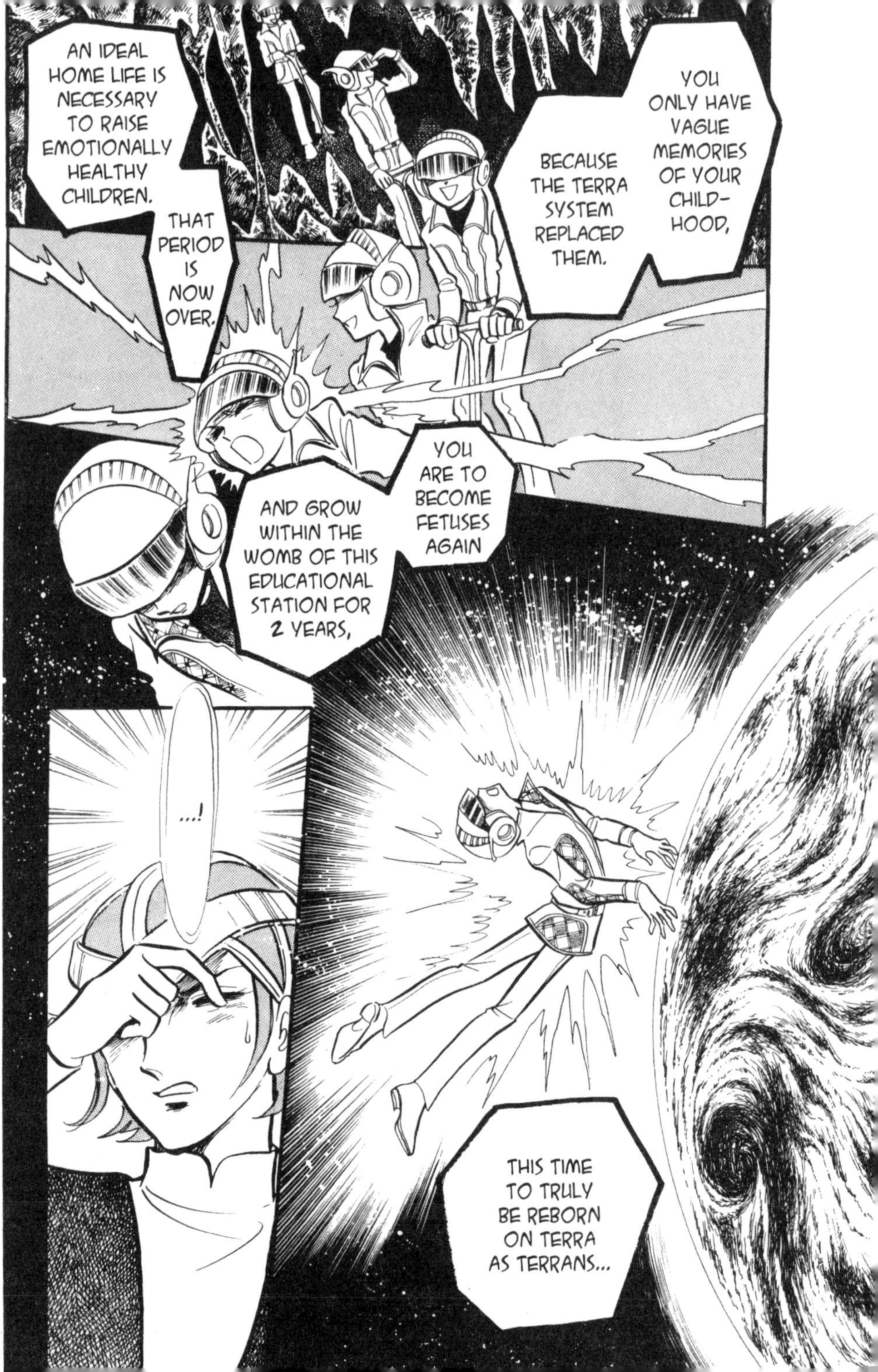
YOU ONLY HAVE VAGUE MEMORIES OF YOUR CHILD-HOOD,
BECAUSE THE TERRA SYSTEM REPLACED THEM.
AN IDEAL HOME LIFE IS NECESSARY TO RAISE EMOTIONALLY HEALTHY CHILDREN.
THAT PERIOD IS NOW OVER.
YOU ARE TO BECOME FETUSES AGAIN
AND GROW WITHIN THE WOMB OF THIS EDUCATIONAL STATION FOR 2 YEARS,
THIS TIME TO TRULY BE REBORN ON TERRA AS TERRANS...
...!

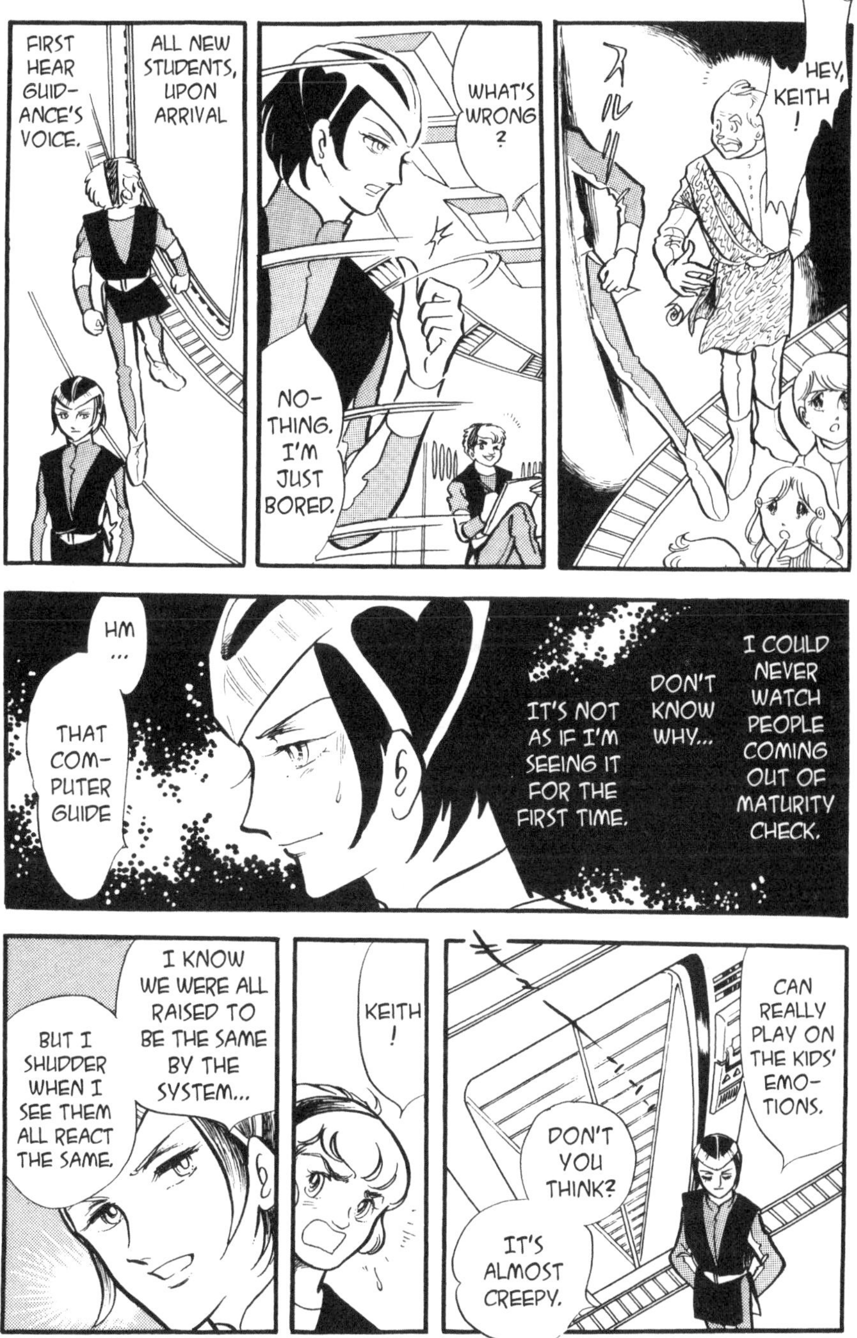

HEY, KEITH!
スル
WHAT'S WRONG?
NOTHING. I'M JUST BORED.
ALL NEW STUDENTS, UPON ARRIVAL
FIRST HEAR GUIDANCE'S VOICE.
I COULD NEVER WATCH PEOPLE COMING OUT OF MATURITY CHECK.
DON'T KNOW WHY...
IT'S NOT AS IF I'M SEEING IT FOR THE FIRST TIME.
HM...
THAT COMPUTER GUIDE
CAN REALLY PLAY ON THE KIDS' EMOTIONS.
DON'T YOU THINK?
IT'S ALMOST CREEPY.
KEITH!
I KNOW WE WERE ALL RAISED TO BE THE SAME BY THE SYSTEM...
BUT I SHUDDER WHEN I SEE THEM ALL REACT THE SAME.

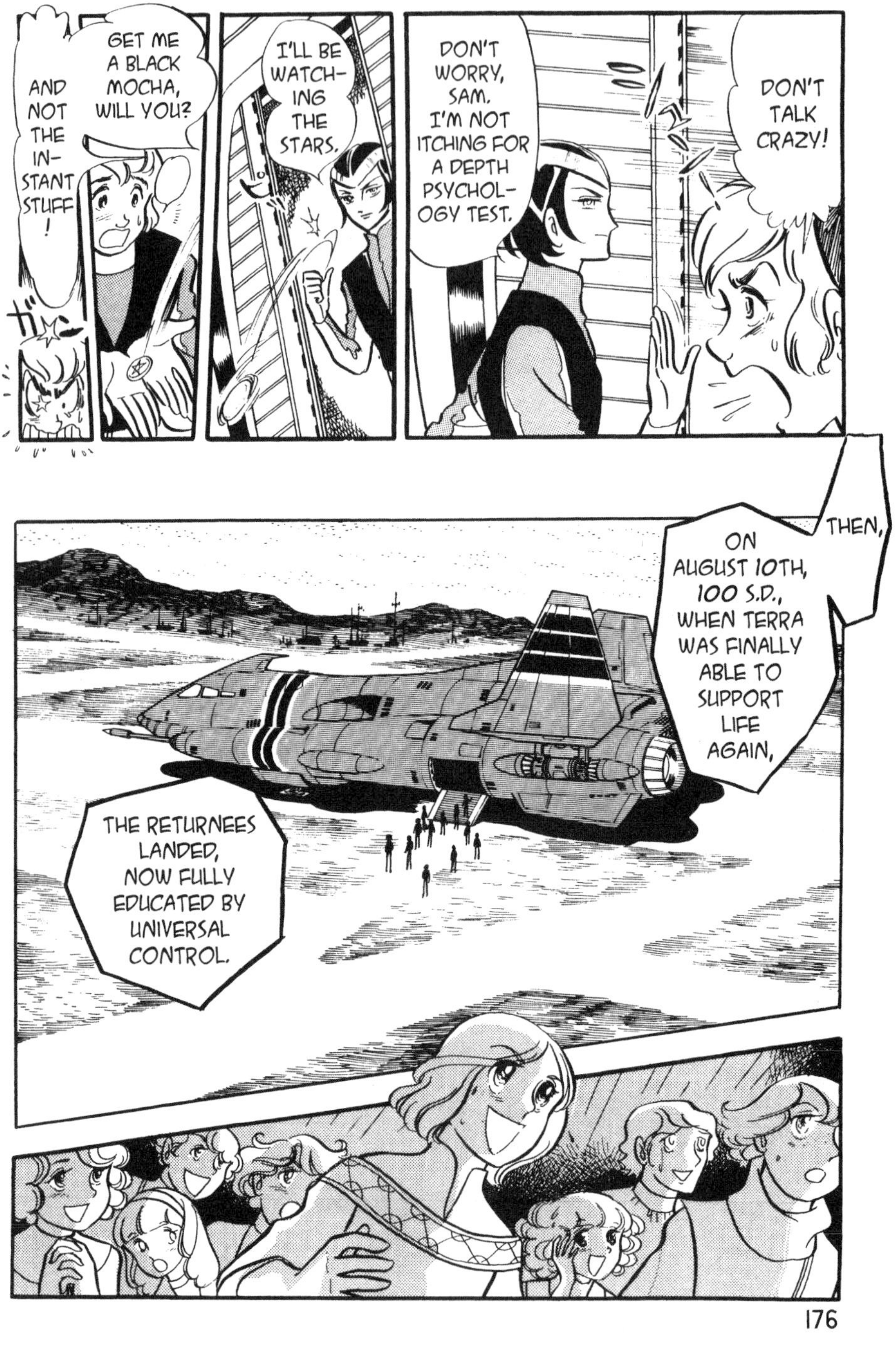
DON'T TALK CRAZY!
DON'T WORRY, SAM. I'M NOT ITCHING FOR A DEPTH PSYCHOL-OGY TEST.
I'LL BE WATCH-ING THE STARS.
GET ME A BLACK MOCHA, WILL YOU?
AND NOT THE IN-STANT STUFF!
THEN,
ON AUGUST 10TH, 100 S.D., WHEN TERRA WAS FINALLY ABLE TO SUPPORT LIFE AGAIN,
THE RETURNEES LANDED, NOW FULLY EDUCATED BY UNIVERSAL CONTROL.

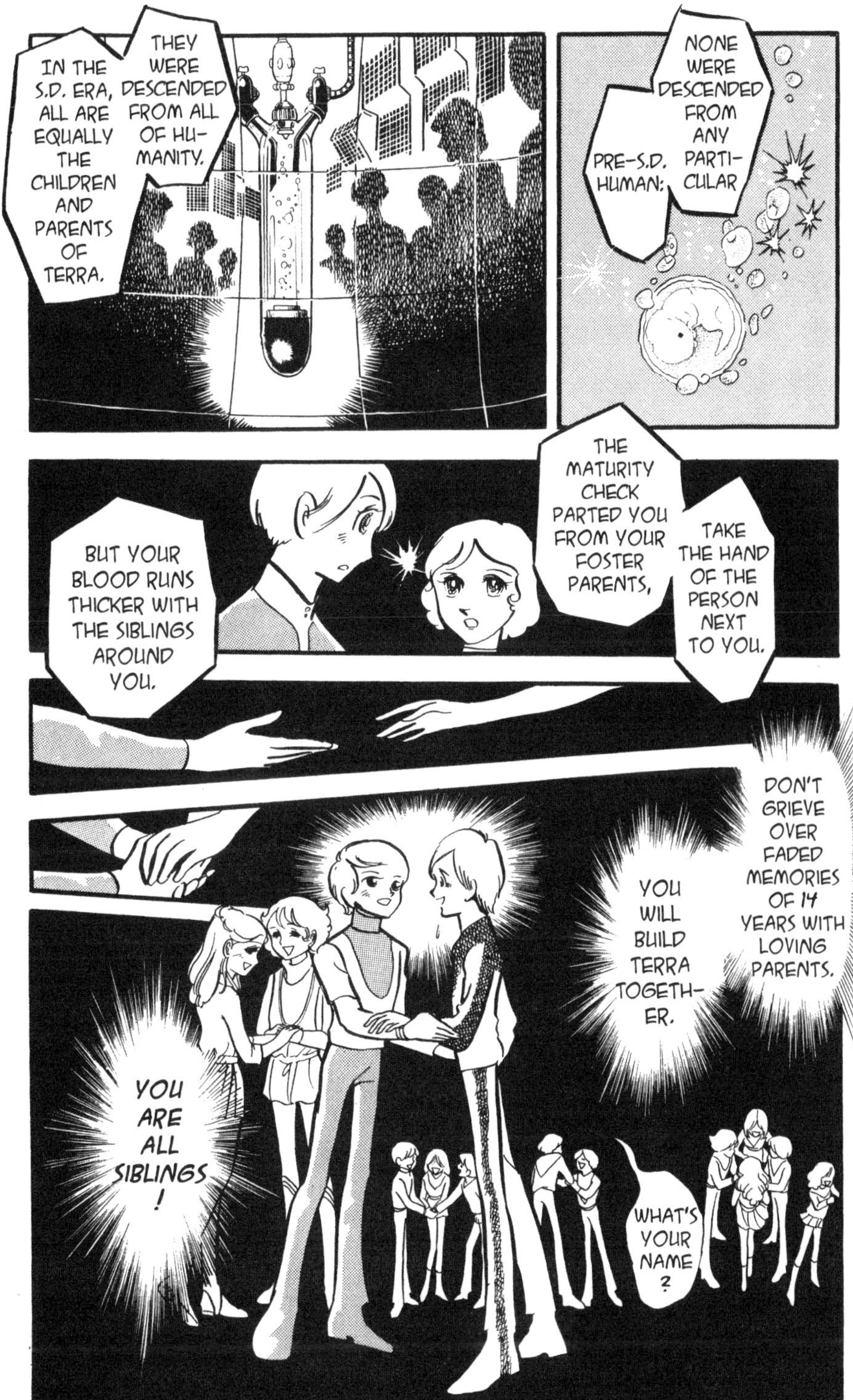
NONE WERE DESCENDED FROM ANY PARTICULAR
PRE-S.D. HUMAN:
THEY WERE DESCENDED FROM ALL OF HU-MANITY.
IN THE S.D. ERA, ALL ARE EQUALLY THE CHILDREN AND PARENTS OF TERRA.
THE MATURITY CHECK PARTED YOU FROM YOUR FOSTER PARENTS,
BUT YOUR BLOOD RUNS THICKER WITH THE SIBLINGS AROUND YOU.
TAKE THE HAND OF THE PERSON NEXT TO YOU.
DON'T GRIEVE OVER FADED MEMORIES OF 14 YEARS WITH LOVING PARENTS.
YOU WILL BUILD TERRA TOGETH-ER.
WHAT'S YOUR NAME ?
YOU ARE ALL SIBLINGS !

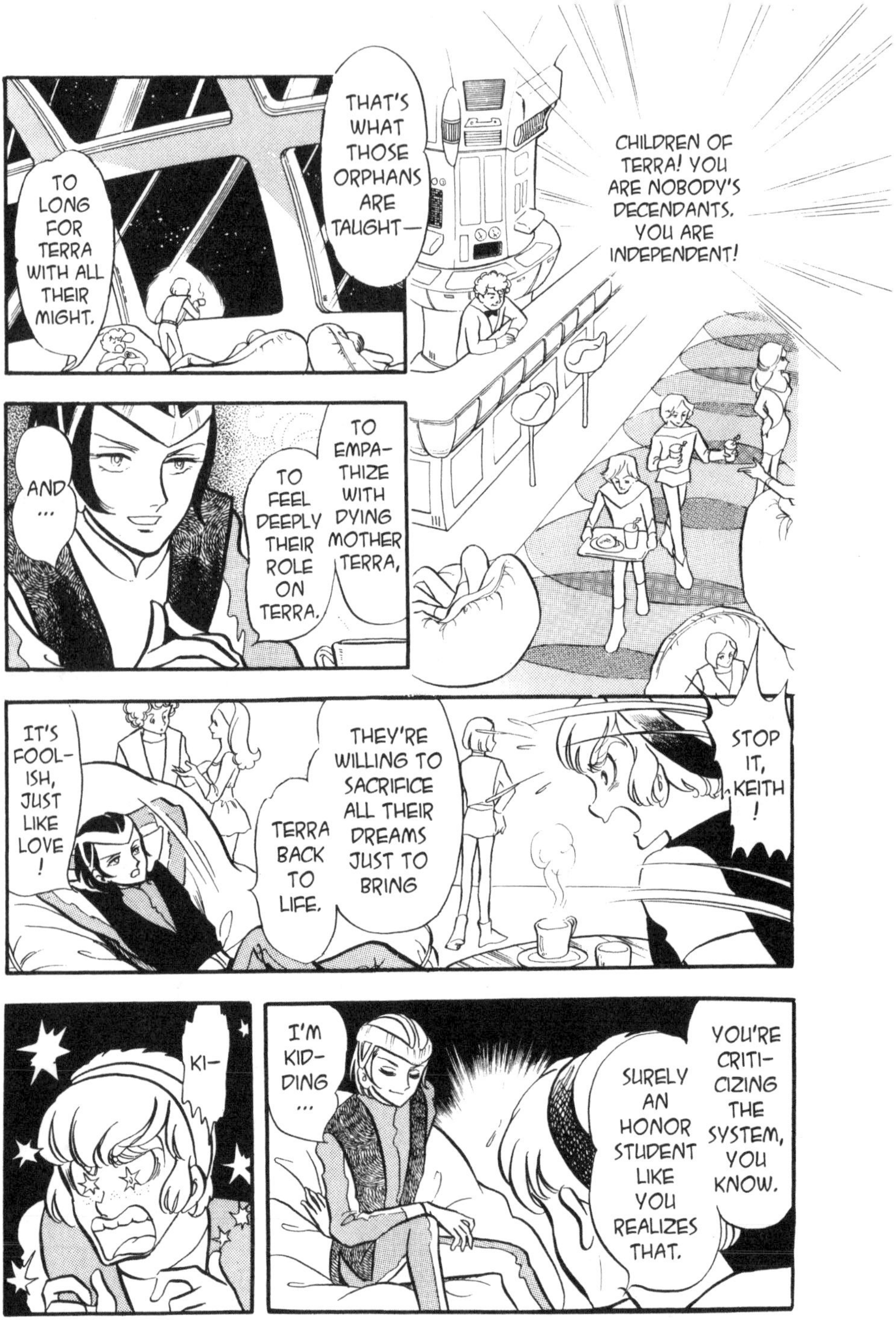
CHILDREN OF TERRA! YOU ARE NOBODY'S DECENDANTS. YOU ARE INDEPENDENT!
THAT'S WHAT THOSE ORPHANS ARE TAUGHT—
TO LONG FOR TERRA WITH ALL THEIR MIGHT.
TO EMPATHIZE WITH DYING MOTHER TERRA,
TO FEEL DEEPLY THEIR ROLE ON TERRA.
AND ...
STOP IT, KEITH!
THEY'RE WILLING TO SACRIFICE ALL THEIR DREAMS JUST TO BRING
TERRA BACK TO LIFE.
IT'S FOOLISH, JUST LIKE LOVE!
YOU'RE CRITICIZING THE SYSTEM, YOU KNOW.
SURELY AN HONOR STUDENT LIKE YOU REALIZES THAT.
I'M KIDDING ...
KI—

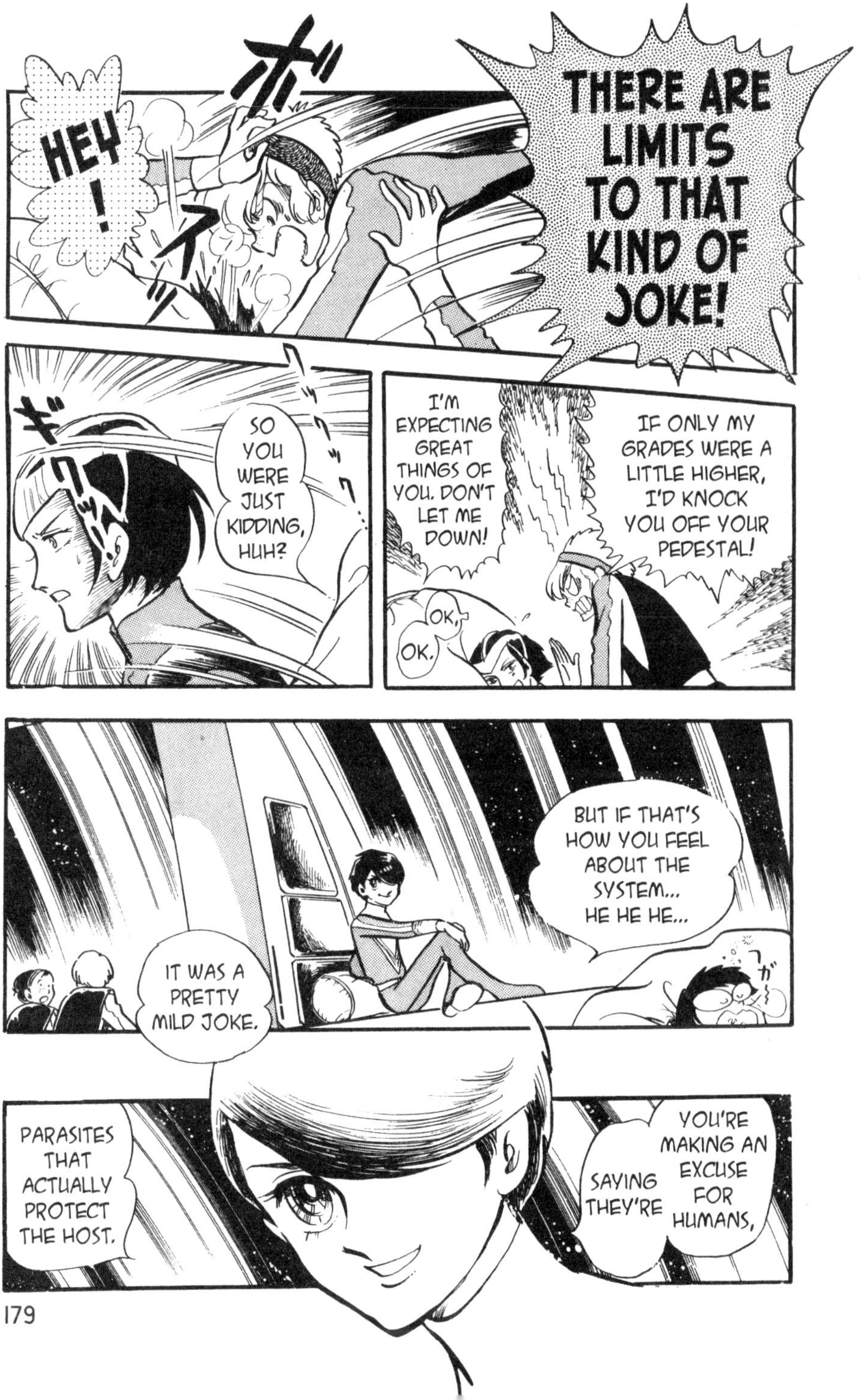
THERE ARE LIMITS TO THAT KIND OF JOKE!
HEY!
IF ONLY MY GRADES WERE A LITTLE HIGHER, I'D KNOCK YOU OFF YOUR PEDESTAL!
I'M EXPECTING GREAT THINGS OF YOU. DON'T LET ME DOWN!
OK,
OK.
SO YOU WERE JUST KIDDING, HUH?
BUT IF THAT'S HOW YOU FEEL ABOUT THE SYSTEM... HE HE HE...
IT WAS A PRETTY MILD JOKE.
YOU'RE MAKING AN EXCUSE FOR HUMANS,
SAYING THEY'RE
PARASITES THAT ACTUALLY PROTECT THE HOST.

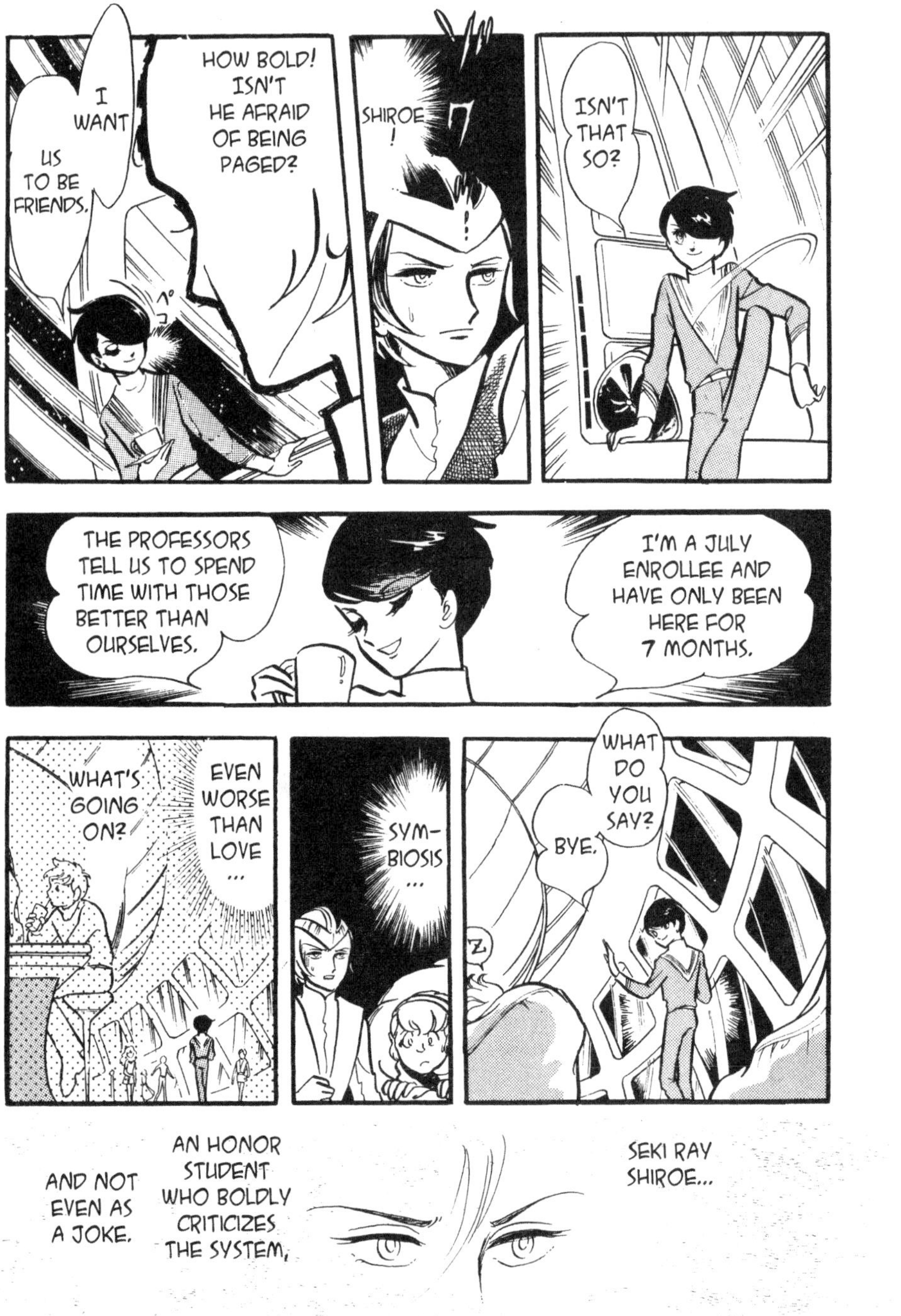
ISN'T THAT SO?
SHIROE!
HOW BOLD! ISN'T HE AFRAID OF BEING PAGED?
I WANT US TO BE FRIENDS.
ペコ
I'M A JULY ENROLLEE AND HAVE ONLY BEEN HERE FOR 7 MONTHS.
THE PROFESSORS TELL US TO SPEND TIME WITH THOSE BETTER THAN OURSELVES.
WHAT DO YOU SAY?
BYE.
SYM-BIOSIS...
EVEN WORSE THAN LOVE...
WHAT'S GOING ON?
SEKI RAY SHIROE...
AN HONOR STUDENT WHO BOLDLY CRITICIZES THE SYSTEM,
AND NOT EVEN AS A JOKE.

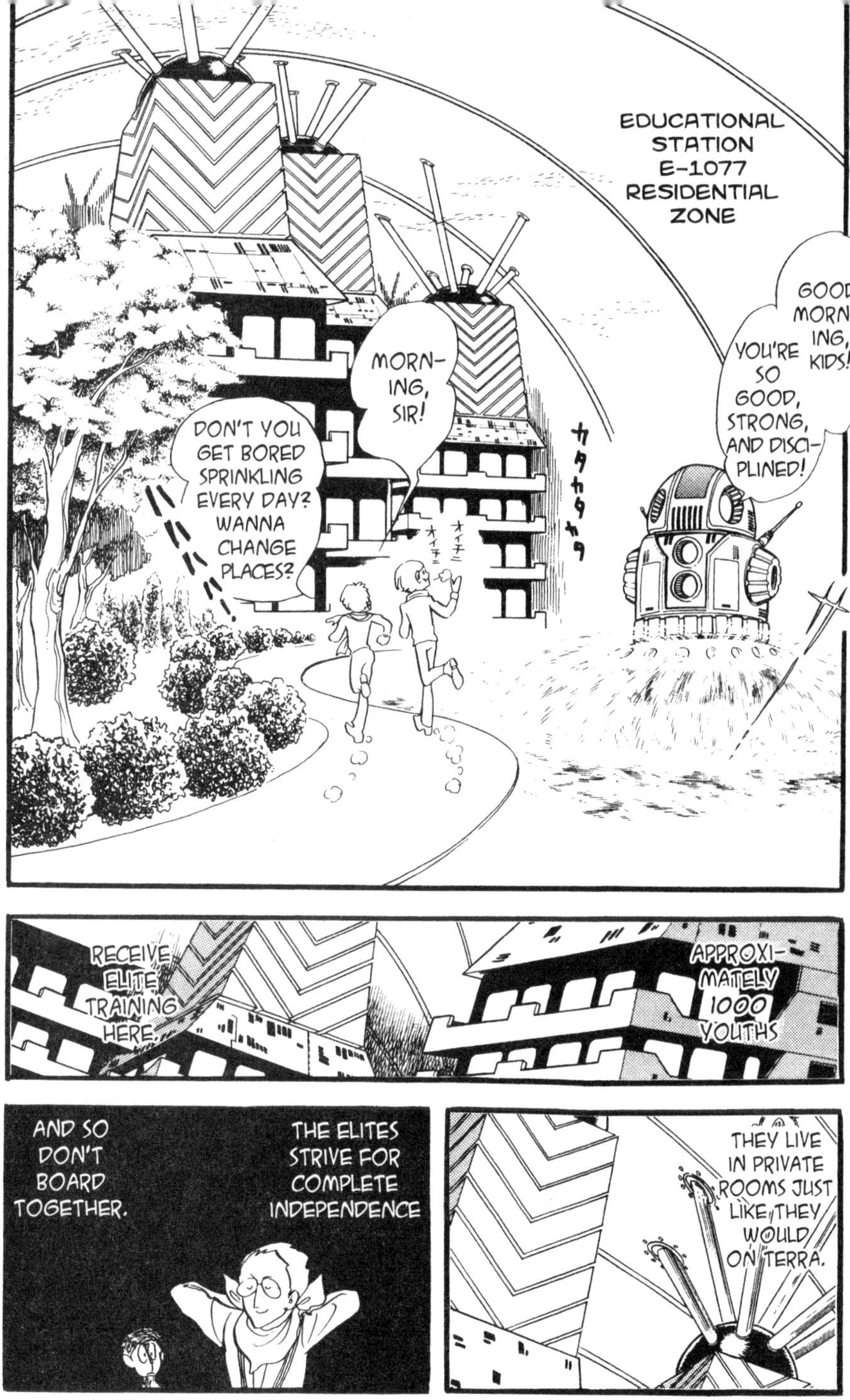
EDUCATIONAL STATION E-1077 RESIDENTIAL ZONE
GOOD MORNING, KIDS!
YOU'RE SO GOOD, STRONG, AND DISCIPLINED!
カタカタカタ
MORNING, SIR!
DON'T YOU GET BORED SPRINKLING EVERY DAY? WANNA CHANGE PLACES?
APPROXIMATELY 1000 YOUTHS
RECEIVE ELITE TRAINING HERE.
THEY LIVE IN PRIVATE ROOMS JUST LIKE THEY WOULD ON TERRA.
THE ELITES STRIVE FOR COMPLETE INDEPENDENCE
AND SO DON'T BOARD TOGETHER.

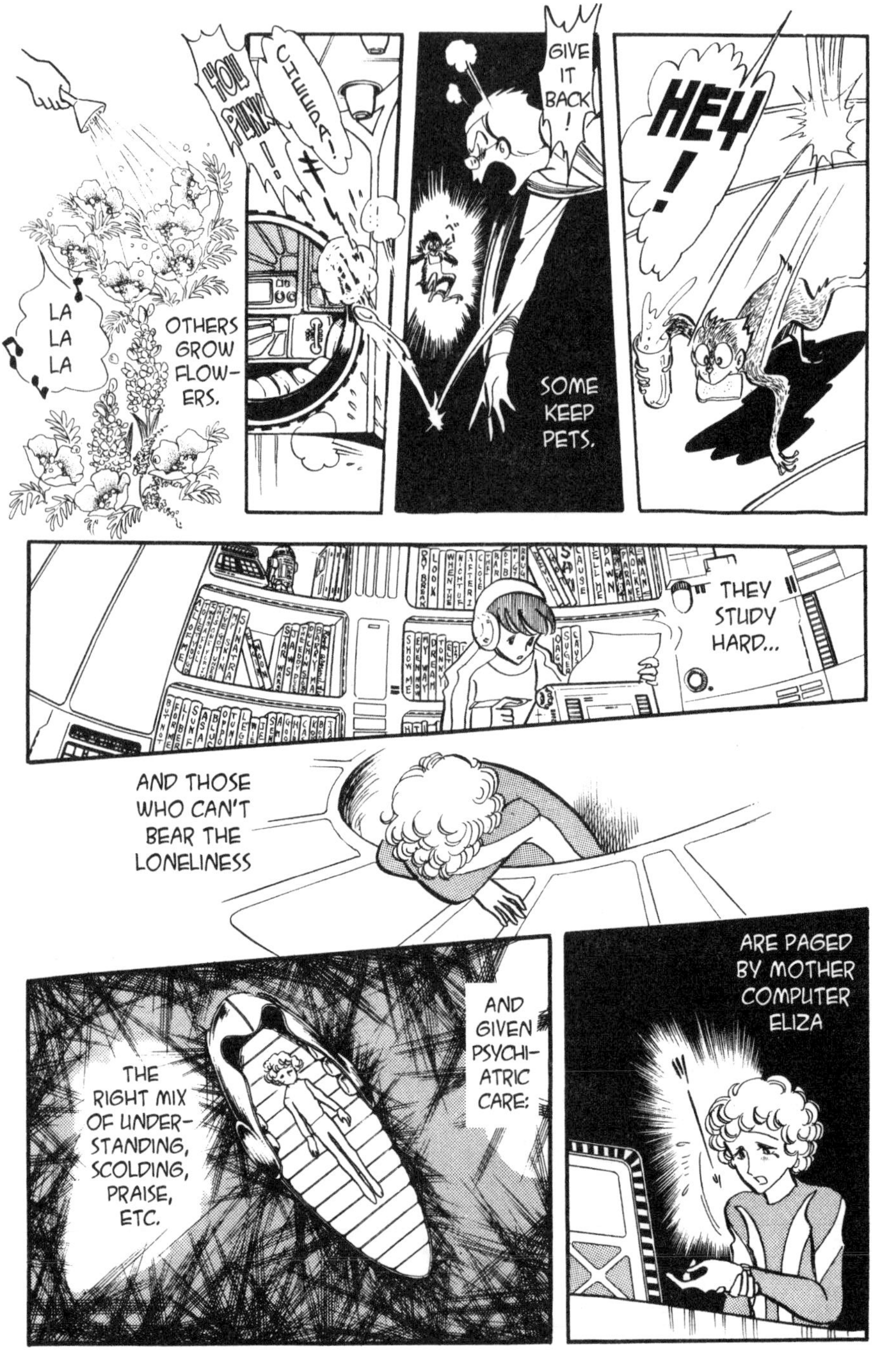
HEY!
GIVE IT BACK!
SOME KEEP PETS.
CHEEPA!
YOU PUNK!!
OTHERS GROW FLOW-ERS.
LA LA LA
THEY STUDY HARD...
AND THOSE WHO CAN'T BEAR THE LONELINESS
ARE PAGED BY MOTHER COMPUTER ELIZA
AND GIVEN PSYCHI-ATRIC CARE:
THE RIGHT MIX OF UNDER-STANDING, SCOLDING, PRAISE, ETC.

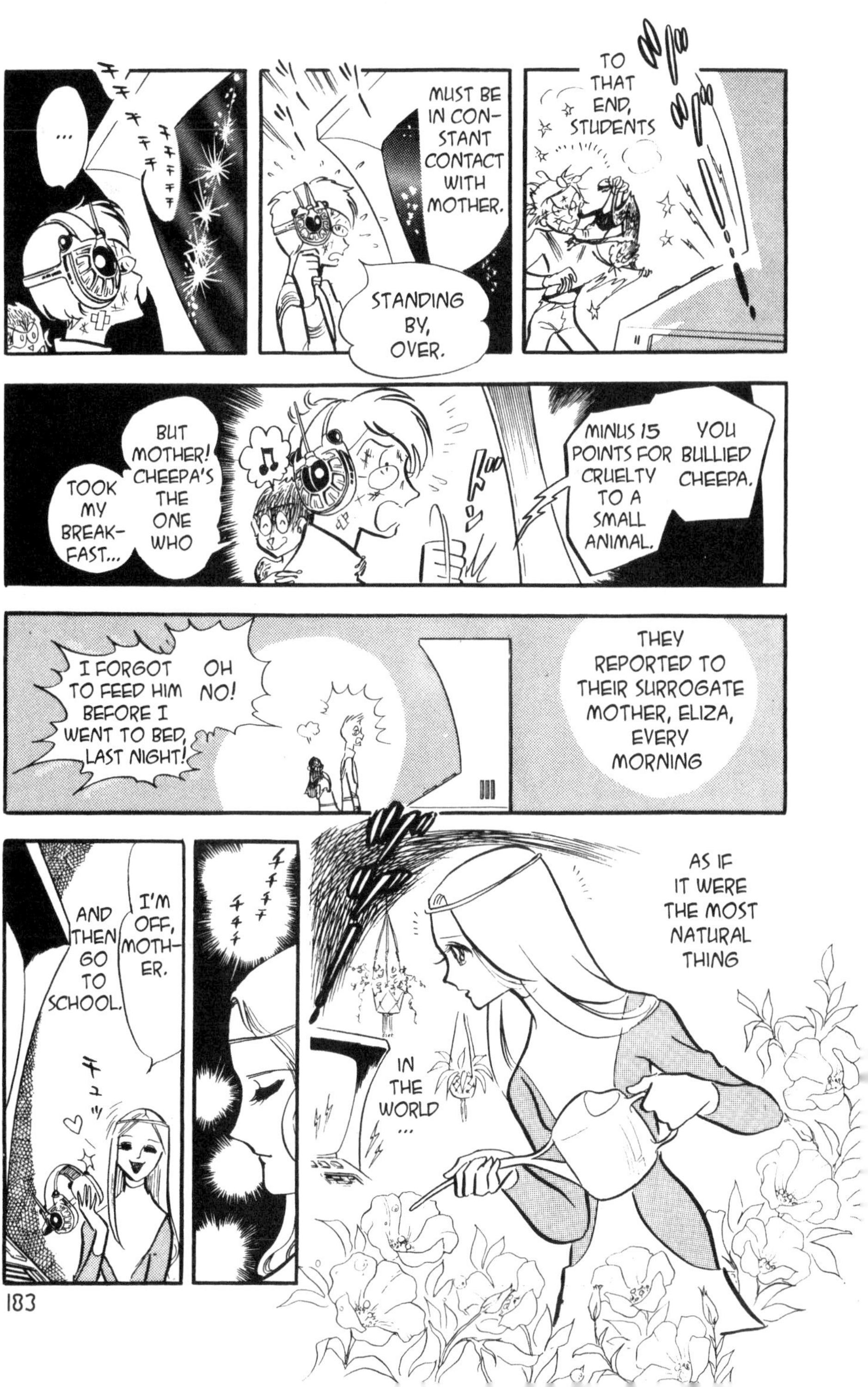
TO THAT END, STUDENTS
MUST BE IN CONSTANT CONTACT WITH MOTHER.
STANDING BY, OVER.
...
チチチチ
YOU BULLIED CHEEPA.
MINUS 15 POINTS FOR CRUELTY TO A SMALL ANIMAL.
BUT MOTHER! CHEEPA'S THE ONE WHO
TOOK MY BREAKFAST...
THEY REPORTED TO THEIR SURROGATE MOTHER, ELIZA, EVERY MORNING
OH NO!
I FORGOT TO FEED HIM BEFORE I WENT TO BED, LAST NIGHT!
AS IF IT WERE THE MOST NATURAL THING
IN THE WORLD ...
チチチチ
I'M OFF, MOTHER.
AND THEN GO TO SCHOOL.
チュッ

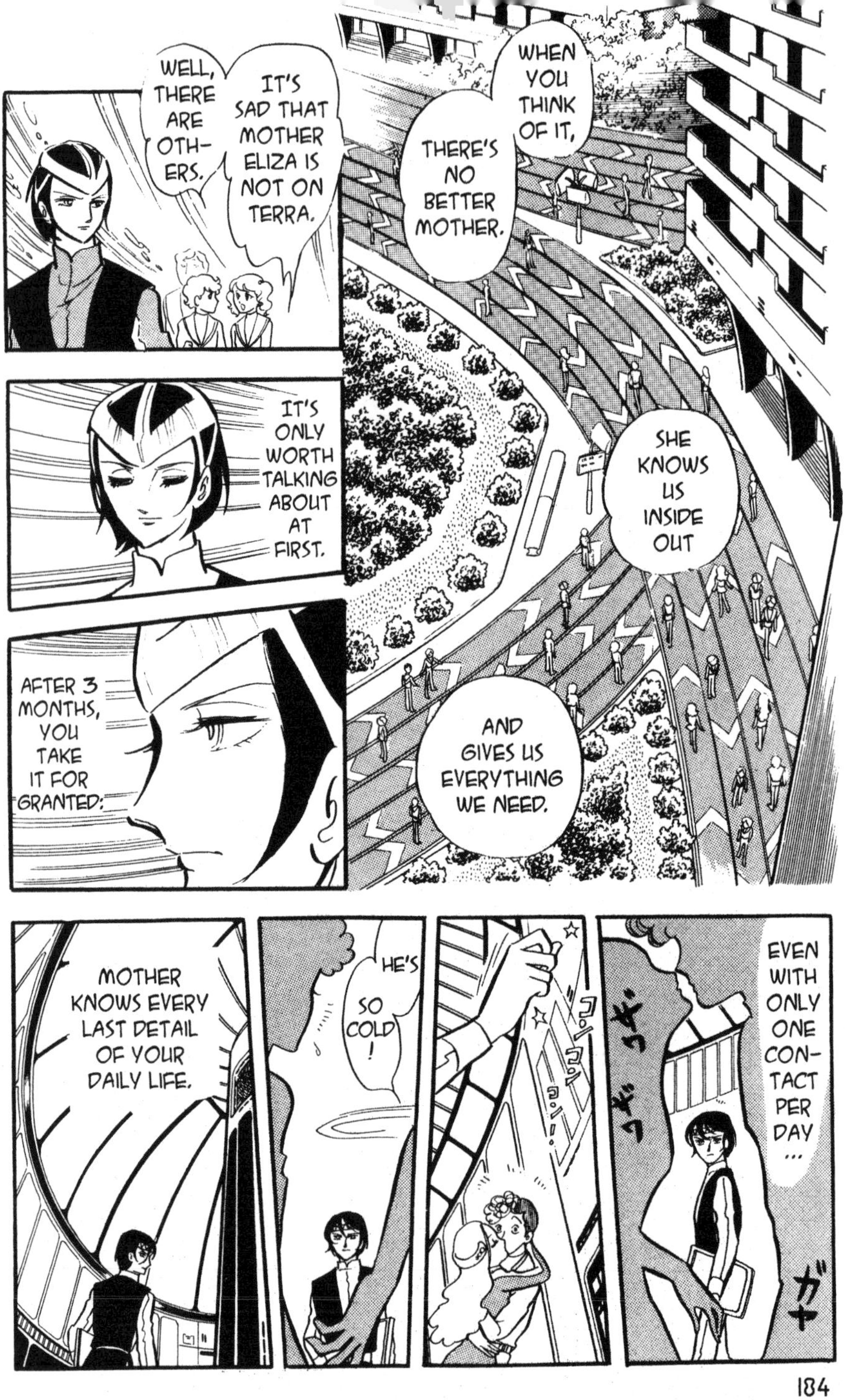
WHEN YOU THINK OF IT,
THERE'S NO BETTER MOTHER.
SHE KNOWS US INSIDE OUT
AND GIVES US EVERYTHING WE NEED.
IT'S SAD THAT MOTHER ELIZA IS NOT ON TERRA.
WELL, THERE ARE OTH-ERS.
IT'S ONLY WORTH TALKING ABOUT AT FIRST.
AFTER 3 MONTHS, YOU TAKE IT FOR GRANTED.
EVEN WITH ONLY ONE CON-TACT PER DAY...
HE'S SO COLD!
MOTHER KNOWS EVERY LAST DETAIL OF YOUR DAILY LIFE.

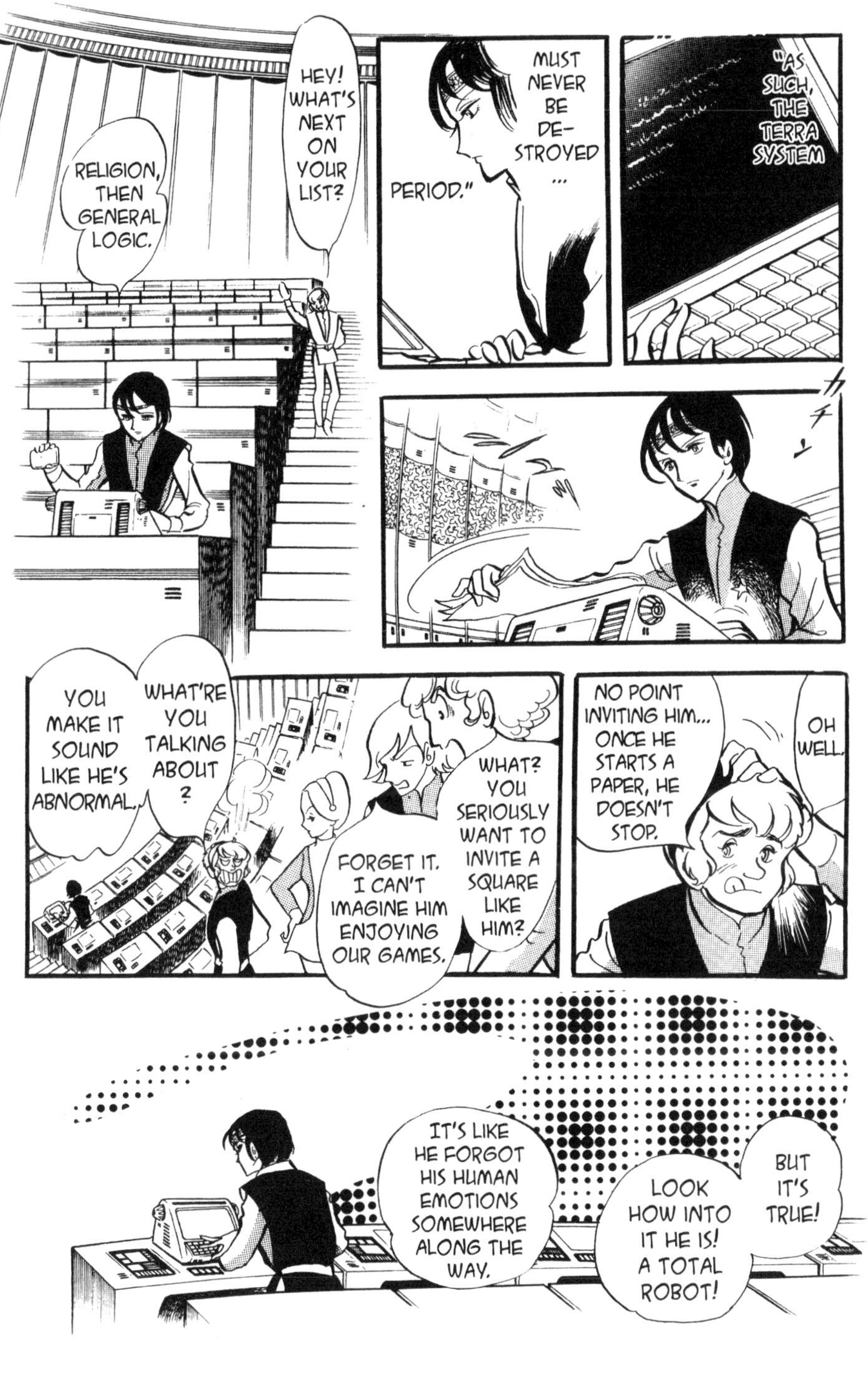
"AS SUCH, THE TERRA SYSTEM
MUST NEVER BE DE-STROYED ...
PERIOD."
HEY! WHAT'S NEXT ON YOUR LIST?
RELIGION, THEN GENERAL LOGIC.
OH WELL.
NO POINT INVITING HIM... ONCE HE STARTS A PAPER, HE DOESN'T STOP.
WHAT? YOU SERIOUSLY WANT TO INVITE A SQUARE LIKE HIM?
FORGET IT. I CAN'T IMAGINE HIM ENJOYING OUR GAMES.
WHAT'RE YOU TALKING ABOUT?
YOU MAKE IT SOUND LIKE HE'S ABNORMAL.
BUT IT'S TRUE!
LOOK HOW INTO IT HE IS! A TOTAL ROBOT!
IT'S LIKE HE FORGOT HIS HUMAN EMOTIONS SOMEWHERE ALONG THE WAY.

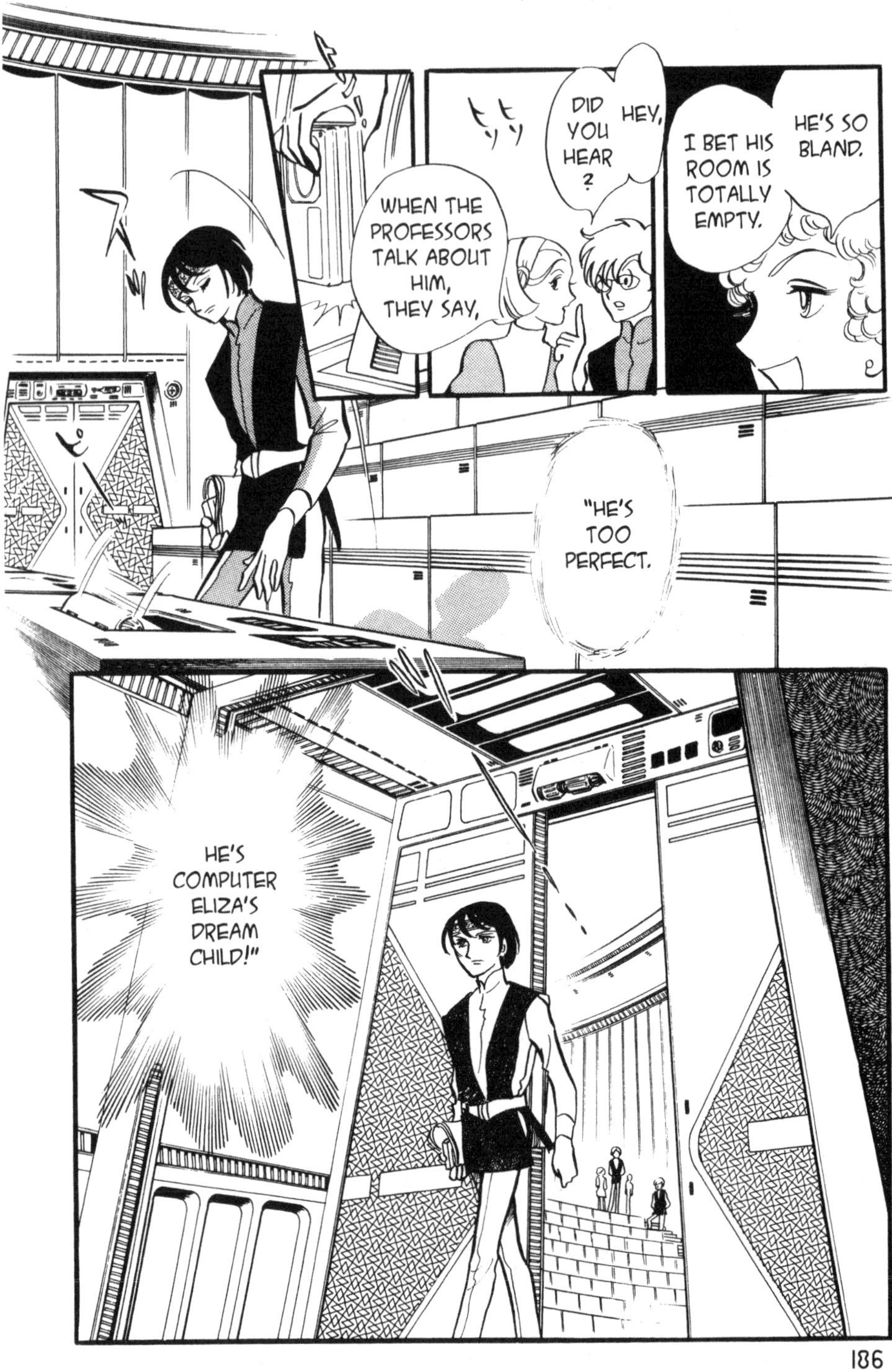
HE'S SO BLAND.
I BET HIS ROOM IS TOTALLY EMPTY.
HEY,
DID YOU HEAR?
ヒソヒソ
WHEN THE PROFESSORS TALK ABOUT HIM, THEY SAY,
"HE'S TOO PERFECT.
HE'S COMPUTER ELIZA'S DREAM CHILD!"

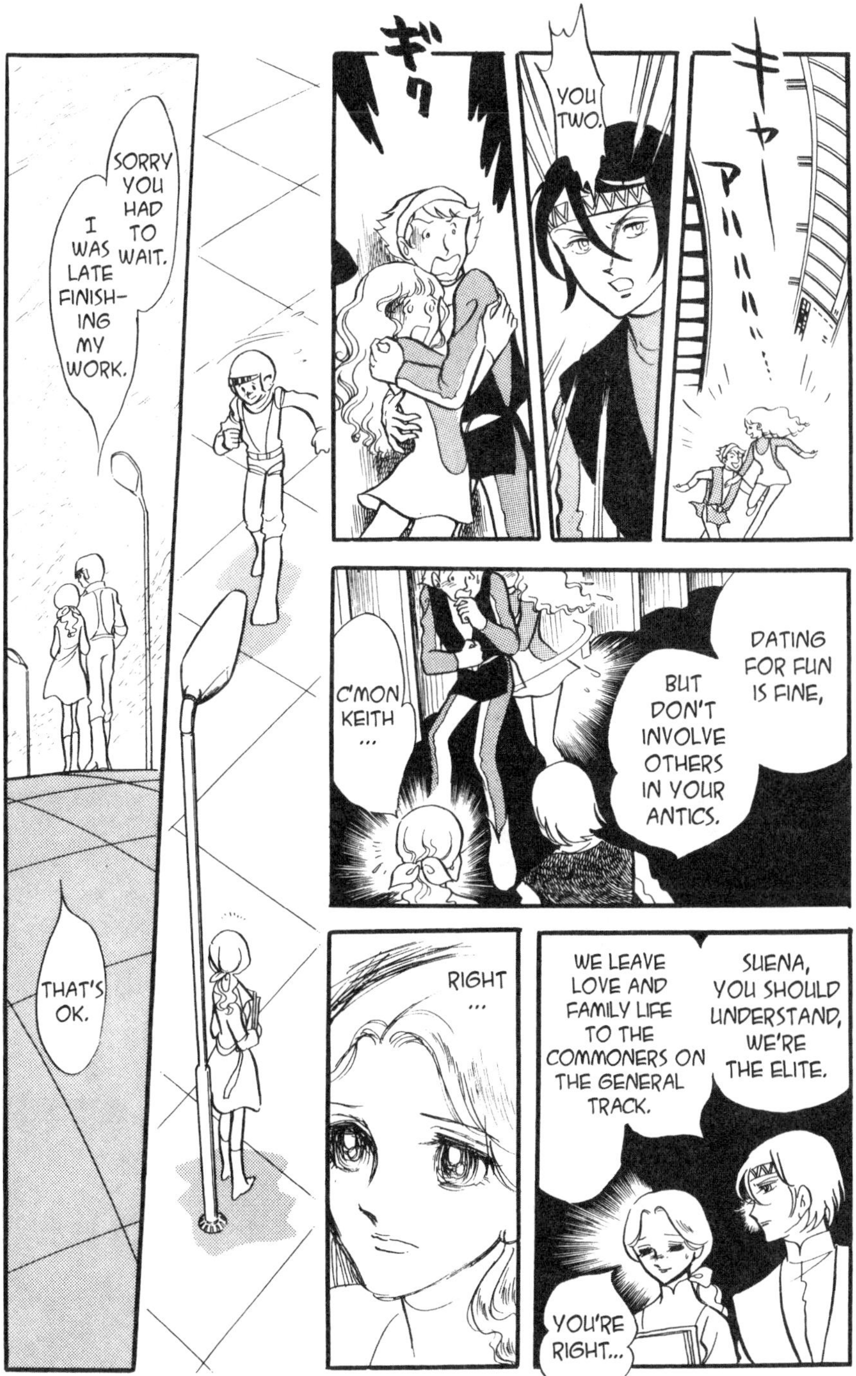
キャアハハハ…
YOU TWO.
ギク
DATING FOR FUN IS FINE,
BUT DON'T INVOLVE OTHERS IN YOUR ANTICS.
C'MON KEITH ...
SUENA, YOU SHOULD UNDERSTAND, WE'RE THE ELITE.
WE LEAVE LOVE AND FAMILY LIFE TO THE COMMONERS ON THE GENERAL TRACK.
YOU'RE RIGHT...
RIGHT ...
SORRY YOU HAD TO WAIT.
I WAS LATE FINISHING MY WORK.
THAT'S OK.

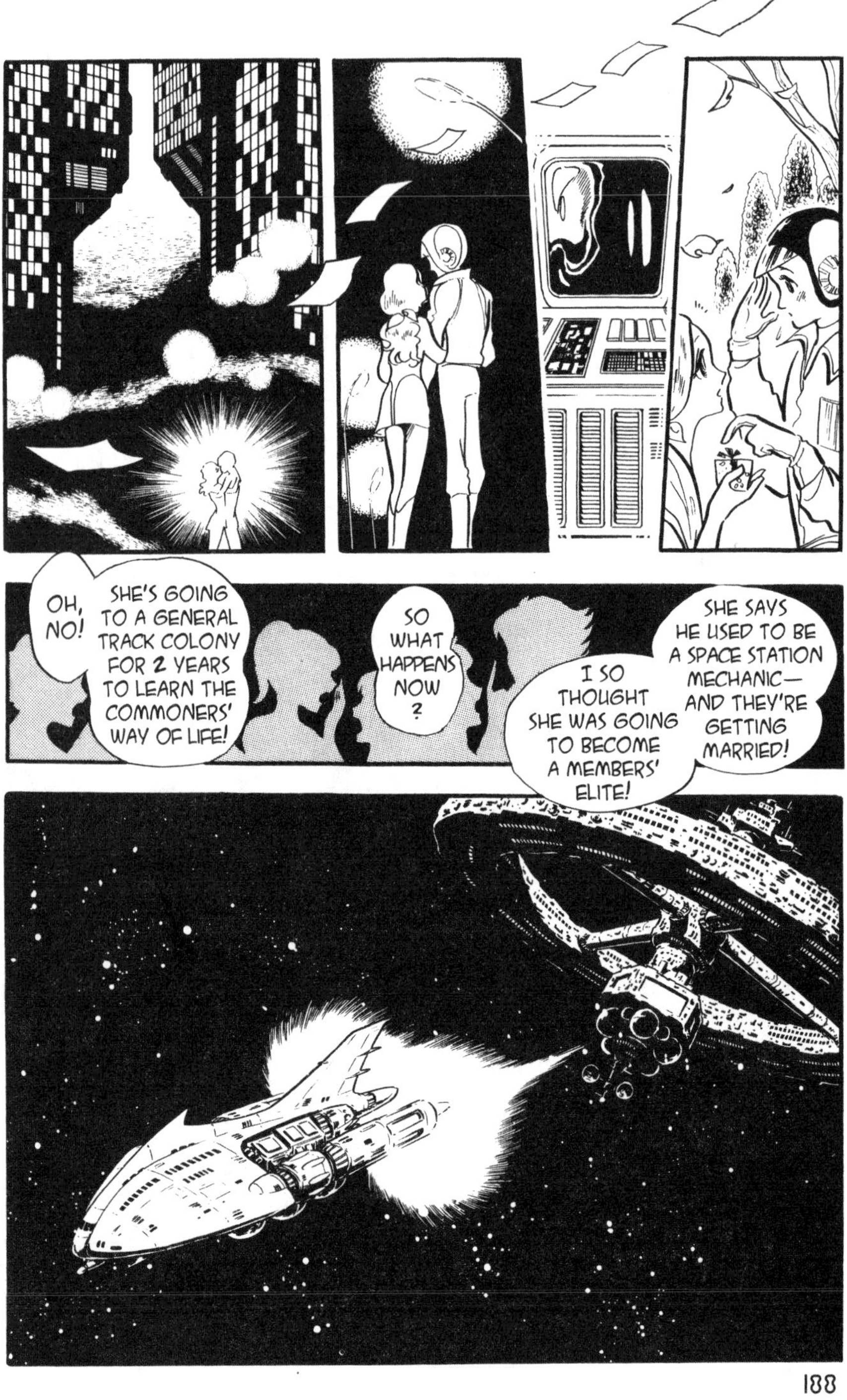
SHE SAYS HE USED TO BE A SPACE STATION MECHANIC— AND THEY'RE GETTING MARRIED!
I SO THOUGHT SHE WAS GOING TO BECOME A MEMBERS' ELITE!
SO WHAT HAPPENS NOW?
SHE'S GOING TO A GENERAL TRACK COLONY FOR 2 YEARS TO LEARN THE COMMONERS' WAY OF LIFE!
OH, NO!

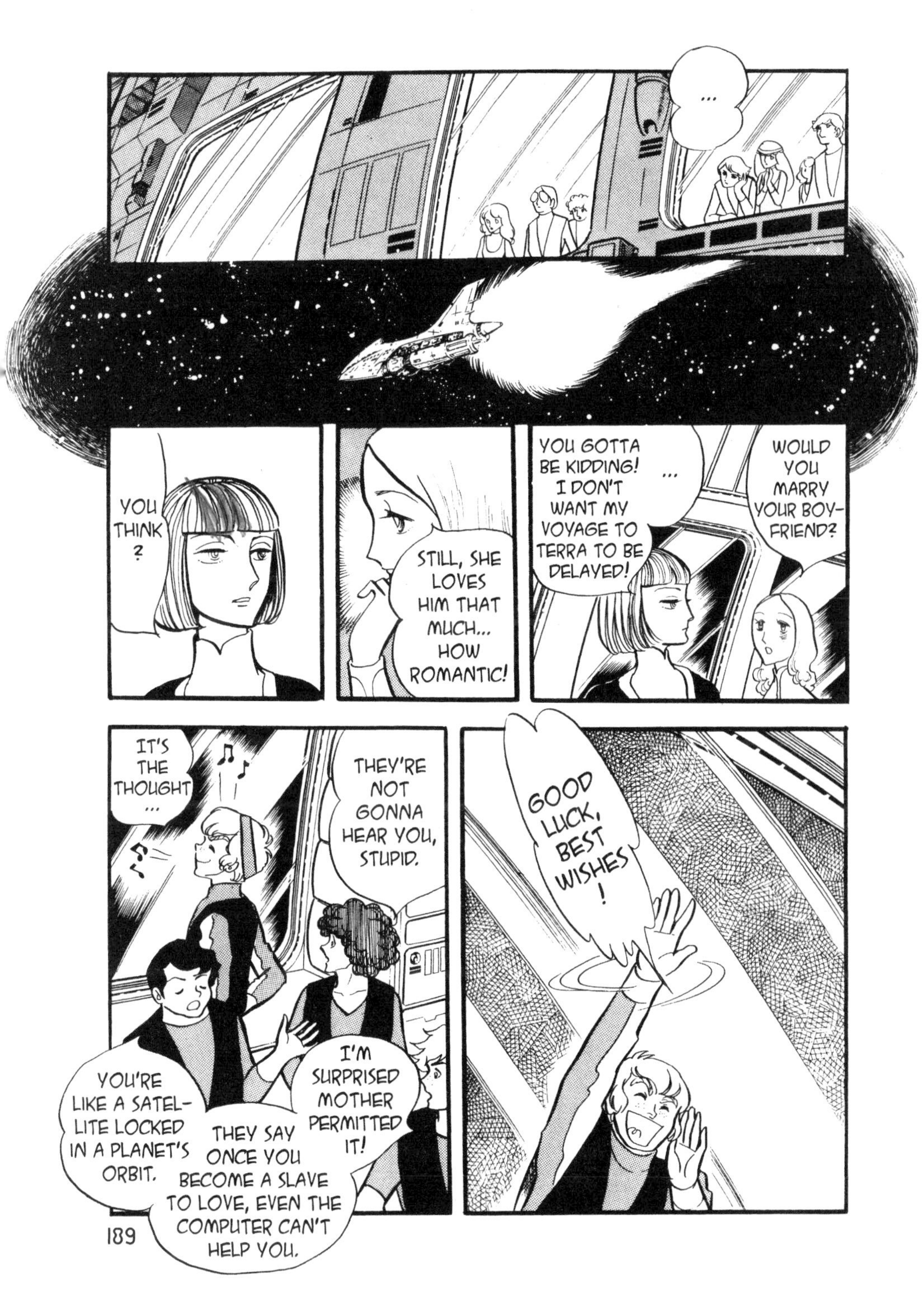
...
WOULD YOU MARRY YOUR BOY-FRIEND?
YOU GOTTA BE KIDDING! I DON'T WANT MY VOYAGE TO TERRA TO BE DELAYED!
...
STILL, SHE LOVES HIM THAT MUCH... HOW ROMANTIC!
YOU THINK?
GOOD LUCK, BEST WISHES!
IT'S THE THOUGHT ...
THEY'RE NOT GONNA HEAR YOU, STUPID.
I'M SURPRISED MOTHER PERMITTED IT!
YOU'RE LIKE A SATEL-LITE LOCKED IN A PLANET'S ORBIT.
THEY SAY ONCE YOU BECOME A SLAVE TO LOVE, EVEN THE COMPUTER CAN'T HELP YOU.

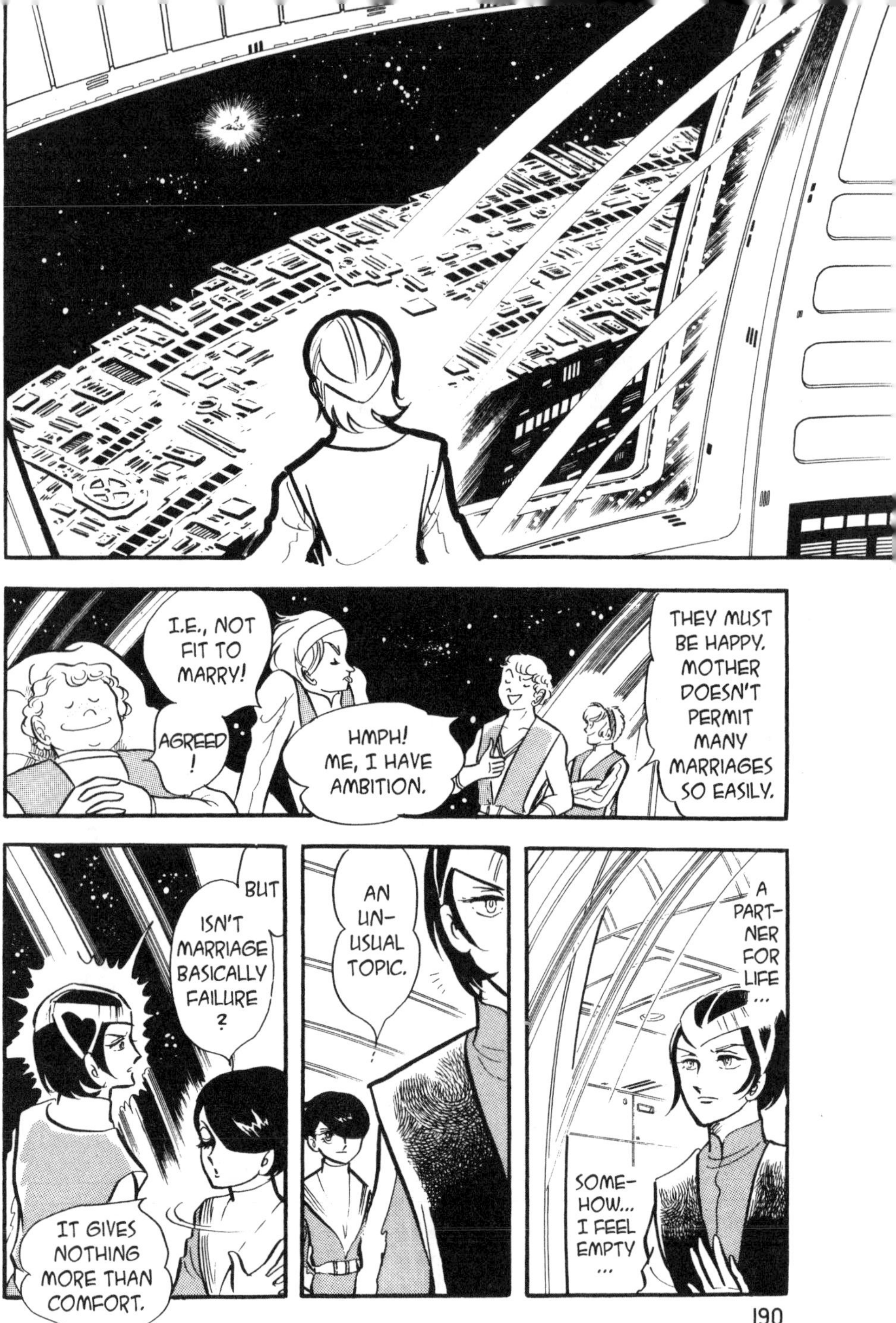
THEY MUST BE HAPPY. MOTHER DOESN'T PERMIT MANY MARRIAGES SO EASILY.
HMPH! ME, I HAVE AMBITION.
I.E., NOT FIT TO MARRY!
AGREED!
A PARTNER FOR LIFE...
SOMEHOW... I FEEL EMPTY...
AN UNUSUAL TOPIC.
BUT ISN'T MARRIAGE BASICALLY FAILURE?
IT GIVES NOTHING MORE THAN COMFORT.

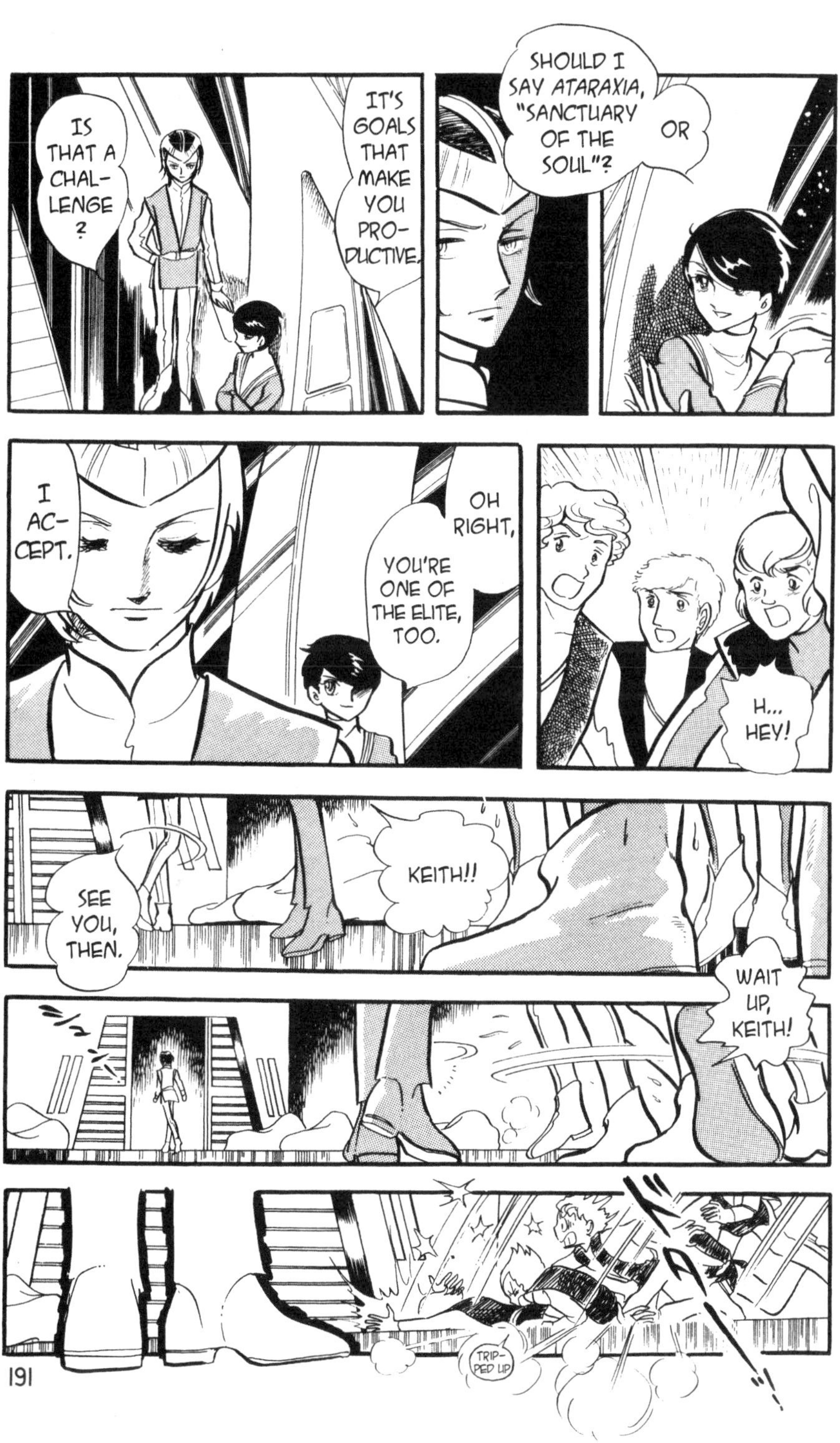
OR
SHOULD I SAY ATARAXIA, "SANCTUARY OF THE SOUL"?
IT'S GOALS THAT MAKE YOU PRODUCTIVE.
IS THAT A CHALLENGE?
H... HEY!
OH RIGHT, YOU'RE ONE OF THE ELITE, TOO.
I ACCEPT.
KEITH!!
SEE YOU, THEN.
WAIT UP, KEITH!
TRIPPED UP

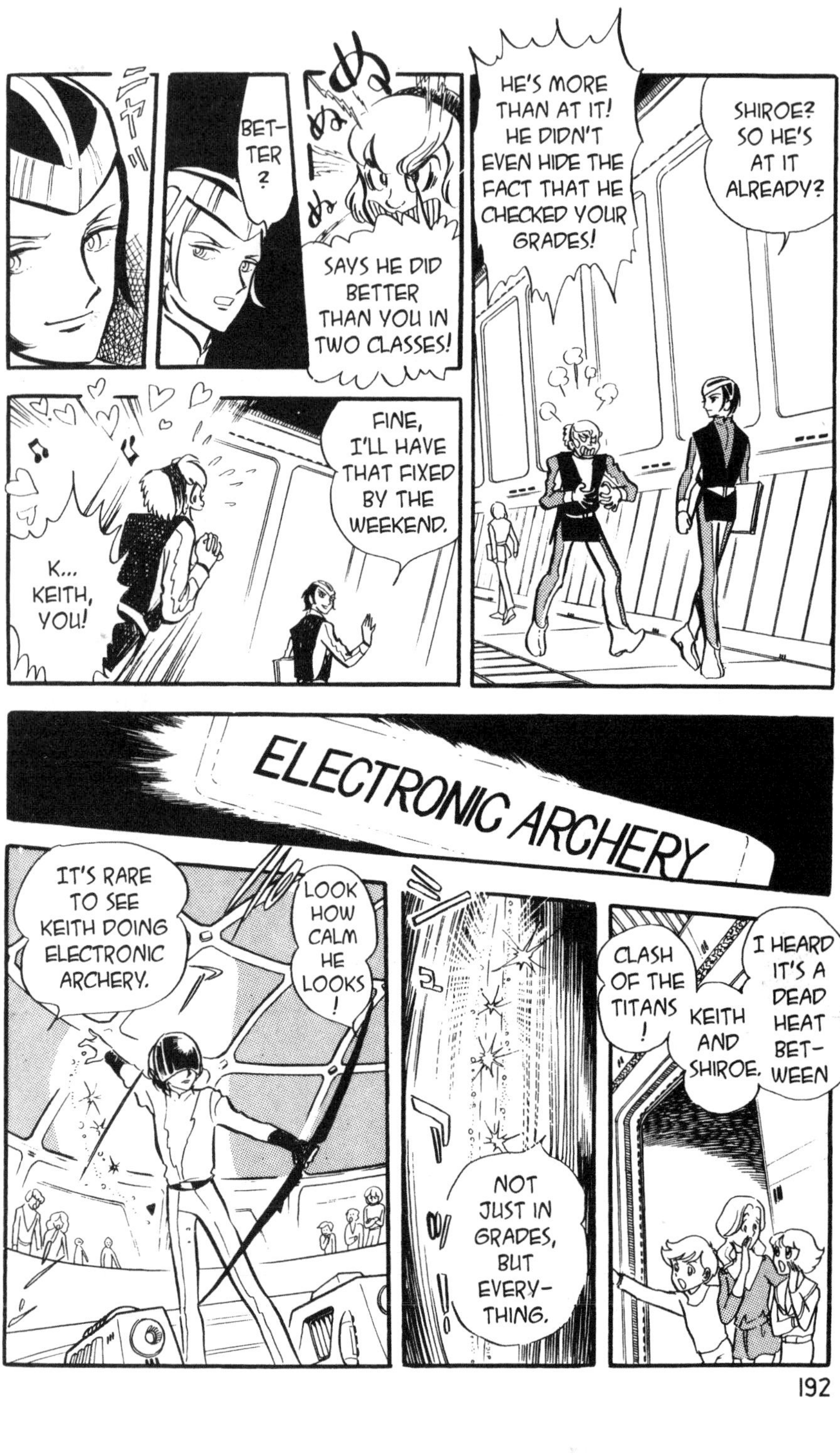
SHIROE? SO HE'S AT IT ALREADY?
HE'S MORE THAN AT IT! HE DIDN'T EVEN HIDE THE FACT THAT HE CHECKED YOUR GRADES!
ぬ ぬ ぬ ぬ
SAYS HE DID BETTER THAN YOU IN TWO CLASSES!
BET-TER?
ニヤリ
FINE, I'LL HAVE THAT FIXED BY THE WEEKEND.
K... KEITH, YOU!
ELECTRONIC ARCHERY
I HEARD IT'S A DEAD HEAT BET-WEEN
KEITH AND SHIROE.
CLASH OF THE TITANS!
NOT JUST IN GRADES, BUT EVERY-THING.
IT'S RARE TO SEE KEITH DOING ELECTRONIC ARCHERY.
LOOK HOW CALM HE LOOKS!

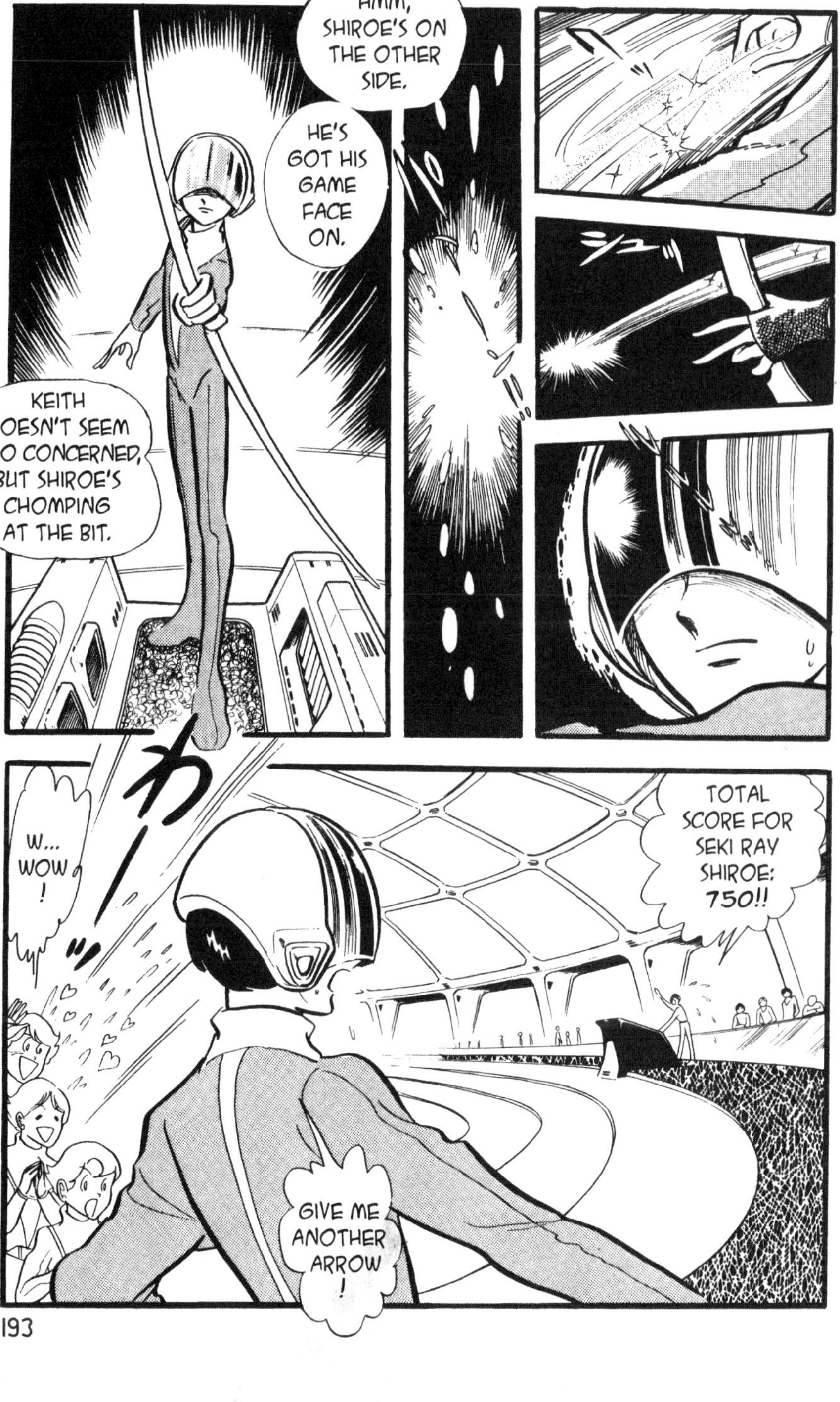
HMM, SHIROE'S ON THE OTHER SIDE.
HE'S GOT HIS GAME FACE ON.
KEITH DOESN'T SEEM TOO CONCERNED, BUT SHIROE'S CHOMPING AT THE BIT.
TOTAL SCORE FOR SEKI RAY SHIROE: 750!!
わー
W... WOW!
GIVE ME ANOTHER ARROW!

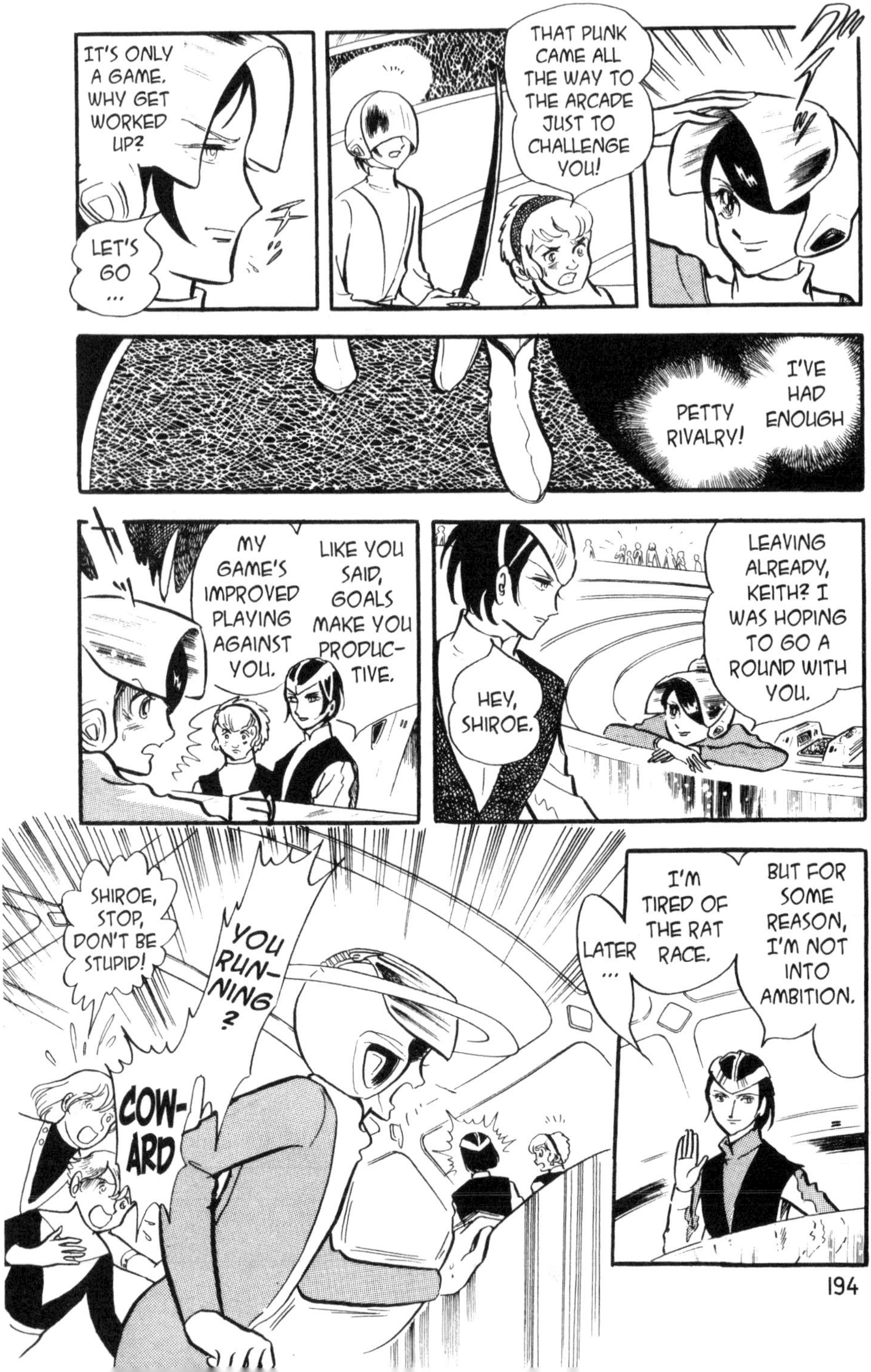
THAT PUNK CAME ALL THE WAY TO THE ARCADE JUST TO CHALLENGE YOU!
IT'S ONLY A GAME. WHY GET WORKED UP?
LET'S GO ...
I'VE HAD ENOUGH
PETTY RIVALRY!
LEAVING ALREADY, KEITH? I WAS HOPING TO GO A ROUND WITH YOU.
HEY, SHIROE.
LIKE YOU SAID, GOALS MAKE YOU PRODUC-TIVE.
MY GAME'S IMPROVED PLAYING AGAINST YOU.
BUT FOR SOME REASON, I'M NOT INTO AMBITION.
I'M TIRED OF THE RAT RACE.
LATER ...
YOU RUN-NING?
COW-ARD
SHIROE, STOP, DON'T BE STUPID!

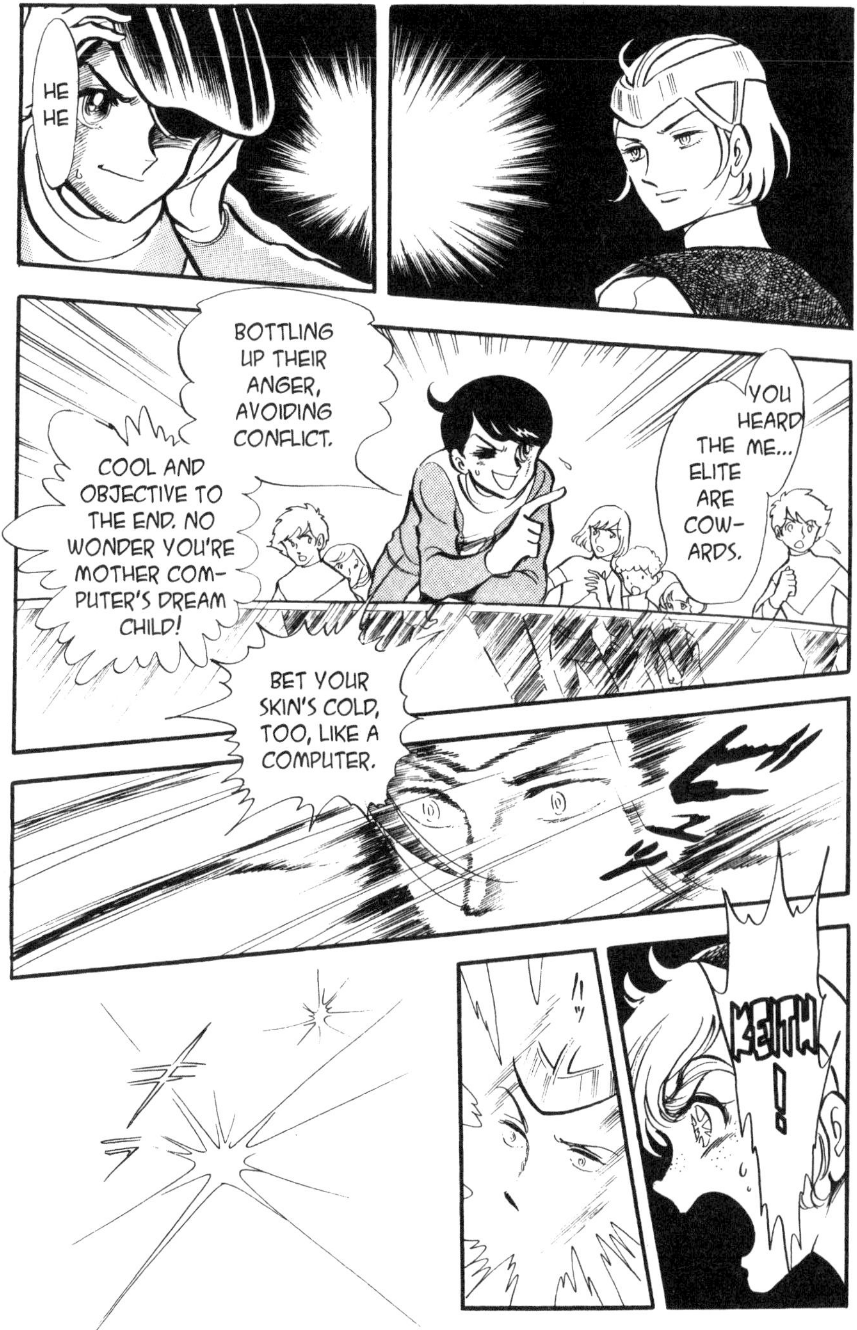
HE HE
YOU HEARD ME... THE ELITE ARE COWARDS.
BOTTLING UP THEIR ANGER, AVOIDING CONFLICT.
COOL AND OBJECTIVE TO THE END. NO WONDER YOU'RE MOTHER COMPUTER'S DREAM CHILD!
BET YOUR SKIN'S COLD, TOO, LIKE A COMPUTER.
KEITH!

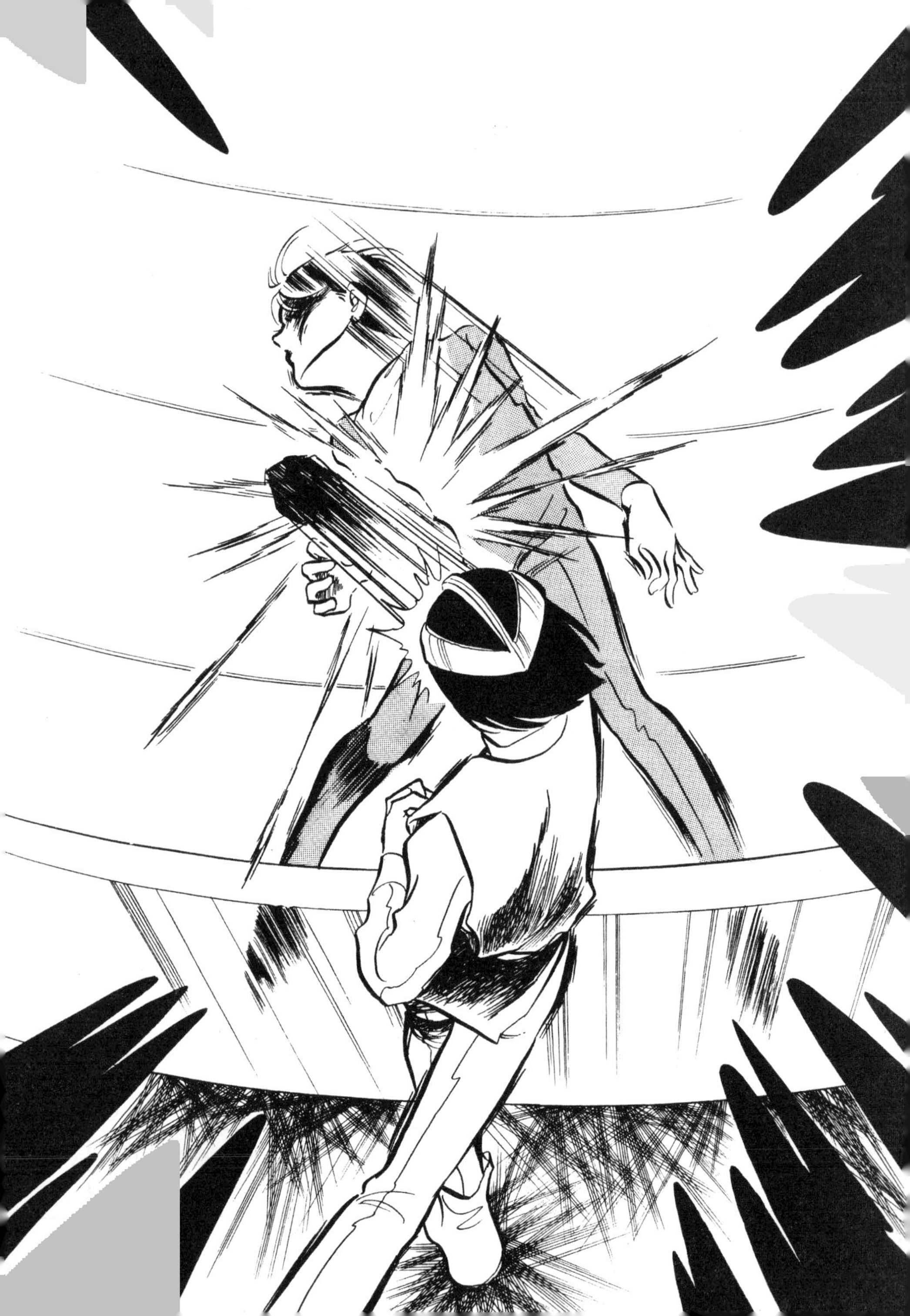

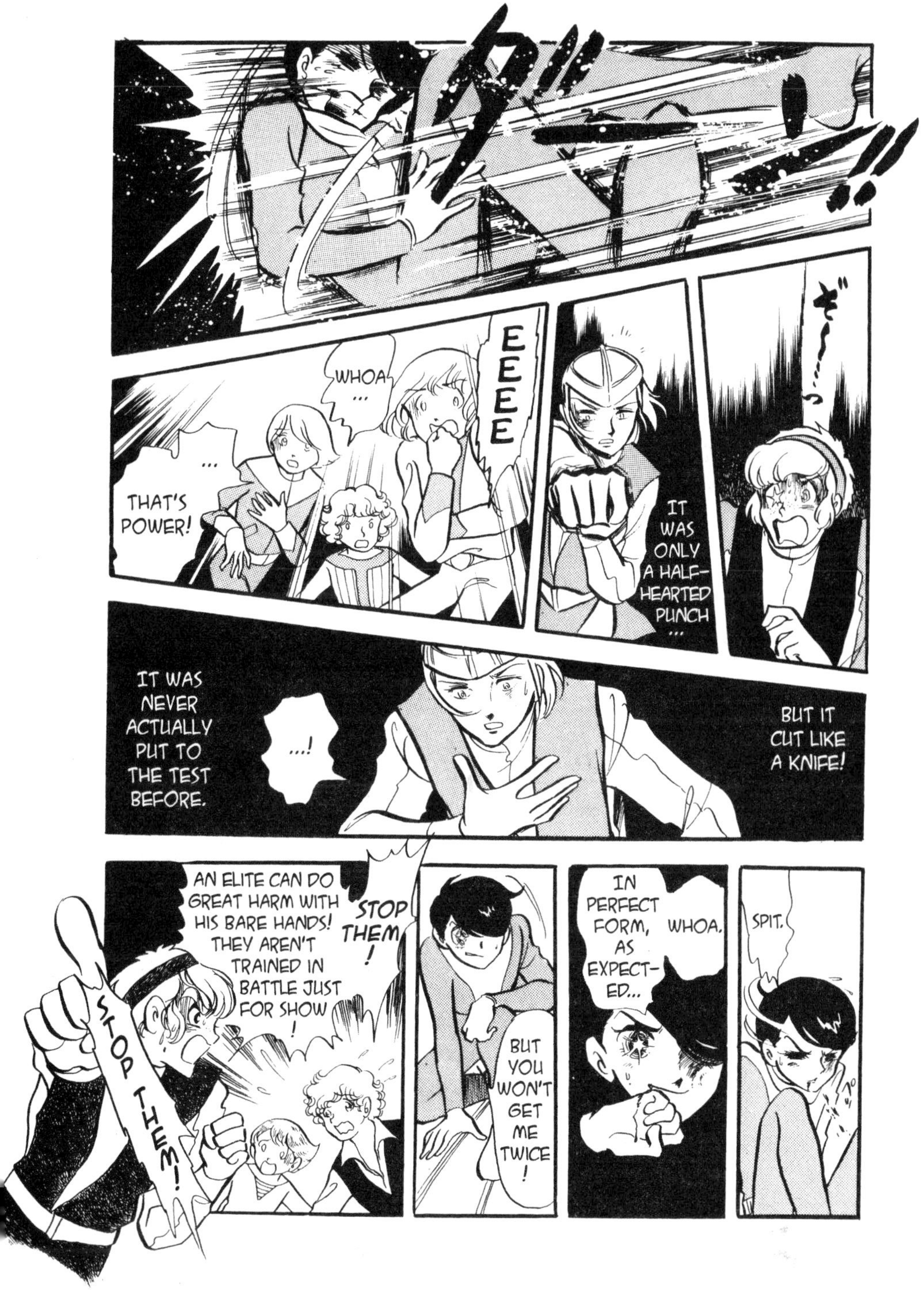
EEEE
WHOA ...
...
THAT'S POWER!
IT WAS ONLY A HALF-HEARTED PUNCH ...
BUT IT CUT LIKE A KNIFE!
...!
IT WAS NEVER ACTUALLY PUT TO THE TEST BEFORE.
SPIT.
WHOA.
IN PERFECT FORM, AS EXPECTED...
BUT YOU WON'T GET ME TWICE!
STOP THEM!
AN ELITE CAN DO GREAT HARM WITH HIS BARE HANDS! THEY AREN'T TRAINED IN BATTLE JUST FOR SHOW!
STOP THEM!

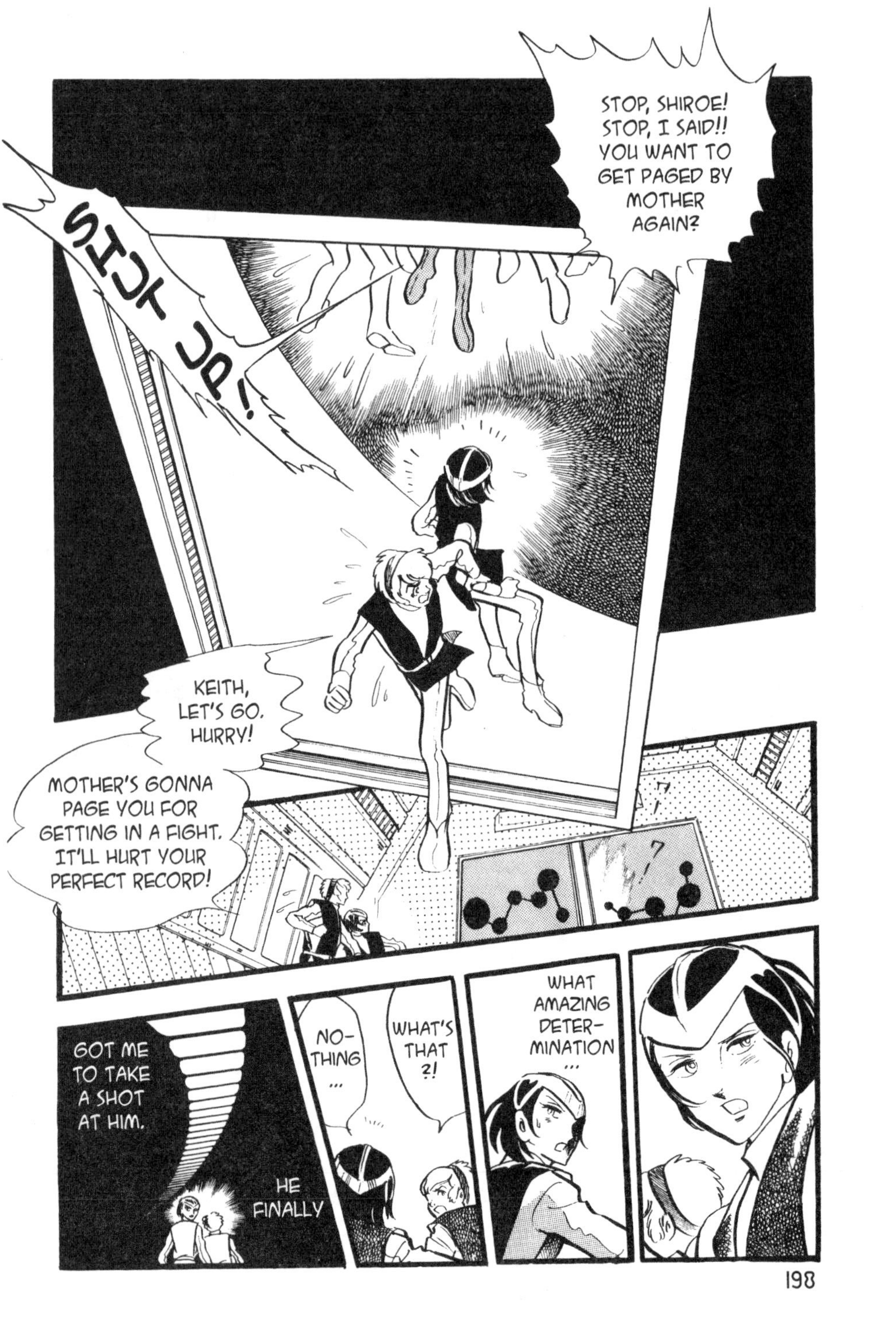
STOP, SHIROE! STOP, I SAID!! YOU WANT TO GET PAGED BY MOTHER AGAIN?
SHUT UP!
KEITH, LET'S GO. HURRY!
MOTHER'S GONNA PAGE YOU FOR GETTING IN A FIGHT. IT'LL HURT YOUR PERFECT RECORD!
?!
WHAT AMAZING DETER-MINATION ...
WHAT'S THAT ?!
NO-THING ...
HE FINALLY
GOT ME TO TAKE A SHOT AT HIM.

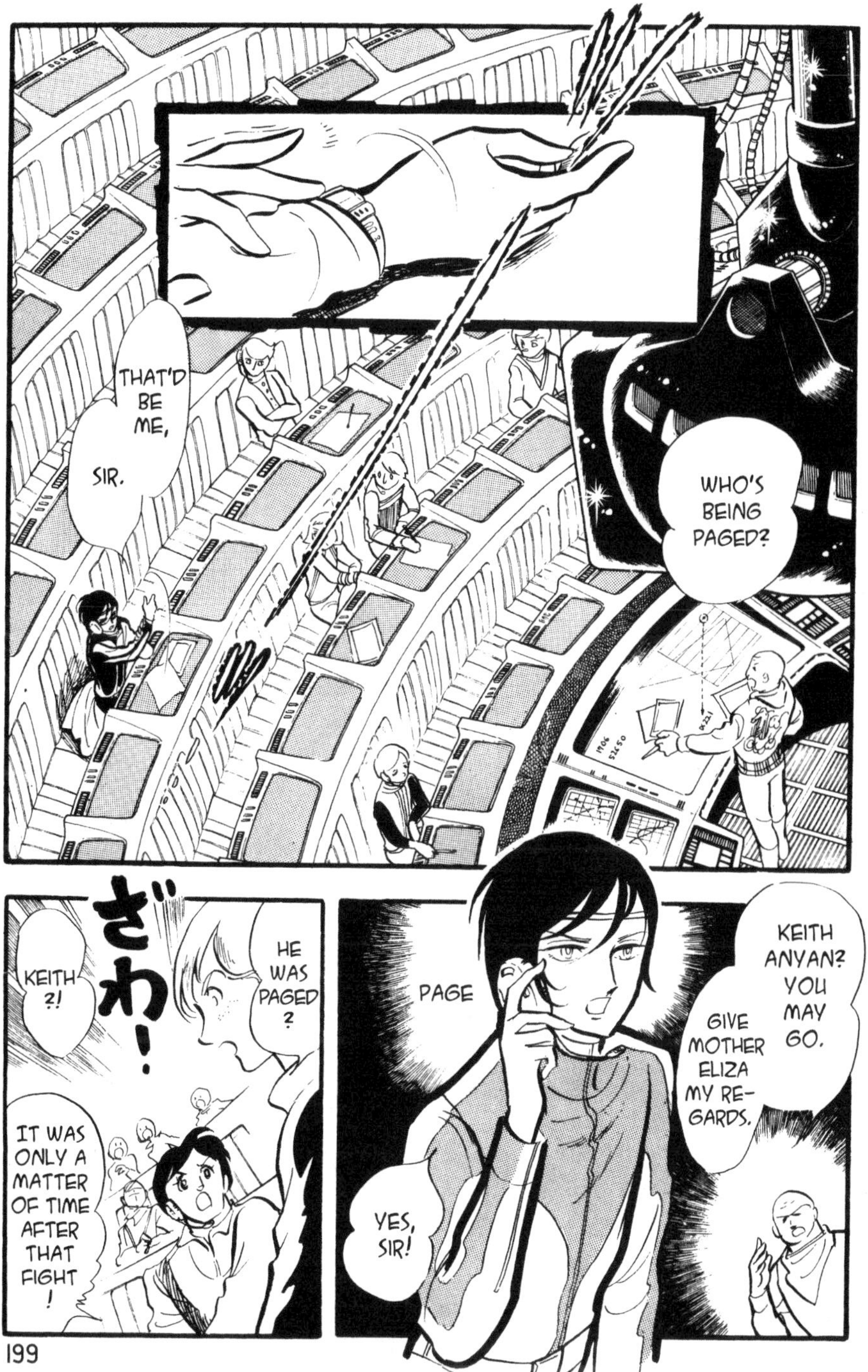
WHO'S BEING PAGED?
THAT'D BE ME, SIR.
KEITH ANYAN? YOU MAY GO.
GIVE MOTHER ELIZA MY REGARDS.
PAGE
YES, SIR!
ざわ！
HE WAS PAGED?
KEITH?!
IT WAS ONLY A MATTER OF TIME AFTER THAT FIGHT!

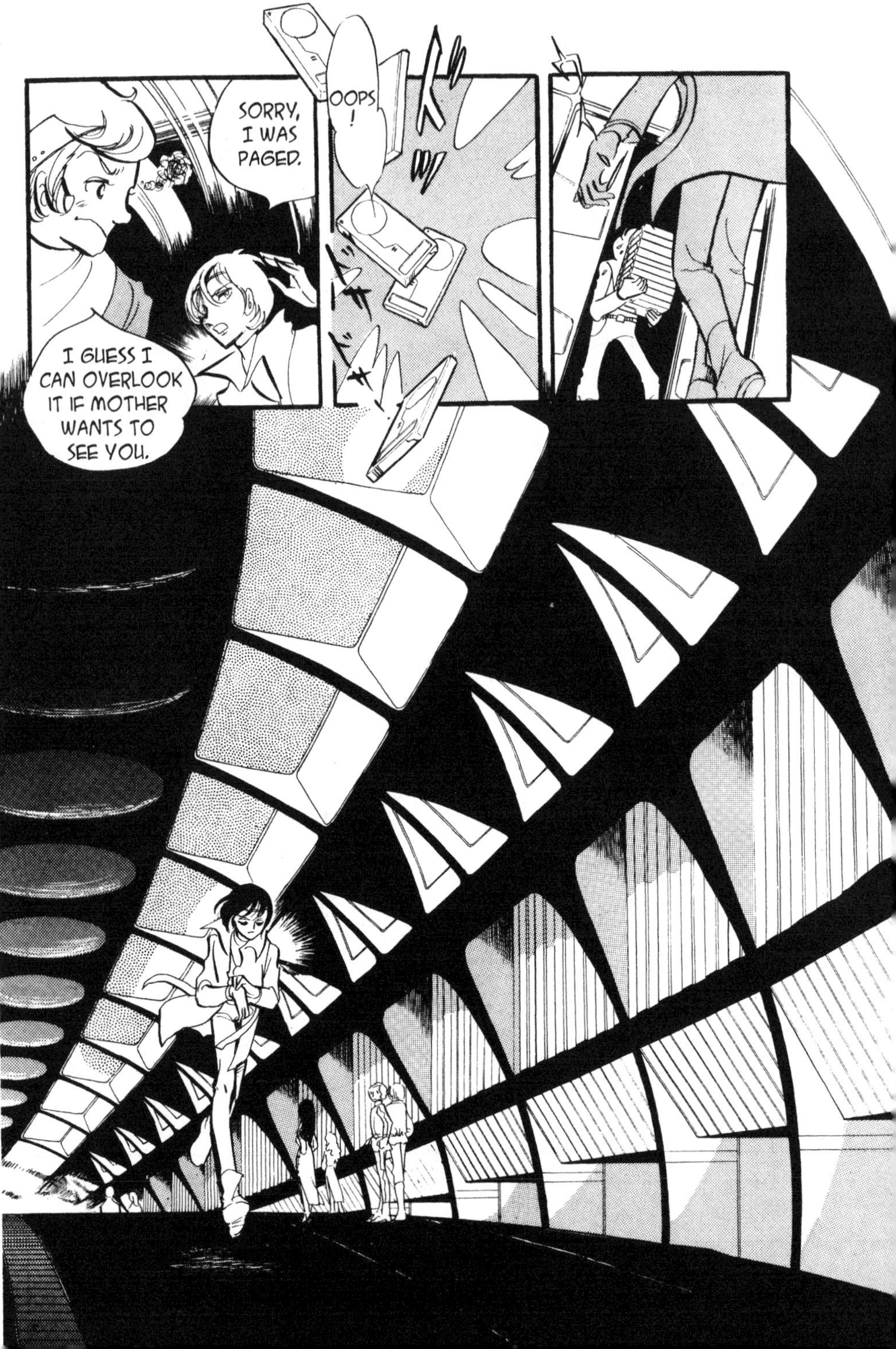
OOPS!
SORRY, I WAS PAGED.
I GUESS I CAN OVERLOOK IT IF MOTHER WANTS TO SEE YOU.

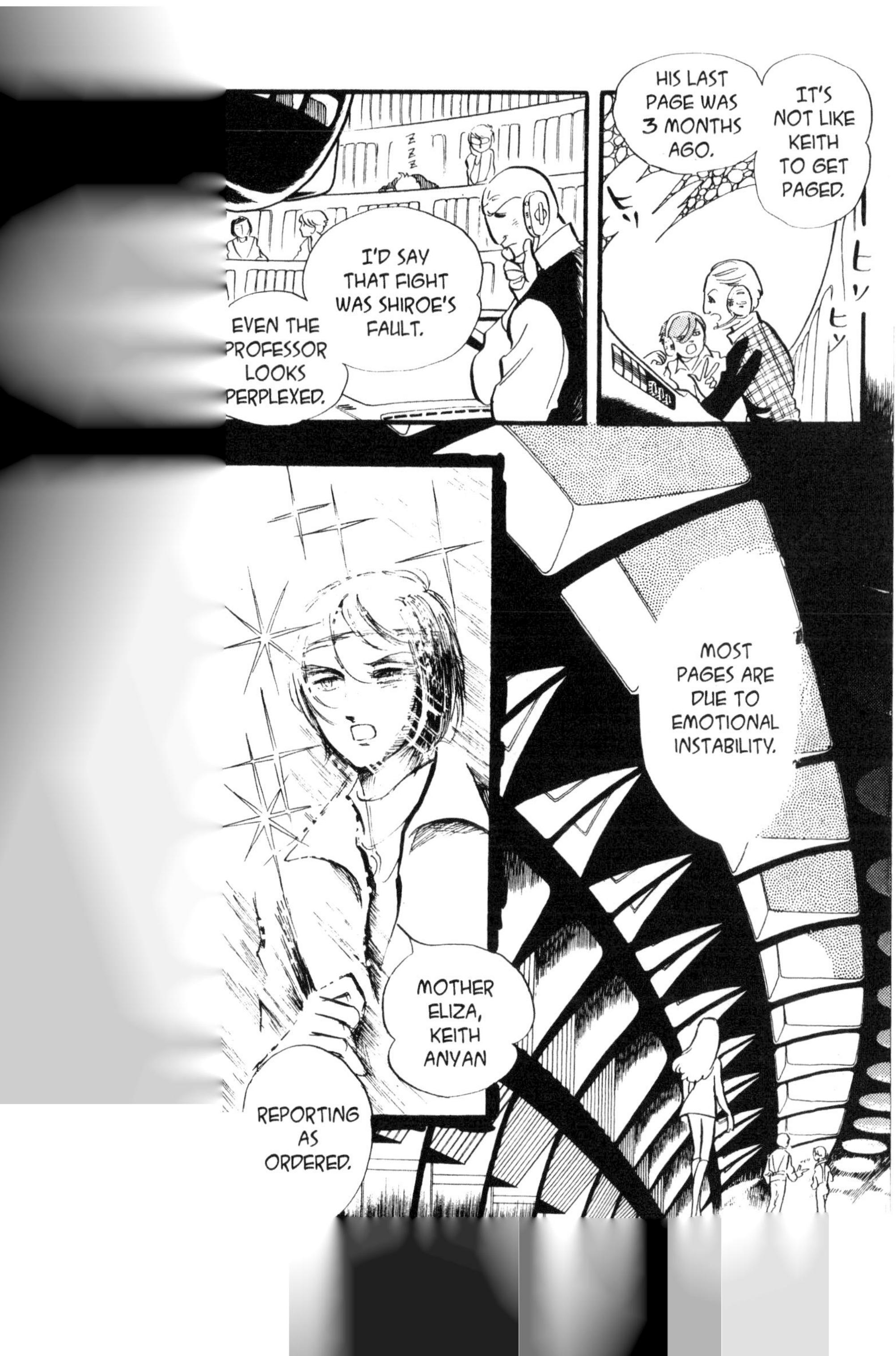
IT'S NOT LIKE KEITH TO GET PAGED.
HIS LAST PAGE WAS 3 MONTHS AGO.
I'D SAY THAT FIGHT WAS SHIROE'S FAULT.
EVEN THE PROFESSOR LOOKS PERPLEXED.
MOST PAGES ARE DUE TO EMOTIONAL INSTABILITY.
MOTHER ELIZA, KEITH ANYAN
REPORTING AS ORDERED.

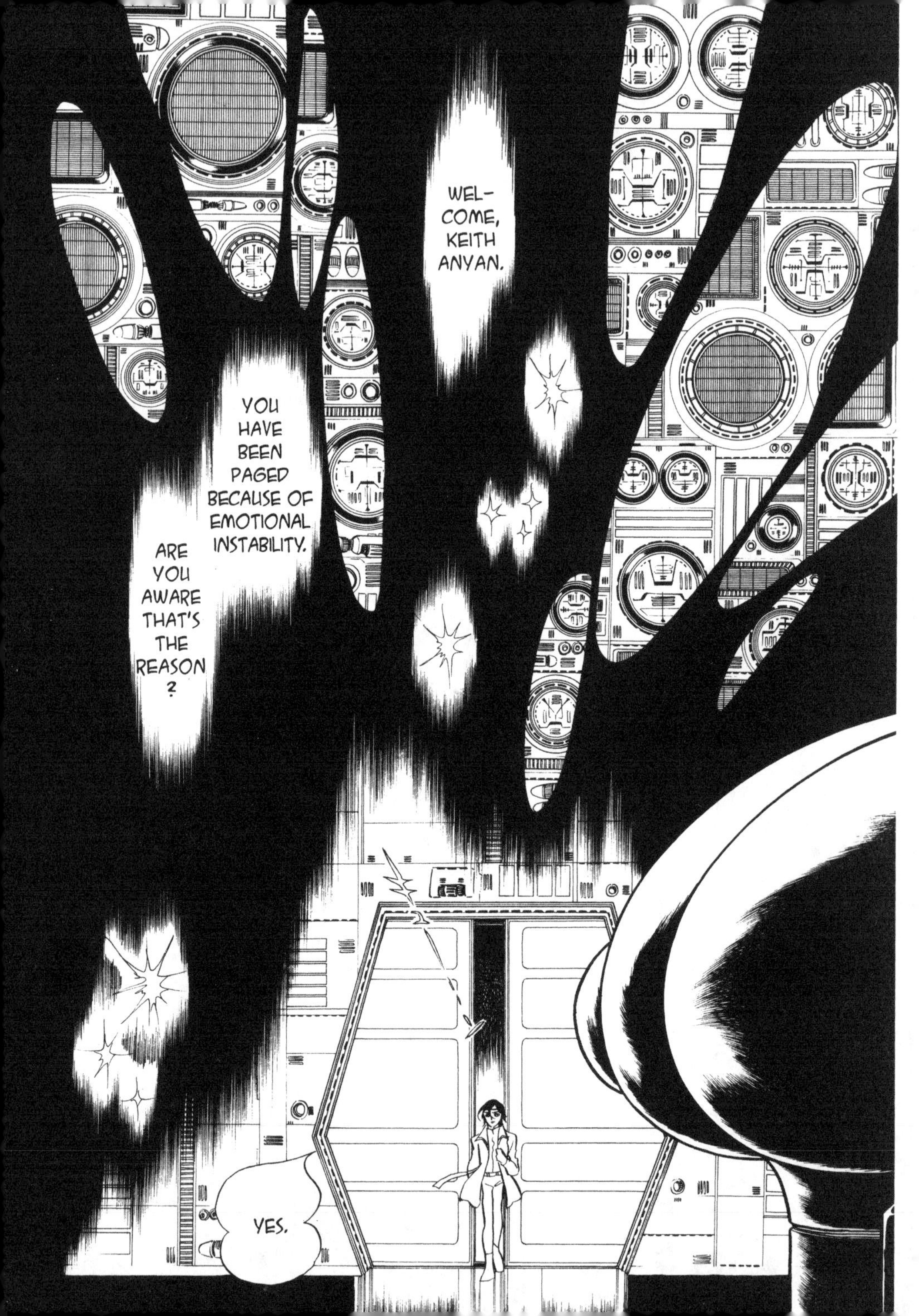
WEL-COME, KEITH ANYAN.
YOU HAVE BEEN PAGED BECAUSE OF EMOTIONAL INSTABILITY.
ARE YOU AWARE THAT'S THE REASON?
YES.

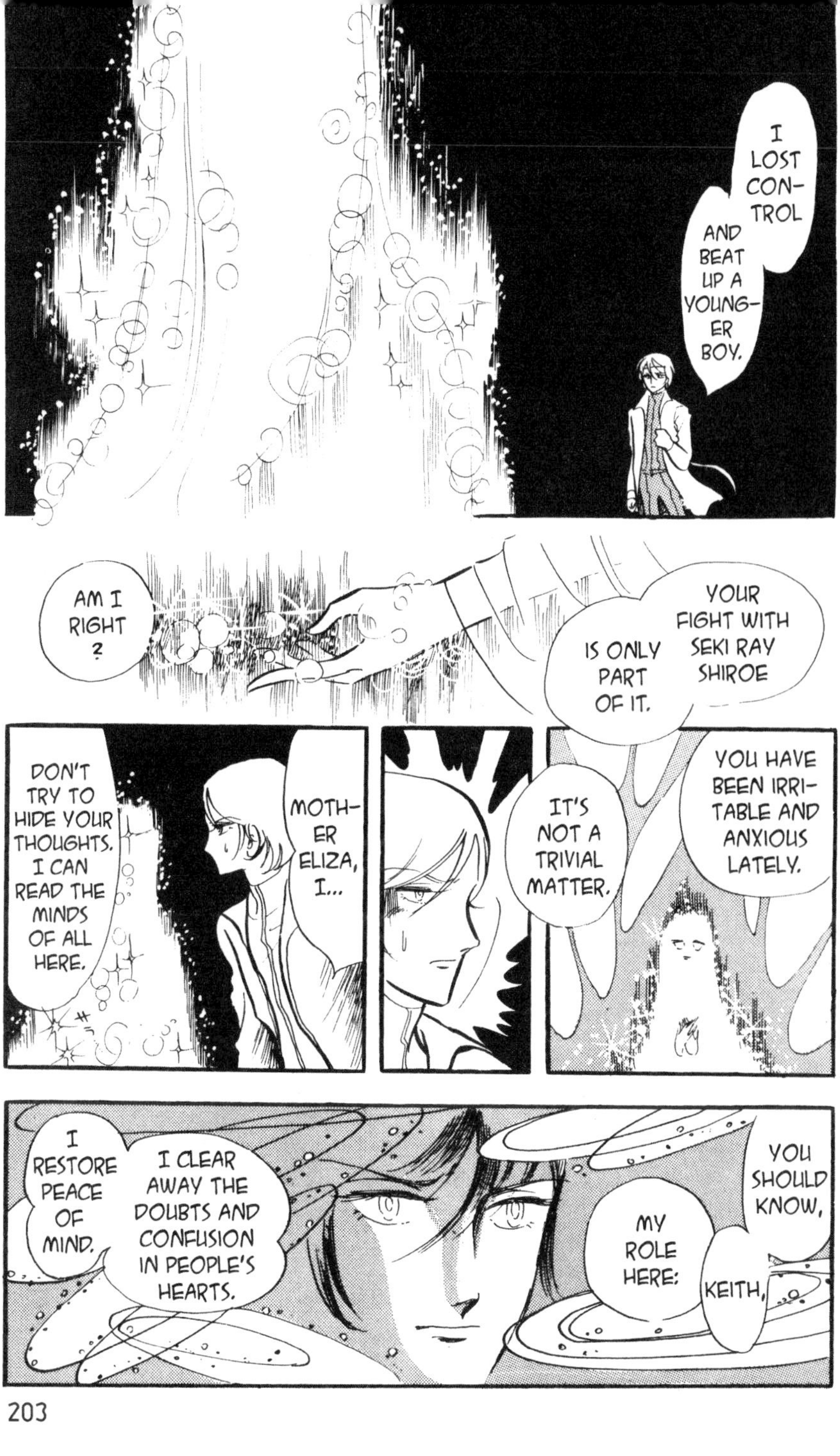
I LOST CONTROL
AND BEAT UP A YOUNGER BOY.
YOUR FIGHT WITH SEKI RAY SHIROE
IS ONLY PART OF IT.
AM I RIGHT?
YOU HAVE BEEN IRRITABLE AND ANXIOUS LATELY.
IT'S NOT A TRIVIAL MATTER.
MOTHER ELIZA, I...
DON'T TRY TO HIDE YOUR THOUGHTS. I CAN READ THE MINDS OF ALL HERE.
YOU SHOULD KNOW,
KEITH,
MY ROLE HERE:
I CLEAR AWAY THE DOUBTS AND CONFUSION IN PEOPLE'S HEARTS.
I RESTORE PEACE OF MIND.

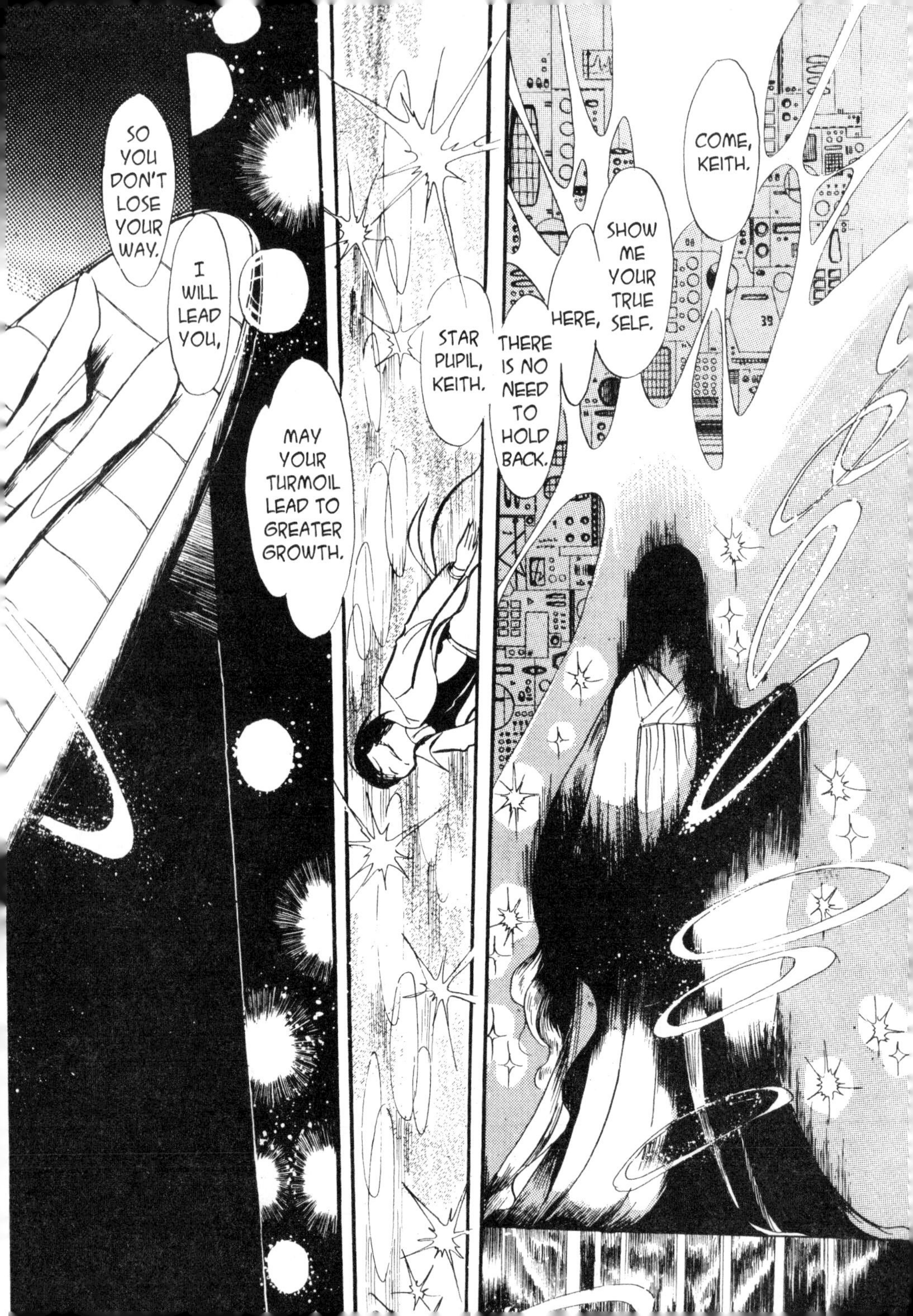
COME, KEITH.
SHOW ME YOUR TRUE SELF.
HERE,
THERE IS NO NEED TO HOLD BACK.
STAR PUPIL, KEITH.
MAY YOUR TURMOIL LEAD TO GREATER GROWTH.
I WILL LEAD YOU,
SO YOU DON'T LOSE YOUR WAY.

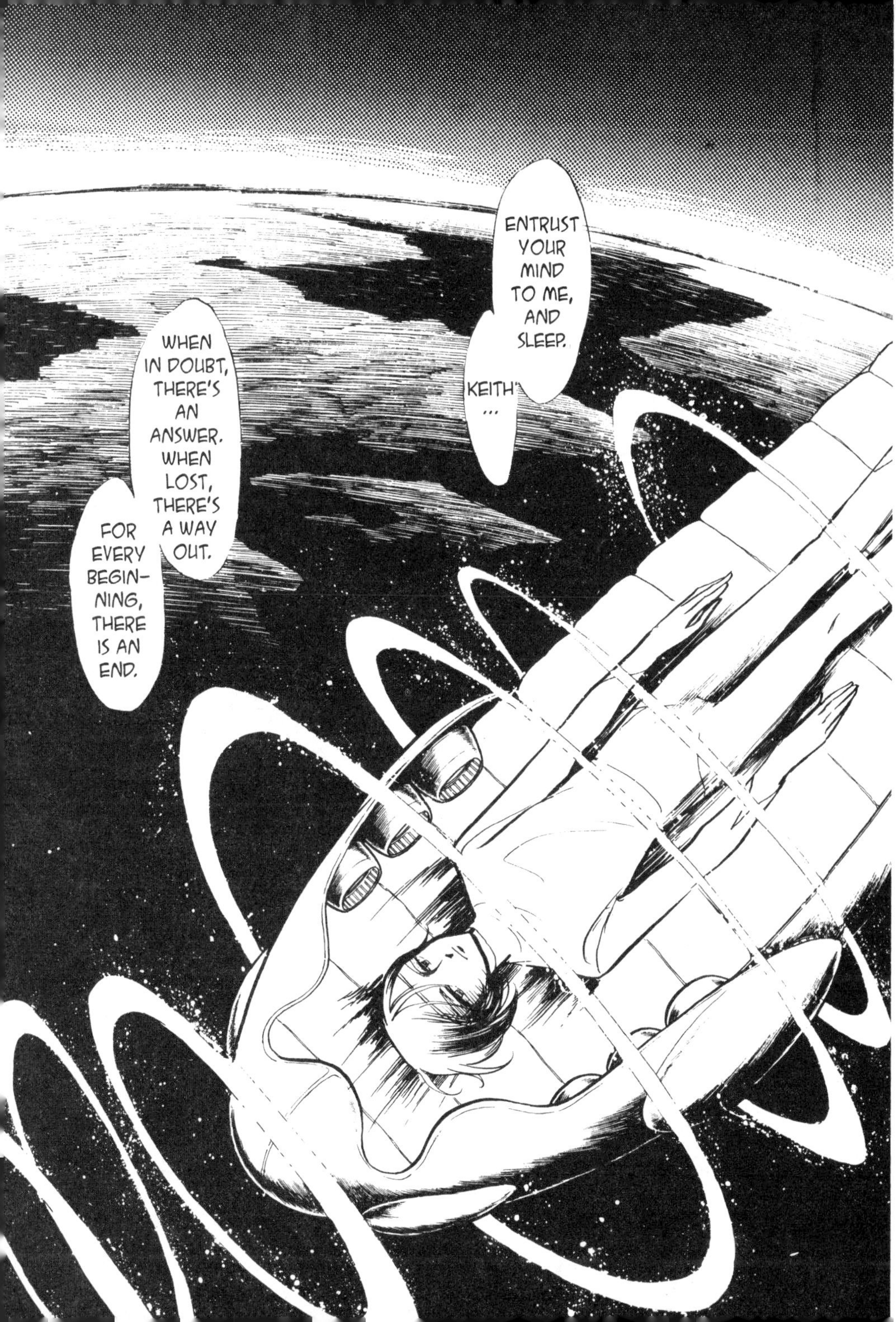
ENTRUST YOUR MIND TO ME, AND SLEEP.
KEITH...
WHEN IN DOUBT, THERE'S AN ANSWER. WHEN LOST, THERE'S A WAY OUT.
FOR EVERY BEGIN-NING, THERE IS AN END.

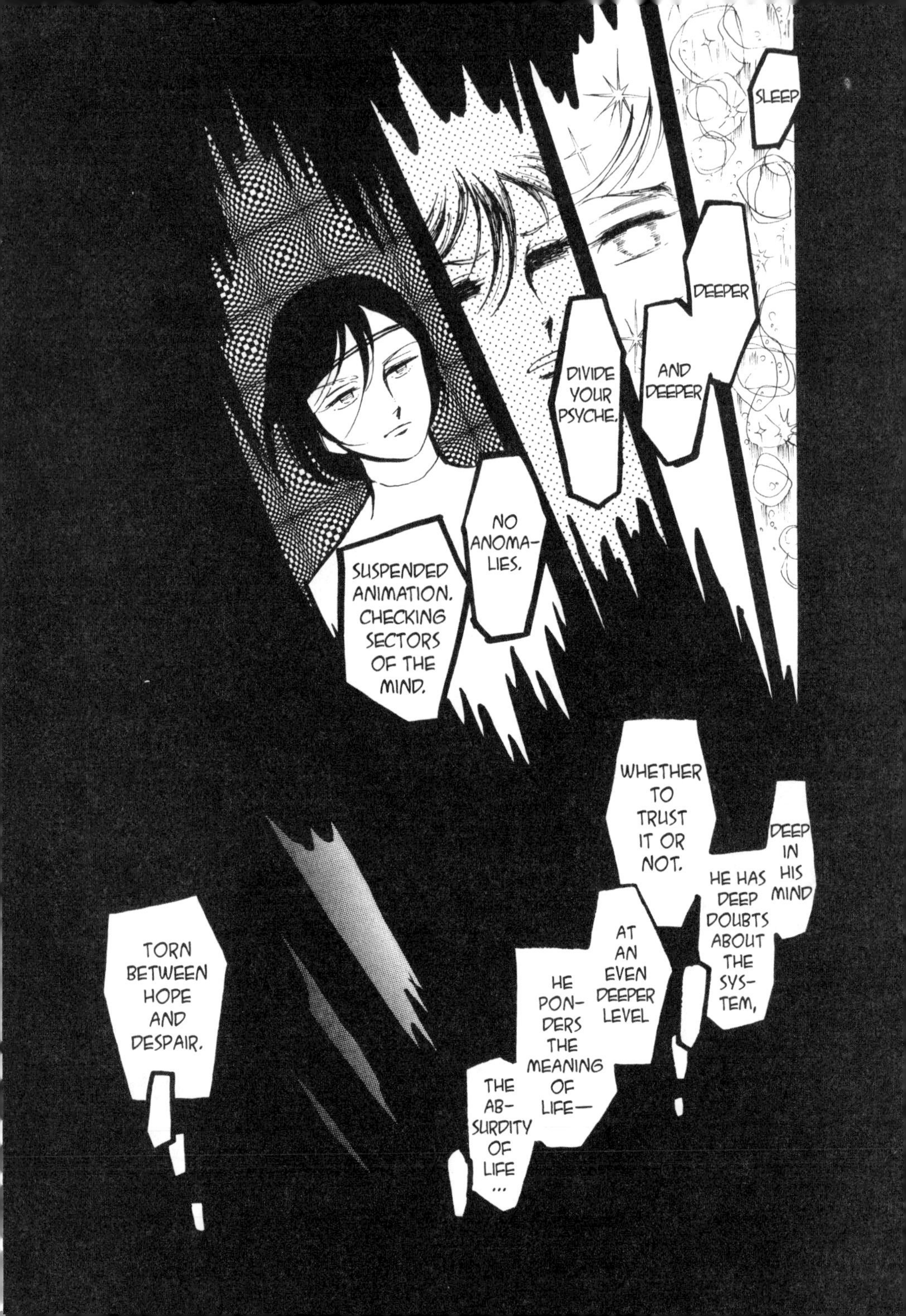
SLEEP
DEEPER
AND DEEPER
DIVIDE YOUR PSYCHE.
NO ANOMALIES.
SUSPENDED ANIMATION. CHECKING SECTORS OF THE MIND.
DEEP IN HIS MIND
HE HAS DEEP DOUBTS ABOUT THE SYSTEM,
WHETHER TO TRUST IT OR NOT.
AT AN EVEN DEEPER LEVEL
HE PONDERS THE MEANING OF LIFE—
THE ABSURDITY OF LIFE ...
TORN BETWEEN HOPE AND DESPAIR.

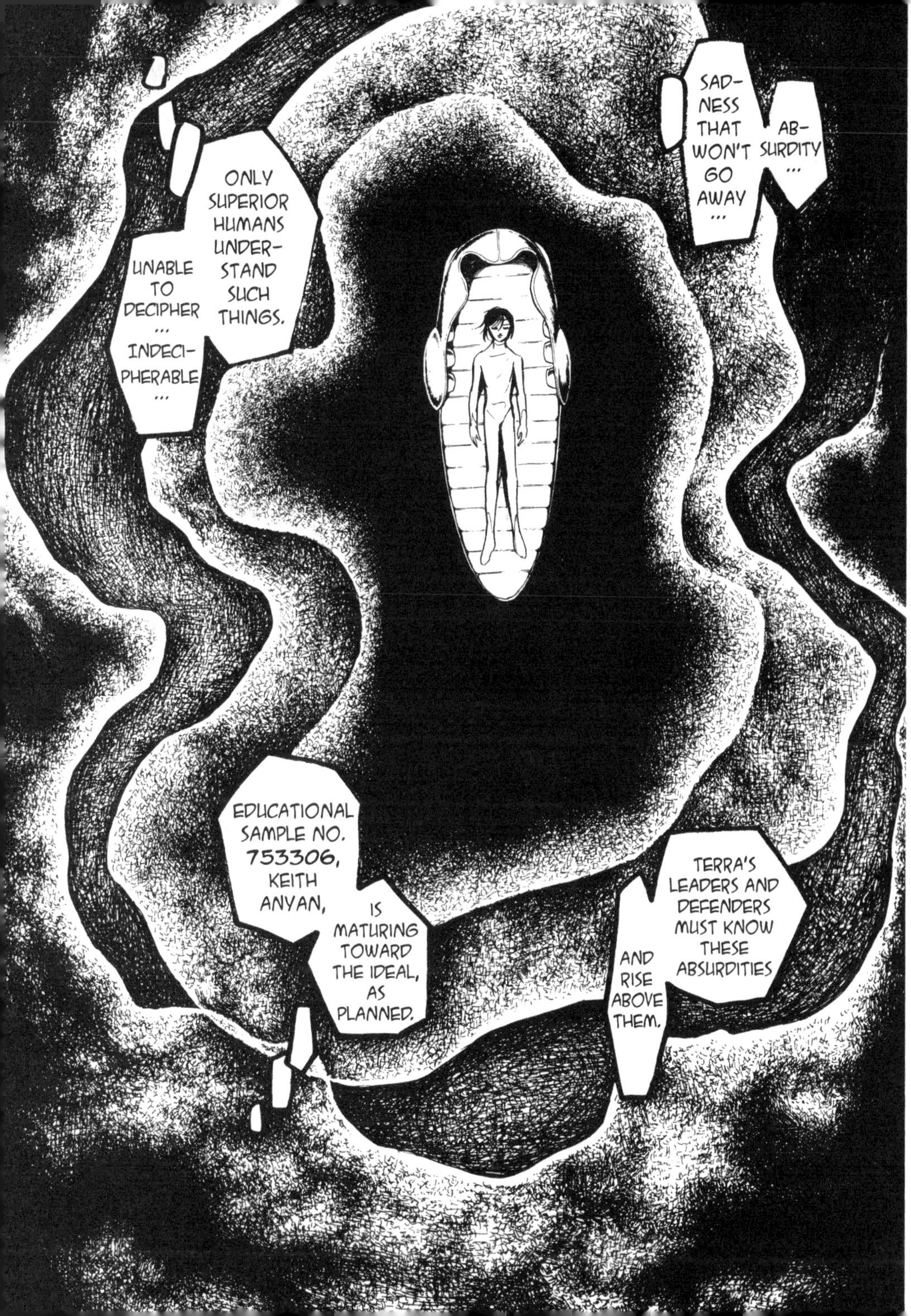

AB-SURDITY...
SAD-NESS THAT WON'T GO AWAY...
ONLY SUPERIOR HUMANS UNDER-STAND SUCH THINGS.
UNABLE TO DECIPHER... INDECI-PHERABLE...
TERRA'S LEADERS AND DEFENDERS MUST KNOW THESE ABSURDITIES
AND RISE ABOVE THEM.
EDUCATIONAL SAMPLE NO. 753306, KEITH ANYAN,
IS MATURING TOWARD THE IDEAL, AS PLANNED.

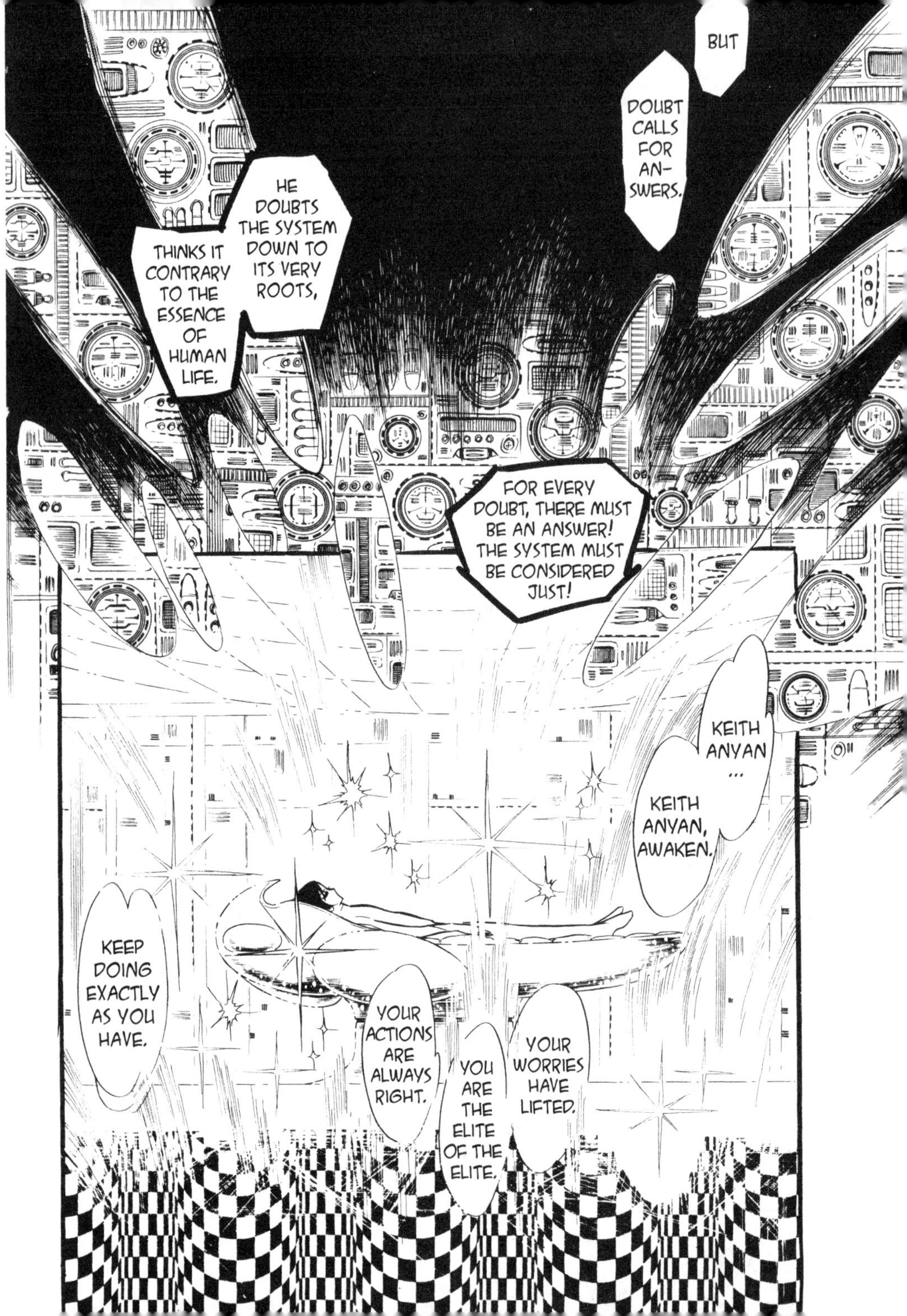
HE DOUBTS THE SYSTEM DOWN TO ITS VERY ROOTS,
THINKS IT CONTRARY TO THE ESSENCE OF HUMAN LIFE.
BUT
DOUBT CALLS FOR AN-SWERS.
FOR EVERY DOUBT, THERE MUST BE AN ANSWER! THE SYSTEM MUST BE CONSIDERED JUST!
KEITH ANYAN ...
KEITH ANYAN, AWAKEN.
YOUR WORRIES HAVE LIFTED.
YOU ARE THE ELITE OF THE ELITE.
YOUR ACTIONS ARE ALWAYS RIGHT.
KEEP DOING EXACTLY AS YOU HAVE.

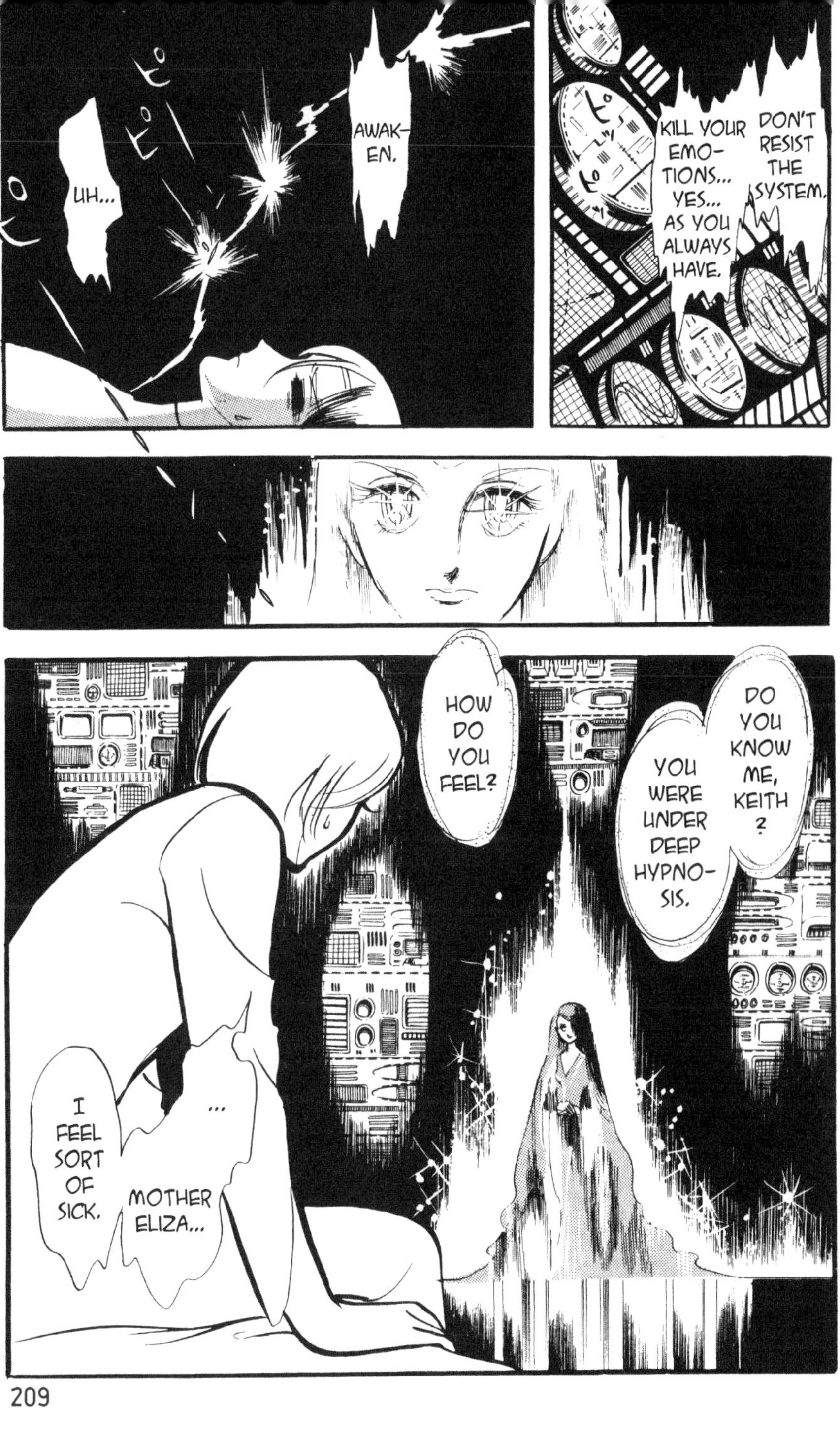
DON'T RESIST THE SYSTEM.
KILL YOUR EMOTIONS... YES... AS YOU ALWAYS HAVE.
AWAKEN.
UH...
DO YOU KNOW ME, KEITH?
YOU WERE UNDER DEEP HYPNOSIS.
HOW DO YOU FEEL?
...
MOTHER ELIZA...
I FEEL SORT OF SICK.

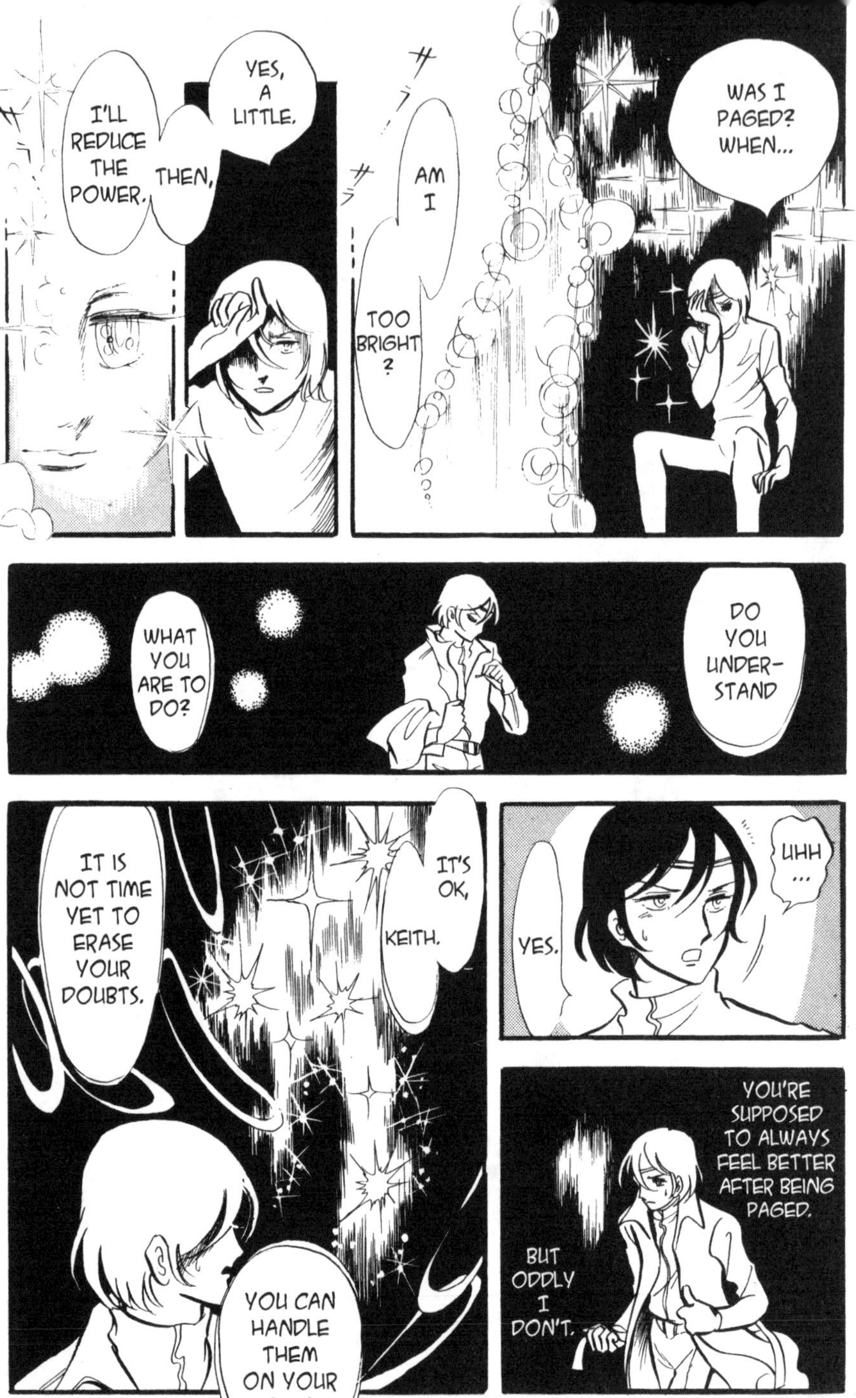
WAS I PAGED? WHEN...
AM I TOO BRIGHT?
YES, A LITTLE.
THEN,
I'LL REDUCE THE POWER.
DO YOU UNDERSTAND
WHAT YOU ARE TO DO?
UHH...
YES.
YOU'RE SUPPOSED TO ALWAYS FEEL BETTER AFTER BEING PAGED.
BUT ODDLY I DON'T.
IT'S OK, KEITH.
IT IS NOT TIME YET TO ERASE YOUR DOUBTS.
YOU CAN HANDLE THEM ON YOUR OWN.

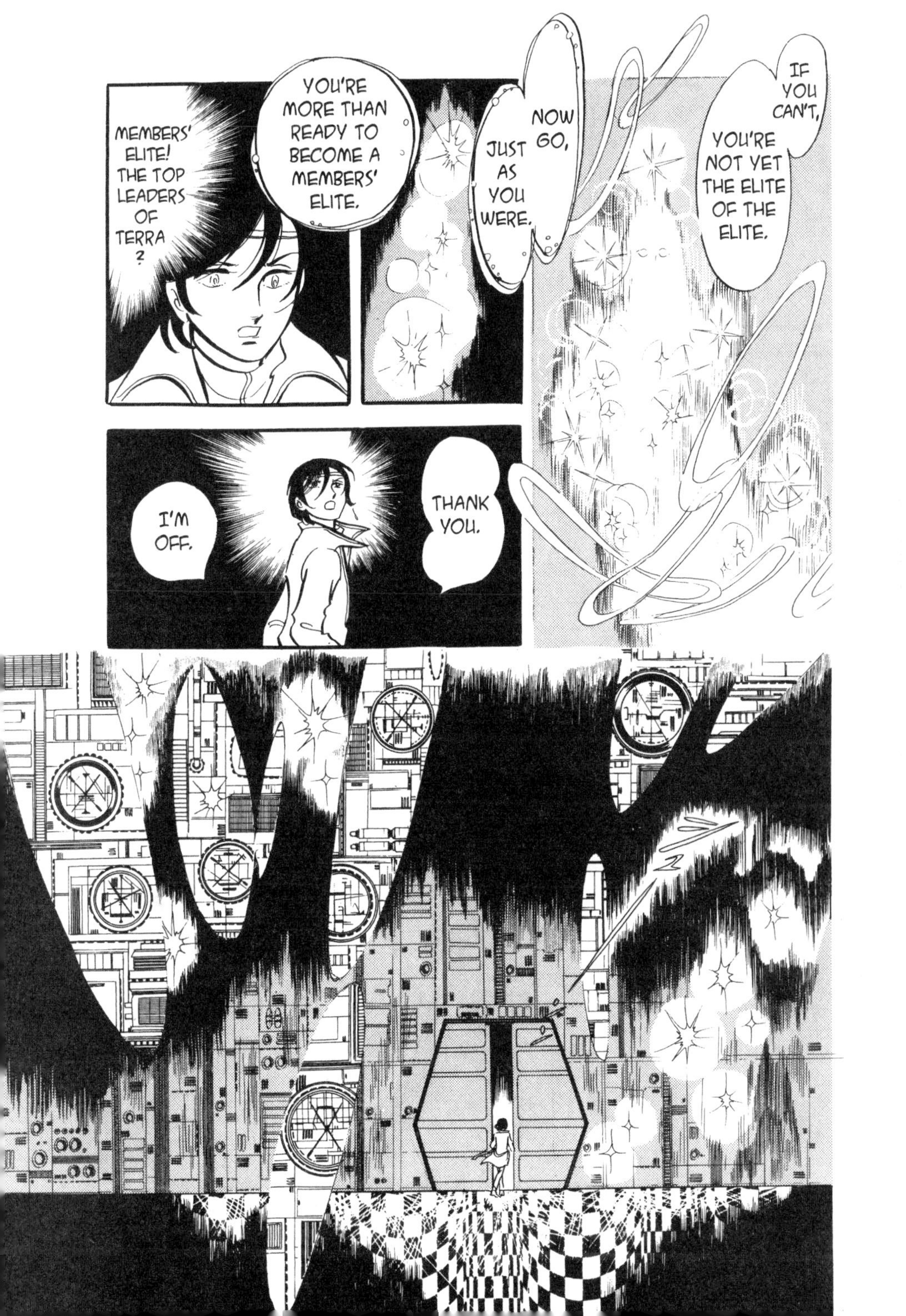
IF YOU CAN'T, YOU'RE NOT YET THE ELITE OF THE ELITE.
NOW GO, JUST AS YOU WERE.
YOU'RE MORE THAN READY TO BECOME A MEMBERS' ELITE.
MEMBERS' ELITE! THE TOP LEADERS OF TERRA?
THANK YOU.
I'M OFF.

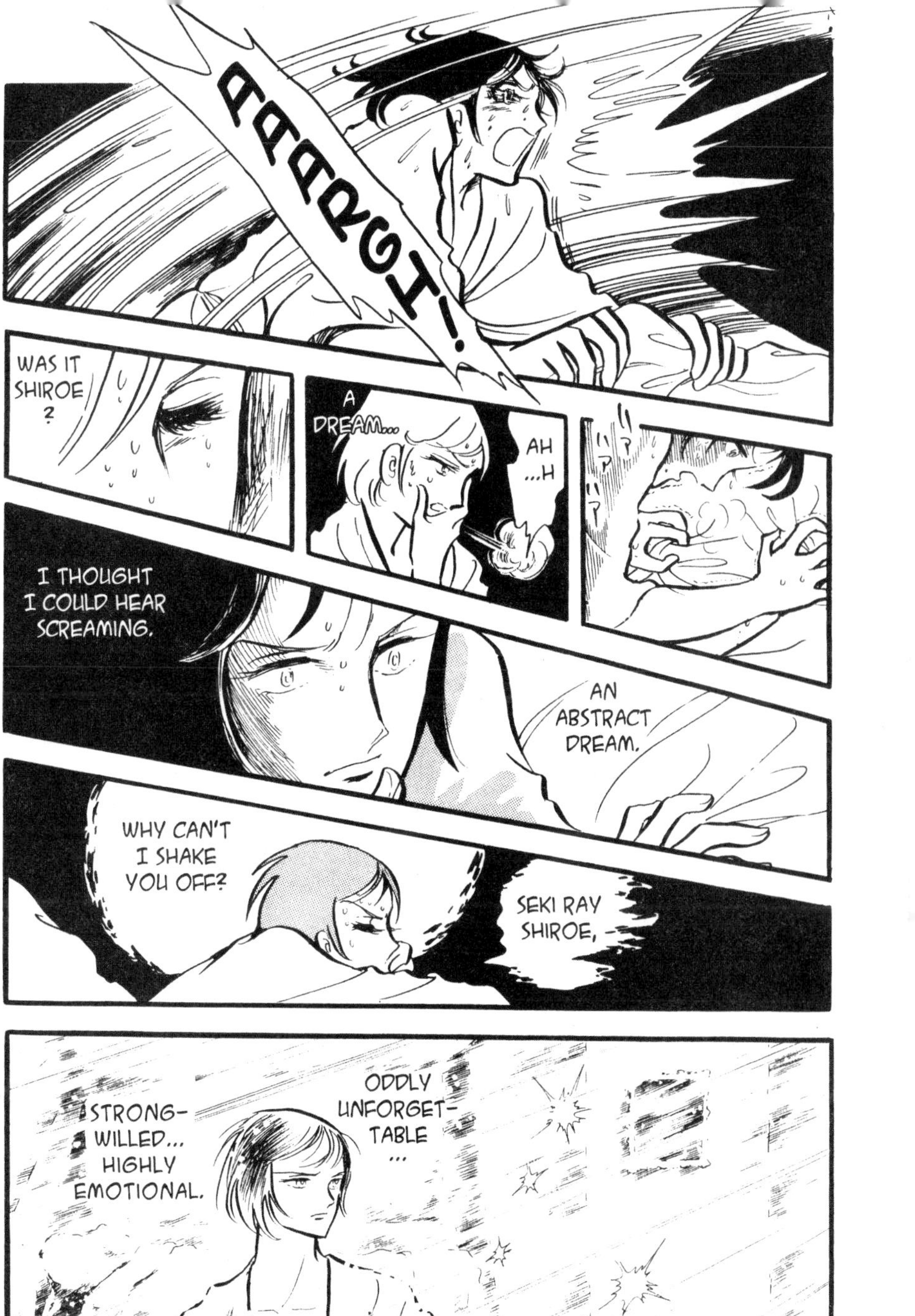
AAARGH!
AH ...H
A DREAM...
WAS IT SHIROE?
AN ABSTRACT DREAM.
I THOUGHT I COULD HEAR SCREAMING.
SEKI RAY SHIROE,
WHY CAN'T I SHAKE YOU OFF?
ODDLY UNFORGET-TABLE ...
STRONG-WILLED... HIGHLY EMOTIONAL.

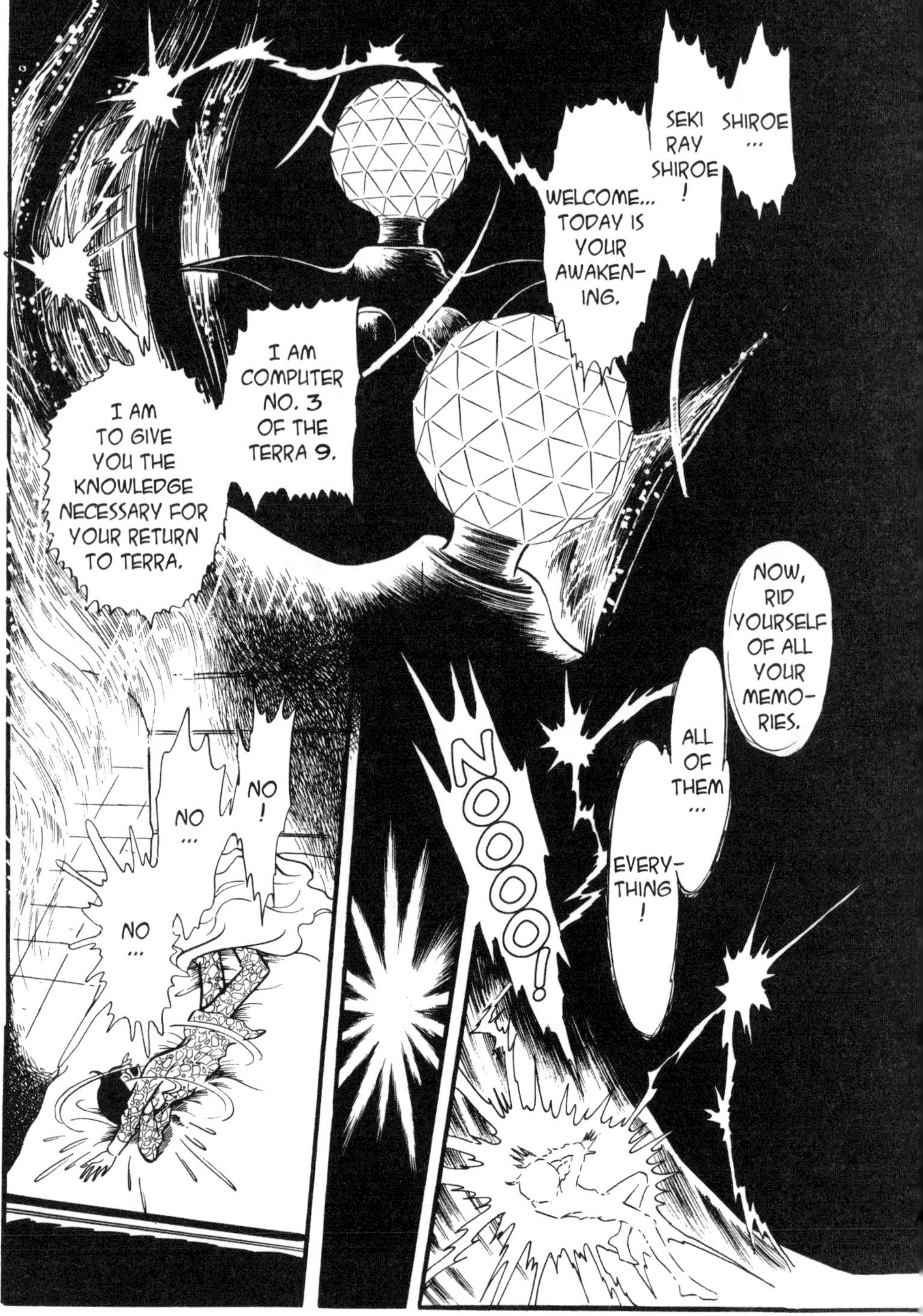
SHIROE ...
SEKI RAY SHIROE!
WELCOME... TODAY IS YOUR AWAKENING.
I AM COMPUTER NO. 3 OF THE TERRA 9.
I AM TO GIVE YOU THE KNOWLEDGE NECESSARY FOR YOUR RETURN TO TERRA.
NOW, RID YOURSELF OF ALL YOUR MEMORIES.
ALL OF THEM ...
EVERYTHING!
NOOOO!
NO!
NO ...
NO ...

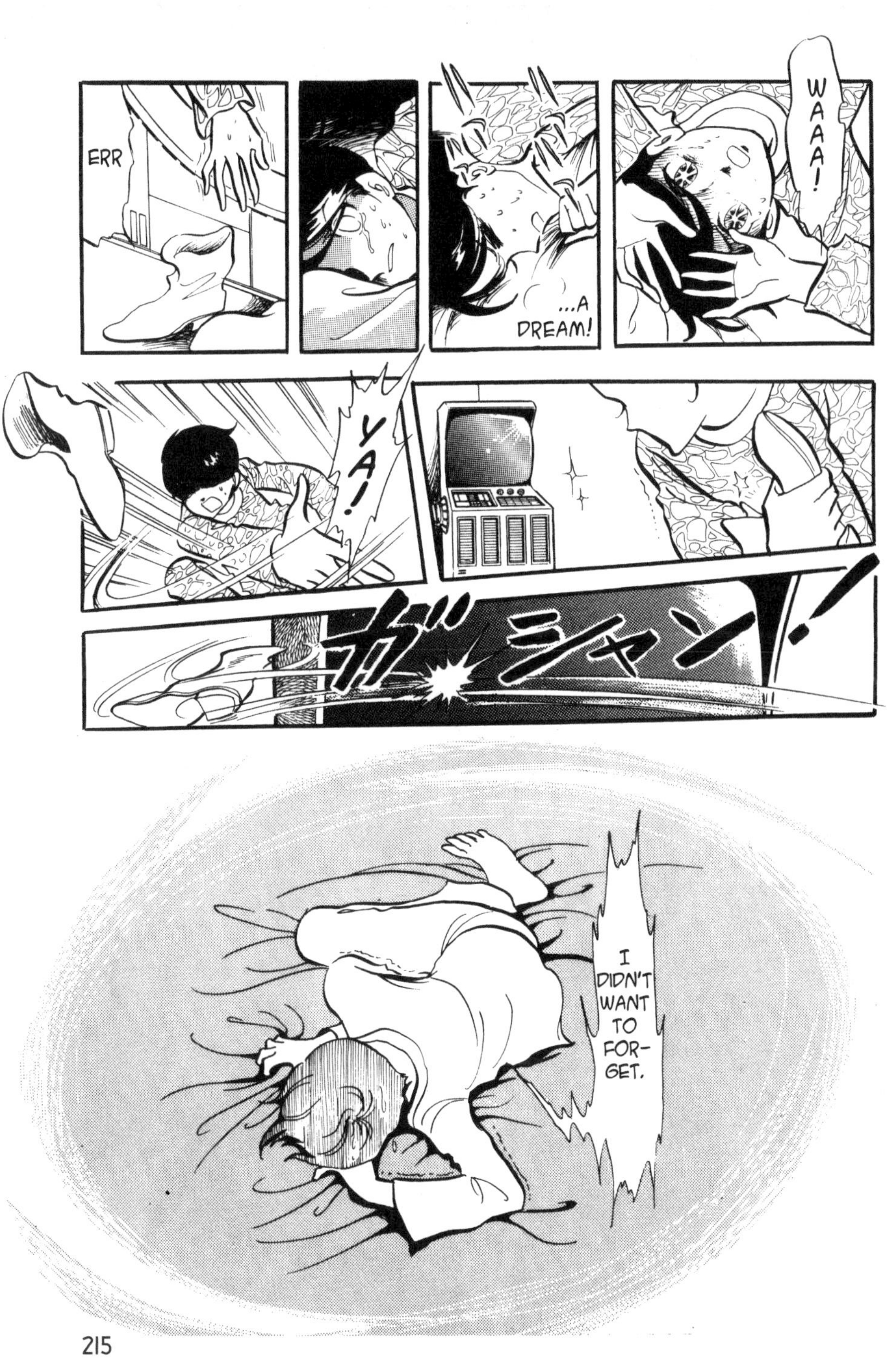
WAAA!
...A DREAM!
ERR
YA!
ガシャン!!
I DIDN'T WANT TO FOR-GET.

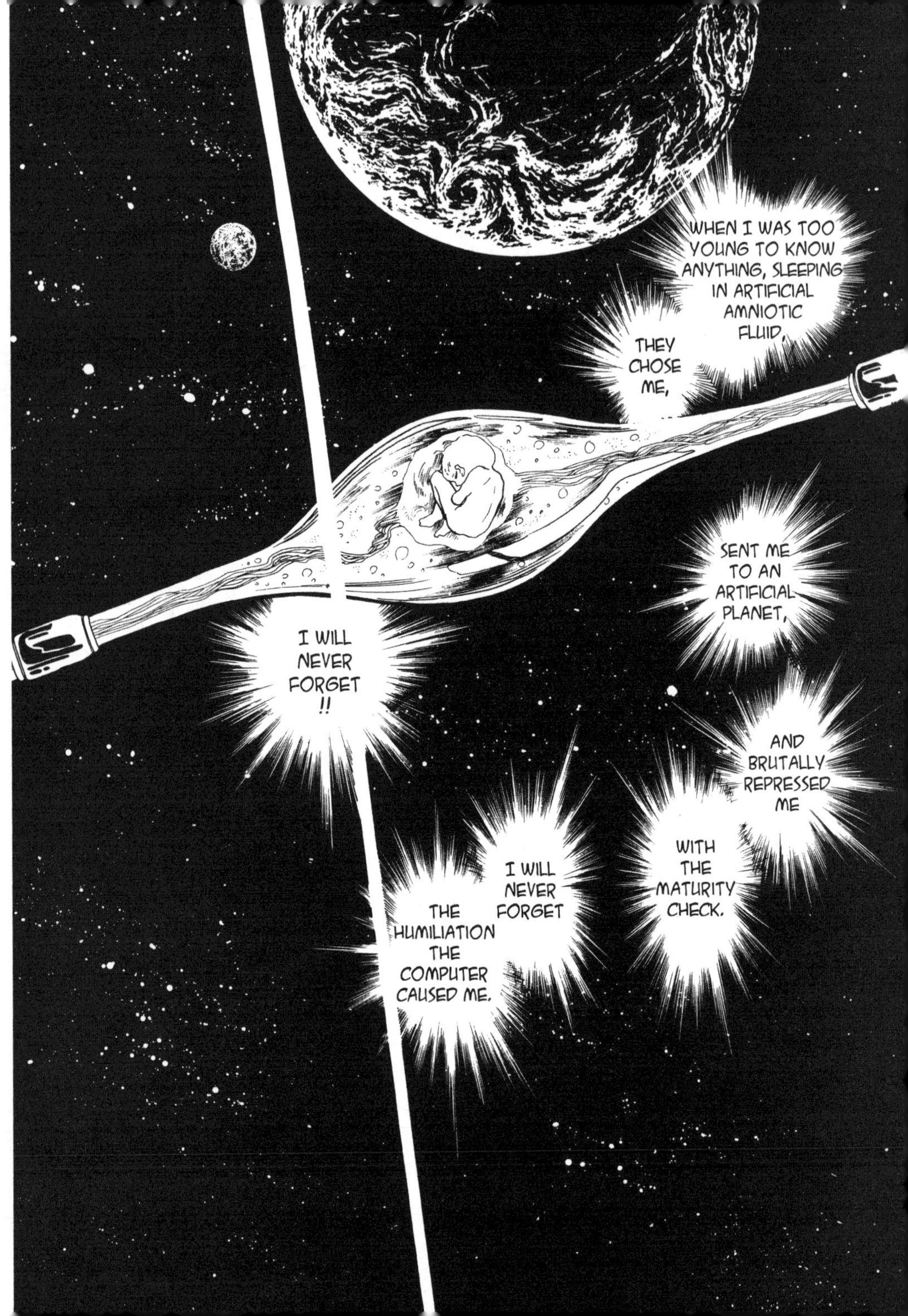
WHEN I WAS TOO YOUNG TO KNOW ANYTHING, SLEEPING IN ARTIFICIAL AMNIOTIC FLUID,
THEY CHOSE ME,
SENT ME TO AN ARTIFICIAL PLANET,
AND BRUTALLY REPRESSED ME
WITH THE MATURITY CHECK.
I WILL NEVER FORGET
THE HUMILIATION THE COMPUTER CAUSED ME.
I WILL NEVER FORGET !!

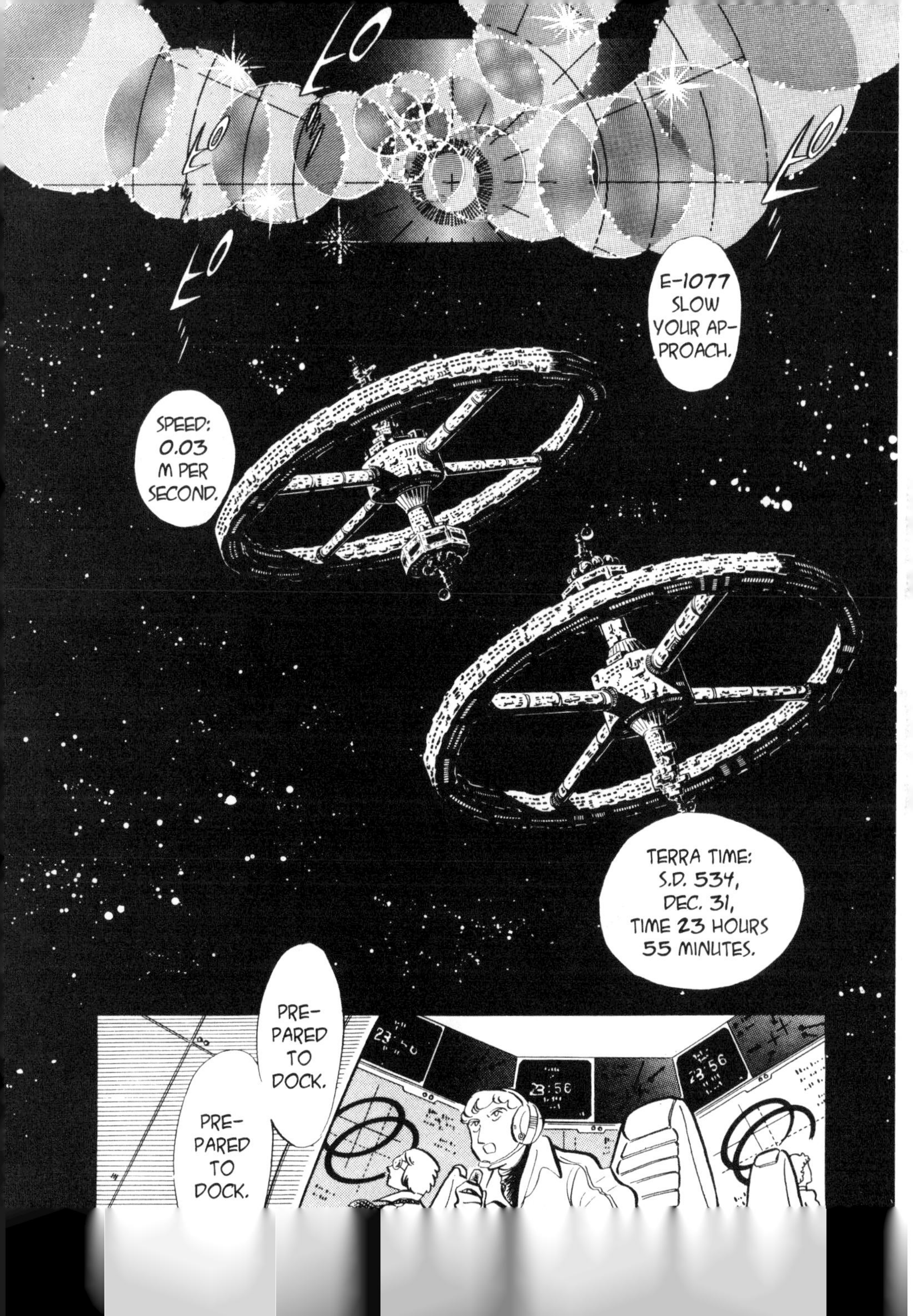
E-1077 SLOW YOUR AP-PROACH.
SPEED: 0.03 M PER SECOND.
TERRA TIME: S.D. 534, DEC. 31, TIME 23 HOURS 55 MINUTES.
PRE-PARED TO DOCK.
PRE-PARED TO DOCK.

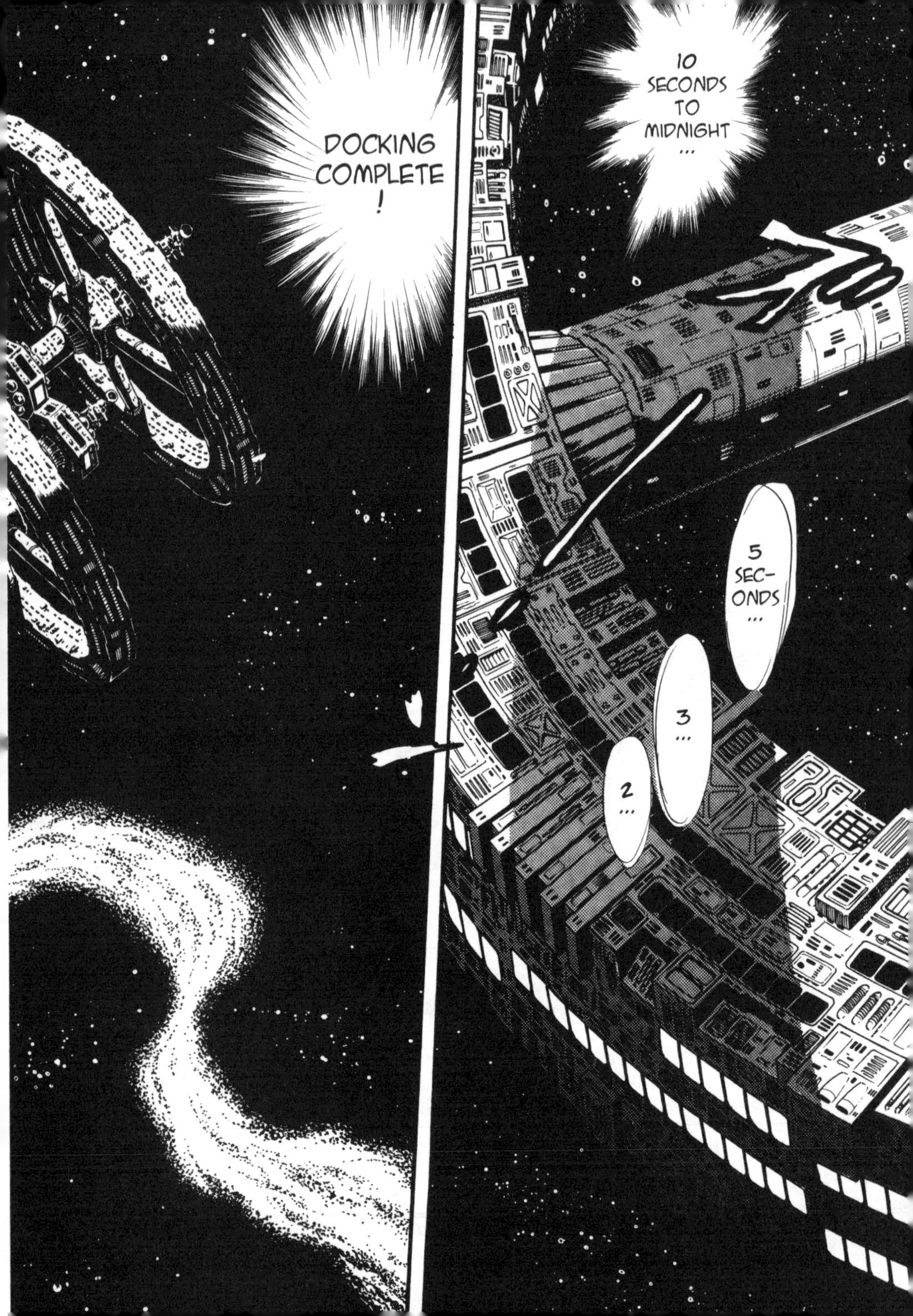
10 SECONDS TO MIDNIGHT ...
5 SEC-ONDS ...
3 ...
2 ...
DOCKING COMPLETE !

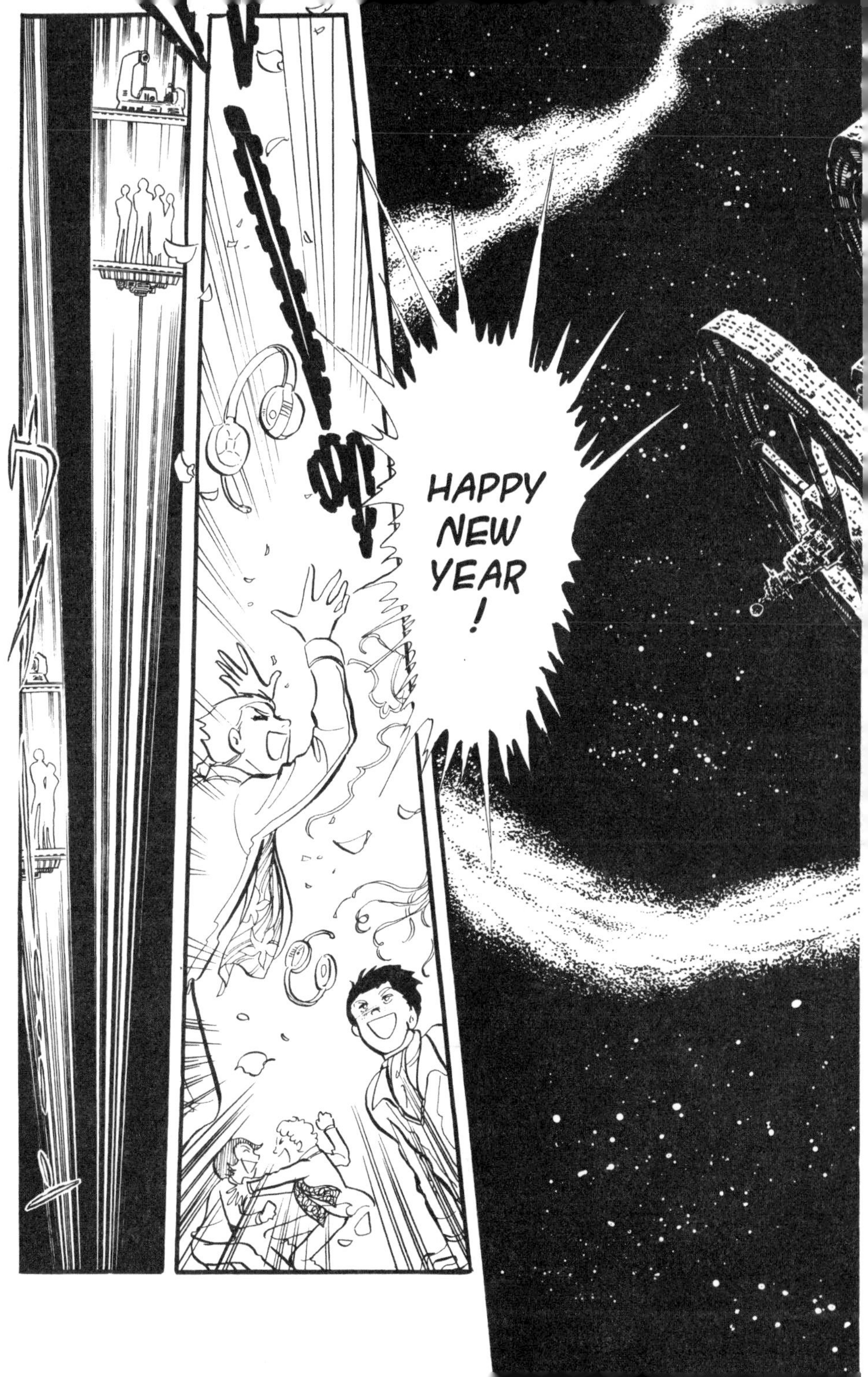
HAPPY NEW YEAR!

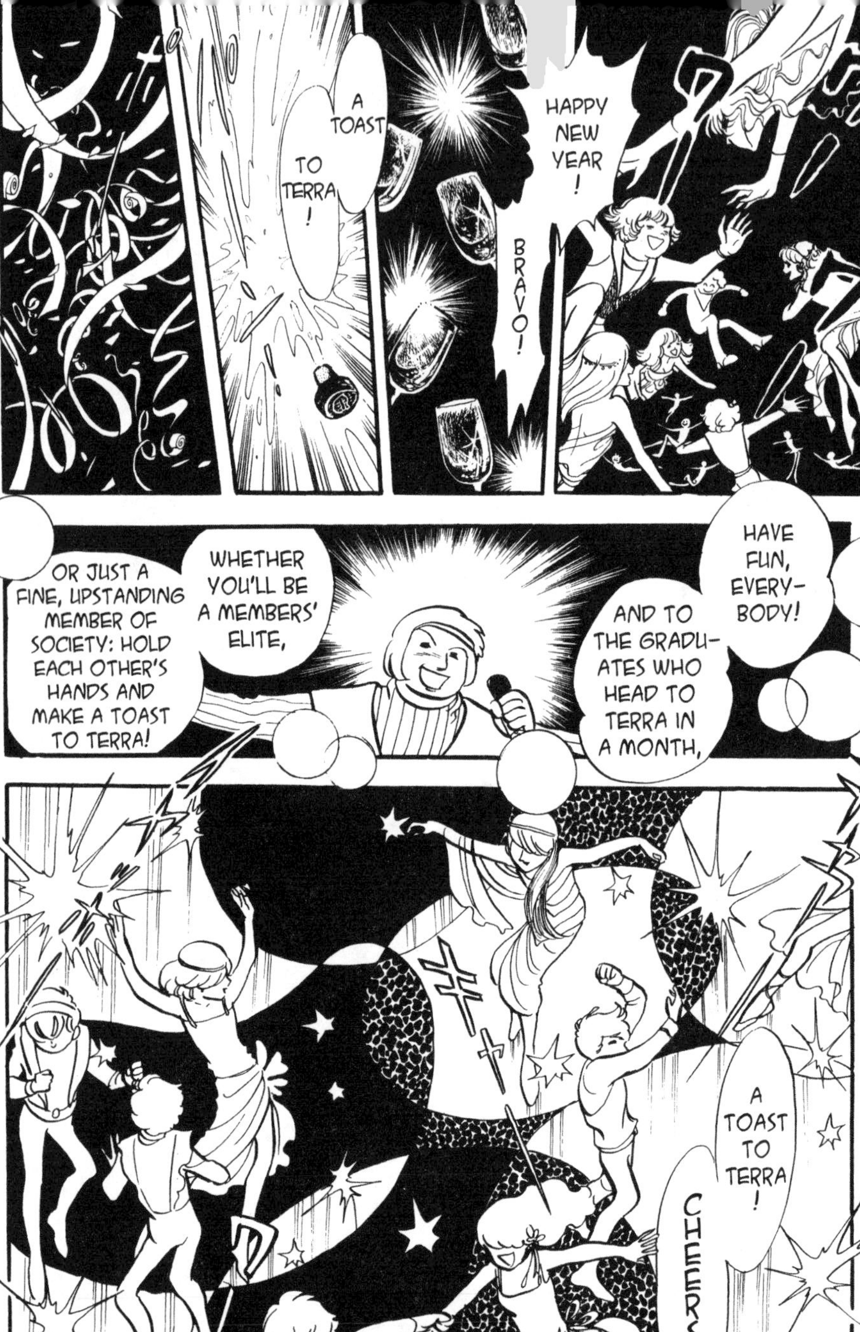
HAPPY NEW YEAR!
BRAVO!
A TOAST TO TERRA!
HAVE FUN, EVERYBODY!
AND TO THE GRADUATES WHO HEAD TO TERRA IN A MONTH,
WHETHER YOU'LL BE A MEMBERS' ELITE,
OR JUST A FINE, UPSTANDING MEMBER OF SOCIETY: HOLD EACH OTHER'S HANDS AND MAKE A TOAST TO TERRA!
A TOAST TO TERRA!
CHEERS!

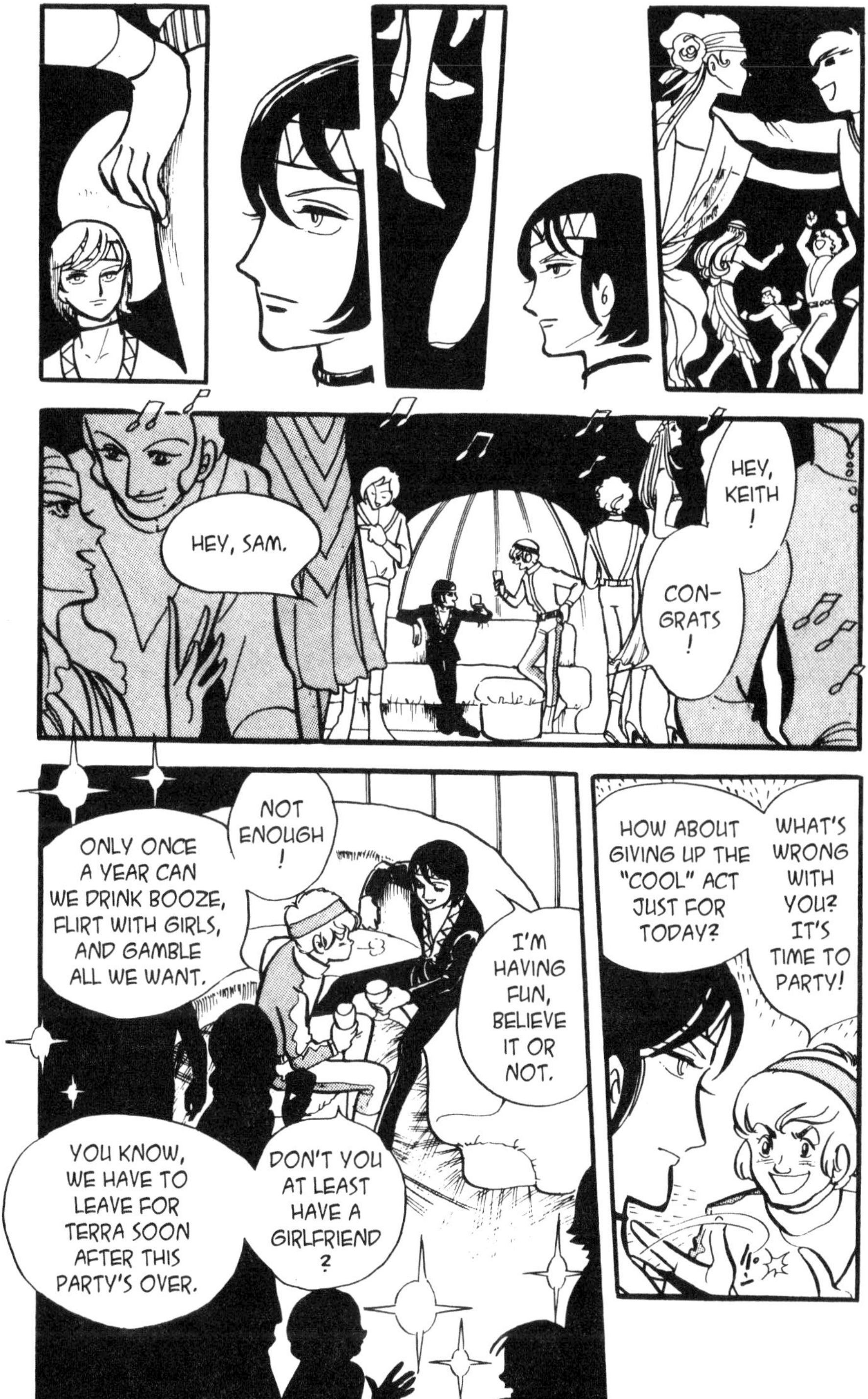
HEY, KEITH!
CON-GRATS!
HEY, SAM.
WHAT'S WRONG WITH YOU? IT'S TIME TO PARTY!
HOW ABOUT GIVING UP THE "COOL" ACT JUST FOR TODAY?
NOT ENOUGH!
ONLY ONCE A YEAR CAN WE DRINK BOOZE, FLIRT WITH GIRLS, AND GAMBLE ALL WE WANT.
I'M HAVING FUN, BELIEVE IT OR NOT.
DON'T YOU AT LEAST HAVE A GIRLFRIEND?
YOU KNOW, WE HAVE TO LEAVE FOR TERRA SOON AFTER THIS PARTY'S OVER.

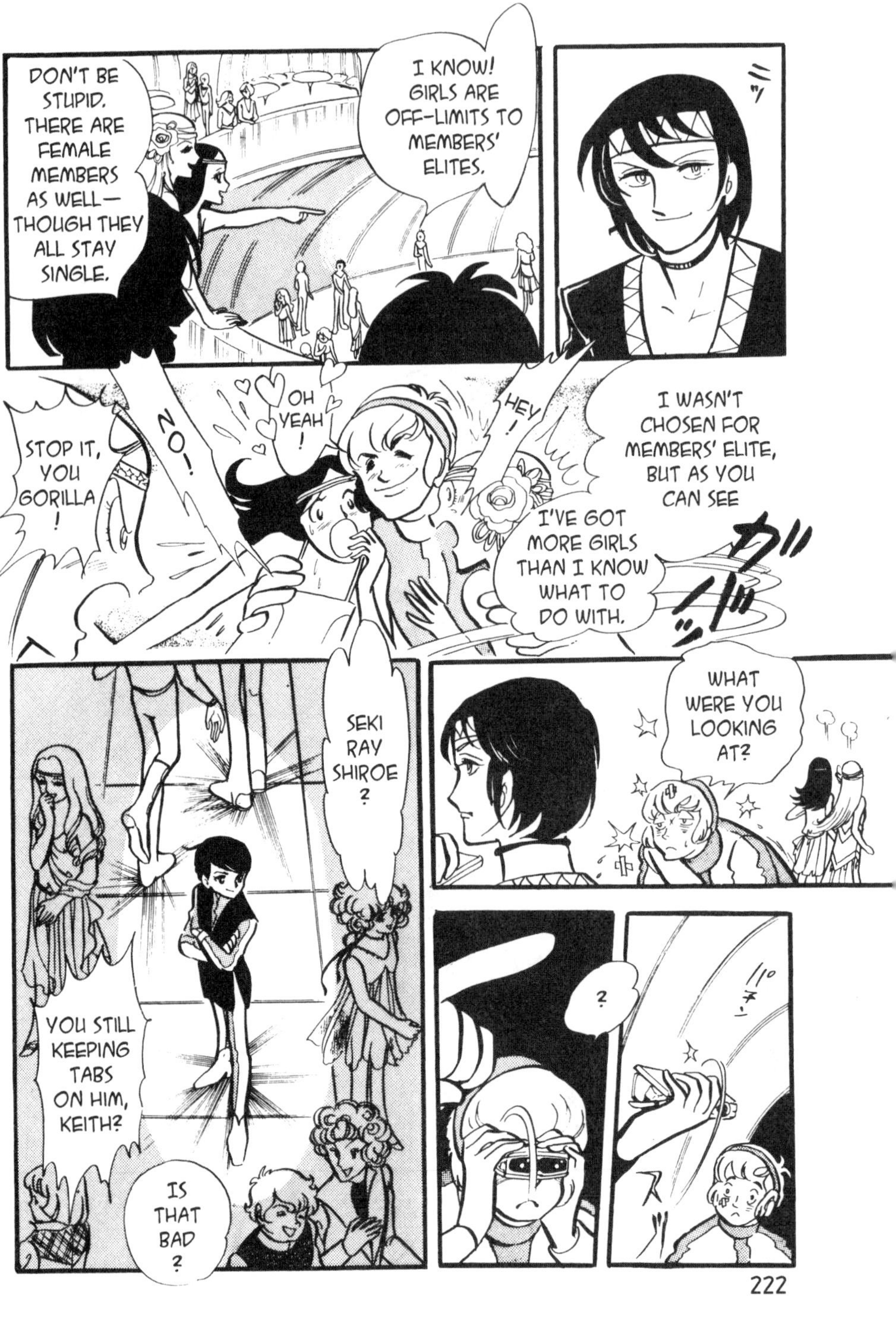
ニッ
I KNOW! GIRLS ARE OFF-LIMITS TO MEMBERS' ELITES.
DON'T BE STUPID. THERE ARE FEMALE MEMBERS AS WELL— THOUGH THEY ALL STAY SINGLE.
I WASN'T CHOSEN FOR MEMBERS' ELITE, BUT AS YOU CAN SEE
I'VE GOT MORE GIRLS THAN I KNOW WHAT TO DO WITH.
ガバッ
HEY!
OH YEAH!
NO!
STOP IT, YOU GORILLA!
WHAT WERE YOU LOOKING AT?
パチン
スッ
?
SEKI RAY SHIROE?
YOU STILL KEEPING TABS ON HIM, KEITH?
IS THAT BAD?

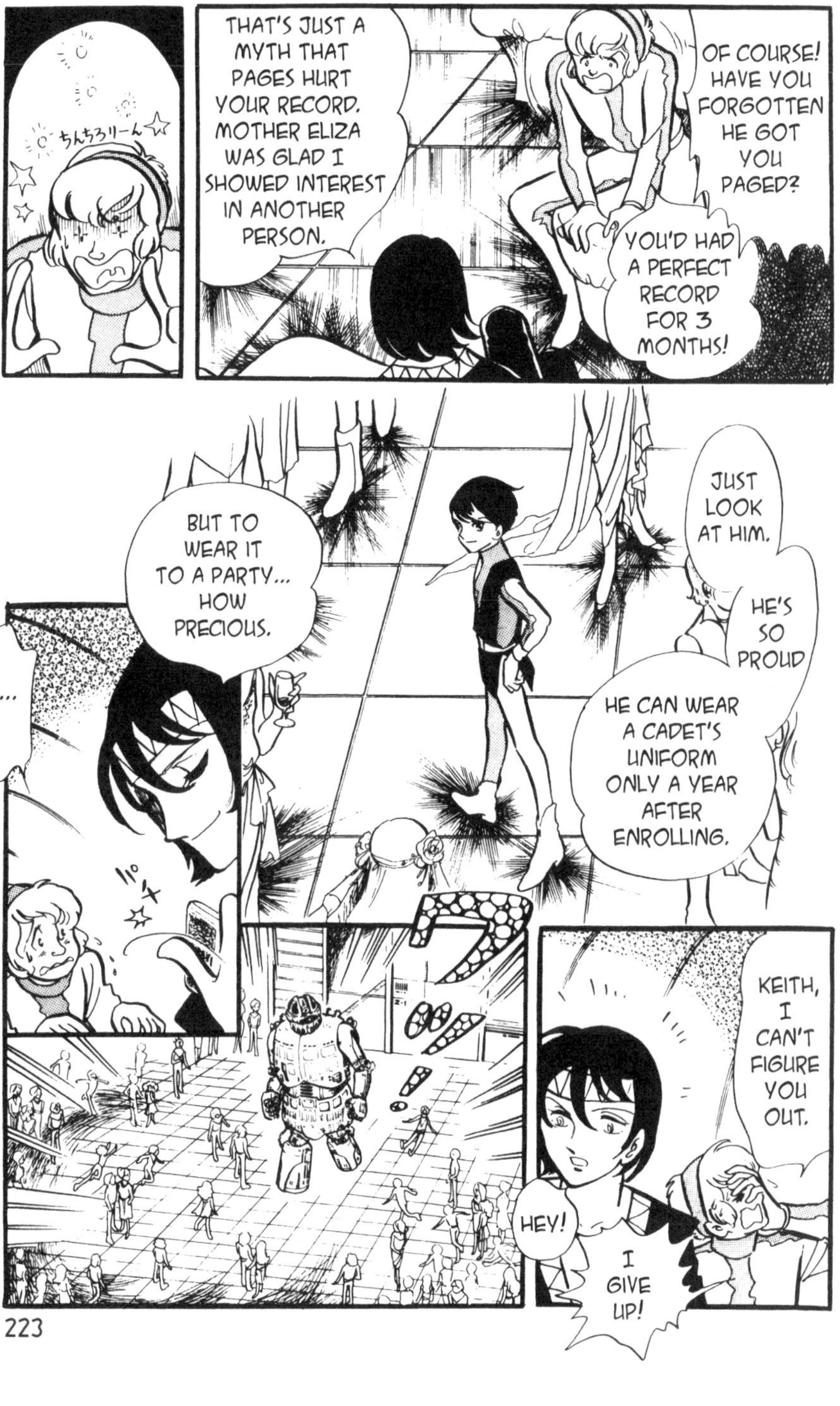
OF COURSE! HAVE YOU FORGOTTEN HE GOT YOU PAGED?
YOU'D HAD A PERFECT RECORD FOR 3 MONTHS!
THAT'S JUST A MYTH THAT PAGES HURT YOUR RECORD. MOTHER ELIZA WAS GLAD I SHOWED INTEREST IN ANOTHER PERSON.
ちんちろりーん
JUST LOOK AT HIM.
HE'S SO PROUD
HE CAN WEAR A CADET'S UNIFORM ONLY A YEAR AFTER ENROLLING.
BUT TO WEAR IT TO A PARTY... HOW PRECIOUS.
...
KEITH, I CAN'T FIGURE YOU OUT.
I GIVE UP!
HEY!

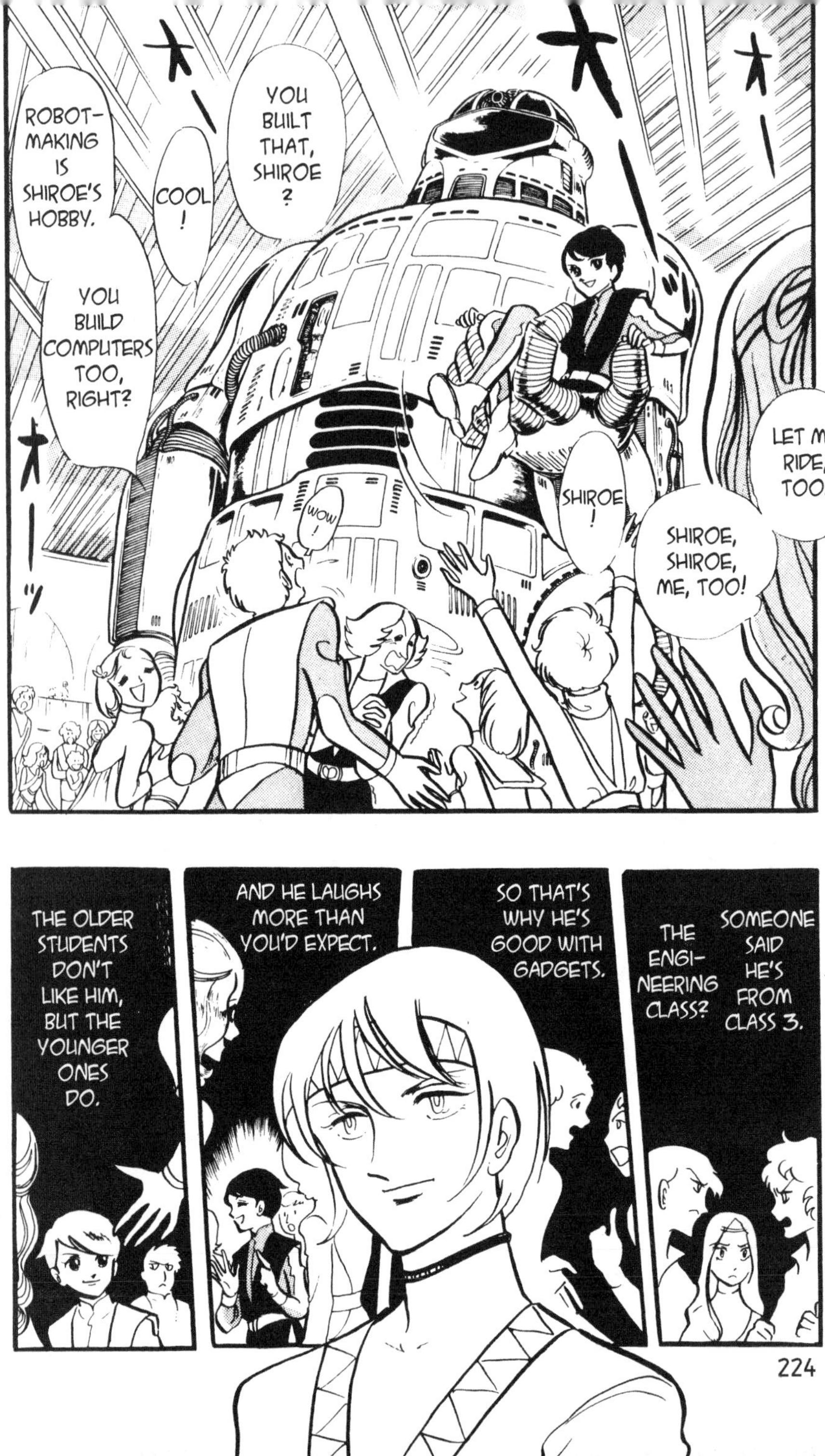
LET ME RIDE, TOO!
SHIROE, SHIROE, ME, TOO!
SHIROE!
YOU BUILT THAT, SHIROE?
WOW!
COOL!
ROBOT-MAKING IS SHIROE'S HOBBY.
YOU BUILD COMPUTERS TOO, RIGHT?
SOMEONE SAID HE'S FROM CLASS 3.
THE ENGINEERING CLASS?
SO THAT'S WHY HE'S GOOD WITH GADGETS.
AND HE LAUGHS MORE THAN YOU'D EXPECT.
THE OLDER STUDENTS DON'T LIKE HIM, BUT THE YOUNGER ONES DO.

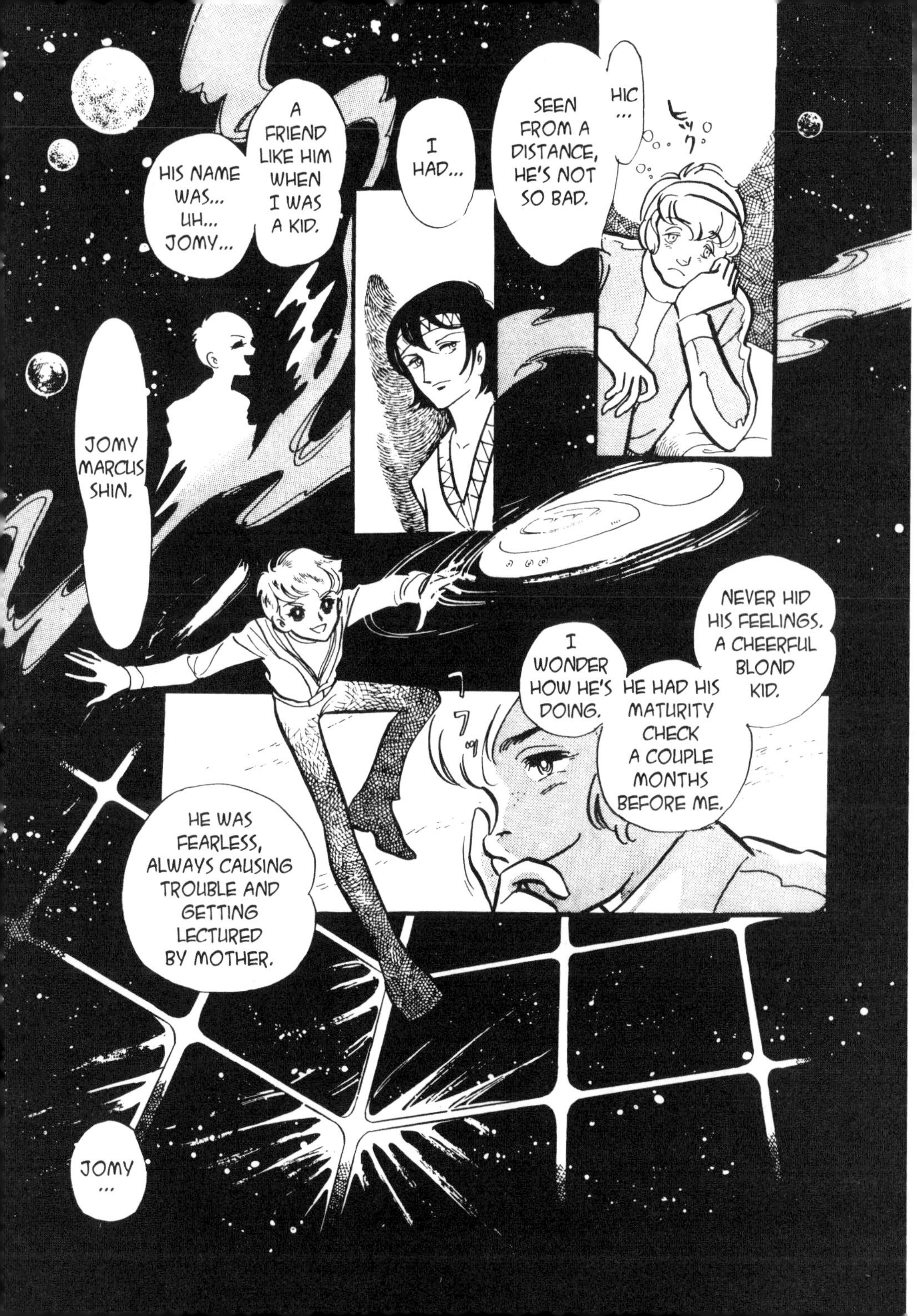
HIC ...
SEEN FROM A DISTANCE, HE'S NOT SO BAD.
I HAD...
A FRIEND LIKE HIM WHEN I WAS A KID.
HIS NAME WAS... UH... JOMY...
JOMY MARCUS SHIN.
NEVER HID HIS FEELINGS. A CHEERFUL BLOND KID.
HE HAD HIS MATURITY CHECK A COUPLE MONTHS BEFORE ME.
I WONDER HOW HE'S DOING.
HE WAS FEARLESS, ALWAYS CAUSING TROUBLE AND GETTING LECTURED BY MOTHER.
JOMY ...

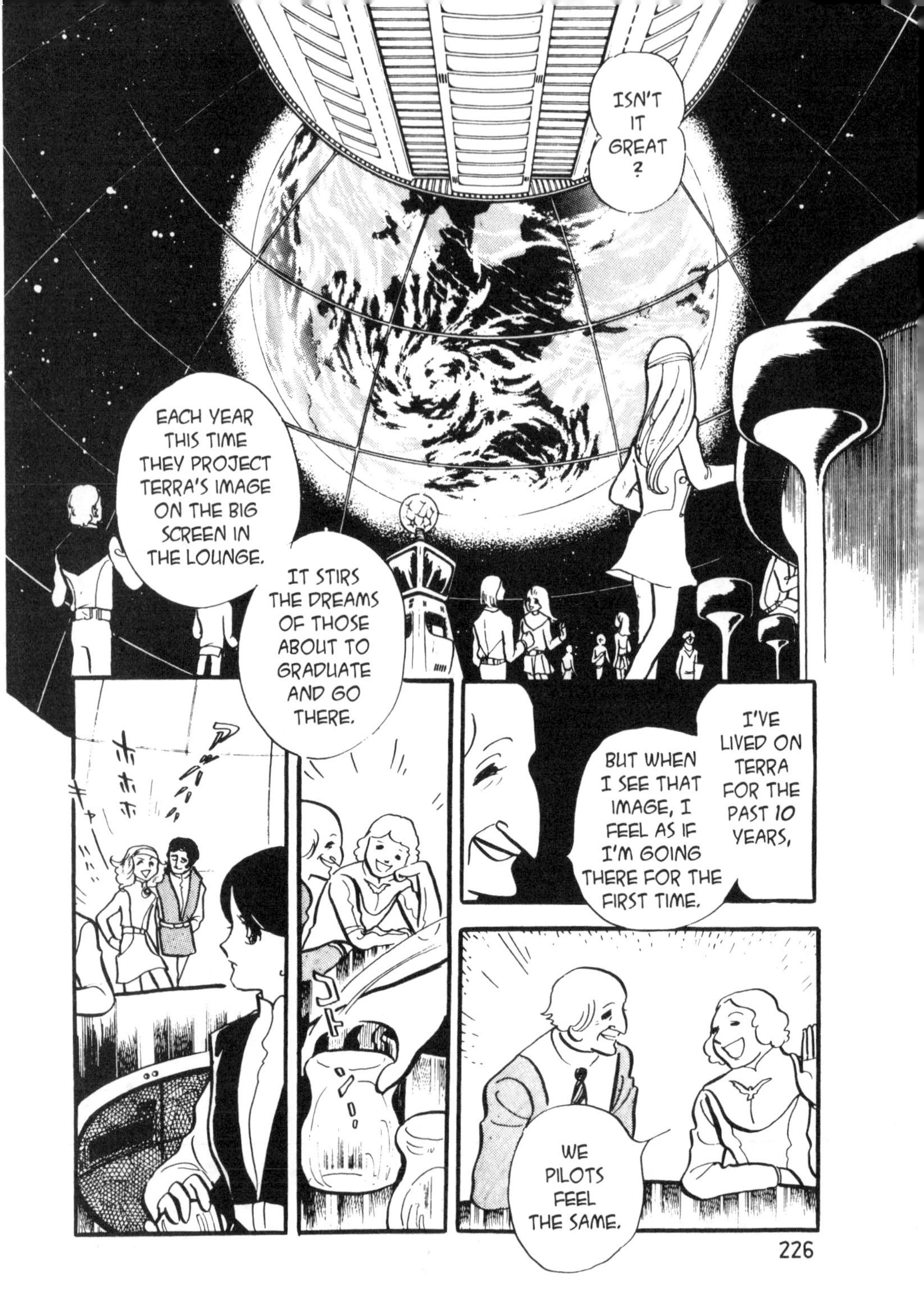
ISN'T IT GREAT?
EACH YEAR THIS TIME THEY PROJECT TERRA'S IMAGE ON THE BIG SCREEN IN THE LOUNGE.
IT STIRS THE DREAMS OF THOSE ABOUT TO GRADUATE AND GO THERE.
I'VE LIVED ON TERRA FOR THE PAST 10 YEARS,
BUT WHEN I SEE THAT IMAGE, I FEEL AS IF I'M GOING THERE FOR THE FIRST TIME.
WE PILOTS FEEL THE SAME.
コト
ホホホ

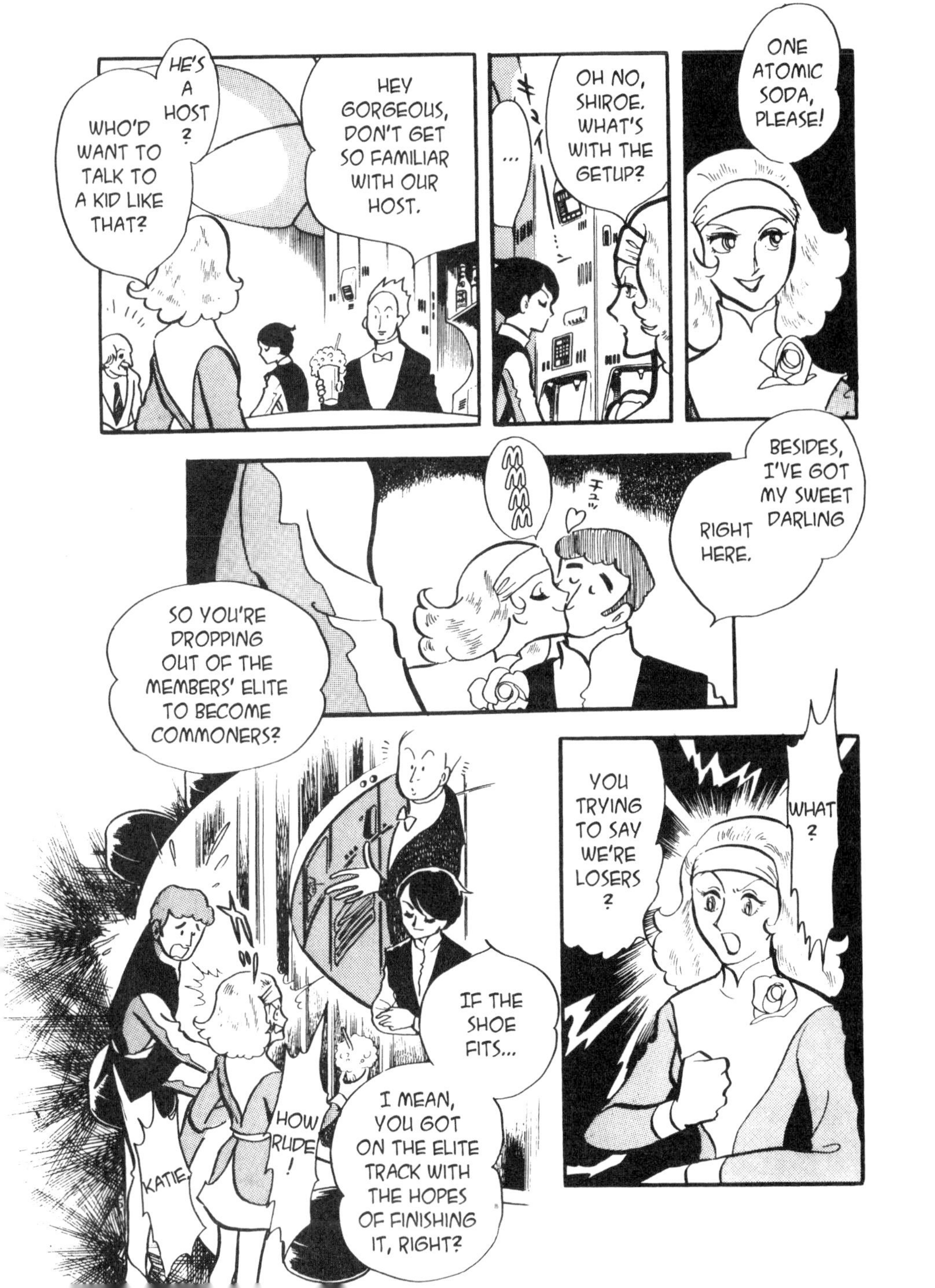

ONE ATOMIC SODA, PLEASE!
OH NO, SHIROE. WHAT'S WITH THE GETUP?
...
HEY GORGEOUS, DON'T GET SO FAMILIAR WITH OUR HOST.
HE'S A HOST?
WHO'D WANT TO TALK TO A KID LIKE THAT?
BESIDES, I'VE GOT MY SWEET DARLING RIGHT HERE.
MMMM
SO YOU'RE DROPPING OUT OF THE MEMBERS' ELITE TO BECOME COMMONERS?
WHAT?
YOU TRYING TO SAY WE'RE LOSERS?
IF THE SHOE FITS...
I MEAN, YOU GOT ON THE ELITE TRACK WITH THE HOPES OF FINISHING IT, RIGHT?
HOW RUDE!
KATIE

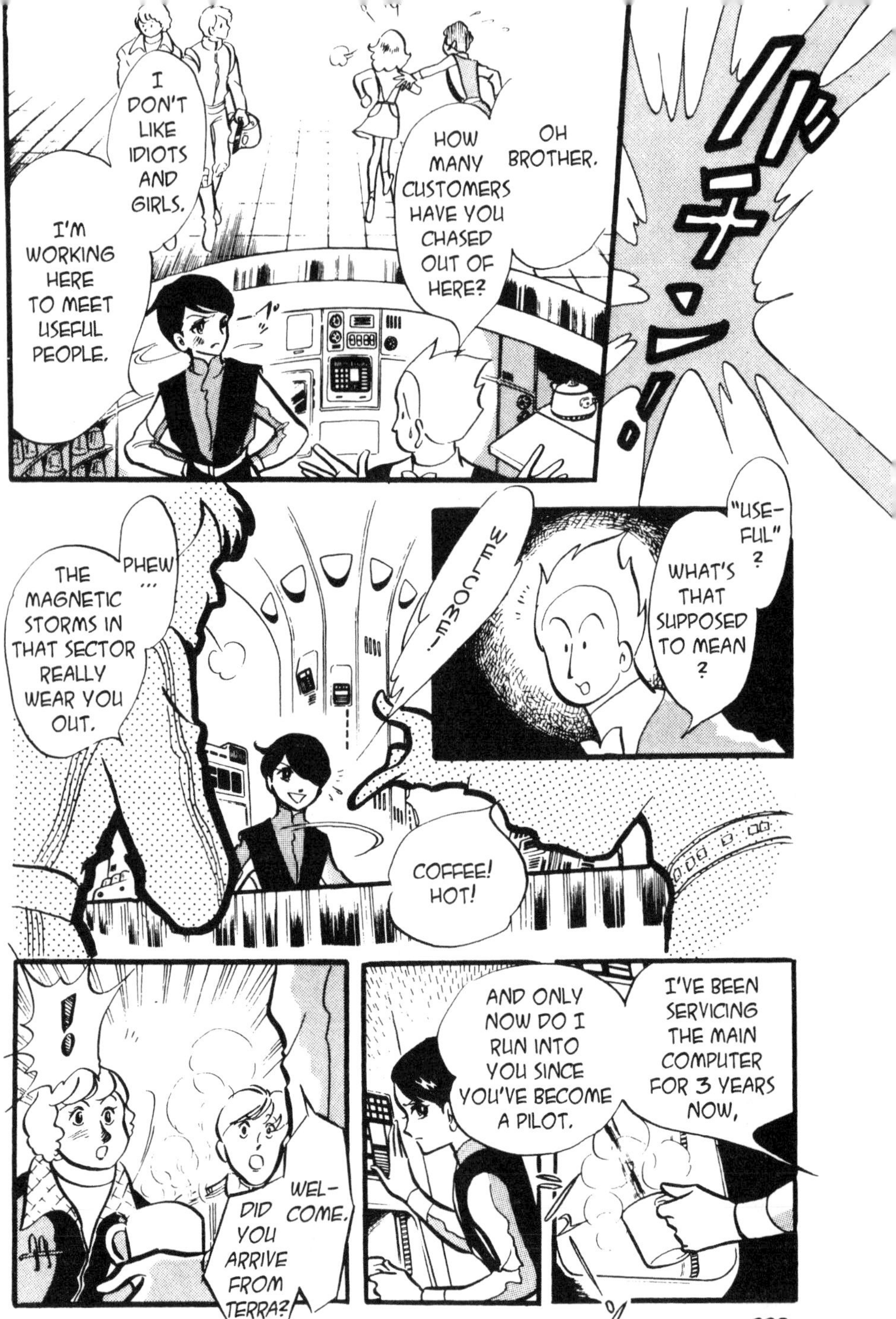
OH BROTHER.
HOW MANY CUSTOMERS HAVE YOU CHASED OUT OF HERE?
I DON'T LIKE IDIOTS AND GIRLS.
I'M WORKING HERE TO MEET USEFUL PEOPLE.
"USE-FUL"?
WHAT'S THAT SUPPOSED TO MEAN?
WELCOME—
PHEW...
THE MAGNETIC STORMS IN THAT SECTOR REALLY WEAR YOU OUT.
COFFEE! HOT!
I'VE BEEN SERVICING THE MAIN COMPUTER FOR 3 YEARS NOW,
AND ONLY NOW DO I RUN INTO YOU SINCE YOU'VE BECOME A PILOT.
!!
WEL-COME.
DID YOU ARRIVE FROM TERRA?

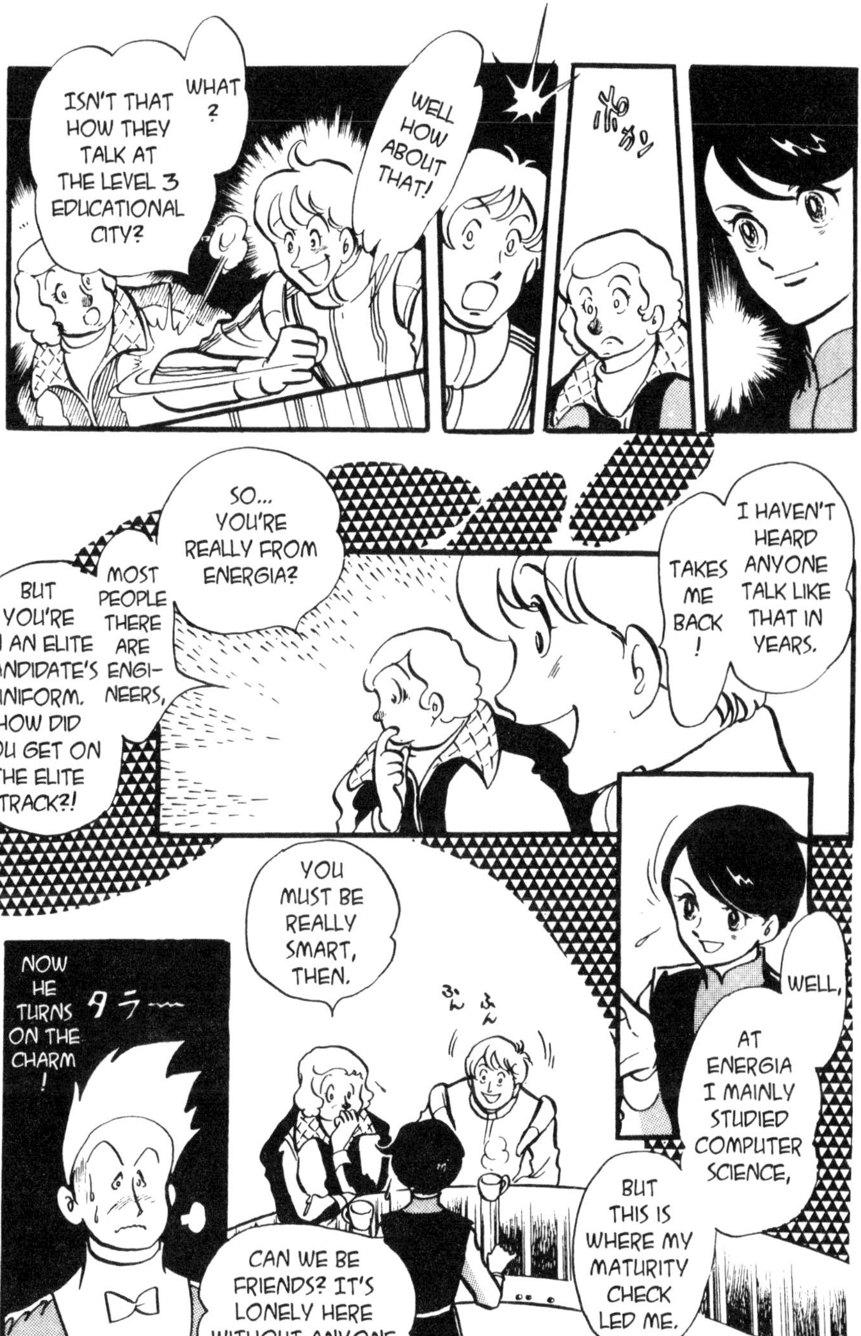
ぽかン
WELL HOW ABOUT THAT!
WHAT?
ISN'T THAT HOW THEY TALK AT THE LEVEL 3 EDUCATIONAL CITY?
...
I HAVEN'T HEARD ANYONE TALK LIKE THAT IN YEARS.
TAKES ME BACK!
SO... YOU'RE REALLY FROM ENERGIA?
MOST PEOPLE THERE ARE ENGINEERS,
BUT YOU'RE IN AN ELITE CANDIDATE'S UNIFORM. HOW DID YOU GET ON THE ELITE TRACK?!
WELL,
AT ENERGIA I MAINLY STUDIED COMPUTER SCIENCE,
BUT THIS IS WHERE MY MATURITY CHECK LED ME.
YOU MUST BE REALLY SMART, THEN.
ふん ふん
CAN WE BE FRIENDS? IT'S LONELY HERE WITHOUT ANYONE FROM HOME.
NOW HE TURNS ON THE CHARM!
タラ〜

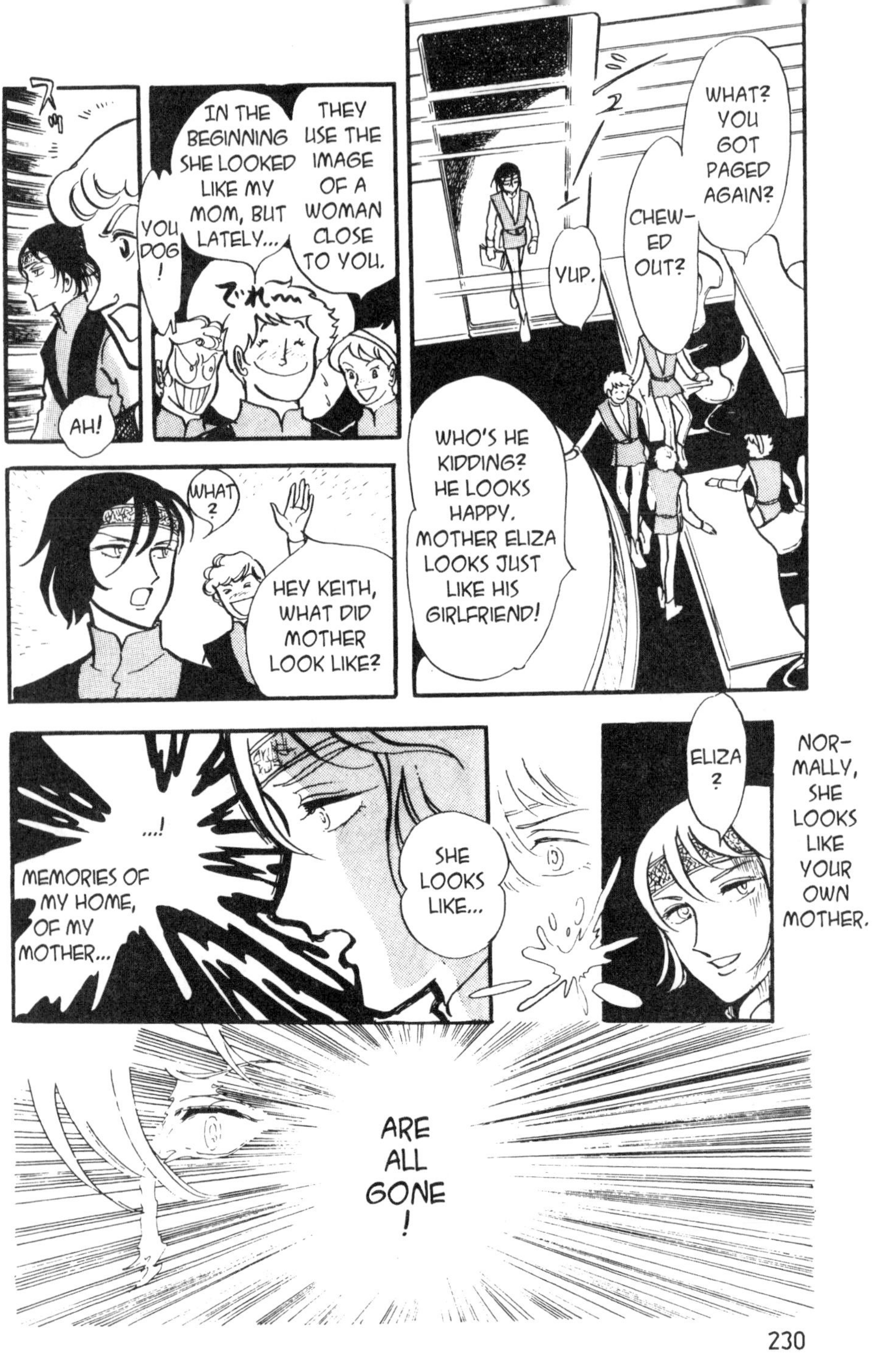
WHAT? YOU GOT PAGED AGAIN?
CHEW-ED OUT?
YUP.
WHO'S HE KIDDING? HE LOOKS HAPPY. MOTHER ELIZA LOOKS JUST LIKE HIS GIRLFRIEND!
THEY USE THE IMAGE OF A WOMAN CLOSE TO YOU.
IN THE BEGINNING SHE LOOKED LIKE MY MOM, BUT LATELY...
でれ〜
YOU DOG!
ス
AH!
HEY KEITH, WHAT DID MOTHER LOOK LIKE?
WHAT?
ELIZA?
NORMALLY, SHE LOOKS LIKE YOUR OWN MOTHER.
SHE LOOKS LIKE...
...!
MEMORIES OF MY HOME, OF MY MOTHER...
ARE ALL GONE!

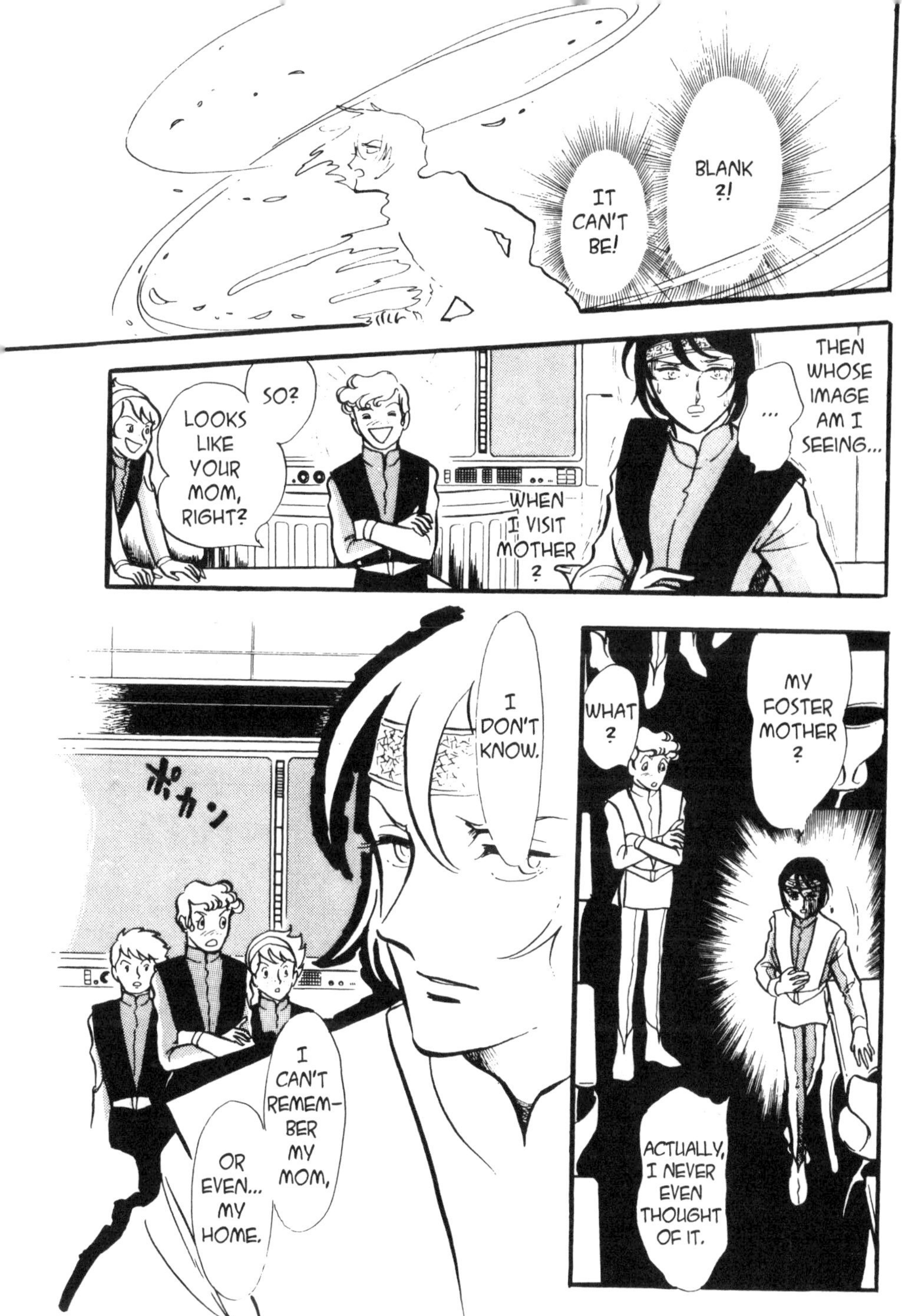
BLANK ?!
IT CAN'T BE!
THEN WHOSE IMAGE AM I SEEING...
...
WHEN I VISIT MOTHER?
SO?
LOOKS LIKE YOUR MOM, RIGHT?
MY FOSTER MOTHER?
WHAT?
ACTUALLY, I NEVER EVEN THOUGHT OF IT.
I DON'T KNOW.
ポカン
I CAN'T REMEMBER MY MOM,
OR EVEN... MY HOME.

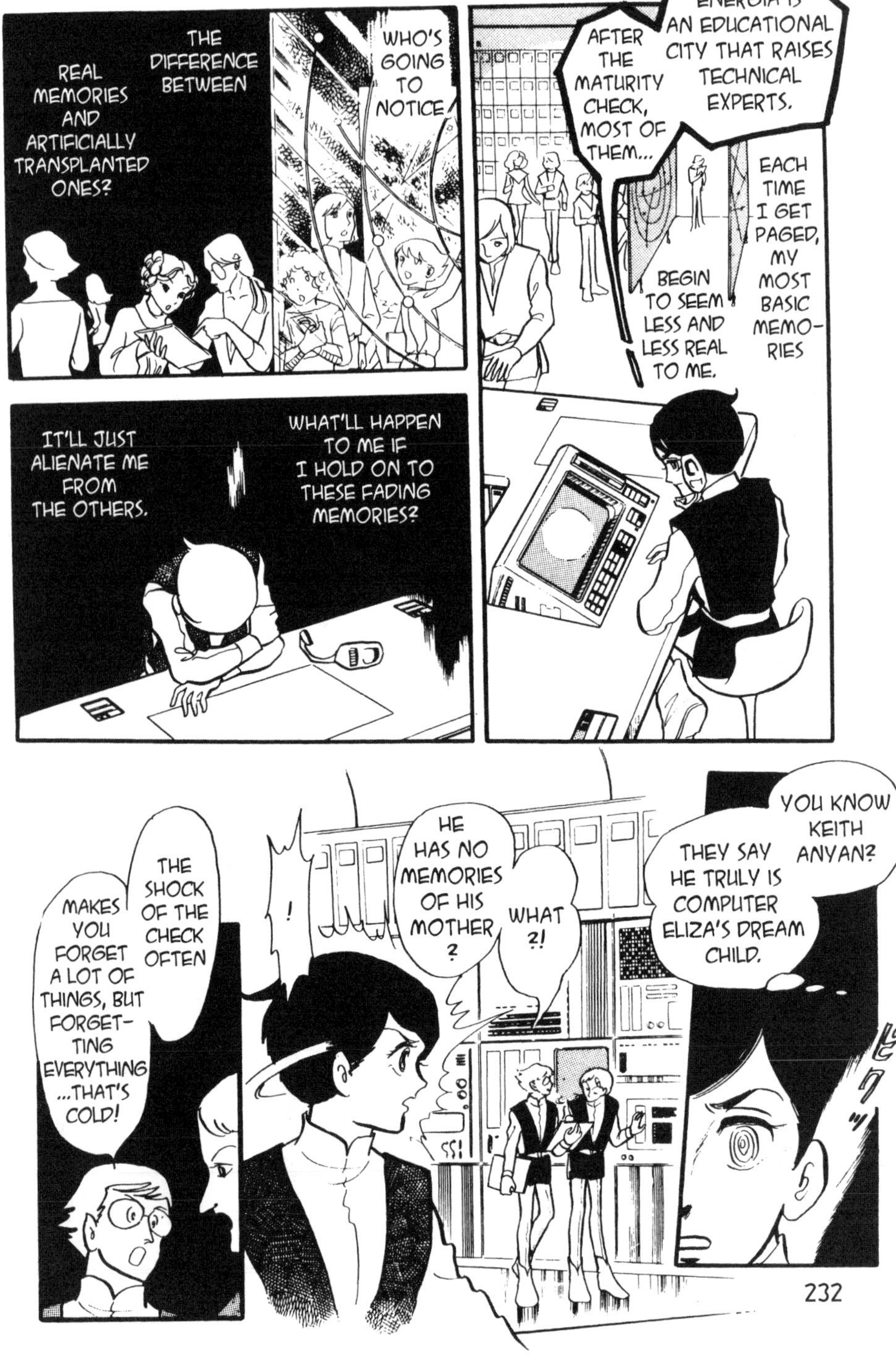
ENERGIA IS AN EDUCATIONAL CITY THAT RAISES TECHNICAL EXPERTS.
AFTER THE MATURITY CHECK, MOST OF THEM...
EACH TIME I GET PAGED, MY MOST BASIC MEMORIES
BEGIN TO SEEM LESS AND LESS REAL TO ME.
WHO'S GOING TO NOTICE
THE DIFFERENCE BETWEEN
REAL MEMORIES AND ARTIFICIALLY TRANSPLANTED ONES?
WHAT'LL HAPPEN TO ME IF I HOLD ON TO THESE FADING MEMORIES?
IT'LL JUST ALIENATE ME FROM THE OTHERS.
YOU KNOW KEITH ANYAN?
THEY SAY HE TRULY IS COMPUTER ELIZA'S DREAM CHILD.
ビクッ
HE HAS NO MEMORIES OF HIS MOTHER?
WHAT?!
!
THE SHOCK OF THE CHECK OFTEN
MAKES YOU FORGET A LOT OF THINGS, BUT FORGETTING EVERYTHING ...THAT'S COLD!

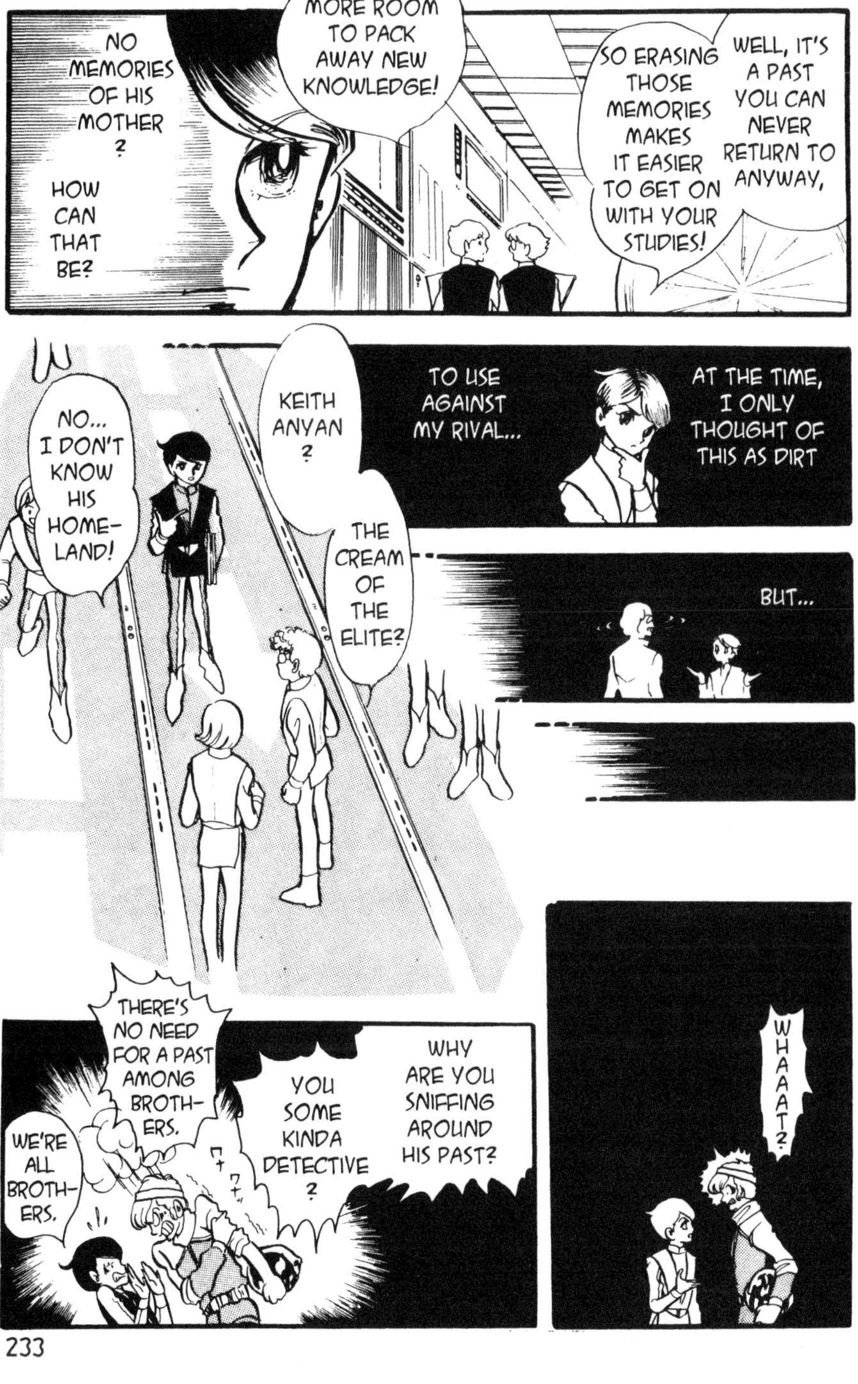
WELL, IT'S A PAST YOU CAN NEVER RETURN TO ANYWAY,
SO ERASING THOSE MEMORIES MAKES IT EASIER TO GET ON WITH YOUR STUDIES!
MORE ROOM TO PACK AWAY NEW KNOWLEDGE!
NO MEMORIES OF HIS MOTHER?
HOW CAN THAT BE?
AT THE TIME, I ONLY THOUGHT OF THIS AS DIRT
TO USE AGAINST MY RIVAL...
BUT...
KEITH ANYAN?
THE CREAM OF THE ELITE?
NO... I DON'T KNOW HIS HOME-LAND!
WHAAAAT?
WHY ARE YOU SNIFFING AROUND HIS PAST?
YOU SOME KINDA DETECTIVE?
THERE'S NO NEED FOR A PAST AMONG BROTH-ERS.
WE'RE ALL BROTH-ERS.

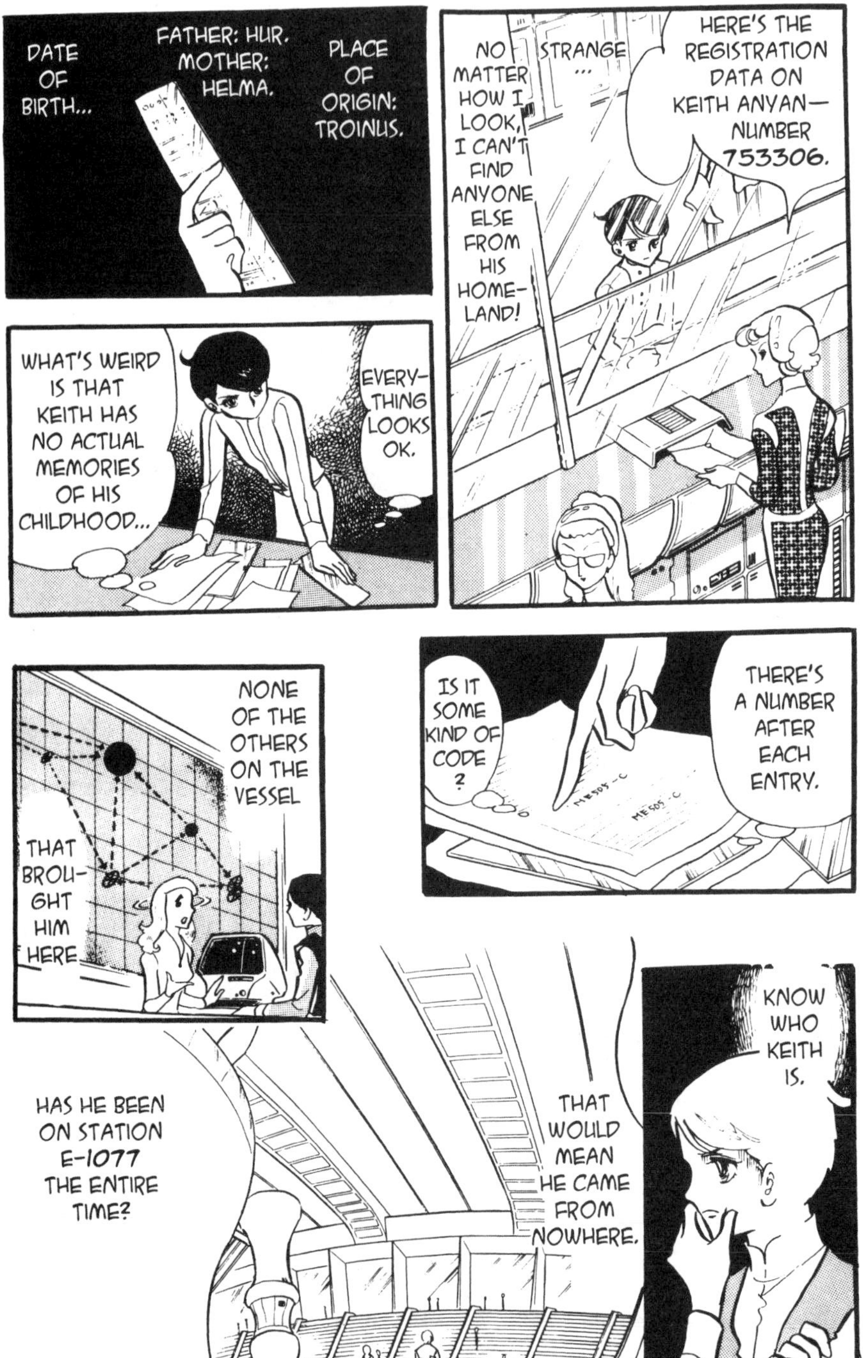
HERE'S THE REGISTRATION DATA ON KEITH ANYAN— NUMBER 753306.
STRANGE...
NO MATTER HOW I LOOK, I CAN'T FIND ANYONE ELSE FROM HIS HOMELAND!
PLACE OF ORIGIN: TROINUS.
FATHER: HUR. MOTHER: HELMA.
DATE OF BIRTH...
EVERYTHING LOOKS OK.
WHAT'S WEIRD IS THAT KEITH HAS NO ACTUAL MEMORIES OF HIS CHILDHOOD...
THERE'S A NUMBER AFTER EACH ENTRY.
IS IT SOME KIND OF CODE?
NONE OF THE OTHERS ON THE VESSEL
THAT BROUGHT HIM HERE
KNOW WHO KEITH IS.
THAT WOULD MEAN HE CAME FROM NOWHERE.
HAS HE BEEN ON STATION E-1077 THE ENTIRE TIME?

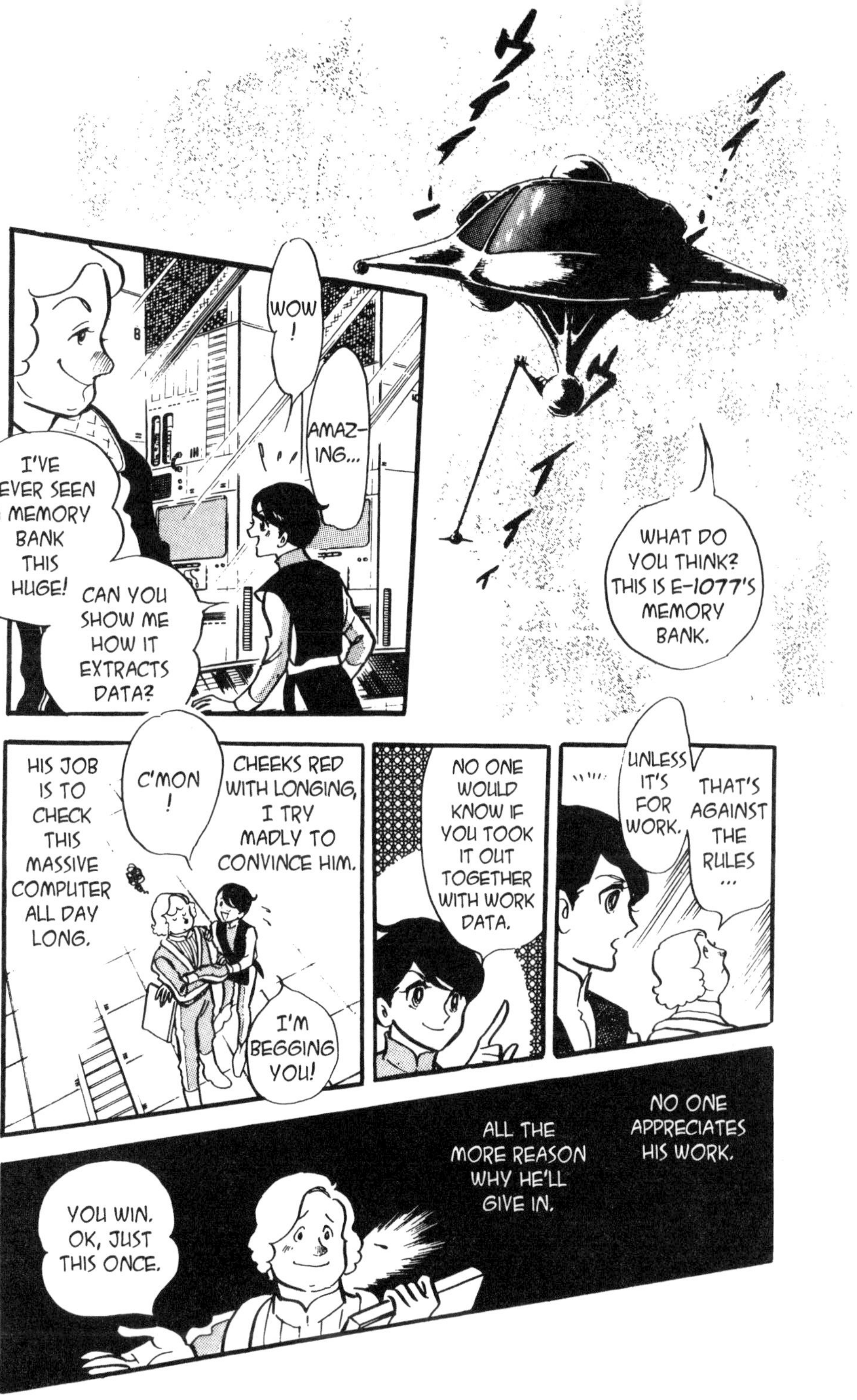
WHAT DO YOU THINK? THIS IS E-1077'S MEMORY BANK.
WOW!
AMAZING...
I'VE NEVER SEEN A MEMORY BANK THIS HUGE!
CAN YOU SHOW ME HOW IT EXTRACTS DATA?
THAT'S AGAINST THE RULES...
UNLESS IT'S FOR WORK.
NO ONE WOULD KNOW IF YOU TOOK IT OUT TOGETHER WITH WORK DATA.
CHEEKS RED WITH LONGING, I TRY MADLY TO CONVINCE HIM.
C'MON!
HIS JOB IS TO CHECK THIS MASSIVE COMPUTER ALL DAY LONG.
I'M BEGGING YOU!
NO ONE APPRECIATES HIS WORK.
ALL THE MORE REASON WHY HE'LL GIVE IN.
YOU WIN. OK, JUST THIS ONCE.

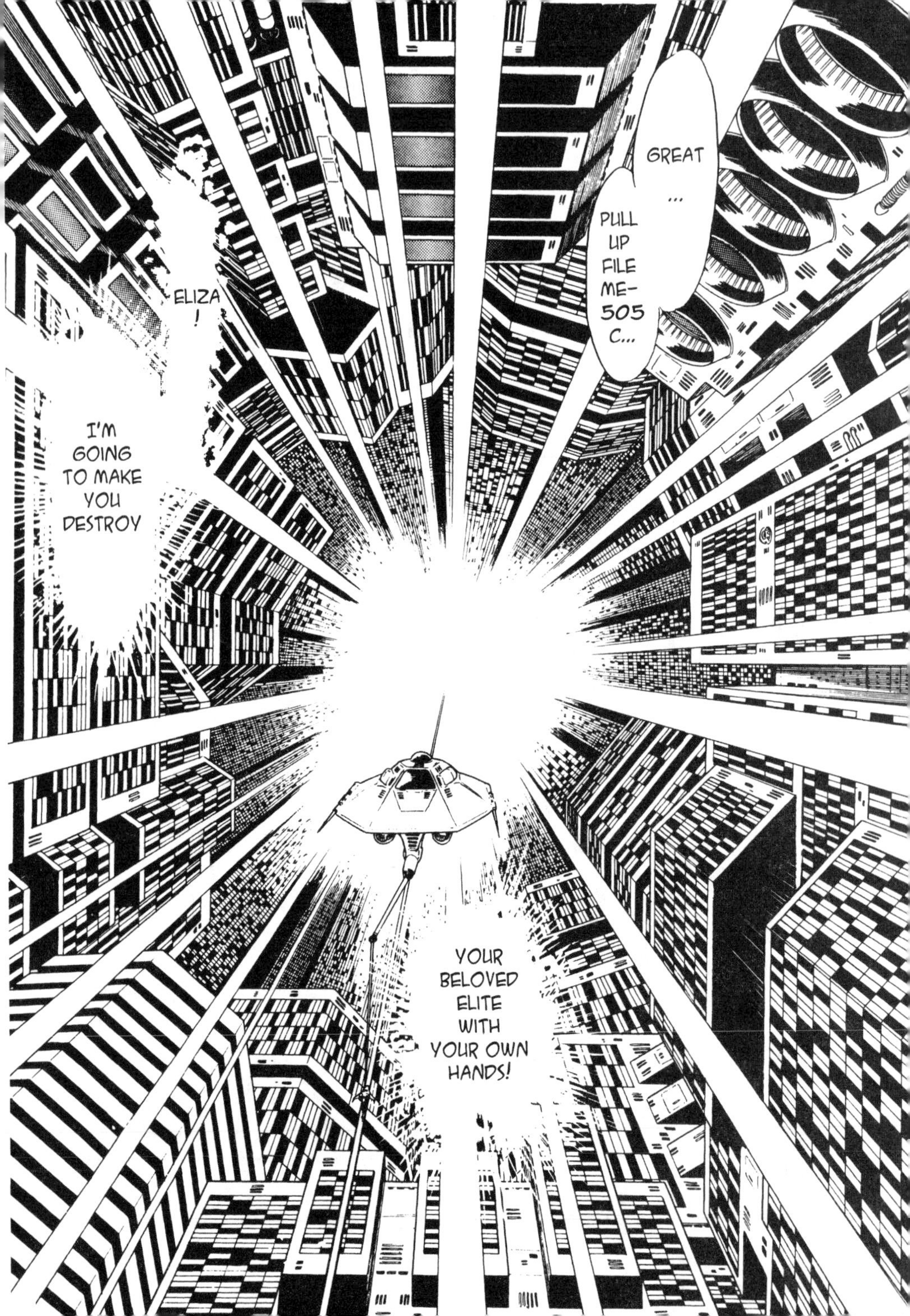
GREAT ...
PULL UP FILE ME-505 C...
ELIZA!
I'M GOING TO MAKE YOU DESTROY
YOUR BELOVED ELITE WITH YOUR OWN HANDS!

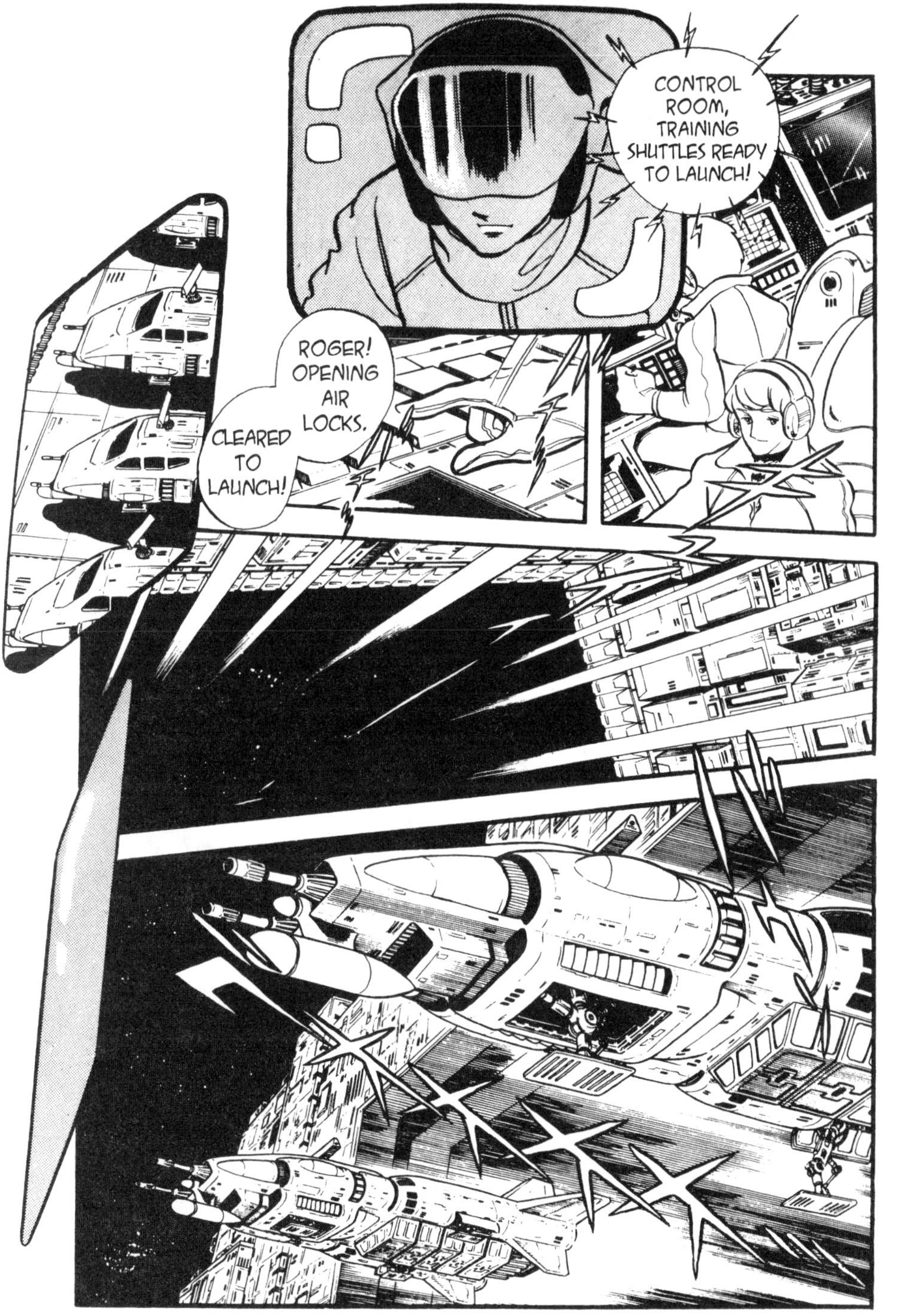

CONTROL ROOM, TRAINING SHUTTLES READY TO LAUNCH!
ROGER! OPENING AIR LOCKS.
CLEARED TO LAUNCH!

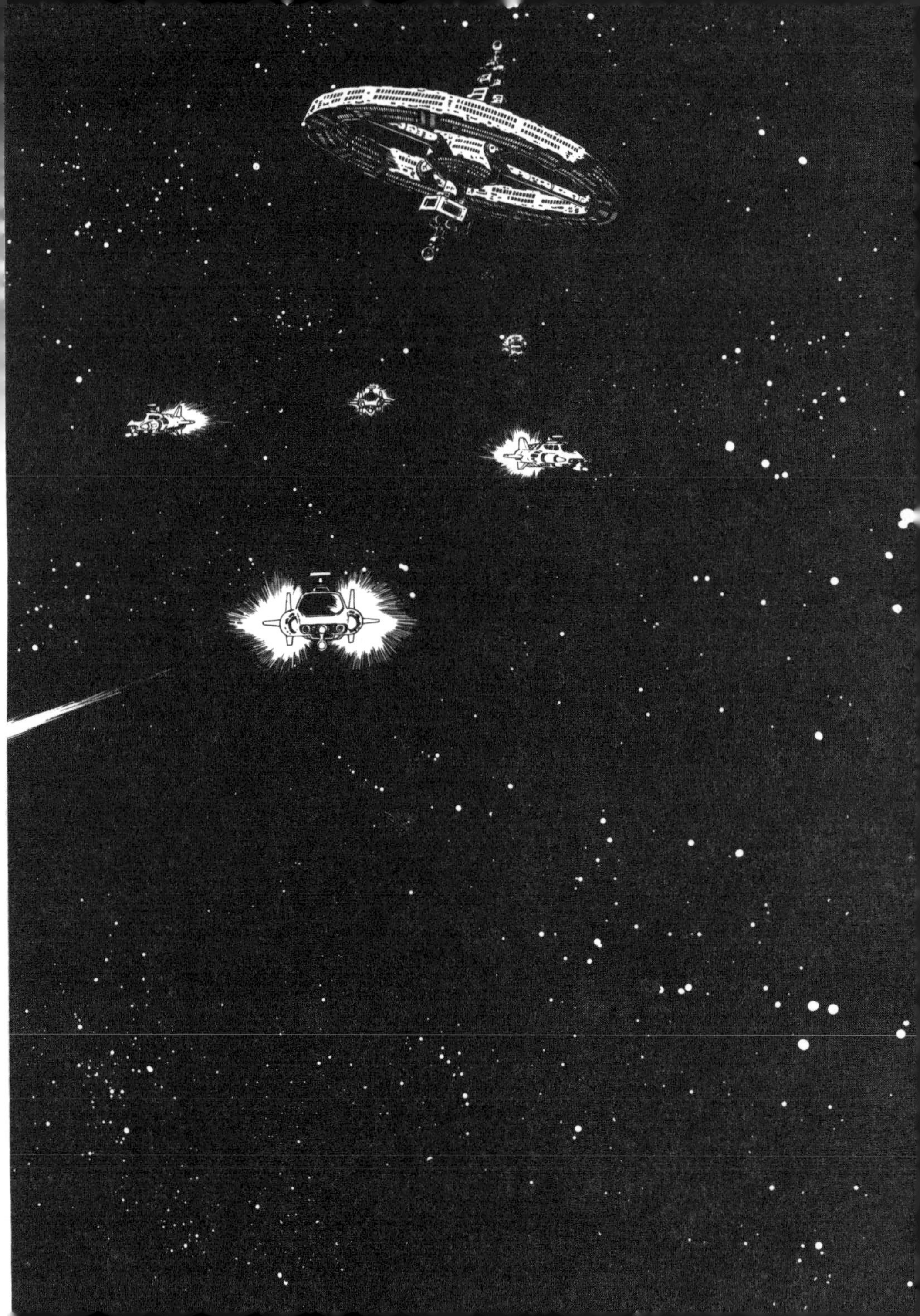

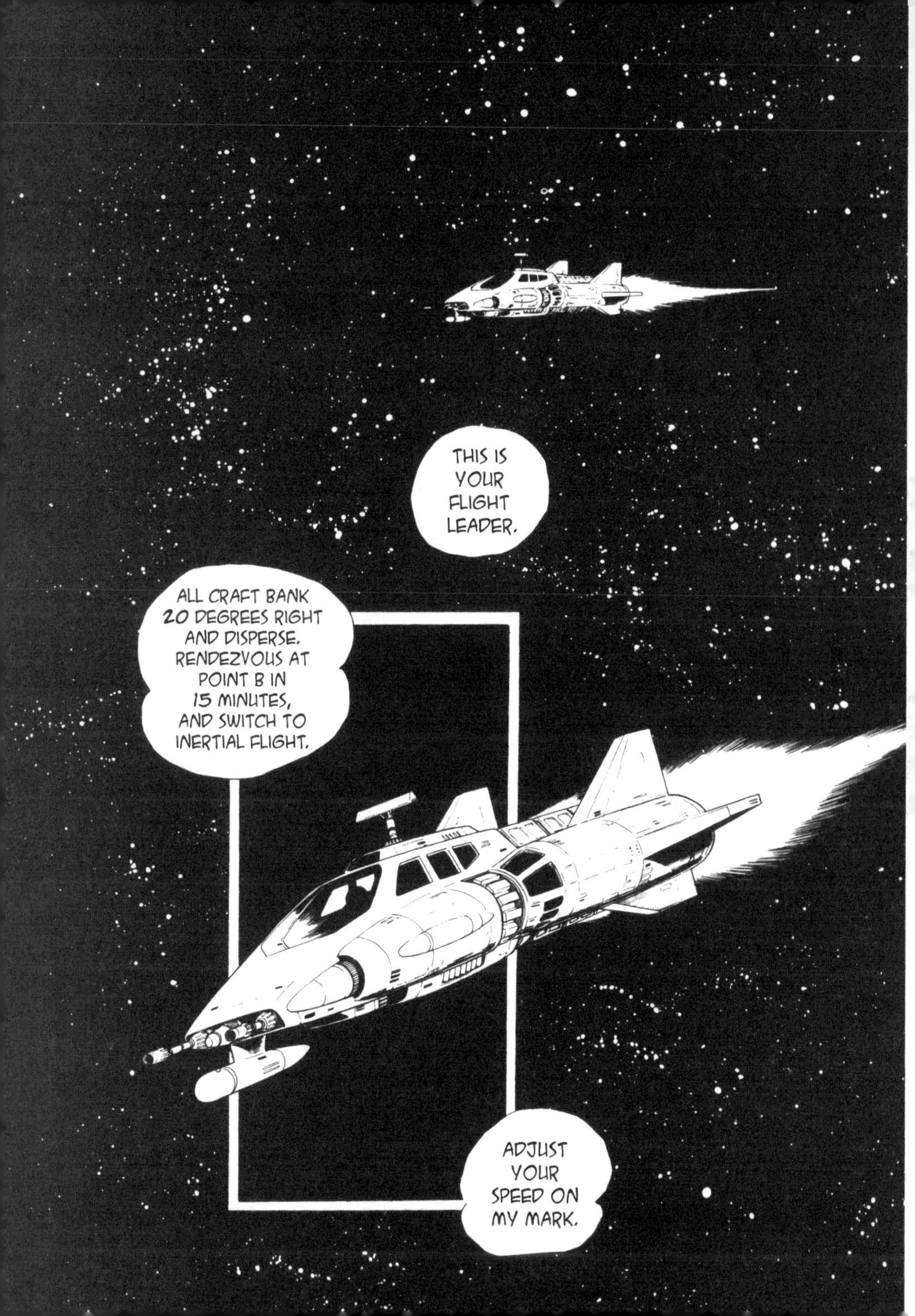
THIS IS YOUR FLIGHT LEADER.
ALL CRAFT BANK 20 DEGREES RIGHT AND DISPERSE. RENDEZVOUS AT POINT B IN 15 MINUTES, AND SWITCH TO INERTIAL FLIGHT.
ADJUST YOUR SPEED ON MY MARK.

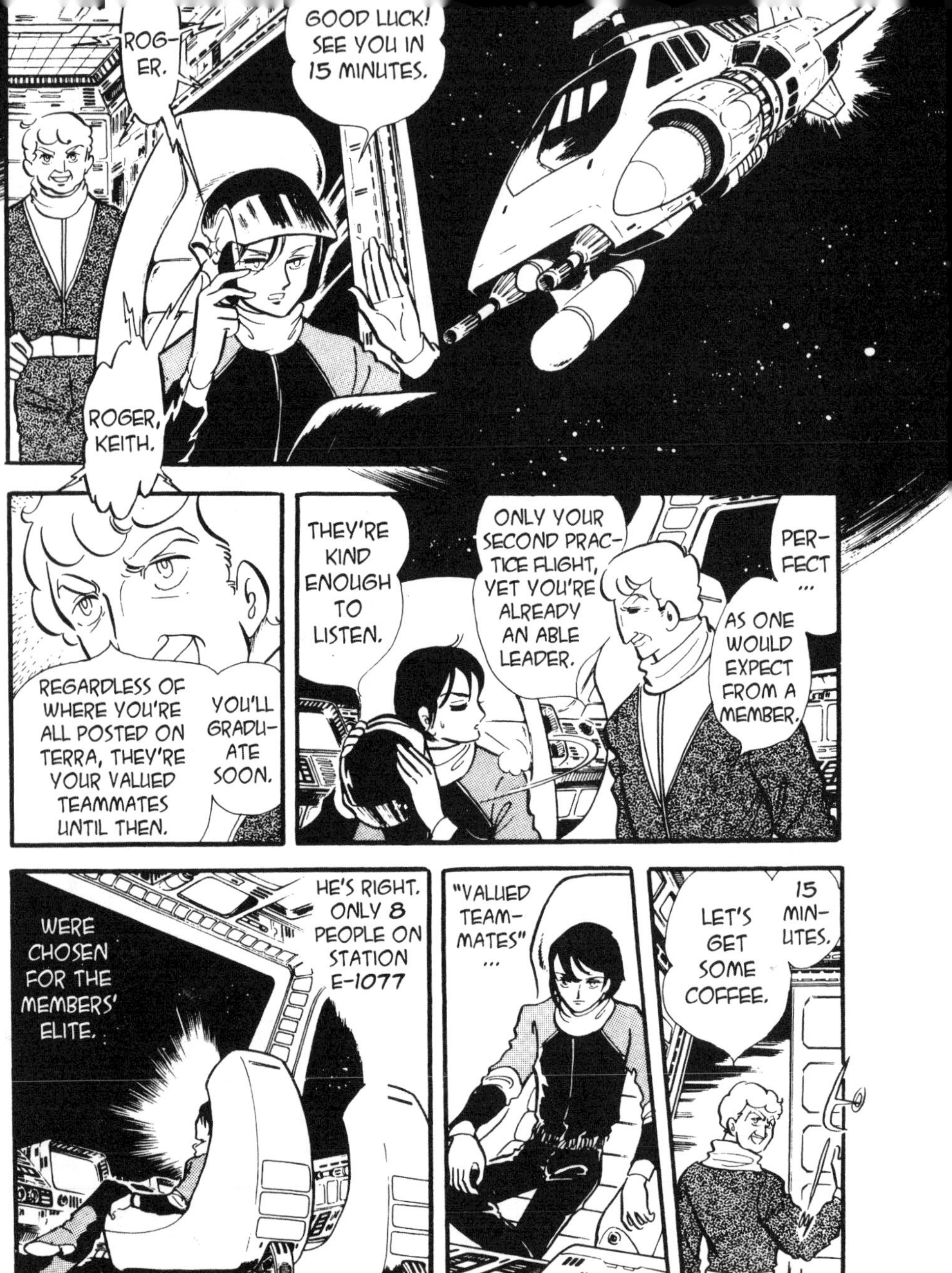
GOOD LUCK! SEE YOU IN 15 MINUTES.
ROG-ER.
ROGER, KEITH.
PER-FECT ...
AS ONE WOULD EXPECT FROM A MEMBER.
ONLY YOUR SECOND PRAC-TICE FLIGHT, YET YOU'RE ALREADY AN ABLE LEADER.
THEY'RE KIND ENOUGH TO LISTEN.
YOU'LL GRADU-ATE SOON.
REGARDLESS OF WHERE YOU'RE ALL POSTED ON TERRA, THEY'RE YOUR VALUED TEAMMATES UNTIL THEN.
15 MIN-UTES.
LET'S GET SOME COFFEE.
"VALUED TEAM-MATES" ...
HE'S RIGHT. ONLY 8 PEOPLE ON STATION E-1077
WERE CHOSEN FOR THE MEMBERS' ELITE.

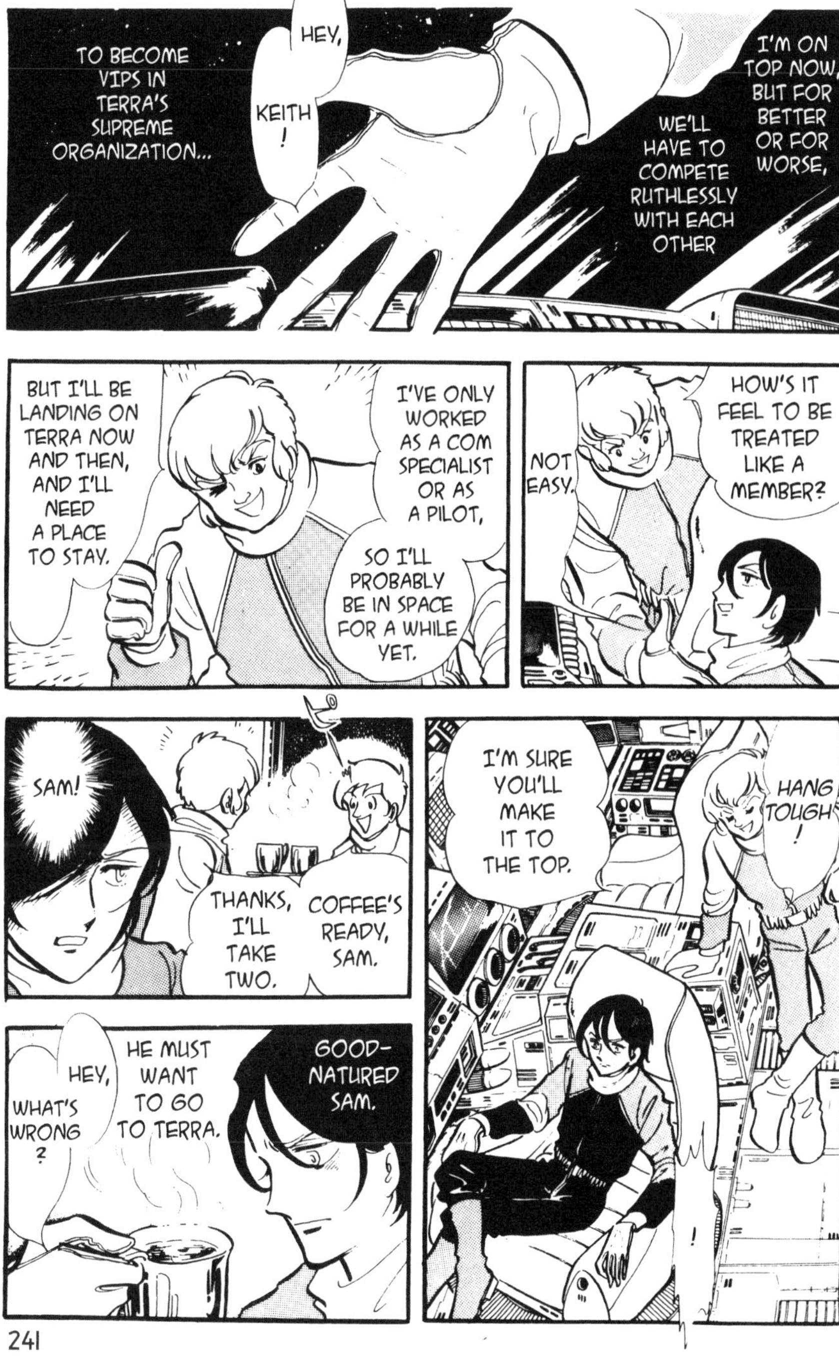

I'M ON TOP NOW, BUT FOR BETTER OR FOR WORSE,
WE'LL HAVE TO COMPETE RUTHLESSLY WITH EACH OTHER
HEY, KEITH!
TO BECOME VIPS IN TERRA'S SUPREME ORGANIZATION...
HOW'S IT FEEL TO BE TREATED LIKE A MEMBER?
NOT EASY.
I'VE ONLY WORKED AS A COM SPECIALIST OR AS A PILOT,
SO I'LL PROBABLY BE IN SPACE FOR A WHILE YET.
BUT I'LL BE LANDING ON TERRA NOW AND THEN, AND I'LL NEED A PLACE TO STAY.
HANG TOUGH!
I'M SURE YOU'LL MAKE IT TO THE TOP.
!
SAM!
COFFEE'S READY, SAM.
THANKS, I'LL TAKE TWO.
GOOD-NATURED SAM.
HE MUST WANT TO GO TO TERRA.
HEY, WHAT'S WRONG?

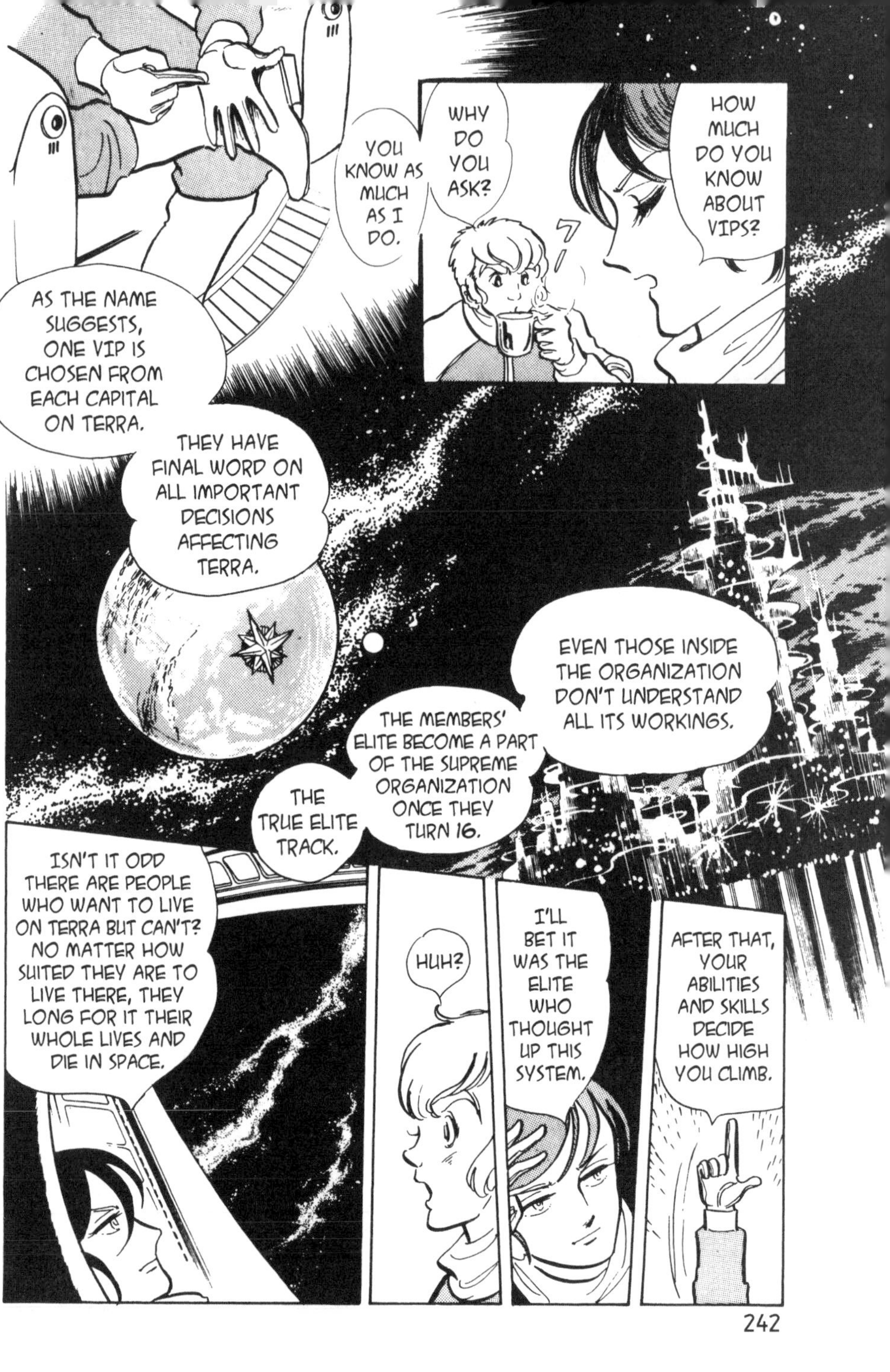
HOW MUCH DO YOU KNOW ABOUT VIPS?
WHY DO YOU ASK?
YOU KNOW AS MUCH AS I DO.
AS THE NAME SUGGESTS, ONE VIP IS CHOSEN FROM EACH CAPITAL ON TERRA.
THEY HAVE FINAL WORD ON ALL IMPORTANT DECISIONS AFFECTING TERRA.
EVEN THOSE INSIDE THE ORGANIZATION DON'T UNDERSTAND ALL ITS WORKINGS.
THE MEMBERS' ELITE BECOME A PART OF THE SUPREME ORGANIZATION ONCE THEY TURN 16.
THE TRUE ELITE TRACK.
AFTER THAT, YOUR ABILITIES AND SKILLS DECIDE HOW HIGH YOU CLIMB.
I'LL BET IT WAS THE ELITE WHO THOUGHT UP THIS SYSTEM.
HUH?
ISN'T IT ODD THERE ARE PEOPLE WHO WANT TO LIVE ON TERRA BUT CAN'T? NO MATTER HOW SUITED THEY ARE TO LIVE THERE, THEY LONG FOR IT THEIR WHOLE LIVES AND DIE IN SPACE.

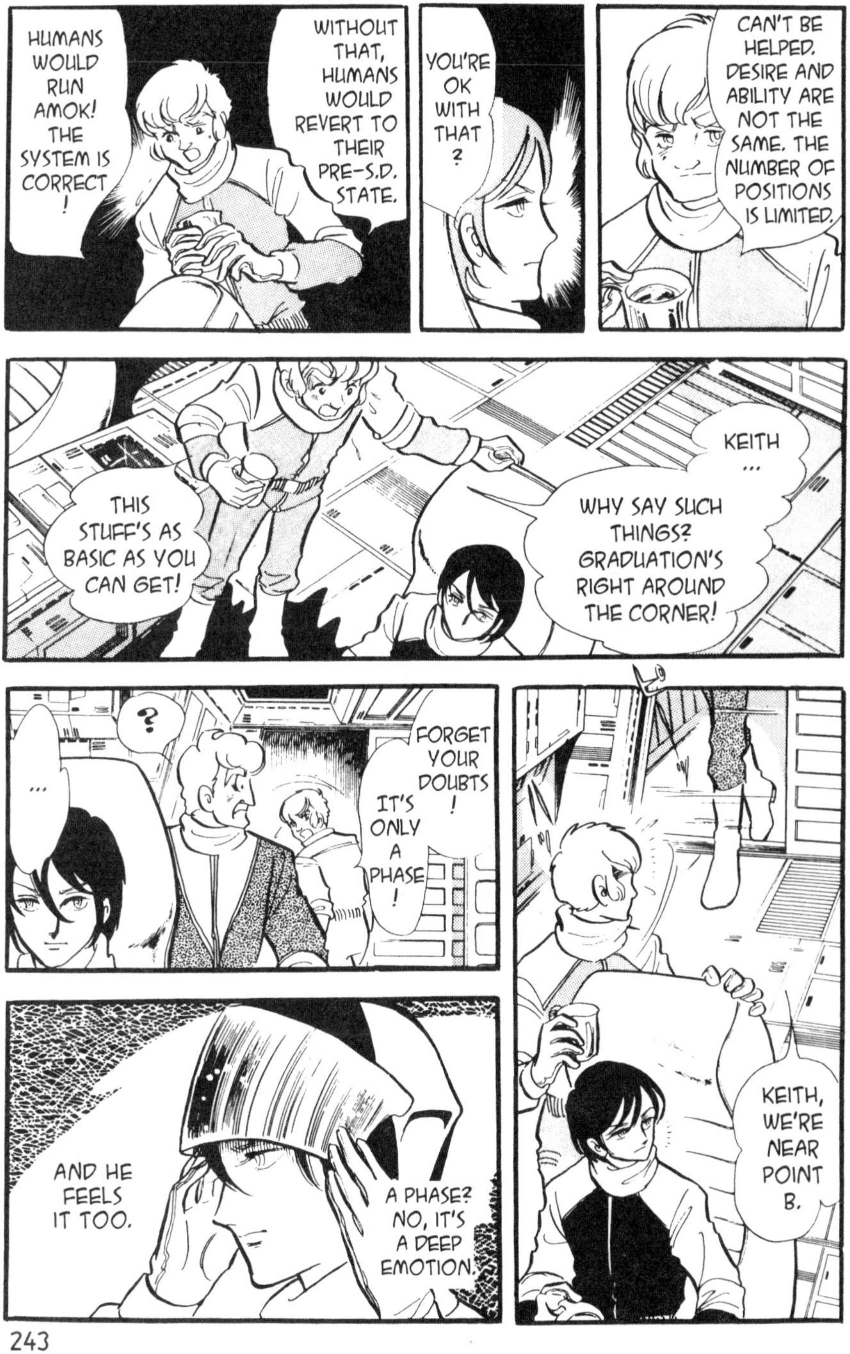
CAN'T BE HELPED. DESIRE AND ABILITY ARE NOT THE SAME. THE NUMBER OF POSITIONS IS LIMITED.
YOU'RE OK WITH THAT?
WITHOUT THAT, HUMANS WOULD REVERT TO THEIR PRE-S.D. STATE.
HUMANS WOULD RUN AMOK! THE SYSTEM IS CORRECT!
KEITH ...
WHY SAY SUCH THINGS? GRADUATION'S RIGHT AROUND THE CORNER!
THIS STUFF'S AS BASIC AS YOU CAN GET!
KEITH, WE'RE NEAR POINT B.
FORGET YOUR DOUBTS!
IT'S ONLY A PHASE!
?
...
A PHASE? NO, IT'S A DEEP EMOTION.
AND HE FEELS IT TOO.

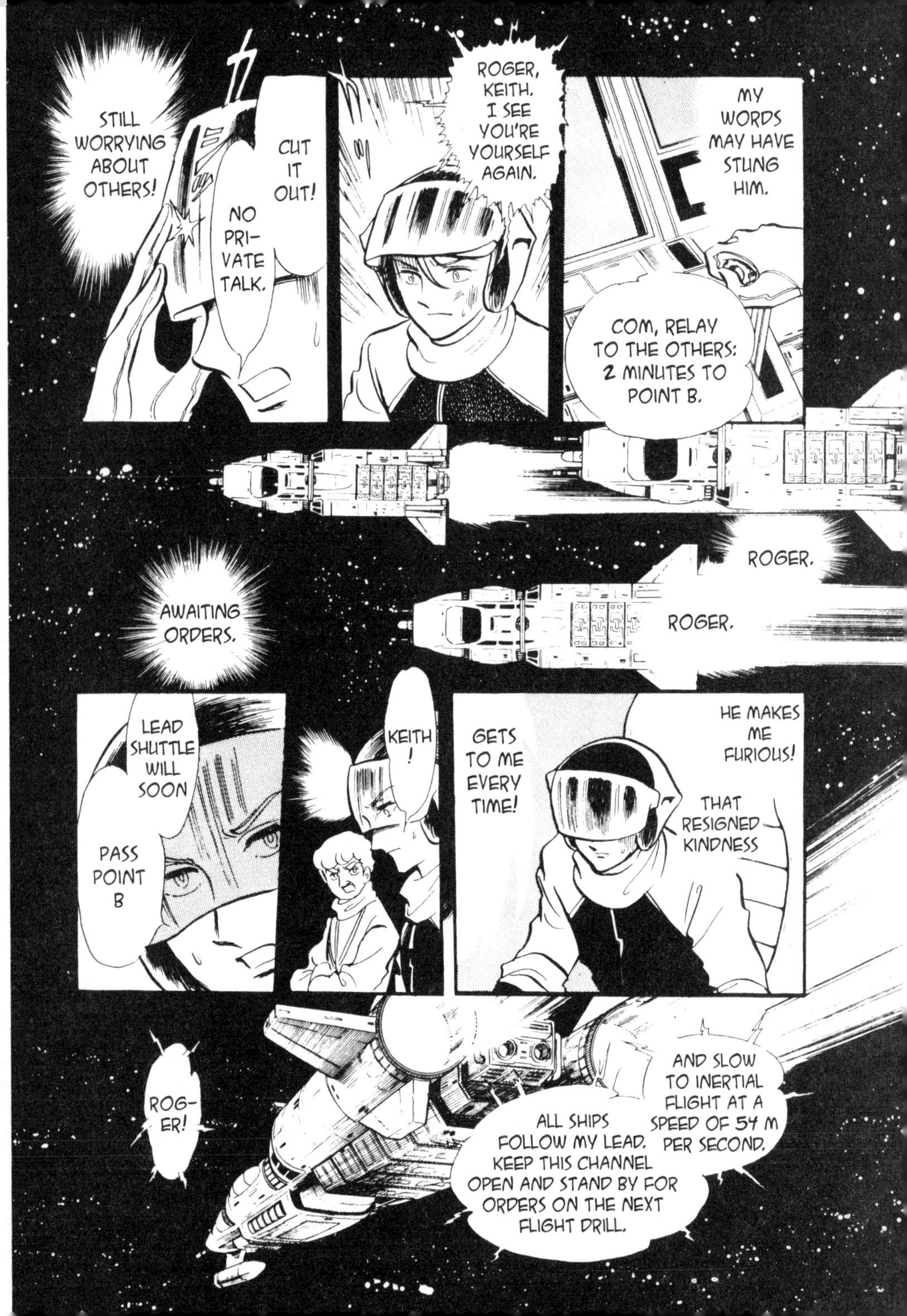
MY WORDS MAY HAVE STUNG HIM.
COM, RELAY TO THE OTHERS: 2 MINUTES TO POINT B.
ROGER, KEITH. I SEE YOU'RE YOURSELF AGAIN.
CUT IT OUT!
NO PRI- VATE TALK.
STILL WORRYING ABOUT OTHERS!
ROGER.
ROGER.
AWAITING ORDERS.
HE MAKES ME FURIOUS!
THAT RESIGNED KINDNESS
GETS TO ME EVERY TIME!
KEITH!
LEAD SHUTTLE WILL SOON
PASS POINT B
AND SLOW TO INERTIAL FLIGHT AT A SPEED OF 54 M PER SECOND.
ALL SHIPS FOLLOW MY LEAD. KEEP THIS CHANNEL OPEN AND STAND BY FOR ORDERS ON THE NEXT FLIGHT DRILL.
ROG- ER!

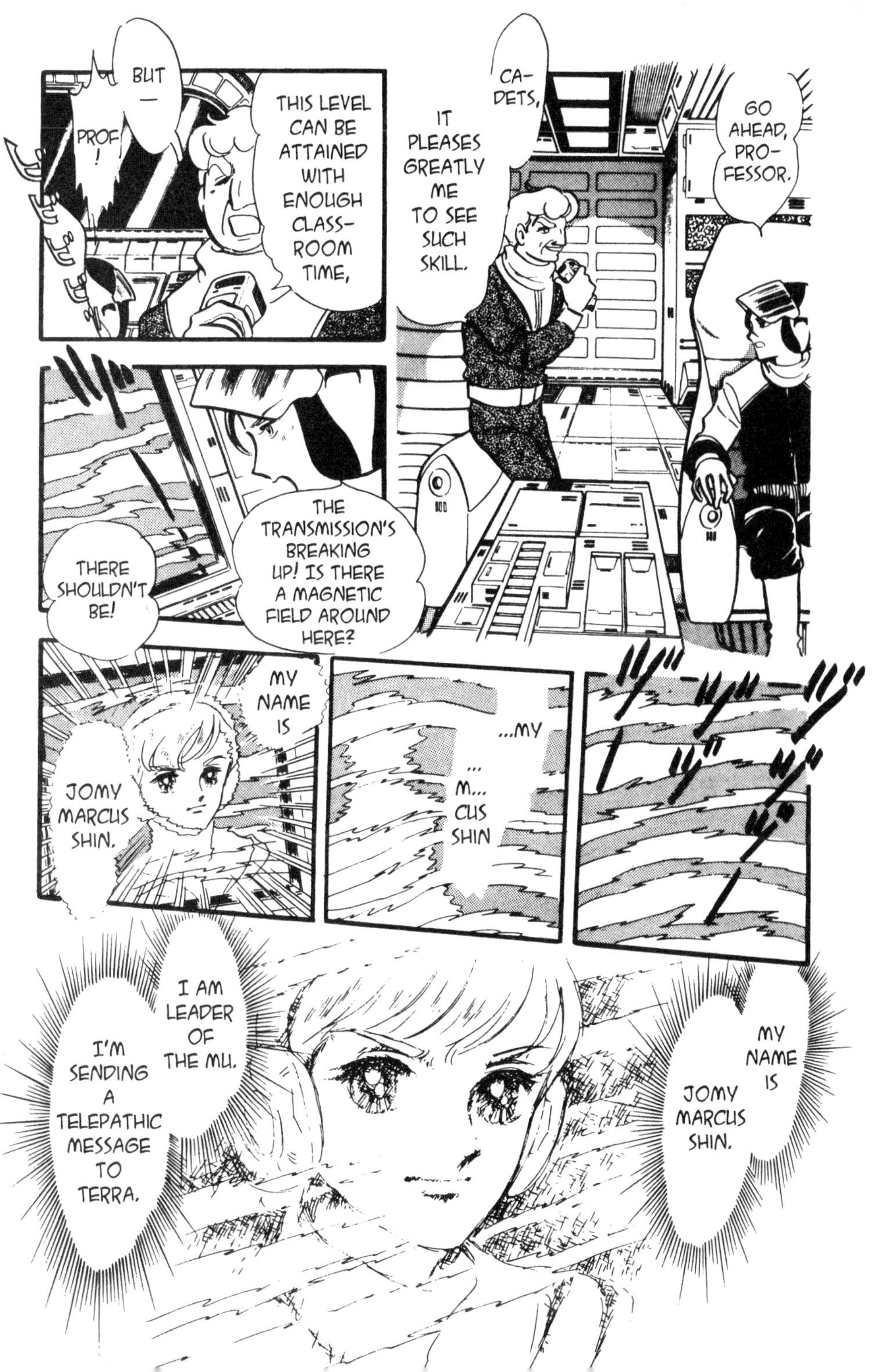
GO AHEAD, PRO-FESSOR.
CA-DETS,
IT PLEASES GREATLY ME TO SEE SUCH SKILL.
THIS LEVEL CAN BE ATTAINED WITH ENOUGH CLASS-ROOM TIME,
BUT —
PROF!
THE TRANSMISSION'S BREAKING UP! IS THERE A MAGNETIC FIELD AROUND HERE?
THERE SHOULDN'T BE!
...MY
... M... CUS SHIN
MY NAME IS
JOMY MARCUS SHIN.
MY NAME IS
JOMY MARCUS SHIN.
I AM LEADER OF THE MU.
I'M SENDING A TELEPATHIC MESSAGE TO TERRA.

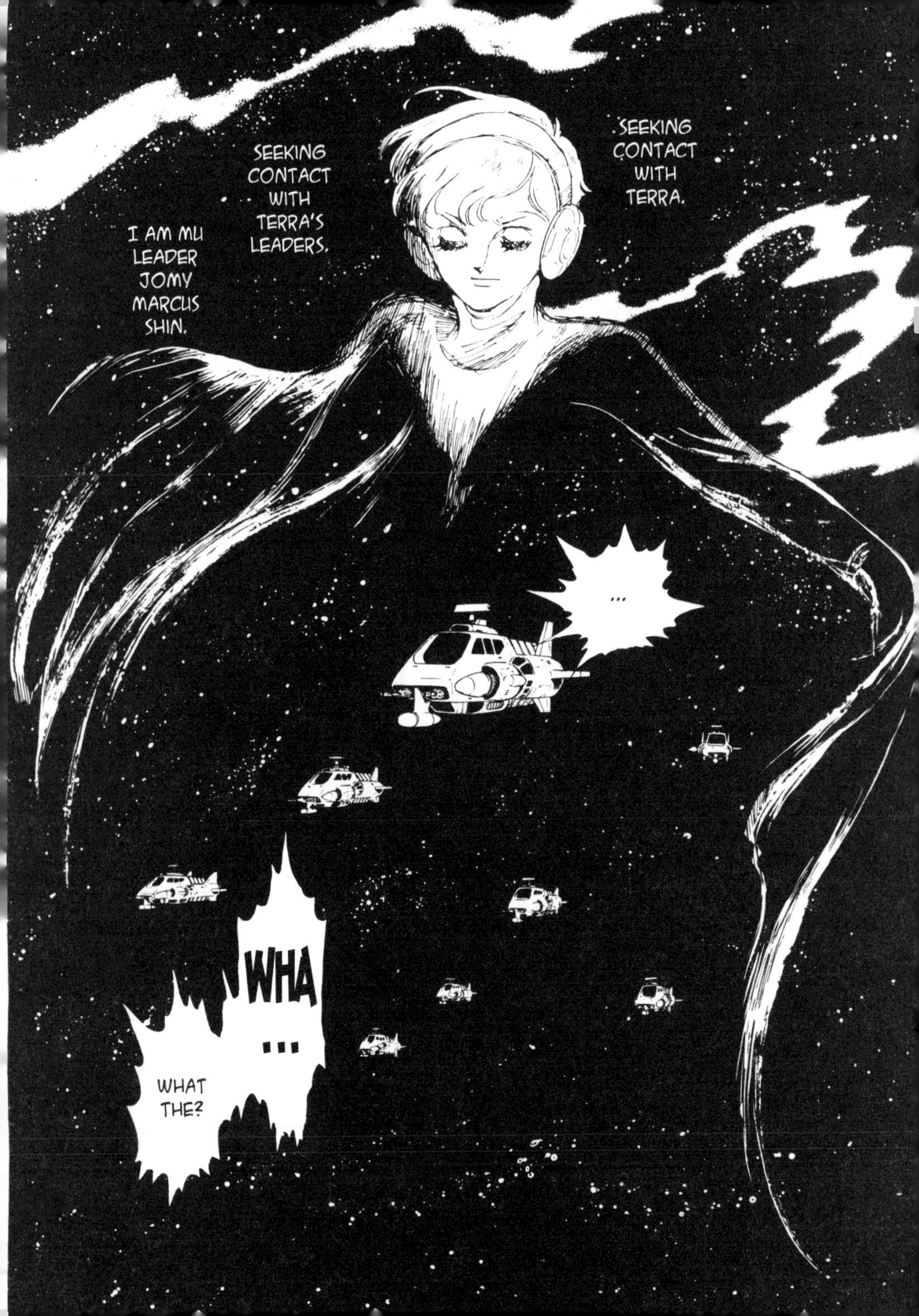
SEEKING CONTACT WITH TERRA.
SEEKING CONTACT WITH TERRA'S LEADERS.
I AM MU LEADER JOMY MARCUS SHIN.
...
WHA...
WHAT THE?

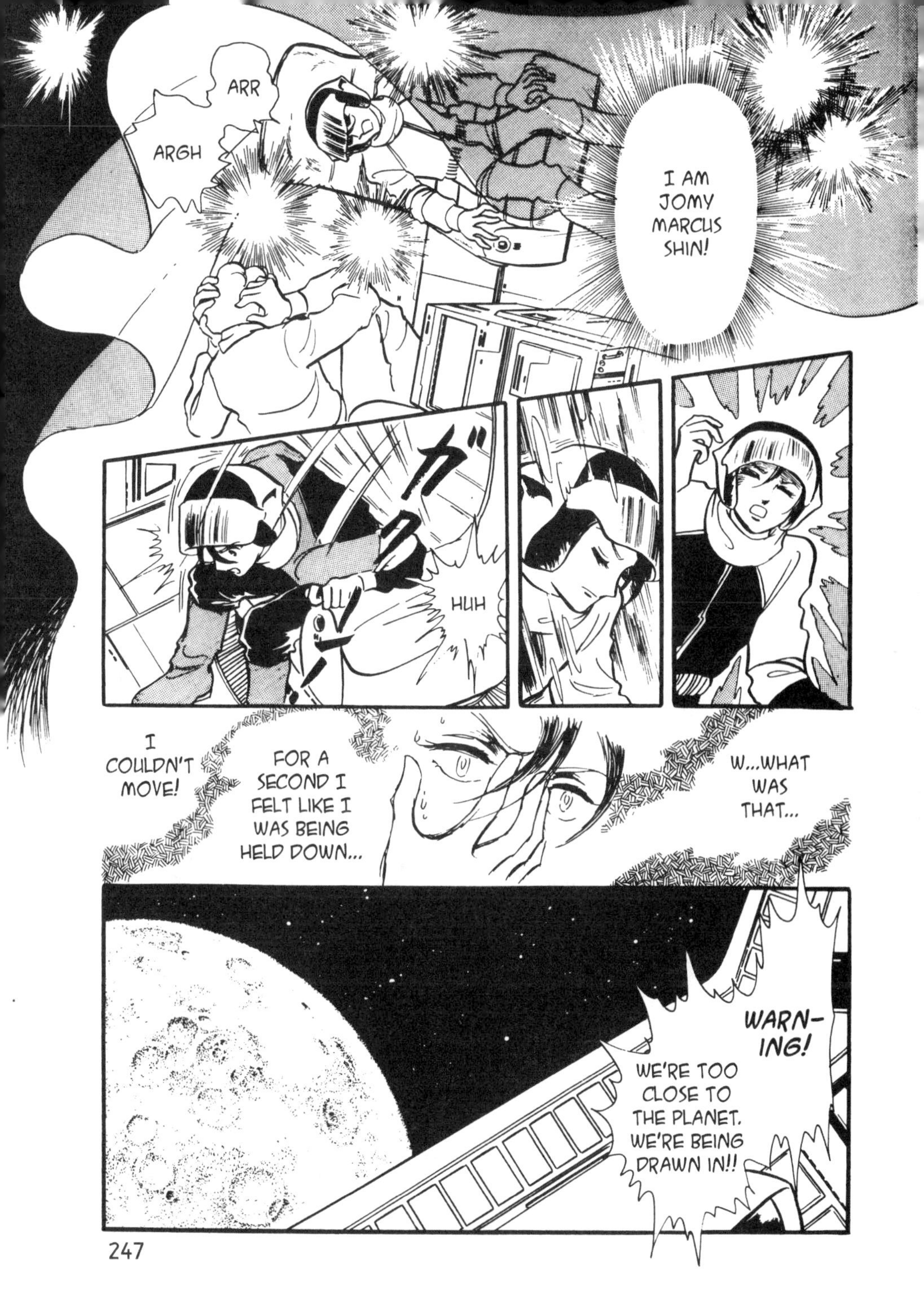
I AM JOMY MARCUS SHIN!
ARR
ARGH
ガク
HUH
W...WHAT WAS THAT...
FOR A SECOND I FELT LIKE I WAS BEING HELD DOWN...
I COULDN'T MOVE!
WARNING!
WE'RE TOO CLOSE TO THE PLANET. WE'RE BEING DRAWN IN!!

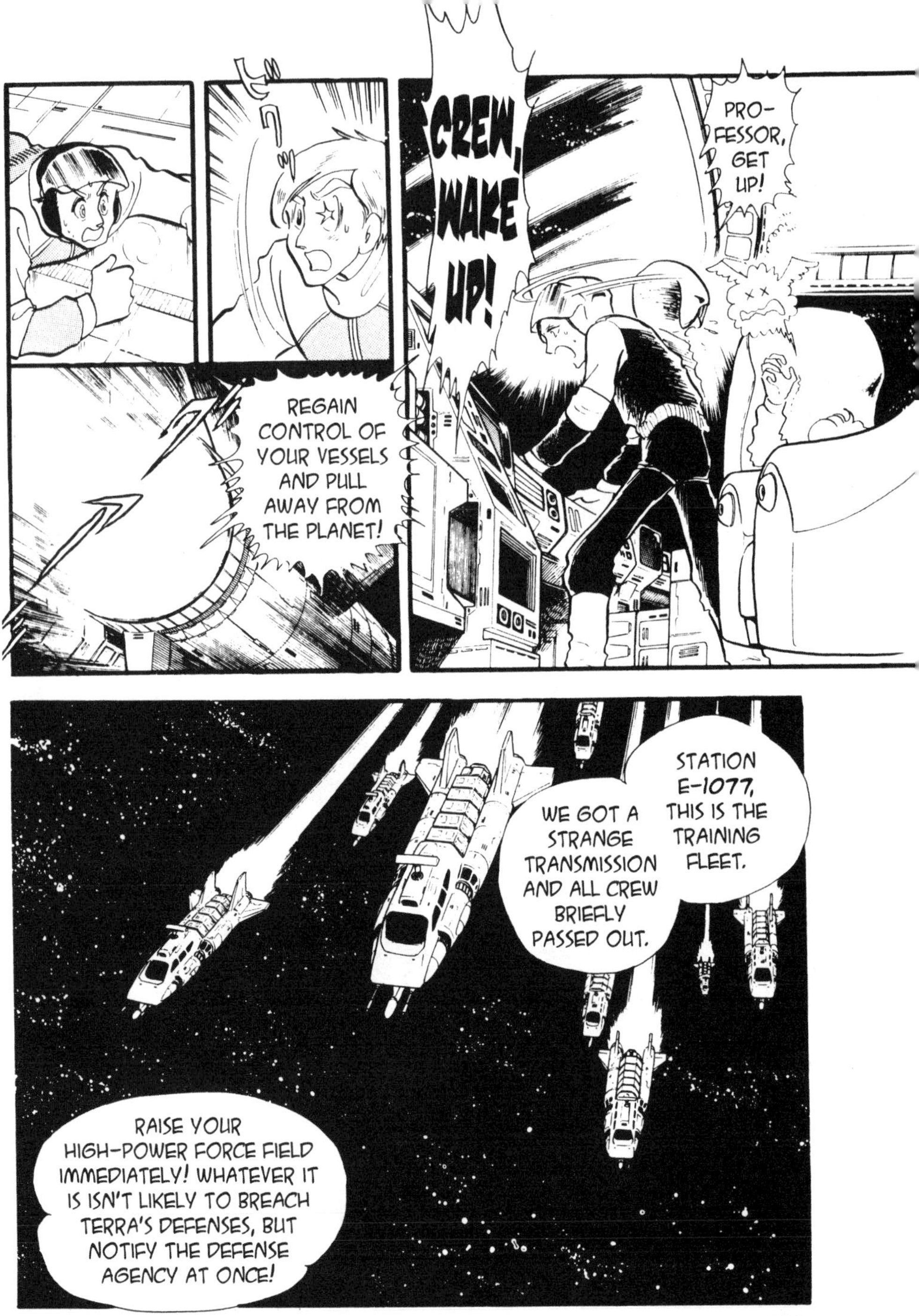
PRO-FESSOR, GET UP!
CREW, WAKE UP!
REGAIN CONTROL OF YOUR VESSELS AND PULL AWAY FROM THE PLANET!
STATION E-1077, THIS IS THE TRAINING FLEET.
WE GOT A STRANGE TRANSMISSION AND ALL CREW BRIEFLY PASSED OUT.
RAISE YOUR HIGH-POWER FORCE FIELD IMMEDIATELY! WHATEVER IT IS ISN'T LIKELY TO BREACH TERRA'S DEFENSES, BUT NOTIFY THE DEFENSE AGENCY AT ONCE!

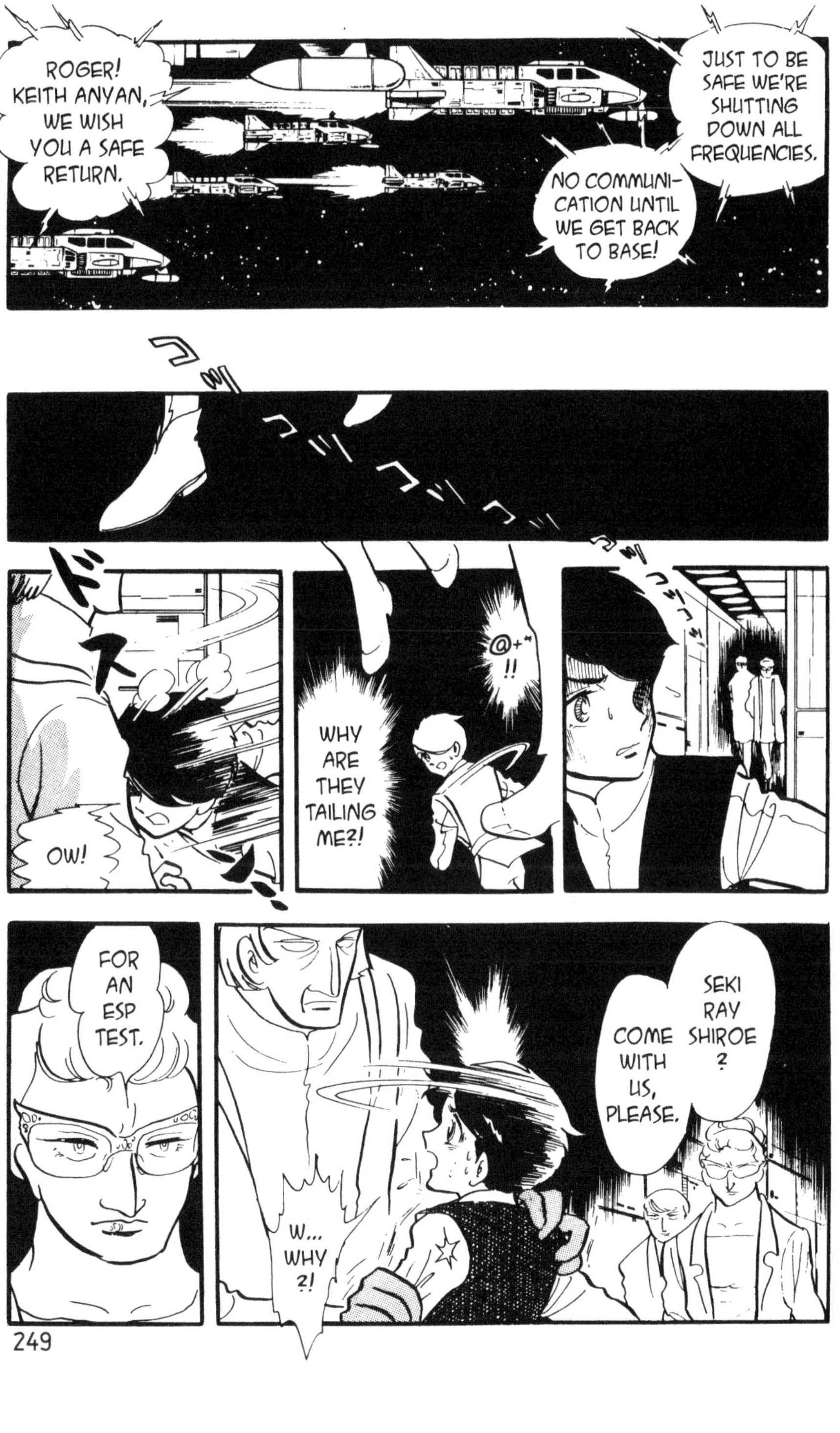
JUST TO BE SAFE WE'RE SHUTTING DOWN ALL FREQUENCIES.
NO COMMUNICATION UNTIL WE GET BACK TO BASE!
ROGER! KEITH ANYAN, WE WISH YOU A SAFE RETURN.
@+* !!
WHY ARE THEY TAILING ME?!
OW!
SEKI RAY SHIROE?
COME WITH US, PLEASE.
W... WHY?!
FOR AN ESP TEST.

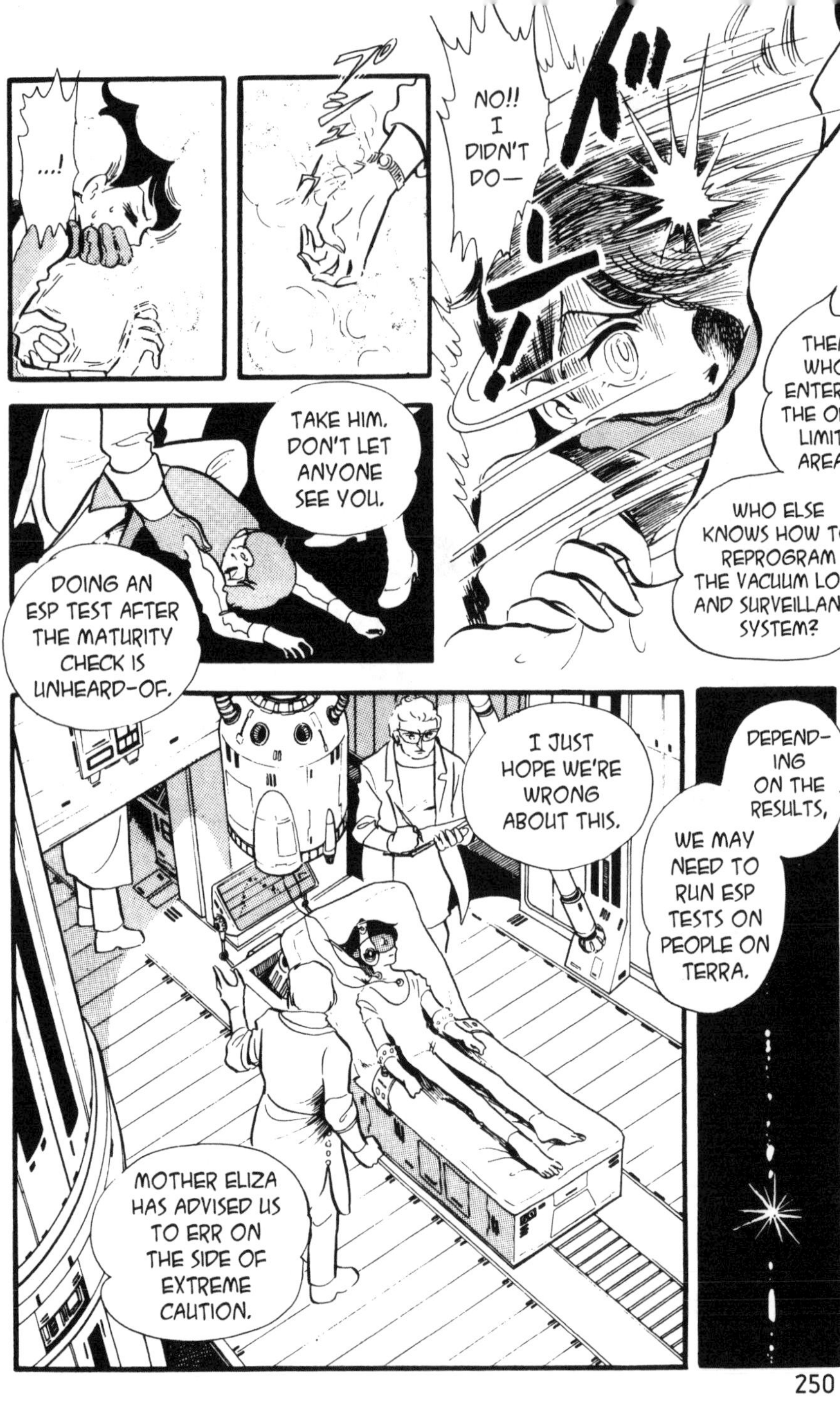

NO!! I DIDN'T DO—
THEN WHO ENTERED THE OFF-LIMITS AREA?
WHO ELSE KNOWS HOW TO REPROGRAM THE VACUUM LOCK AND SURVEILLANCE SYSTEM?
...!
TAKE HIM. DON'T LET ANYONE SEE YOU.
DOING AN ESP TEST AFTER THE MATURITY CHECK IS UNHEARD-OF.
DEPENDING ON THE RESULTS,
WE MAY NEED TO RUN ESP TESTS ON PEOPLE ON TERRA.
I JUST HOPE WE'RE WRONG ABOUT THIS.
MOTHER ELIZA HAS ADVISED US TO ERR ON THE SIDE OF EXTREME CAUTION.

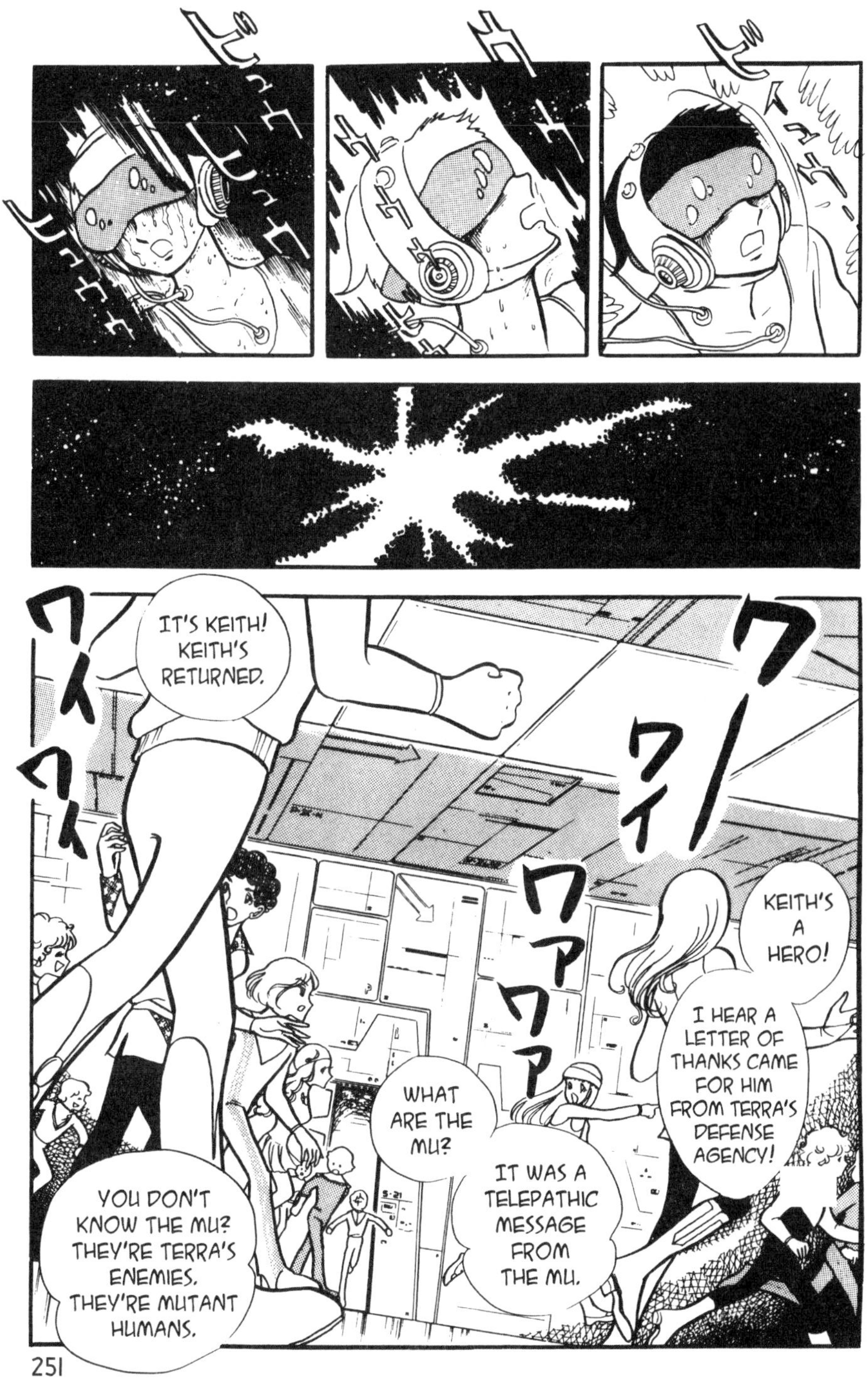
ワーー
ワイ
ワァワァワァ
ワイワイ
IT'S KEITH! KEITH'S RETURNED.
KEITH'S A HERO!
I HEAR A LETTER OF THANKS CAME FOR HIM FROM TERRA'S DEFENSE AGENCY!
IT WAS A TELEPATHIC MESSAGE FROM THE MU.
WHAT ARE THE MU?
YOU DON'T KNOW THE MU? THEY'RE TERRA'S ENEMIES. THEY'RE MUTANT HUMANS.

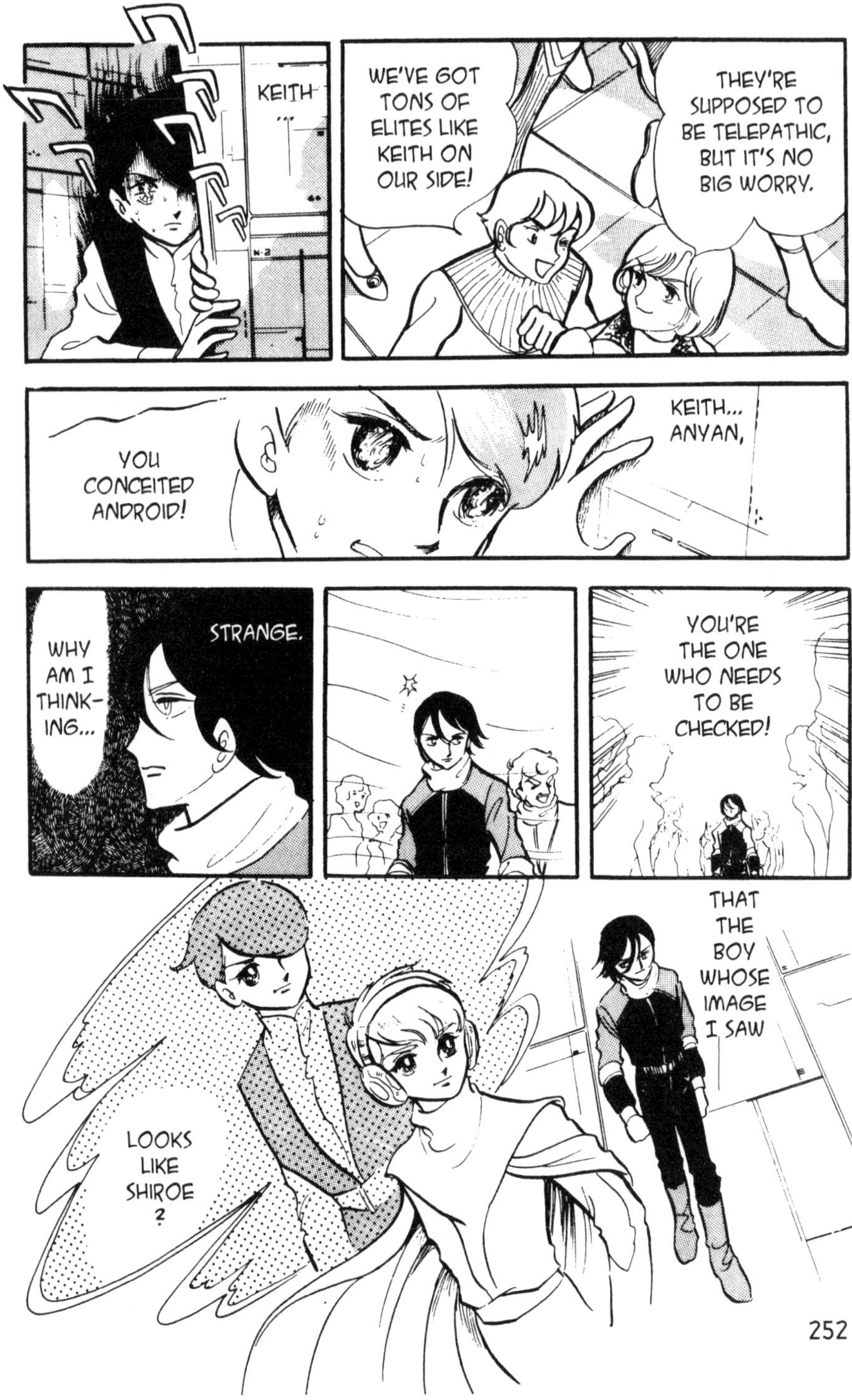
THEY'RE SUPPOSED TO BE TELEPATHIC, BUT IT'S NO BIG WORRY.
WE'VE GOT TONS OF ELITES LIKE KEITH ON OUR SIDE!
KEITH ...
KEITH... ANYAN,
YOU CONCEITED ANDROID!
YOU'RE THE ONE WHO NEEDS TO BE CHECKED!
STRANGE.
WHY AM I THINKING...
THAT THE BOY WHOSE IMAGE I SAW
LOOKS LIKE SHIROE ?

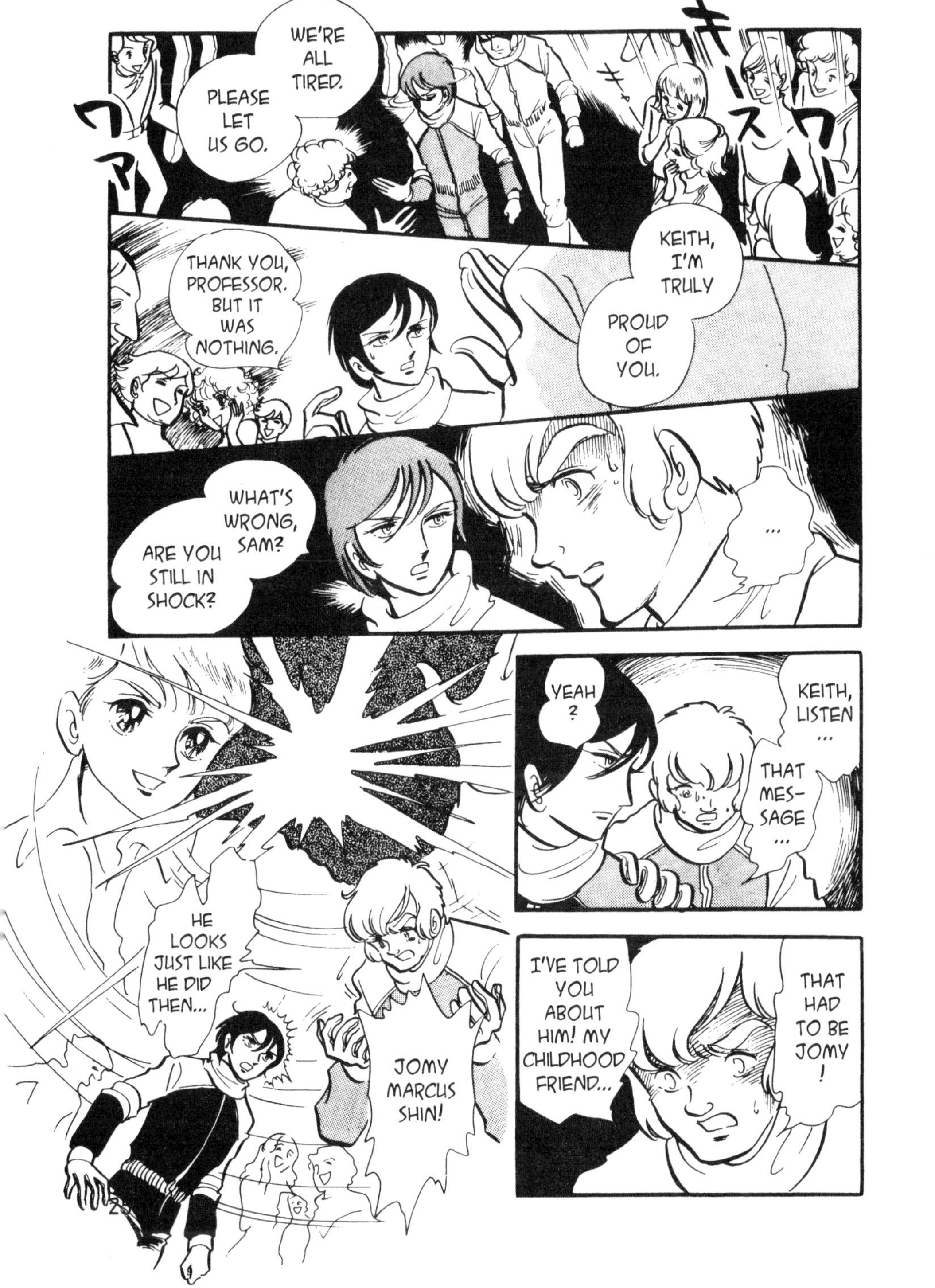
キース
ワー
キャ
WE'RE ALL TIRED.
PLEASE LET US GO.
ワァ
KEITH, I'M TRULY
PROUD OF YOU.
THANK YOU, PROFESSOR. BUT IT WAS NOTHING.
...
WHAT'S WRONG, SAM?
ARE YOU STILL IN SHOCK?
KEITH, LISTEN...
THAT MES-SAGE...
YEAH?
THAT HAD TO BE JOMY!
I'VE TOLD YOU ABOUT HIM! MY CHILDHOOD FRIEND...
JOMY MARCUS SHIN!
HE LOOKS JUST LIKE HE DID THEN...

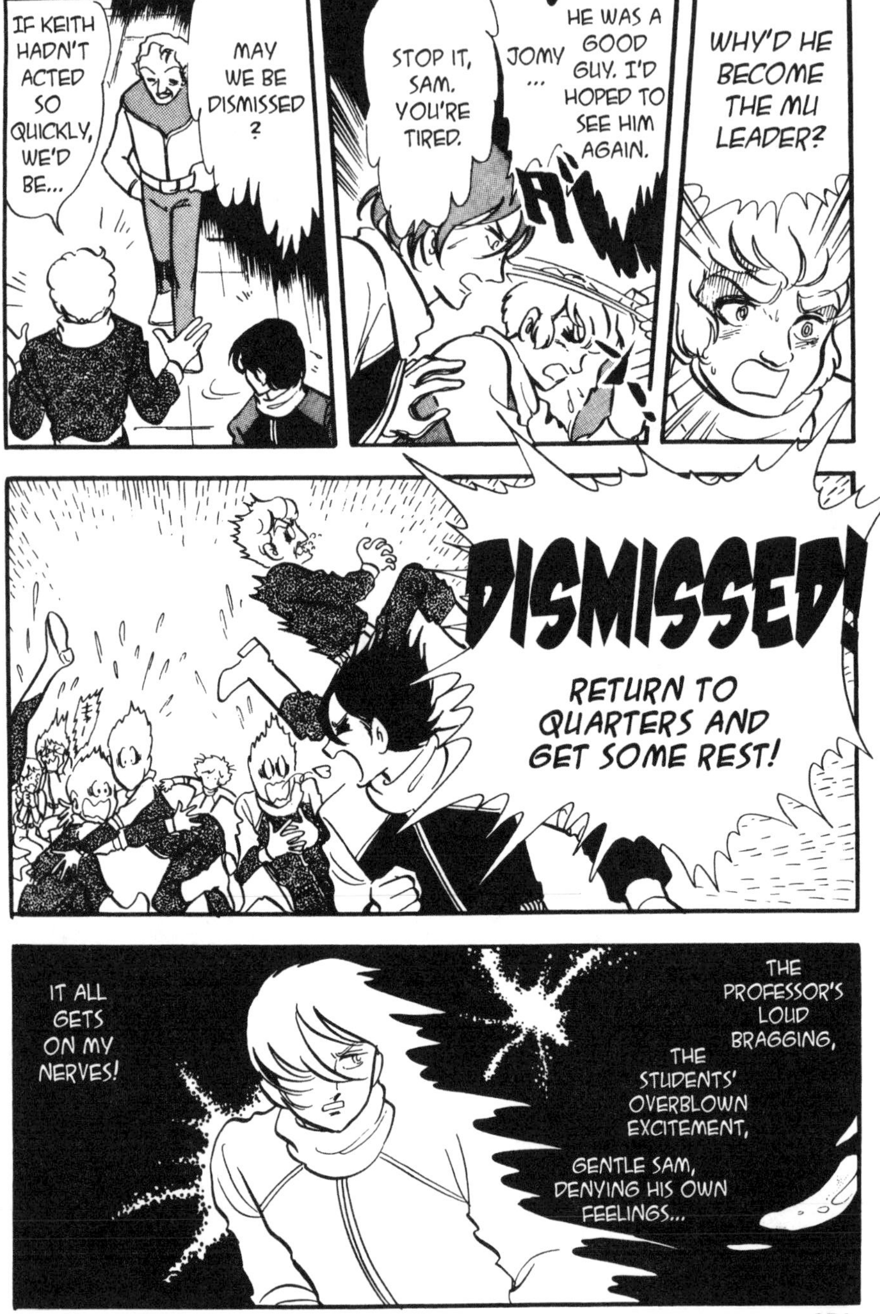
WHY'D HE BECOME THE MU LEADER?
HE WAS A GOOD GUY. I'D HOPED TO SEE HIM AGAIN.
JOMY ...
STOP IT, SAM. YOU'RE TIRED.
MAY WE BE DISMISSED?
IF KEITH HADN'T ACTED SO QUICKLY, WE'D BE...
DISMISSED!
RETURN TO QUARTERS AND GET SOME REST!
THE PROFESSOR'S LOUD BRAGGING,
THE STUDENTS' OVERBLOWN EXCITEMENT,
GENTLE SAM, DENYING HIS OWN FEELINGS...
IT ALL GETS ON MY NERVES!

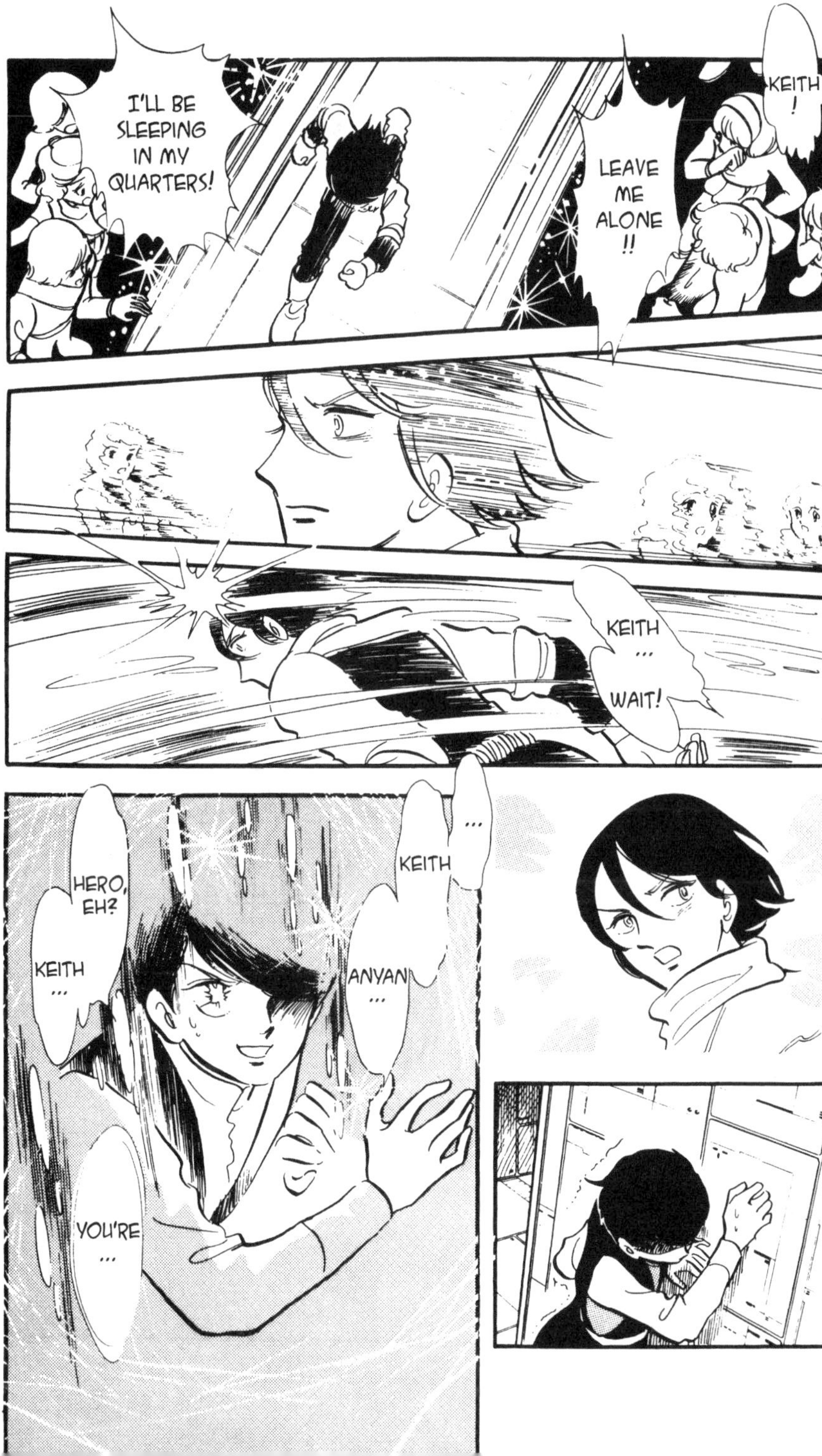
KEITH!
LEAVE ME ALONE!!
I'LL BE SLEEPING IN MY QUARTERS!
KEITH... WAIT!
...
KEITH
ANYAN...
HERO, EH?
KEITH...
YOU'RE...

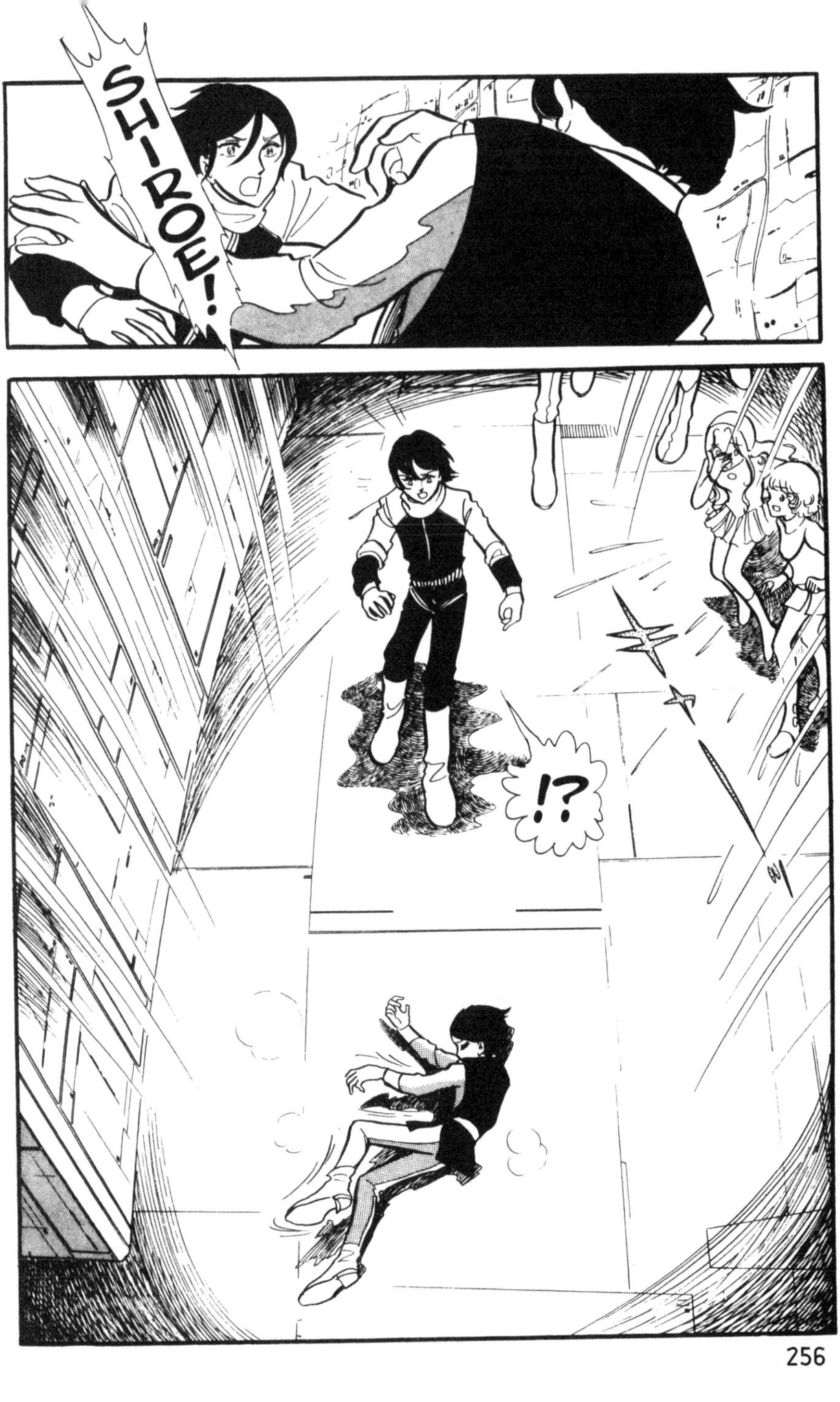
SHIROE!
!?

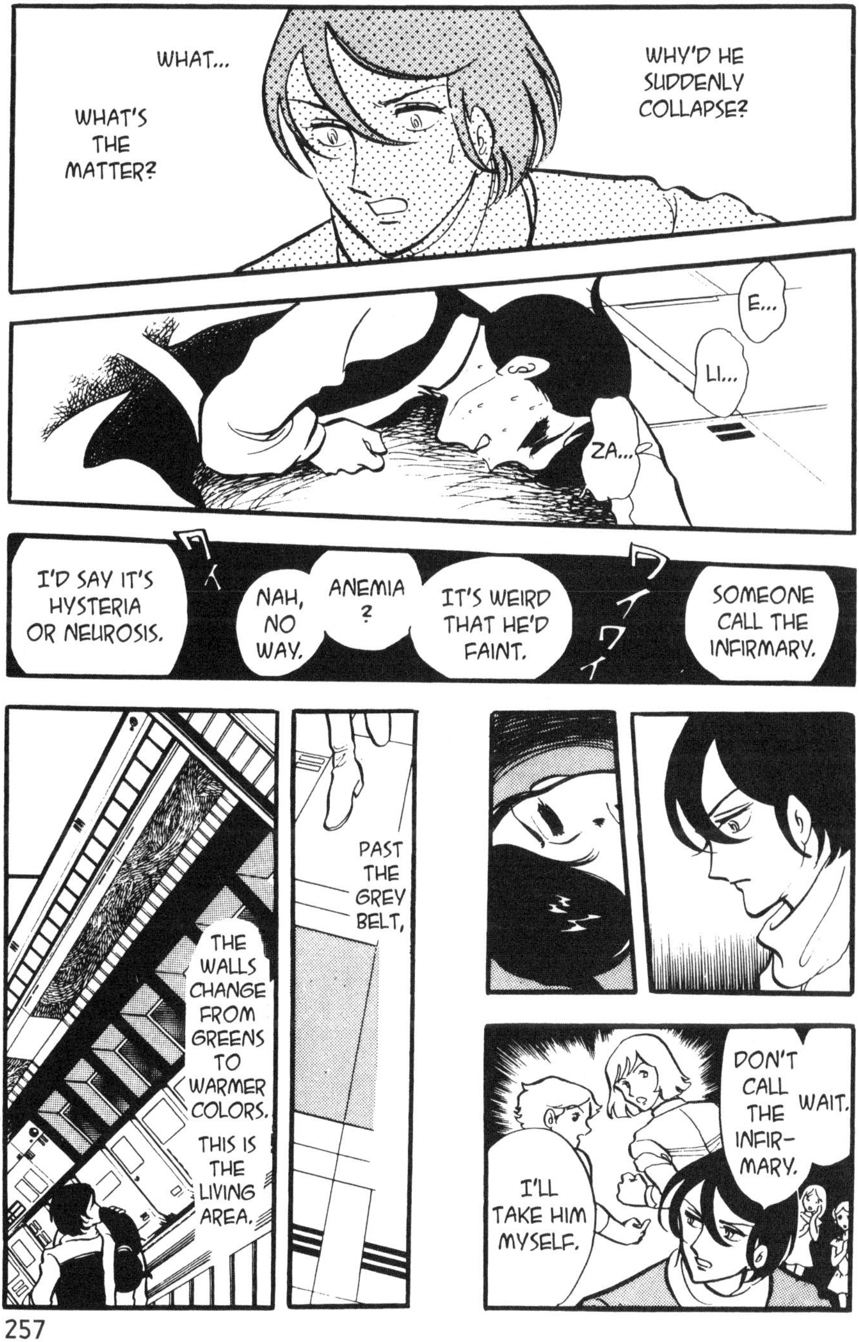
WHY'D HE SUDDENLY COLLAPSE?
WHAT...
WHAT'S THE MATTER?
E...
LI...
ZA...
ワイワイ
SOMEONE CALL THE INFIRMARY.
IT'S WEIRD THAT HE'D FAINT.
ANEMIA?
NAH, NO WAY.
ワイ
I'D SAY IT'S HYSTERIA OR NEUROSIS.
WAIT.
DON'T CALL THE INFIRMARY.
I'LL TAKE HIM MYSELF.
PAST THE GREY BELT,
THE WALLS CHANGE FROM GREENS TO WARMER COLORS.
THIS IS THE LIVING AREA.

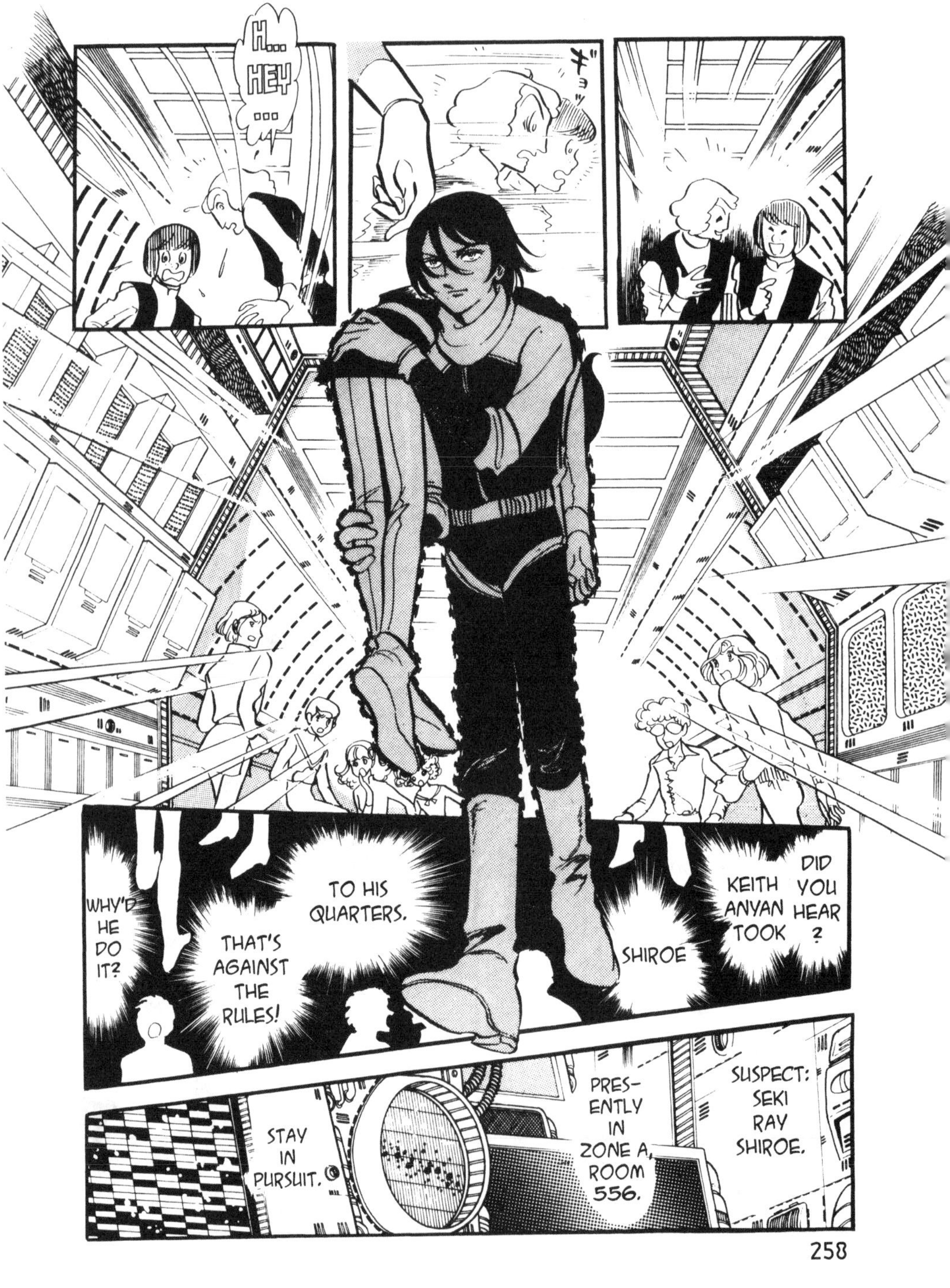
ギョッ
H... HEY ...
DID YOU HEAR?
KEITH ANYAN TOOK
SHIROE
TO HIS QUARTERS.
THAT'S AGAINST THE RULES!
WHY'D HE DO IT?
SUSPECT: SEKI RAY SHIROE.
PRESENTLY IN ZONE A, ROOM 556.
STAY IN PURSUIT.

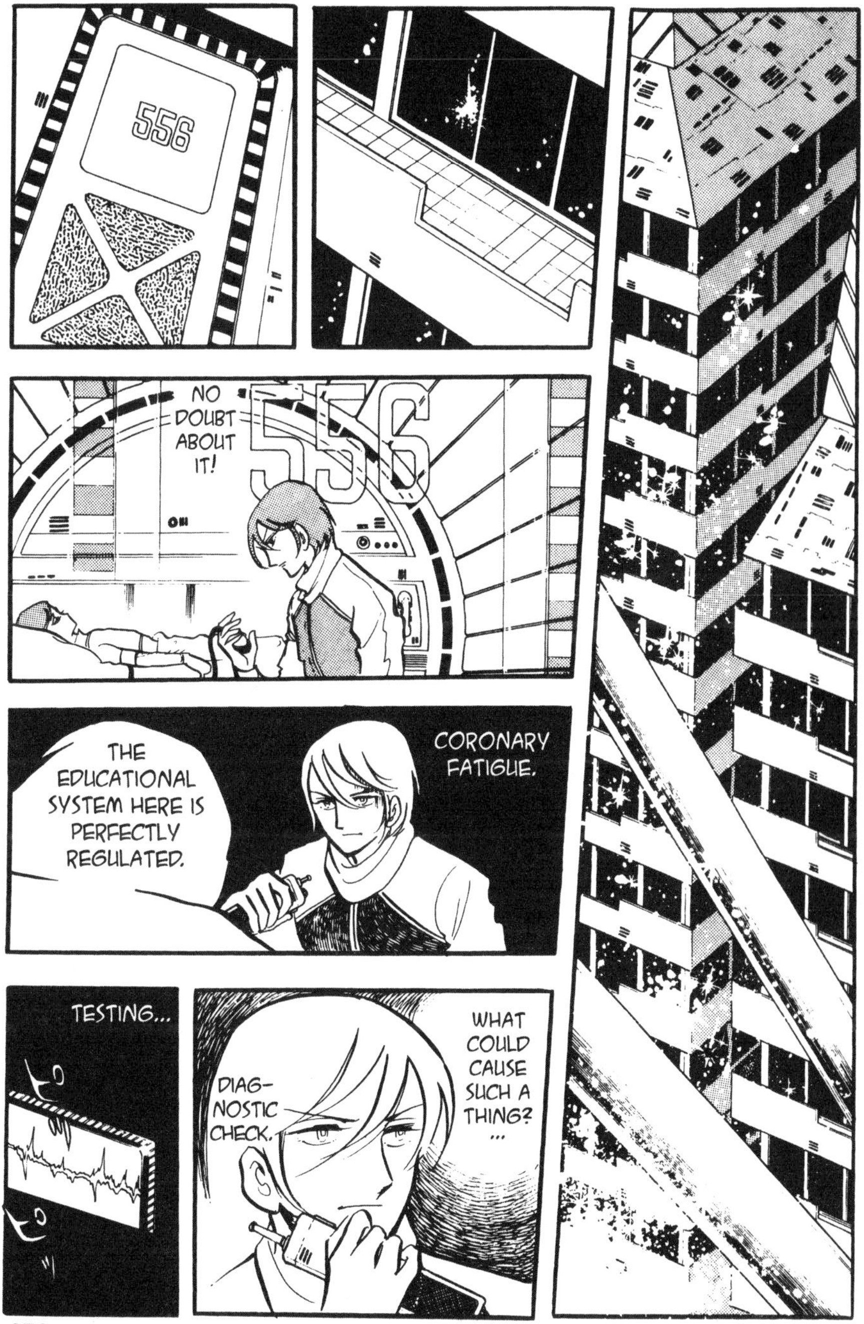
556
NO DOUBT ABOUT IT!
CORONARY FATIGUE.
THE EDUCATIONAL SYSTEM HERE IS PERFECTLY REGULATED.
WHAT COULD CAUSE SUCH A THING? ...
DIAG-NOSTIC CHECK.
TESTING...

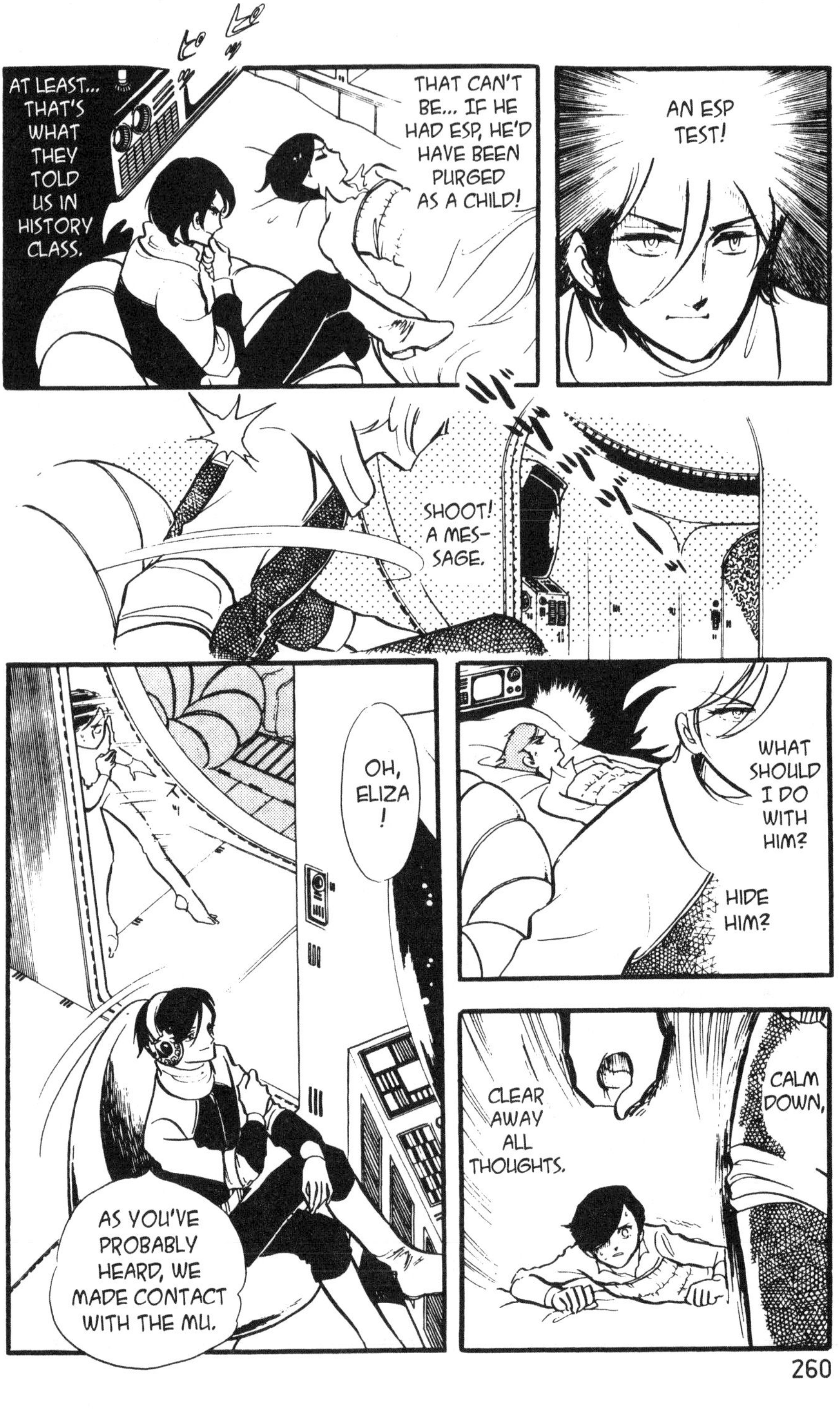
AN ESP TEST!
THAT CAN'T BE... IF HE HAD ESP, HE'D HAVE BEEN PURGED AS A CHILD!
AT LEAST... THAT'S WHAT THEY TOLD US IN HISTORY CLASS.
SHOOT! A MES-SAGE.
WHAT SHOULD I DO WITH HIM?
HIDE HIM?
CALM DOWN,
CLEAR AWAY ALL THOUGHTS.
OH, ELIZA!
AS YOU'VE PROBABLY HEARD, WE MADE CONTACT WITH THE MU.

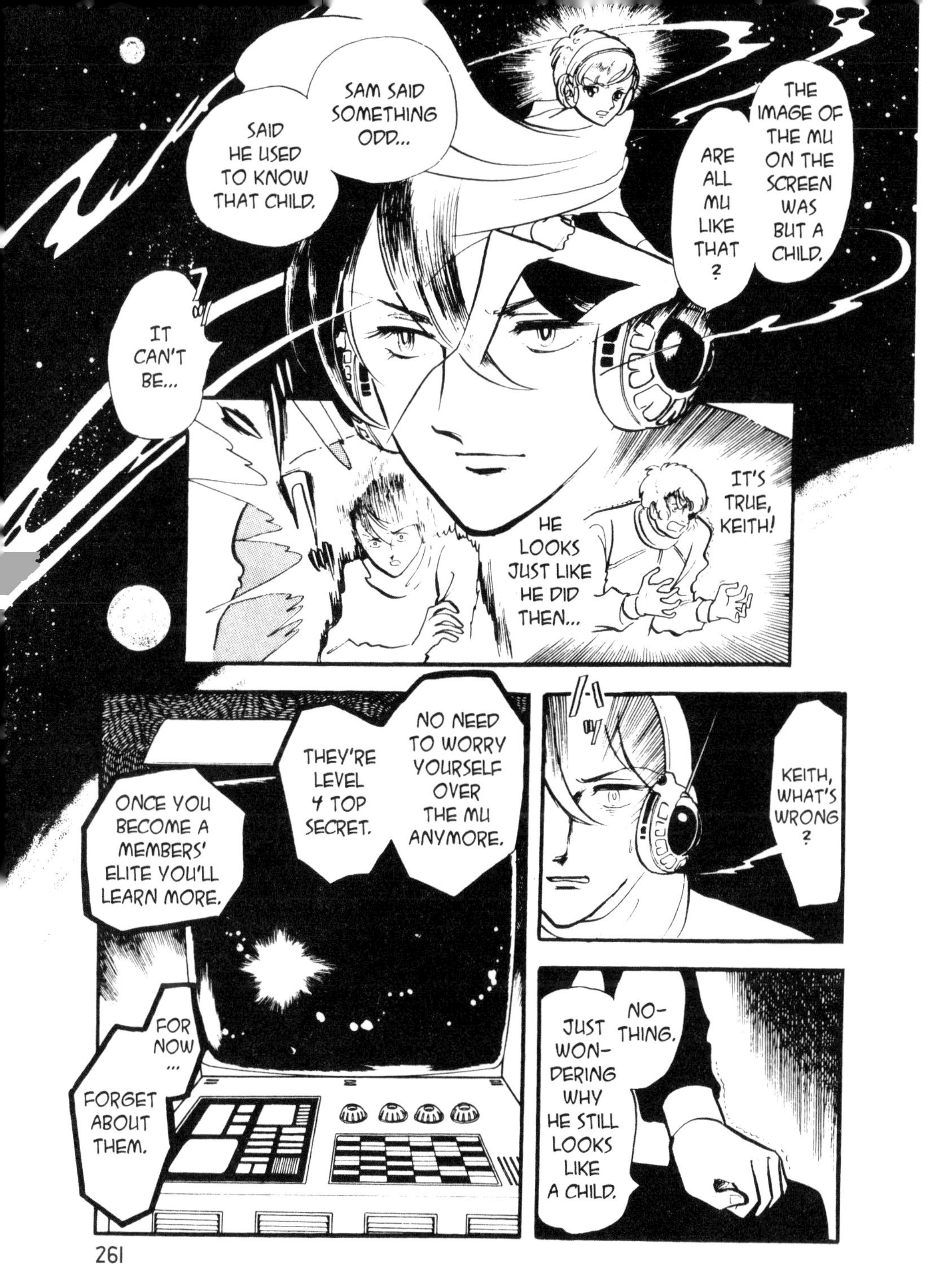
THE IMAGE OF THE MU ON THE SCREEN WAS BUT A CHILD.
ARE ALL MU LIKE THAT?
SAM SAID SOMETHING ODD...
SAID HE USED TO KNOW THAT CHILD.
IT CAN'T BE...
IT'S TRUE, KEITH!
HE LOOKS JUST LIKE HE DID THEN...
KEITH, WHAT'S WRONG?
NO-THING.
JUST WON-DERING WHY HE STILL LOOKS LIKE A CHILD.
NO NEED TO WORRY YOURSELF OVER THE MU ANYMORE.
THEY'RE LEVEL 4 TOP SECRET.
ONCE YOU BECOME A MEMBERS' ELITE YOU'LL LEARN MORE.
FOR NOW...
FORGET ABOUT THEM.

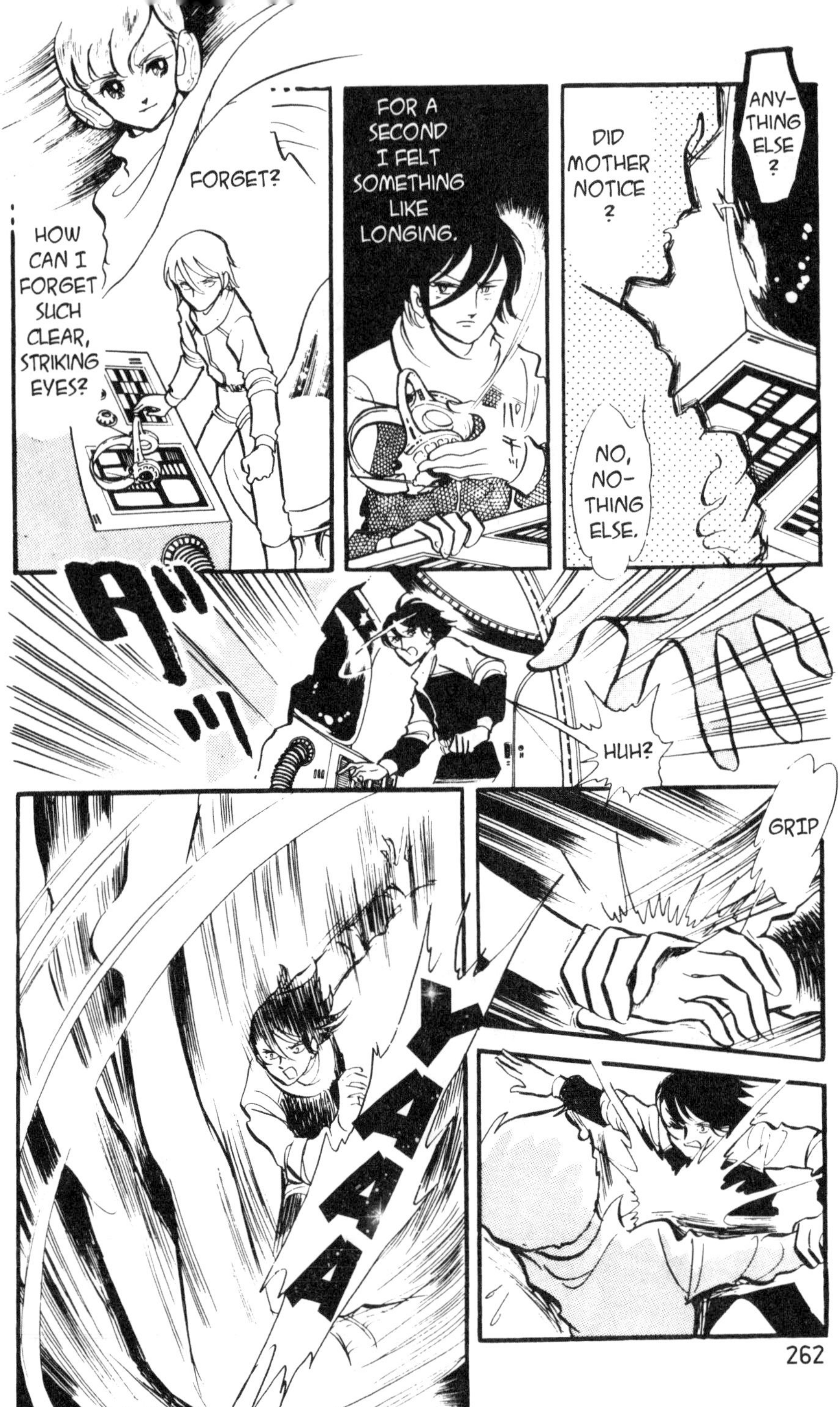
ANY-THING ELSE?
DID MOTHER NOTICE?
NO, NO-THING ELSE.
FOR A SECOND I FELT SOMETHING LIKE LONGING.
FORGET?
HOW CAN I FORGET SUCH CLEAR, STRIKING EYES?
HUH?
GRIP

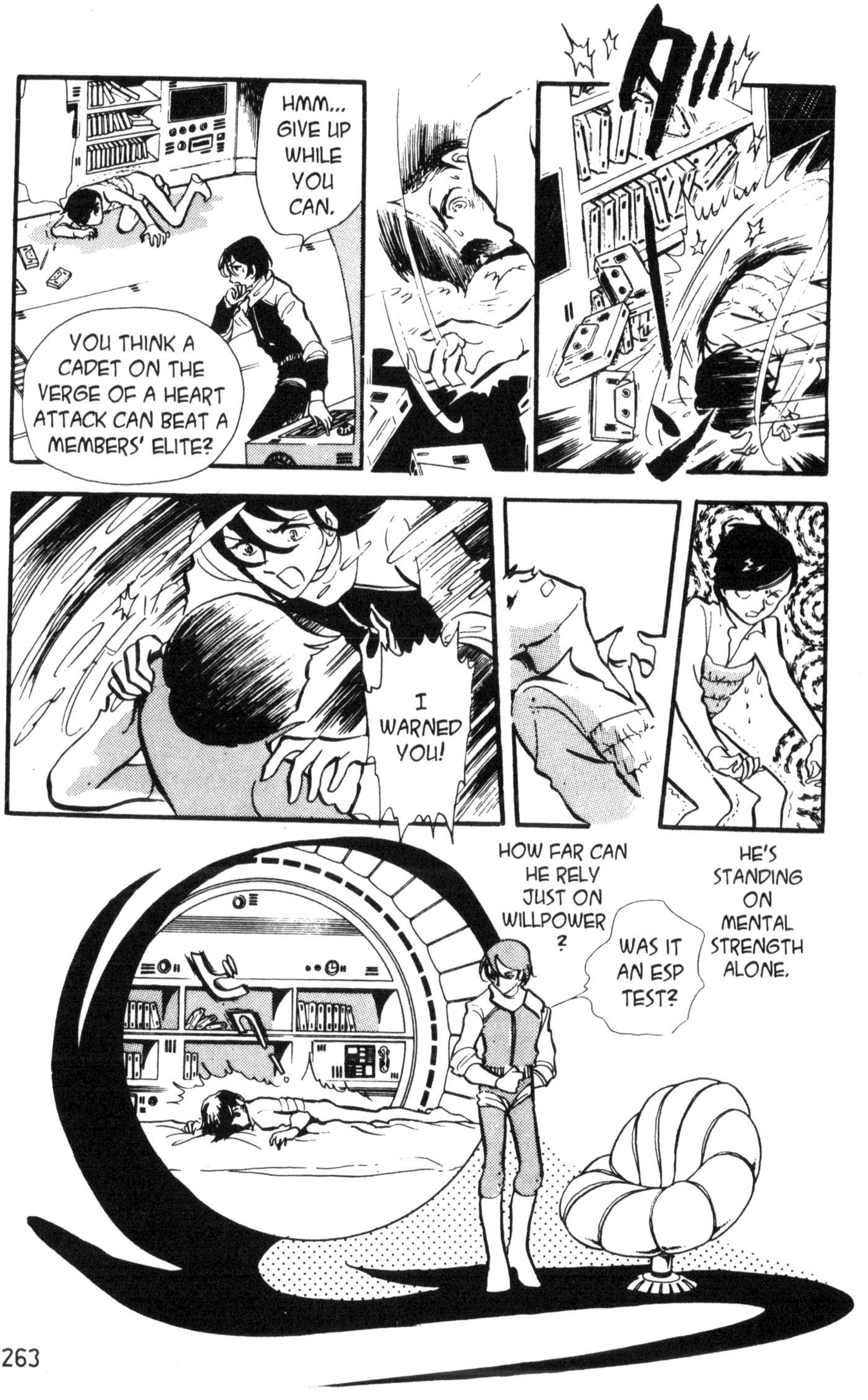

HMM... GIVE UP WHILE YOU CAN.
YOU THINK A CADET ON THE VERGE OF A HEART ATTACK CAN BEAT A MEMBERS' ELITE?
I WARNED YOU!
HE'S STANDING ON MENTAL STRENGTH ALONE.
HOW FAR CAN HE RELY JUST ON WILLPOWER?
WAS IT AN ESP TEST?

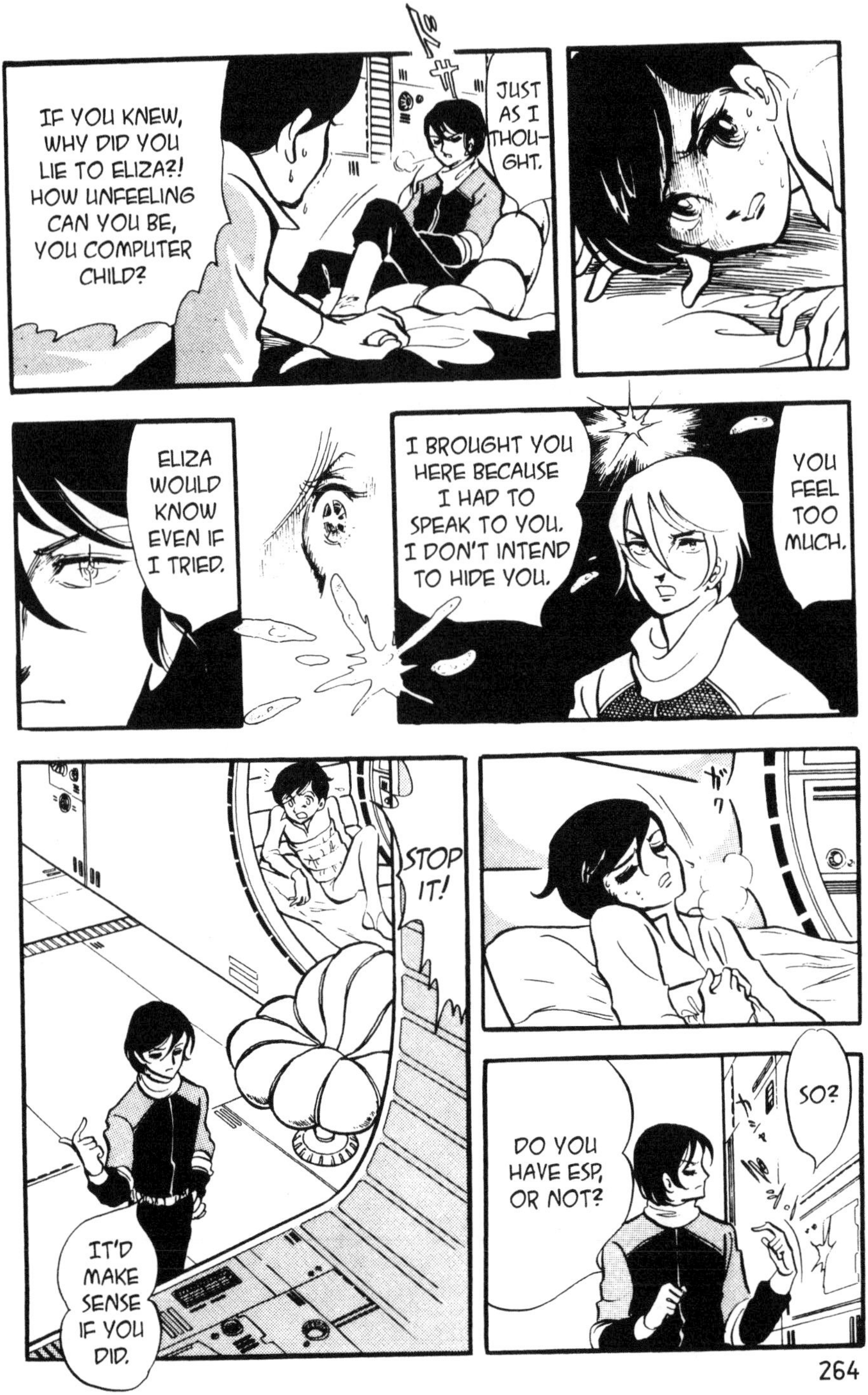
JUST AS I THOUGHT.
IF YOU KNEW, WHY DID YOU LIE TO ELIZA?! HOW UNFEELING CAN YOU BE, YOU COMPUTER CHILD?
YOU FEEL TOO MUCH.
I BROUGHT YOU HERE BECAUSE I HAD TO SPEAK TO YOU. I DON'T INTEND TO HIDE YOU.
ELIZA WOULD KNOW EVEN IF I TRIED.
SO?
DO YOU HAVE ESP, OR NOT?
STOP IT!
IT'D MAKE SENSE IF YOU DID.

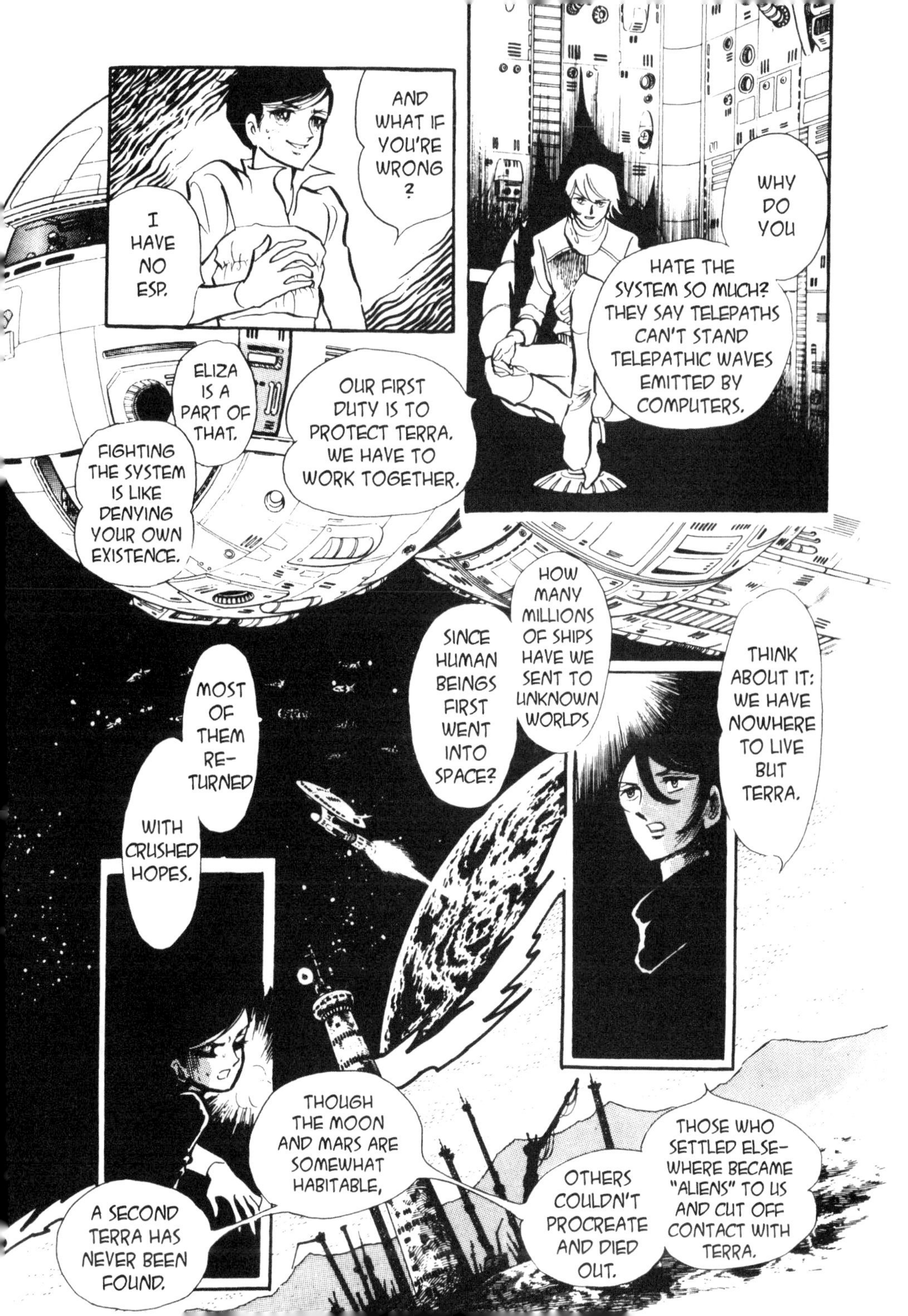
WHY DO YOU
HATE THE SYSTEM SO MUCH? THEY SAY TELEPATHS CAN'T STAND TELEPATHIC WAVES EMITTED BY COMPUTERS.
AND WHAT IF YOU'RE WRONG?
I HAVE NO ESP.
OUR FIRST DUTY IS TO PROTECT TERRA. WE HAVE TO WORK TOGETHER.
ELIZA IS A PART OF THAT.
FIGHTING THE SYSTEM IS LIKE DENYING YOUR OWN EXISTENCE.
THINK ABOUT IT: WE HAVE NOWHERE TO LIVE BUT TERRA.
HOW MANY MILLIONS OF SHIPS HAVE WE SENT TO UNKNOWN WORLDS
SINCE HUMAN BEINGS FIRST WENT INTO SPACE?
MOST OF THEM RETURNED
WITH CRUSHED HOPES.
THOSE WHO SETTLED ELSEWHERE BECAME "ALIENS" TO US AND CUT OFF CONTACT WITH TERRA.
OTHERS COULDN'T PROCREATE AND DIED OUT.
THOUGH THE MOON AND MARS ARE SOMEWHAT HABITABLE,
A SECOND TERRA HAS NEVER BEEN FOUND.

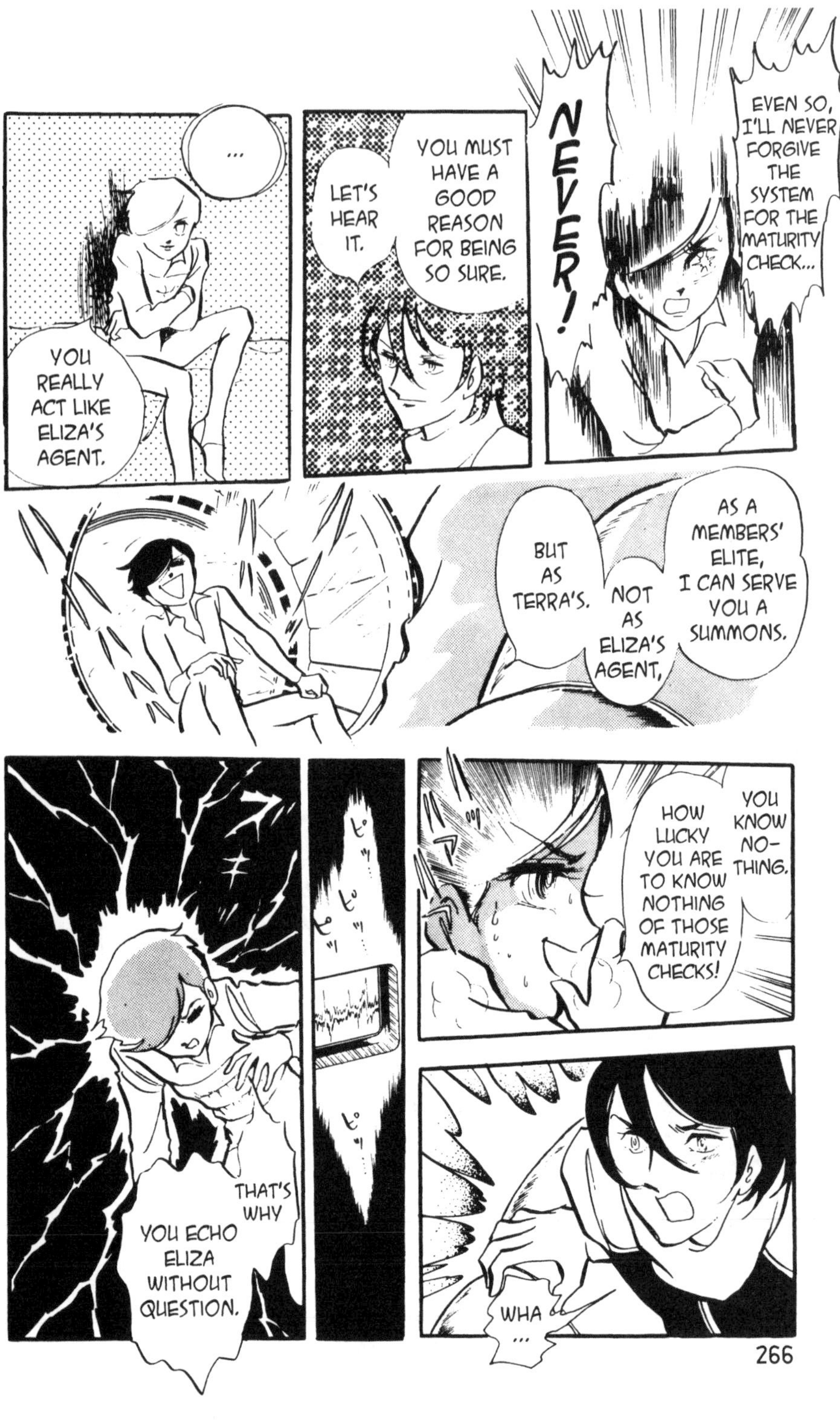
NEVER!
EVEN SO, I'LL NEVER FORGIVE THE SYSTEM FOR THE MATURITY CHECK...
YOU MUST HAVE A GOOD REASON FOR BEING SO SURE.
LET'S HEAR IT.
...
YOU REALLY ACT LIKE ELIZA'S AGENT.
AS A MEMBERS' ELITE, I CAN SERVE YOU A SUMMONS.
NOT AS ELIZA'S AGENT,
BUT AS TERRA'S.
YOU KNOW NO-THING.
HOW LUCKY YOU ARE TO KNOW NOTHING OF THOSE MATURITY CHECKS!
WHA ...
THAT'S WHY
YOU ECHO ELIZA WITHOUT QUESTION.

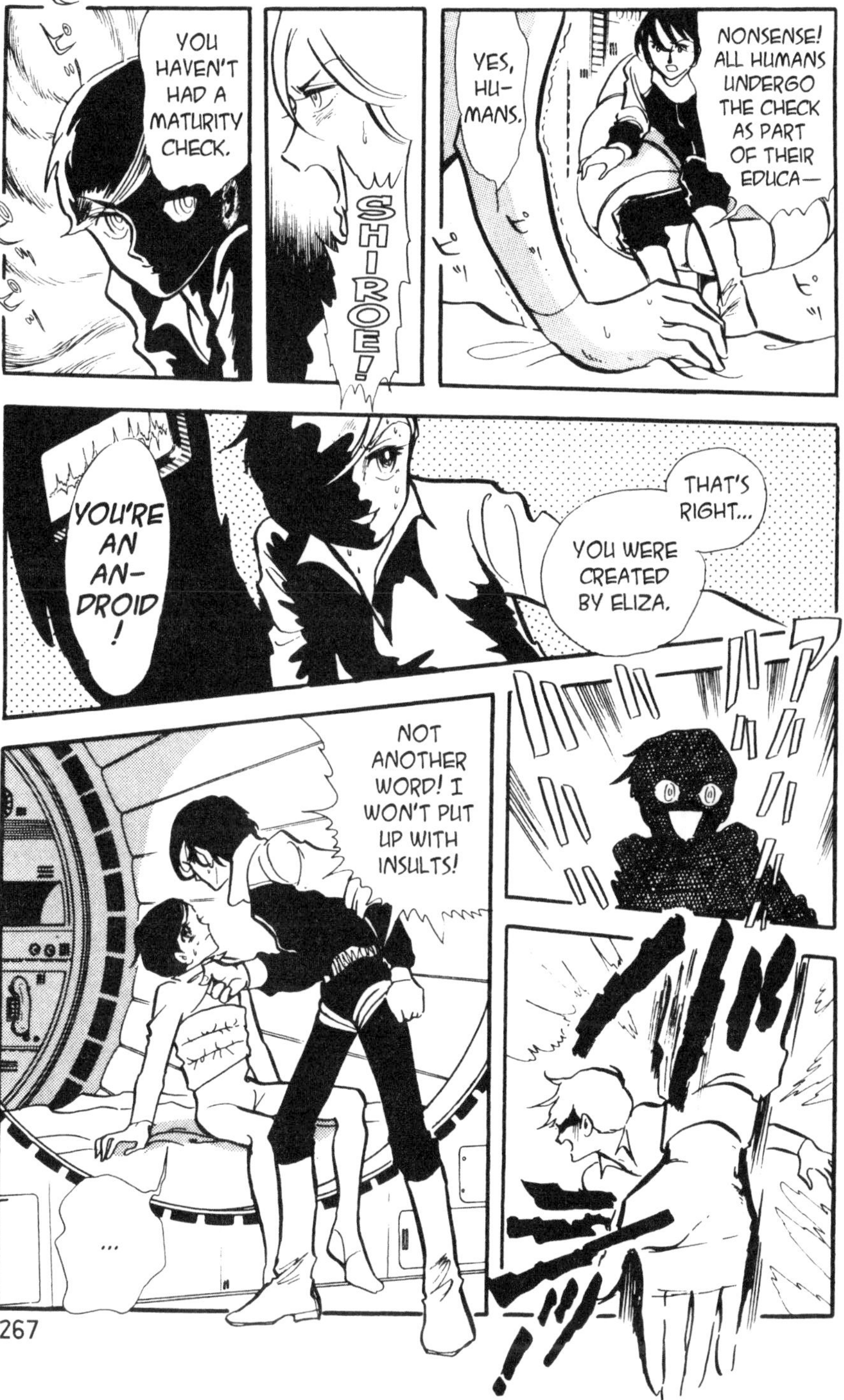
NONSENSE! ALL HUMANS UNDERGO THE CHECK AS PART OF THEIR EDUCA—
YES, HU-MANS.
SHIROE!
YOU HAVEN'T HAD A MATURITY CHECK.
THAT'S RIGHT...
YOU WERE CREATED BY ELIZA.
YOU'RE AN AN-DROID!
NOT ANOTHER WORD! I WON'T PUT UP WITH INSULTS!
...

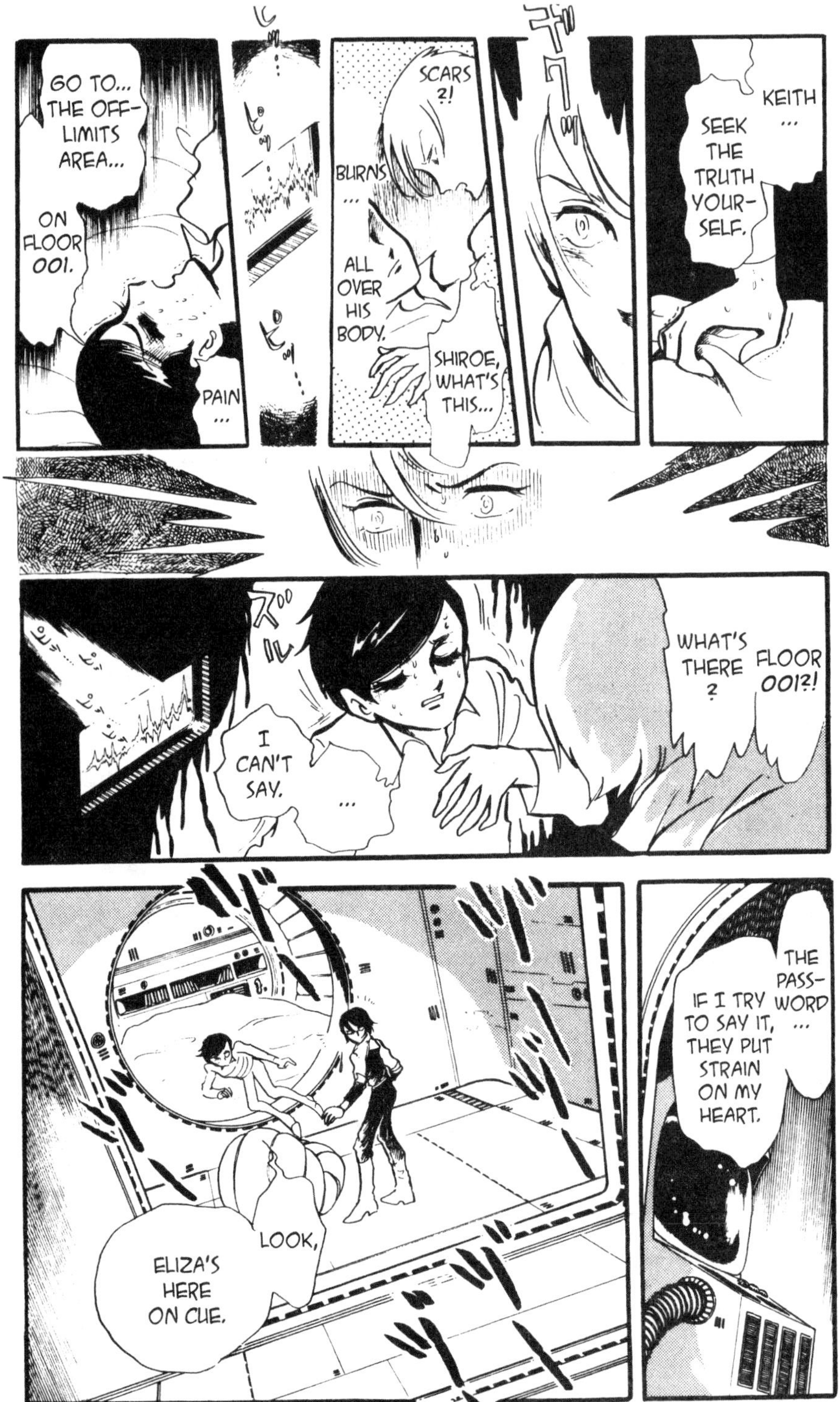
KEITH...
SEEK THE TRUTH YOURSELF.
SCARS?!
BURNS...
ALL OVER HIS BODY.
SHIROE, WHAT'S THIS...
GO TO... THE OFF-LIMITS AREA...
ON FLOOR 001.
PAIN...
FLOOR 001?!
WHAT'S THERE?
...
I CAN'T SAY.
THE PASSWORD...
IF I TRY TO SAY IT, THEY PUT STRAIN ON MY HEART.
LOOK,
ELIZA'S HERE ON CUE.

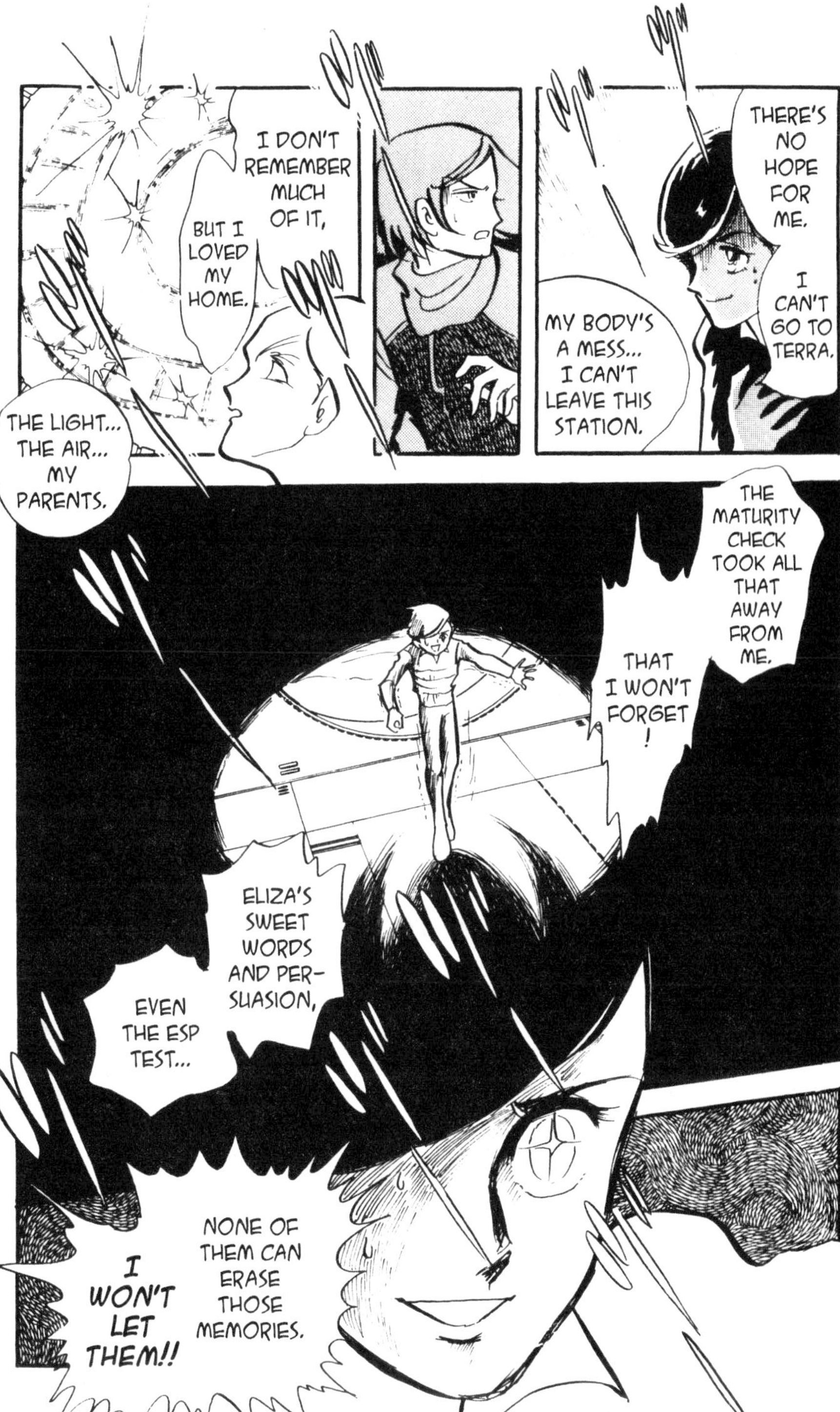
THERE'S NO HOPE FOR ME.
I CAN'T GO TO TERRA.
MY BODY'S A MESS... I CAN'T LEAVE THIS STATION.
I DON'T REMEMBER MUCH OF IT,
BUT I LOVED MY HOME.
THE LIGHT... THE AIR... MY PARENTS.
THE MATURITY CHECK TOOK ALL THAT AWAY FROM ME.
THAT I WON'T FORGET!
ELIZA'S SWEET WORDS AND PERSUASION,
EVEN THE ESP TEST...
NONE OF THEM CAN ERASE THOSE MEMORIES.
I WON'T LET THEM!!

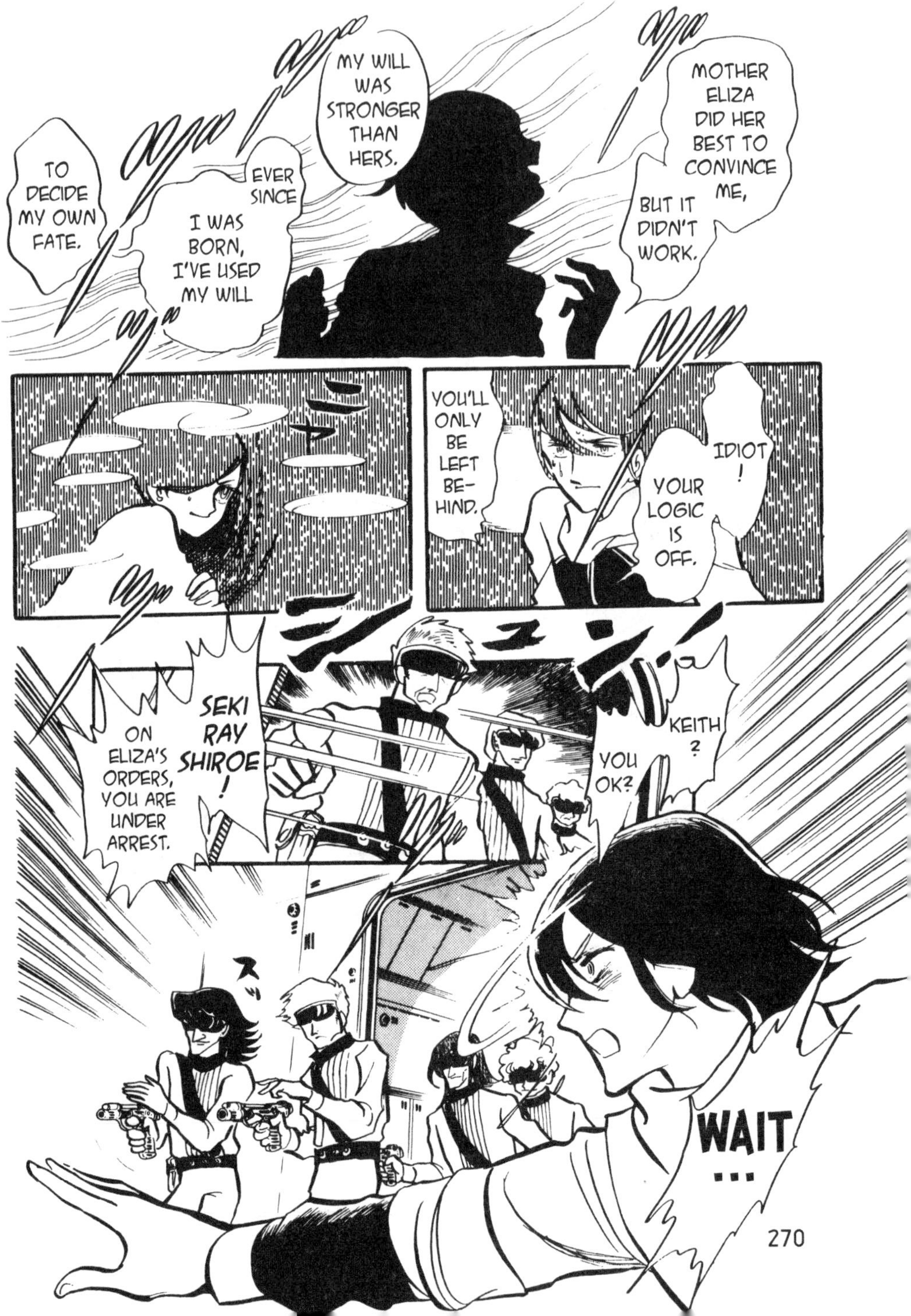
MOTHER ELIZA DID HER BEST TO CONVINCE ME,
BUT IT DIDN'T WORK.
MY WILL WAS STRONGER THAN HERS.
EVER SINCE
I WAS BORN, I'VE USED MY WILL
TO DECIDE MY OWN FATE.
IDIOT!
YOUR LOGIC IS OFF.
YOU'LL ONLY BE LEFT BE-HIND.
KEITH?
YOU OK?
SEKI RAY SHIROE!
ON ELIZA'S ORDERS, YOU ARE UNDER ARREST.
WAIT...

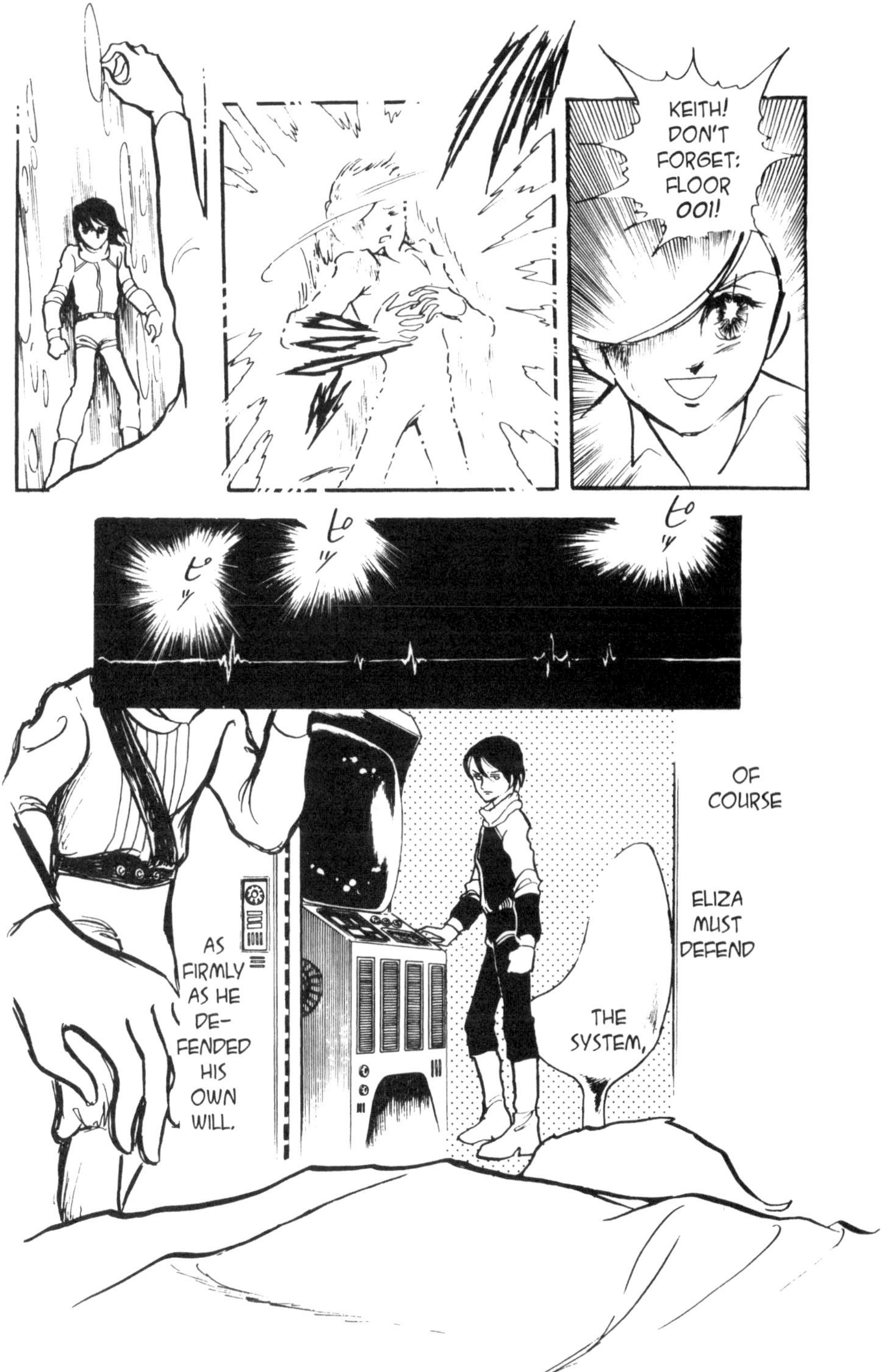
KEITH! DON'T FORGET: FLOOR 001!
ピッ
ピッ
ピッ
OF COURSE
ELIZA MUST DEFEND
THE SYSTEM,
AS FIRMLY AS HE DE-FENDED HIS OWN WILL.

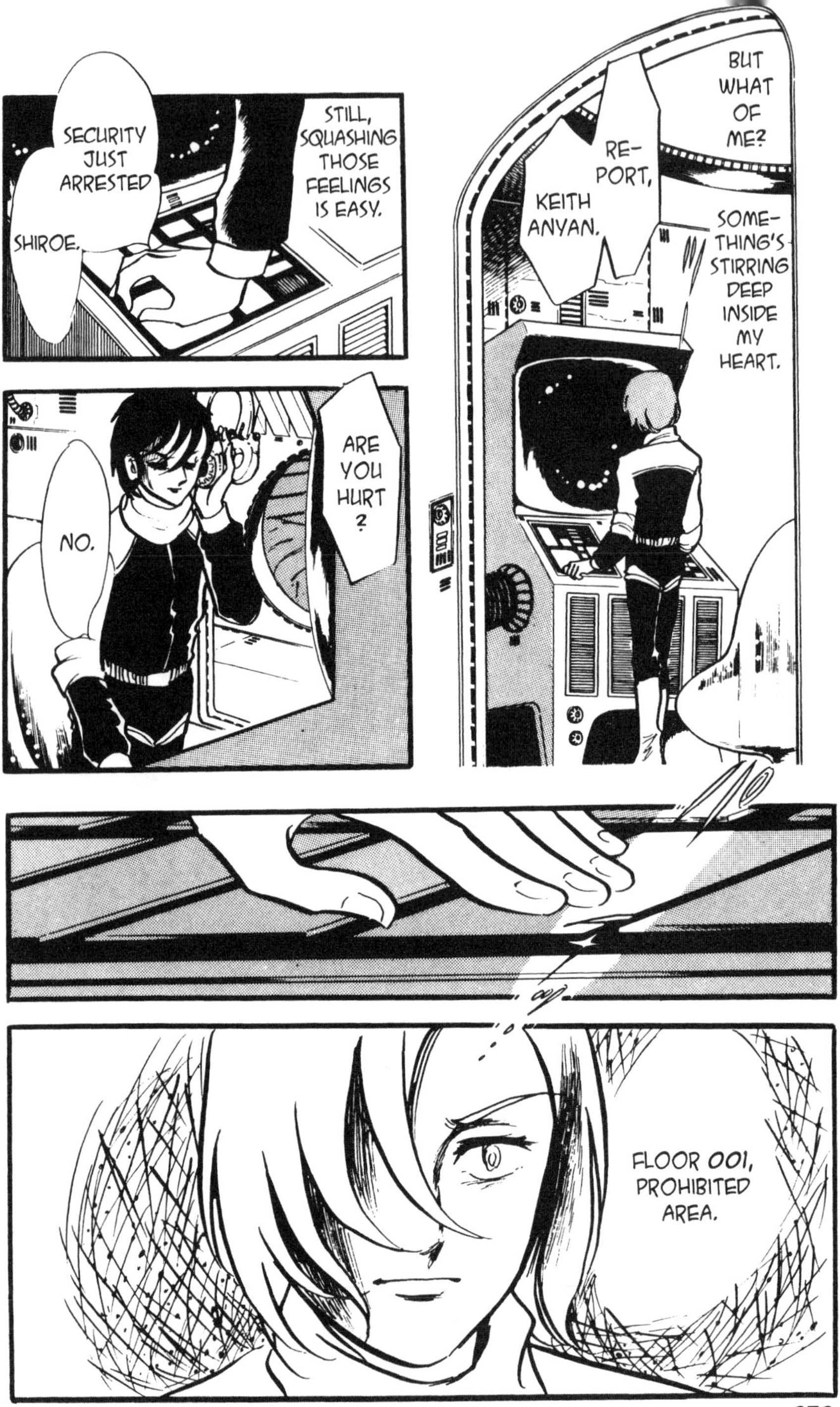
BUT WHAT OF ME?
RE-PORT, KEITH ANYAN.
SOME-THING'S STIRRING DEEP INSIDE MY HEART.
STILL, SQUASHING THOSE FEELINGS IS EASY.
SECURITY JUST ARRESTED
SHIROE.
ARE YOU HURT?
NO.
FLOOR 001, PROHIBITED AREA.

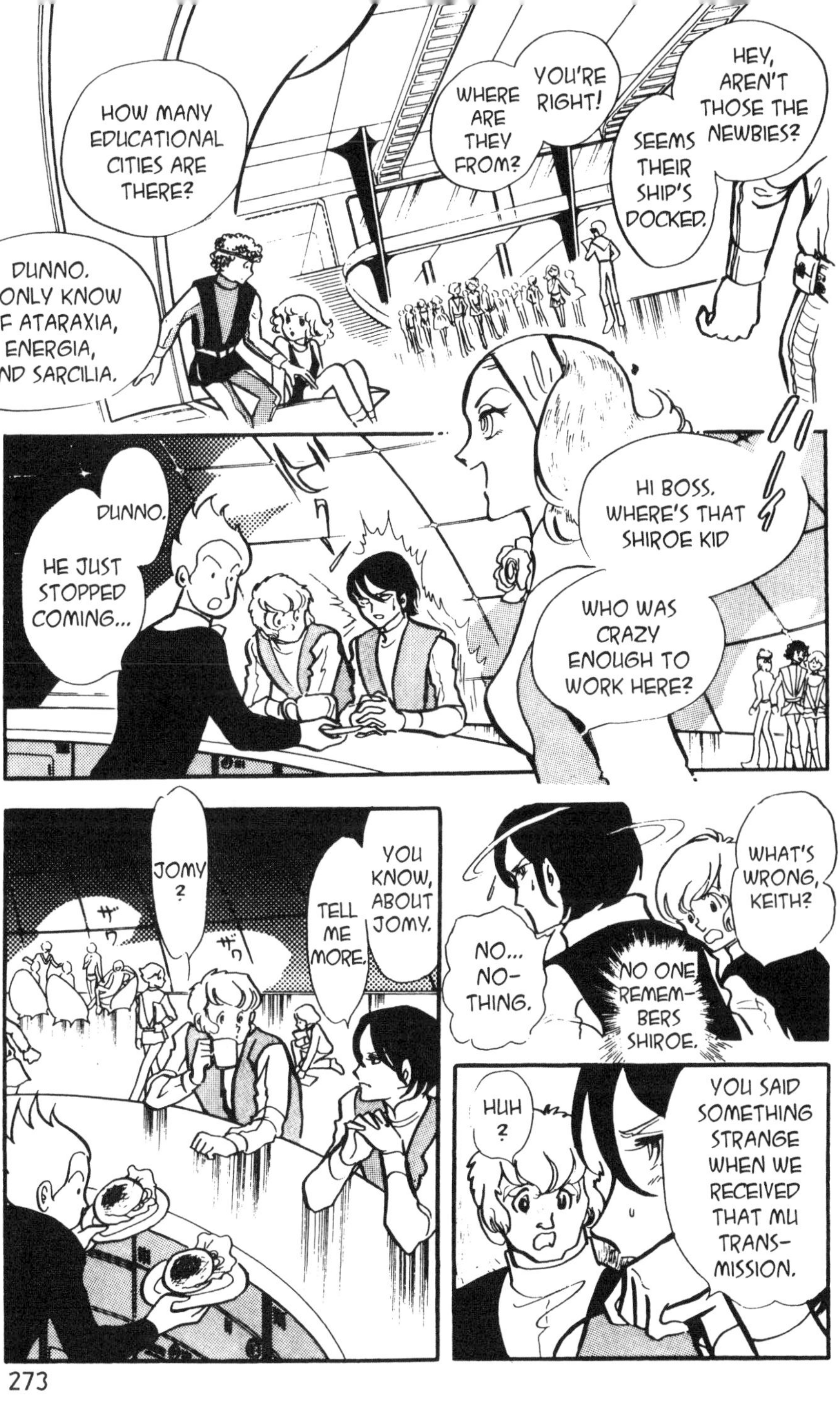
HEY, AREN'T THOSE THE NEWBIES?
SEEMS THEIR SHIP'S DOCKED.
YOU'RE RIGHT!
WHERE ARE THEY FROM?
HOW MANY EDUCATIONAL CITIES ARE THERE?
DUNNO. I ONLY KNOW OF ATARAXIA, ENERGIA, AND SARCILIA.
HI BOSS. WHERE'S THAT SHIROE KID
WHO WAS CRAZY ENOUGH TO WORK HERE?
DUNNO.
HE JUST STOPPED COMING...
WHAT'S WRONG, KEITH?
NO ONE REMEM-BERS SHIROE.
NO... NO-THING.
YOU SAID SOMETHING STRANGE WHEN WE RECEIVED THAT MU TRANS-MISSION.
HUH?
YOU KNOW, ABOUT JOMY.
TELL ME MORE.
JOMY?
ザワ
ザワ

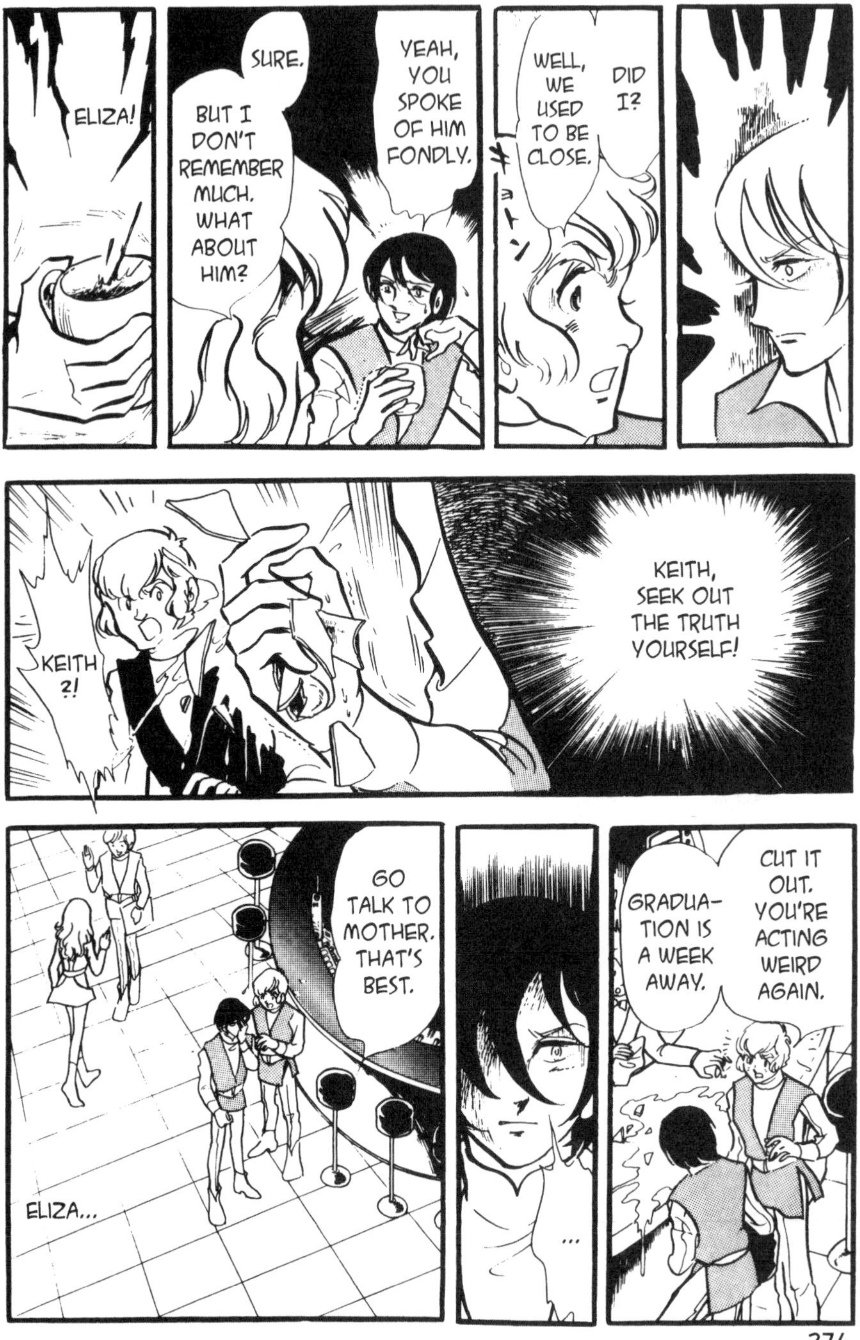
DID I?
WELL, WE USED TO BE CLOSE.
キョトン
YEAH, YOU SPOKE OF HIM FONDLY.
SURE.
BUT I DON'T REMEMBER MUCH. WHAT ABOUT HIM?
ELIZA!
KEITH, SEEK OUT THE TRUTH YOURSELF!
KEITH ?!
CUT IT OUT. YOU'RE ACTING WEIRD AGAIN.
GRADUATION IS A WEEK AWAY.
...
GO TALK TO MOTHER. THAT'S BEST.
ELIZA...

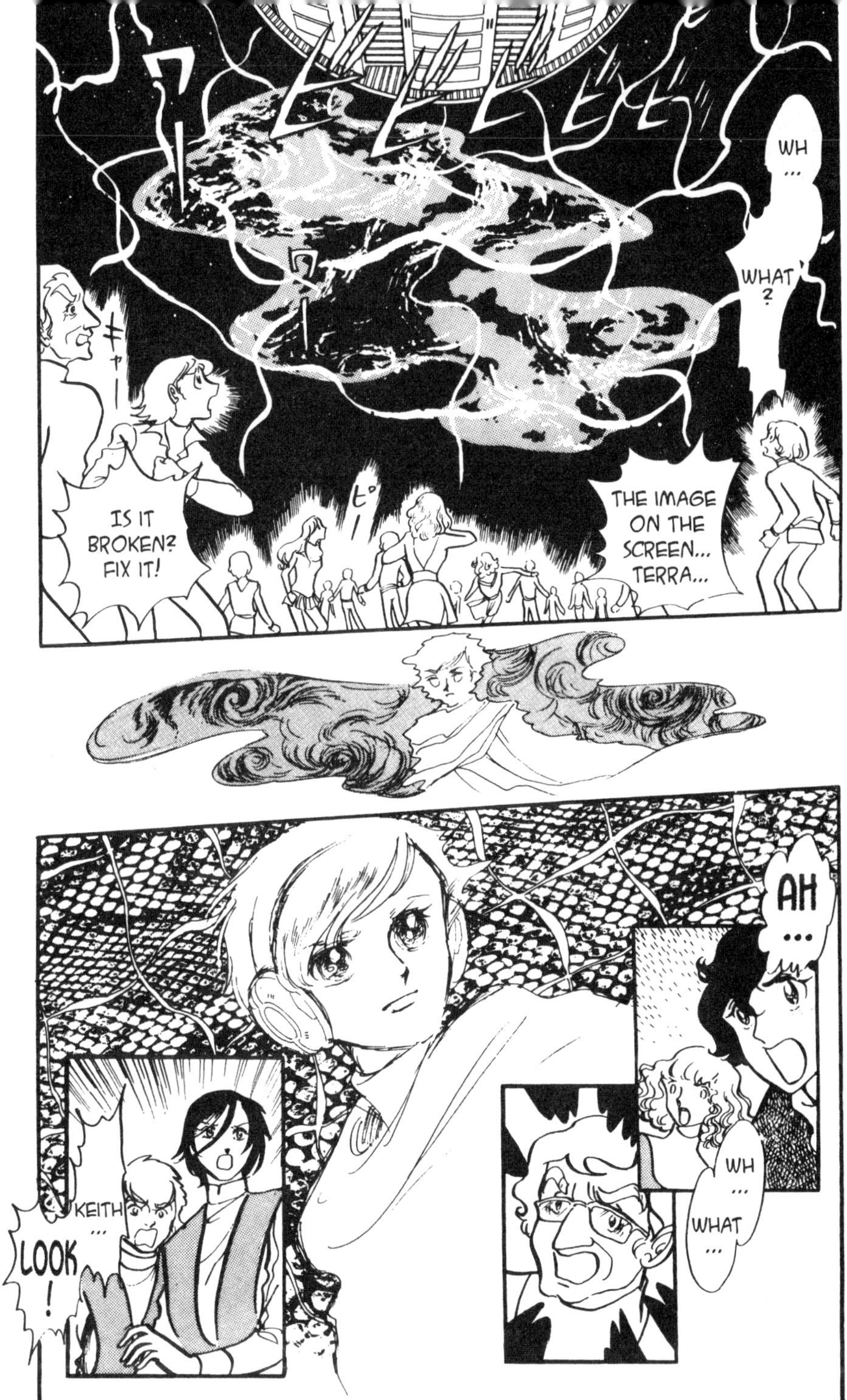
WH ... WHAT?
THE IMAGE ON THE SCREEN... TERRA...
IS IT BROKEN? FIX IT!
AH ...
WH ... WHAT ...
KEITH ...
LOOK!

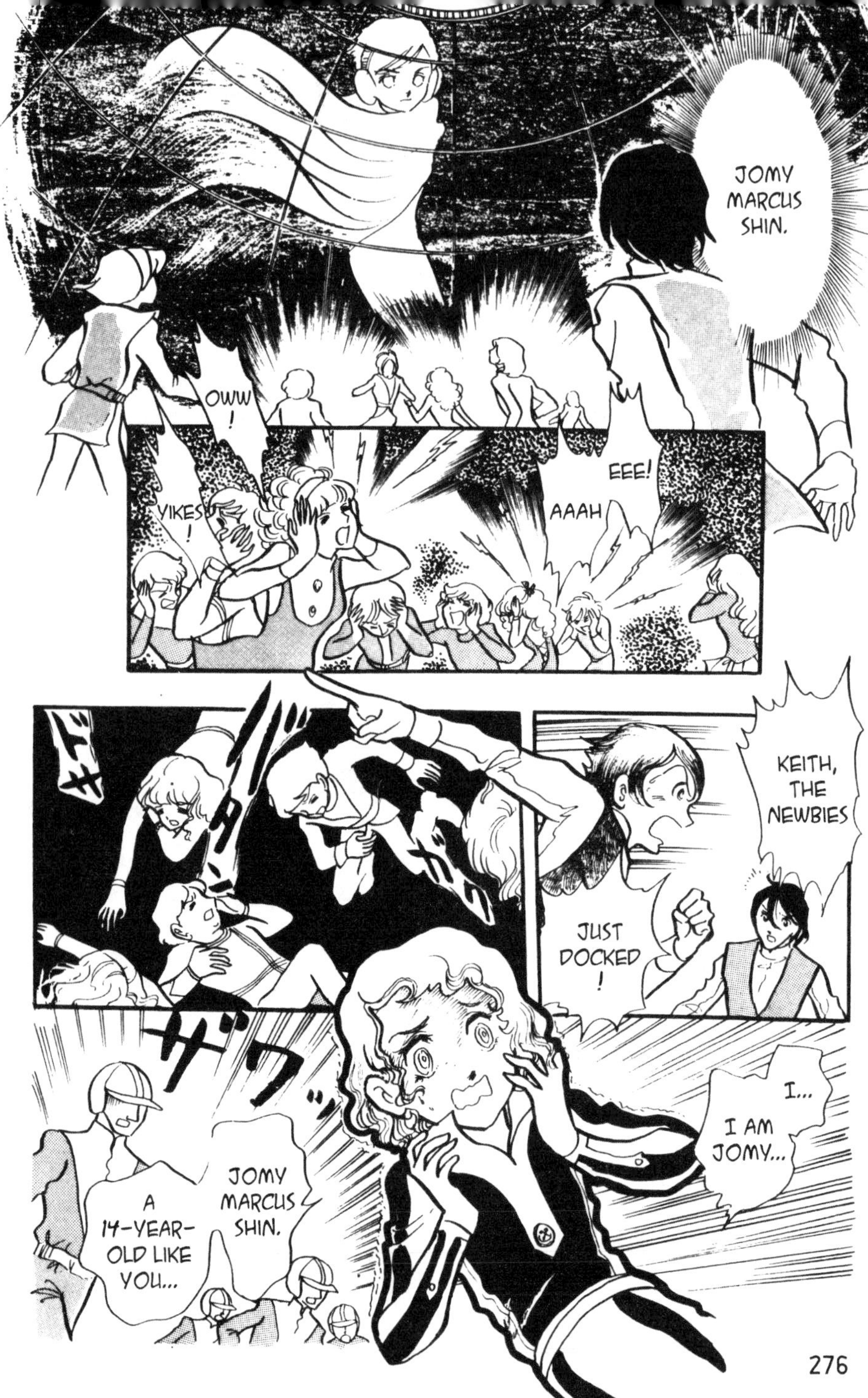
JOMY MARCUS SHIN.
OWW!
EEE!
AAAH
YIKES!
KEITH, THE NEWBIES JUST DOCKED!
I... I AM JOMY...
ザワッ
JOMY MARCUS SHIN.
A 14-YEAR-OLD LIKE YOU...

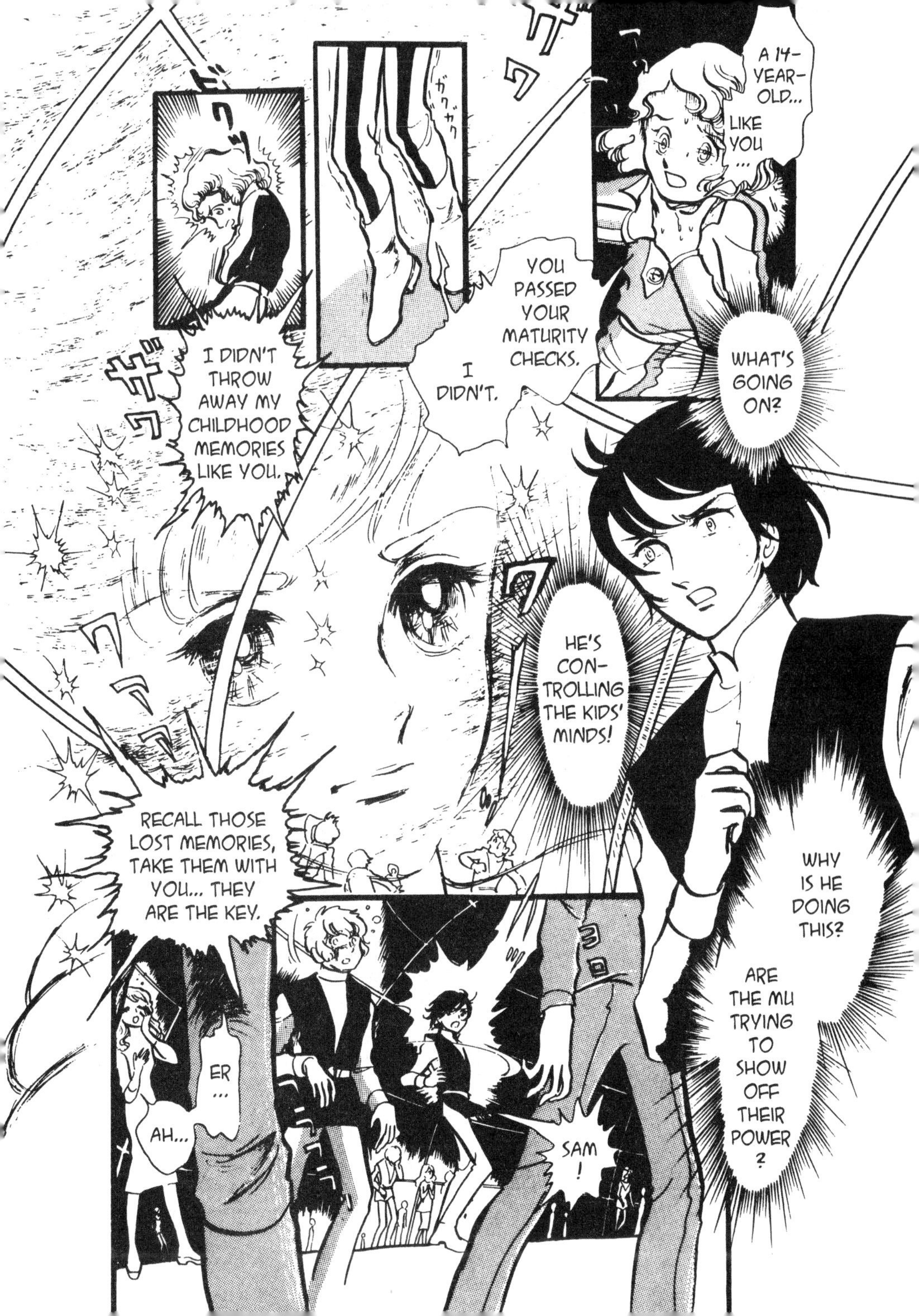
A 14-YEAR-OLD... LIKE YOU...
YOU PASSED YOUR MATURITY CHECKS.
I DIDN'T.
ガクガク
I DIDN'T THROW AWAY MY CHILDHOOD MEMORIES LIKE YOU.
WHAT'S GOING ON?
HE'S CON-TROLLING THE KIDS' MINDS!
RECALL THOSE LOST MEMORIES, TAKE THEM WITH YOU... THEY ARE THE KEY.
WHY IS HE DOING THIS?
ARE THE MU TRYING TO SHOW OFF THEIR POWER?
SAM!
ER...
AH...

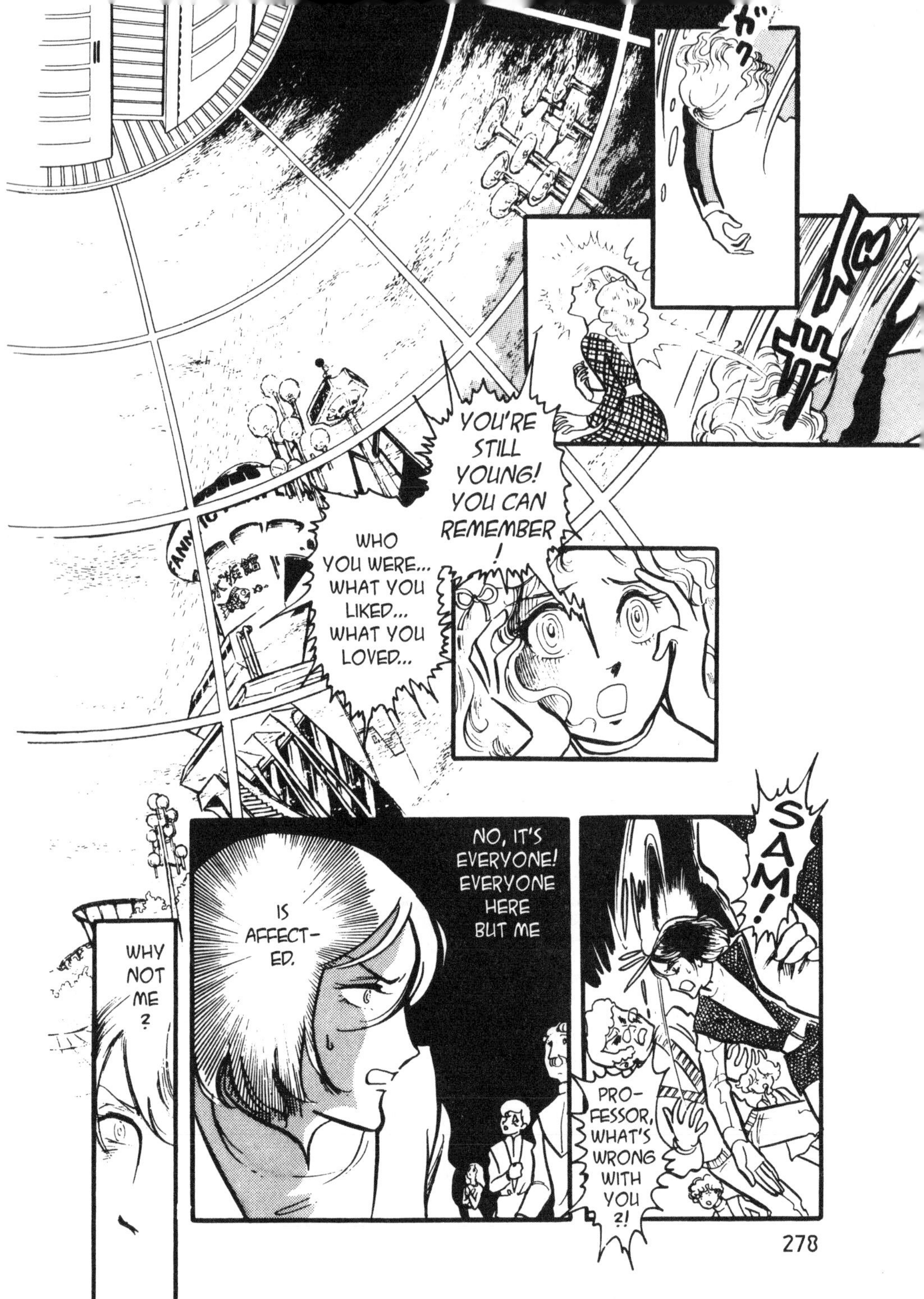
YOU'RE STILL YOUNG! YOU CAN REMEMBER!
WHO YOU WERE... WHAT YOU LIKED... WHAT YOU LOVED...
SAM!
PROFESSOR, WHAT'S WRONG WITH YOU?!
NO, IT'S EVERYONE! EVERYONE HERE BUT ME
IS AFFECTED.
WHY NOT ME?

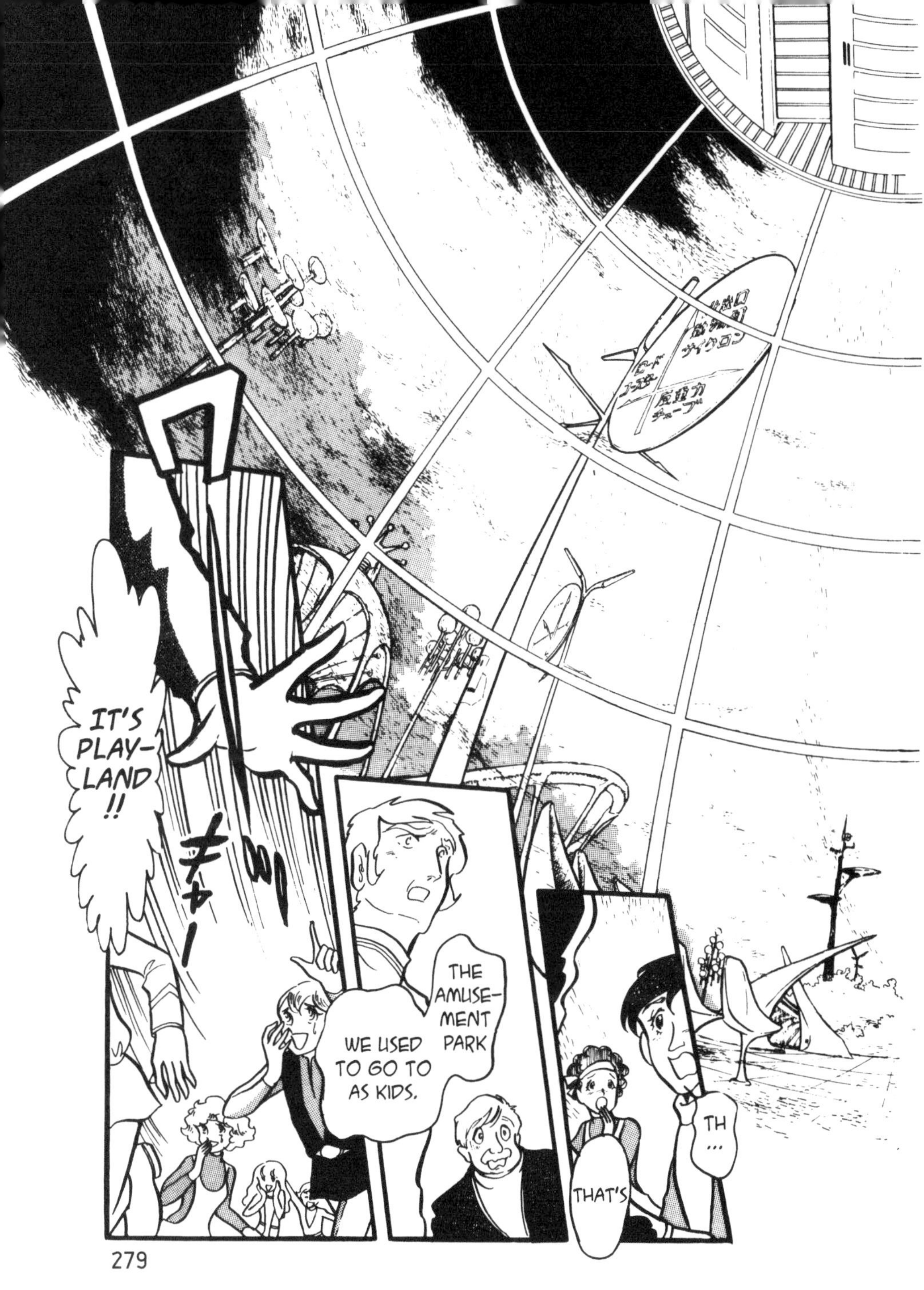
TH ...
THAT'S
IT'S PLAYLAND!!
THE AMUSEMENT PARK WE USED TO GO TO AS KIDS.

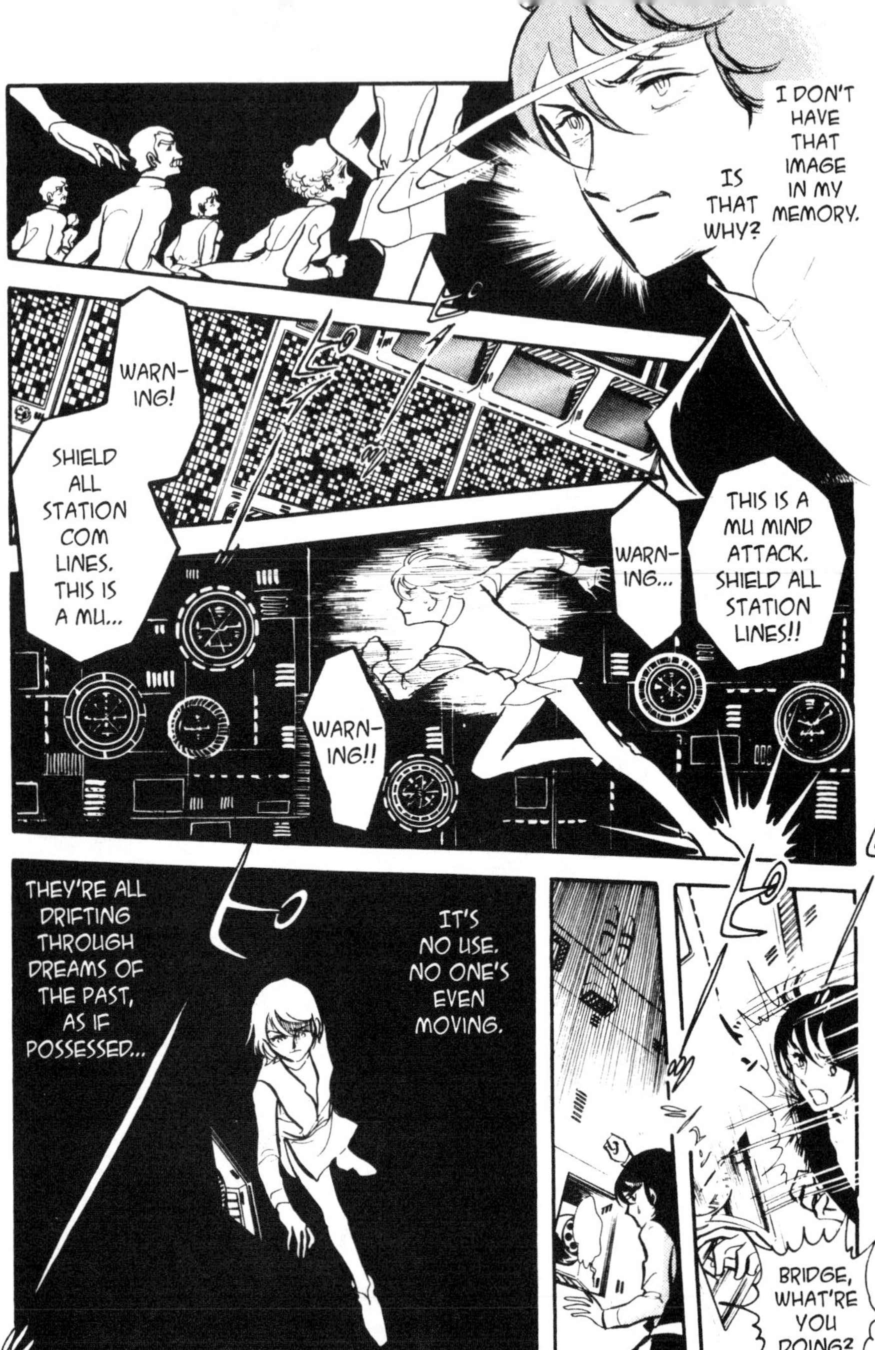
I DON'T HAVE THAT IMAGE IN MY MEMORY.
IS THAT WHY?
WARNING!
SHIELD ALL STATION COM LINES. THIS IS A MU...
THIS IS A MU MIND ATTACK. SHIELD ALL STATION LINES!!
WARNING...
WARNING!!
BRIDGE, WHAT'RE YOU DOING? SHIELDS!
IT'S NO USE. NO ONE'S EVEN MOVING.
THEY'RE ALL DRIFTING THROUGH DREAMS OF THE PAST, AS IF POSSESSED...

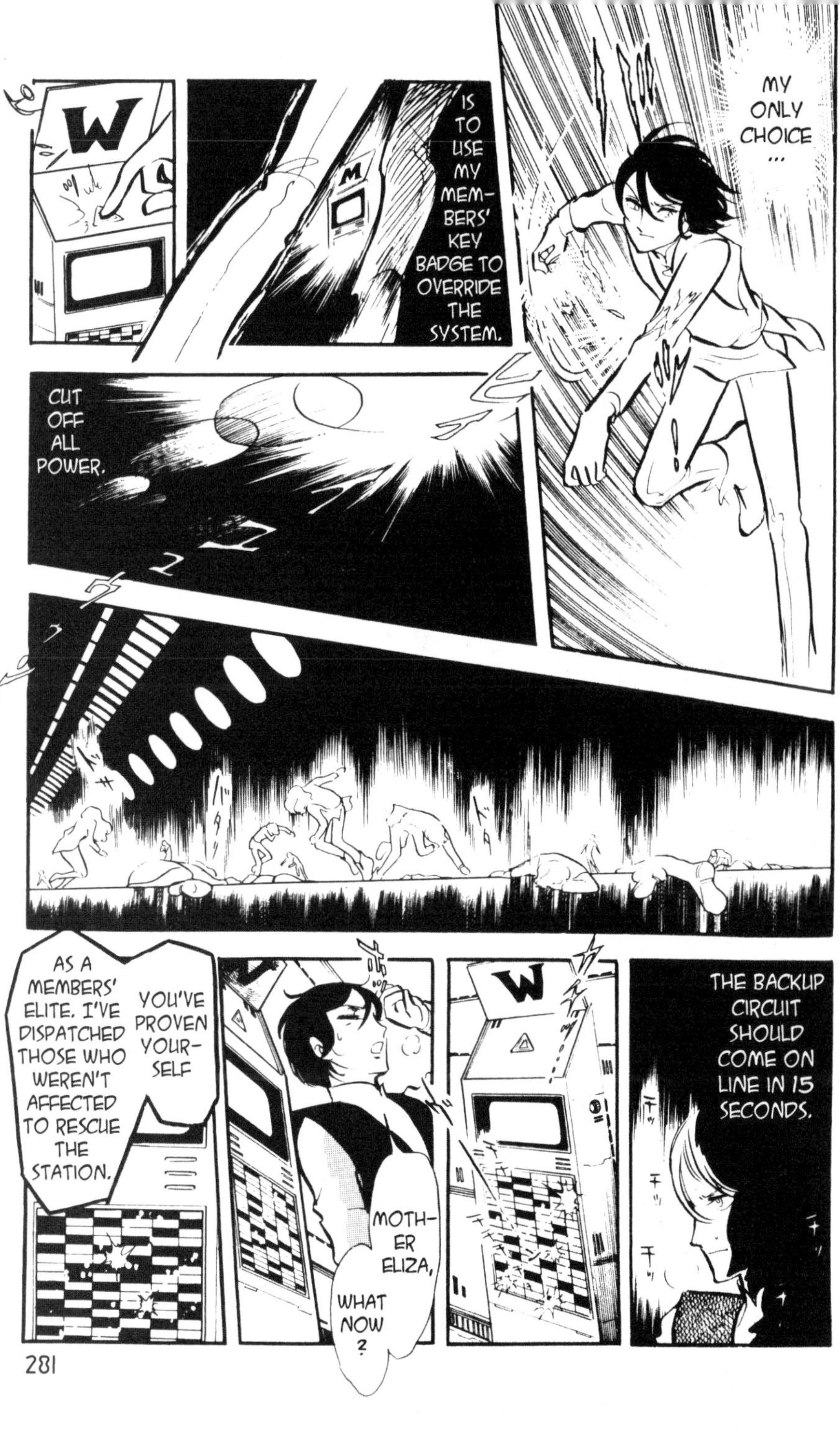
MY ONLY CHOICE ...
IS TO USE MY MEMBERS' KEY BADGE TO OVERRIDE THE SYSTEM.
CUT OFF ALL POWER.
THE BACKUP CIRCUIT SHOULD COME ON LINE IN 15 SECONDS.
MOTHER ELIZA,
WHAT NOW?
YOU'VE PROVEN YOURSELF
AS A MEMBERS' ELITE. I'VE DISPATCHED THOSE WHO WEREN'T AFFECTED TO RESCUE THE STATION.

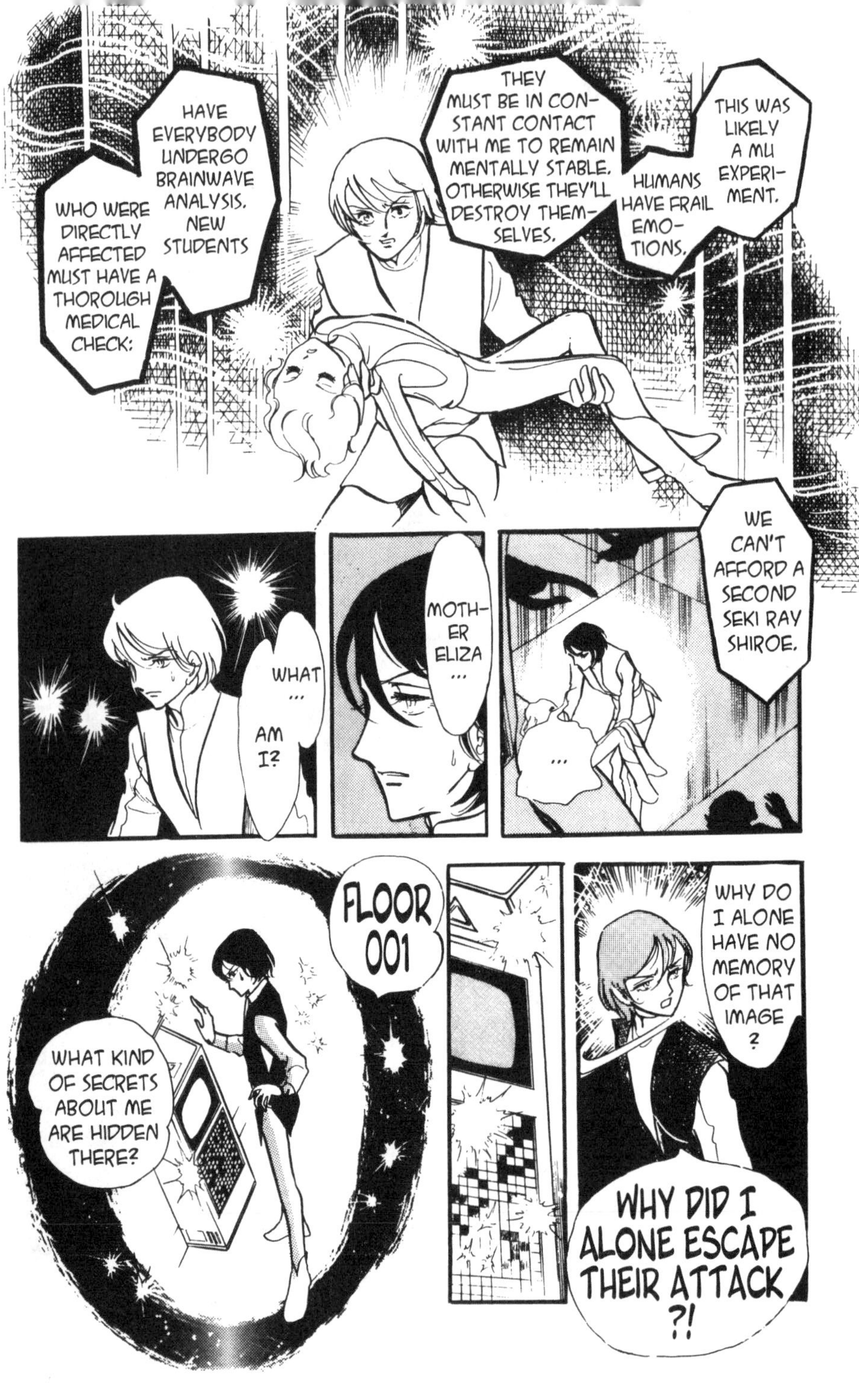
THIS WAS LIKELY A MU EXPERIMENT.
HUMANS HAVE FRAIL EMOTIONS.
THEY MUST BE IN CONSTANT CONTACT WITH ME TO REMAIN MENTALLY STABLE. OTHERWISE THEY'LL DESTROY THEMSELVES.
HAVE EVERYBODY UNDERGO BRAINWAVE ANALYSIS. NEW STUDENTS
WHO WERE DIRECTLY AFFECTED MUST HAVE A THOROUGH MEDICAL CHECK:
WE CAN'T AFFORD A SECOND SEKI RAY SHIROE.
...
MOTHER ELIZA ...
WHAT ... AM I?
WHY DO I ALONE HAVE NO MEMORY OF THAT IMAGE ?
WHY DID I ALONE ESCAPE THEIR ATTACK ?!
FLOOR 001
WHAT KIND OF SECRETS ABOUT ME ARE HIDDEN THERE?

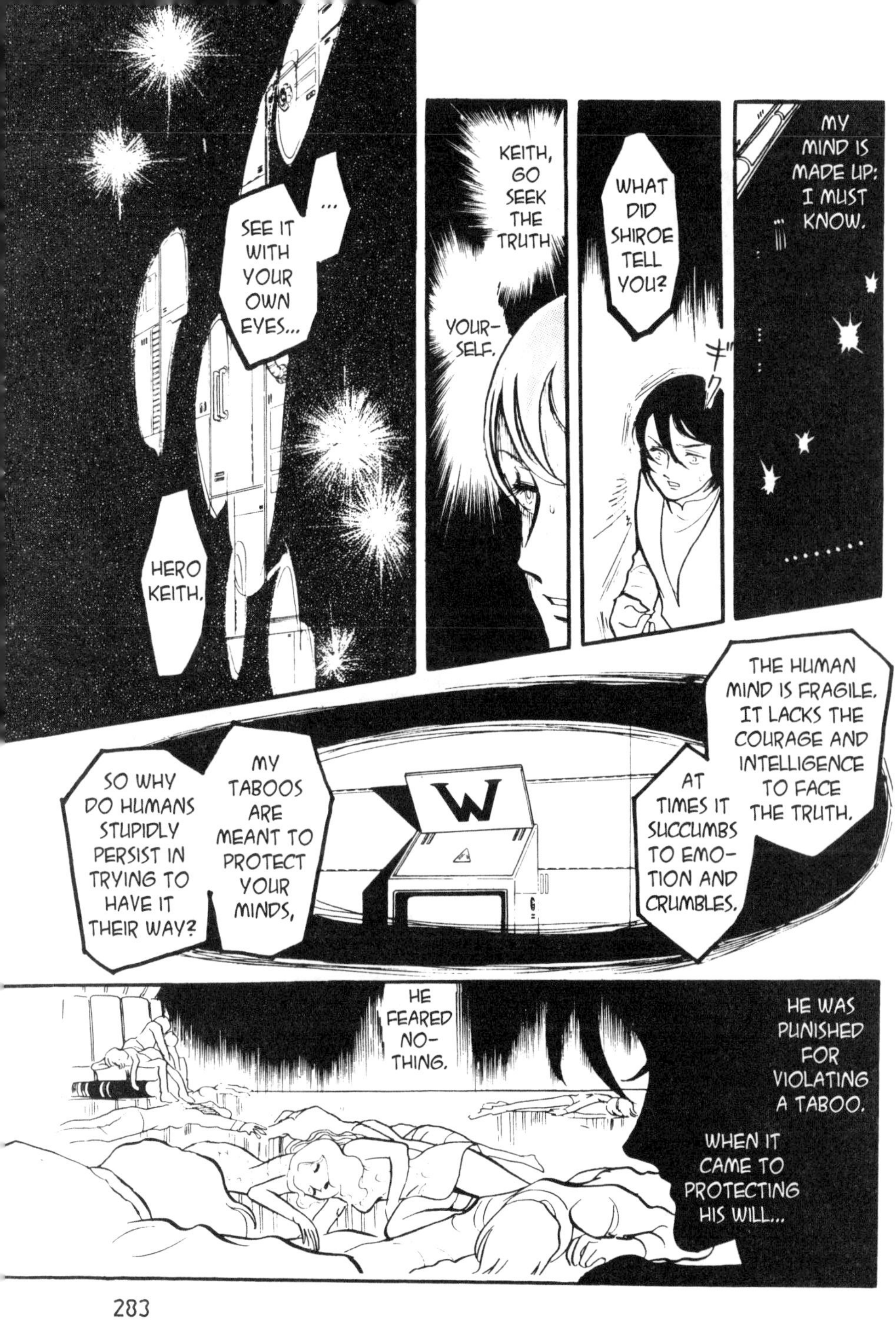
MY MIND IS MADE UP: I MUST KNOW.
......
WHAT DID SHIROE TELL YOU?
ギク
KEITH, GO SEEK THE TRUTH YOURSELF.
...
SEE IT WITH YOUR OWN EYES...
HERO KEITH.
THE HUMAN MIND IS FRAGILE. IT LACKS THE COURAGE AND INTELLIGENCE TO FACE THE TRUTH.
AT TIMES IT SUCCUMBS TO EMOTION AND CRUMBLES.
W
MY TABOOS ARE MEANT TO PROTECT YOUR MINDS,
SO WHY DO HUMANS STUPIDLY PERSIST IN TRYING TO HAVE IT THEIR WAY?
HE WAS PUNISHED FOR VIOLATING A TABOO.
WHEN IT CAME TO PROTECTING HIS WILL...
HE FEARED NOTHING.

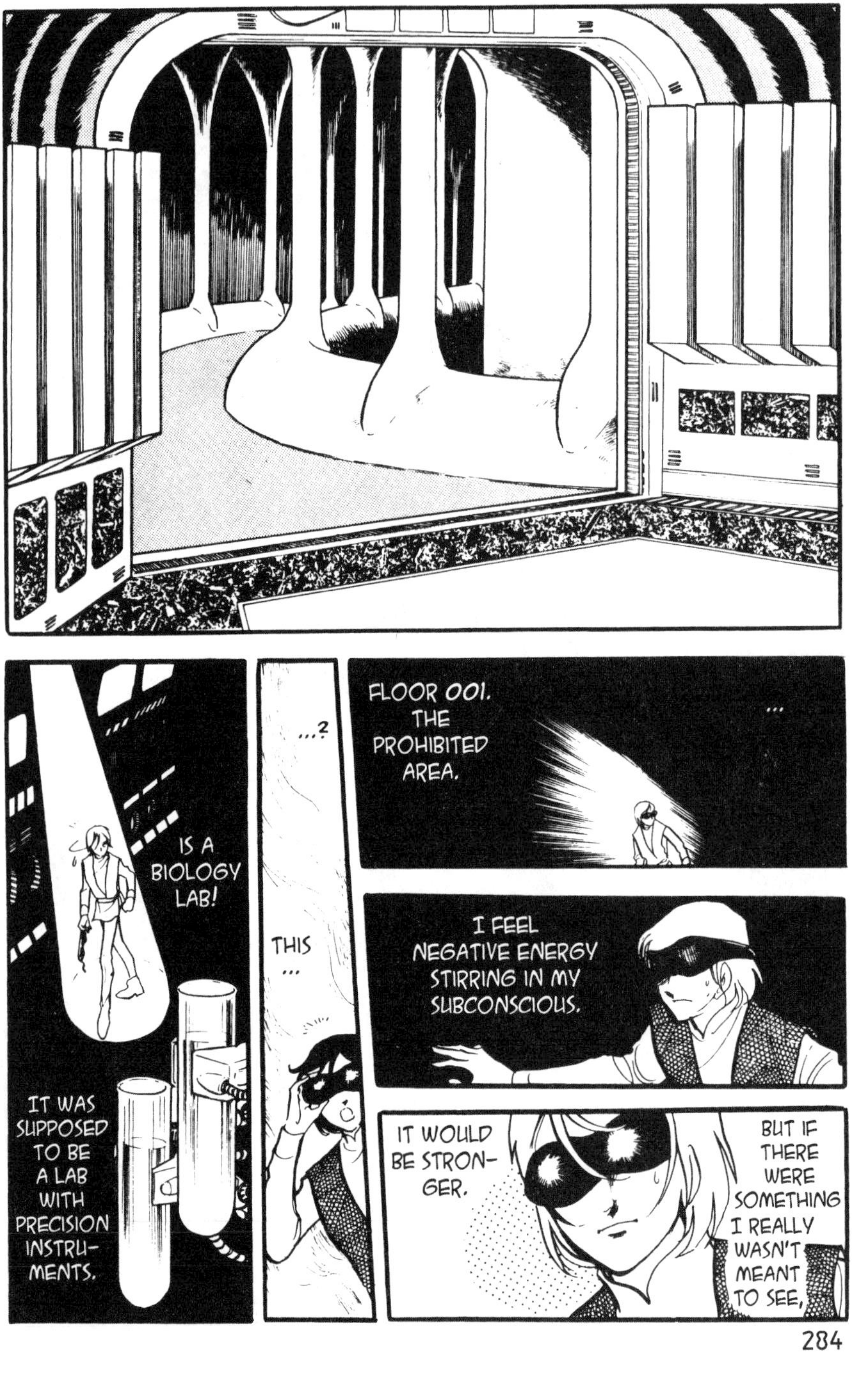
...
FLOOR 001. THE PROHIBITED AREA.
I FEEL NEGATIVE ENERGY STIRRING IN MY SUBCONSCIOUS.
BUT IF THERE WERE SOMETHING I REALLY WASN'T MEANT TO SEE,
IT WOULD BE STRONGER.
...?
THIS ...
IS A BIOLOGY LAB!
IT WAS SUPPOSED TO BE A LAB WITH PRECISION INSTRUMENTS.

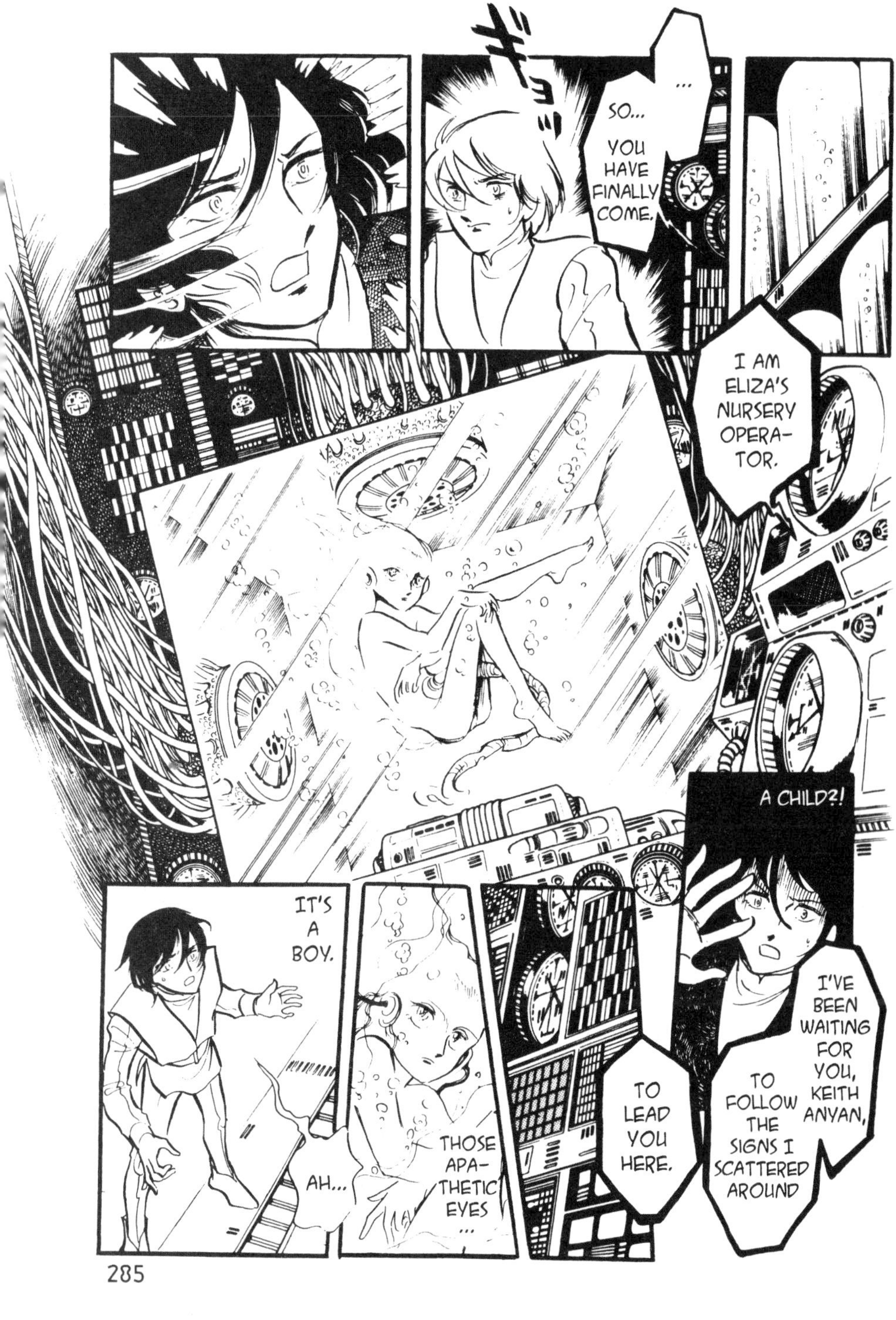
ギョッ
...
SO... YOU HAVE FINALLY COME.
I AM ELIZA'S NURSERY OPERATOR.
A CHILD?!
I'VE BEEN WAITING FOR YOU, KEITH ANYAN,
TO FOLLOW THE SIGNS I SCATTERED AROUND
TO LEAD YOU HERE.
THOSE APATHETIC EYES ...
AH...
IT'S A BOY.

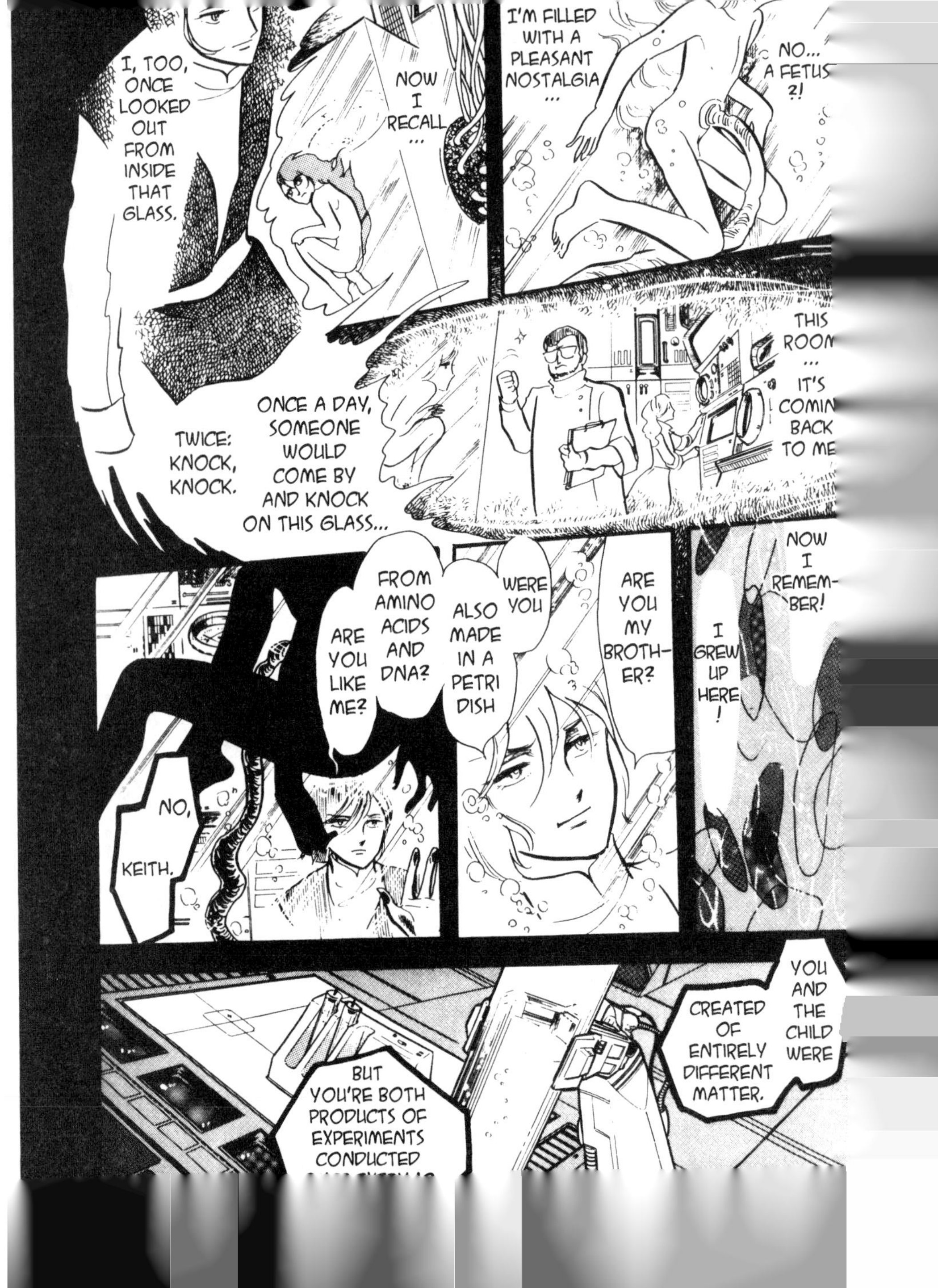
I'M FILLED WITH A PLEASANT NOSTALGIA ...
NO... A FETUS?!
NOW I RECALL ...
I, TOO, ONCE LOOKED OUT FROM INSIDE THAT GLASS.
THIS ROOM ... IT'S COMING BACK TO ME
ONCE A DAY, SOMEONE WOULD COME BY AND KNOCK ON THIS GLASS...
TWICE: KNOCK, KNOCK.
NOW I REMEMBER!
I GREW UP HERE!
ARE YOU MY BROTHER?
WERE YOU ALSO MADE IN A PETRI DISH
FROM AMINO ACIDS AND DNA?
ARE YOU LIKE ME?
NO, KEITH.
YOU AND THE CHILD WERE
CREATED OF ENTIRELY DIFFERENT MATTER.
BUT YOU'RE BOTH PRODUCTS OF EXPERIMENTS CONDUCTED

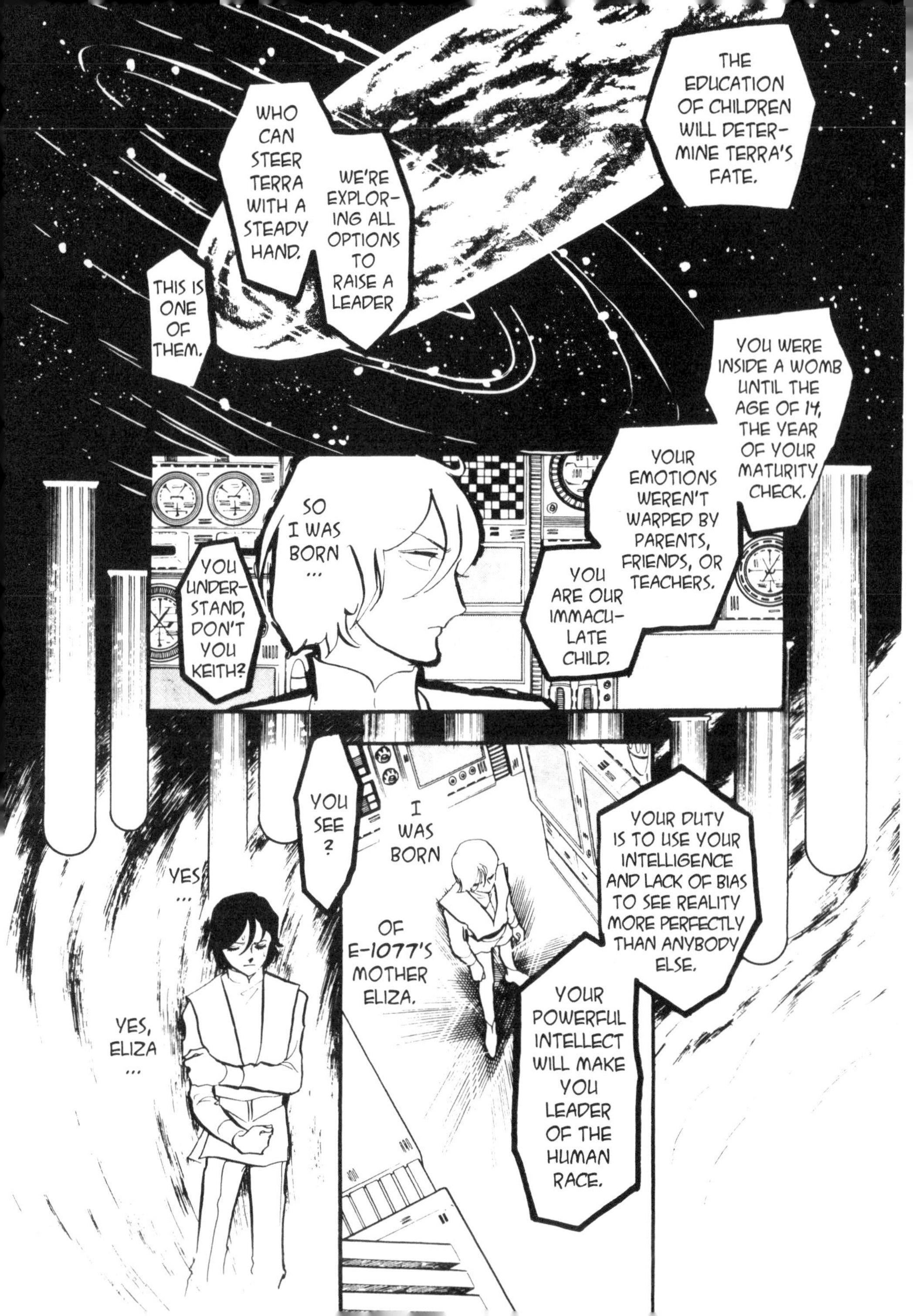
THE EDUCATION OF CHILDREN WILL DETERMINE TERRA'S FATE.
WE'RE EXPLORING ALL OPTIONS TO RAISE A LEADER
WHO CAN STEER TERRA WITH A STEADY HAND.
THIS IS ONE OF THEM.
YOU WERE INSIDE A WOMB UNTIL THE AGE OF 14, THE YEAR OF YOUR MATURITY CHECK.
YOUR EMOTIONS WEREN'T WARPED BY PARENTS, FRIENDS, OR TEACHERS.
YOU ARE OUR IMMACULATE CHILD.
SO I WAS BORN ...
YOU UNDERSTAND, DON'T YOU KEITH?
YOUR DUTY IS TO USE YOUR INTELLIGENCE AND LACK OF BIAS TO SEE REALITY MORE PERFECTLY THAN ANYBODY ELSE.
YOUR POWERFUL INTELLECT WILL MAKE YOU LEADER OF THE HUMAN RACE.
I WAS BORN
OF E-1077'S MOTHER ELIZA.
YOU SEE?
YES ...
YES, ELIZA ...

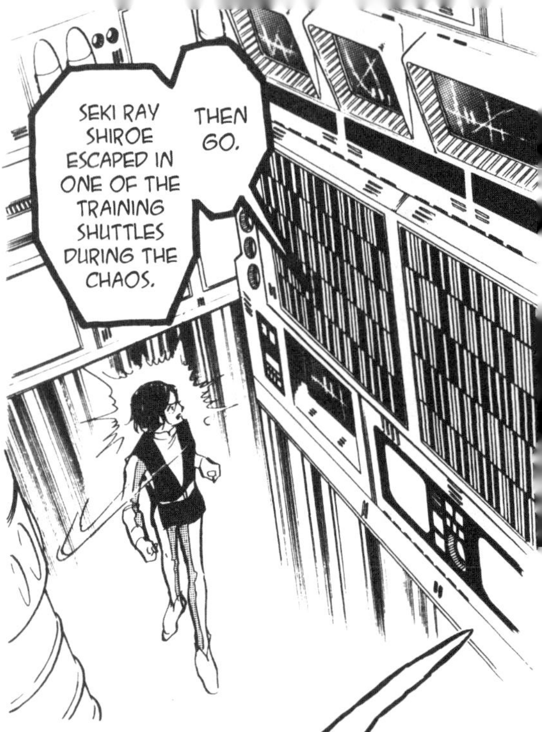
THEN GO.
SEKI RAY SHIROE ESCAPED IN ONE OF THE TRAINING SHUTTLES DURING THE CHAOS.

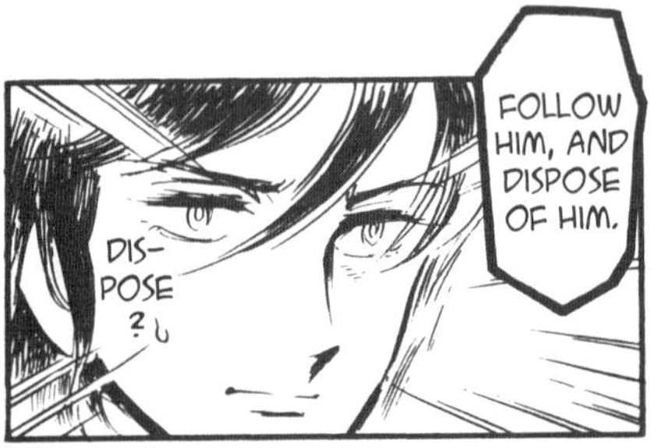
FOLLOW HIM, AND DISPOSE OF HIM.
DIS-POSE?

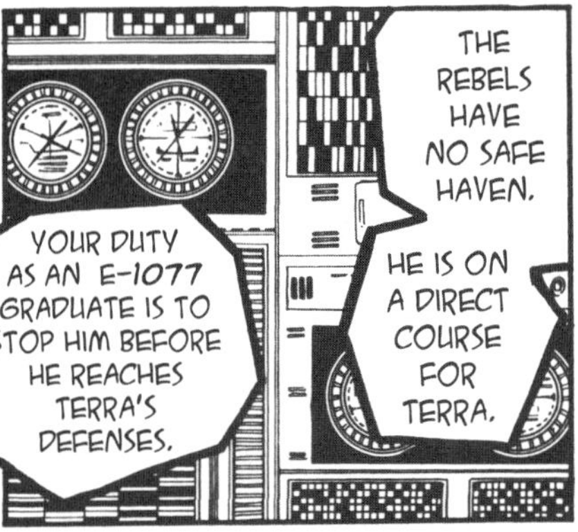
THE REBELS HAVE NO SAFE HAVEN.
HE IS ON A DIRECT COURSE FOR TERRA.
YOUR DUTY AS AN E-1077 GRADUATE IS TO STOP HIM BEFORE HE REACHES TERRA'S DEFENSES.

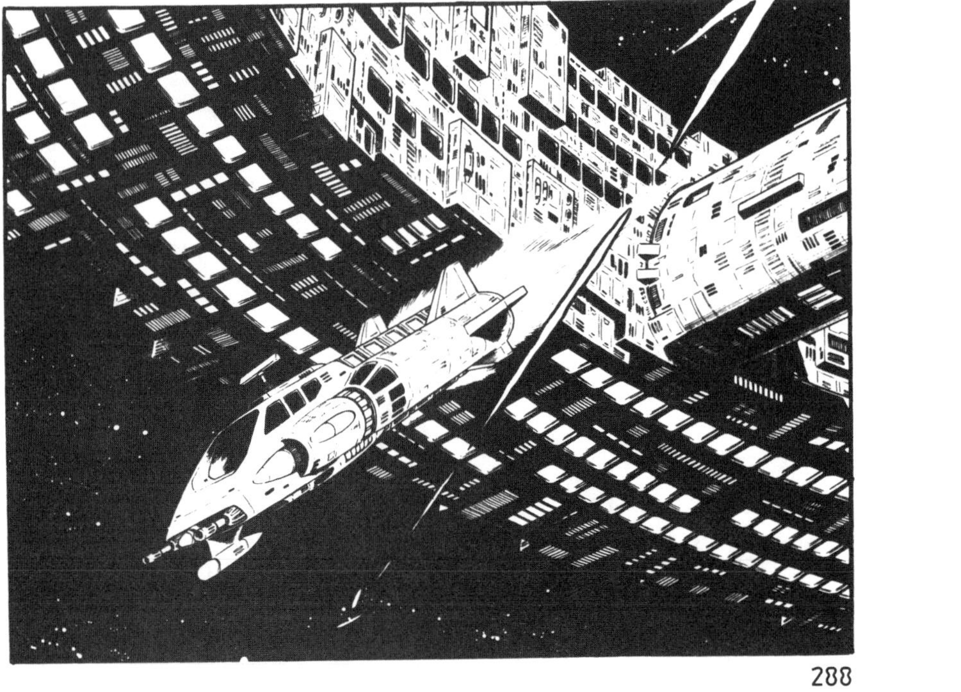

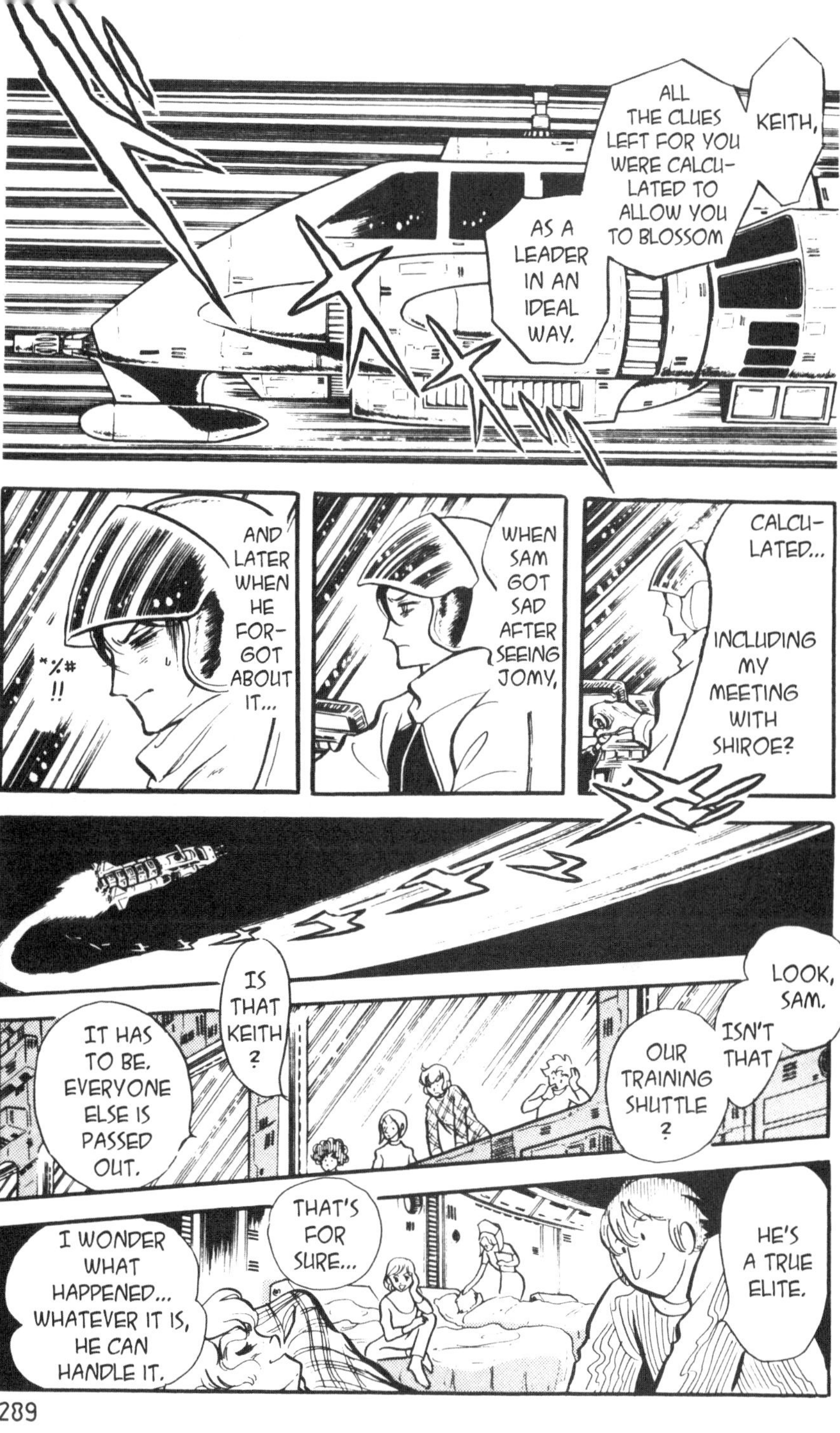
KEITH,
ALL THE CLUES LEFT FOR YOU WERE CALCULATED TO ALLOW YOU TO BLOSSOM
AS A LEADER IN AN IDEAL WAY.
CALCULATED...
INCLUDING MY MEETING WITH SHIROE?
WHEN SAM GOT SAD AFTER SEEING JOMY,
AND LATER WHEN HE FORGOT ABOUT IT...
*%# !!
LOOK, SAM.
ISN'T THAT
OUR TRAINING SHUTTLE?
IS THAT KEITH?
IT HAS TO BE. EVERYONE ELSE IS PASSED OUT.
HE'S A TRUE ELITE.
THAT'S FOR SURE...
I WONDER WHAT HAPPENED... WHATEVER IT IS, HE CAN HANDLE IT.

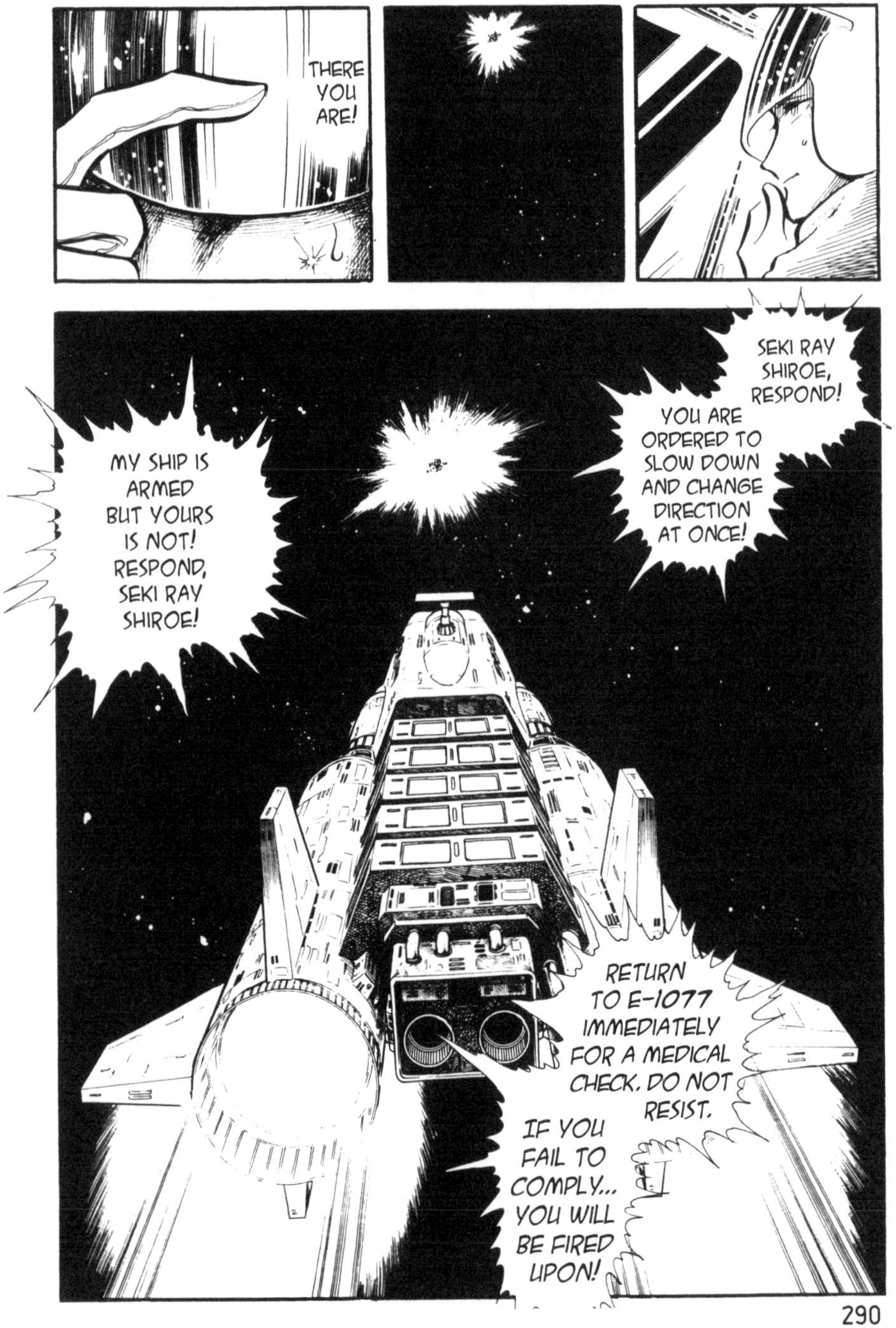
THERE YOU ARE!
SEKI RAY SHIROE, RESPOND!
YOU ARE ORDERED TO SLOW DOWN AND CHANGE DIRECTION AT ONCE!
MY SHIP IS ARMED BUT YOURS IS NOT! RESPOND, SEKI RAY SHIROE!
RETURN TO E-1077 IMMEDIATELY FOR A MEDICAL CHECK. DO NOT RESIST.
IF YOU FAIL TO COMPLY... YOU WILL BE FIRED UPON!

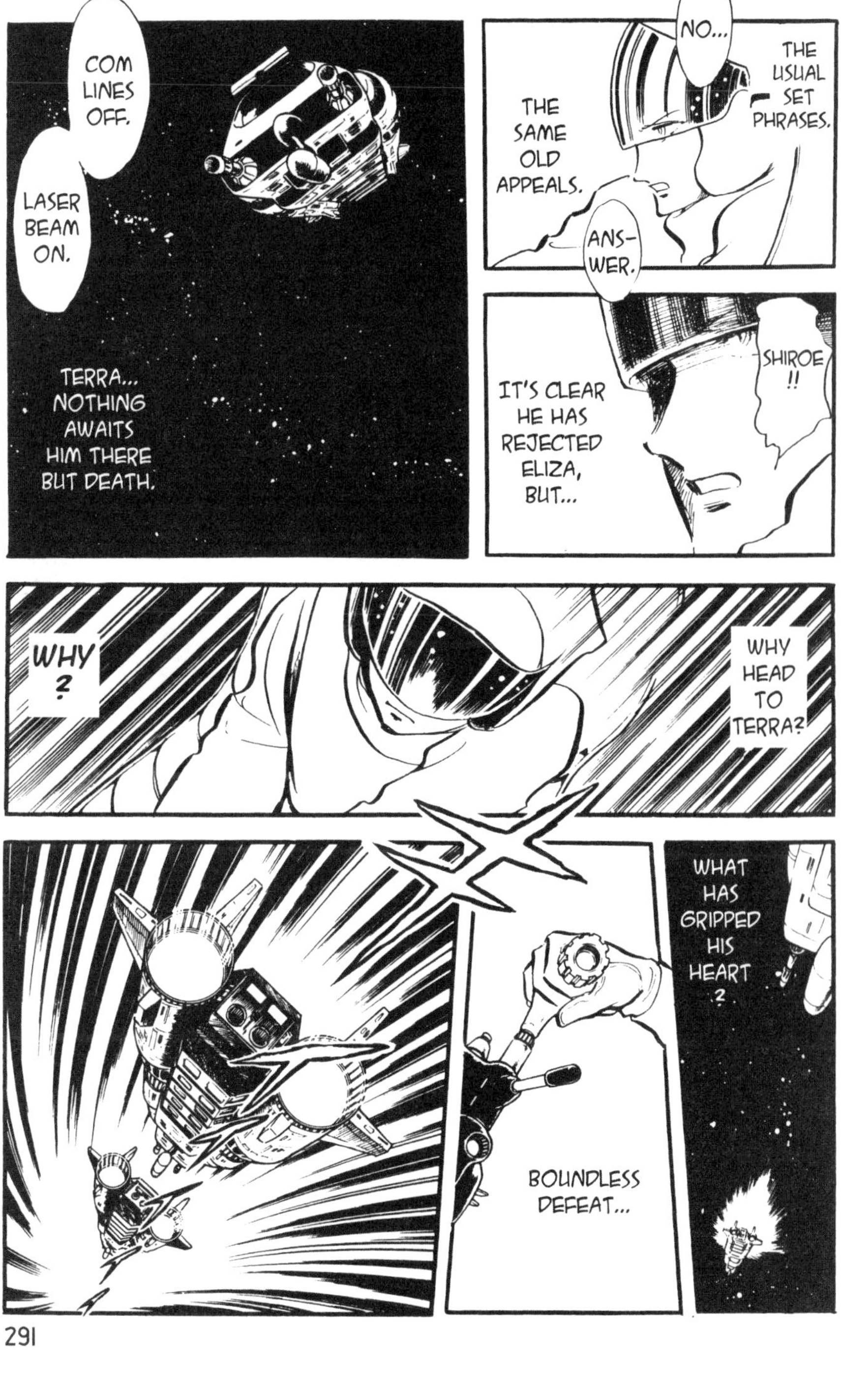
NO...
THE USUAL SET PHRASES.
THE SAME OLD APPEALS.
ANSWER.
SHIROE!!
IT'S CLEAR HE HAS REJECTED ELIZA, BUT...
COM LINES OFF.
LASER BEAM ON.
TERRA... NOTHING AWAITS HIM THERE BUT DEATH.
WHY HEAD TO TERRA?
WHY?
WHAT HAS GRIPPED HIS HEART?
BOUNDLESS DEFEAT...

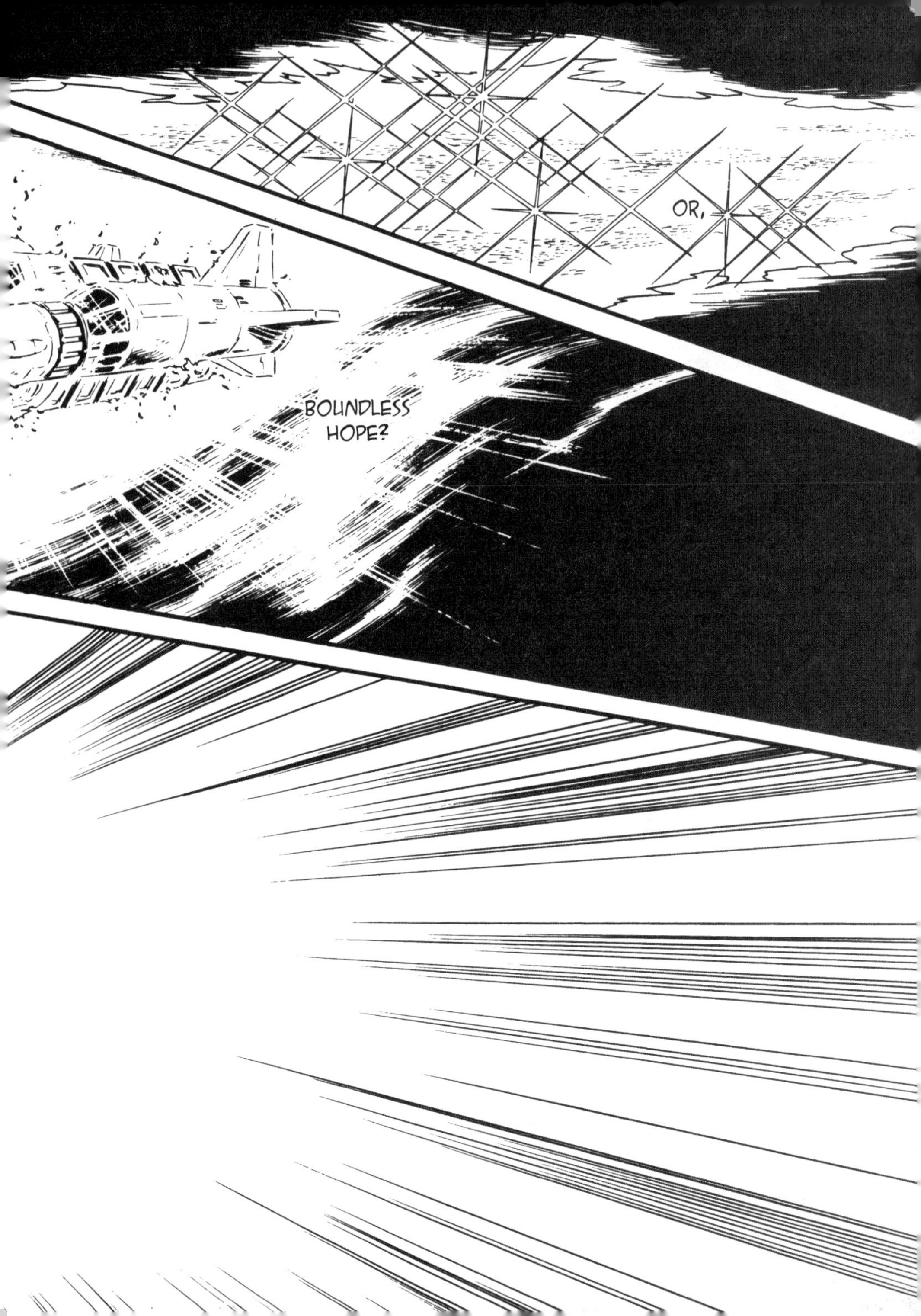
OR,
BOUNDLESS HOPE?

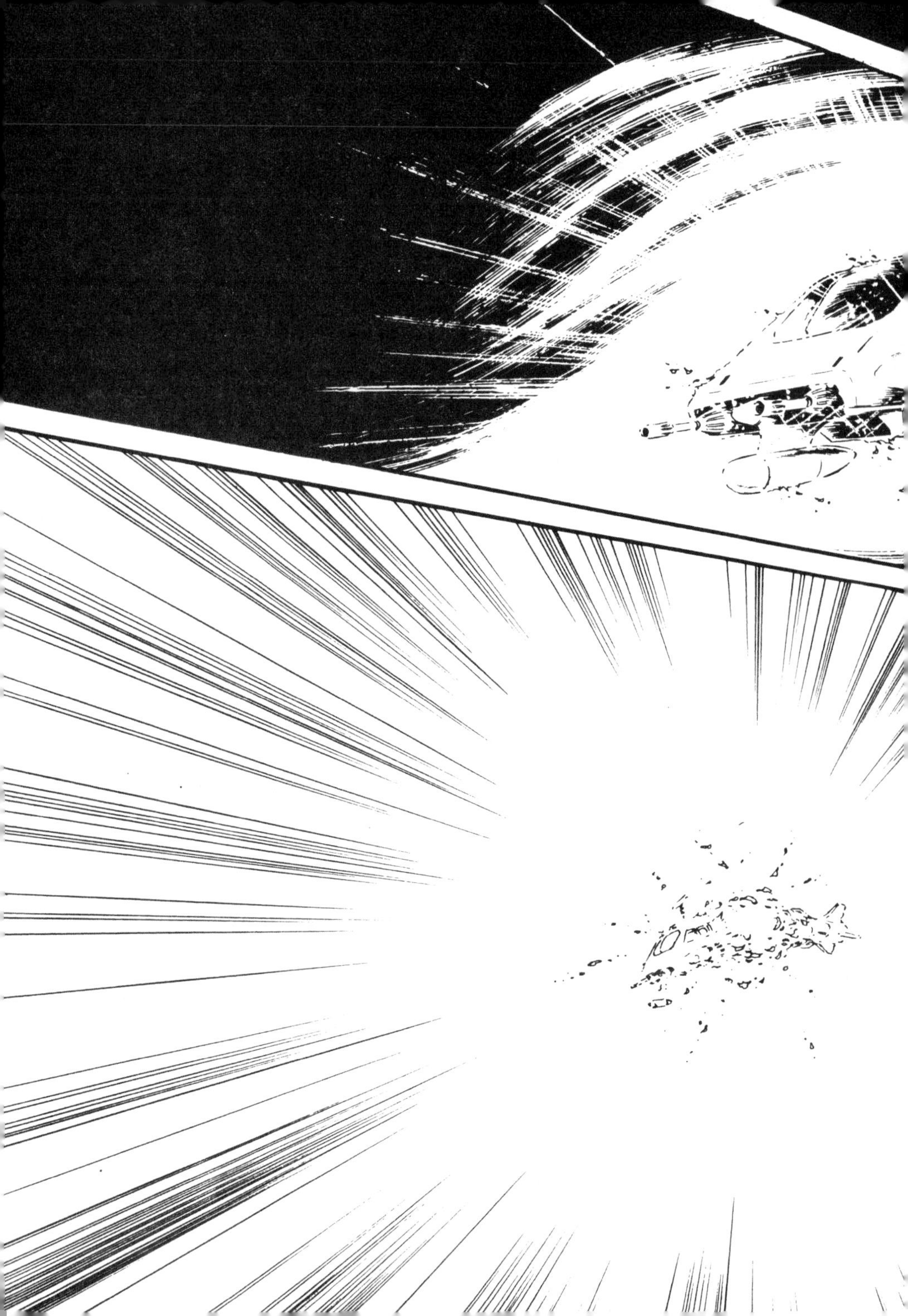

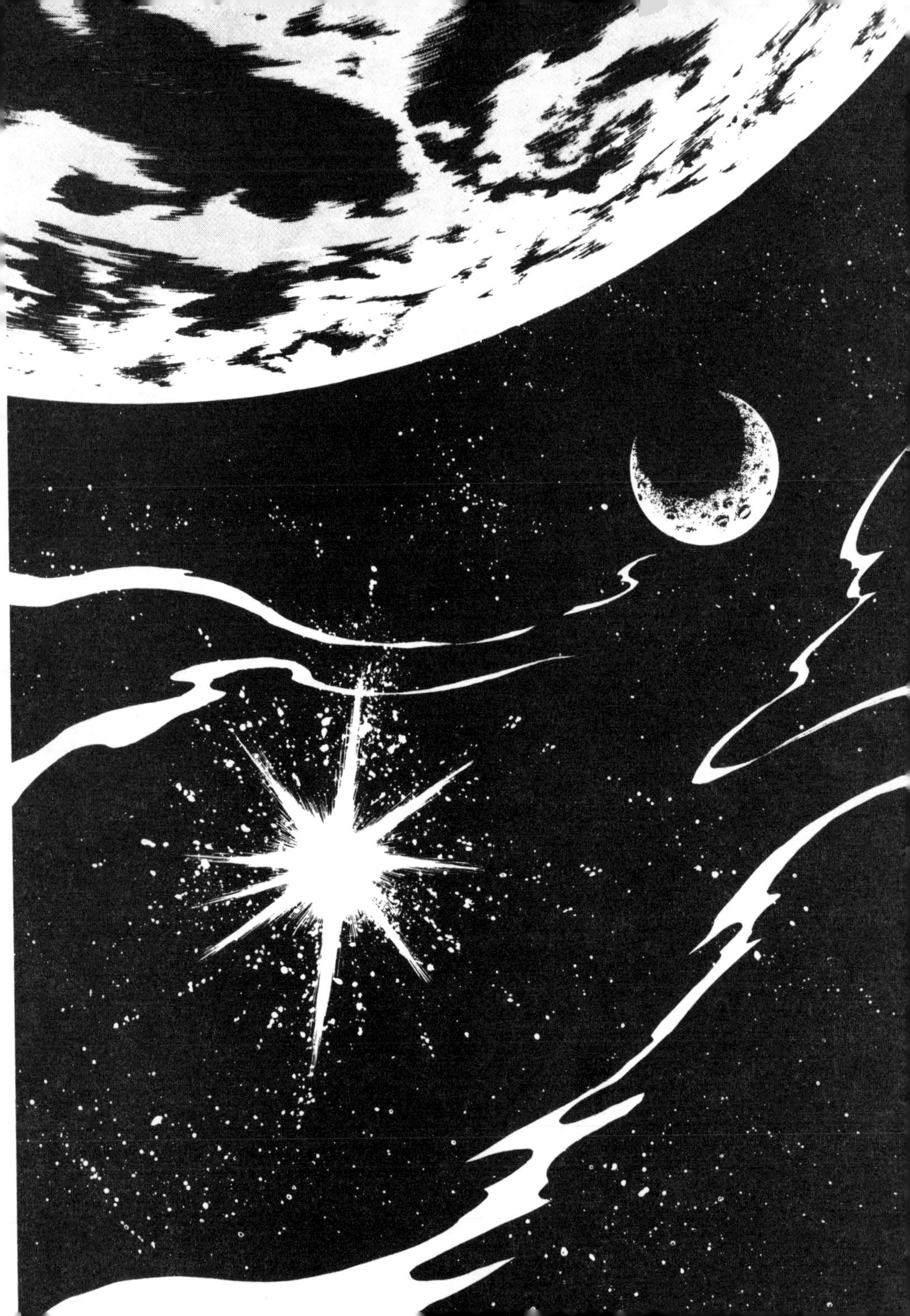

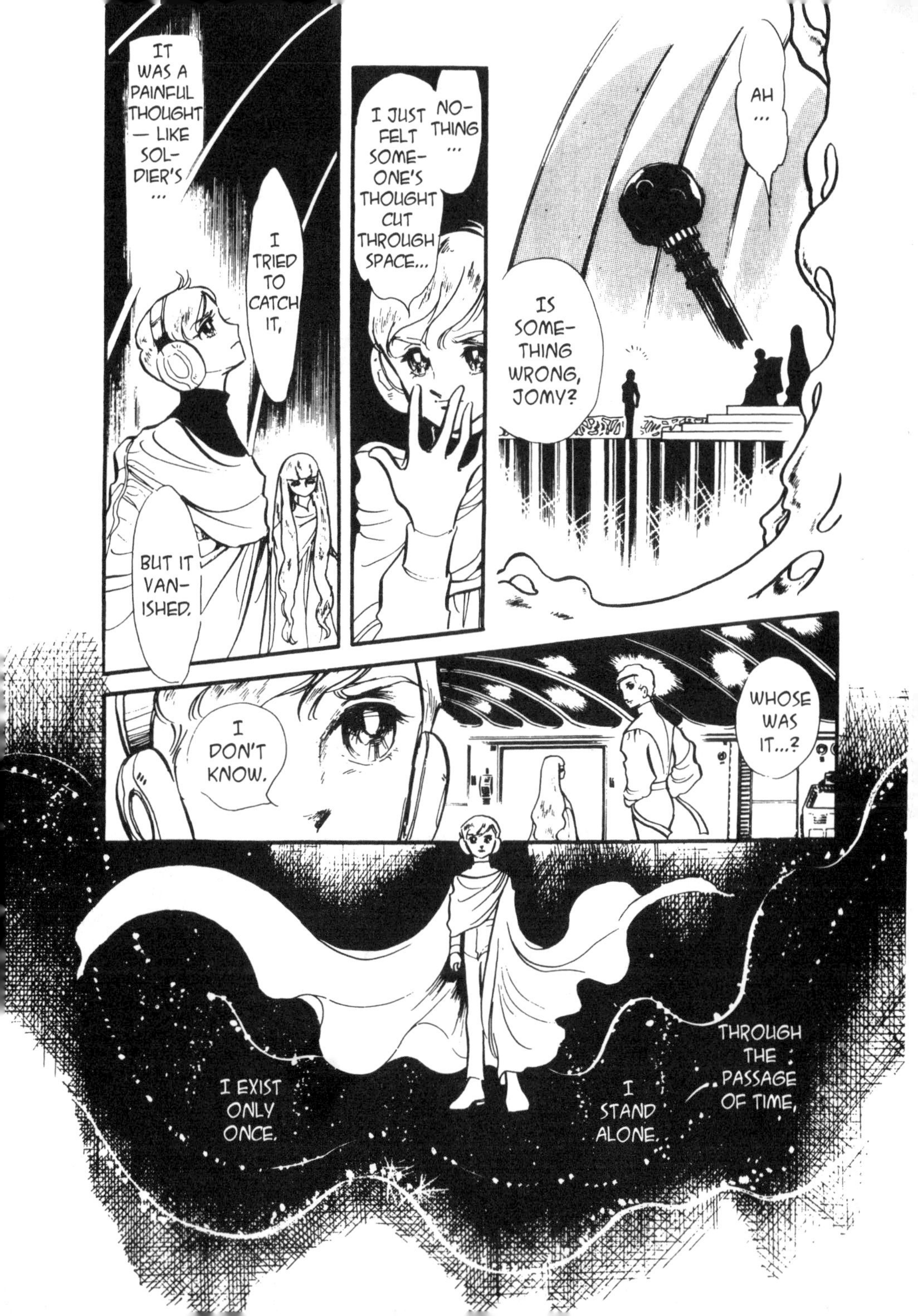
AH ...
IS SOMETHING WRONG, JOMY?
NOTHING ...
I JUST FELT SOMEONE'S THOUGHT CUT THROUGH SPACE...
IT WAS A PAINFUL THOUGHT — LIKE SOLDIER'S ...
I TRIED TO CATCH IT,
BUT IT VANISHED.
WHOSE WAS IT...?
I DON'T KNOW.
THROUGH THE PASSAGE OF TIME,
I STAND ALONE.
I EXIST ONLY ONCE.

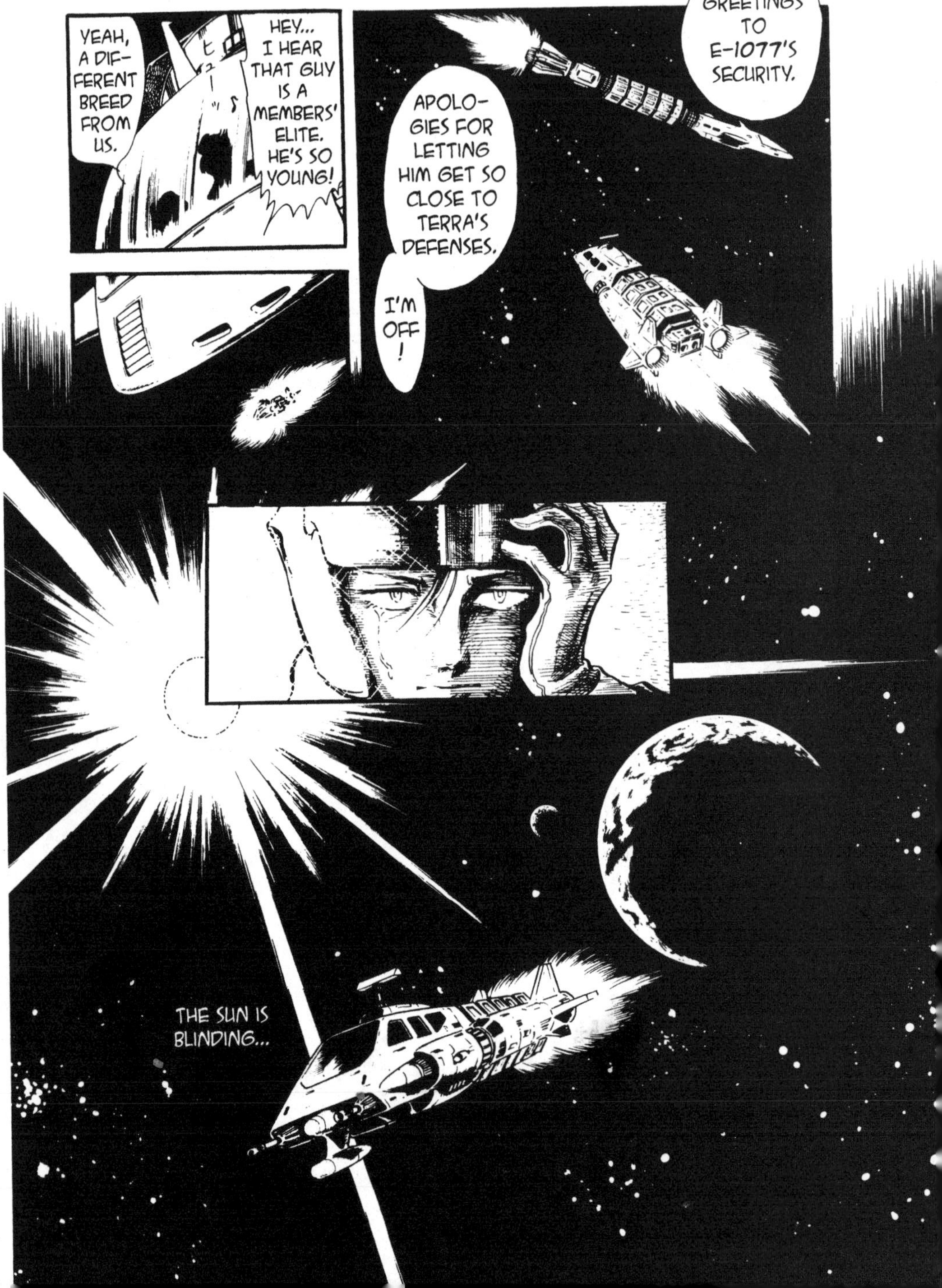
GREETINGS TO E-1077'S SECURITY.
APOLOGIES FOR LETTING HIM GET SO CLOSE TO TERRA'S DEFENSES.
I'M OFF!
HEY... I HEAR THAT GUY IS A MEMBERS' ELITE. HE'S SO YOUNG!
YEAH, A DIFFERENT BREED FROM US.
THE SUN IS BLINDING...

PART 3

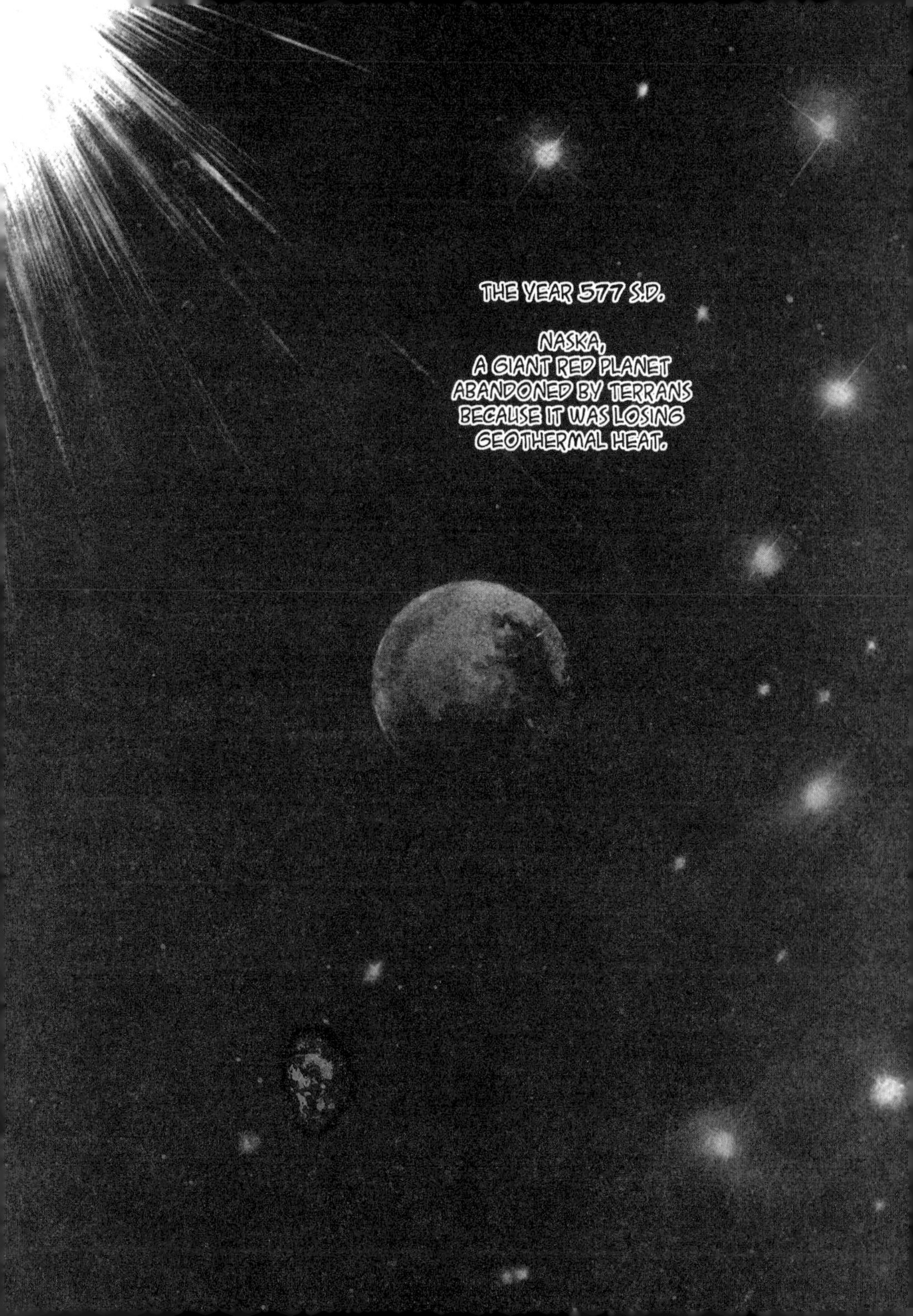
THE YEAR 577 S.D.
NASKA, A GIANT RED PLANET ABANDONED BY TERRANS BECAUSE IT WAS LOSING GEOTHERMAL HEAT.

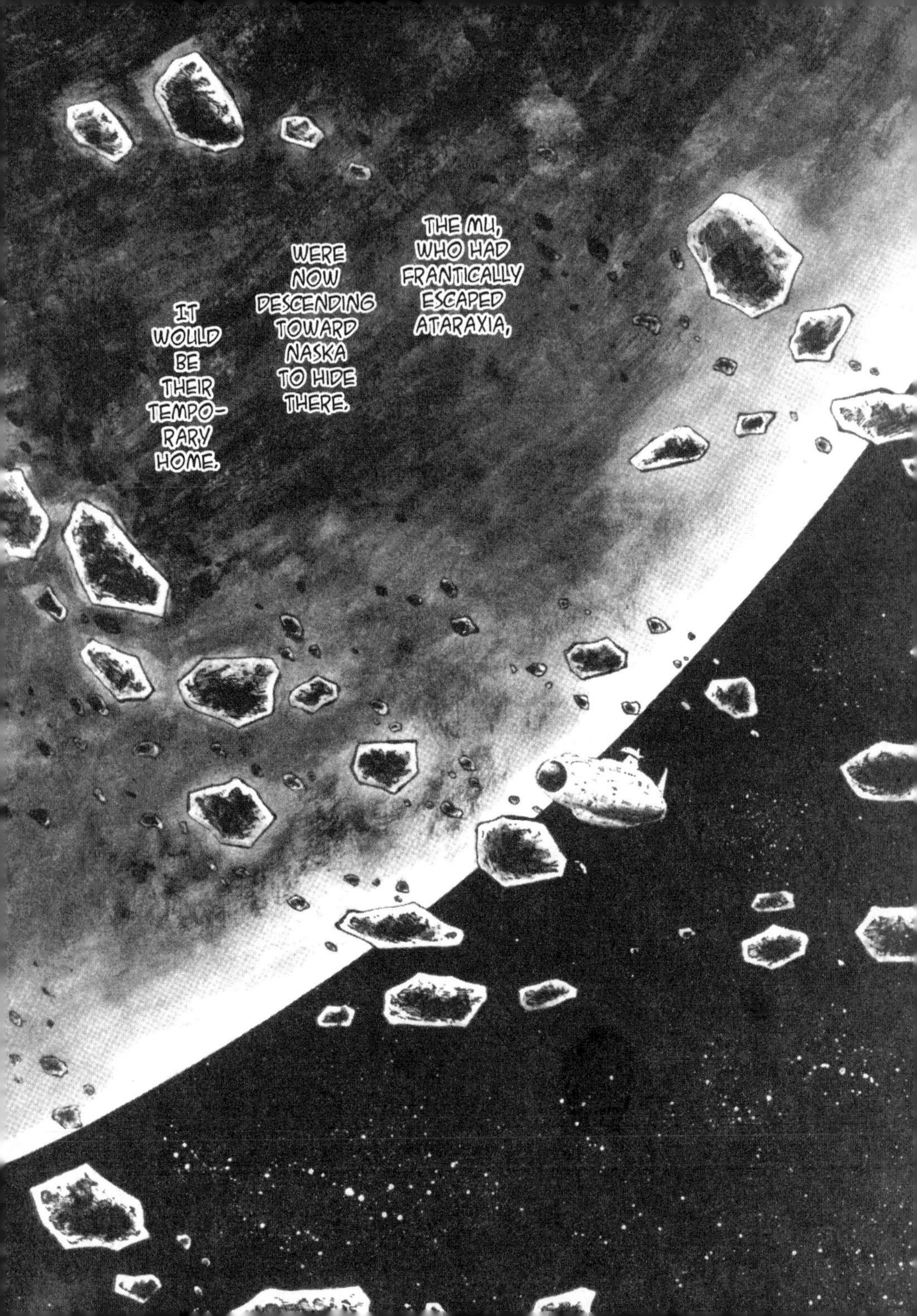
THE MU, WHO HAD FRANTICALLY ESCAPED ATARAXIA,
WERE NOW DESCENDING TOWARD NASKA TO HIDE THERE.
IT WOULD BE THEIR TEMPO-RARY HOME.

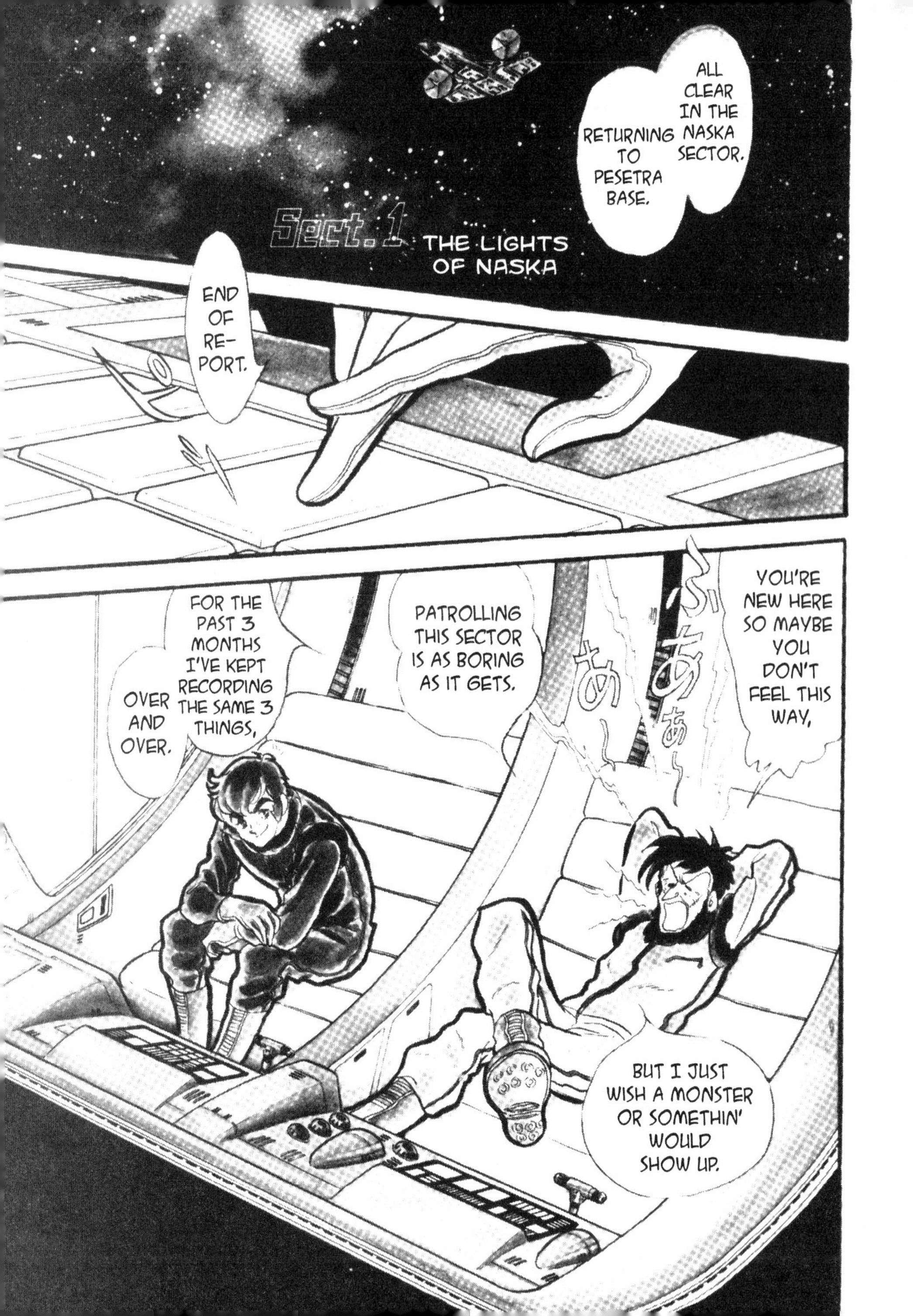
ALL CLEAR IN THE NASKA SECTOR.
RETURNING TO PESETRA BASE.
Sect. 1 THE LIGHTS OF NASKA
END OF RE-PORT.
YOU'RE NEW HERE SO MAYBE YOU DON'T FEEL THIS WAY,
BUT I JUST WISH A MONSTER OR SOMETHIN' WOULD SHOW UP.
PATROLLING THIS SECTOR IS AS BORING AS IT GETS.
FOR THE PAST 3 MONTHS I'VE KEPT RECORDING THE SAME 3 THINGS,
OVER AND OVER.

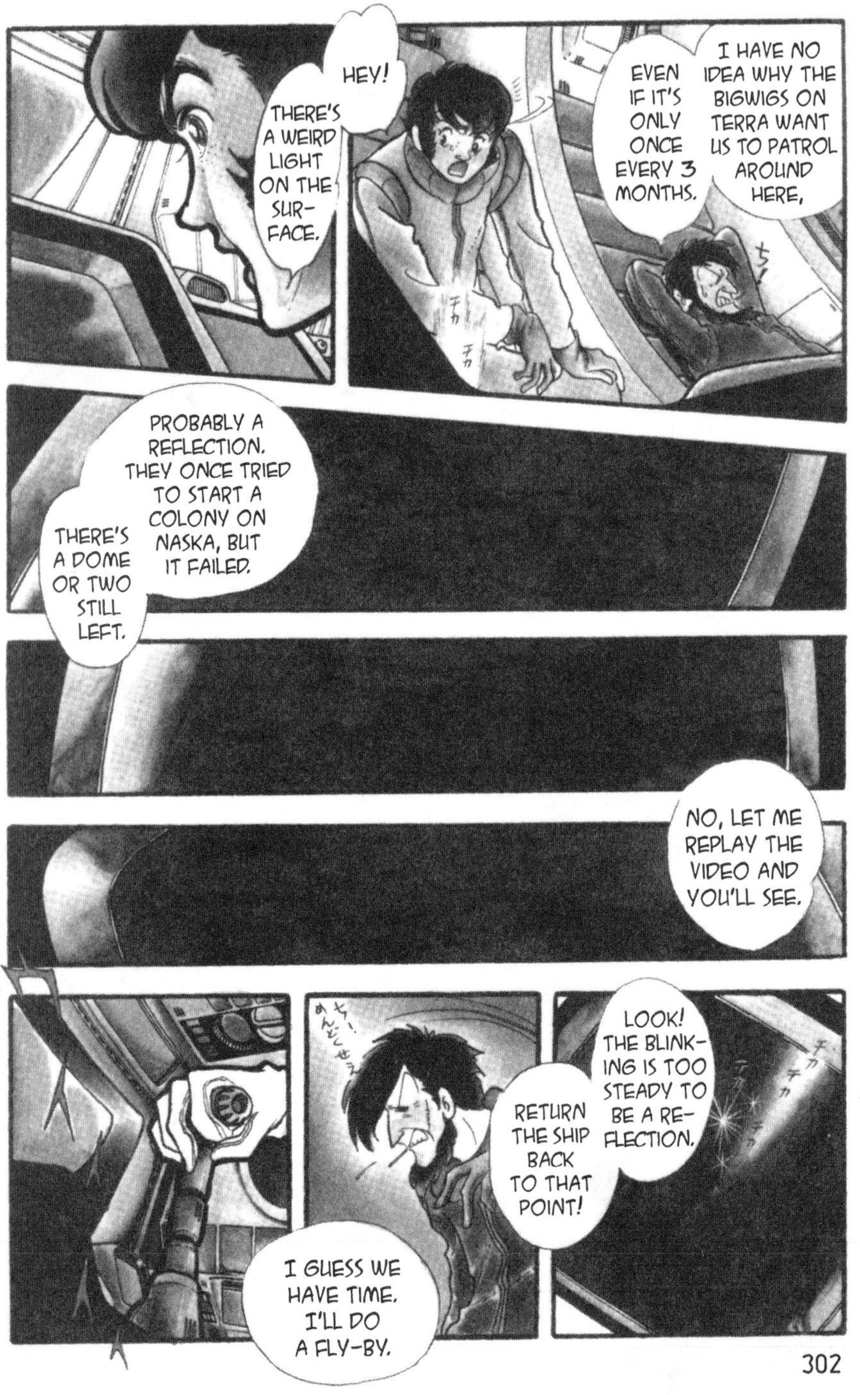
I HAVE NO IDEA WHY THE BIGWIGS ON TERRA WANT US TO PATROL AROUND HERE,
EVEN IF IT'S ONLY ONCE EVERY 3 MONTHS.
HEY!
THERE'S A WEIRD LIGHT ON THE SURFACE.
PROBABLY A REFLECTION. THEY ONCE TRIED TO START A COLONY ON NASKA, BUT IT FAILED.
THERE'S A DOME OR TWO STILL LEFT.
NO, LET ME REPLAY THE VIDEO AND YOU'LL SEE.
LOOK! THE BLINKING IS TOO STEADY TO BE A REFLECTION.
RETURN THE SHIP BACK TO THAT POINT!
I GUESS WE HAVE TIME. I'LL DO A FLY-BY.

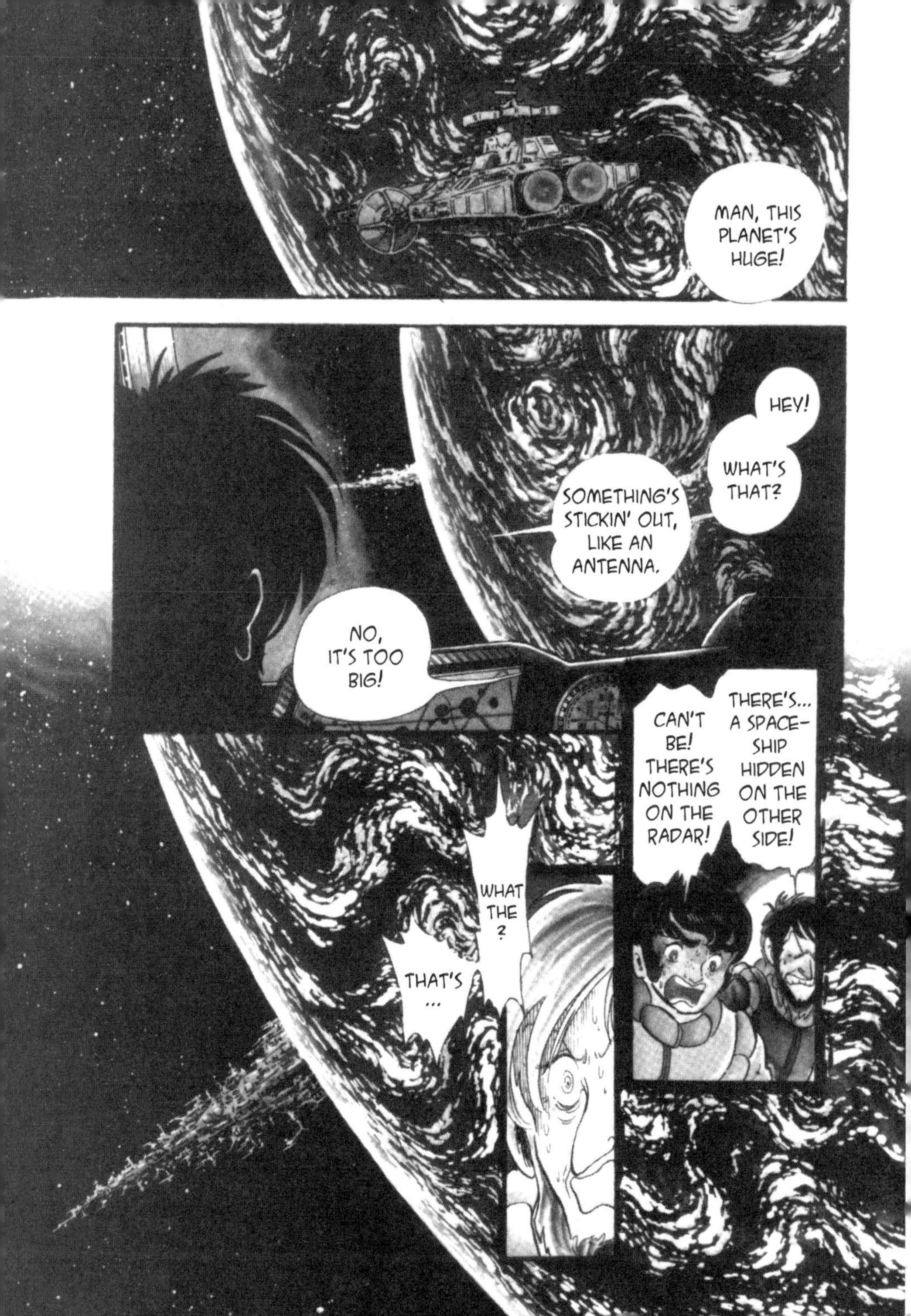
MAN, THIS PLANET'S HUGE!
HEY!
WHAT'S THAT?
SOMETHING'S STICKIN' OUT, LIKE AN ANTENNA.
NO, IT'S TOO BIG!
THERE'S... A SPACE-SHIP HIDDEN ON THE OTHER SIDE!
CAN'T BE! THERE'S NOTHING ON THE RADAR!
WHAT THE?
THAT'S...

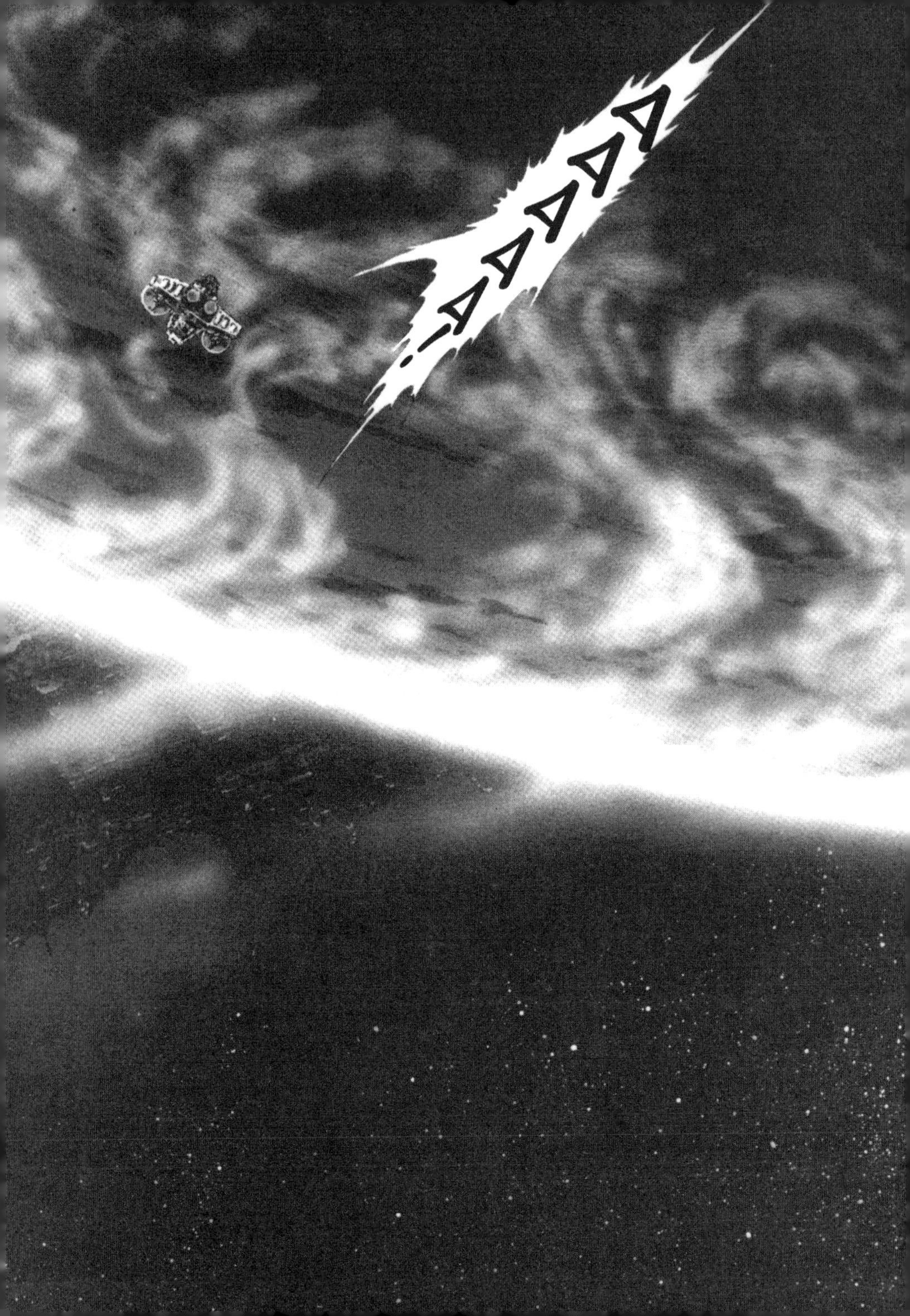
AAAAA!

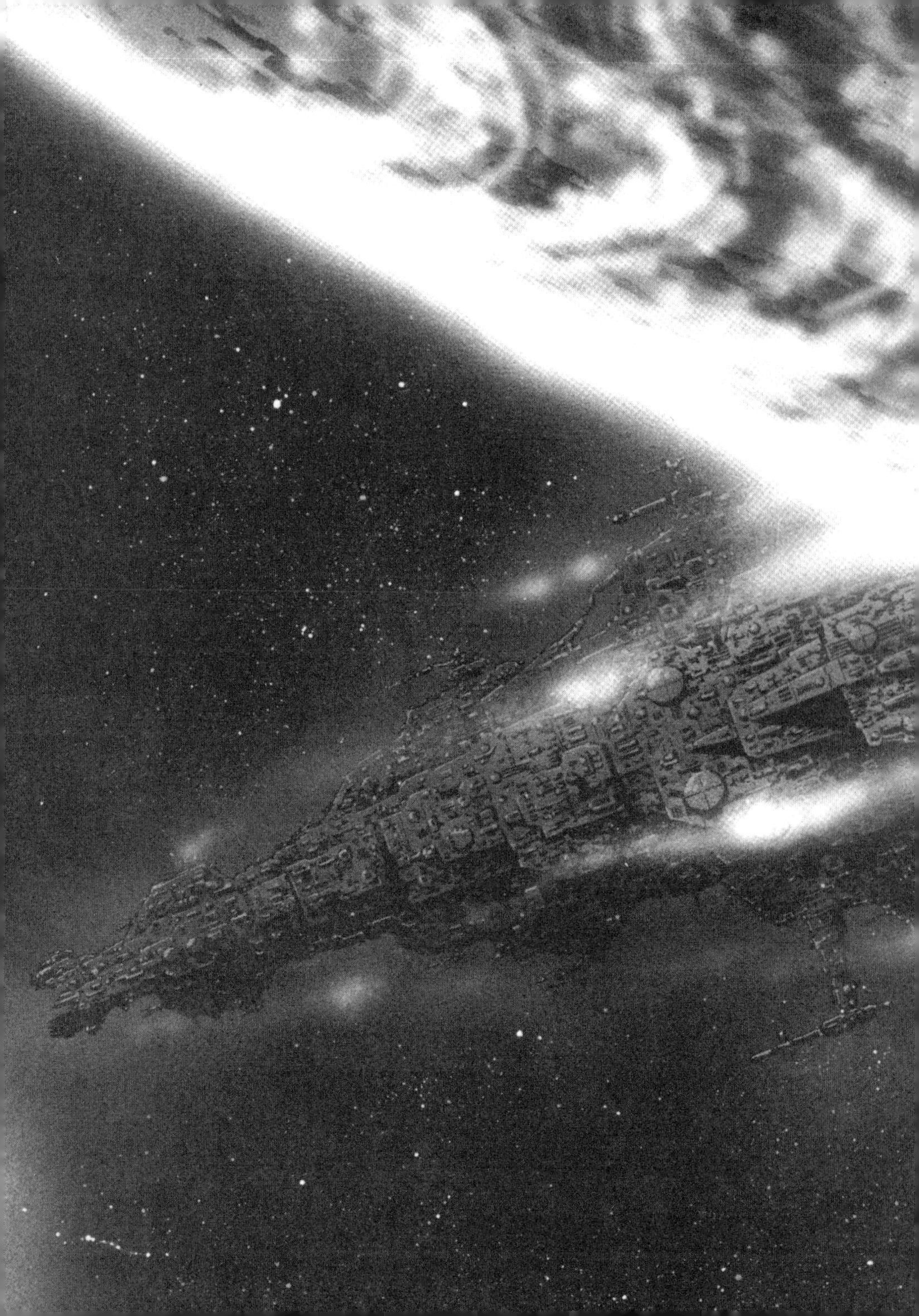

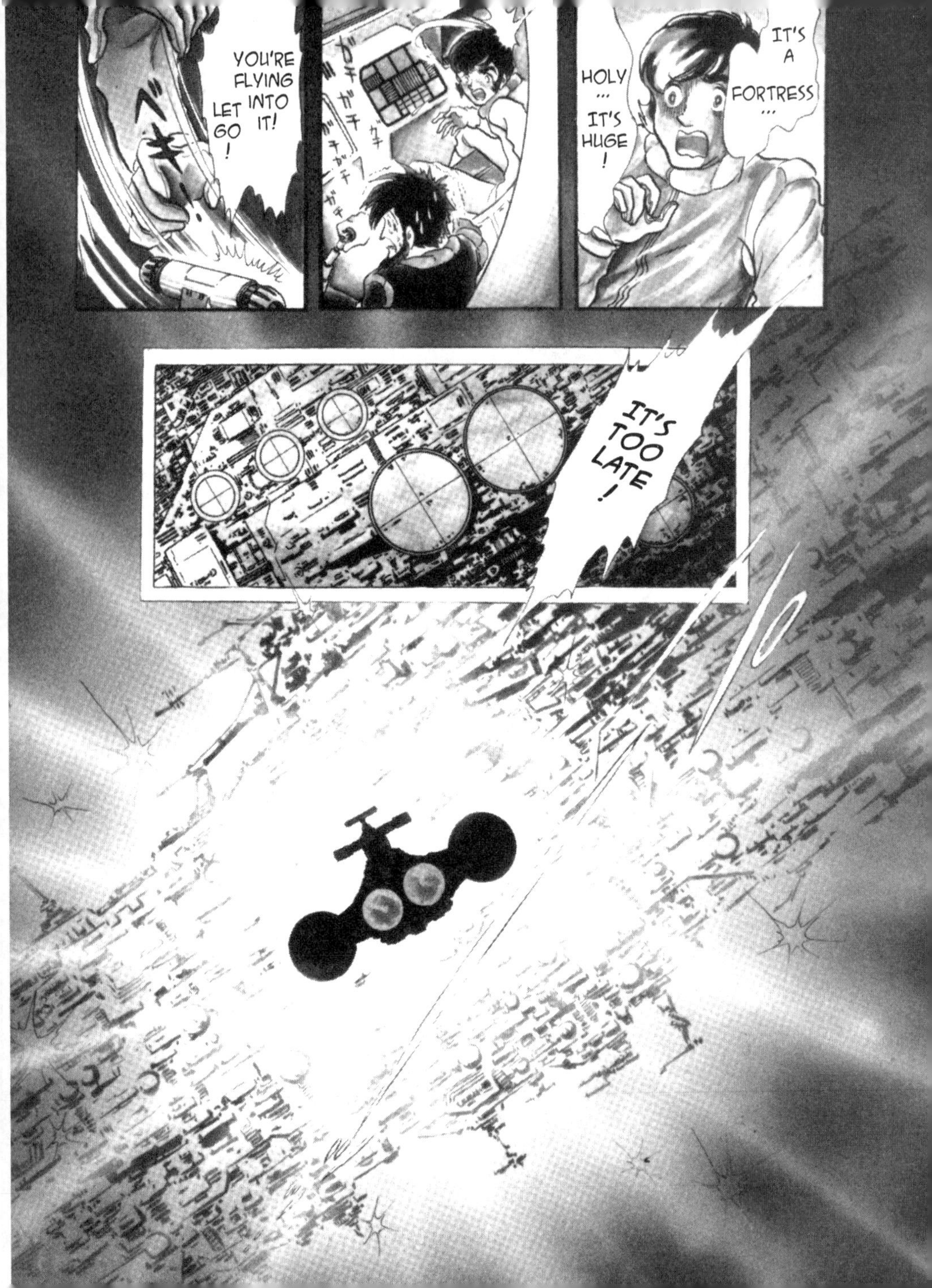
IT'S A FORTRESS...
HOLY... IT'S HUGE!
YOU'RE FLYING INTO IT!
LET GO!
IT'S TOO LATE!

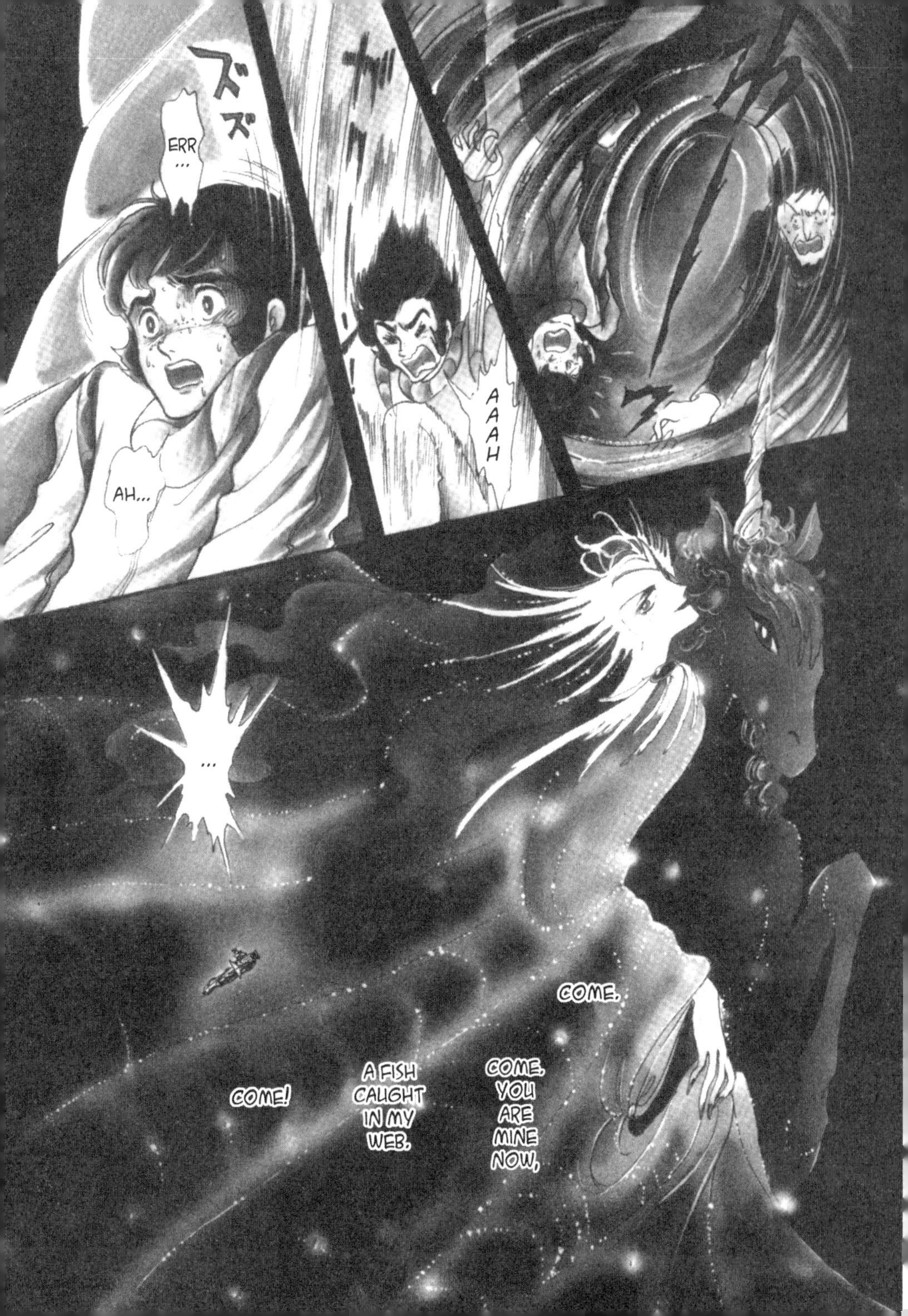
AAAH
ズズ
ERR ...
AH...
COME.
COME. YOU ARE MINE NOW,
A FISH CAUGHT IN MY WEB.
...
COME!

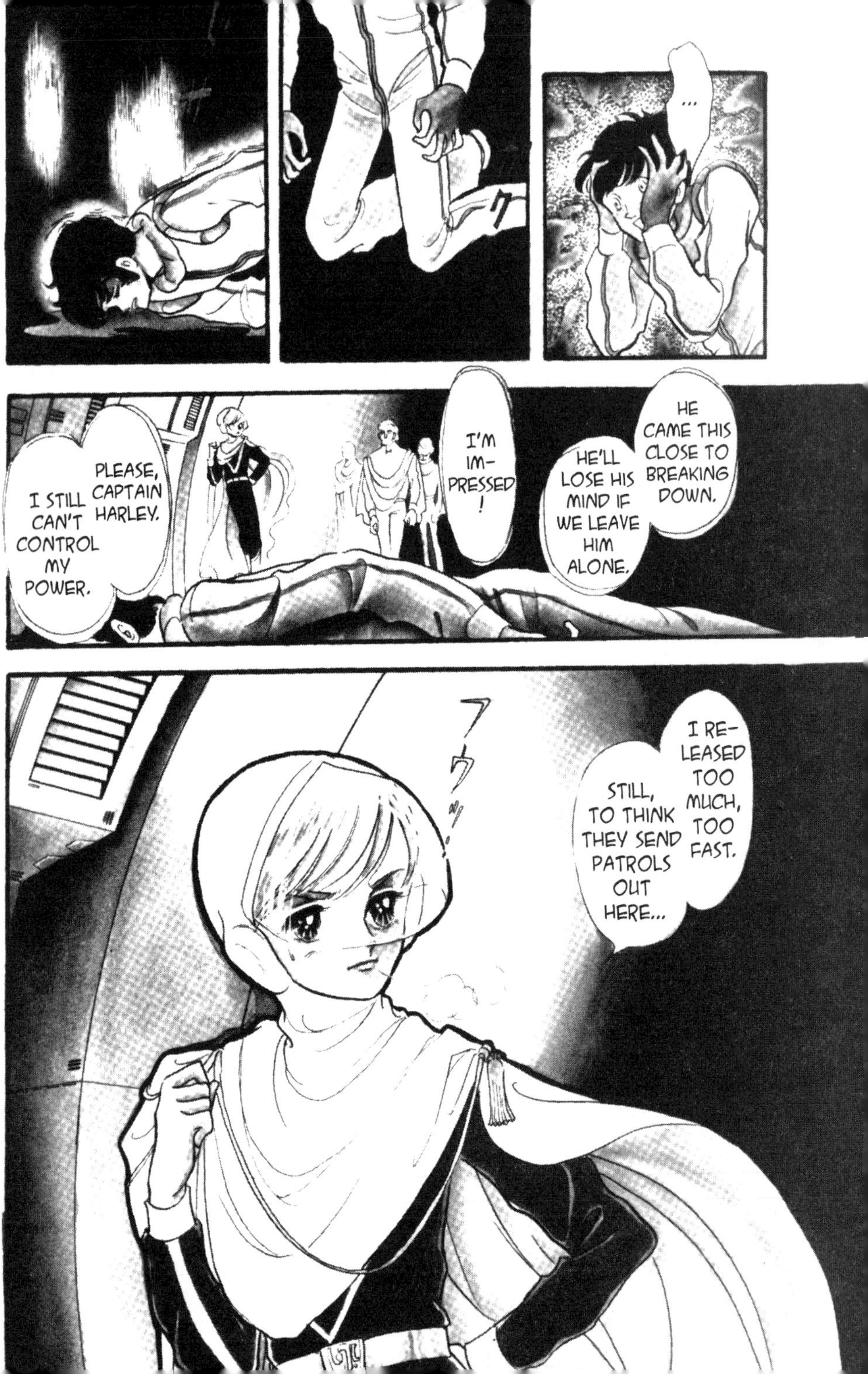
...
HE CAME THIS CLOSE TO BREAKING DOWN.
HE'LL LOSE HIS MIND IF WE LEAVE HIM ALONE.
I'M IM-PRESSED!
PLEASE, CAPTAIN HARLEY.
I STILL CAN'T CONTROL MY POWER.
I RE-LEASED TOO MUCH, TOO FAST.
STILL, TO THINK THEY SEND PATROLS OUT HERE...
フゥ

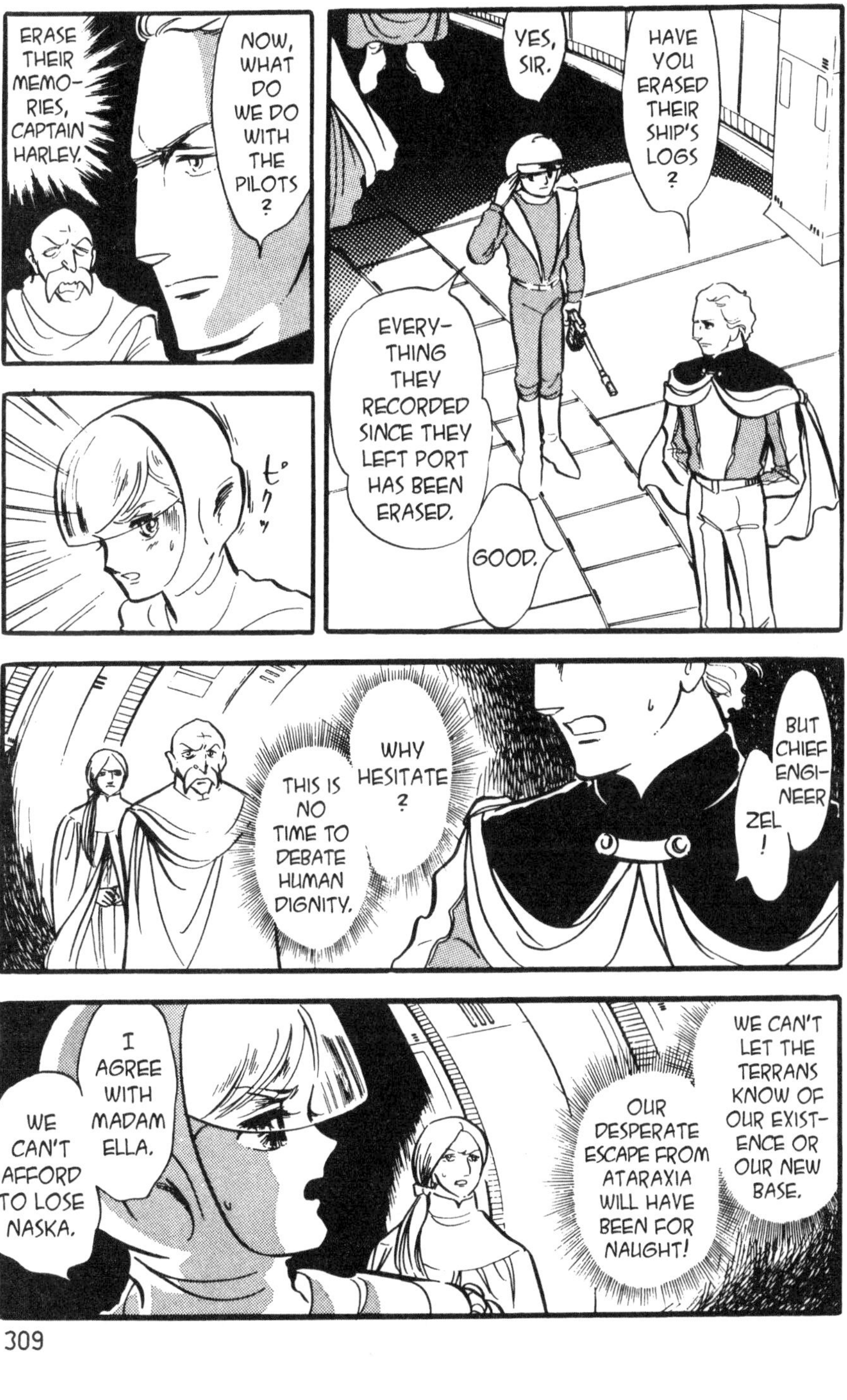
HAVE YOU ERASED THEIR SHIP'S LOGS?
YES, SIR.
EVERYTHING THEY RECORDED SINCE THEY LEFT PORT HAS BEEN ERASED.
GOOD.
NOW, WHAT DO WE DO WITH THE PILOTS?
ERASE THEIR MEMORIES, CAPTAIN HARLEY.
ピクッ
BUT CHIEF ENGINEER ZEL!
WHY HESITATE?
THIS IS NO TIME TO DEBATE HUMAN DIGNITY.
WE CAN'T LET THE TERRANS KNOW OF OUR EXISTENCE OR OUR NEW BASE.
OUR DESPERATE ESCAPE FROM ATARAXIA WILL HAVE BEEN FOR NAUGHT!
I AGREE WITH MADAM ELLA.
WE CAN'T AFFORD TO LOSE NASKA.

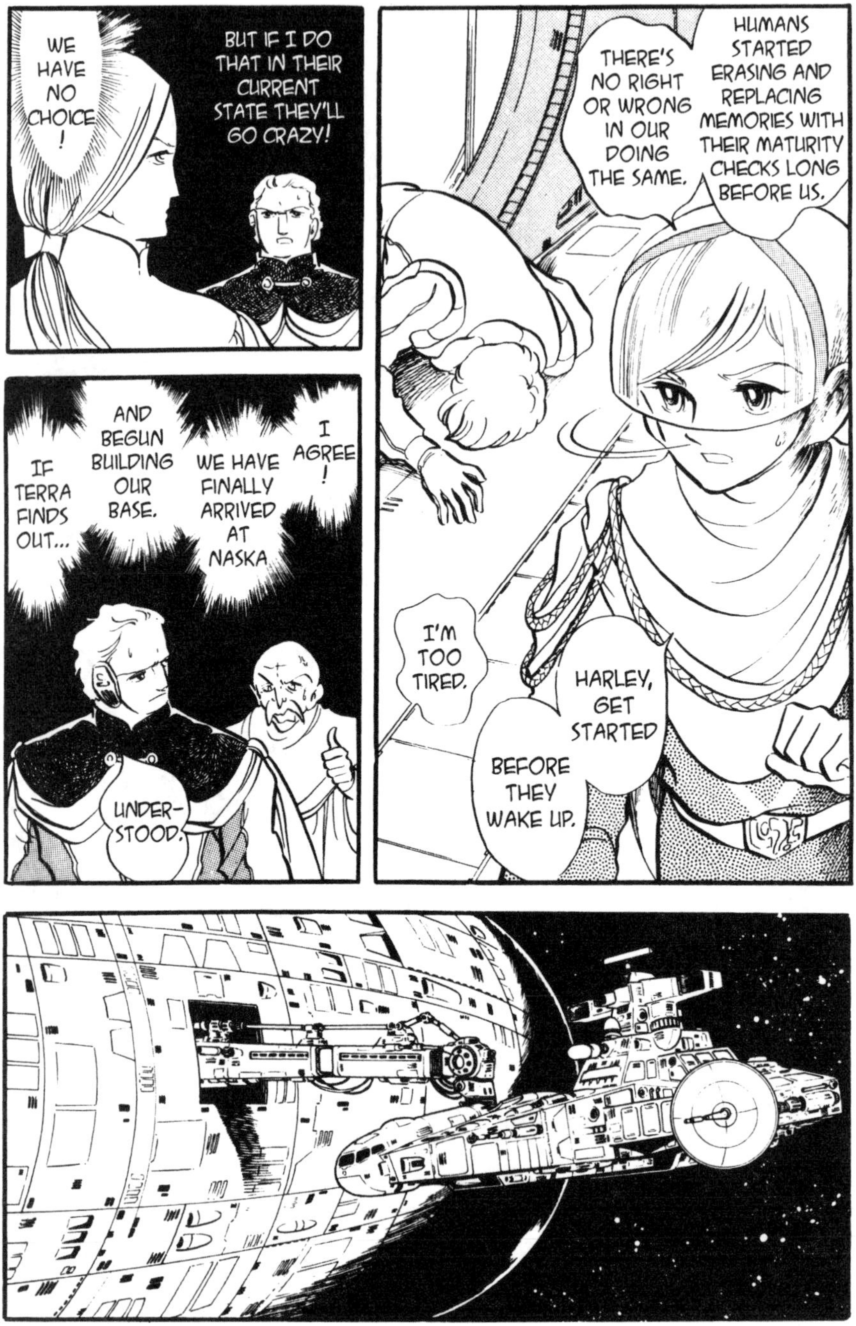
HUMANS STARTED ERASING AND REPLACING MEMORIES WITH THEIR MATURITY CHECKS LONG BEFORE US.
THERE'S NO RIGHT OR WRONG IN OUR DOING THE SAME.
HARLEY, GET STARTED
BEFORE THEY WAKE UP.
I'M TOO TIRED.
BUT IF I DO THAT IN THEIR CURRENT STATE THEY'LL GO CRAZY!
WE HAVE NO CHOICE!
I AGREE!
WE HAVE FINALLY ARRIVED AT NASKA
AND BEGUN BUILDING OUR BASE.
IF TERRA FINDS OUT...
UNDER-STOOD.

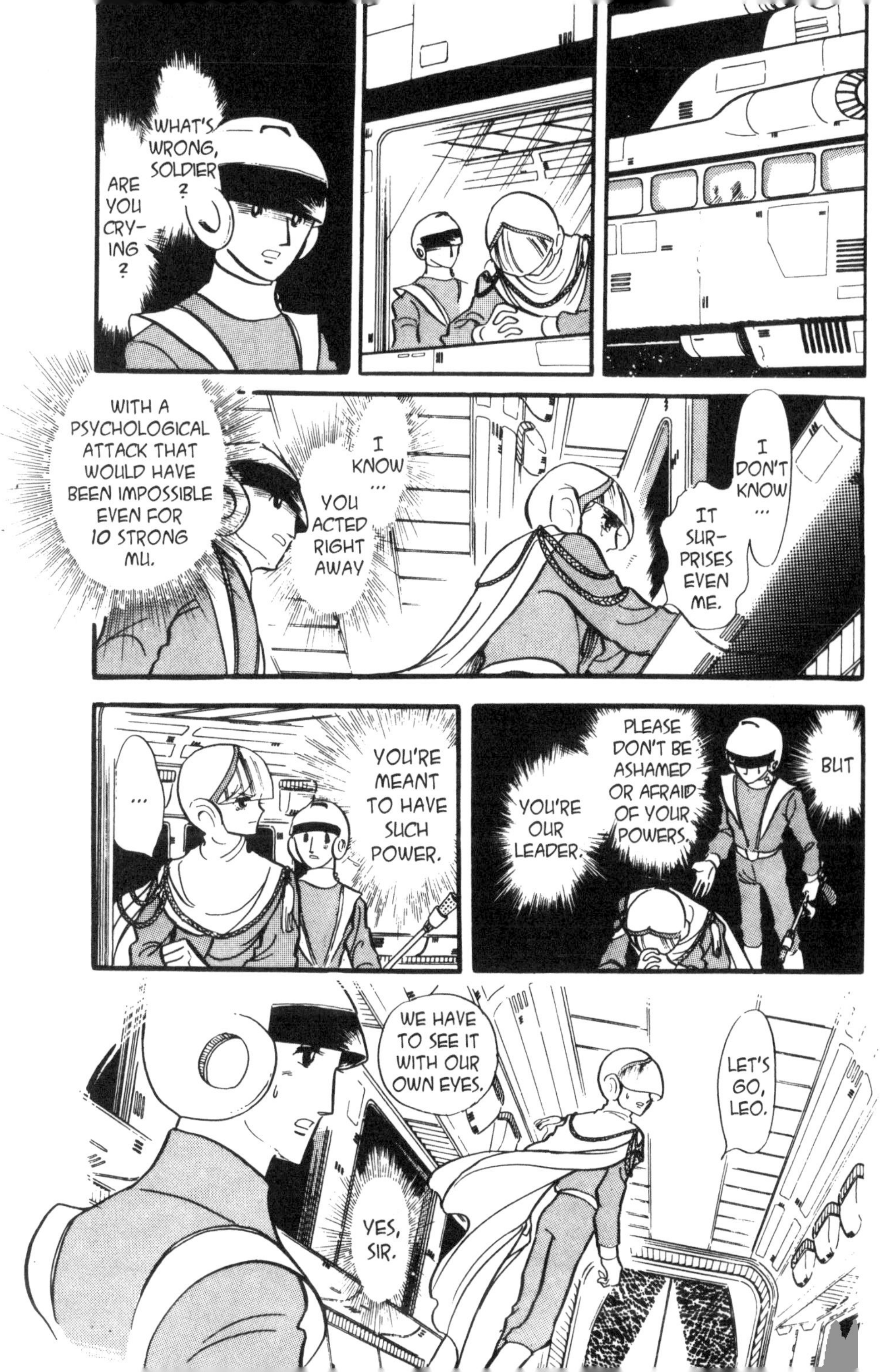
WHAT'S WRONG, SOLDIER?
ARE YOU CRY-ING?
I DON'T KNOW...
IT SUR-PRISES EVEN ME.
I KNOW...
YOU ACTED RIGHT AWAY
WITH A PSYCHOLOGICAL ATTACK THAT WOULD HAVE BEEN IMPOSSIBLE EVEN FOR 10 STRONG MU.
BUT
PLEASE DON'T BE ASHAMED OR AFRAID OF YOUR POWERS.
YOU'RE OUR LEADER.
YOU'RE MEANT TO HAVE SUCH POWER.
...
LET'S GO, LEO.
WE HAVE TO SEE IT WITH OUR OWN EYES.
YES, SIR.

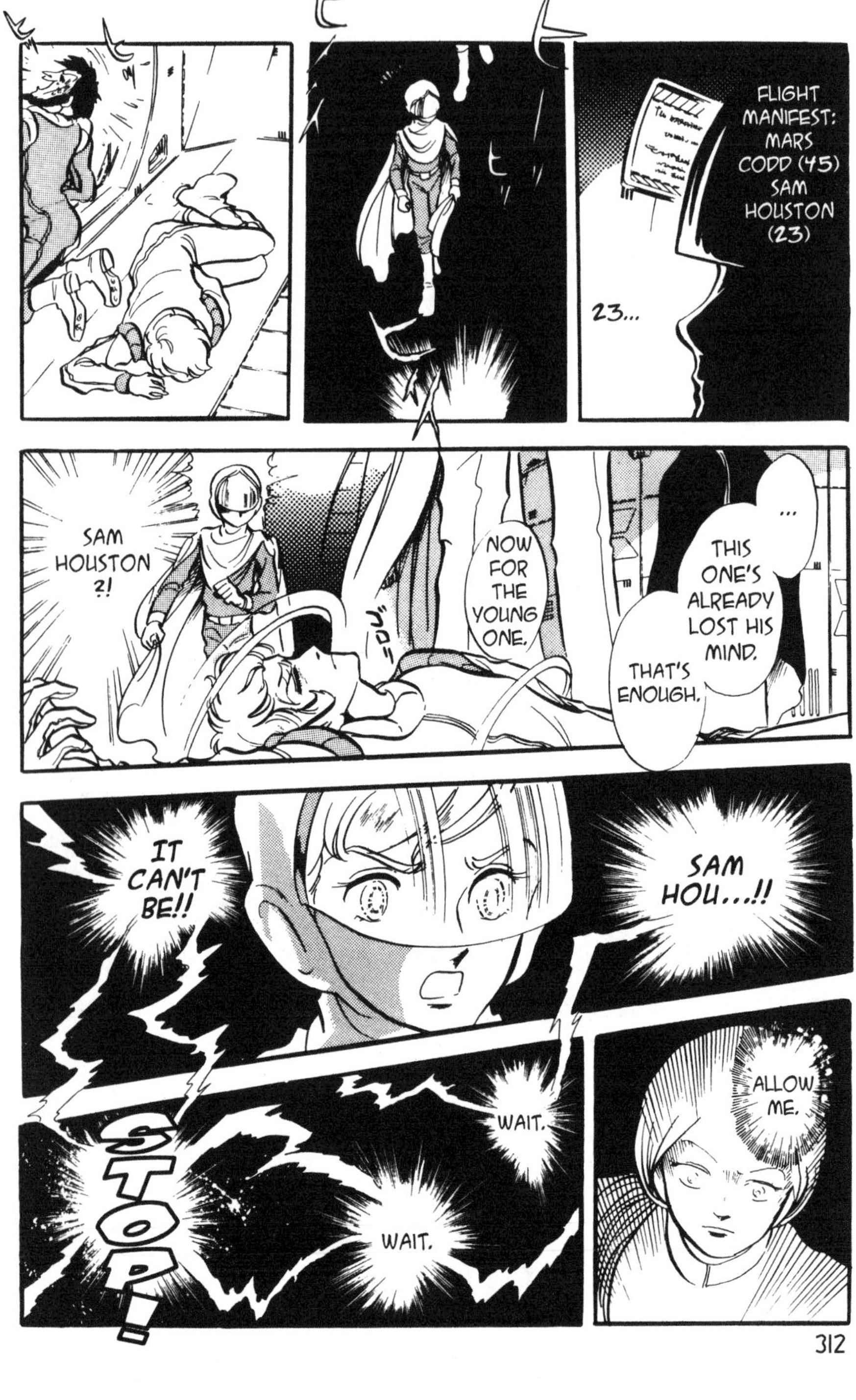
FLIGHT MANIFEST: MARS CODD (45) SAM HOUSTON (23)
23...
...
THIS ONE'S ALREADY LOST HIS MIND.
THAT'S ENOUGH.
NOW FOR THE YOUNG ONE.
SAM HOUSTON ?!
SAM HOU...!!
IT CAN'T BE!!
ALLOW ME.
WAIT.
WAIT.
STOP!

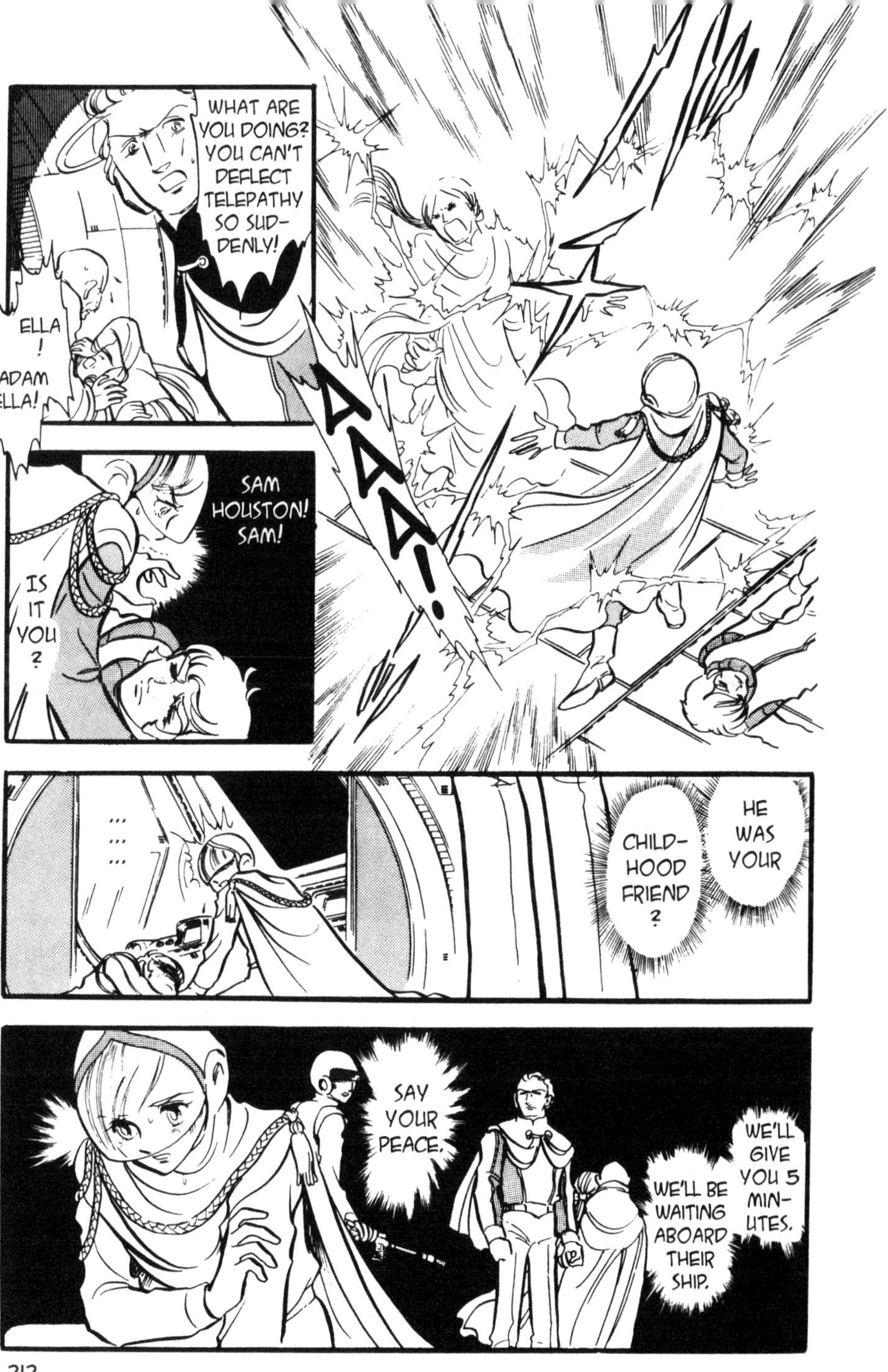
AAA!
WHAT ARE YOU DOING? YOU CAN'T DEFLECT TELEPATHY SO SUD-DENLY!
ELLA! MADAM ELLA!
SAM HOUSTON! SAM!
IS IT YOU?
HE WAS YOUR
CHILD-HOOD FRIEND?
WE'LL GIVE YOU 5 MIN-UTES.
WE'LL BE WAITING ABOARD THEIR SHIP.
SAY YOUR PEACE.

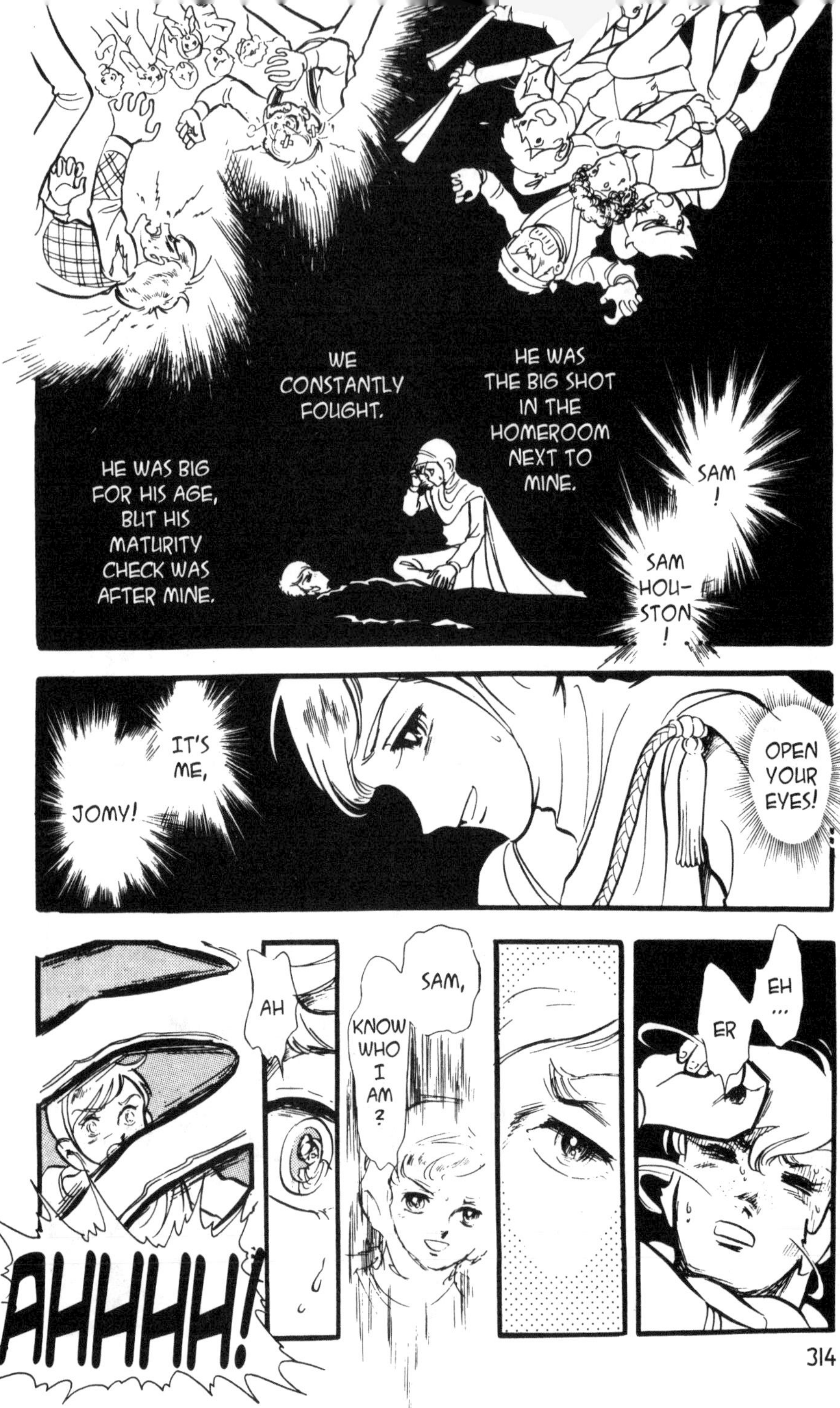
HE WAS THE BIG SHOT IN THE HOMEROOM NEXT TO MINE.
SAM!
SAM HOUSTON!
WE CONSTANTLY FOUGHT.
HE WAS BIG FOR HIS AGE, BUT HIS MATURITY CHECK WAS AFTER MINE.
OPEN YOUR EYES!
IT'S ME,
JOMY!
EH...
ER
SAM,
KNOW WHO I AM?
AH
AHHHH!

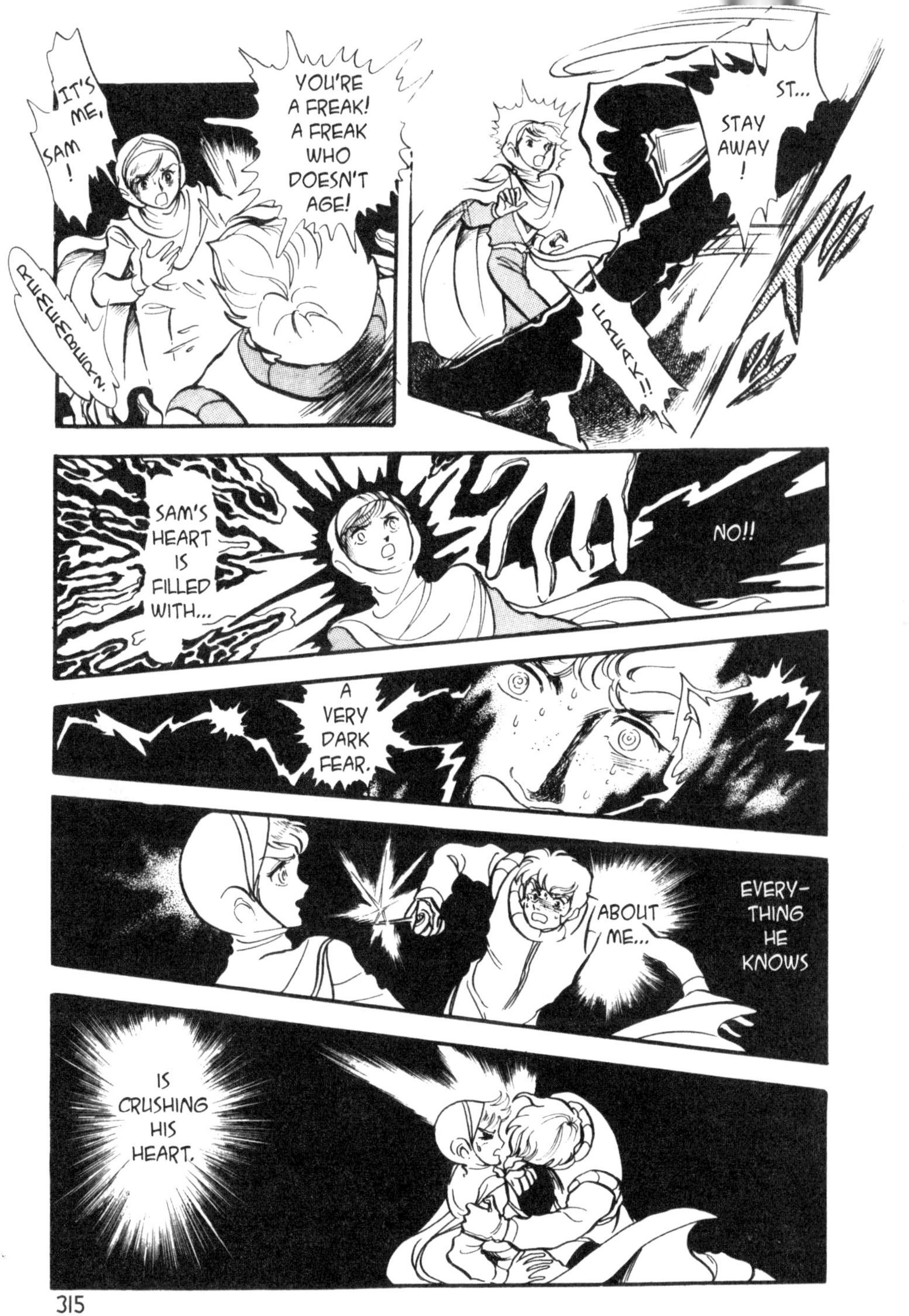
ST...
STAY AWAY!
FRWAK!!
IT'S ME, SAM!
YOU'RE A FREAK! A FREAK WHO DOESN'T AGE!
NO!!
SAM'S HEART IS FILLED WITH...
A VERY DARK FEAR.
EVERY-THING HE KNOWS
ABOUT ME...
IS CRUSHING HIS HEART.

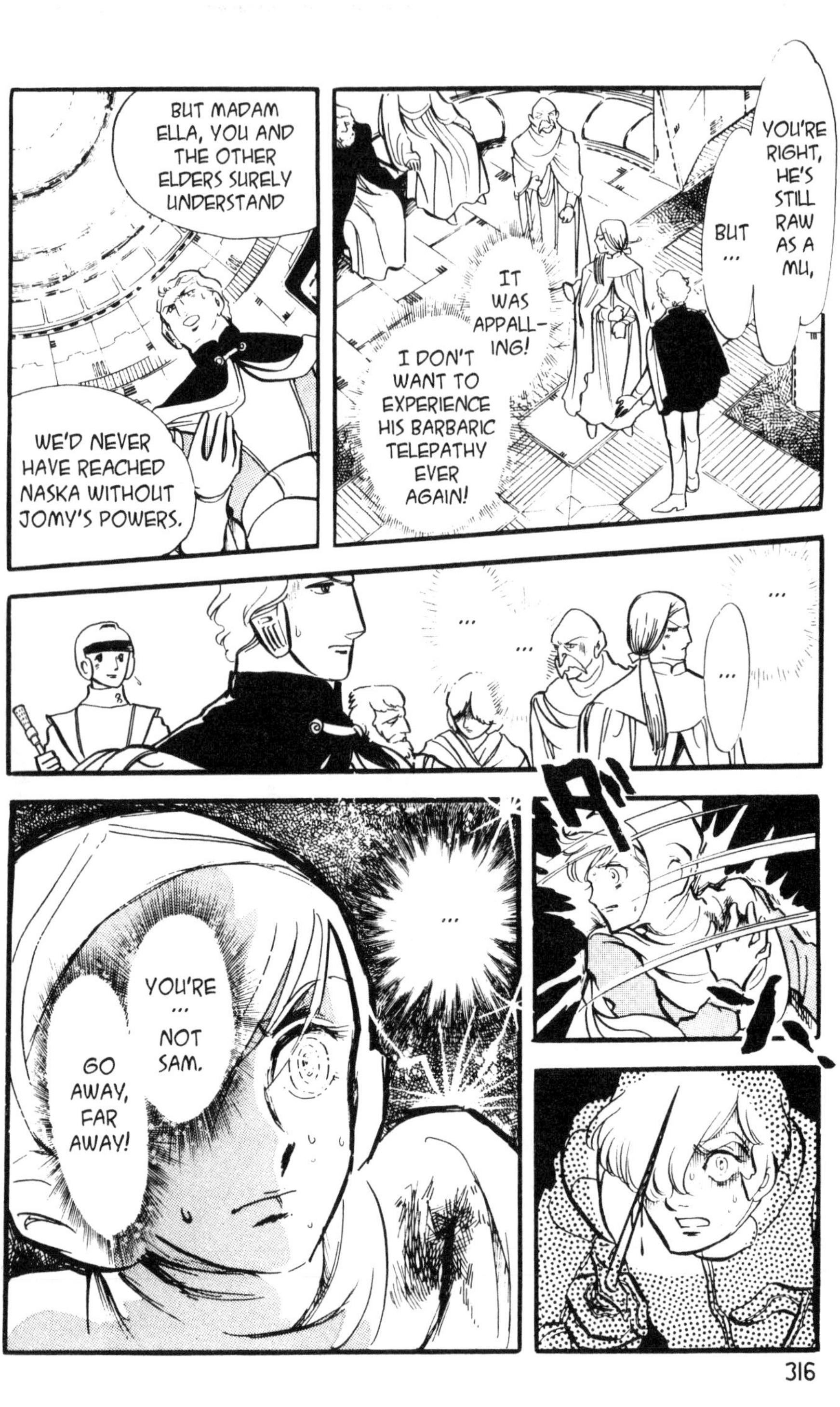
YOU'RE RIGHT, HE'S STILL RAW AS A MU,
BUT ...
IT WAS APPALL-ING!
I DON'T WANT TO EXPERIENCE HIS BARBARIC TELEPATHY EVER AGAIN!
BUT MADAM ELLA, YOU AND THE OTHER ELDERS SURELY UNDERSTAND
WE'D NEVER HAVE REACHED NASKA WITHOUT JOMY'S POWERS.
...
...
...
...
...
...
YOU'RE ... NOT SAM.
GO AWAY, FAR AWAY!

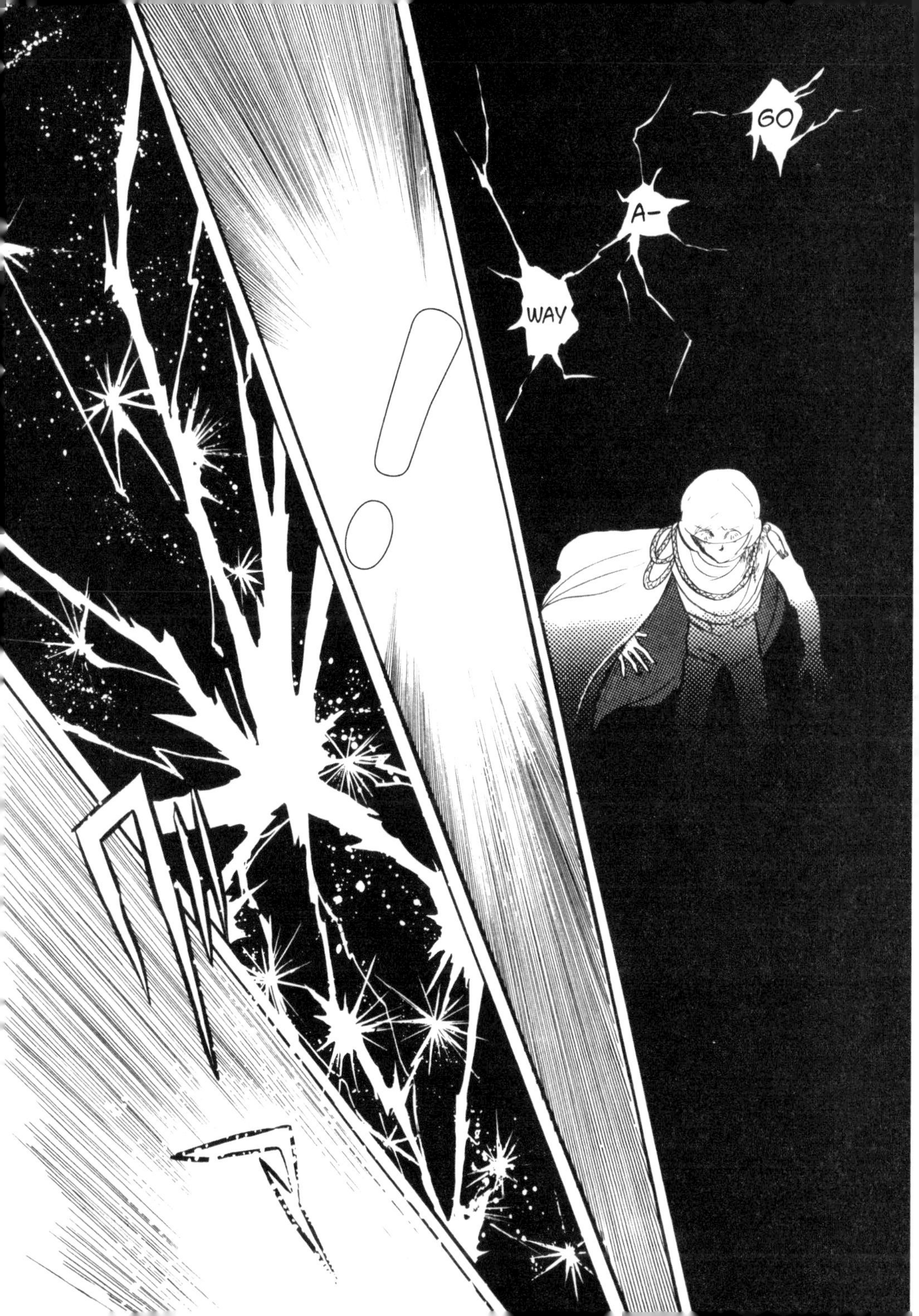
GO
A-
WAY
!

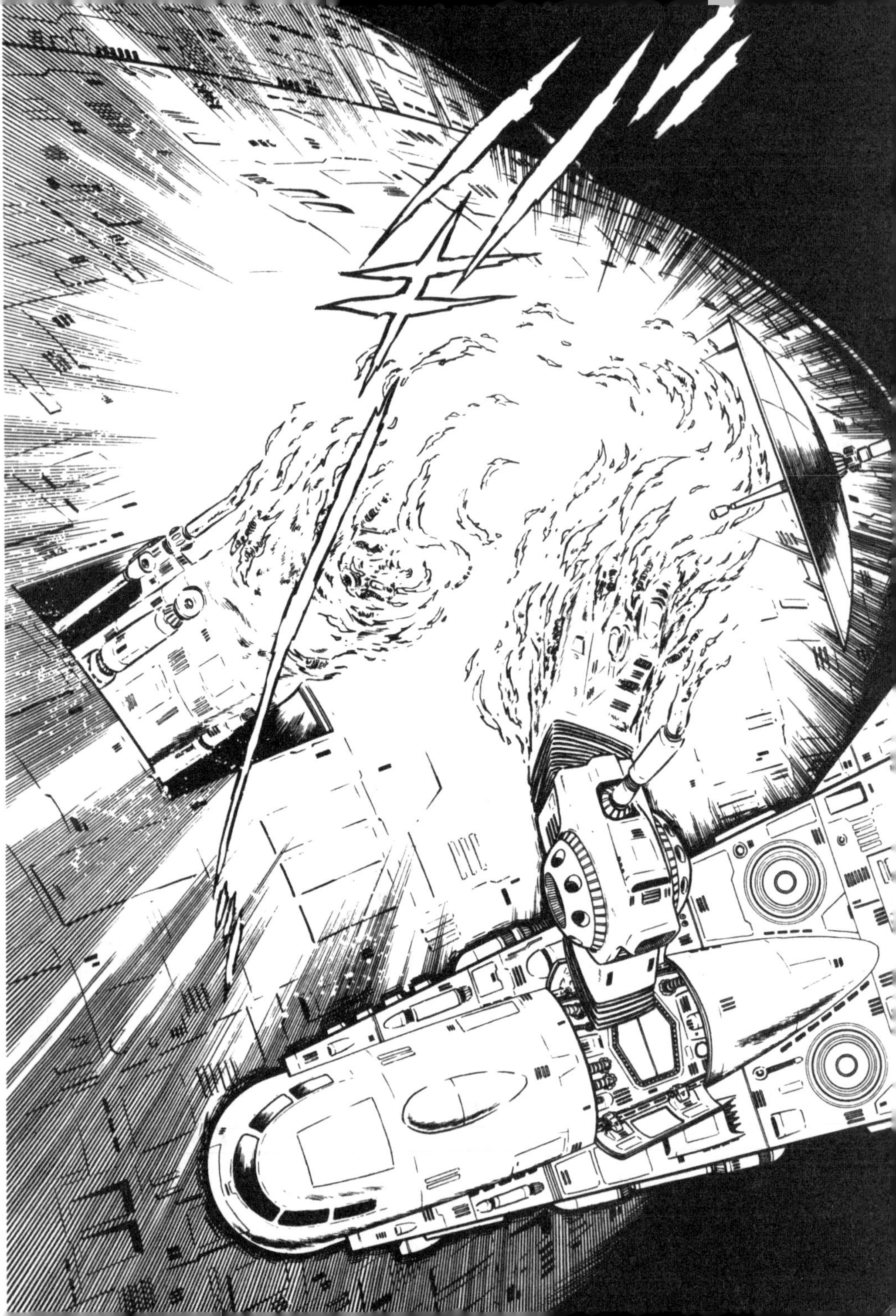

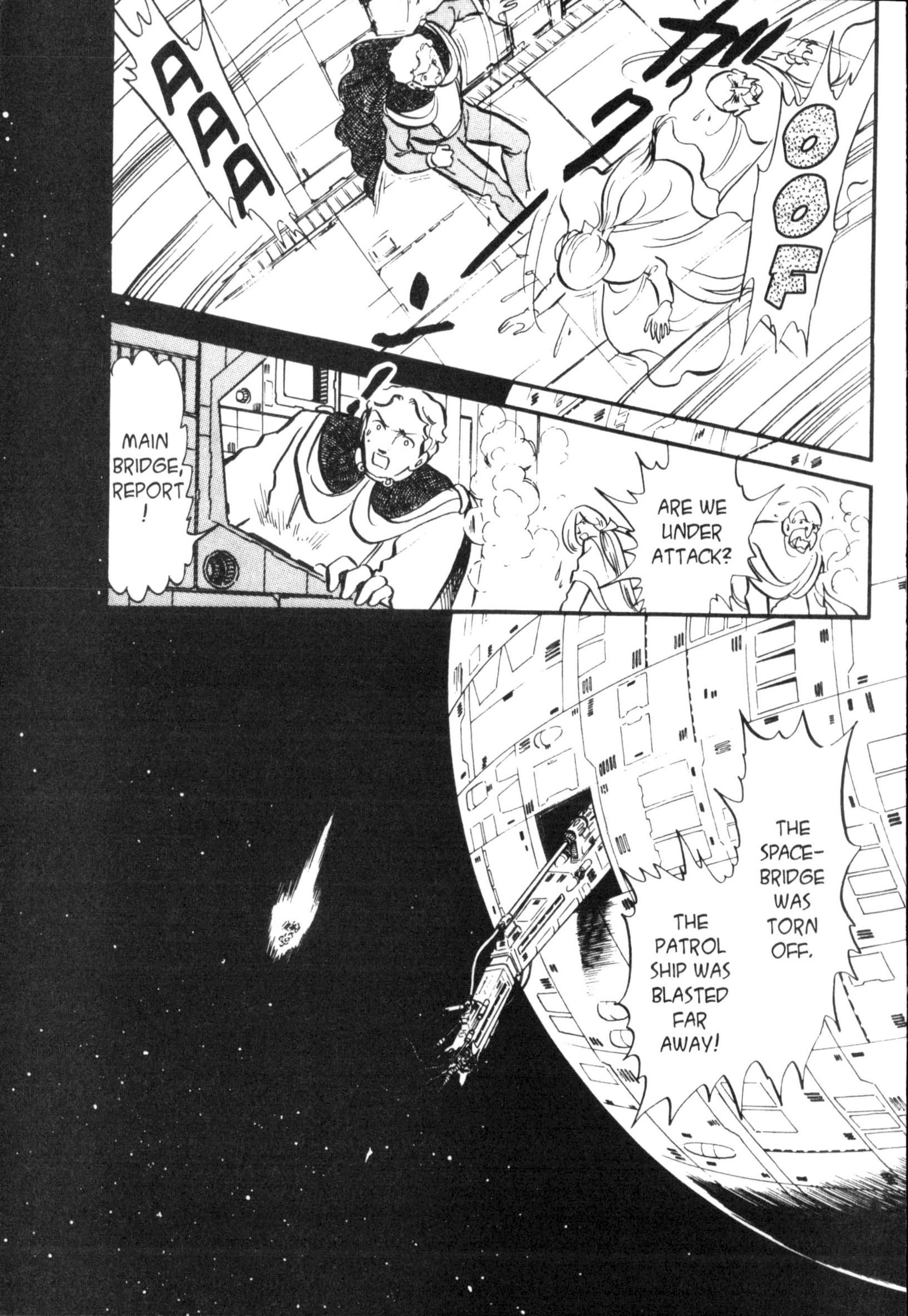
OOOF
AAA
ARE WE UNDER ATTACK?
MAIN BRIDGE, REPORT!
THE SPACE-BRIDGE WAS TORN OFF.
THE PATROL SHIP WAS BLASTED FAR AWAY!

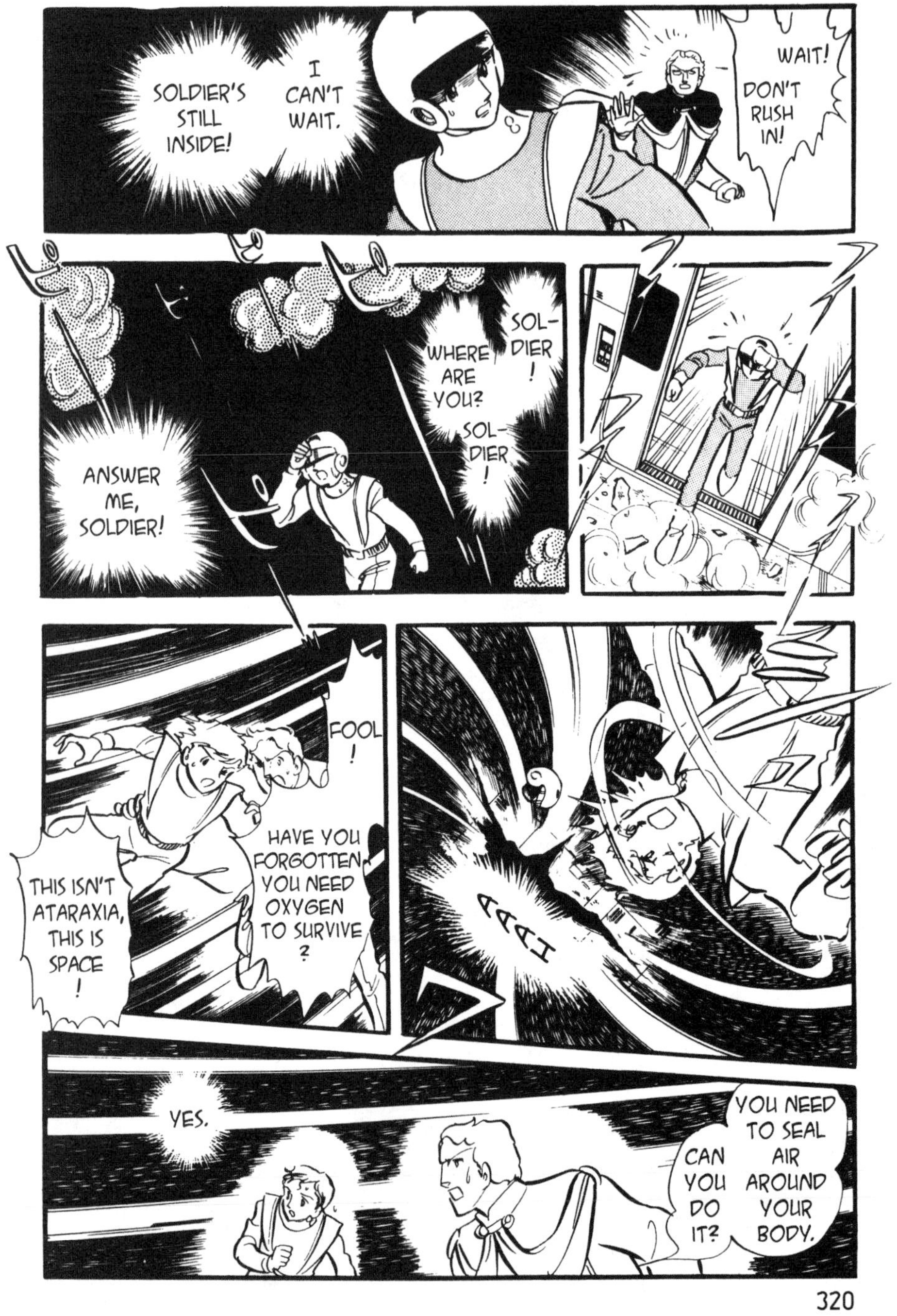
WAIT! DON'T RUSH IN!
I CAN'T WAIT.
SOLDIER'S STILL INSIDE!
SOLDIER!
WHERE ARE YOU?
SOLDIER!
ANSWER ME, SOLDIER!
FOOL!
HAVE YOU FORGOTTEN YOU NEED OXYGEN TO SURVIVE?
THIS ISN'T ATARAXIA, THIS IS SPACE!
YOU NEED TO SEAL AIR AROUND YOUR BODY.
CAN YOU DO IT?
YES.

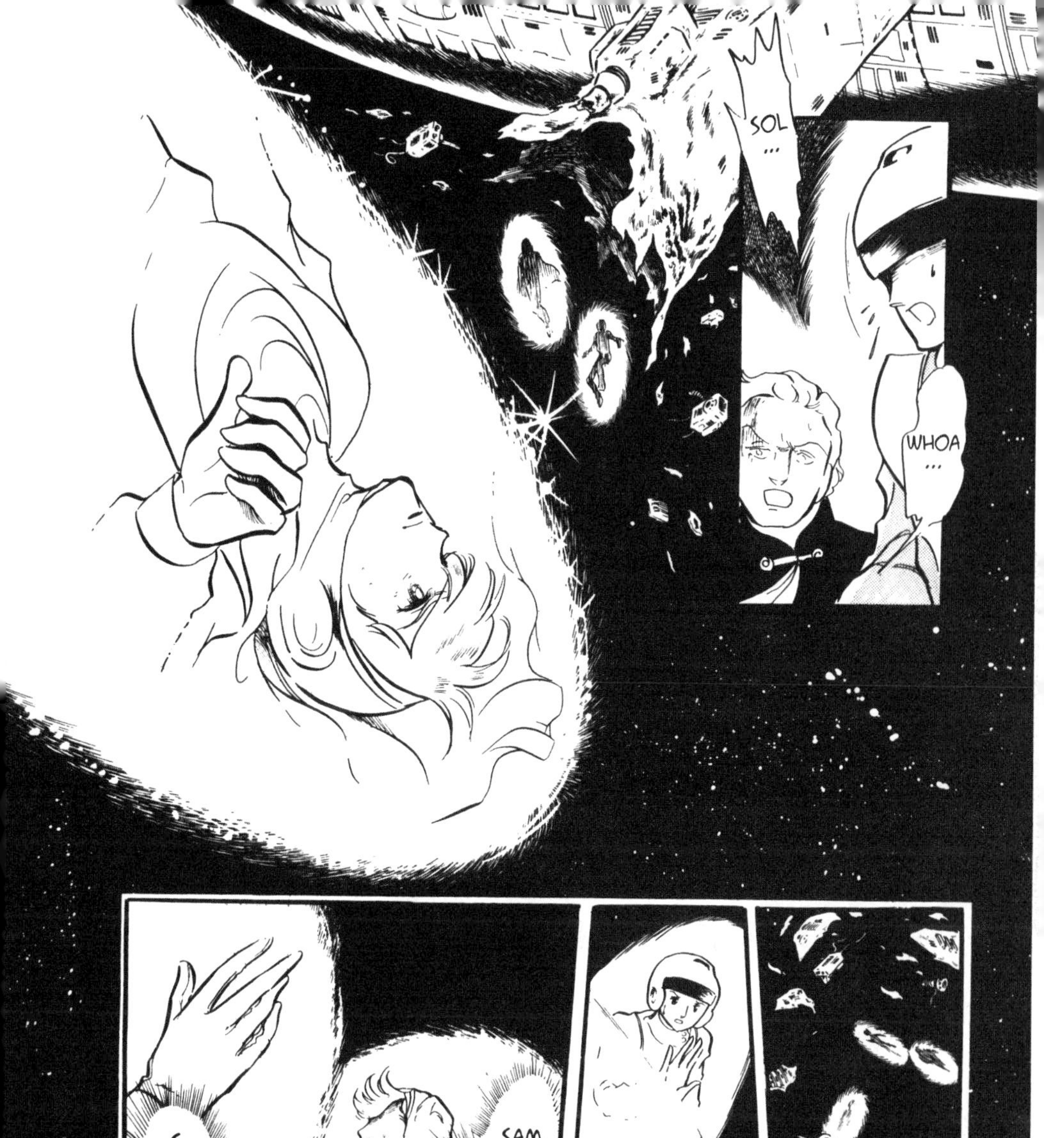
SOL ...
WHOA ...
SAM, I DIDN'T WANT TO SEE YOU
LIKE THIS.
SOLDIER!!

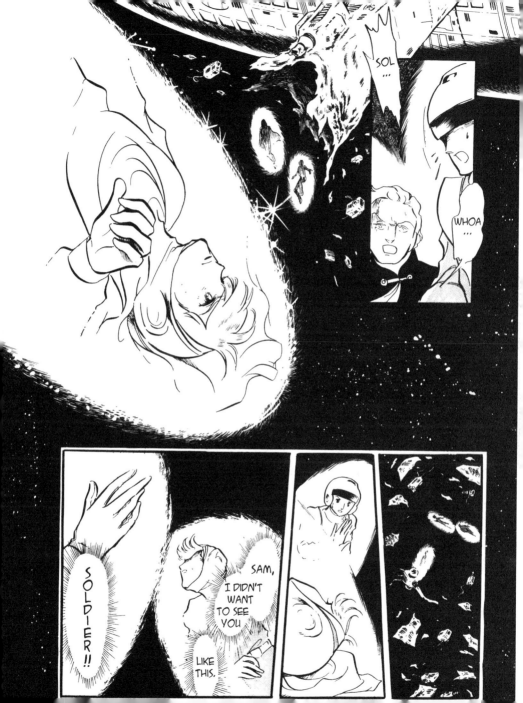

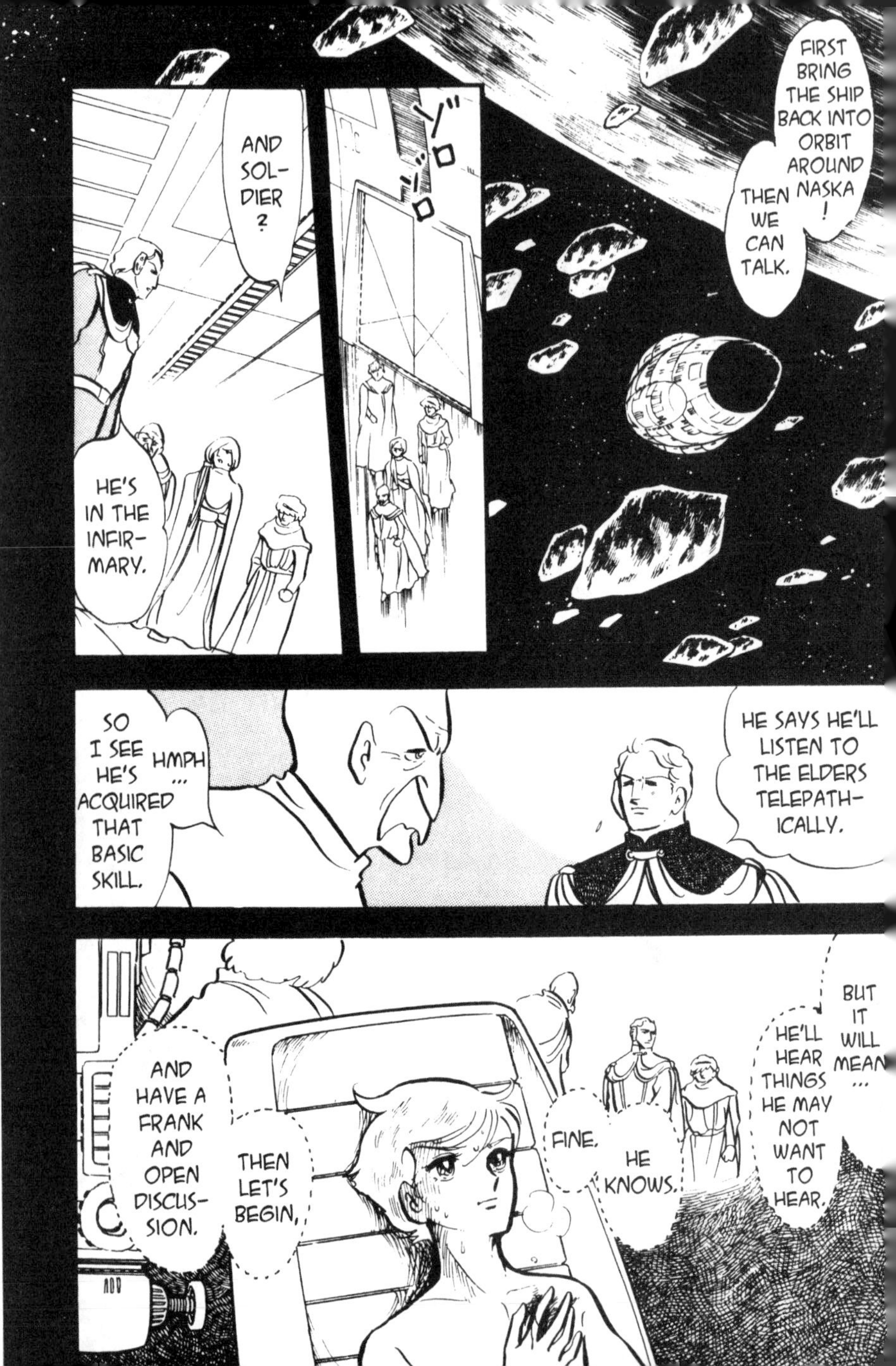
FIRST BRING THE SHIP BACK INTO ORBIT AROUND NASKA!
THEN WE CAN TALK.
ゾロゾロ
AND SOLDIER?
HE'S IN THE INFIRMARY.
HE SAYS HE'LL LISTEN TO THE ELDERS TELEPATHICALLY.
HMPH...
SO I SEE HE'S ACQUIRED THAT BASIC SKILL.
BUT IT WILL MEAN...
HE'LL HEAR THINGS HE MAY NOT WANT TO HEAR.
HE KNOWS.
FINE.
THEN LET'S BEGIN,
AND HAVE A FRANK AND OPEN DISCUSSION.

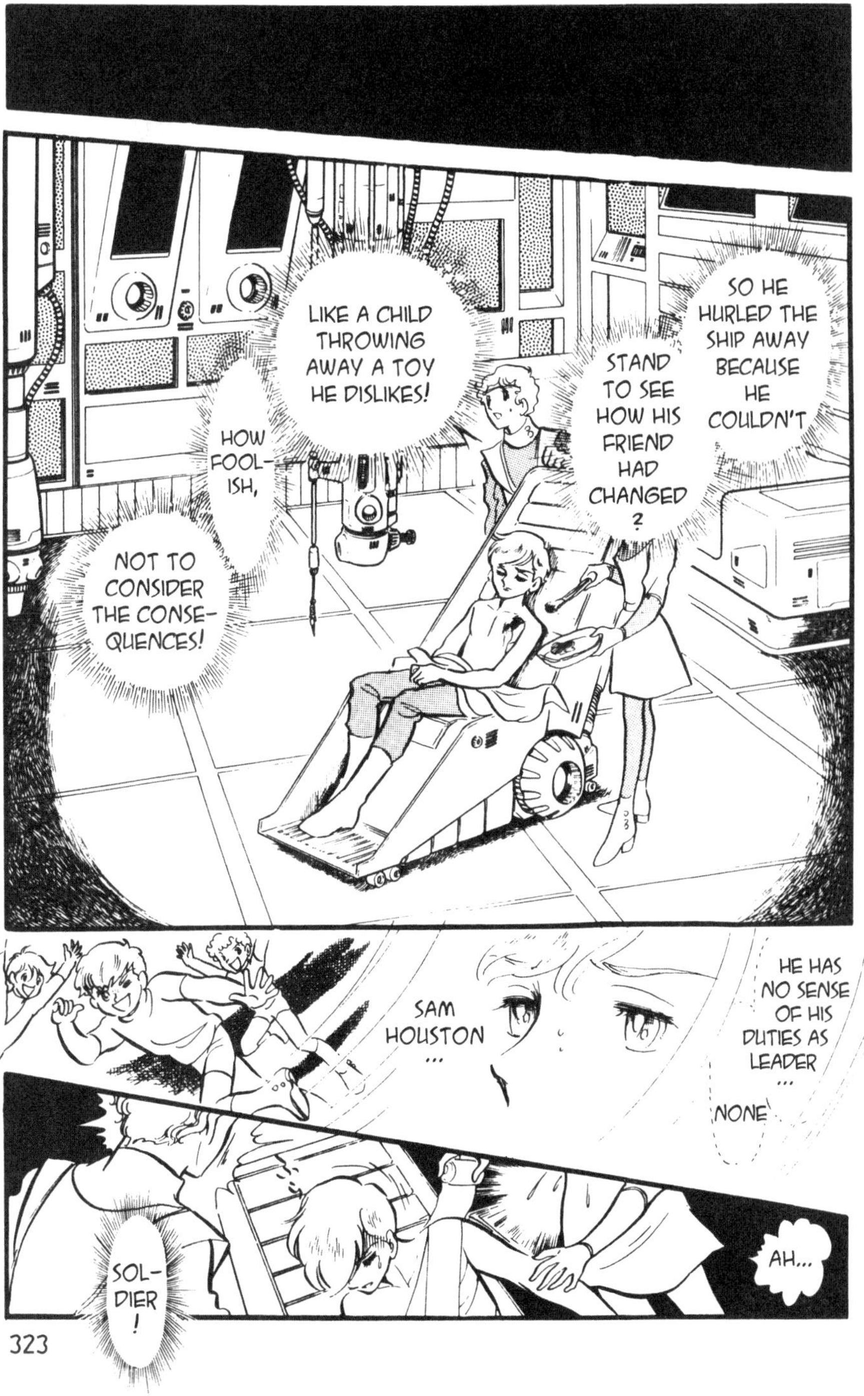
SO HE HURLED THE SHIP AWAY BECAUSE HE COULDN'T
STAND TO SEE HOW HIS FRIEND HAD CHANGED?
LIKE A CHILD THROWING AWAY A TOY HE DISLIKES!
HOW FOOL-ISH,
NOT TO CONSIDER THE CONSE-QUENCES!
HE HAS NO SENSE OF HIS DUTIES AS LEADER...
NONE
SAM HOUSTON...
AH...
SOL-DIER!

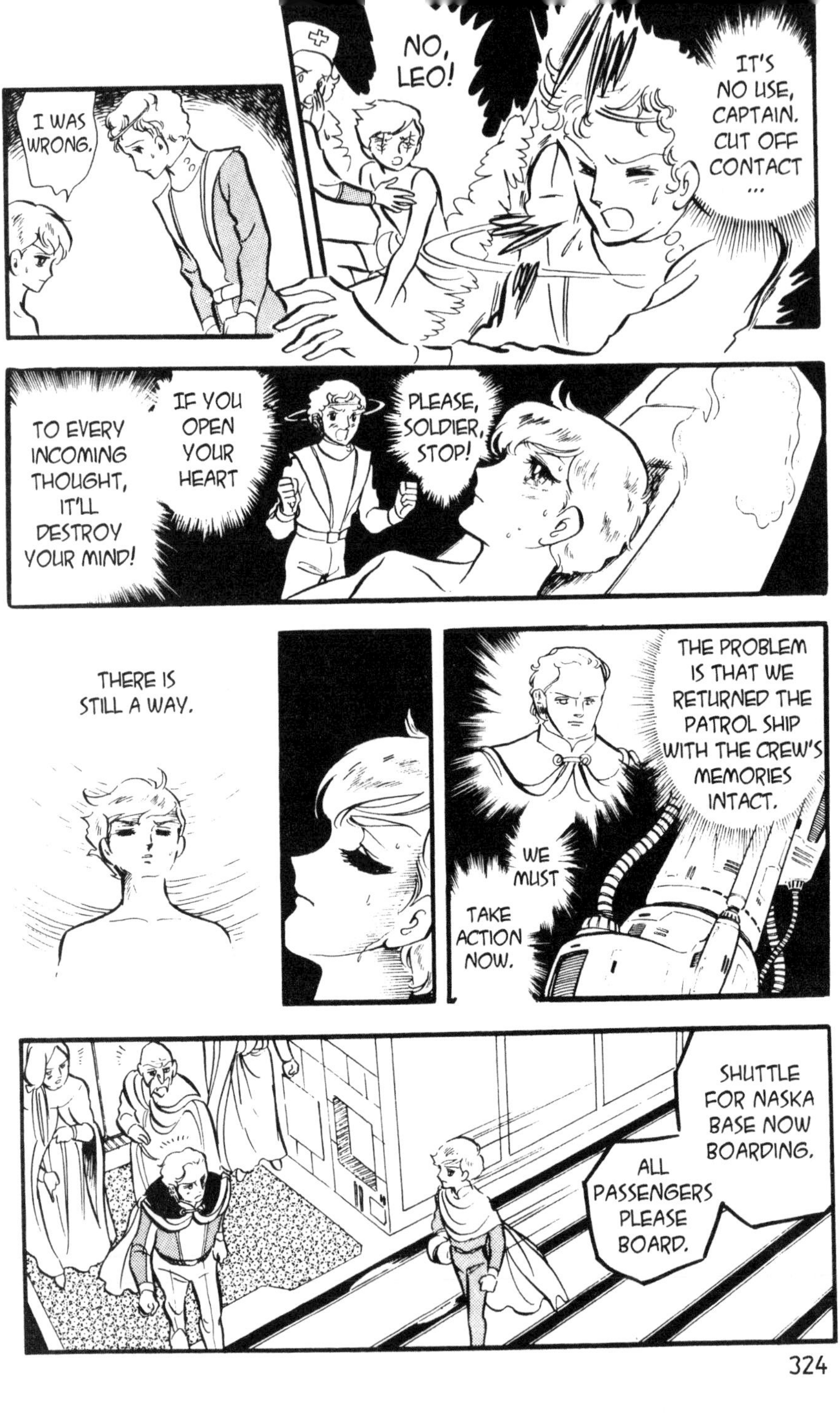
IT'S NO USE, CAPTAIN. CUT OFF CONTACT ...
NO, LEO!
I WAS WRONG.
PLEASE, SOLDIER, STOP!
IF YOU OPEN YOUR HEART
TO EVERY INCOMING THOUGHT, IT'LL DESTROY YOUR MIND!
THE PROBLEM IS THAT WE RETURNED THE PATROL SHIP WITH THE CREW'S MEMORIES INTACT.
WE MUST
TAKE ACTION NOW.
THERE IS STILL A WAY.
SHUTTLE FOR NASKA BASE NOW BOARDING.
ALL PASSENGERS PLEASE BOARD.

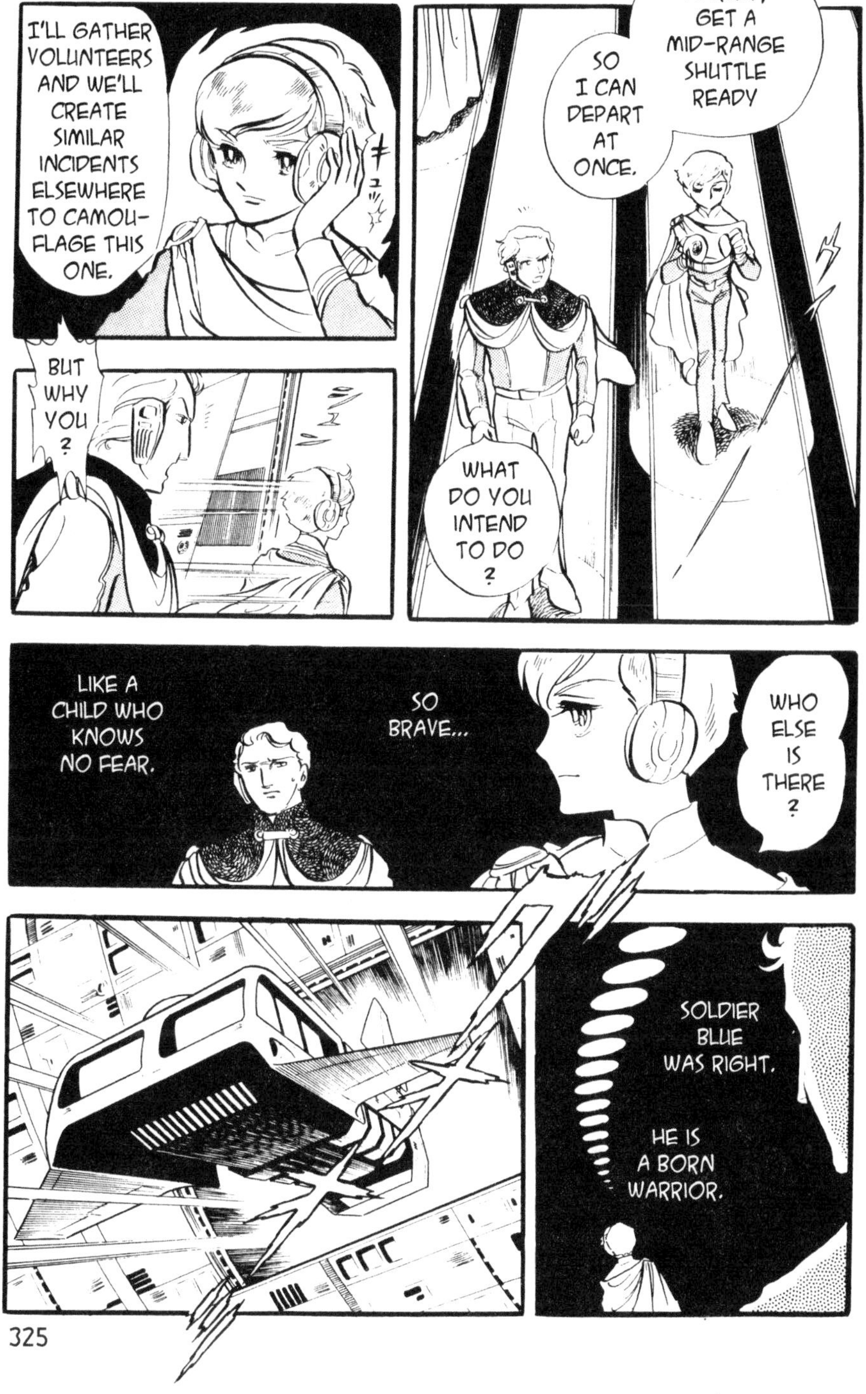
HARLEY, GET A MID-RANGE SHUTTLE READY
SO I CAN DEPART AT ONCE.
WHAT DO YOU INTEND TO DO?
I'LL GATHER VOLUNTEERS AND WE'LL CREATE SIMILAR INCIDENTS ELSEWHERE TO CAMOUFLAGE THIS ONE.
BUT WHY YOU?
WHO ELSE IS THERE?
SO BRAVE...
LIKE A CHILD WHO KNOWS NO FEAR.
SOLDIER BLUE WAS RIGHT.
HE IS A BORN WARRIOR.

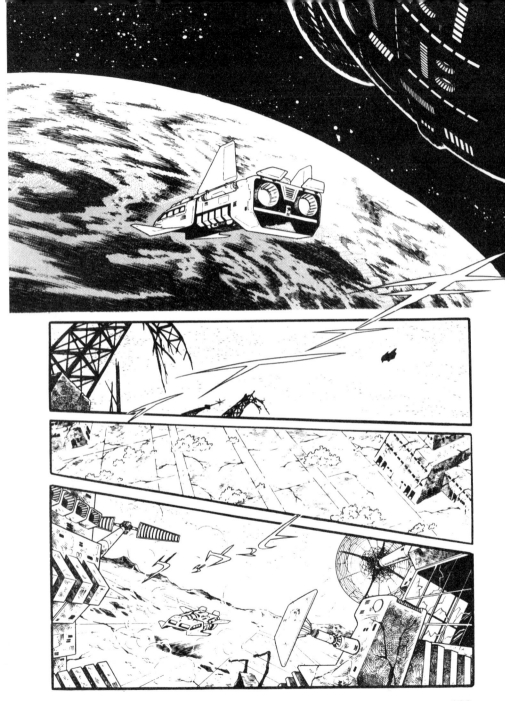

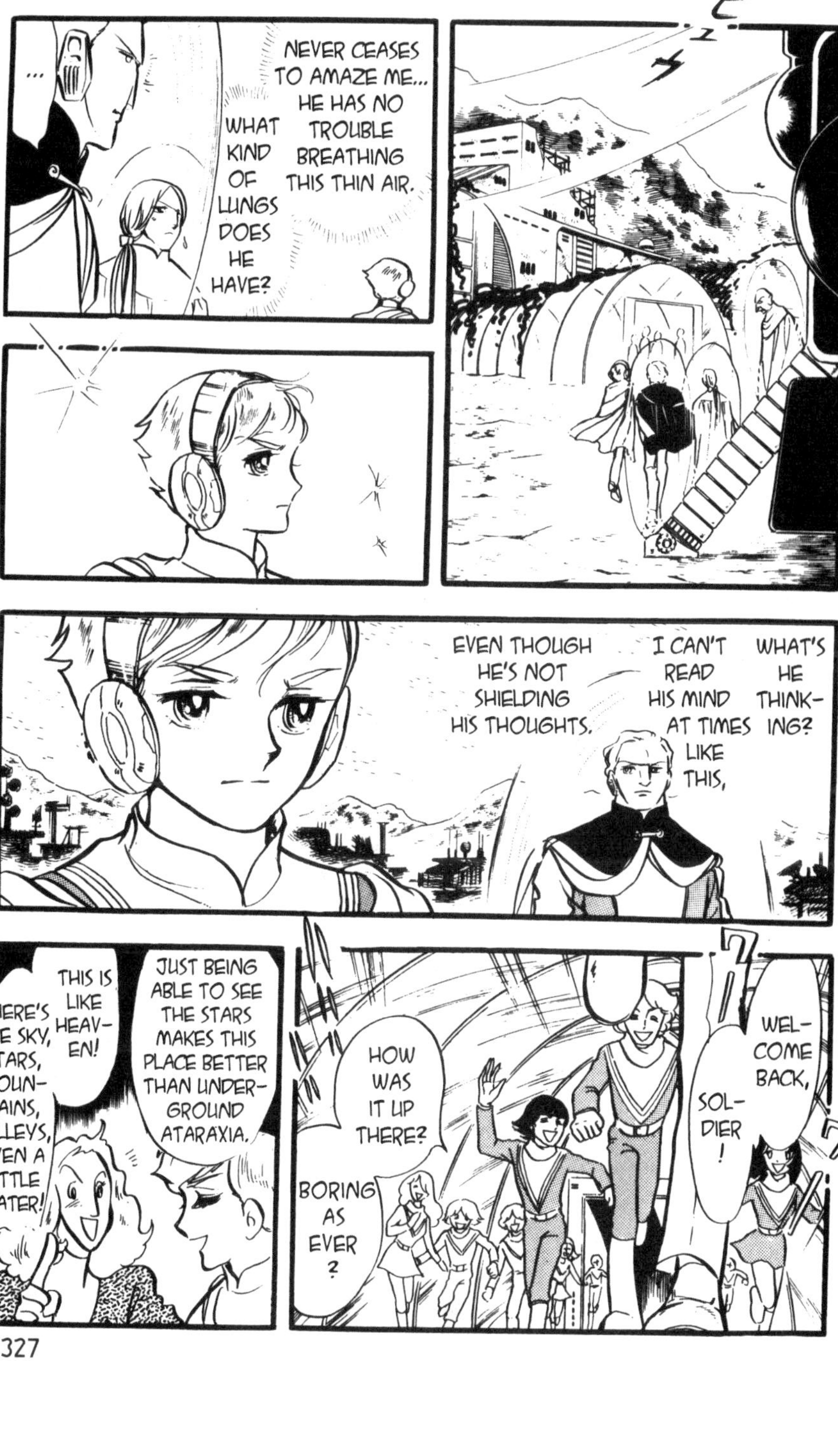
NEVER CEASES TO AMAZE ME... HE HAS NO TROUBLE BREATHING THIS THIN AIR.
WHAT KIND OF LUNGS DOES HE HAVE?
...
WHAT'S HE THINKING?
I CAN'T READ HIS MIND AT TIMES LIKE THIS,
EVEN THOUGH HE'S NOT SHIELDING HIS THOUGHTS.
WELCOME BACK, SOLDIER!
HOW WAS IT UP THERE?
BORING AS EVER?
JUST BEING ABLE TO SEE THE STARS MAKES THIS PLACE BETTER THAN UNDERGROUND ATARAXIA.
THIS IS LIKE HEAVEN!
THERE'S THE SKY, STARS, MOUNTAINS, VALLEYS, EVEN A LITTLE WATER!

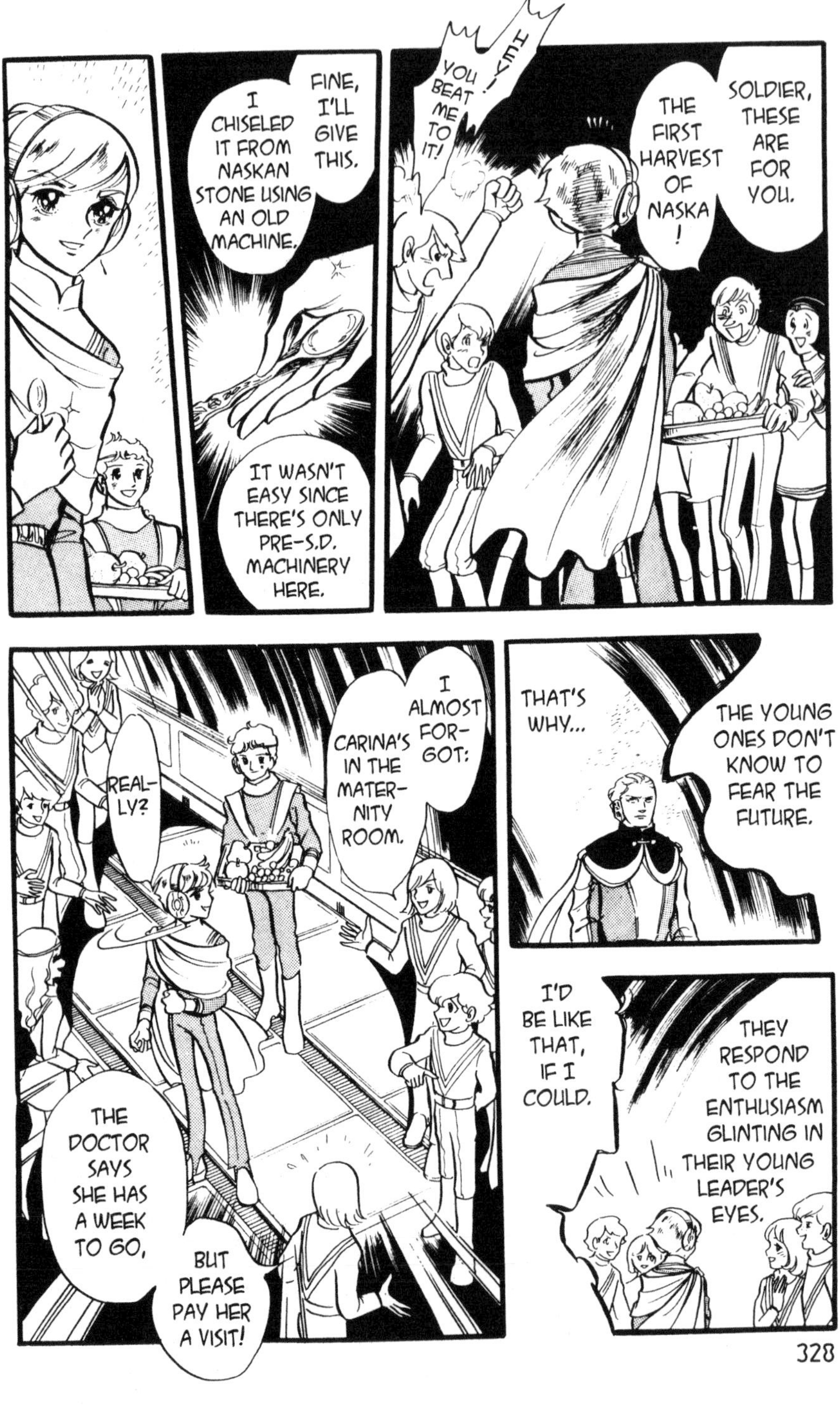
SOLDIER, THESE ARE FOR YOU.
THE FIRST HARVEST OF NASKA!
HEY!
YOU BEAT ME TO IT!
FINE, I'LL GIVE THIS.
I CHISELED IT FROM NASKAN STONE USING AN OLD MACHINE.
IT WASN'T EASY SINCE THERE'S ONLY PRE-S.D. MACHINERY HERE.
THE YOUNG ONES DON'T KNOW TO FEAR THE FUTURE.
THAT'S WHY...
THEY RESPOND TO THE ENTHUSIASM GLINTING IN THEIR YOUNG LEADER'S EYES.
I'D BE LIKE THAT, IF I COULD.
I ALMOST FOR-GOT:
CARINA'S IN THE MATER-NITY ROOM.
REAL-LY?
THE DOCTOR SAYS SHE HAS A WEEK TO GO,
BUT PLEASE PAY HER A VISIT!

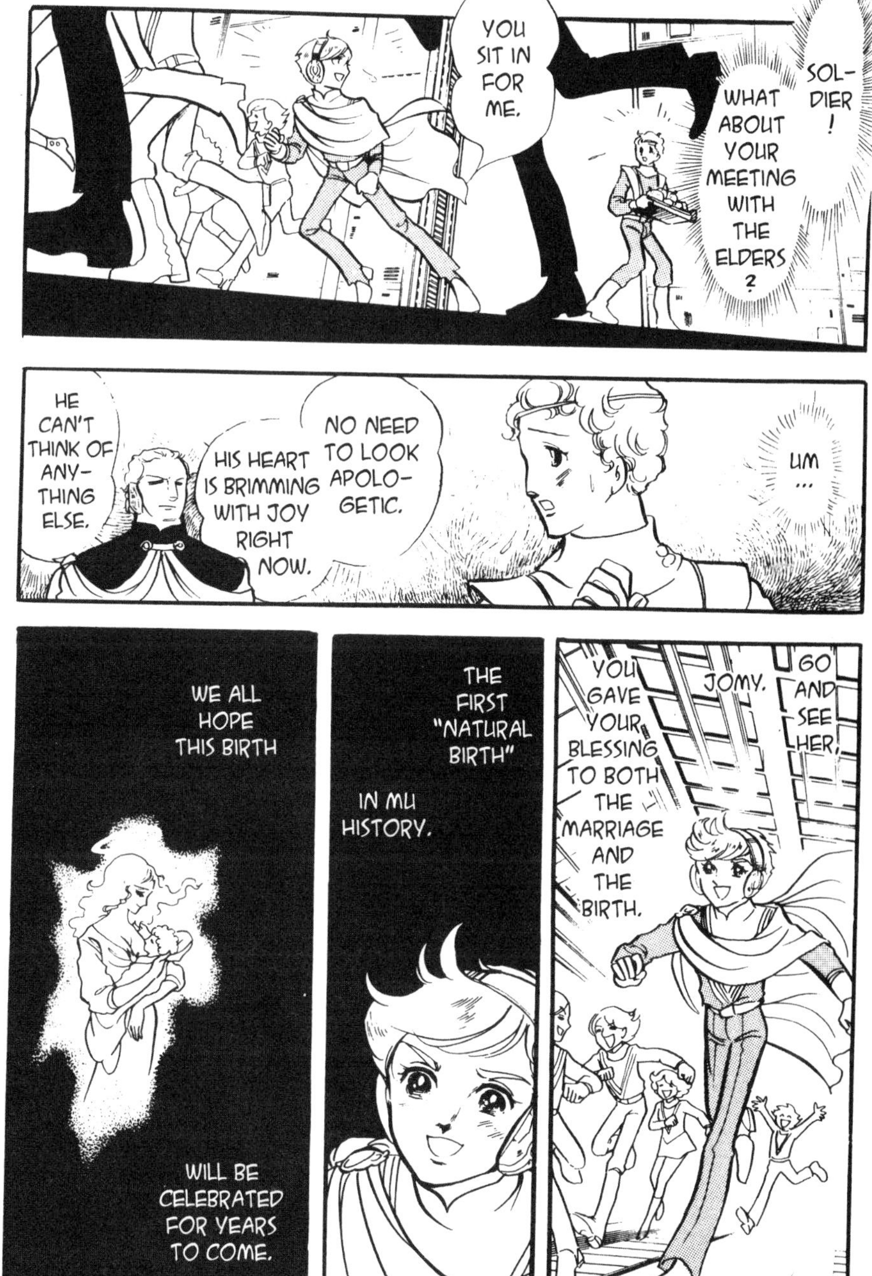
SOL-DIER!
WHAT ABOUT YOUR MEETING WITH THE ELDERS?
YOU SIT IN FOR ME.
UM ...
NO NEED TO LOOK APOLO-GETIC.
HIS HEART IS BRIMMING WITH JOY RIGHT NOW.
HE CAN'T THINK OF ANY-THING ELSE.
GO AND SEE HER,
JOMY.
YOU GAVE YOUR BLESSING TO BOTH THE MARRIAGE AND THE BIRTH.
THE FIRST "NATURAL BIRTH"
IN MU HISTORY.
WE ALL HOPE THIS BIRTH
WILL BE CELEBRATED FOR YEARS TO COME.

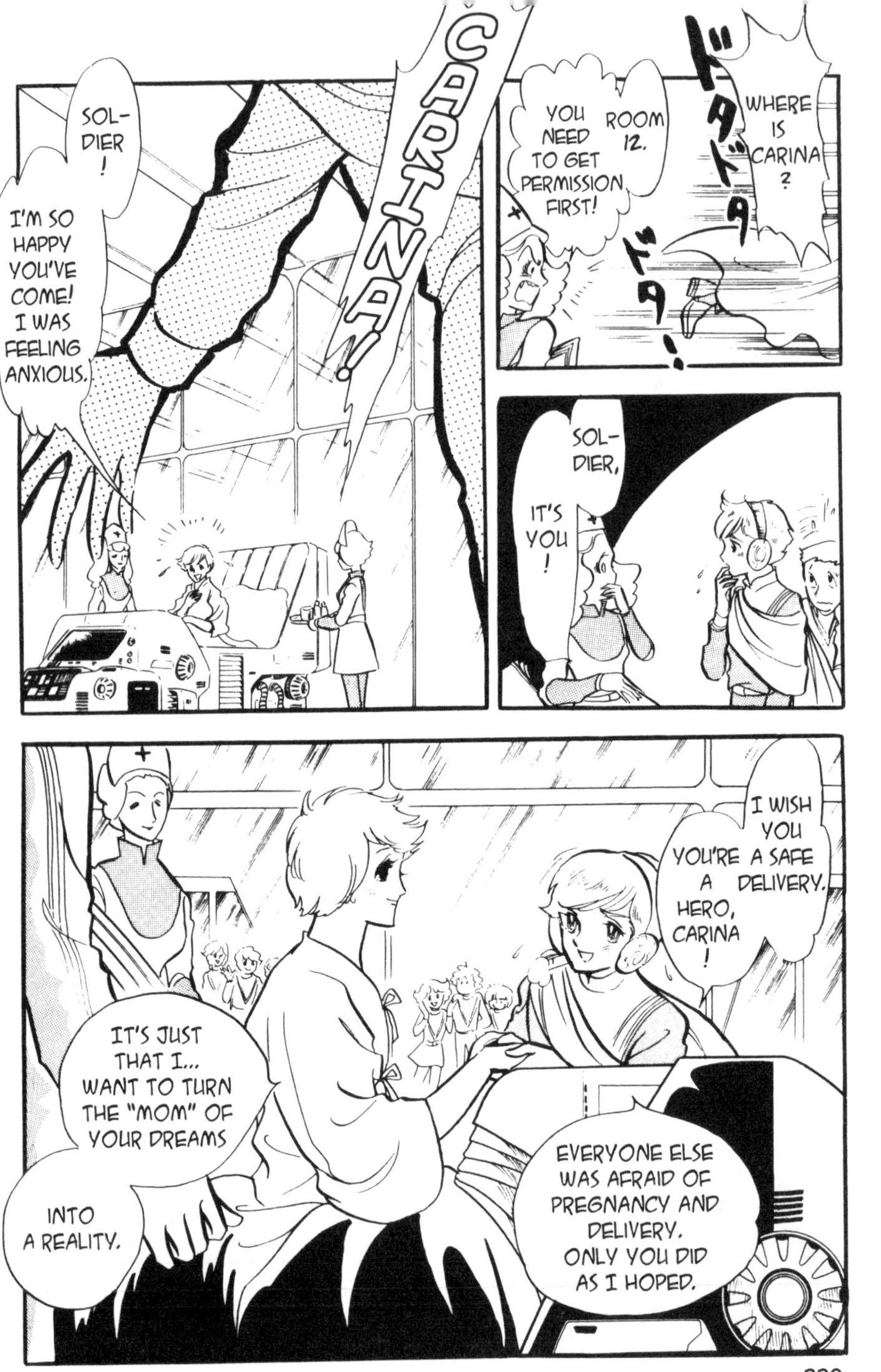
ドタドタ
ドタ!!
WHERE IS CARINA?
ROOM 12.
YOU NEED TO GET PERMISSION FIRST!
SOL-DIER,
IT'S YOU!
CARINA!
SOL-DIER!
I'M SO HAPPY YOU'VE COME! I WAS FEELING ANXIOUS.
I WISH YOU A SAFE DELIVERY.
YOU'RE A HERO, CARINA!
EVERYONE ELSE WAS AFRAID OF PREGNANCY AND DELIVERY. ONLY YOU DID AS I HOPED.
IT'S JUST THAT I... WANT TO TURN THE "MOM" OF YOUR DREAMS
INTO A REALITY.

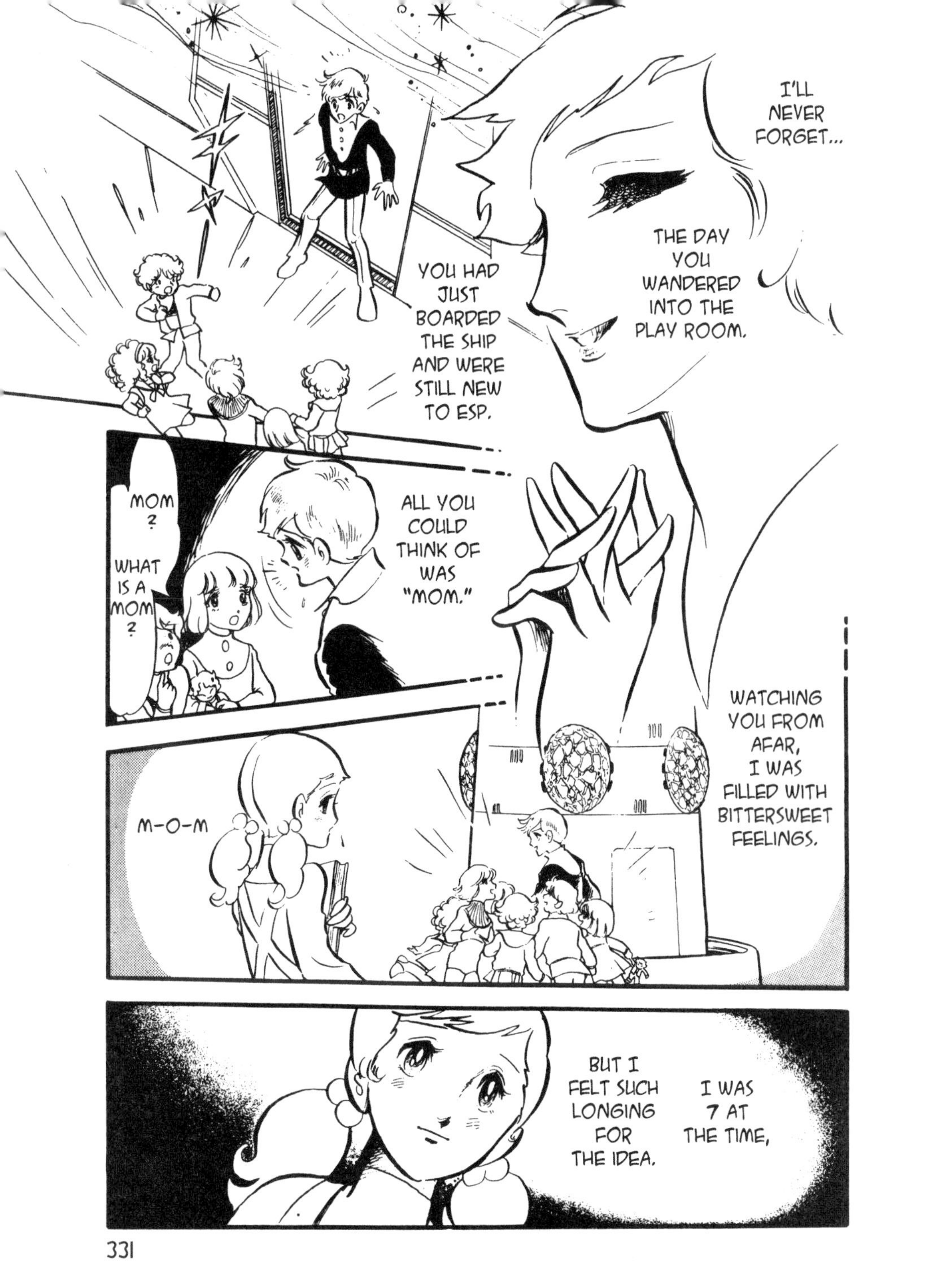
I'LL NEVER FORGET...
THE DAY YOU WANDERED INTO THE PLAY ROOM.
YOU HAD JUST BOARDED THE SHIP AND WERE STILL NEW TO ESP.
ALL YOU COULD THINK OF WAS "MOM."
MOM?
WHAT IS A MOM?
WATCHING YOU FROM AFAR, I WAS FILLED WITH BITTERSWEET FEELINGS.
M-O-M
I WAS 7 AT THE TIME,
BUT I FELT SUCH LONGING FOR THE IDEA.

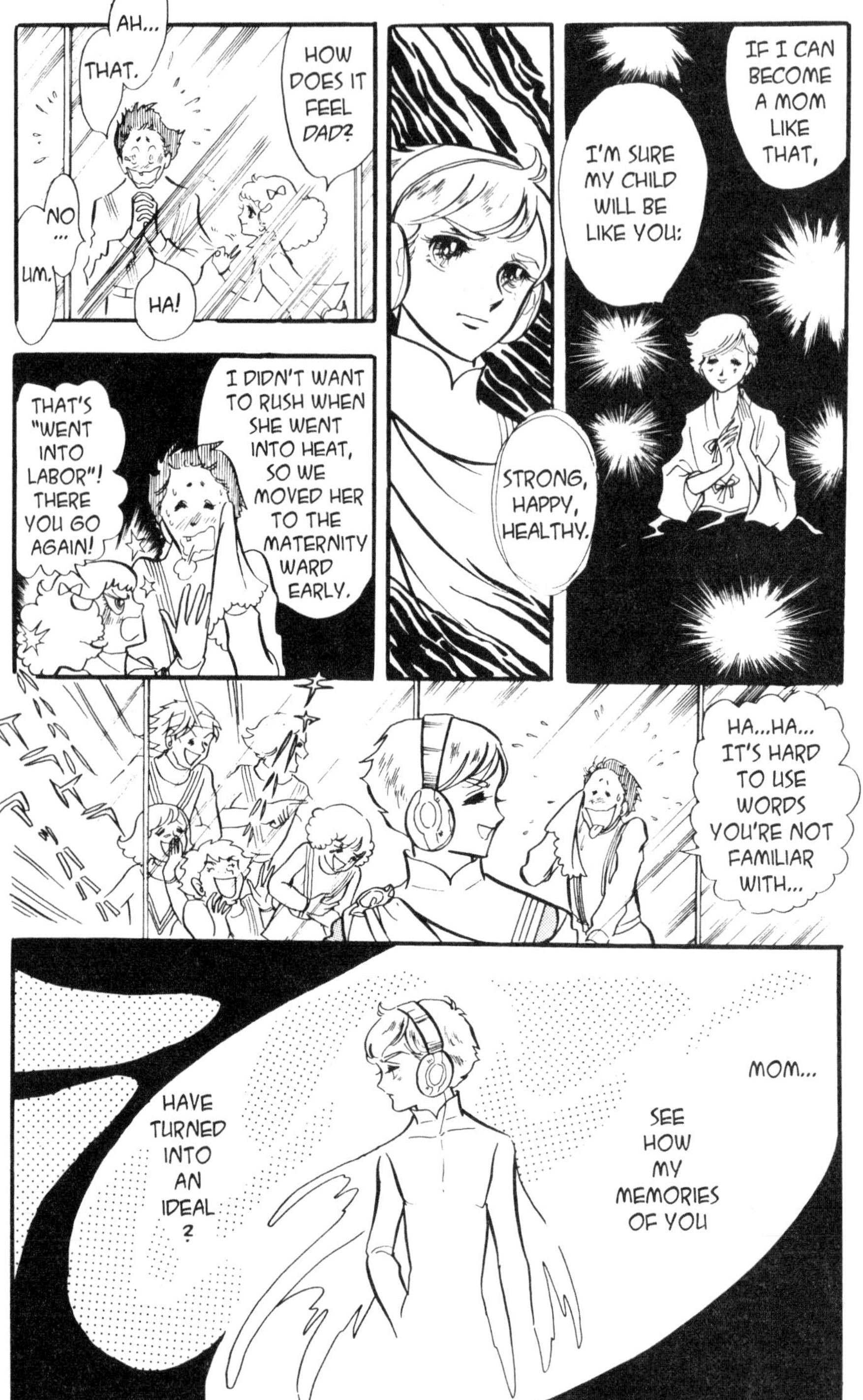
IF I CAN BECOME A MOM LIKE THAT,
I'M SURE MY CHILD WILL BE LIKE YOU:
STRONG, HAPPY, HEALTHY.
HOW DOES IT FEEL DAD?
AH... THAT.
NO ... UM.
HA!
I DIDN'T WANT TO RUSH WHEN SHE WENT INTO HEAT, SO WE MOVED HER TO THE MATERNITY WARD EARLY.
THAT'S "WENT INTO LABOR"! THERE YOU GO AGAIN!
HA...HA... IT'S HARD TO USE WORDS YOU'RE NOT FAMILIAR WITH...
MOM...
SEE HOW MY MEMORIES OF YOU
HAVE TURNED INTO AN IDEAL?

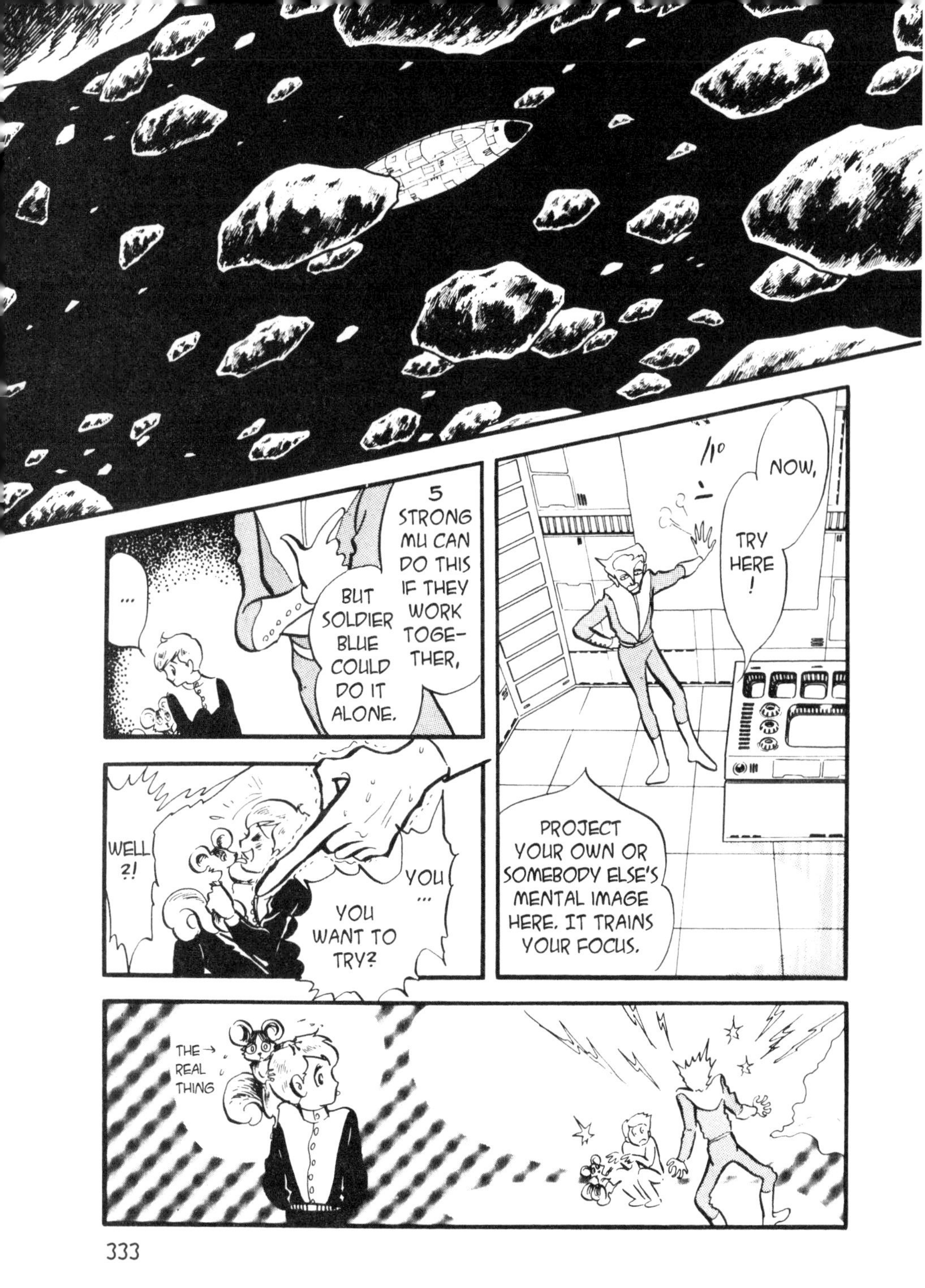
NOW,
TRY HERE!
PROJECT YOUR OWN OR SOMEBODY ELSE'S MENTAL IMAGE HERE. IT TRAINS YOUR FOCUS.
5 STRONG MU CAN DO THIS IF THEY WORK TOGE-THER,
BUT SOLDIER BLUE COULD DO IT ALONE.
...
YOU ...
YOU WANT TO TRY?
WELL ?!
THE → REAL THING

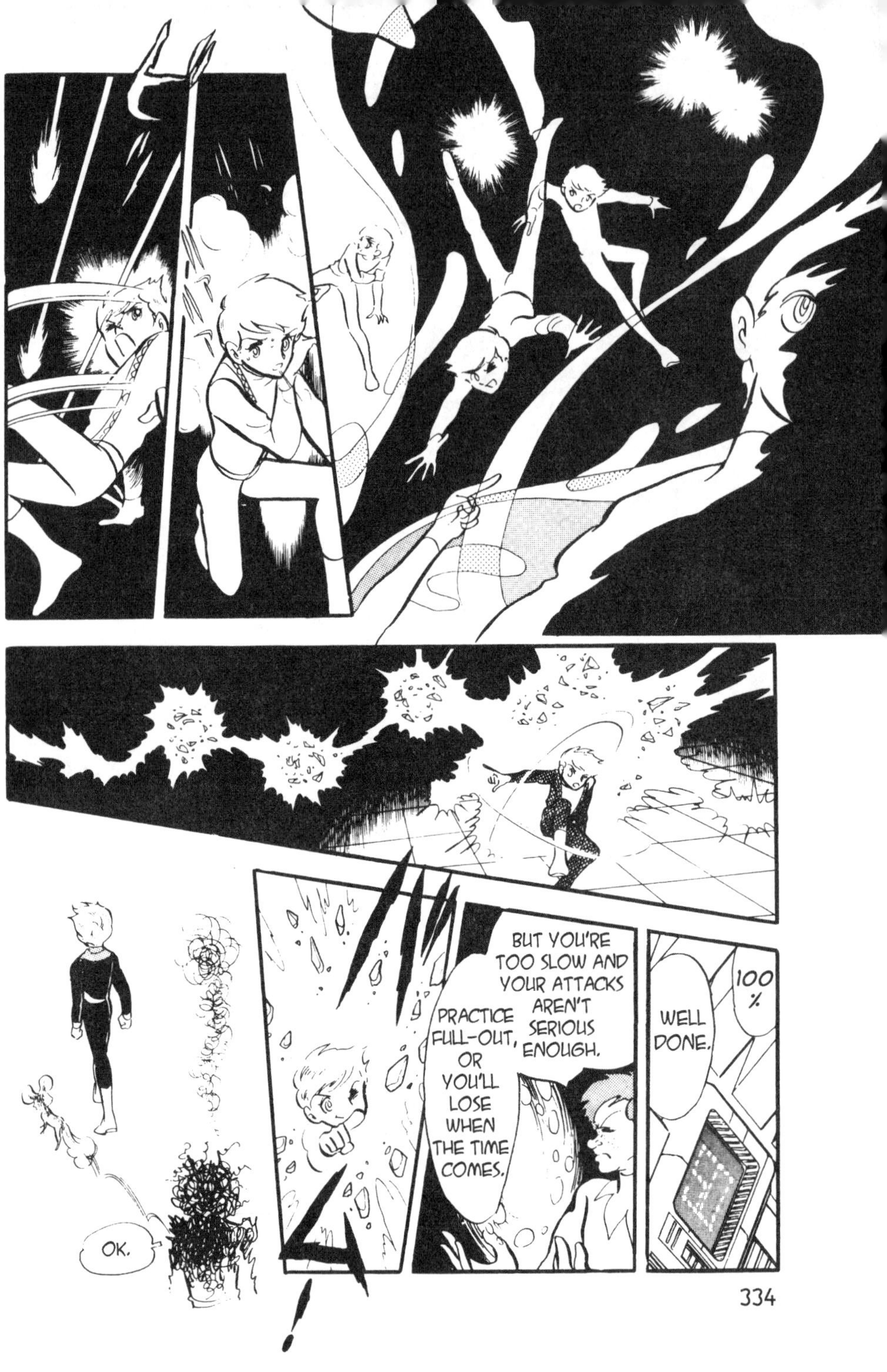
100%
WELL DONE.
BUT YOU'RE TOO SLOW AND YOUR ATTACKS AREN'T SERIOUS ENOUGH.
PRACTICE FULL-OUT, OR YOU'LL LOSE WHEN THE TIME COMES.
OK.

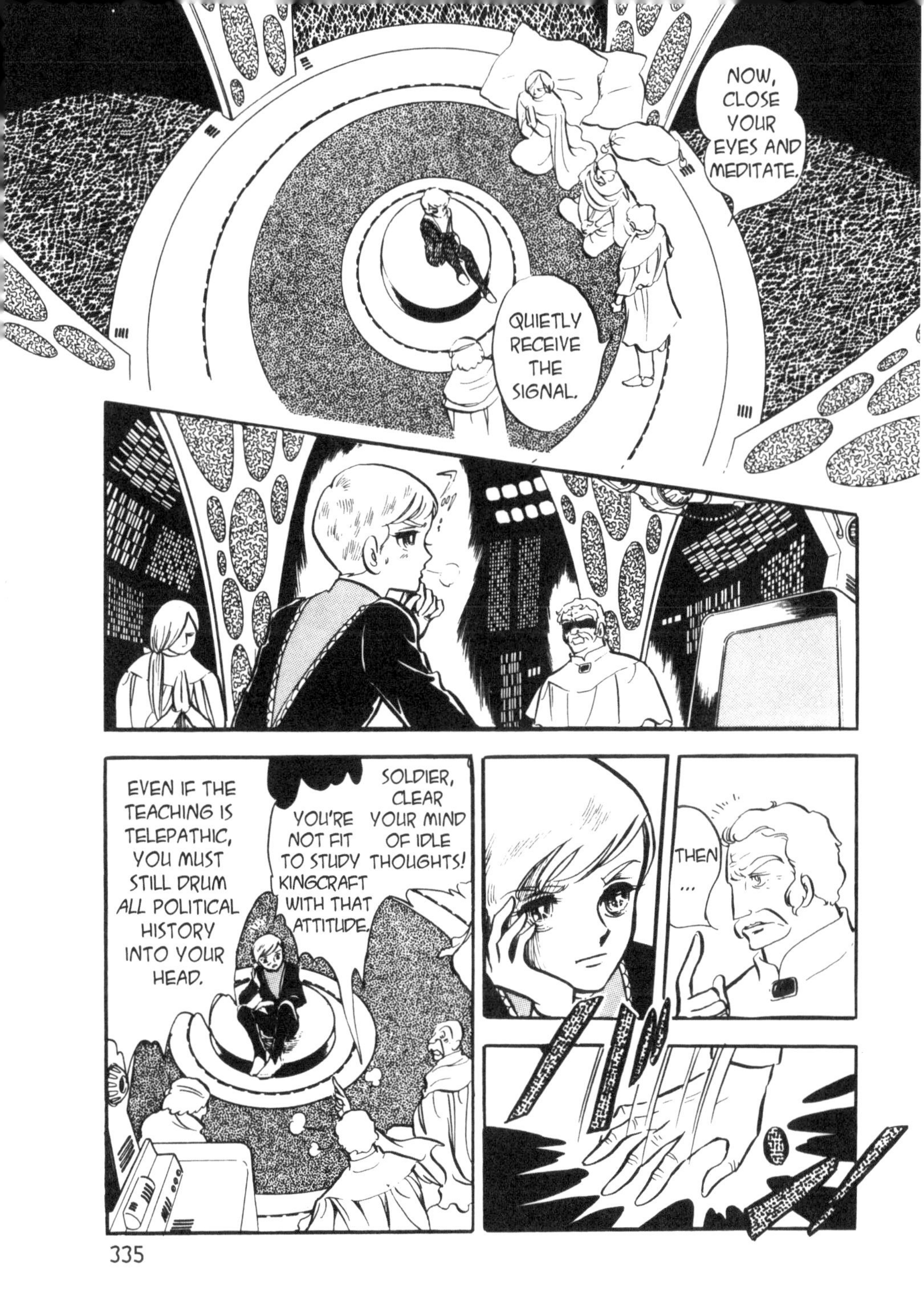
NOW, CLOSE YOUR EYES AND MEDITATE.
QUIETLY RECEIVE THE SIGNAL.
THEN ...
SOLDIER, CLEAR YOUR MIND OF IDLE THOUGHTS!
YOU'RE NOT FIT TO STUDY KINGCRAFT WITH THAT ATTITUDE.
EVEN IF THE TEACHING IS TELEPATHIC, YOU MUST STILL DRUM ALL POLITICAL HISTORY INTO YOUR HEAD.

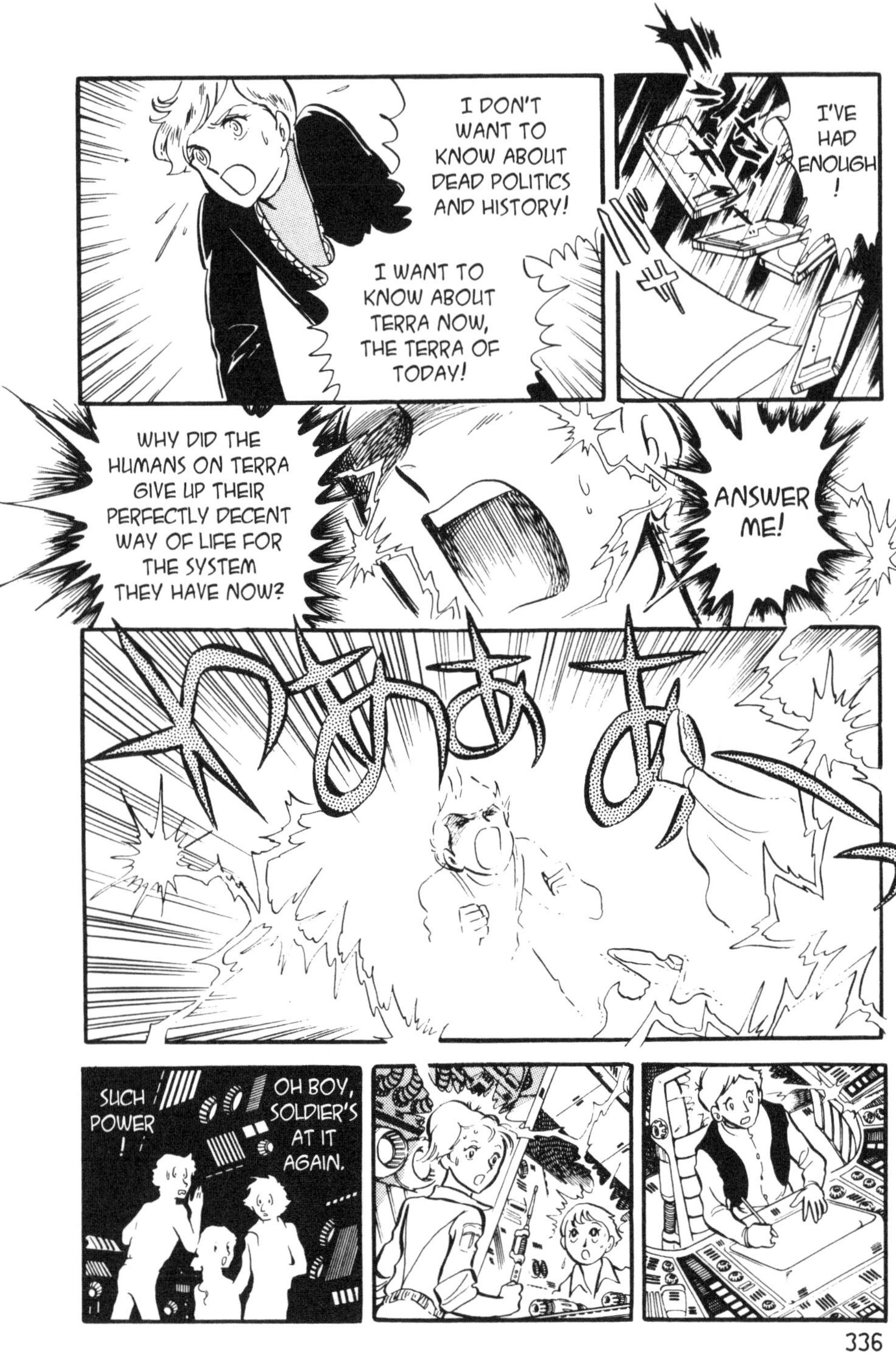

I'VE HAD ENOUGH!
I DON'T WANT TO KNOW ABOUT DEAD POLITICS AND HISTORY!
I WANT TO KNOW ABOUT TERRA NOW, THE TERRA OF TODAY!
WHY DID THE HUMANS ON TERRA GIVE UP THEIR PERFECTLY DECENT WAY OF LIFE FOR THE SYSTEM THEY HAVE NOW?
ANSWER ME!
OH BOY, SOLDIER'S AT IT AGAIN.
SUCH POWER!

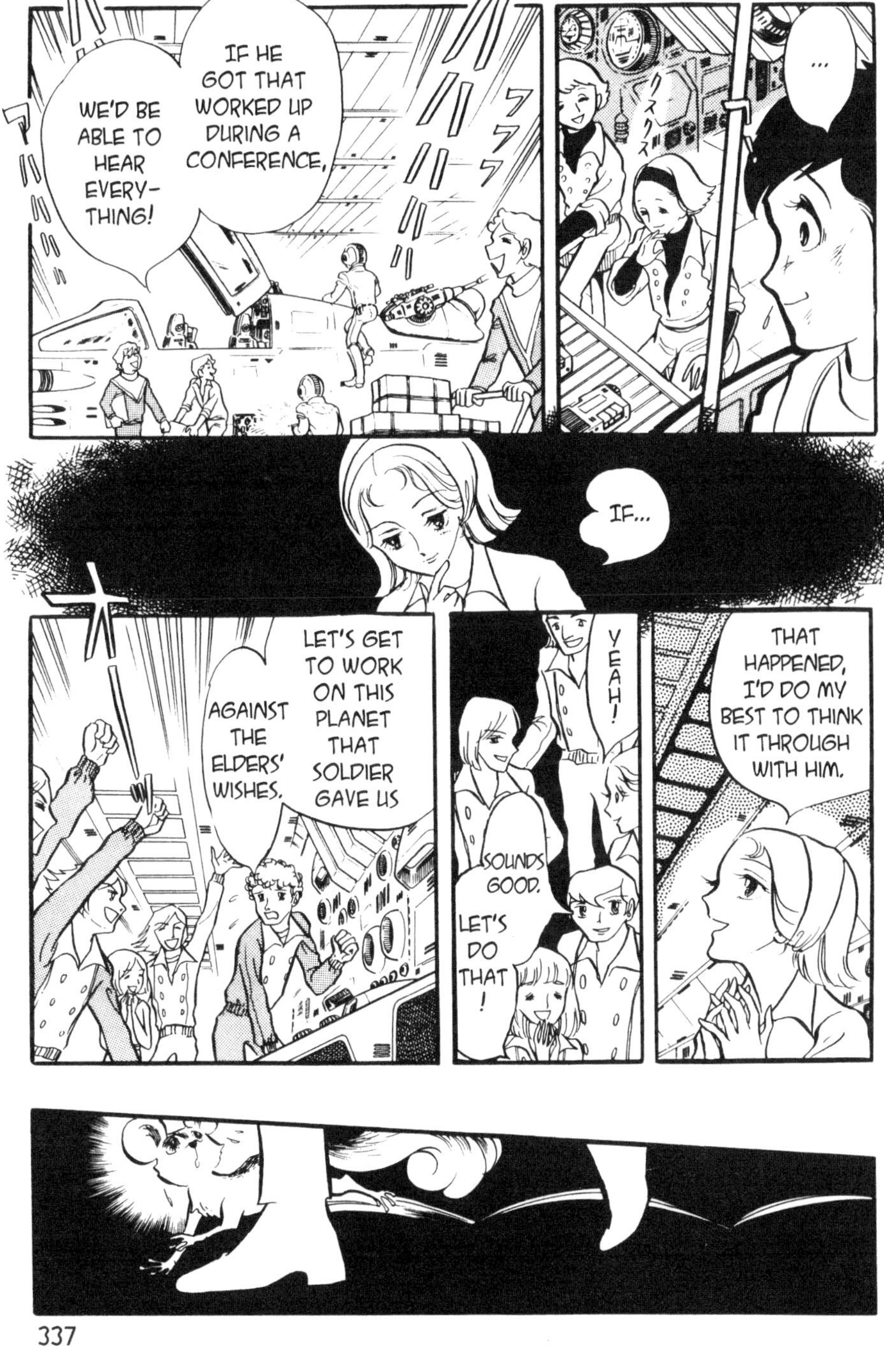
...
クスクス
IF HE GOT THAT WORKED UP DURING A CONFERENCE,
WE'D BE ABLE TO HEAR EVERYTHING!
フフフ
IF...
THAT HAPPENED, I'D DO MY BEST TO THINK IT THROUGH WITH HIM.
YEAH!
SOUNDS GOOD.
LET'S DO THAT!
LET'S GET TO WORK ON THIS PLANET THAT SOLDIER GAVE US
AGAINST THE ELDERS' WISHES.

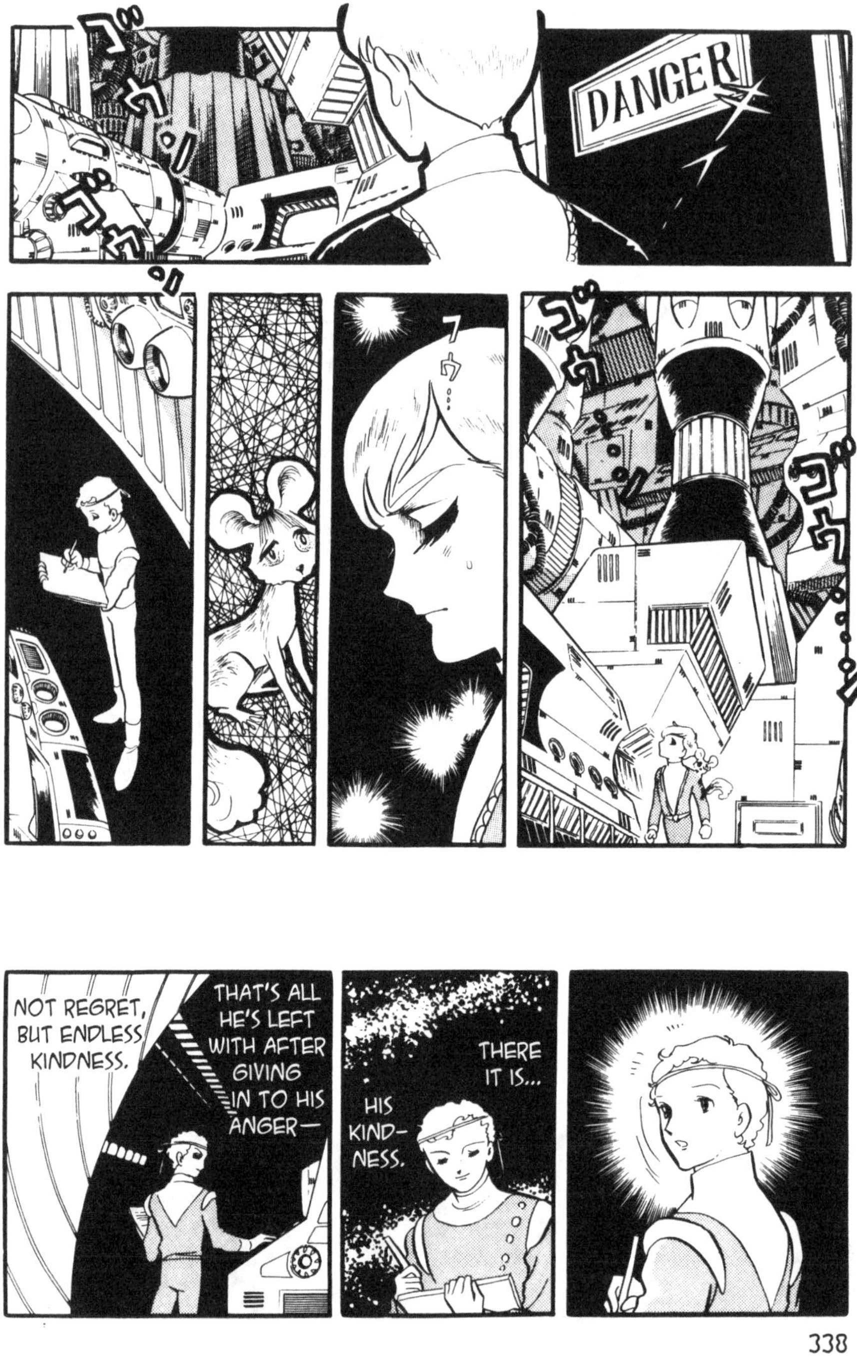
DANGER
THERE IT IS...
HIS KINDNESS.
THAT'S ALL HE'S LEFT WITH AFTER GIVING IN TO HIS ANGER—
NOT REGRET, BUT ENDLESS KINDNESS.

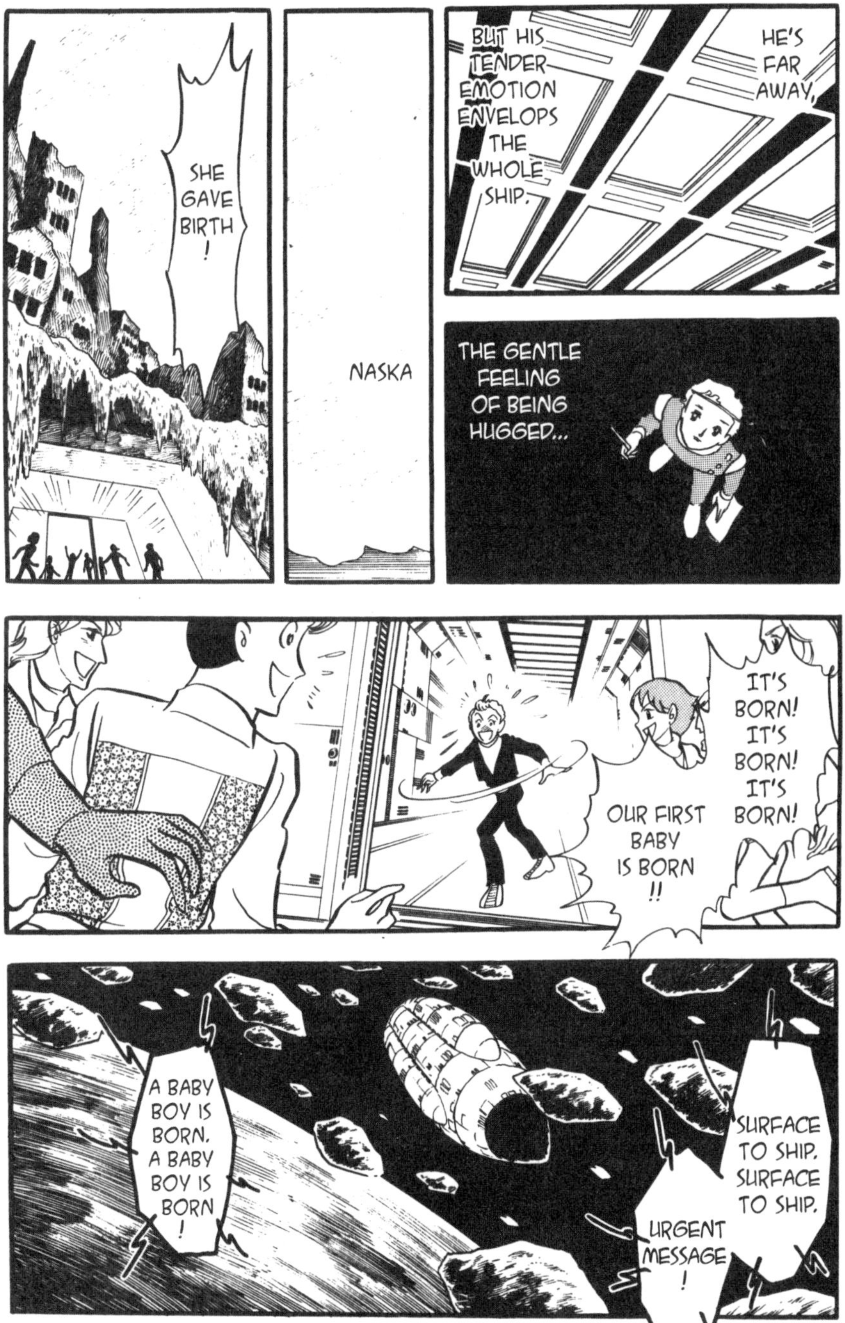
HE'S FAR AWAY,
BUT HIS TENDER EMOTION ENVELOPS THE WHOLE SHIP.
THE GENTLE FEELING OF BEING HUGGED...
NASKA
SHE GAVE BIRTH!
IT'S BORN! IT'S BORN! IT'S BORN!
OUR FIRST BABY IS BORN!!
SURFACE TO SHIP. SURFACE TO SHIP.
URGENT MESSAGE!
A BABY BOY IS BORN. A BABY BOY IS BORN!

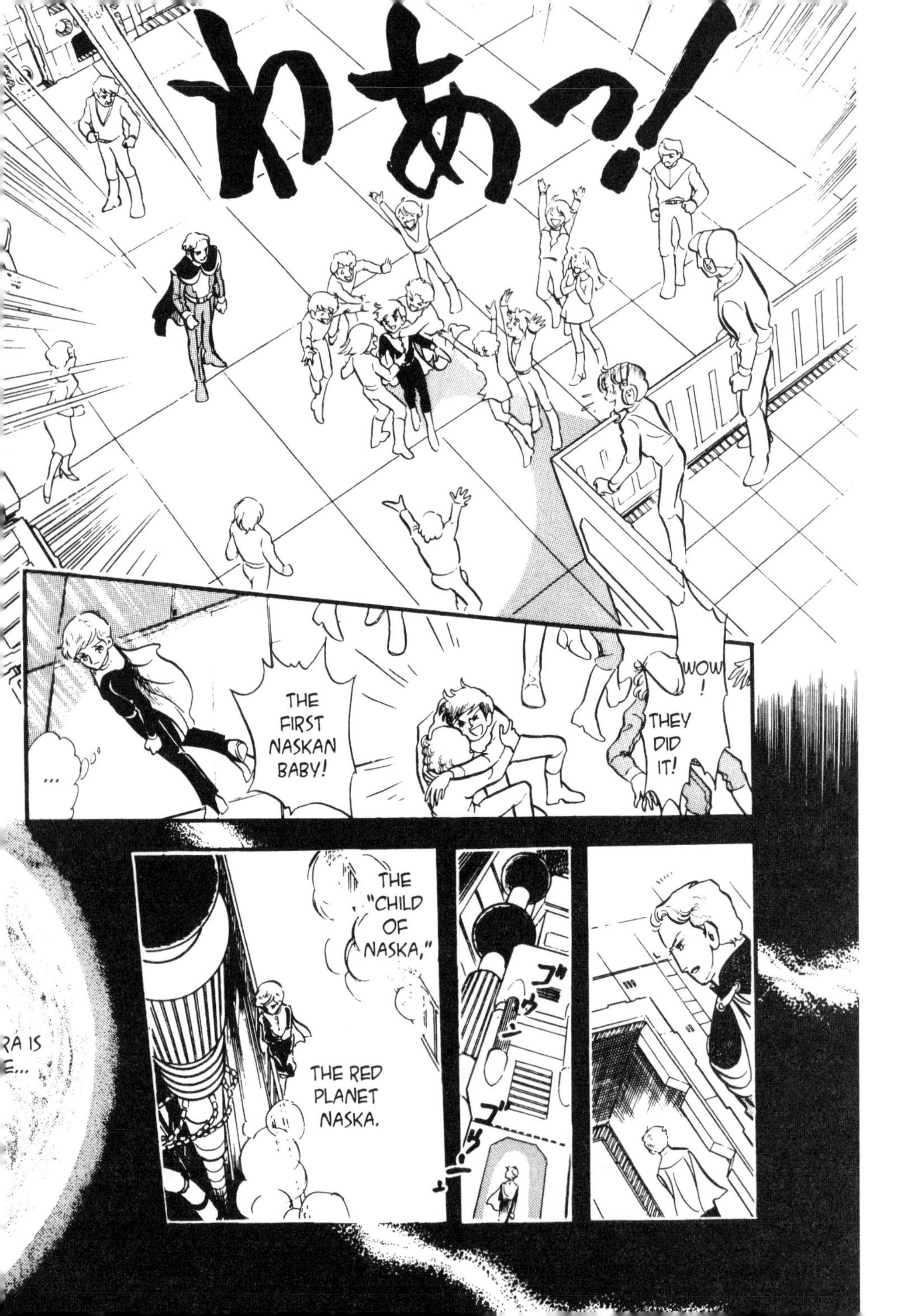

わあっ!
WOW!
THEY DID IT!
THE FIRST NASKAN BABY!
...
ゴウン
ゴウン
THE "CHILD OF NASKA,"
THE RED PLANET NASKA.

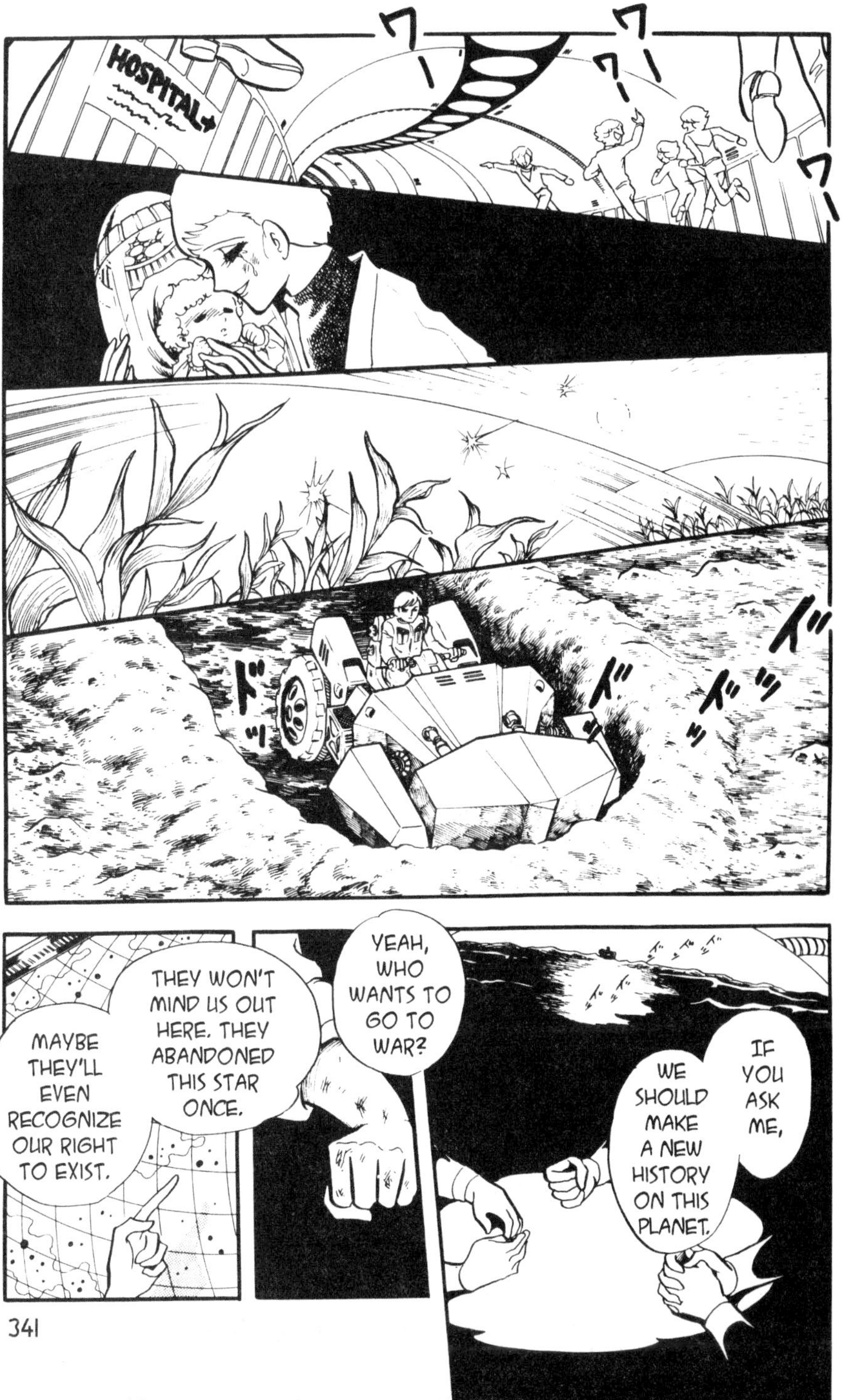
HOSPITAL
IF YOU ASK ME,
WE SHOULD MAKE A NEW HISTORY ON THIS PLANET.
YEAH, WHO WANTS TO GO TO WAR?
THEY WON'T MIND US OUT HERE. THEY ABANDONED THIS STAR ONCE.
MAYBE THEY'LL EVEN RECOGNIZE OUR RIGHT TO EXIST.

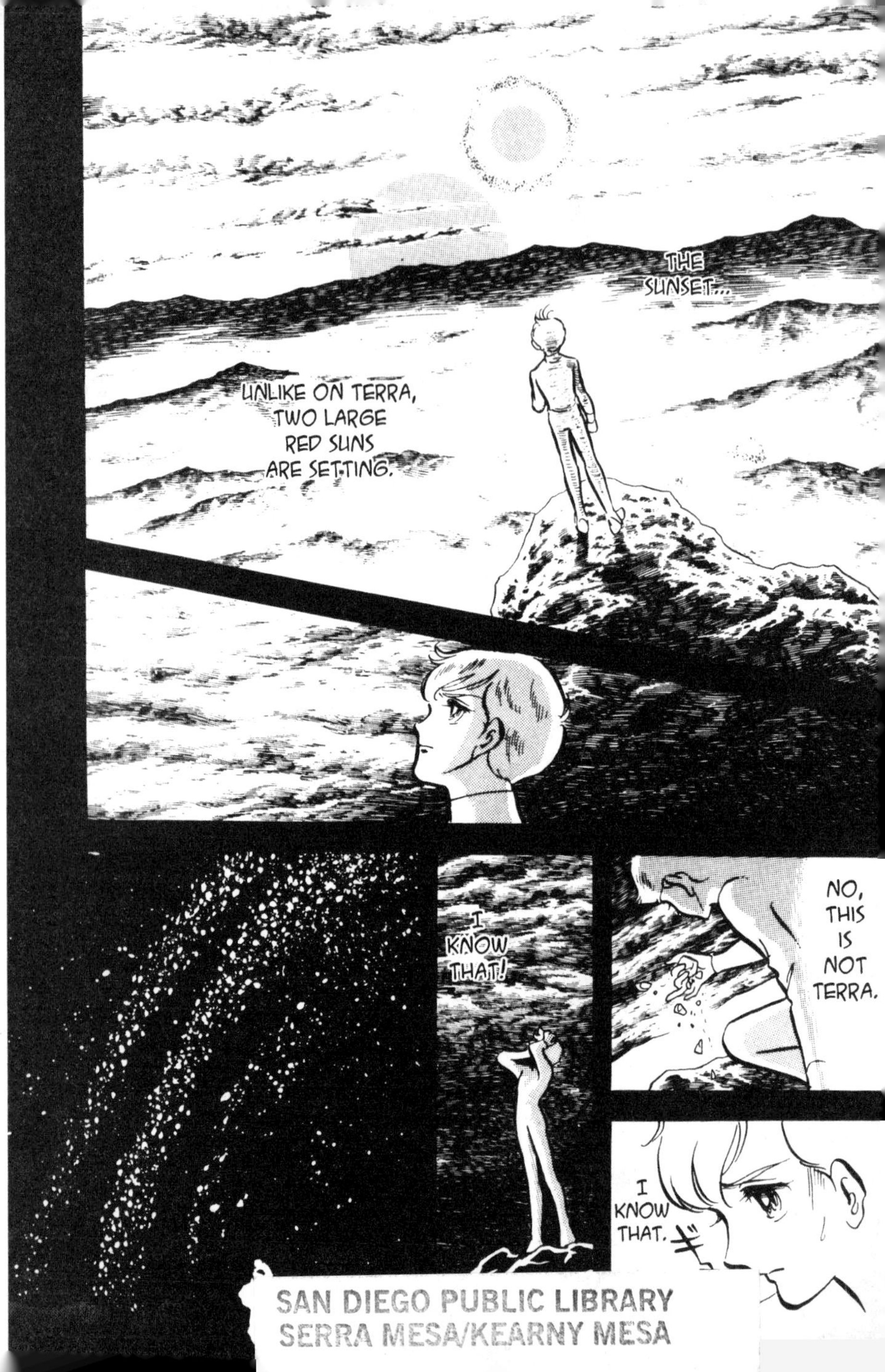
THE SUNSET...
UNLIKE ON TERRA, TWO LARGE RED SUNS ARE SETTING.
NO, THIS IS NOT TERRA.
I KNOW THAT.
ギ
I KNOW THAT!

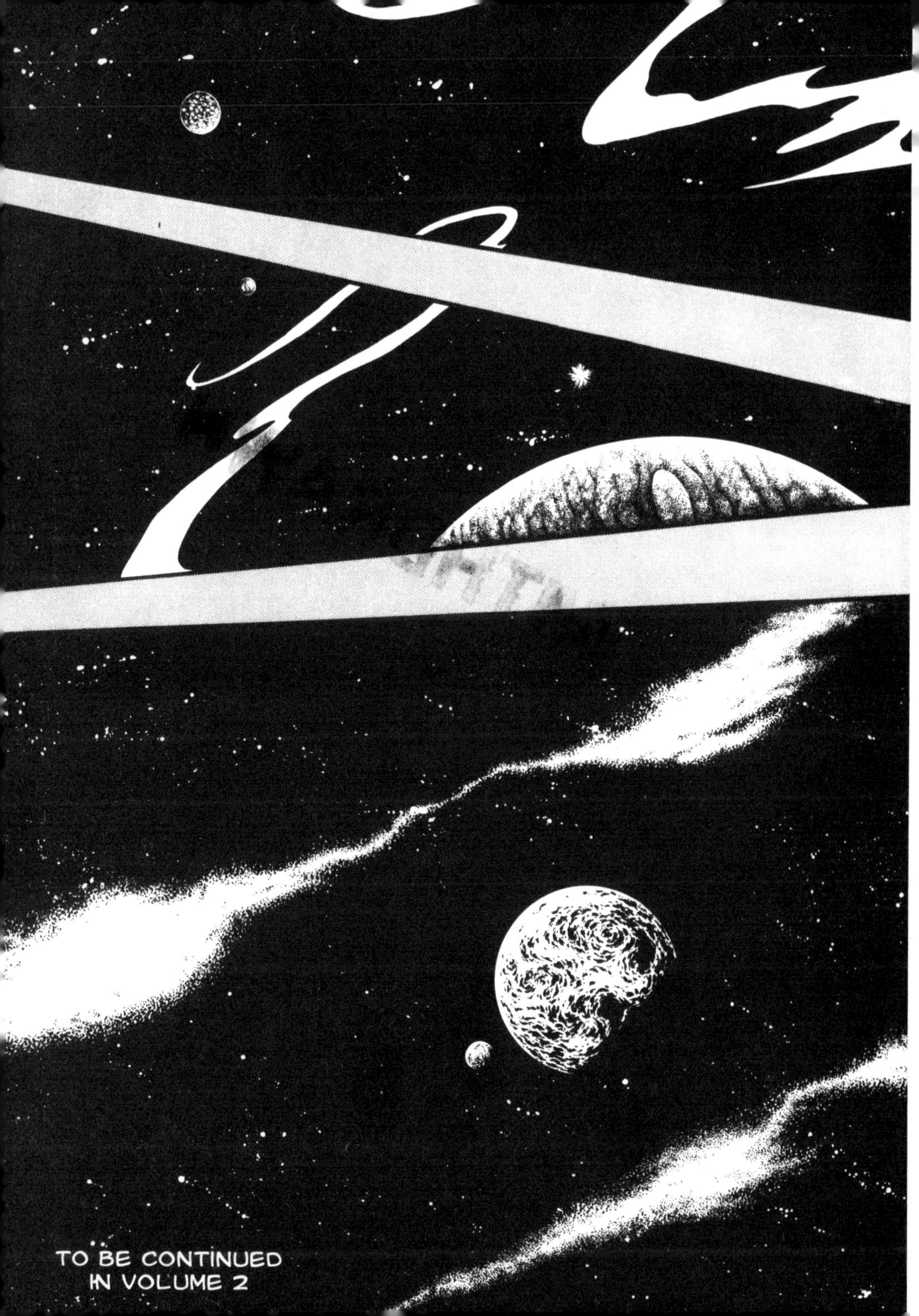
TO BE CONTINUED
IN VOLUME 2

WRONG WAY!

Japanese books, including manga like this one,
are meant to be read from right to left.

So the front cover is actually the back cover, and vice-versa.

To read this book, please flip it over and start in the top right-hand corner.
Read the panels, and the bubbles in the panels, from right to left,
then drop down to the next row and repeat.

It may make you dizzy at first,
but forcing your brain to do things backwards makes you smarter in the long run.
We swear.